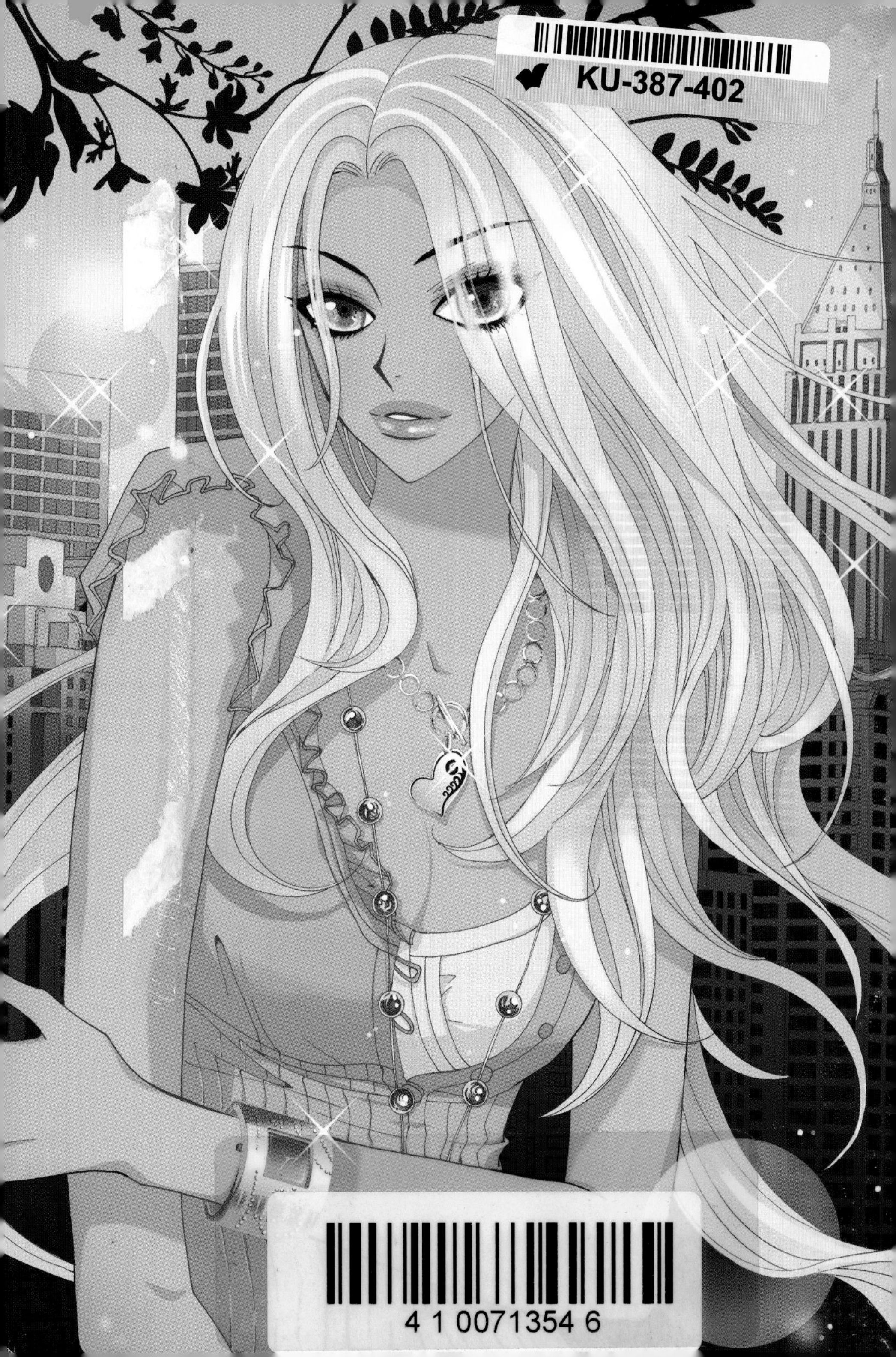

gossip girl

FOR YOUR EYES ONLY

CHAPTER 1 3
CHAPTER 2 45
CHAPTER 3 87
CHAPTER 4 129
CHAPTER 5 173
CHAPTER 6 207

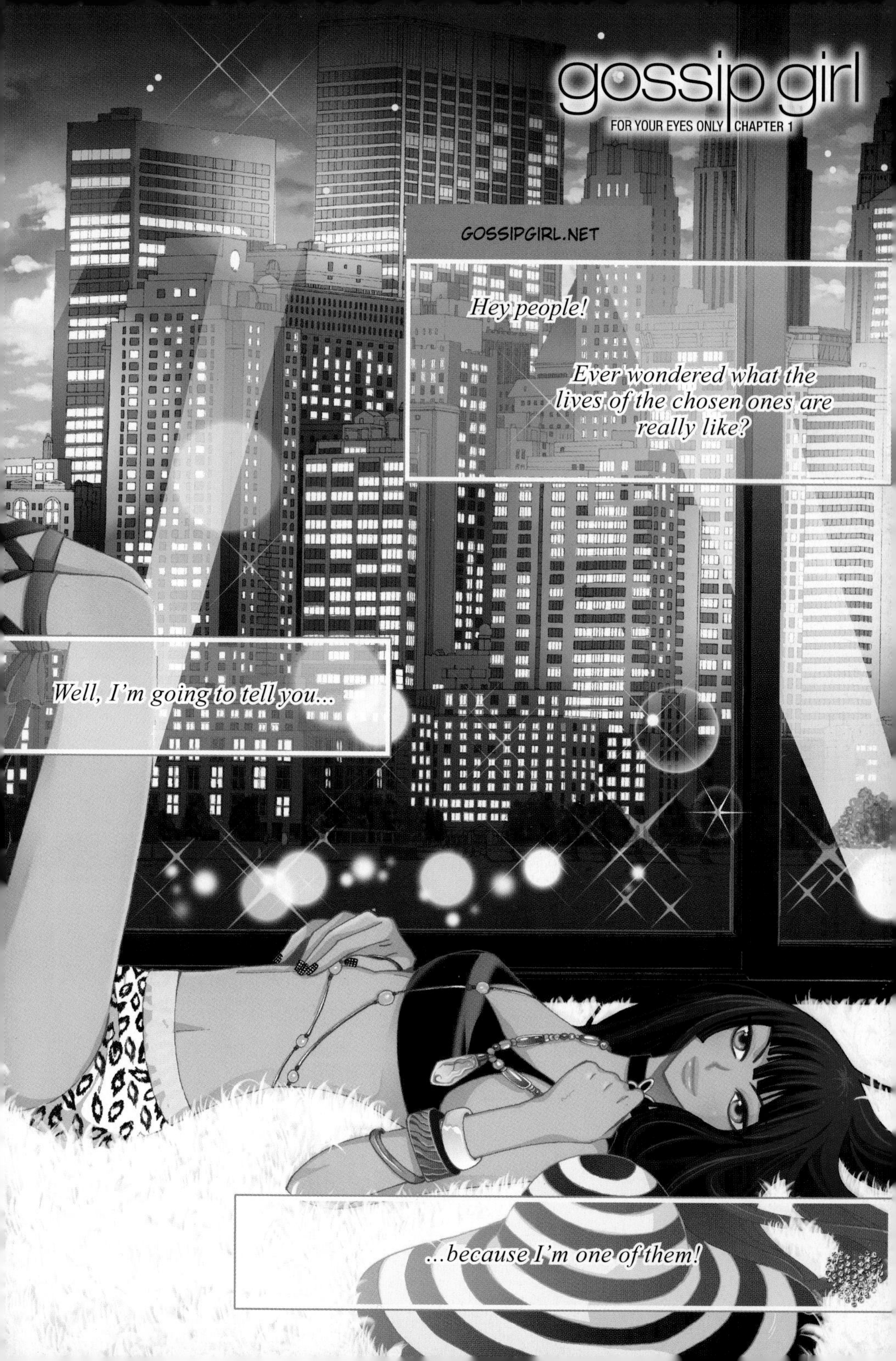
gossip girl
FOR YOUR EYES ONLY | CHAPTER 1
GOSSIPGIRL.NET
Hey people!
Ever wondered what the lives of the chosen ones are really like?
Well, I'm going to tell you...
...because I'm one of them!

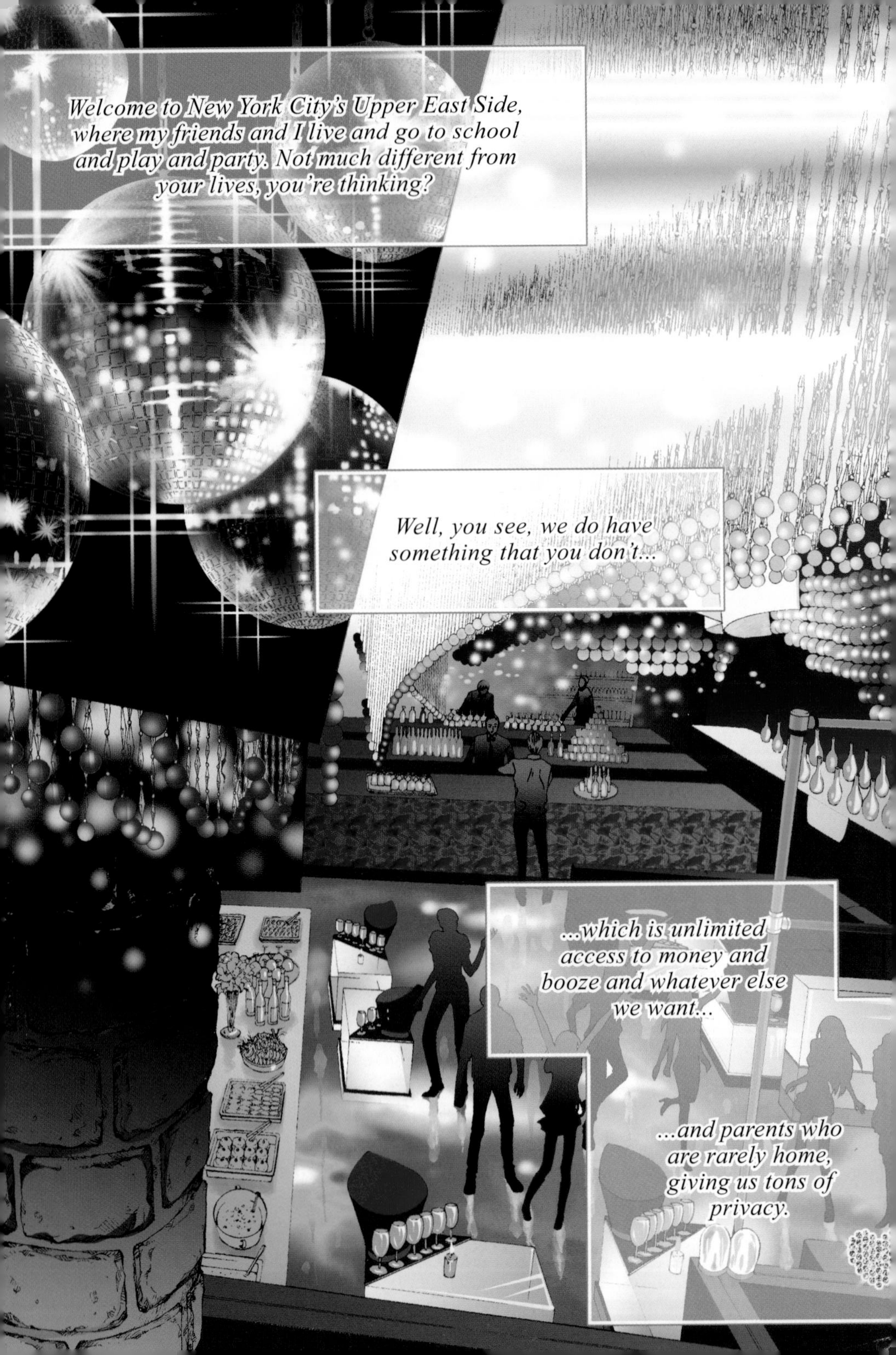
Welcome to New York City's Upper East Side, where my friends and I live and go to school and play and party. Not much different from your lives, you're thinking?
Well, you see, we do have something that you don't...
...which is unlimited access to money and booze and whatever else we want...
...and parents who are rarely home, giving us tons of privacy.

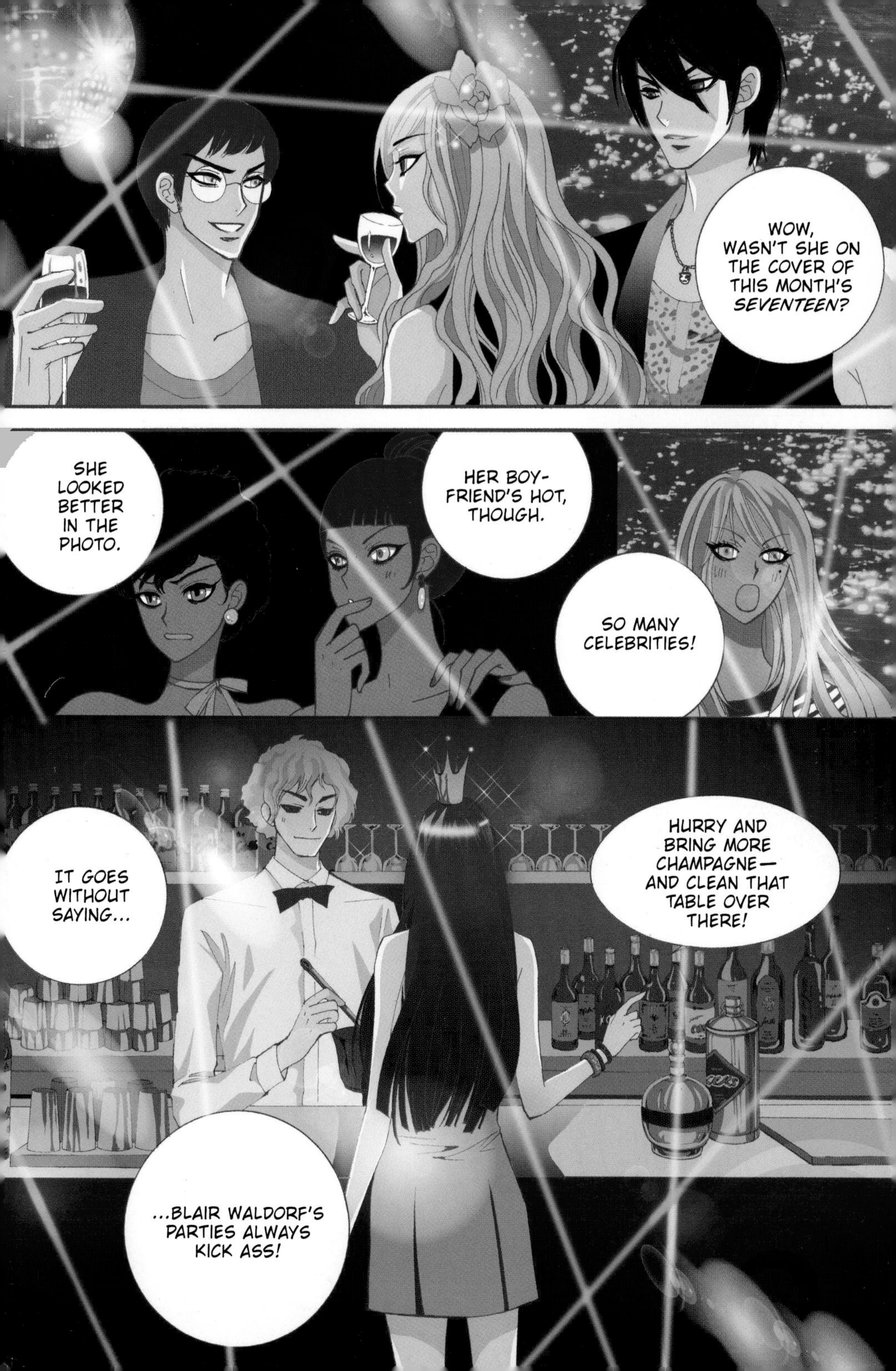
WOW, WASN'T SHE ON THE COVER OF THIS MONTH'S *SEVENTEEN*?
SHE LOOKED BETTER IN THE PHOTO.
HER BOY-FRIEND'S HOT, THOUGH.
SO MANY CELEBRITIES!
IT GOES WITHOUT SAYING...
HURRY AND BRING MORE CHAMPAGNE— AND CLEAN THAT TABLE OVER THERE!
...BLAIR WALDORF'S PARTIES ALWAYS KICK ASS!

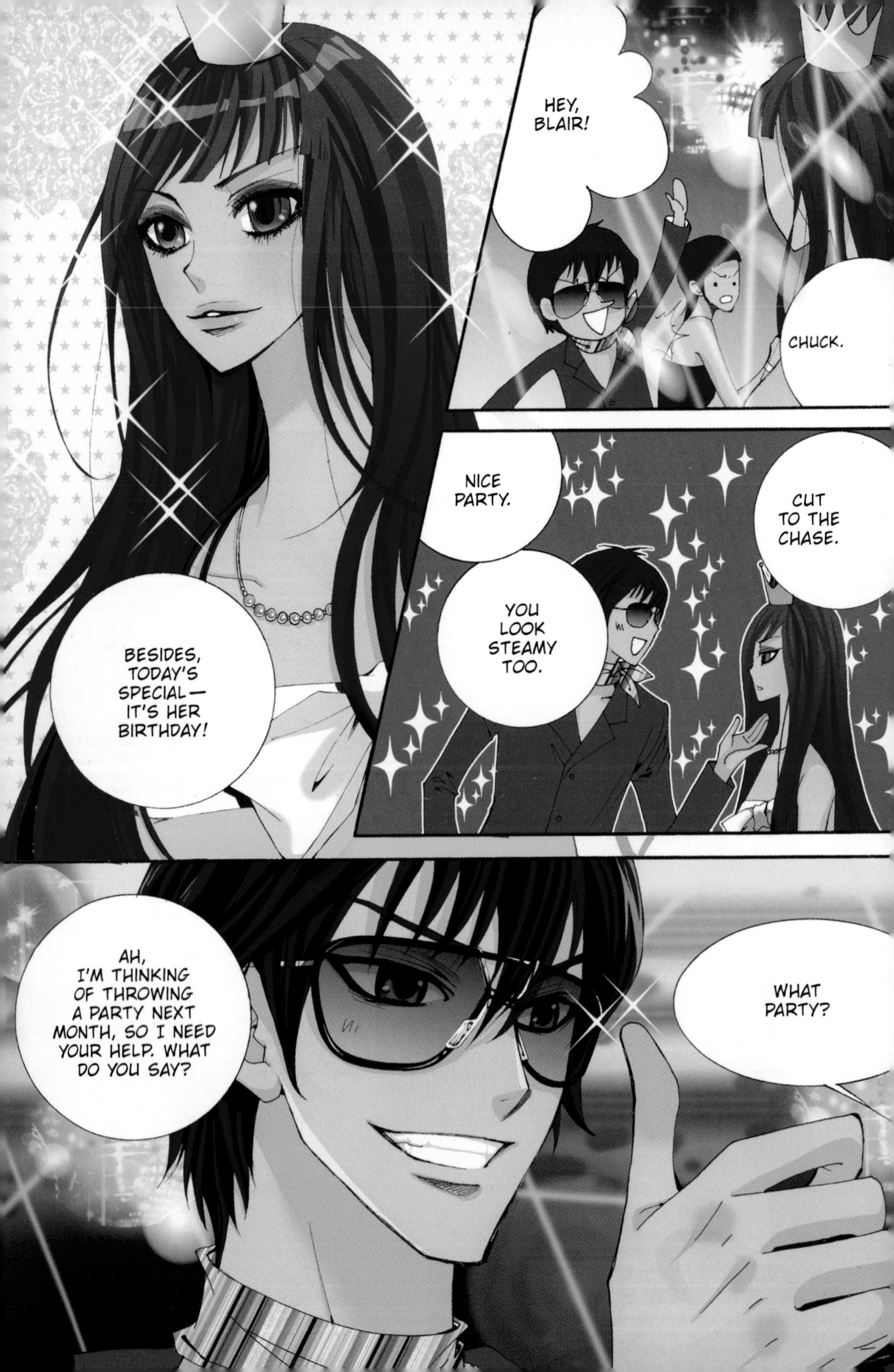
BESIDES, TODAY'S SPECIAL— IT'S HER BIRTHDAY!
HEY, BLAIR!
CHUCK.
NICE PARTY.
YOU LOOK STEAMY TOO.
CUT TO THE CHASE.
AH, I'M THINKING OF THROWING A PARTY NEXT MONTH, SO I NEED YOUR HELP. WHAT DO YOU SAY?
WHAT PARTY?

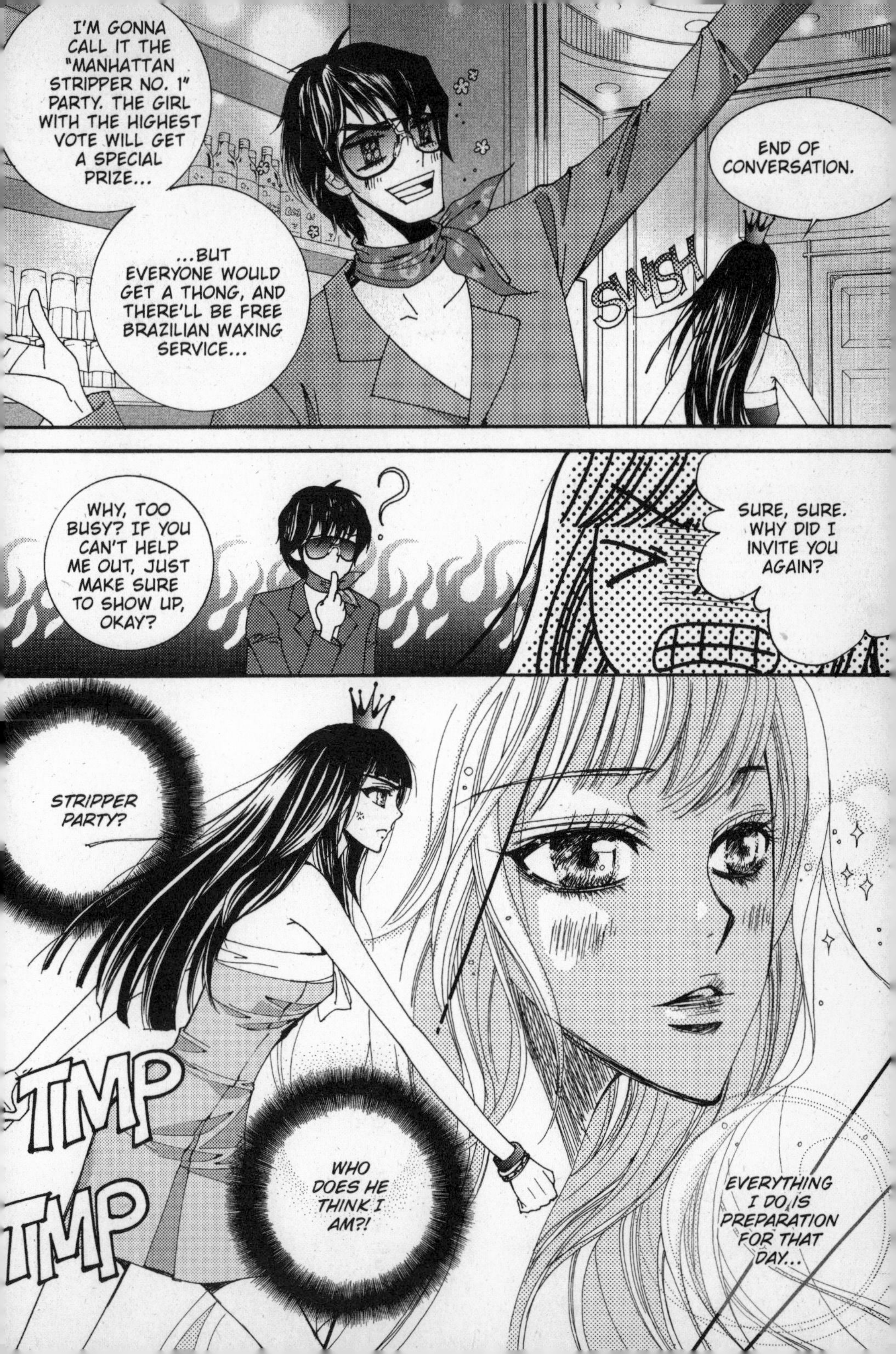
I'M GONNA CALL IT THE "MANHATTAN STRIPPER NO. 1" PARTY. THE GIRL WITH THE HIGHEST VOTE WILL GET A SPECIAL PRIZE...
...BUT EVERYONE WOULD GET A THONG, AND THERE'LL BE FREE BRAZILIAN WAXING SERVICE...
SWISH
END OF CONVERSATION.
WHY, TOO BUSY? IF YOU CAN'T HELP ME OUT, JUST MAKE SURE TO SHOW UP, OKAY?
SURE, SURE. WHY DID I INVITE YOU AGAIN?
STRIPPER PARTY?
TMP
TMP
WHO DOES HE THINK I AM?!
EVERYTHING I DO IS PREPARATION FOR THAT DAY...

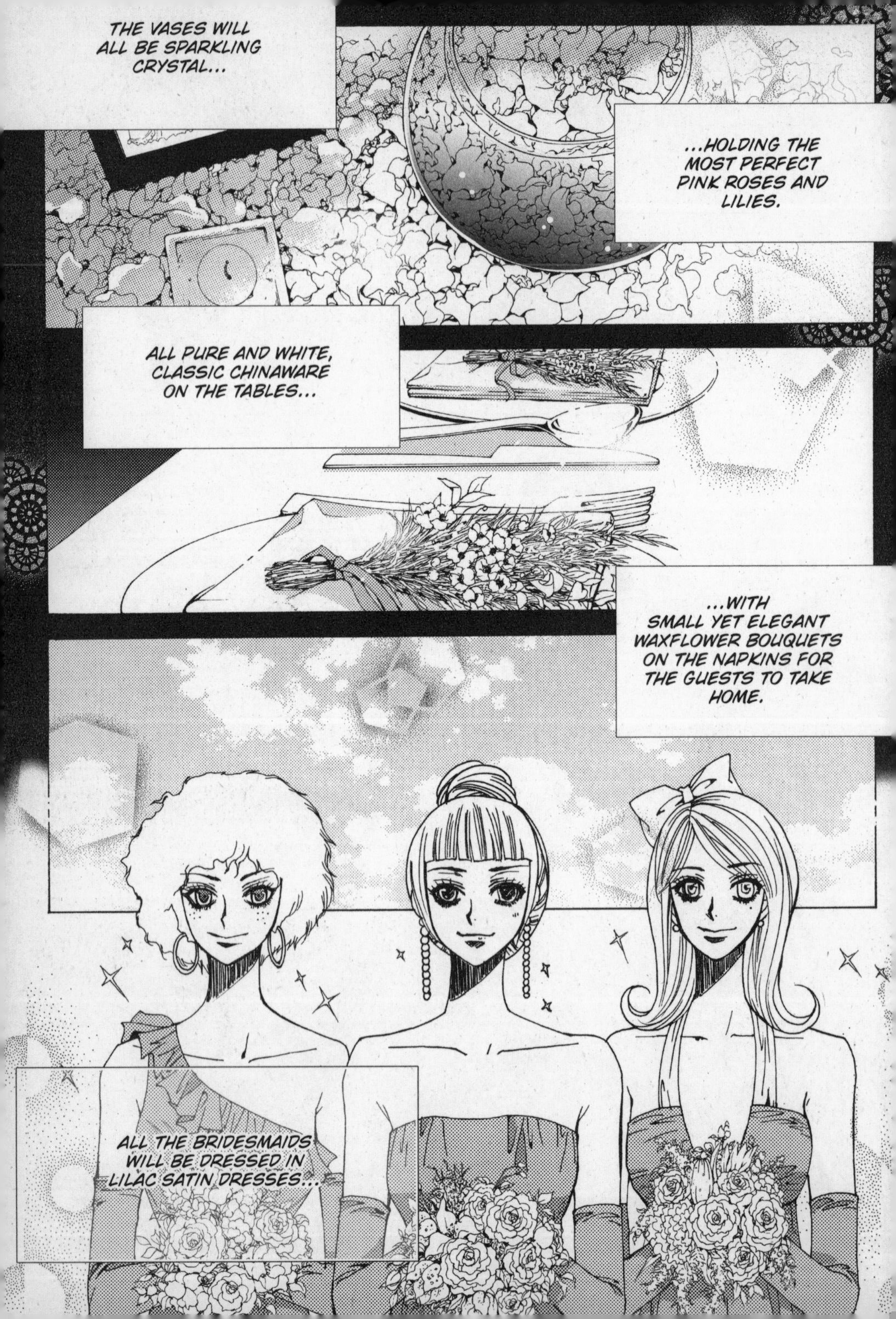
THE VASES WILL ALL BE SPARKLING CRYSTAL...
...HOLDING THE MOST PERFECT PINK ROSES AND LILIES.
ALL PURE AND WHITE, CLASSIC CHINAWARE ON THE TABLES...
...WITH SMALL YET ELEGANT WAXFLOWER BOUQUETS ON THE NAPKINS FOR THE GUESTS TO TAKE HOME.
ALL THE BRIDESMAIDS WILL BE DRESSED IN LILAC SATIN DRESSES...

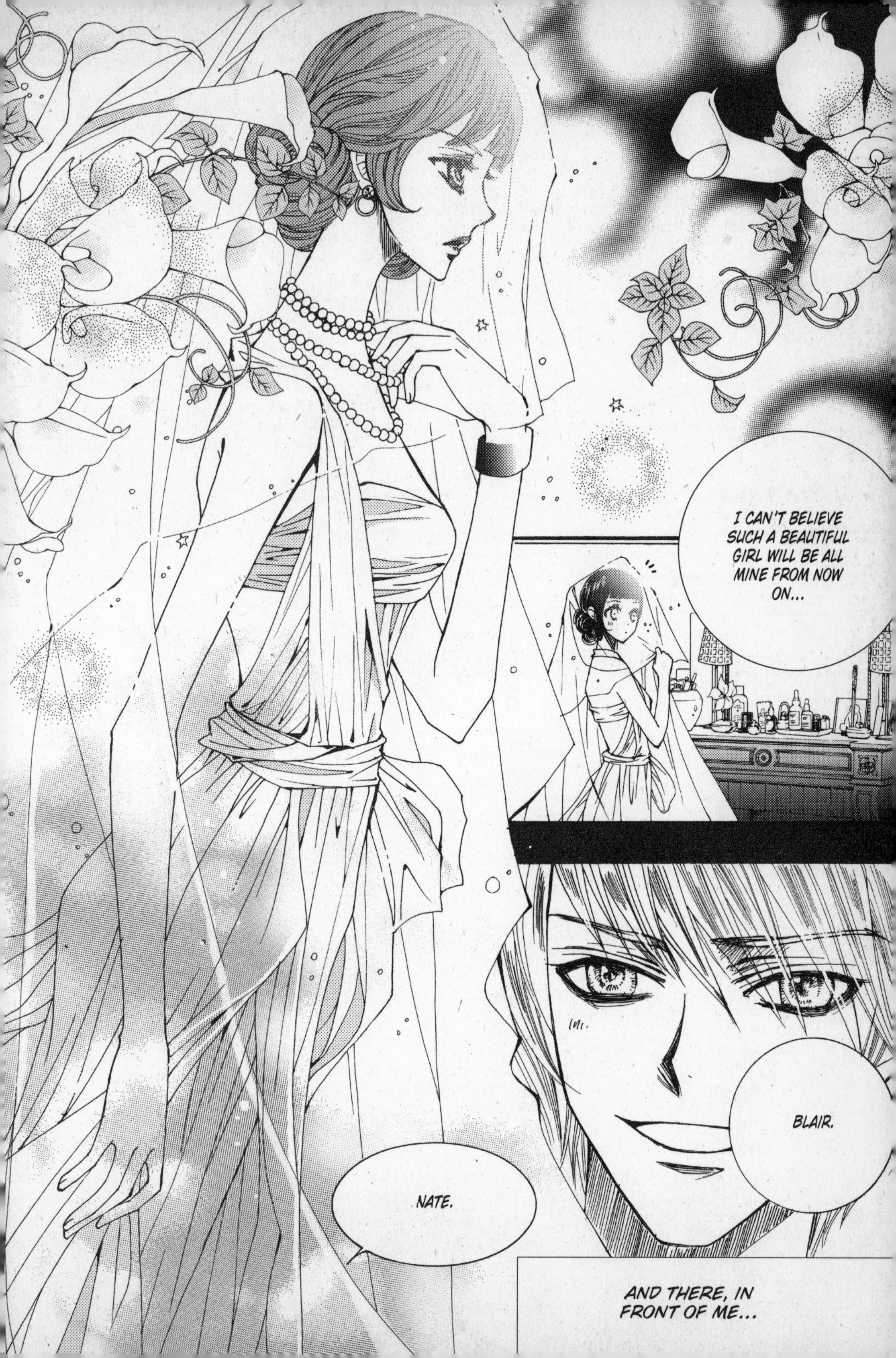
NATE.
I CAN'T BELIEVE SUCH A BEAUTIFUL GIRL WILL BE ALL MINE FROM NOW ON...
BLAIR.
AND THERE, IN FRONT OF ME...

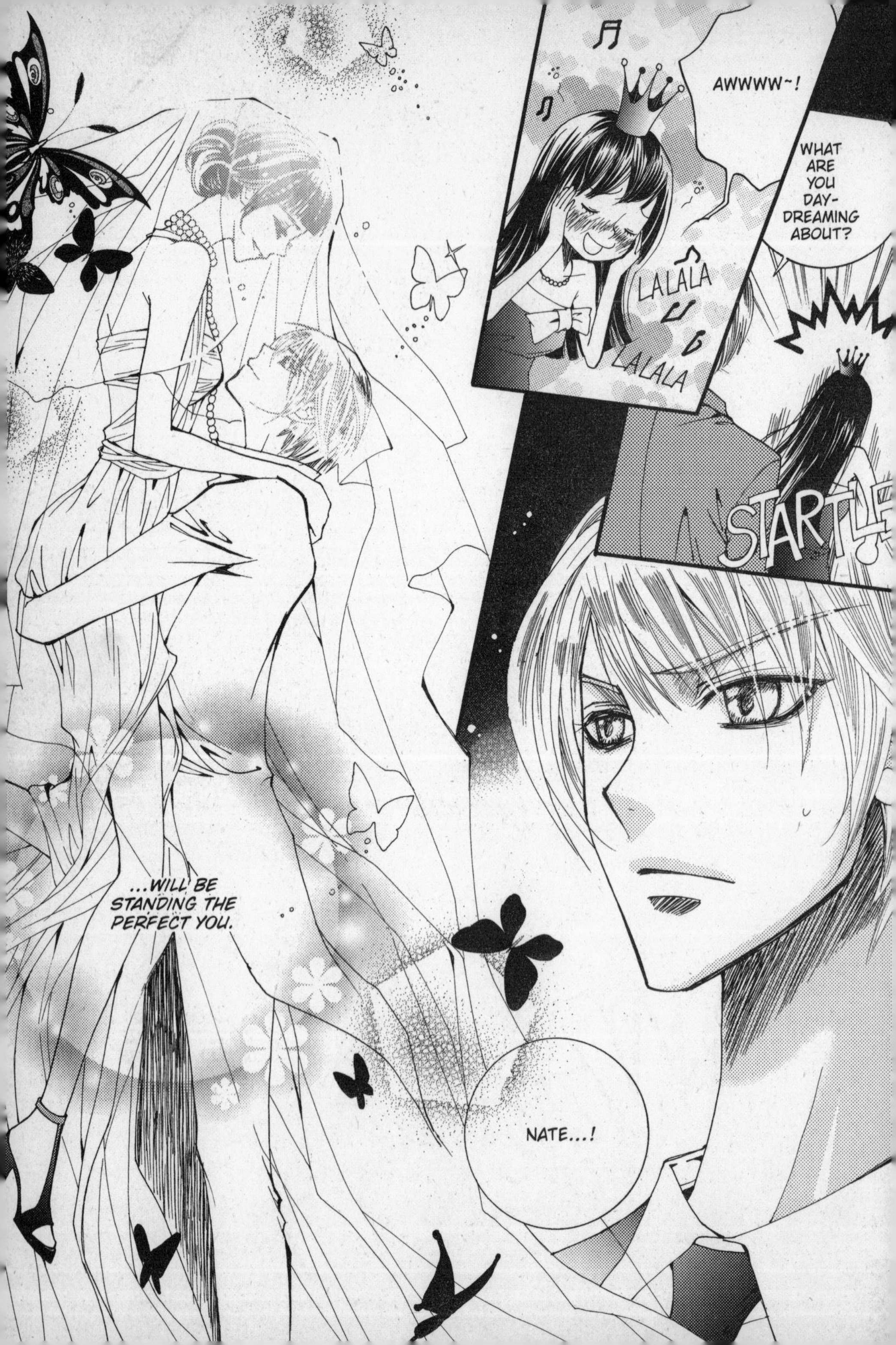
...WILL BE STANDING THE PERFECT YOU.
NATE...!
LALALA
LALALA
AWWWW~!
WHAT ARE YOU DAY-DREAMING ABOUT?
STARTLE

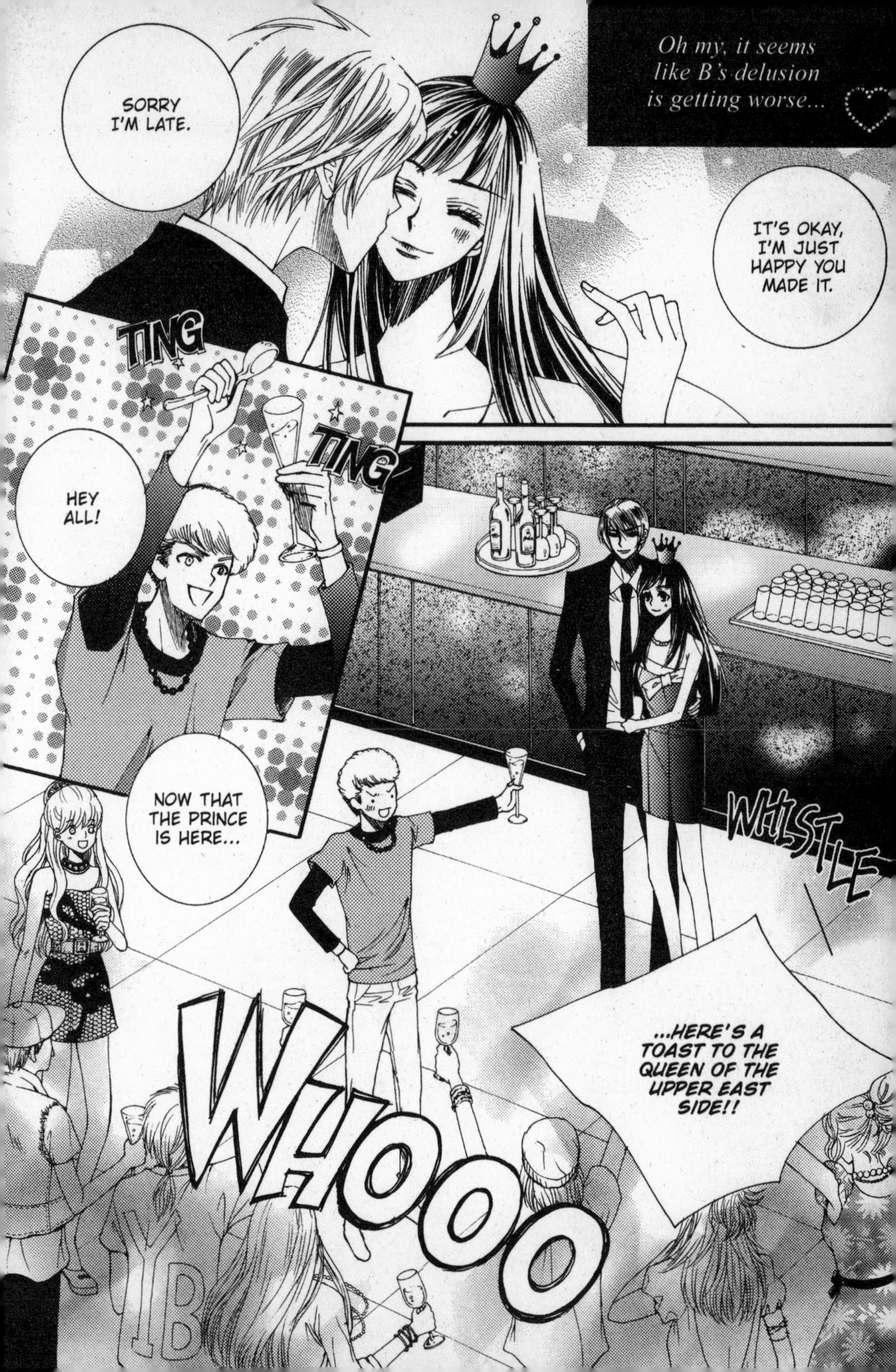
SORRY I'M LATE.
Oh my, it seems like B's delusion is getting worse...
IT'S OKAY, I'M JUST HAPPY YOU MADE IT.
TING
TING
HEY ALL!
NOW THAT THE PRINCE IS HERE...
WHISTLE
...HERE'S A TOAST TO THE QUEEN OF THE UPPER EAST SIDE!!
WHOOO

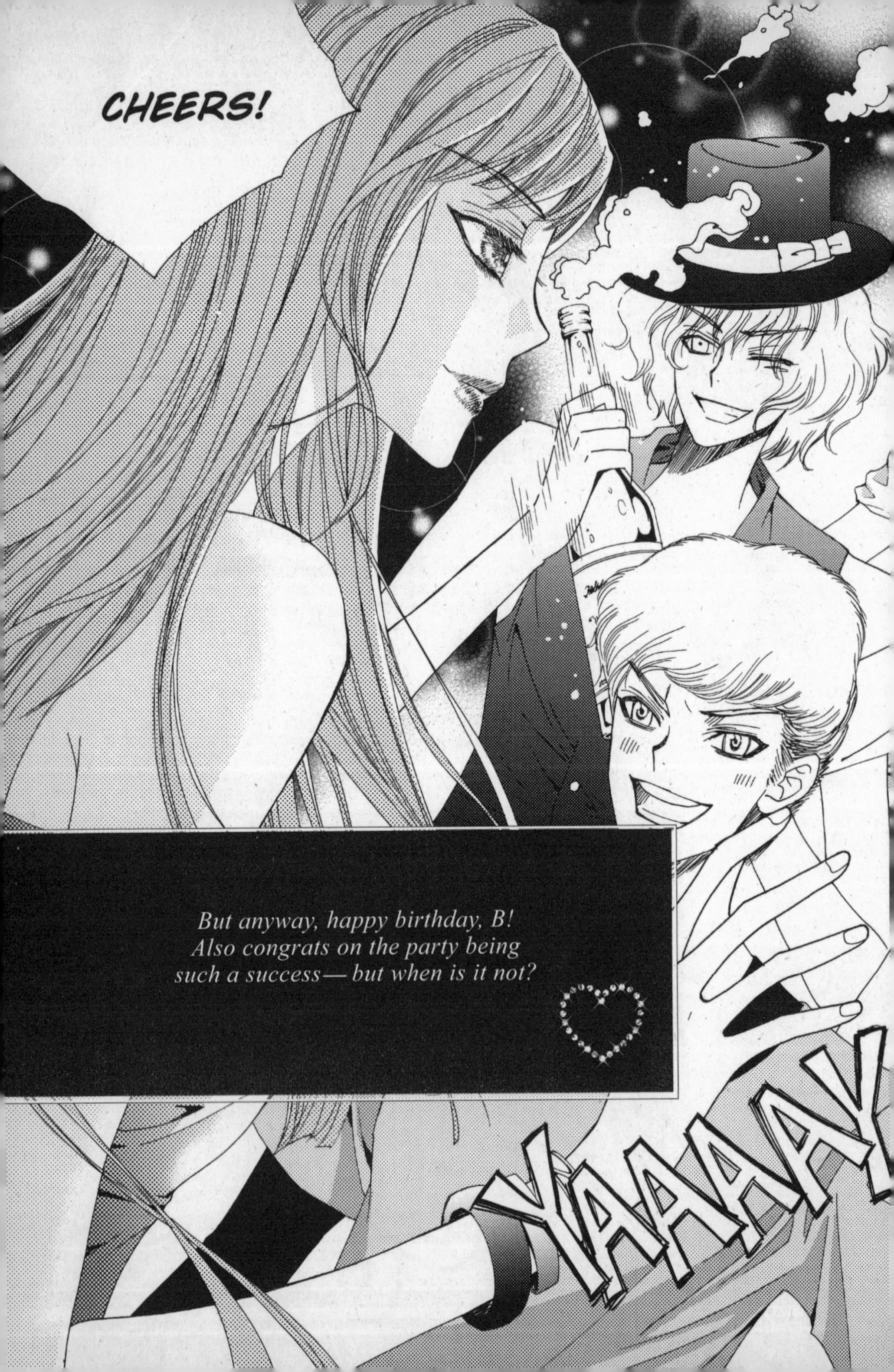
CHEERS!
But anyway, happy birthday, B! Also congrats on the party being such a success— but when is it not?
YAAAAY

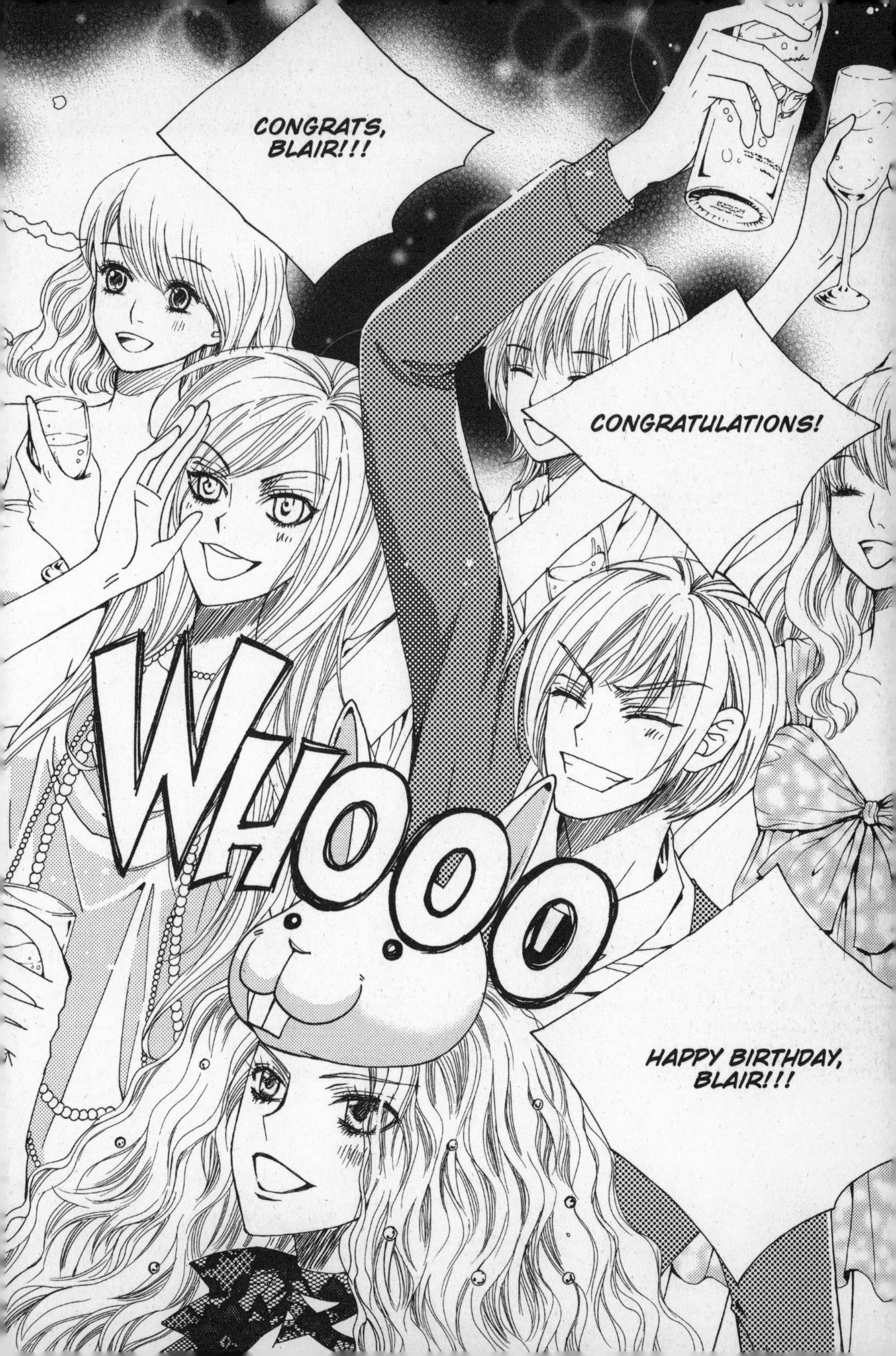
CONGRATS, BLAIR!!!
CONGRATULATIONS!
WHOOOO
HAPPY BIRTHDAY, BLAIR!!!

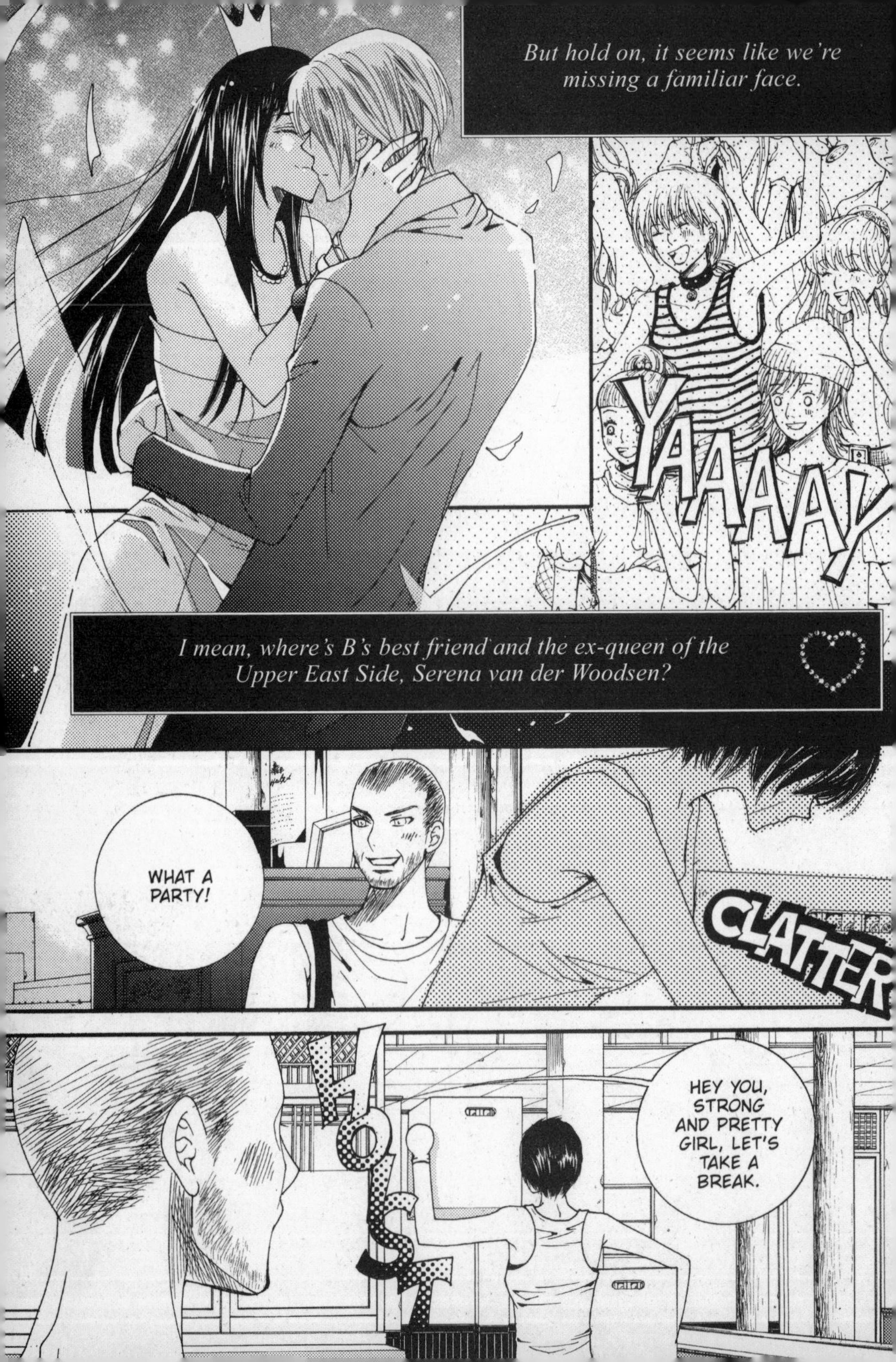

But hold on, it seems like we're missing a familiar face.
YAAAAY
I mean, where's B's best friend and the ex-queen of the Upper East Side, Serena van der Woodsen?
WHAT A PARTY!
CLATTER
HOIST
HEY YOU, STRONG AND PRETTY GIRL, LET'S TAKE A BREAK.

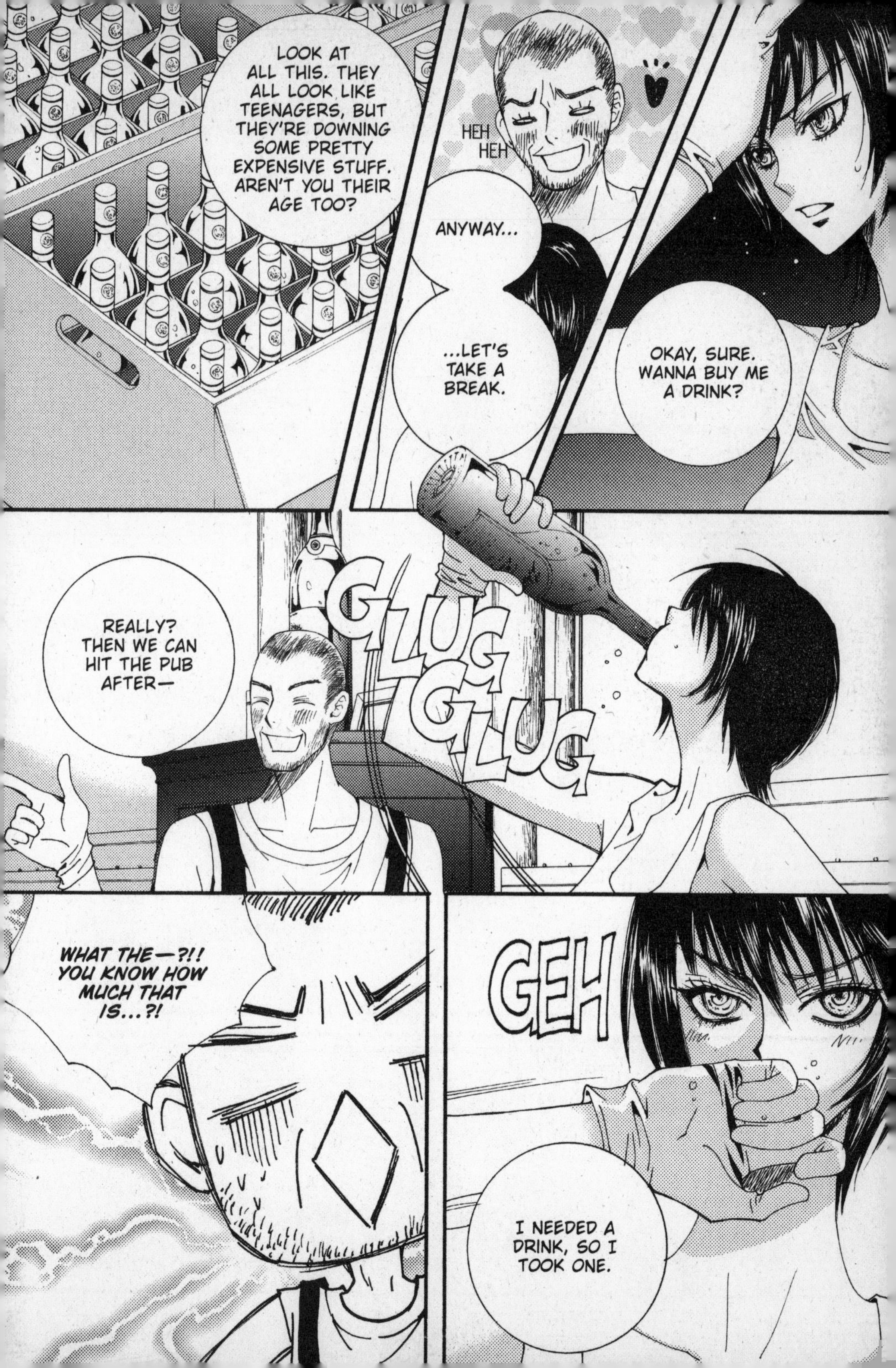
LOOK AT ALL THIS. THEY ALL LOOK LIKE TEENAGERS, BUT THEY'RE DOWNING SOME PRETTY EXPENSIVE STUFF. AREN'T YOU THEIR AGE TOO?
HEH HEH
ANYWAY...
...LET'S TAKE A BREAK.
OKAY, SURE. WANNA BUY ME A DRINK?
REALLY? THEN WE CAN HIT THE PUB AFTER—
GLUG GLUG
WHAT THE—?!! YOU KNOW HOW MUCH THAT IS...?!
GEH
I NEEDED A DRINK, SO I TOOK ONE.

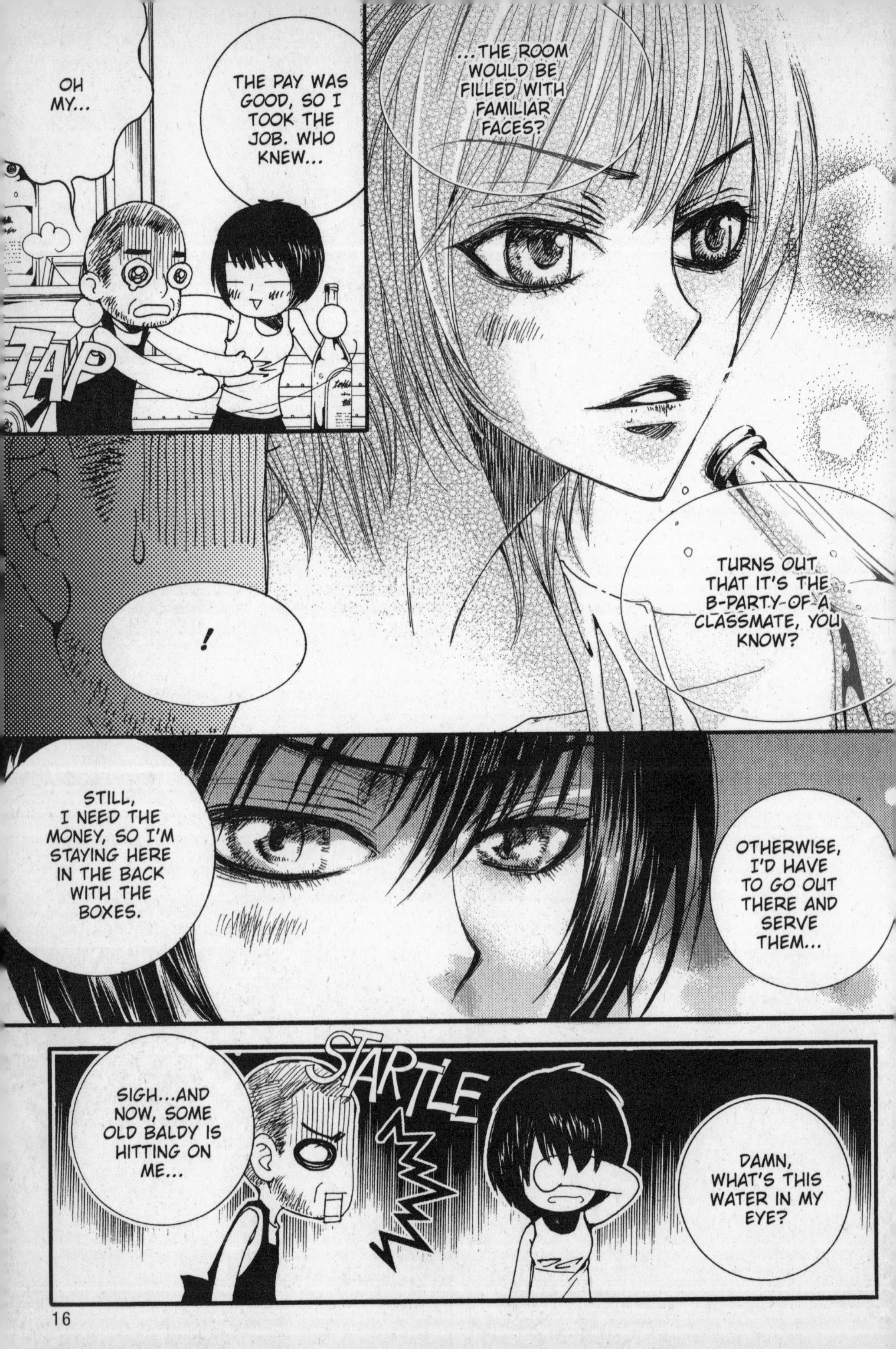
OH MY...
THE PAY WAS GOOD, SO I TOOK THE JOB. WHO KNEW...
TAP
!
...THE ROOM WOULD BE FILLED WITH FAMILIAR FACES?
TURNS OUT THAT IT'S THE B-PARTY OF A CLASSMATE, YOU KNOW?
STILL, I NEED THE MONEY, SO I'M STAYING HERE IN THE BACK WITH THE BOXES.
OTHERWISE, I'D HAVE TO GO OUT THERE AND SERVE THEM...
SIGH...AND NOW, SOME OLD BALDY IS HITTING ON ME...
STARTLE
DAMN, WHAT'S THIS WATER IN MY EYE?

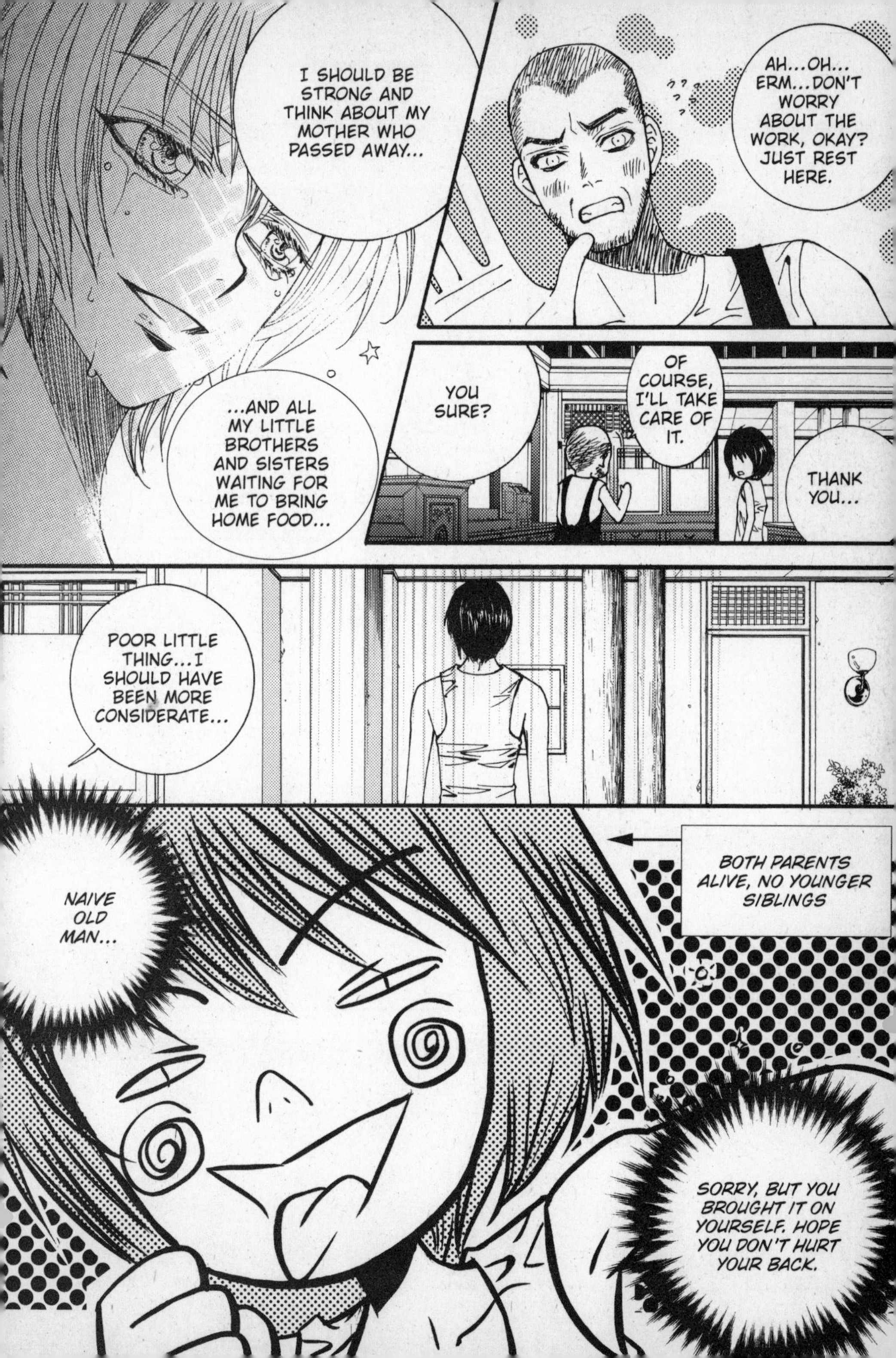
I SHOULD BE STRONG AND THINK ABOUT MY MOTHER WHO PASSED AWAY...
...AND ALL MY LITTLE BROTHERS AND SISTERS WAITING FOR ME TO BRING HOME FOOD...
AH...OH... ERM...DON'T WORRY ABOUT THE WORK, OKAY? JUST REST HERE.
YOU SURE?
OF COURSE, I'LL TAKE CARE OF IT.
THANK YOU...
POOR LITTLE THING...I SHOULD HAVE BEEN MORE CONSIDERATE...
NAIVE OLD MAN...
BOTH PARENTS ALIVE, NO YOUNGER SIBLINGS
SORRY, BUT YOU BROUGHT IT ON YOURSELF. HOPE YOU DON'T HURT YOUR BACK.

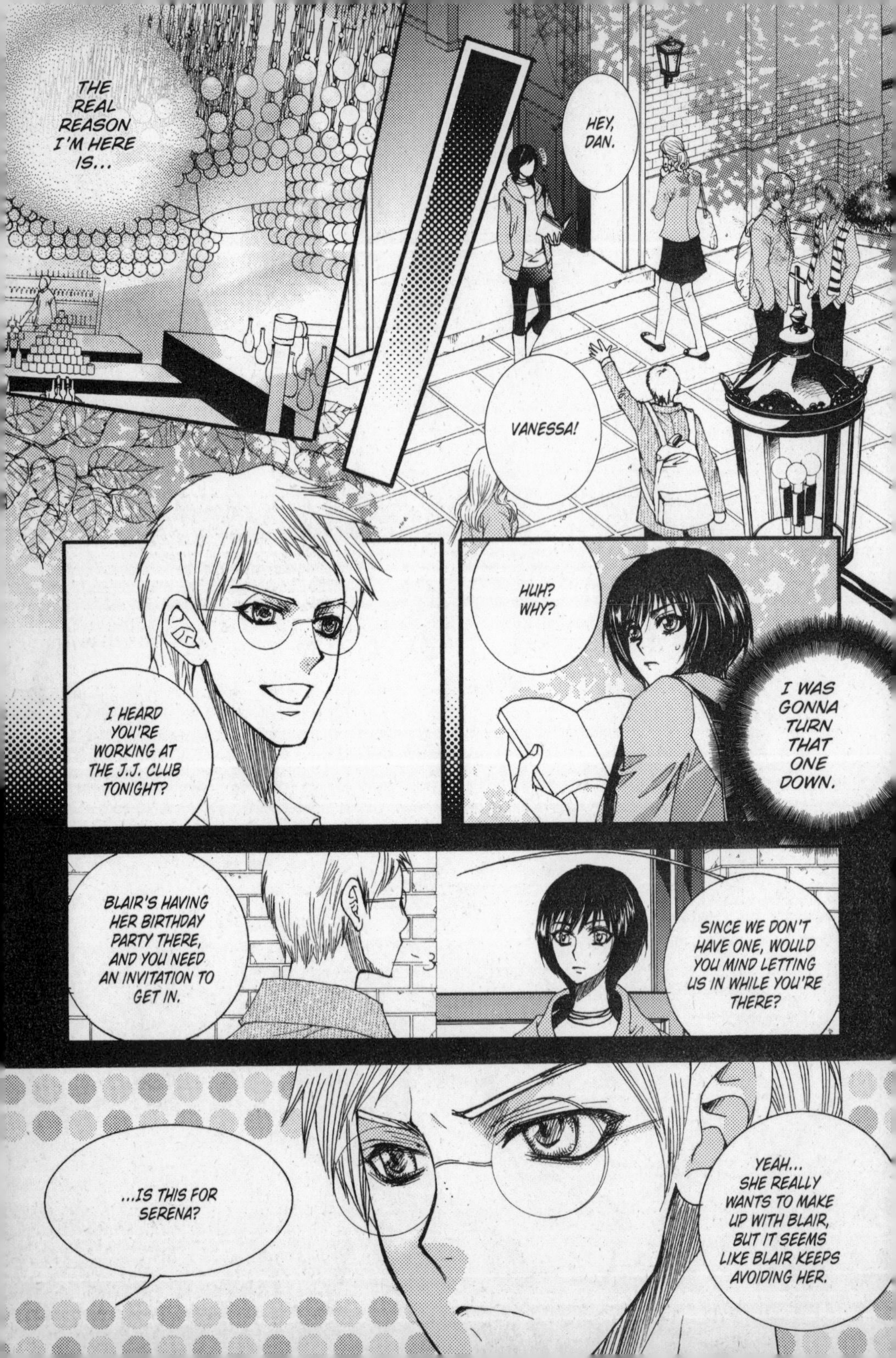
THE REAL REASON I'M HERE IS...
HEY, DAN.
VANESSA!
I HEARD YOU'RE WORKING AT THE J.J. CLUB TONIGHT?
HUH? WHY?
I WAS GONNA TURN THAT ONE DOWN.
BLAIR'S HAVING HER BIRTHDAY PARTY THERE, AND YOU NEED AN INVITATION TO GET IN.
SINCE WE DON'T HAVE ONE, WOULD YOU MIND LETTING US IN WHILE YOU'RE THERE?
...IS THIS FOR SERENA?
YEAH... SHE REALLY WANTS TO MAKE UP WITH BLAIR, BUT IT SEEMS LIKE BLAIR KEEPS AVOIDING HER.

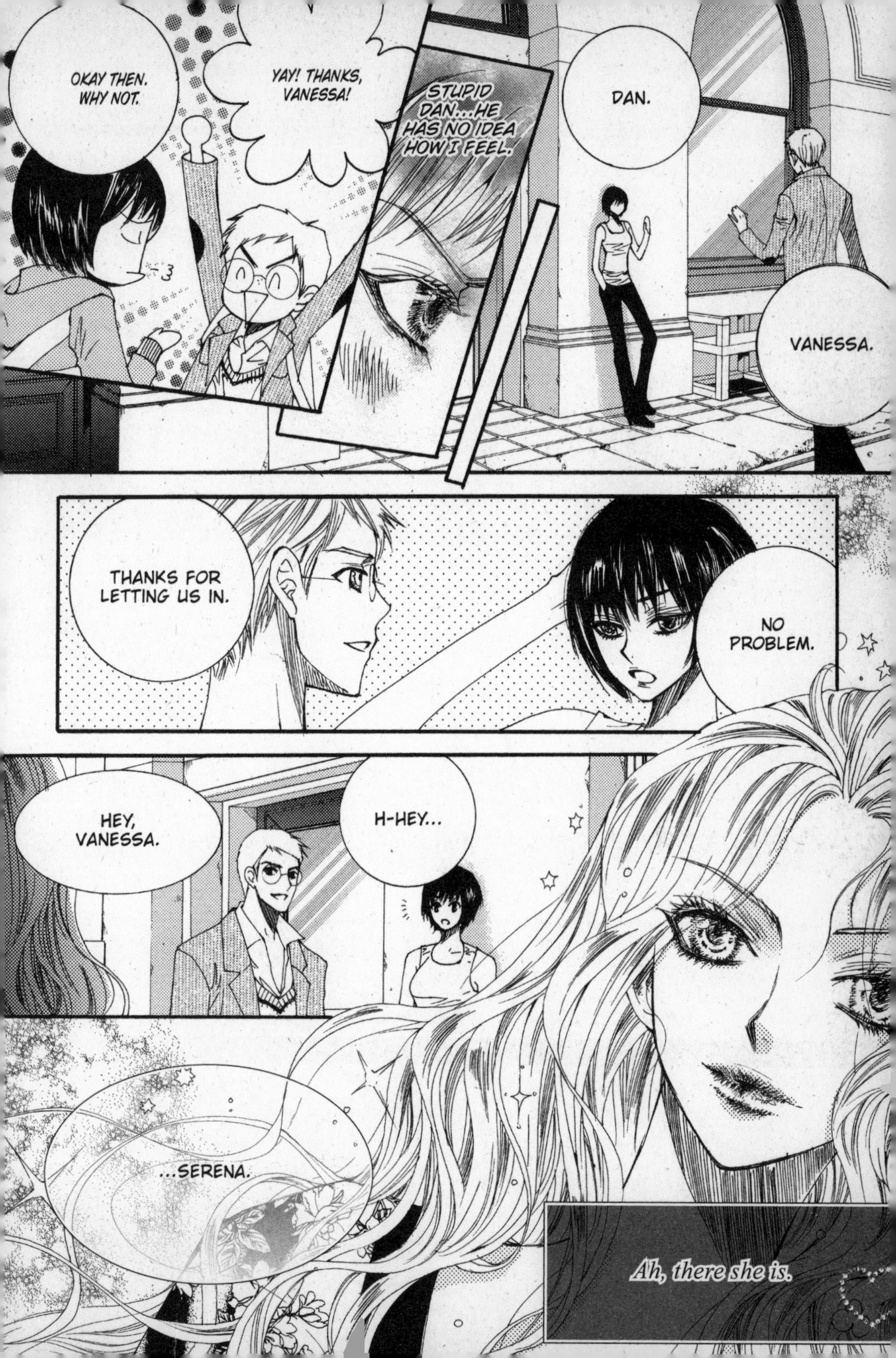

OKAY THEN. WHY NOT.
YAY! THANKS, VANESSA!
STUPID DAN...HE HAS NO IDEA HOW I FEEL.
DAN.
VANESSA.
THANKS FOR LETTING US IN.
NO PROBLEM.
HEY, VANESSA.
H-HEY...
...SERENA.
Ah, there she is.

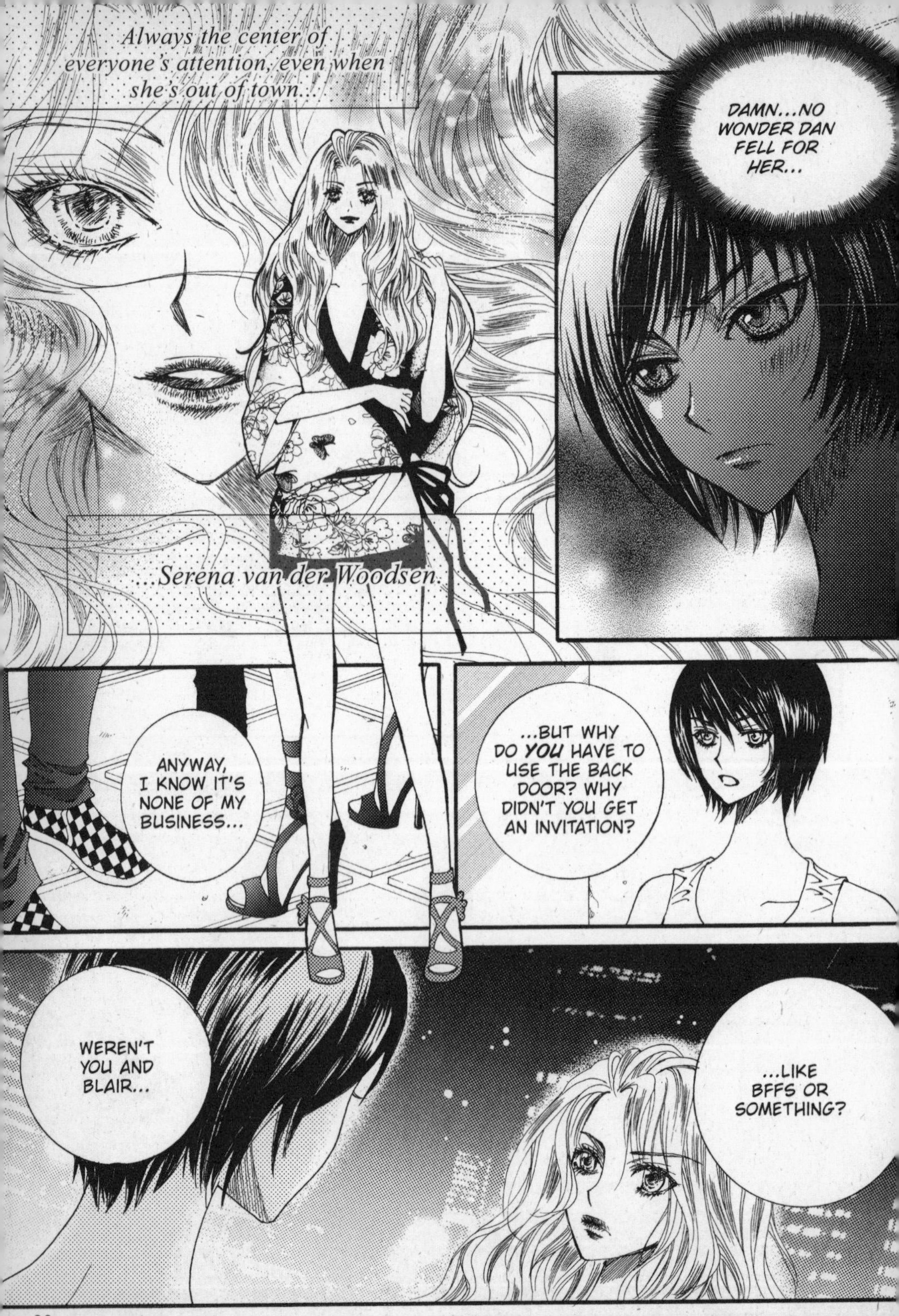
Always the center of everyone's attention, even when she's out of town...
...Serena van der Woodsen.
DAMN...NO WONDER DAN FELL FOR HER...
ANYWAY, I KNOW IT'S NONE OF MY BUSINESS...
...BUT WHY DO *YOU* HAVE TO USE THE BACK DOOR? WHY DIDN'T YOU GET AN INVITATION?
WEREN'T YOU AND BLAIR...
...LIKE BFFS OR SOMETHING?

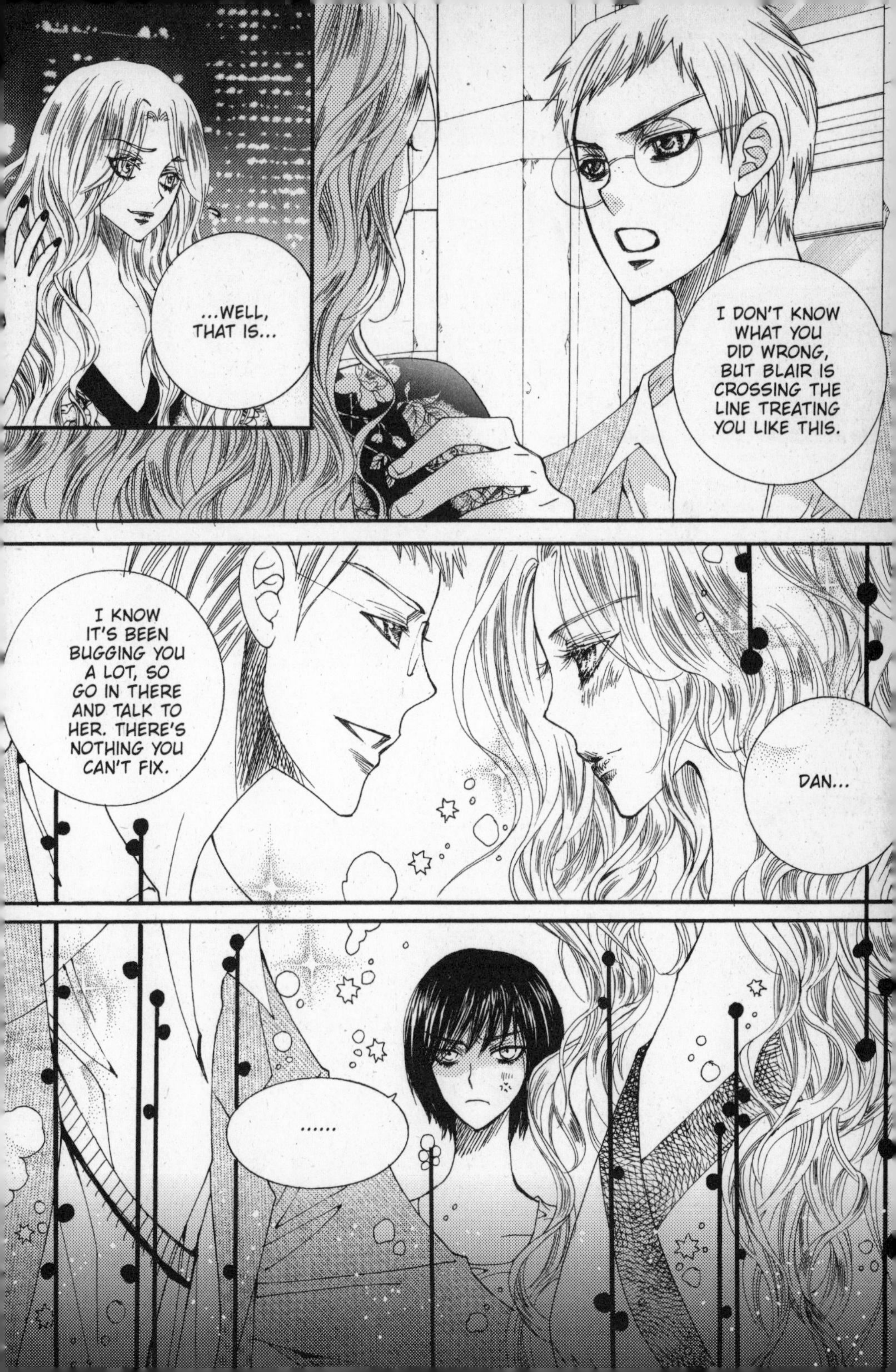
...WELL, THAT IS...
I DON'T KNOW WHAT YOU DID WRONG, BUT BLAIR IS CROSSING THE LINE TREATING YOU LIKE THIS.
I KNOW IT'S BEEN BUGGING YOU A LOT, SO GO IN THERE AND TALK TO HER. THERE'S NOTHING YOU CAN'T FIX.
DAN...
......

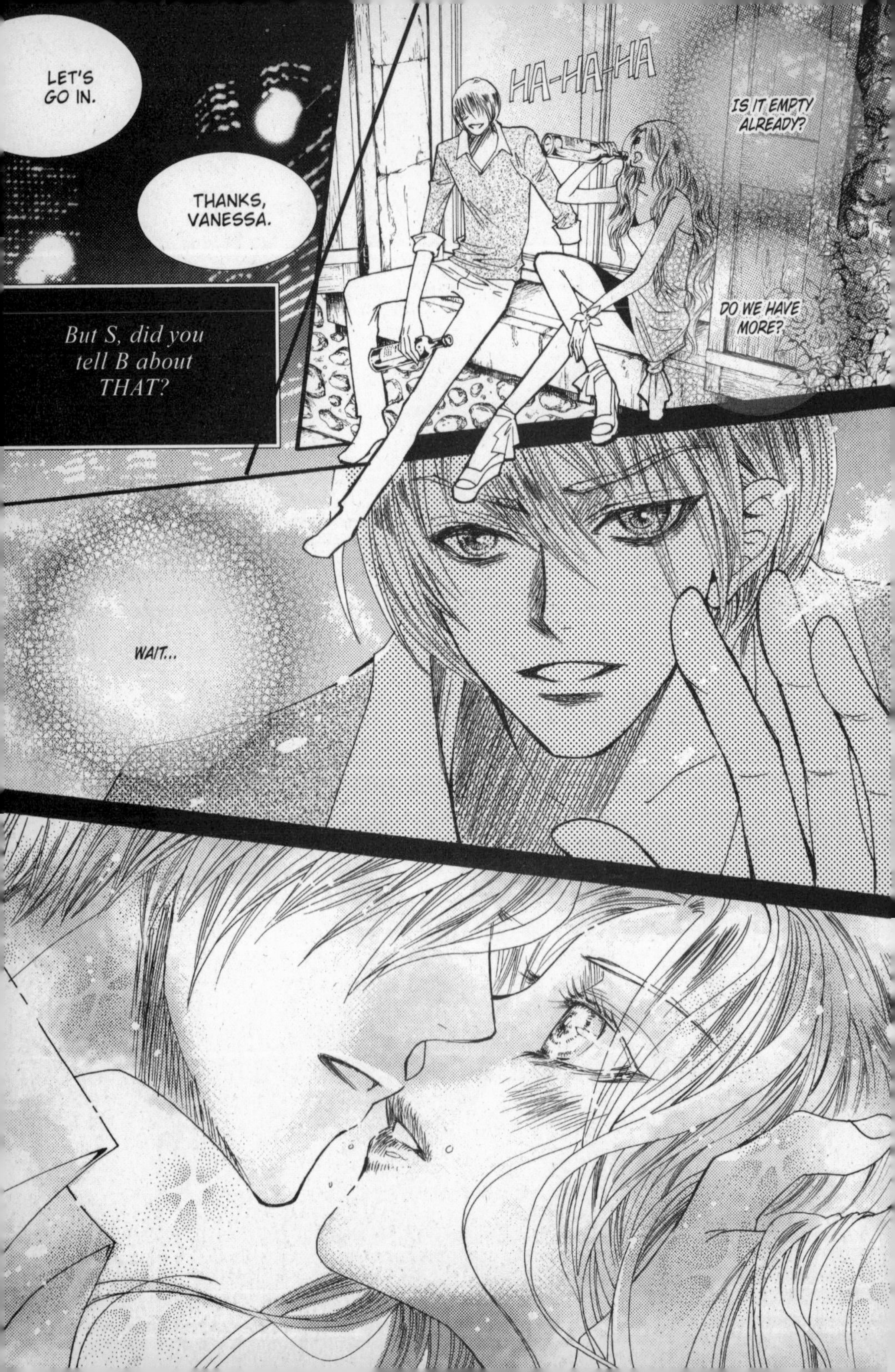

LET'S GO IN.
THANKS, VANESSA.
But S, did you tell B about THAT?
HA-HA-HA
IS IT EMPTY ALREADY?
DO WE HAVE MORE?
WAIT...

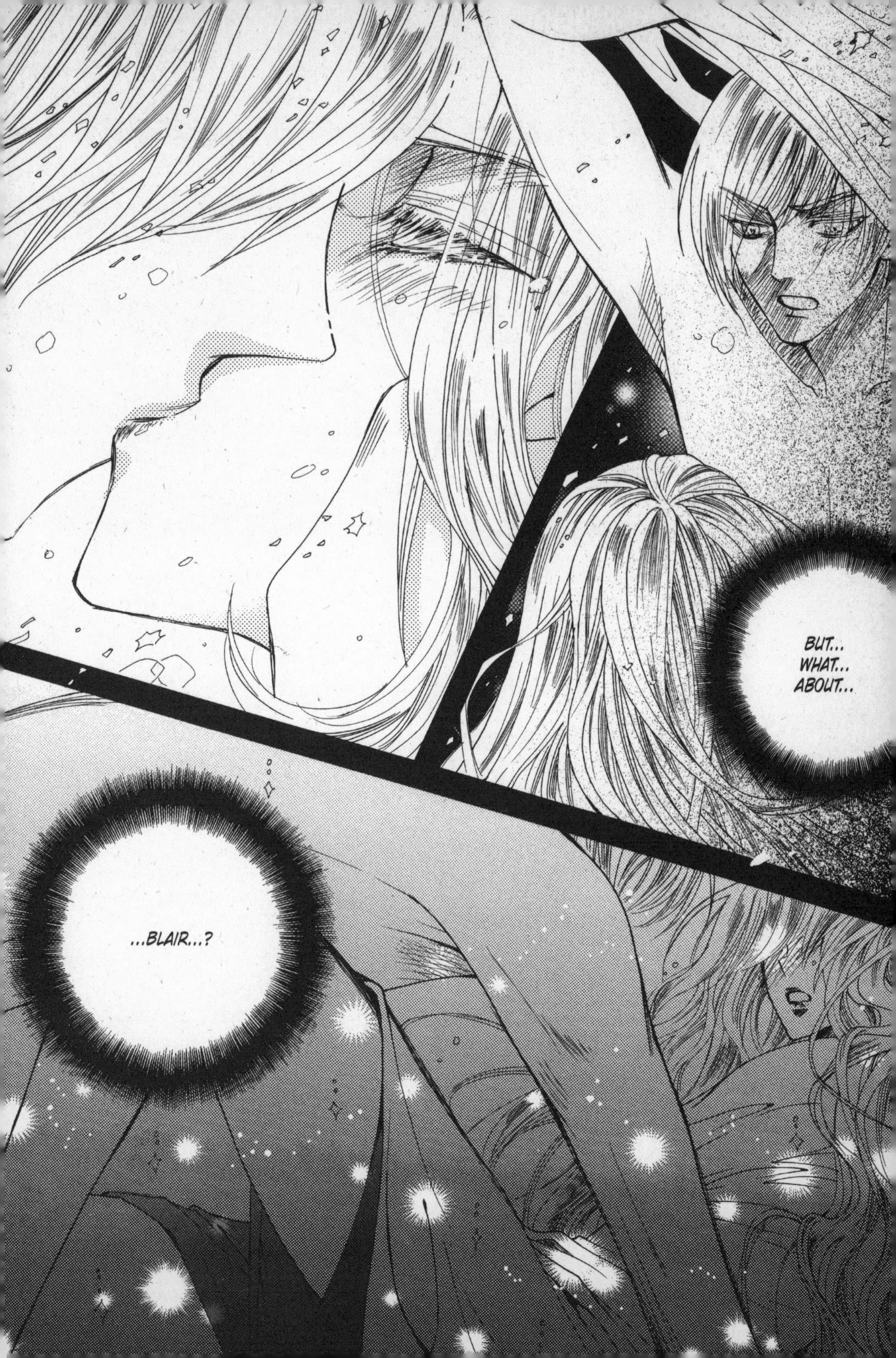
BUT... WHAT... ABOUT...
...BLAIR...?

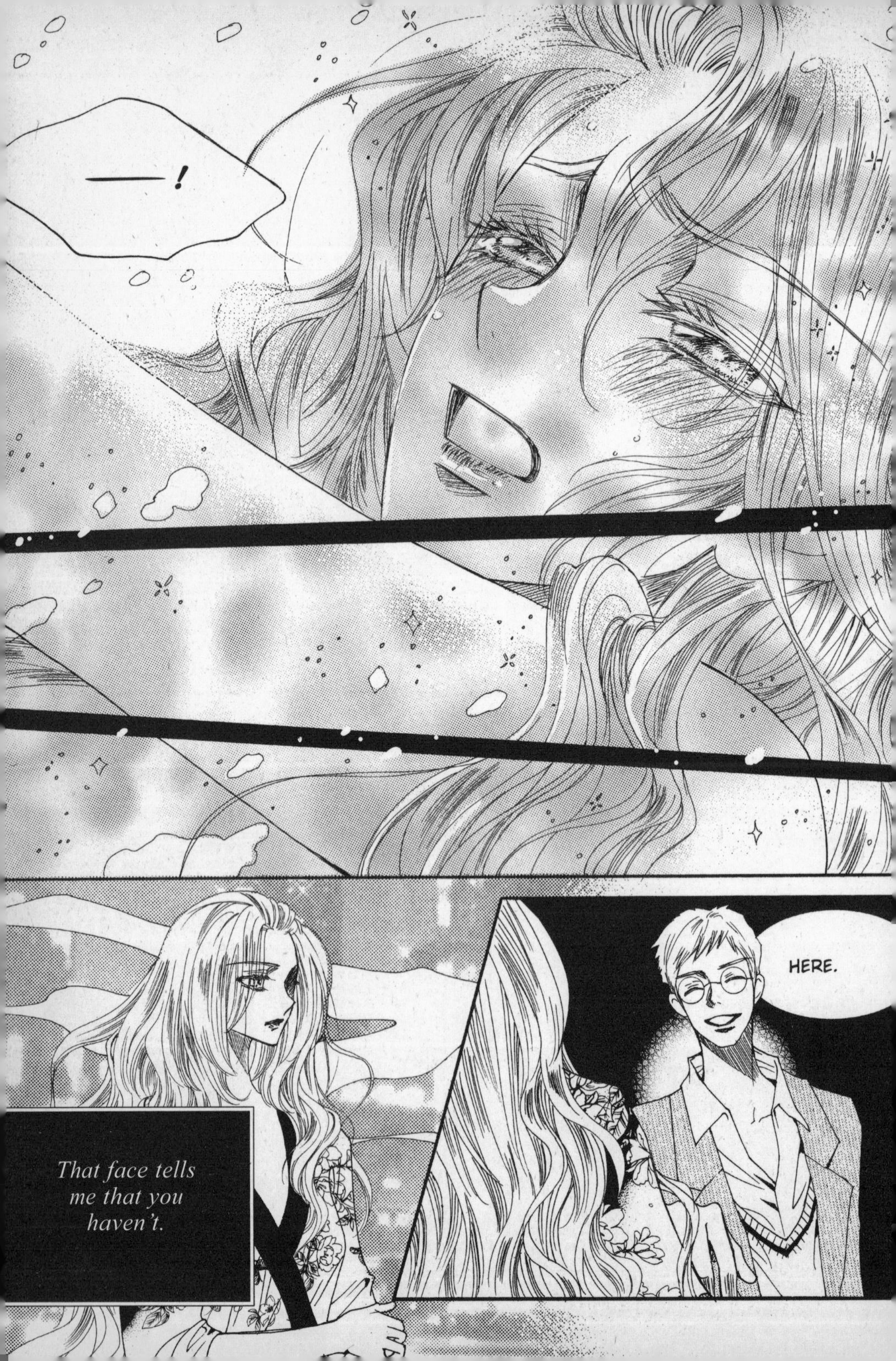
—!
That face tells me that you haven't.
HERE.

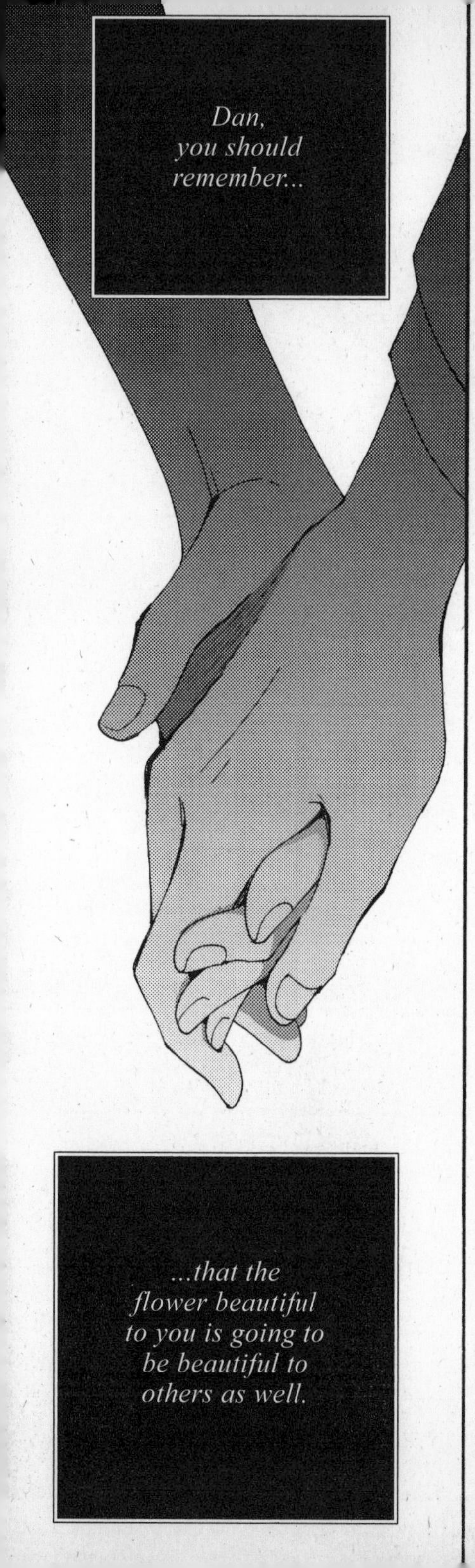
Dan, you should remember...
...that the flower beautiful to you is going to be beautiful to others as well.

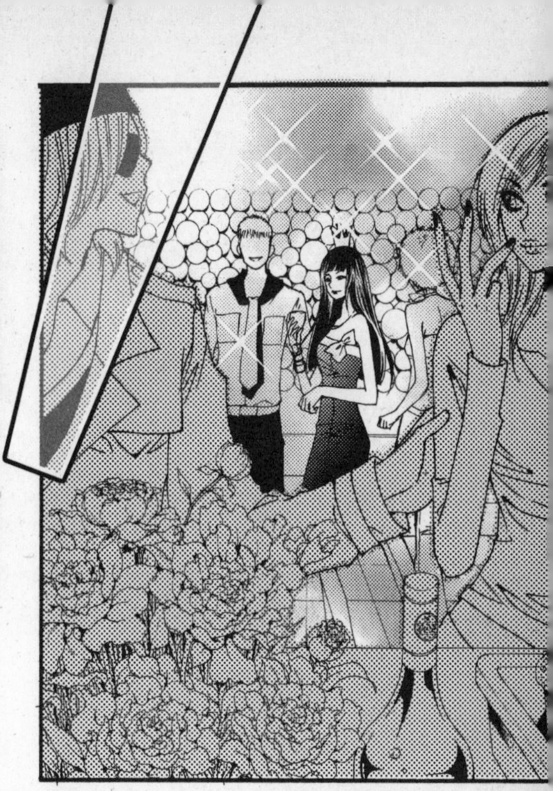

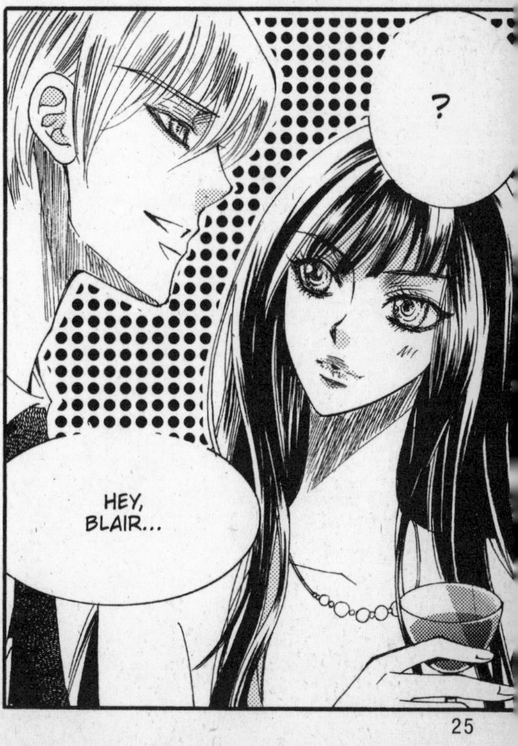
?
HEY, BLAIR...

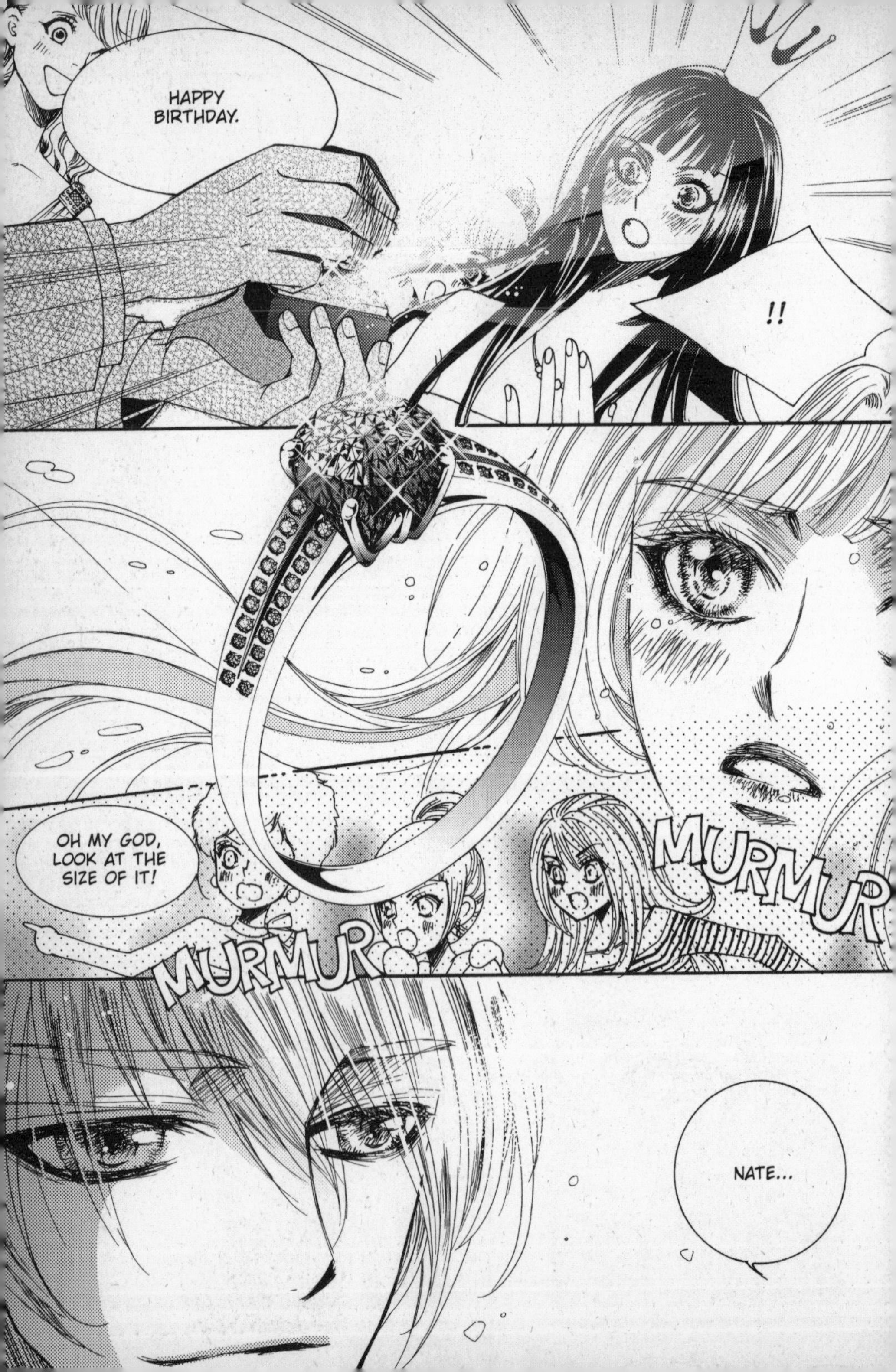
HAPPY BIRTHDAY.
!!
OH MY GOD, LOOK AT THE SIZE OF IT!
MURMUR
MURMUR
NATE...

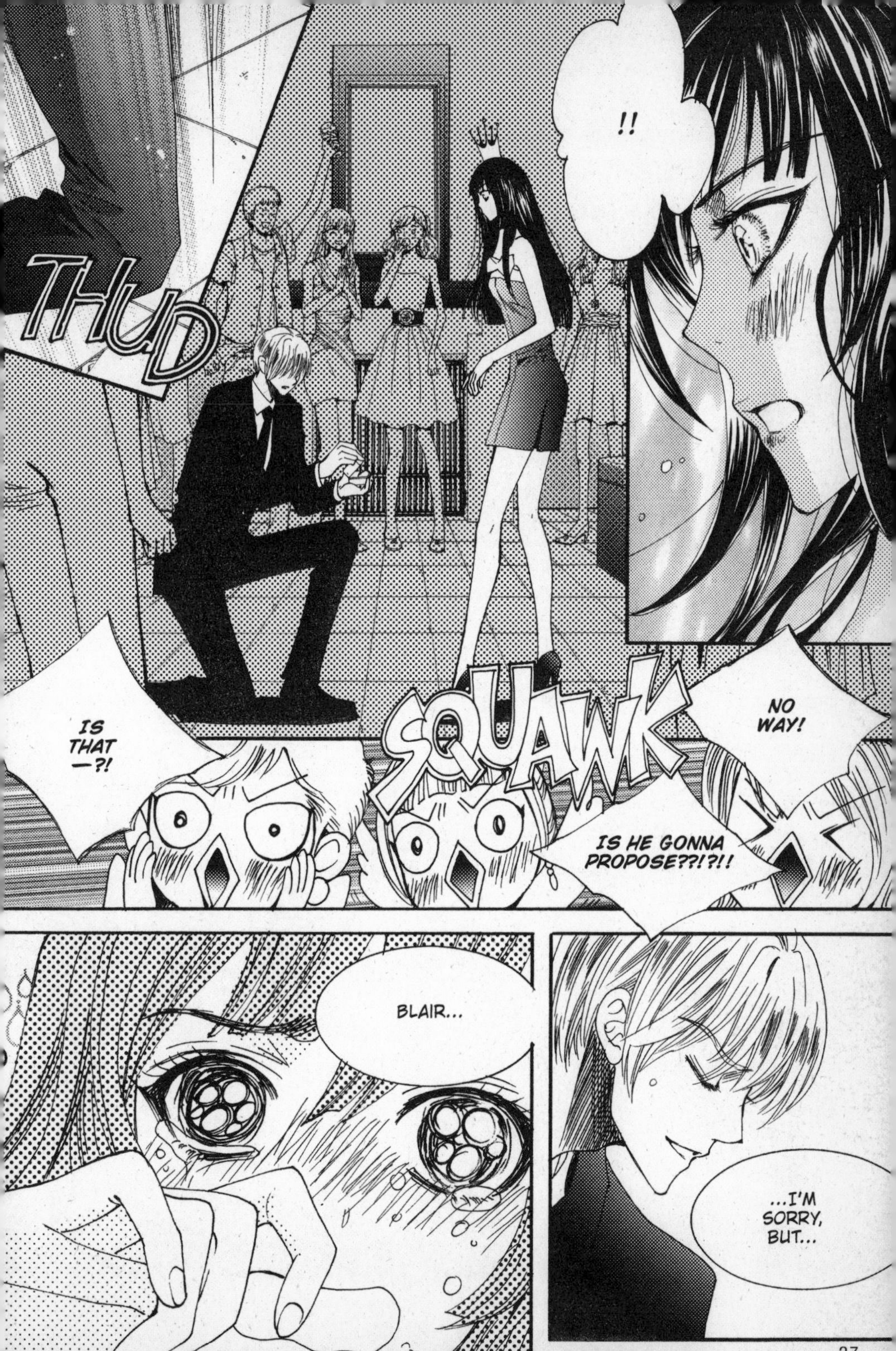
THUD
!!
IS THAT—?!
SQUAWK
NO WAY!
IS HE GONNA PROPOSE??!?!!
BLAIR...
...I'M SORRY, BUT...

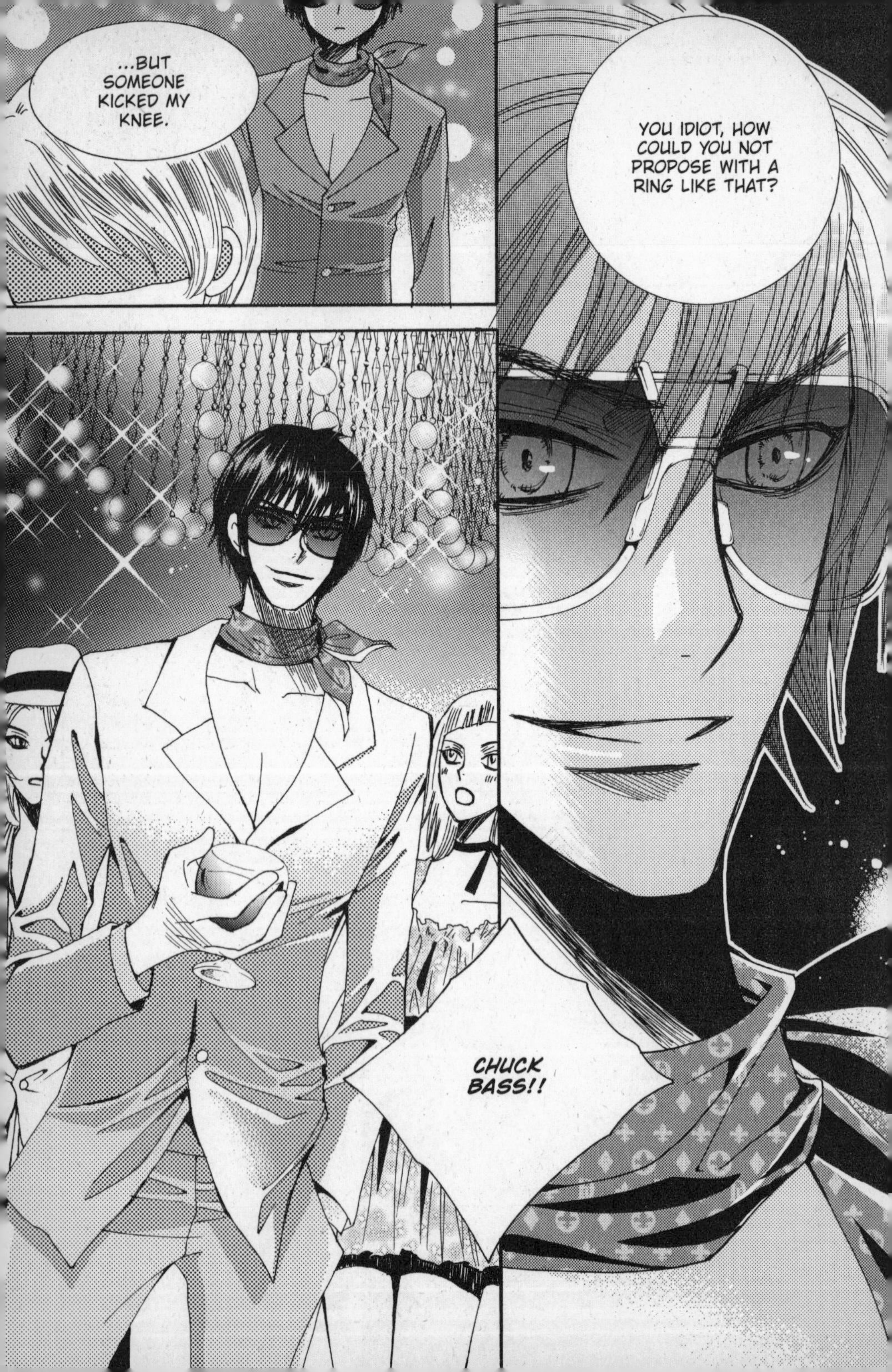
...BUT SOMEONE KICKED MY KNEE.
CHUCK BASS!!
YOU IDIOT, HOW COULD YOU NOT PROPOSE WITH A RING LIKE THAT?

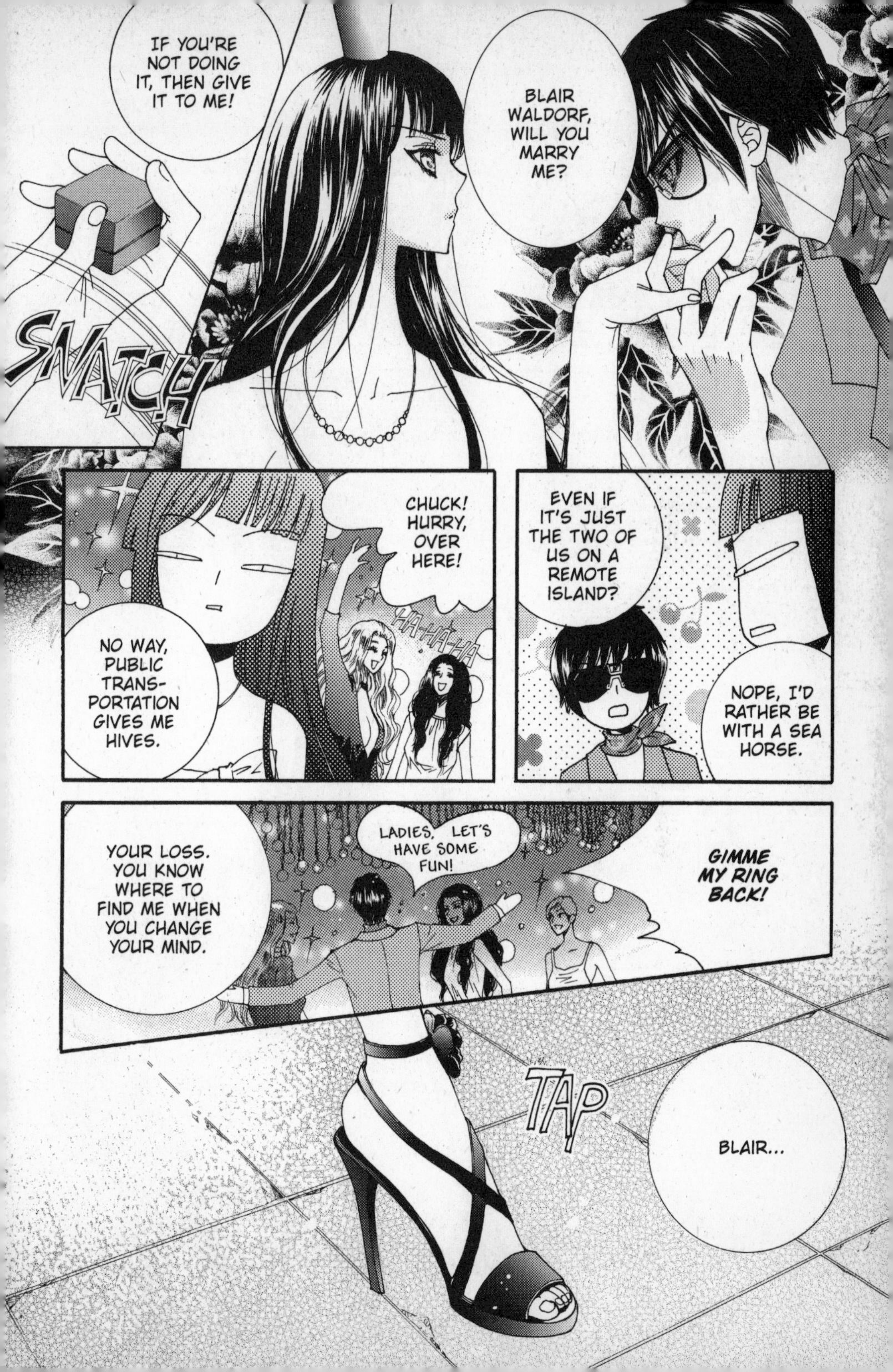
IF YOU'RE NOT DOING IT, THEN GIVE IT TO ME!
BLAIR WALDORF, WILL YOU MARRY ME?
SNATCH
CHUCK! HURRY, OVER HERE!
HA-HA-HA
NO WAY, PUBLIC TRANS-PORTATION GIVES ME HIVES.
EVEN IF IT'S JUST THE TWO OF US ON A REMOTE ISLAND?
NOPE, I'D RATHER BE WITH A SEA HORSE.
YOUR LOSS. YOU KNOW WHERE TO FIND ME WHEN YOU CHANGE YOUR MIND.
LADIES, LET'S HAVE SOME FUN!
GIMME MY RING BACK!
TAP
BLAIR...

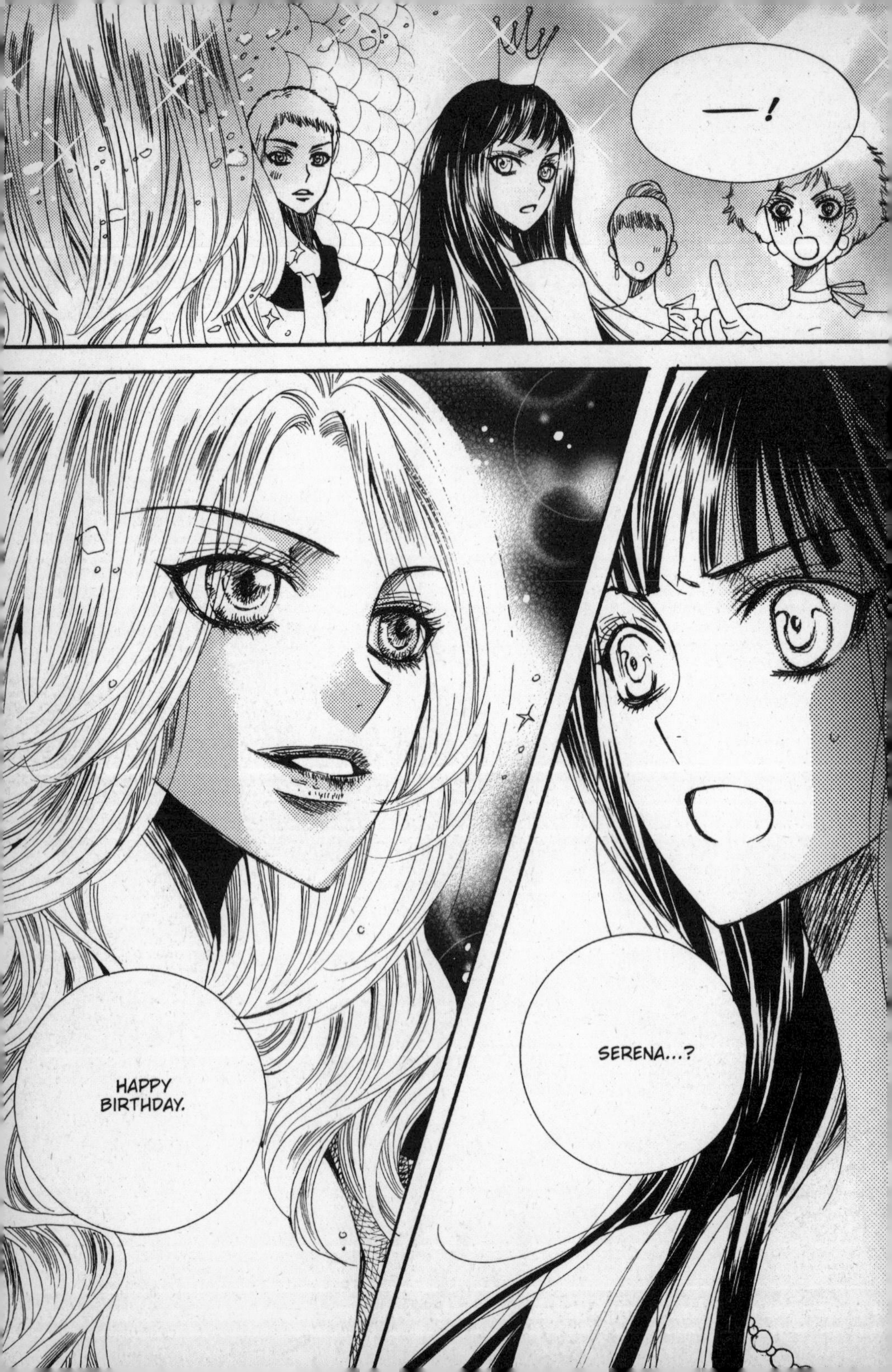
—!
HAPPY BIRTHDAY.
SERENA...?

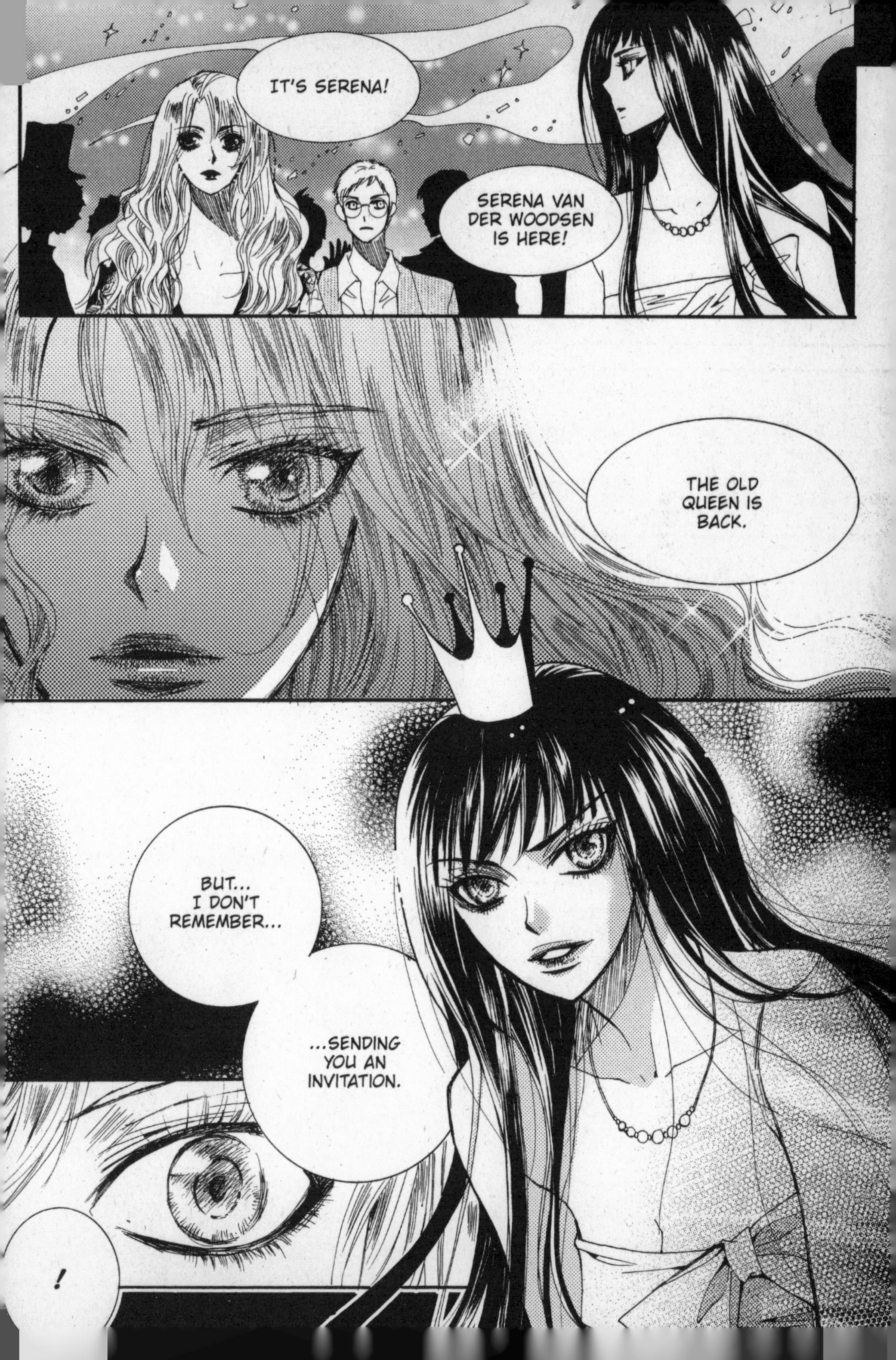
IT'S SERENA!
SERENA VAN DER WOODSEN IS HERE!
THE OLD QUEEN IS BACK.
BUT... I DON'T REMEMBER...
...SENDING YOU AN INVITATION.
!

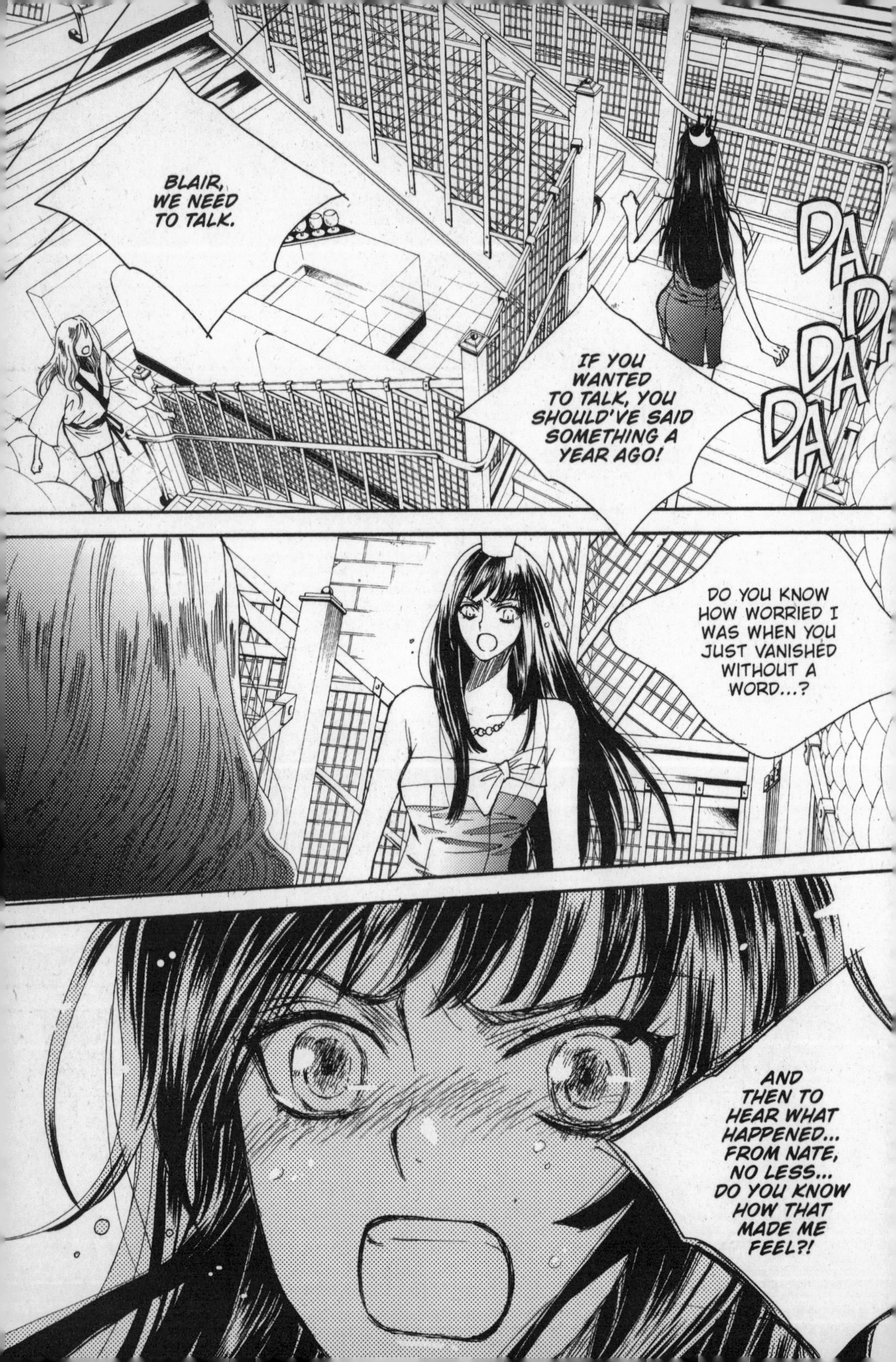
BLAIR, WE NEED TO TALK.
IF YOU WANTED TO TALK, YOU SHOULD'VE SAID SOMETHING A YEAR AGO!
DA DA DA DA
DO YOU KNOW HOW WORRIED I WAS WHEN YOU JUST VANISHED WITHOUT A WORD...?
AND THEN TO HEAR WHAT HAPPENED... FROM NATE, NO LESS... DO YOU KNOW HOW THAT MADE ME FEEL?!

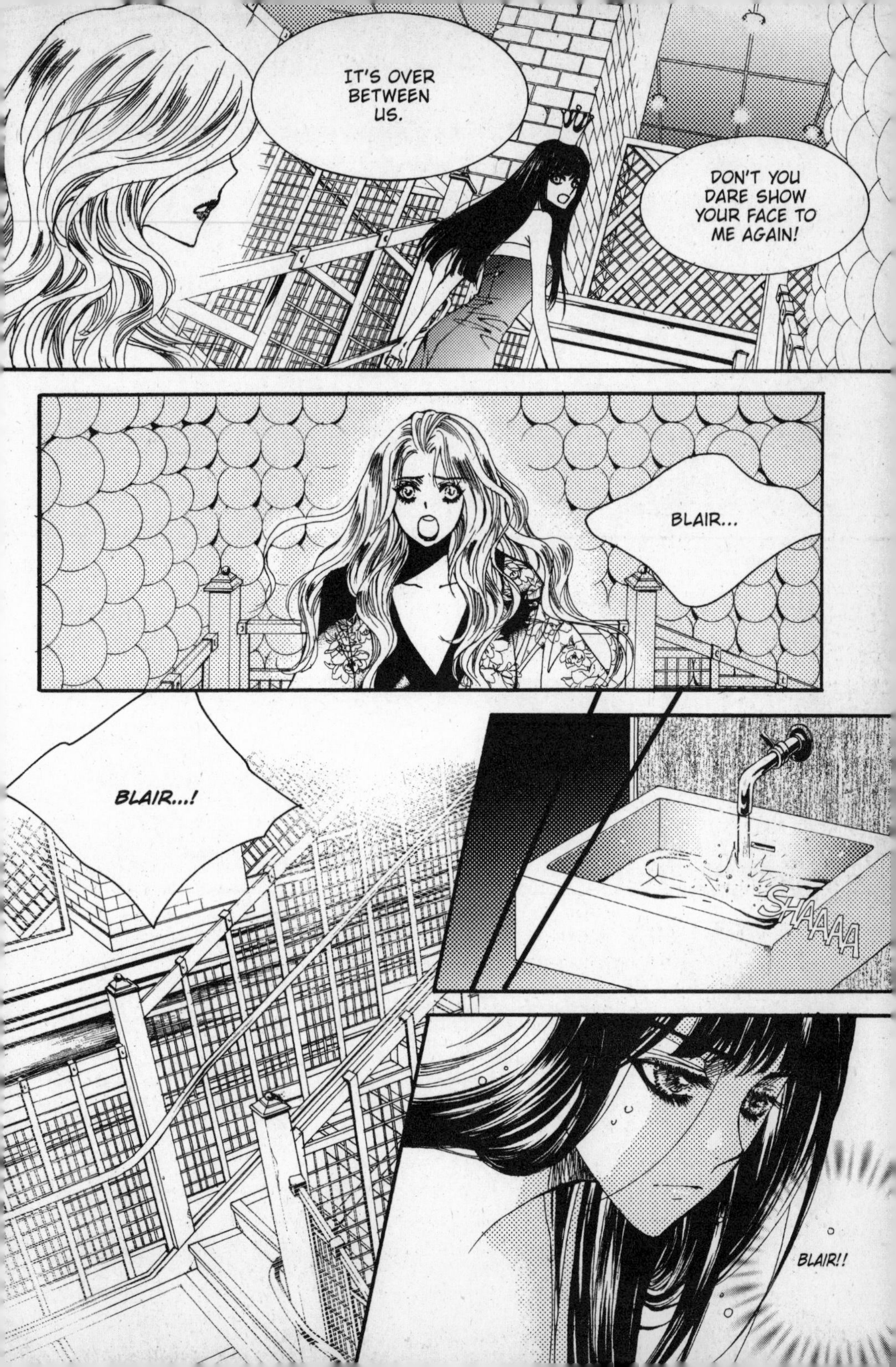
IT'S OVER BETWEEN US.
DON'T YOU DARE SHOW YOUR FACE TO ME AGAIN!
BLAIR...
BLAIR...!
SHAAAAA
BLAIR!!

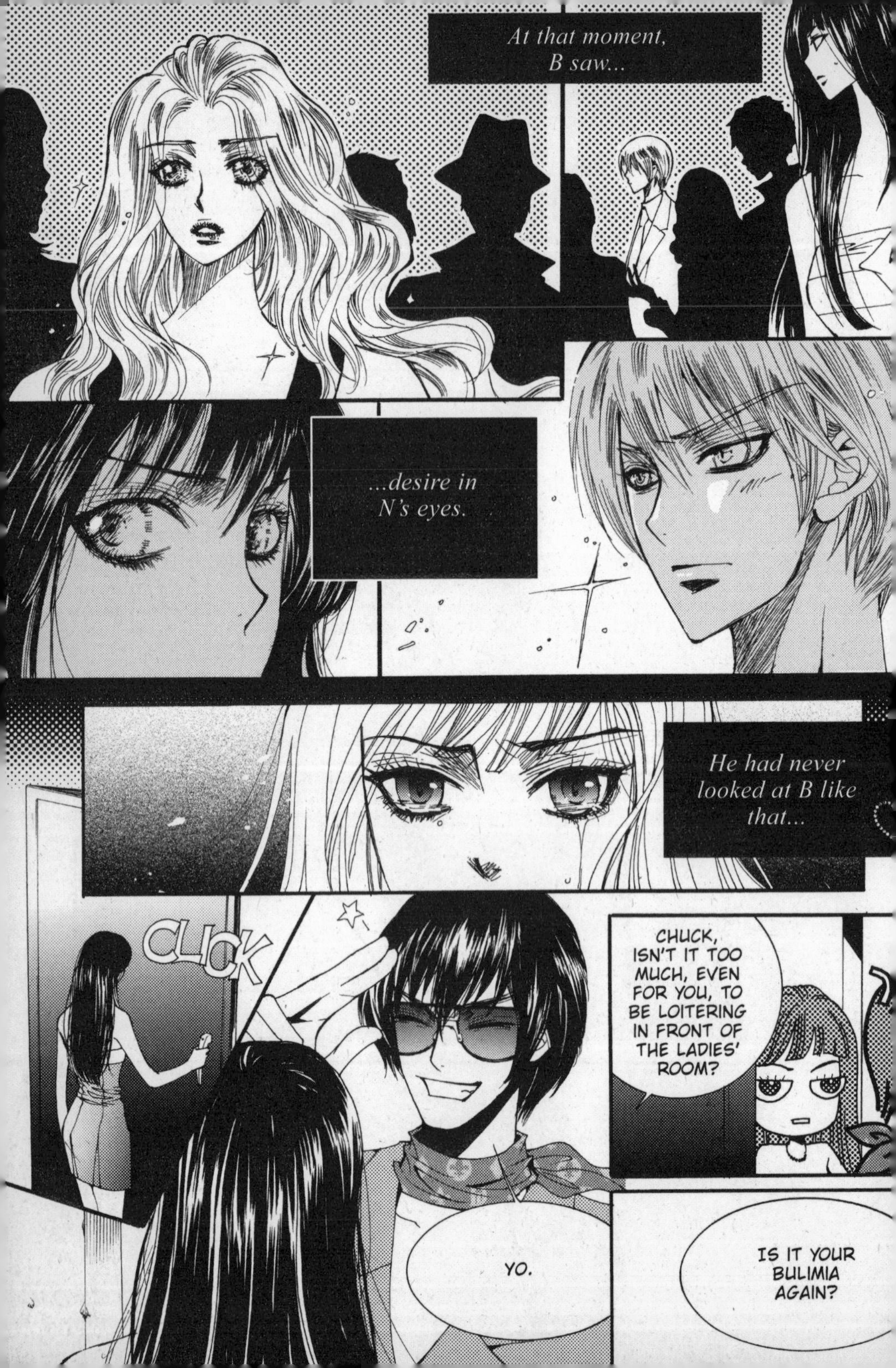
At that moment, B saw...
...desire in N's eyes.
He had never looked at B like that...
CLICK
YO.
CHUCK, ISN'T IT TOO MUCH, EVEN FOR YOU, TO BE LOITERING IN FRONT OF THE LADIES' ROOM?
IS IT YOUR BULIMIA AGAIN?

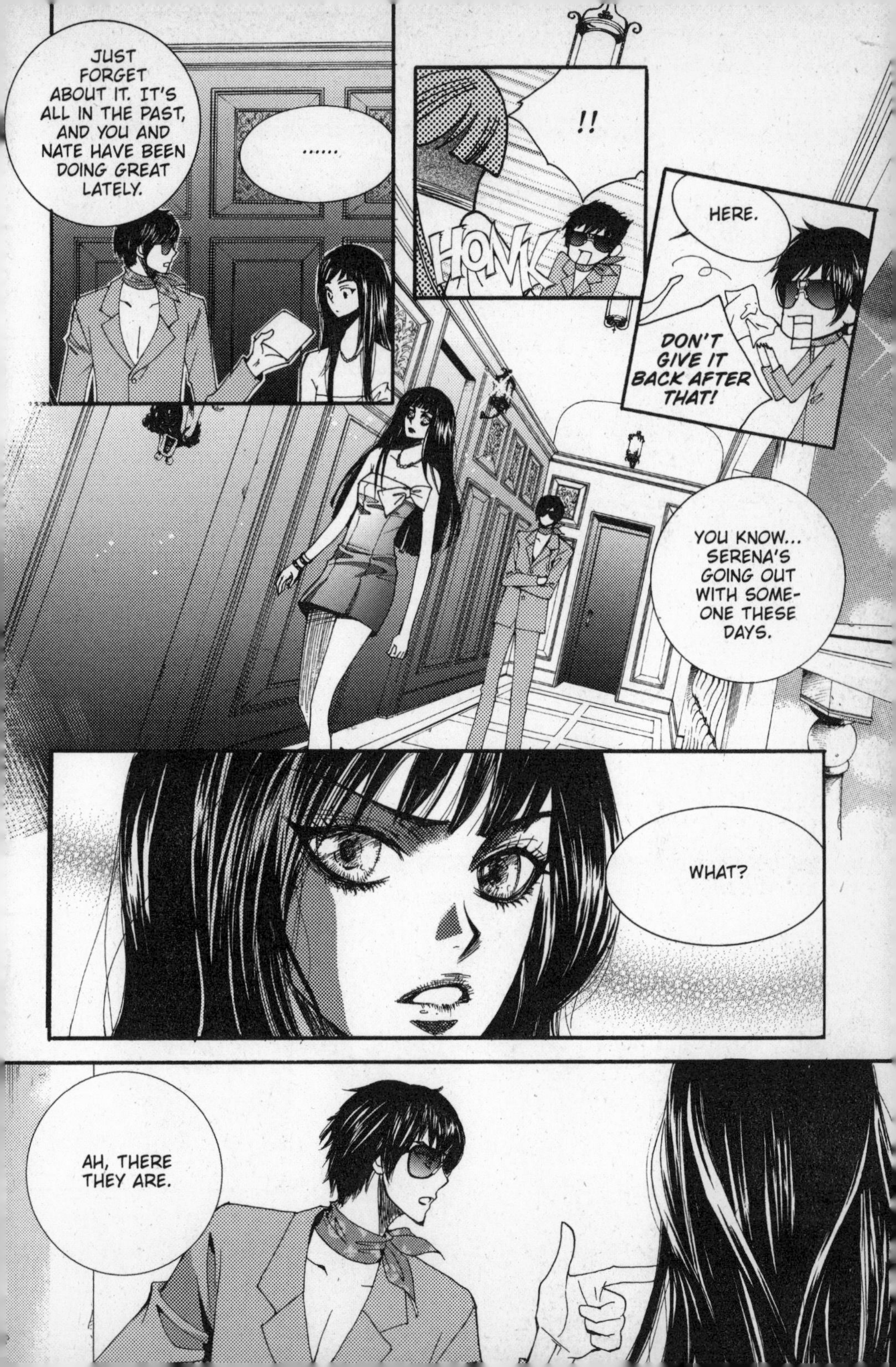
JUST FORGET ABOUT IT. IT'S ALL IN THE PAST, AND YOU AND NATE HAVE BEEN DOING GREAT LATELY.
......
!!
HONK
HERE.
DON'T GIVE IT BACK AFTER THAT!
YOU KNOW... SERENA'S GOING OUT WITH SOME-ONE THESE DAYS.
WHAT?
AH, THERE THEY ARE.

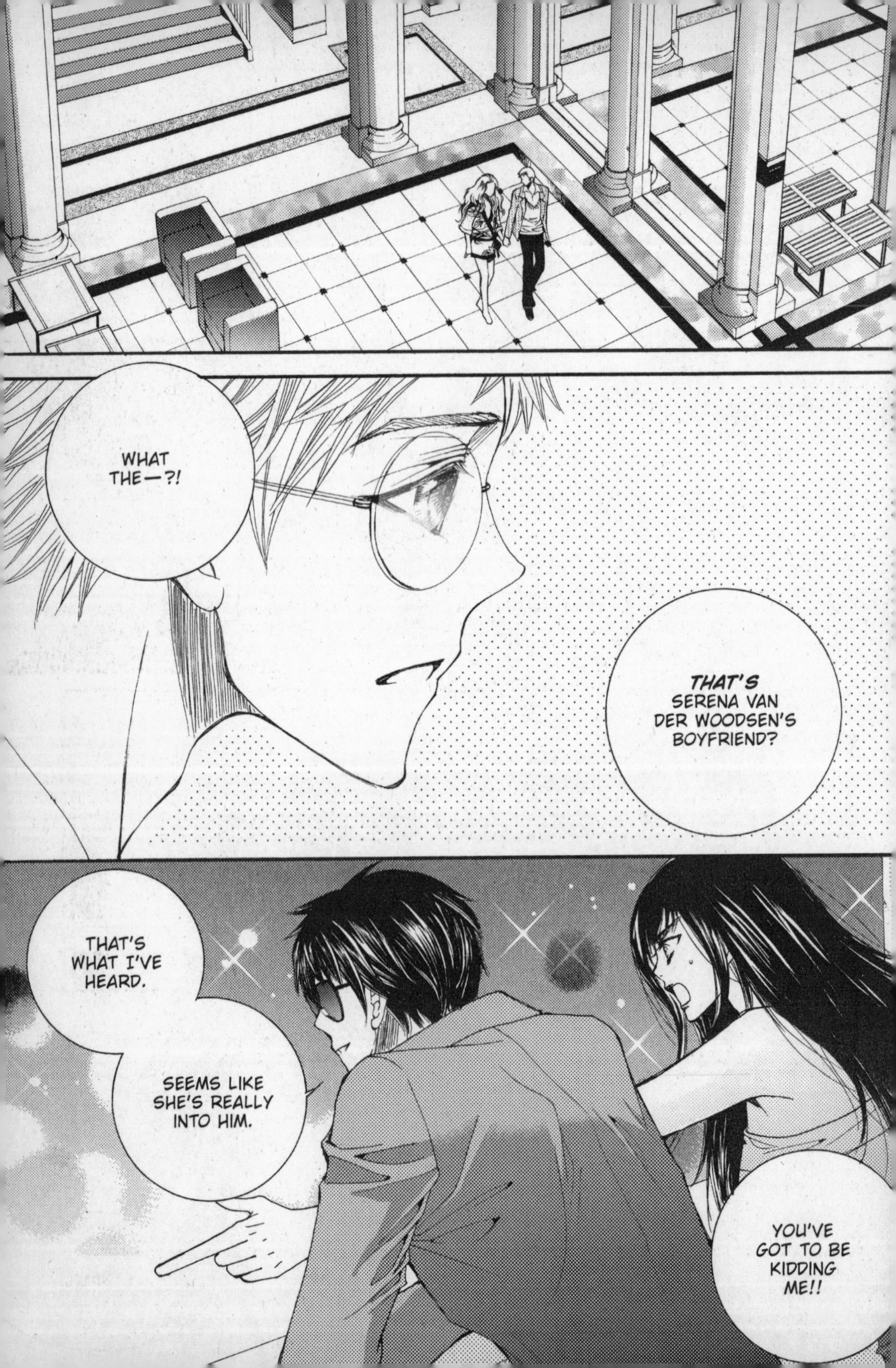
WHAT THE—?!
THAT'S SERENA VAN DER WOODSEN'S BOYFRIEND?
THAT'S WHAT I'VE HEARD.
SEEMS LIKE SHE'S REALLY INTO HIM.
YOU'VE GOT TO BE KIDDING ME!!

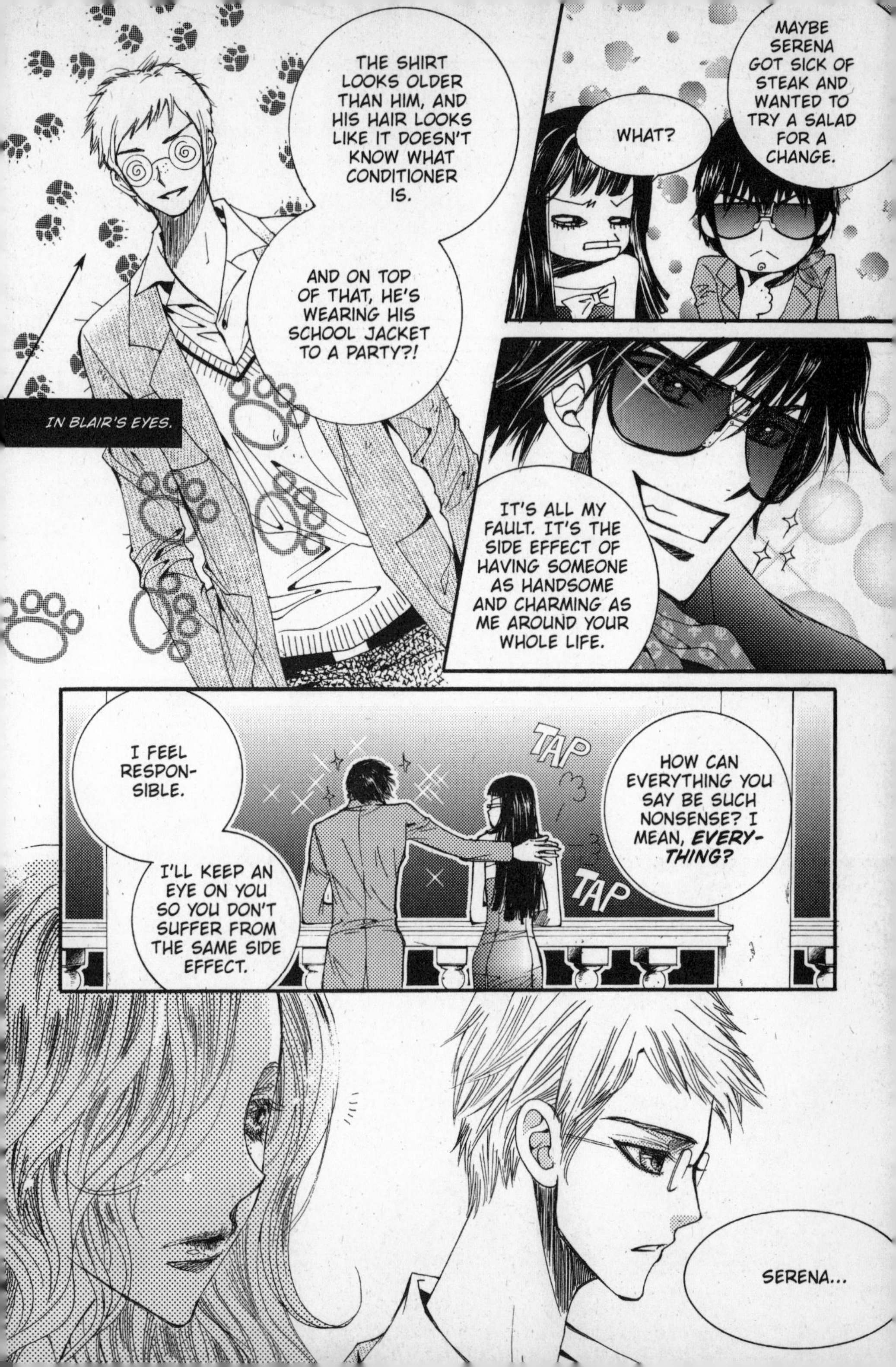
THE SHIRT LOOKS OLDER THAN HIM, AND HIS HAIR LOOKS LIKE IT DOESN'T KNOW WHAT CONDITIONER IS.
AND ON TOP OF THAT, HE'S WEARING HIS SCHOOL JACKET TO A PARTY?!
IN BLAIR'S EYES.
WHAT?
MAYBE SERENA GOT SICK OF STEAK AND WANTED TO TRY A SALAD FOR A CHANGE.
IT'S ALL MY FAULT. IT'S THE SIDE EFFECT OF HAVING SOMEONE AS HANDSOME AND CHARMING AS ME AROUND YOUR WHOLE LIFE.
I FEEL RESPONSIBLE.
I'LL KEEP AN EYE ON YOU SO YOU DON'T SUFFER FROM THE SAME SIDE EFFECT.
TAP
TAP
HOW CAN EVERYTHING YOU SAY BE SUCH NONSENSE? I MEAN, EVERYTHING?
SERENA...

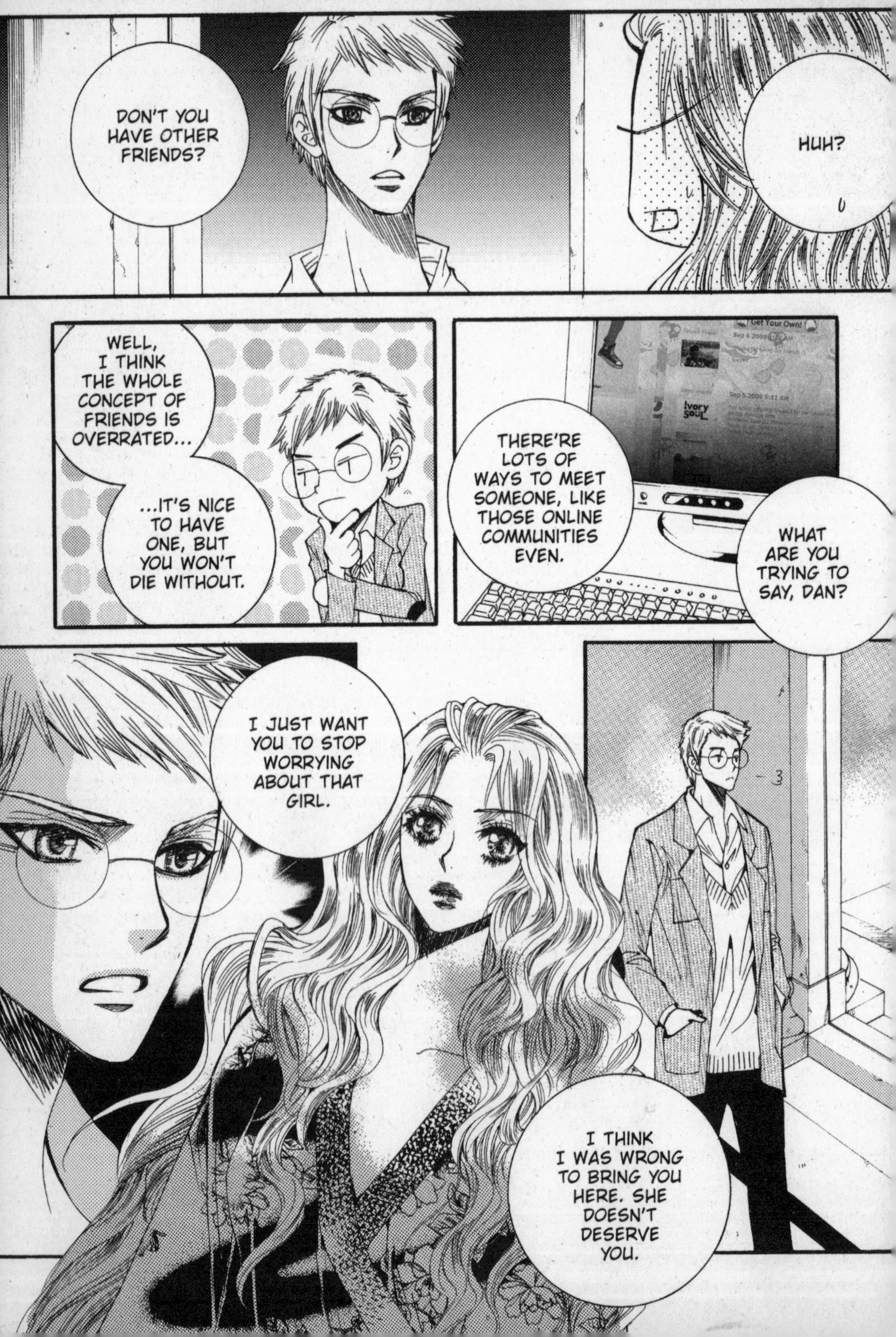
DON'T YOU HAVE OTHER FRIENDS?
HUH?
WELL, I THINK THE WHOLE CONCEPT OF FRIENDS IS OVERRATED...
...IT'S NICE TO HAVE ONE, BUT YOU WON'T DIE WITHOUT.
Get Your Own!
Ivory Soul
THERE'RE LOTS OF WAYS TO MEET SOMEONE, LIKE THOSE ONLINE COMMUNITIES EVEN.
WHAT ARE YOU TRYING TO SAY, DAN?
I JUST WANT YOU TO STOP WORRYING ABOUT THAT GIRL.
I THINK I WAS WRONG TO BRING YOU HERE. SHE DOESN'T DESERVE YOU.

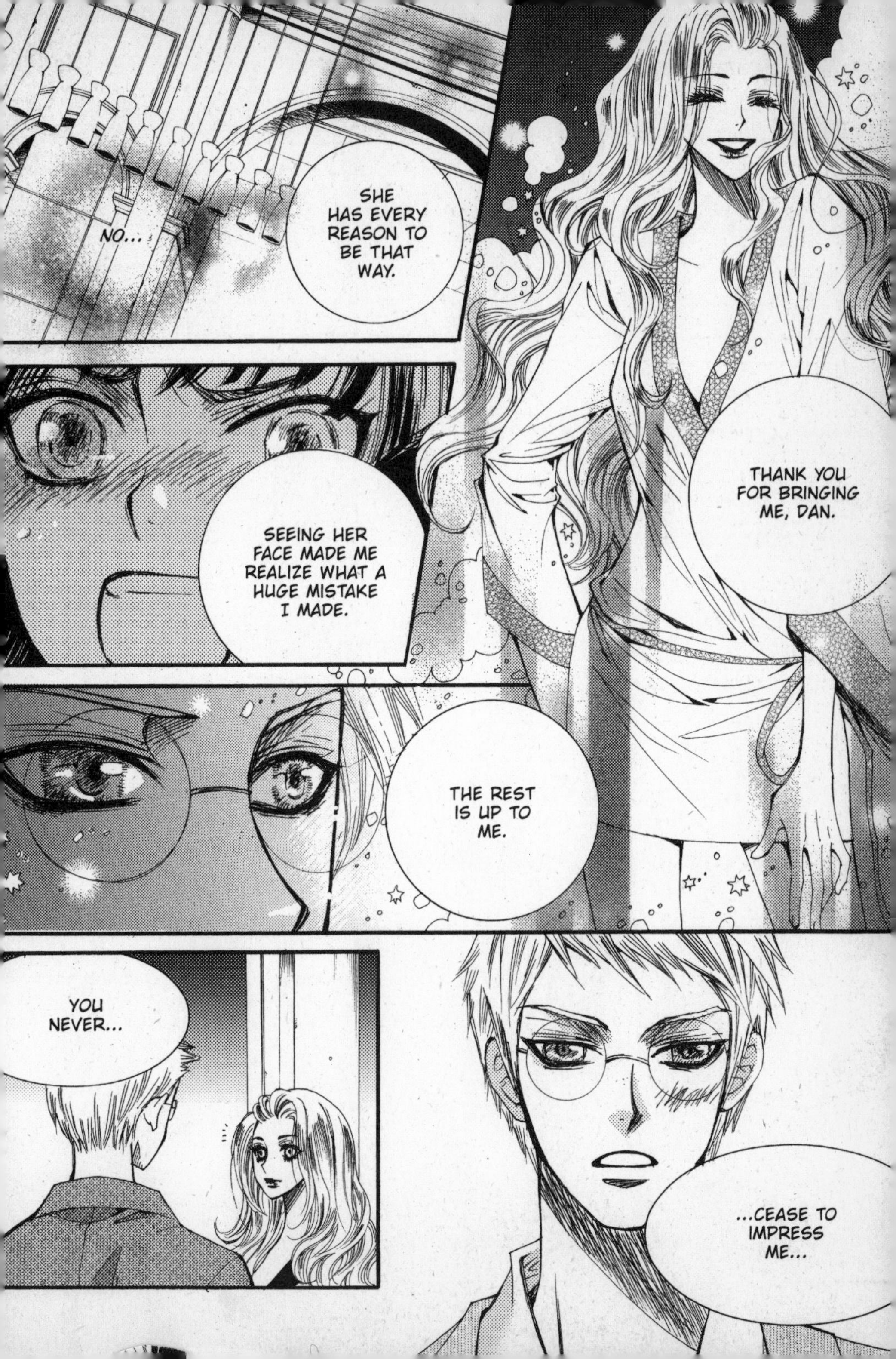
NO...
SHE HAS EVERY REASON TO BE THAT WAY.
SEEING HER FACE MADE ME REALIZE WHAT A HUGE MISTAKE I MADE.
THE REST IS UP TO ME.
THANK YOU FOR BRINGING ME, DAN.
YOU NEVER...
...CEASE TO IMPRESS ME...

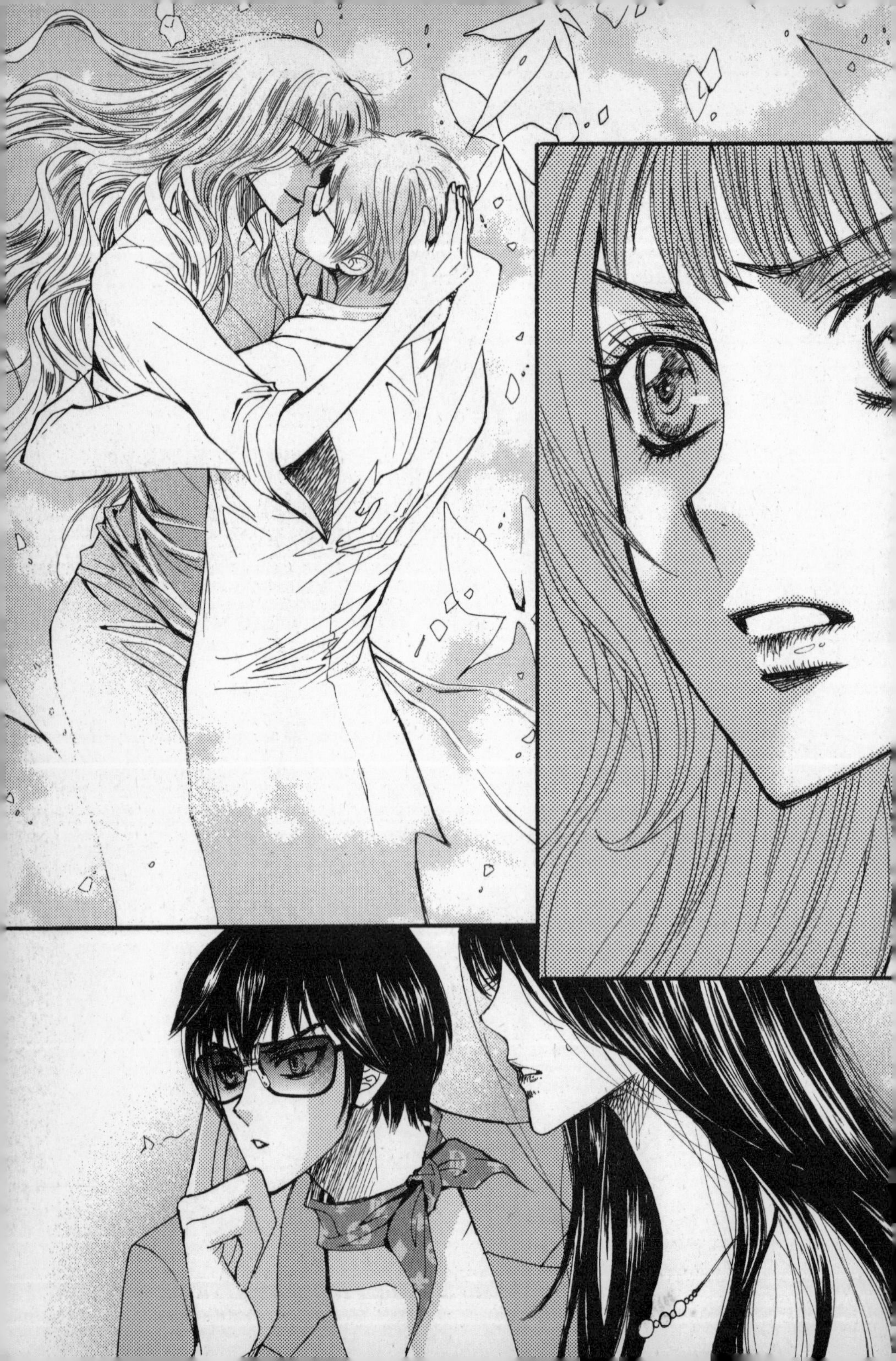

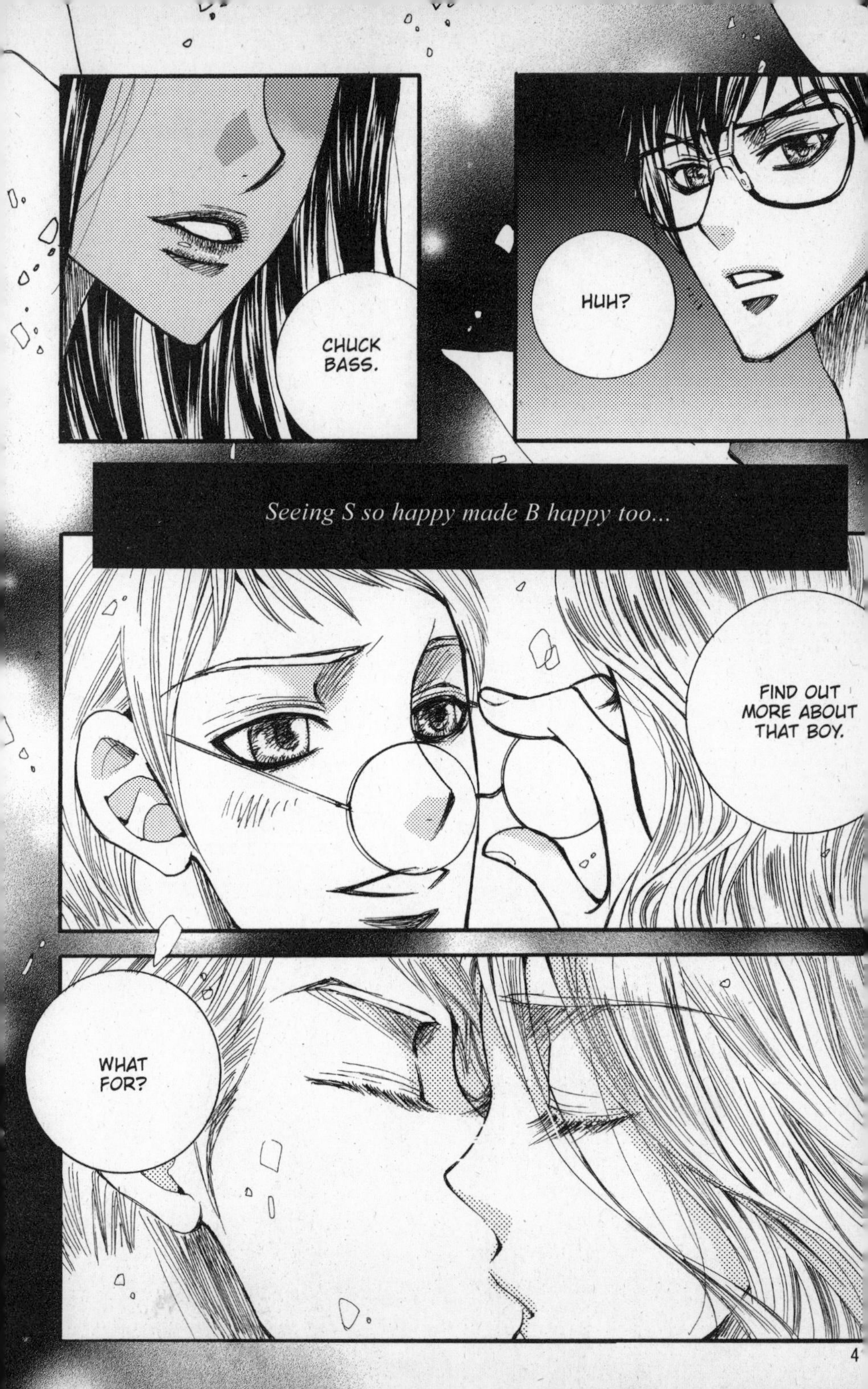
CHUCK BASS.
HUH?
Seeing S so happy made B happy too...
FIND OUT MORE ABOUT THAT BOY.
WHAT FOR?

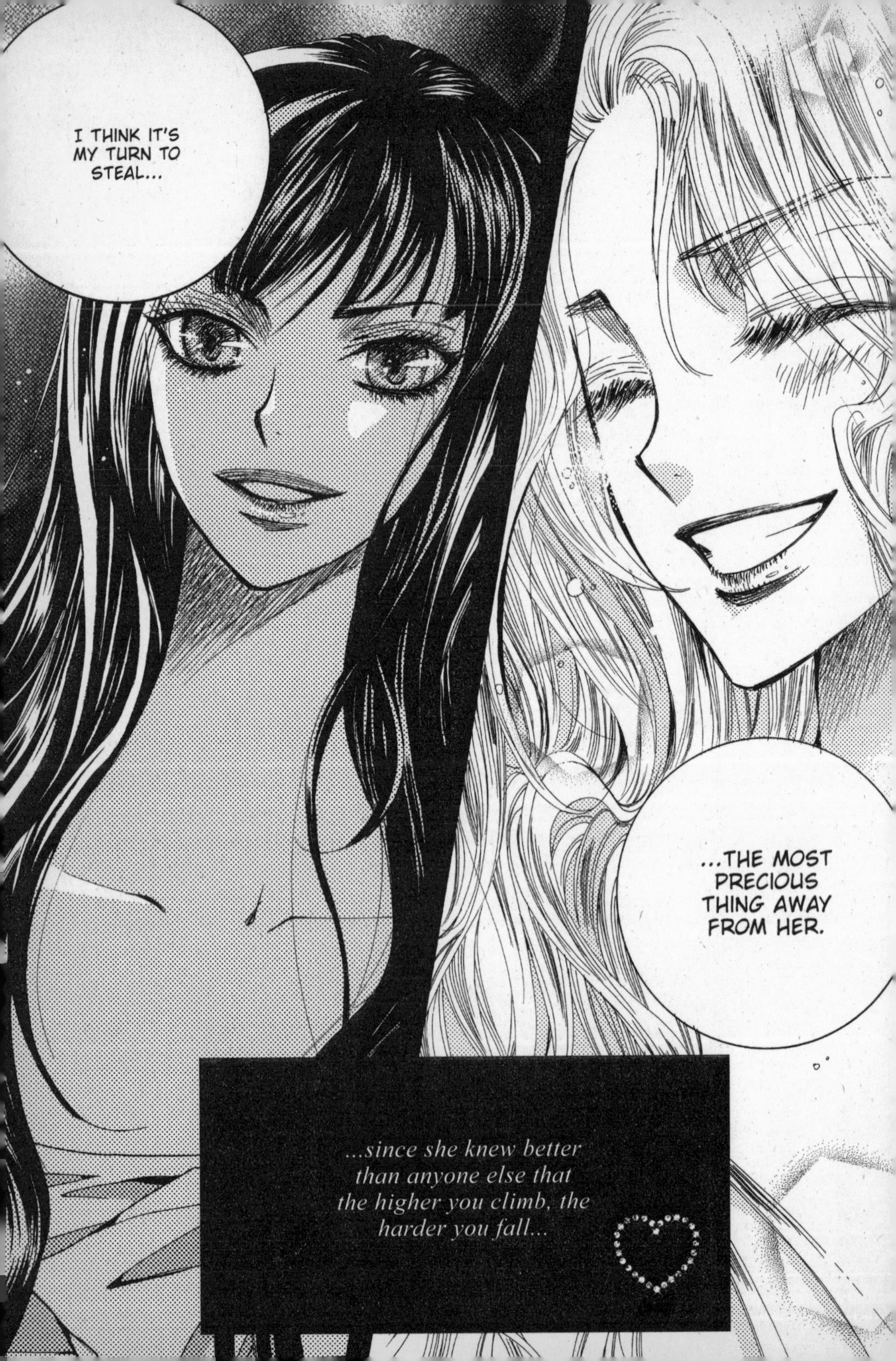
I THINK IT'S MY TURN TO STEAL...
...THE MOST PRECIOUS THING AWAY FROM HER.
...since she knew better than anyone else that the higher you climb, the harder you fall...

gossip girl

FOR YOUR EYES ONLY

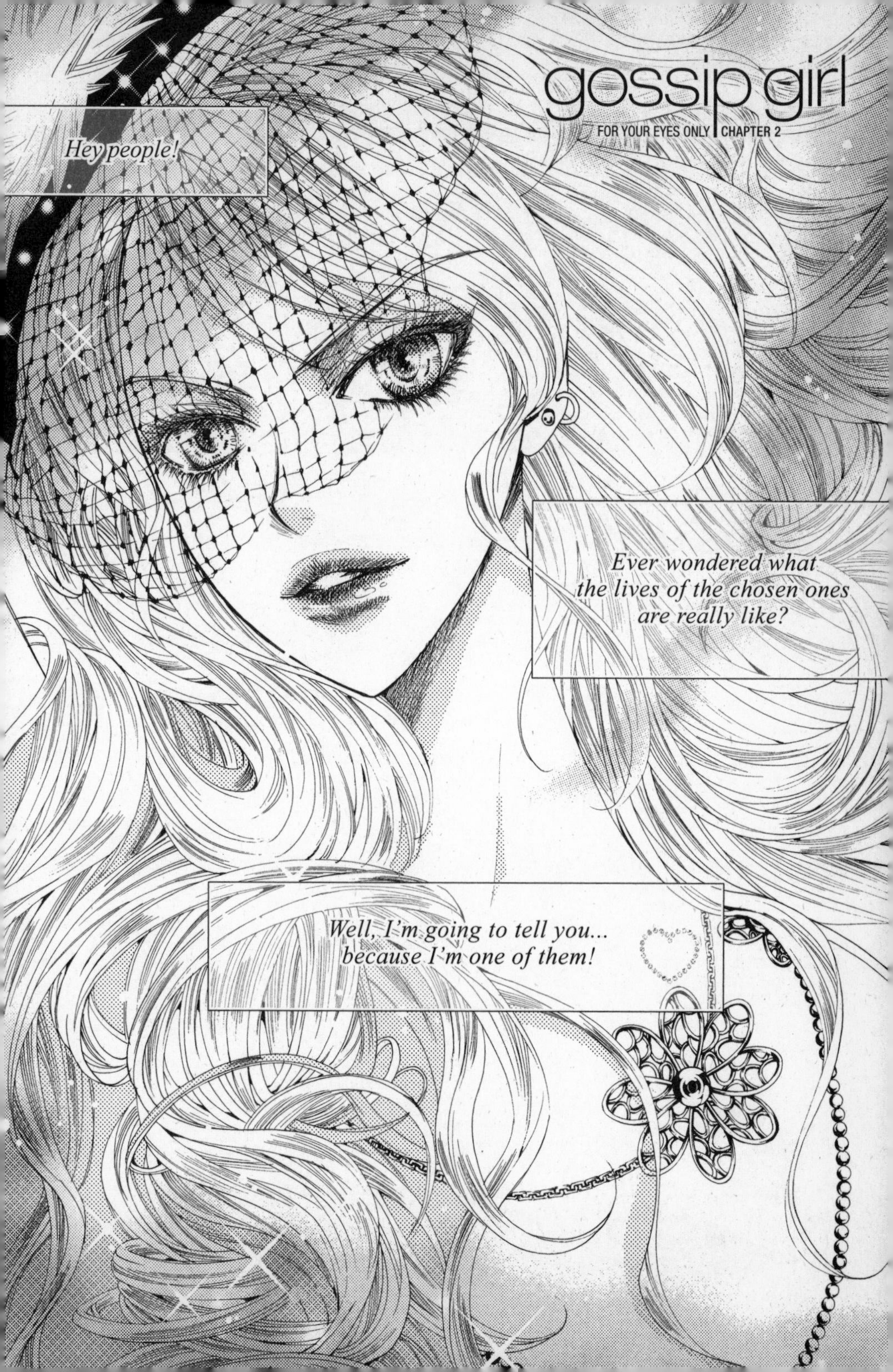
gossip girl
FOR YOUR EYES ONLY | CHAPTER 2
Hey people!
Ever wondered what the lives of the chosen ones are really like?
Well, I'm going to tell you... because I'm one of them!

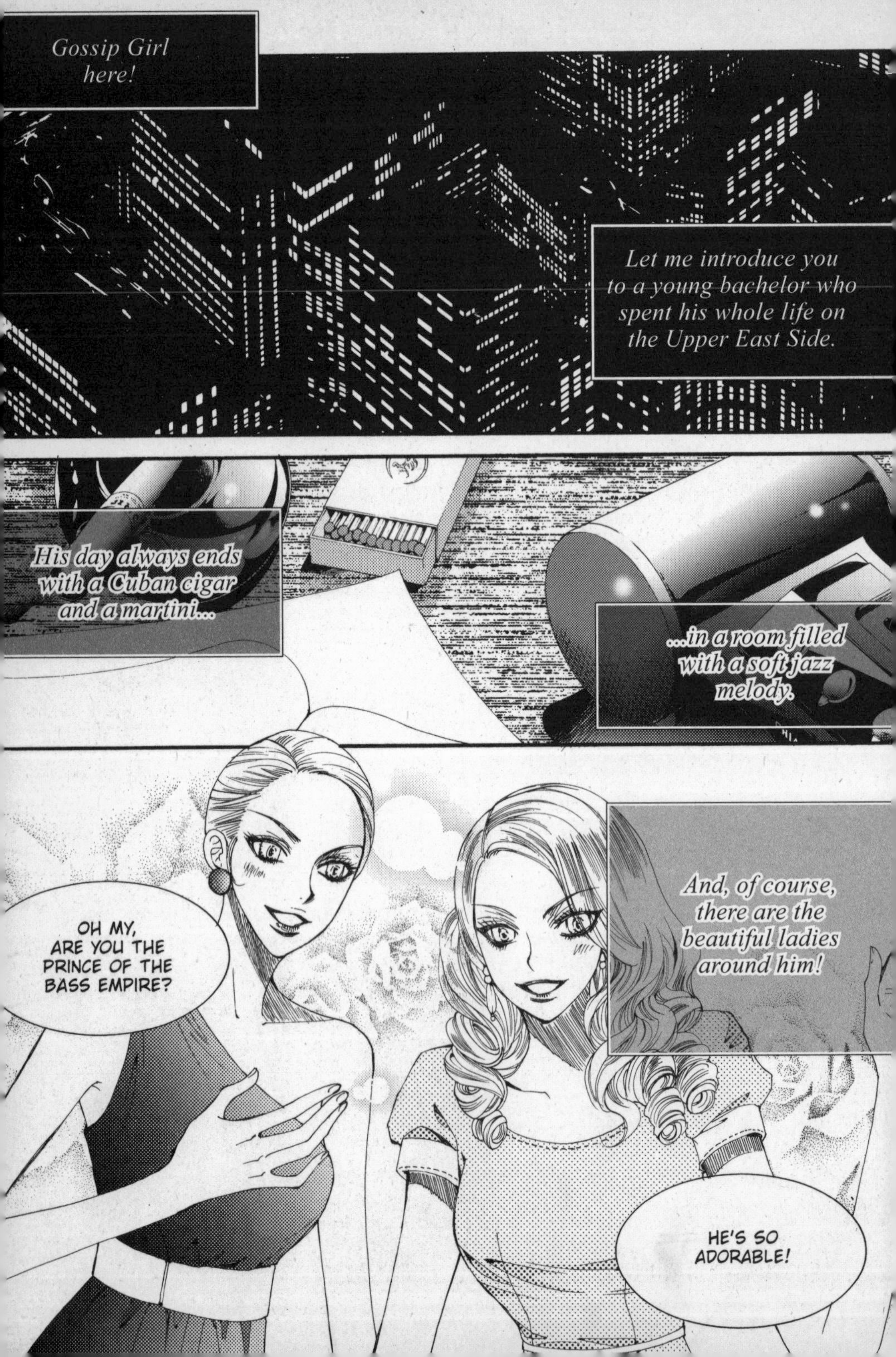
Gossip Girl here!
Let me introduce you to a young bachelor who spent his whole life on the Upper East Side.
His day always ends with a Cuban cigar and a martini...
...in a room filled with a soft jazz melody.
OH MY, ARE YOU THE PRINCE OF THE BASS EMPIRE?
And, of course, there are the beautiful ladies around him!
HE'S SO ADORABLE!

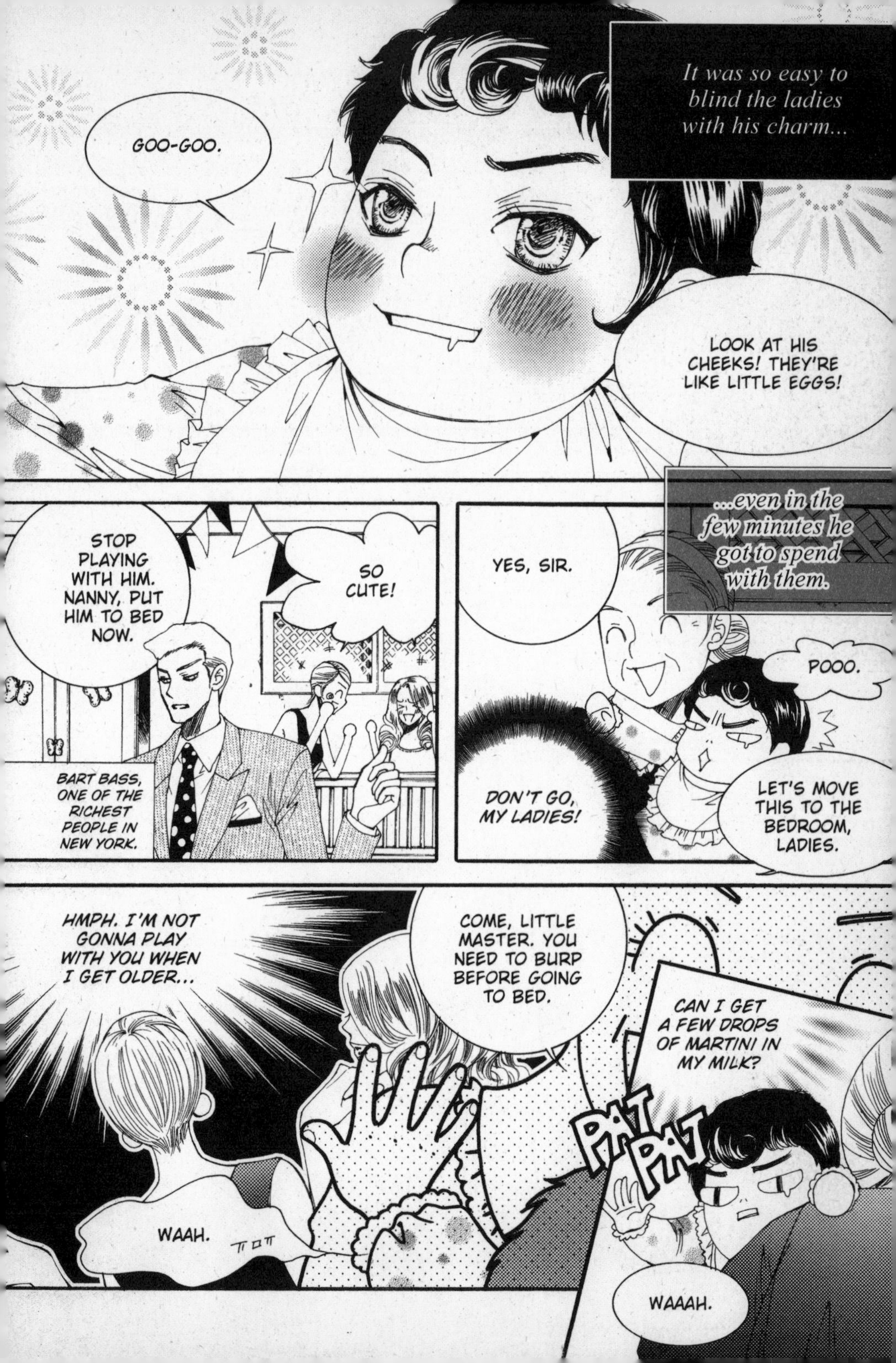
It was so easy to blind the ladies with his charm...
GOO-GOO.
LOOK AT HIS CHEEKS! THEY'RE LIKE LITTLE EGGS!
STOP PLAYING WITH HIM. NANNY, PUT HIM TO BED NOW.
SO CUTE!
BART BASS, ONE OF THE RICHEST PEOPLE IN NEW YORK.
...even in the few minutes he got to spend with them.
YES, SIR.
POOO.
DON'T GO, MY LADIES!
LET'S MOVE THIS TO THE BEDROOM, LADIES.
HMPH. I'M NOT GONNA PLAY WITH YOU WHEN I GET OLDER...
COME, LITTLE MASTER. YOU NEED TO BURP BEFORE GOING TO BED.
CAN I GET A FEW DROPS OF MARTINI IN MY MILK?
PAT PAT
WAAH.
WAAAH.

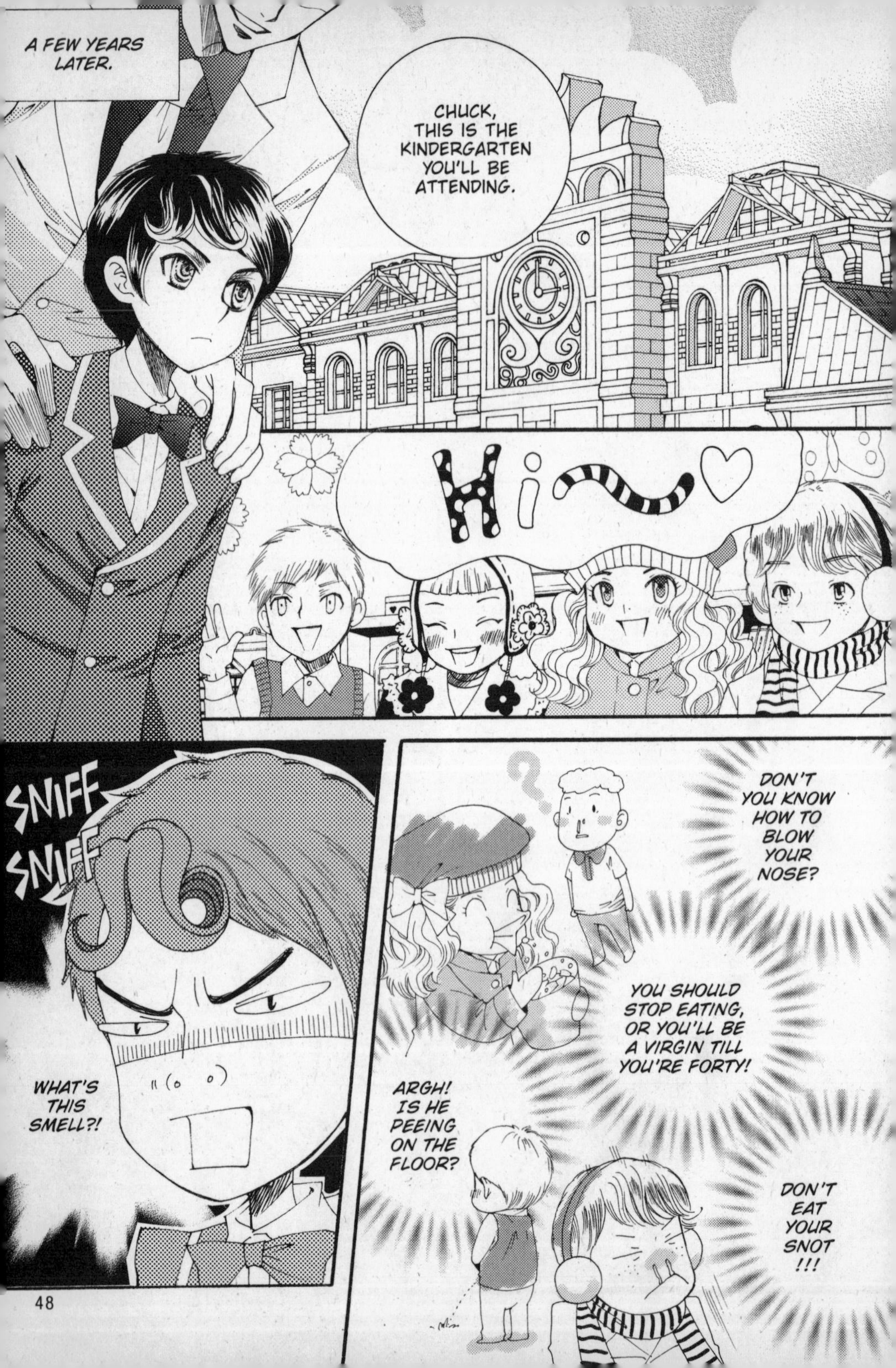
A FEW YEARS LATER.
CHUCK, THIS IS THE KINDERGARTEN YOU'LL BE ATTENDING.
Hi~♥
SNIFF SNIFF
WHAT'S THIS SMELL?!
DON'T YOU KNOW HOW TO BLOW YOUR NOSE?
YOU SHOULD STOP EATING, OR YOU'LL BE A VIRGIN TILL YOU'RE FORTY!
ARGH! IS HE PEEING ON THE FLOOR?
DON'T EAT YOUR SNOT !!!

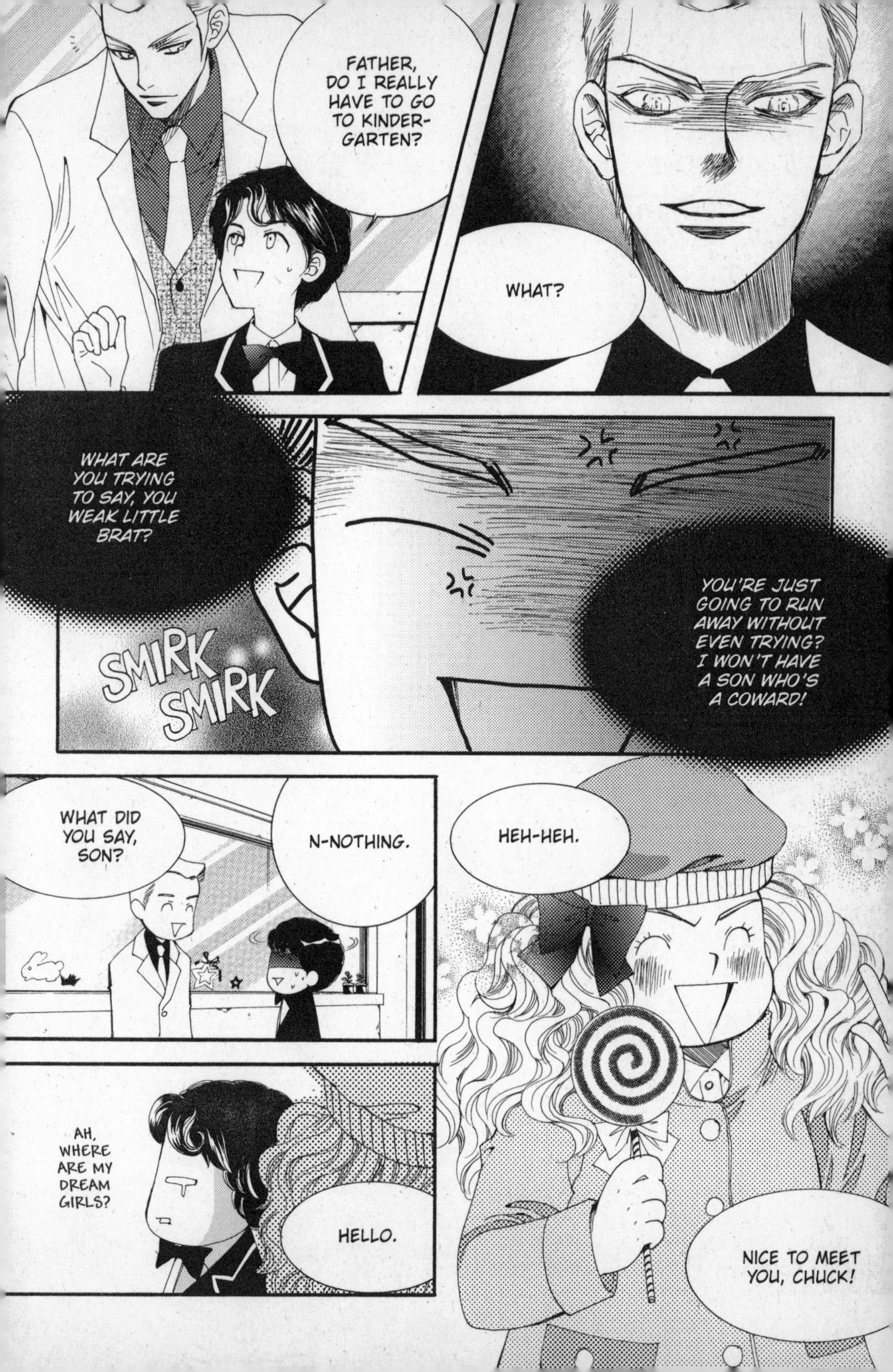
FATHER, DO I REALLY HAVE TO GO TO KINDER-GARTEN?
WHAT?
WHAT ARE YOU TRYING TO SAY, YOU WEAK LITTLE BRAT?
SMIRK SMIRK
YOU'RE JUST GOING TO RUN AWAY WITHOUT EVEN TRYING? I WON'T HAVE A SON WHO'S A COWARD!
WHAT DID YOU SAY, SON?
N-NOTHING.
HEH-HEH.
AH, WHERE ARE MY DREAM GIRLS?
HELLO.
NICE TO MEET YOU, CHUCK!

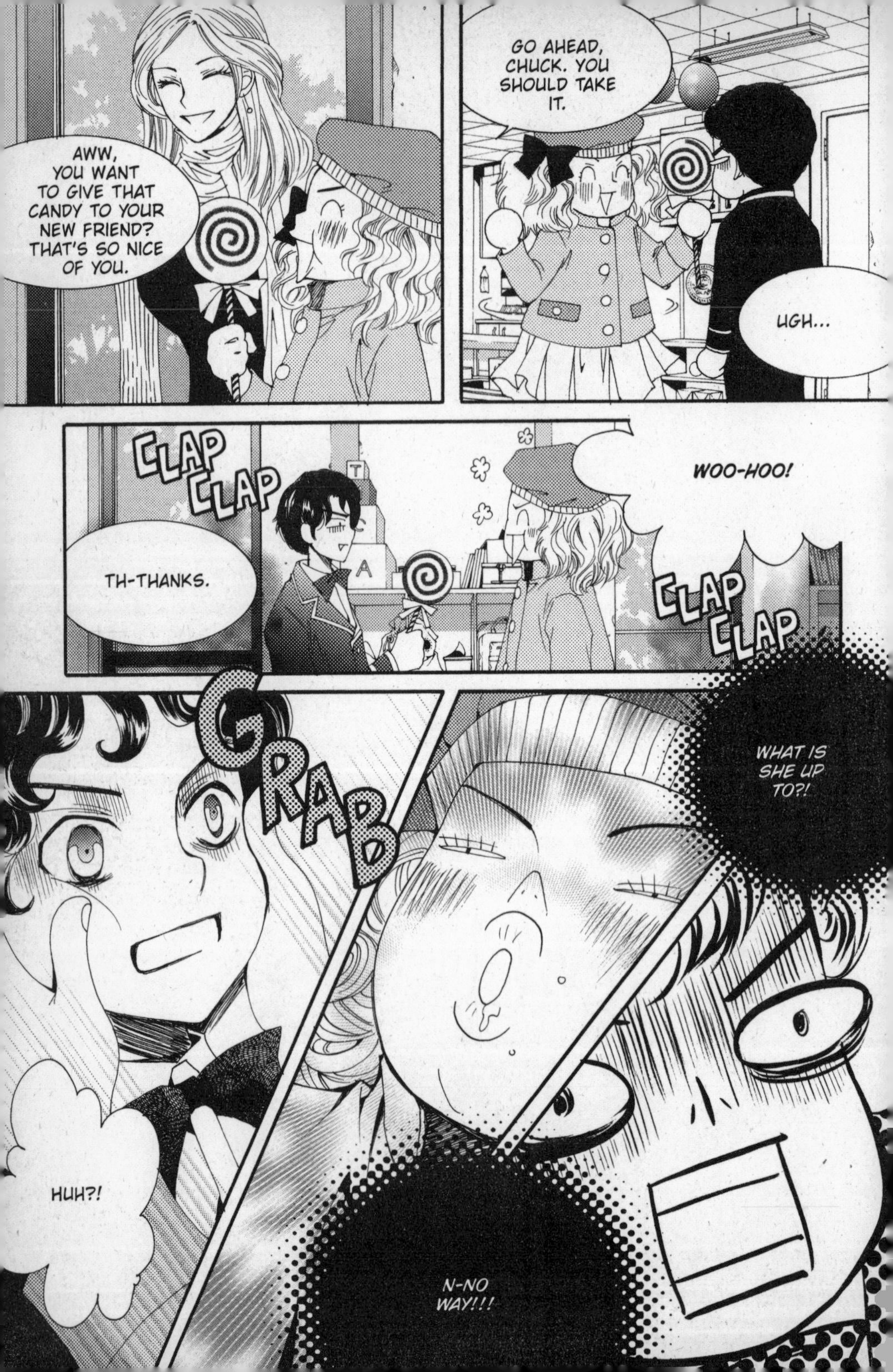
AWW, YOU WANT TO GIVE THAT CANDY TO YOUR NEW FRIEND? THAT'S SO NICE OF YOU.
GO AHEAD, CHUCK. YOU SHOULD TAKE IT.
UGH...
CLAP CLAP
TH-THANKS.
WOO-HOO!
CLAP CLAP
GRAB
WHAT IS SHE UP TO?!
HUH?!
N-NO WAY!!!

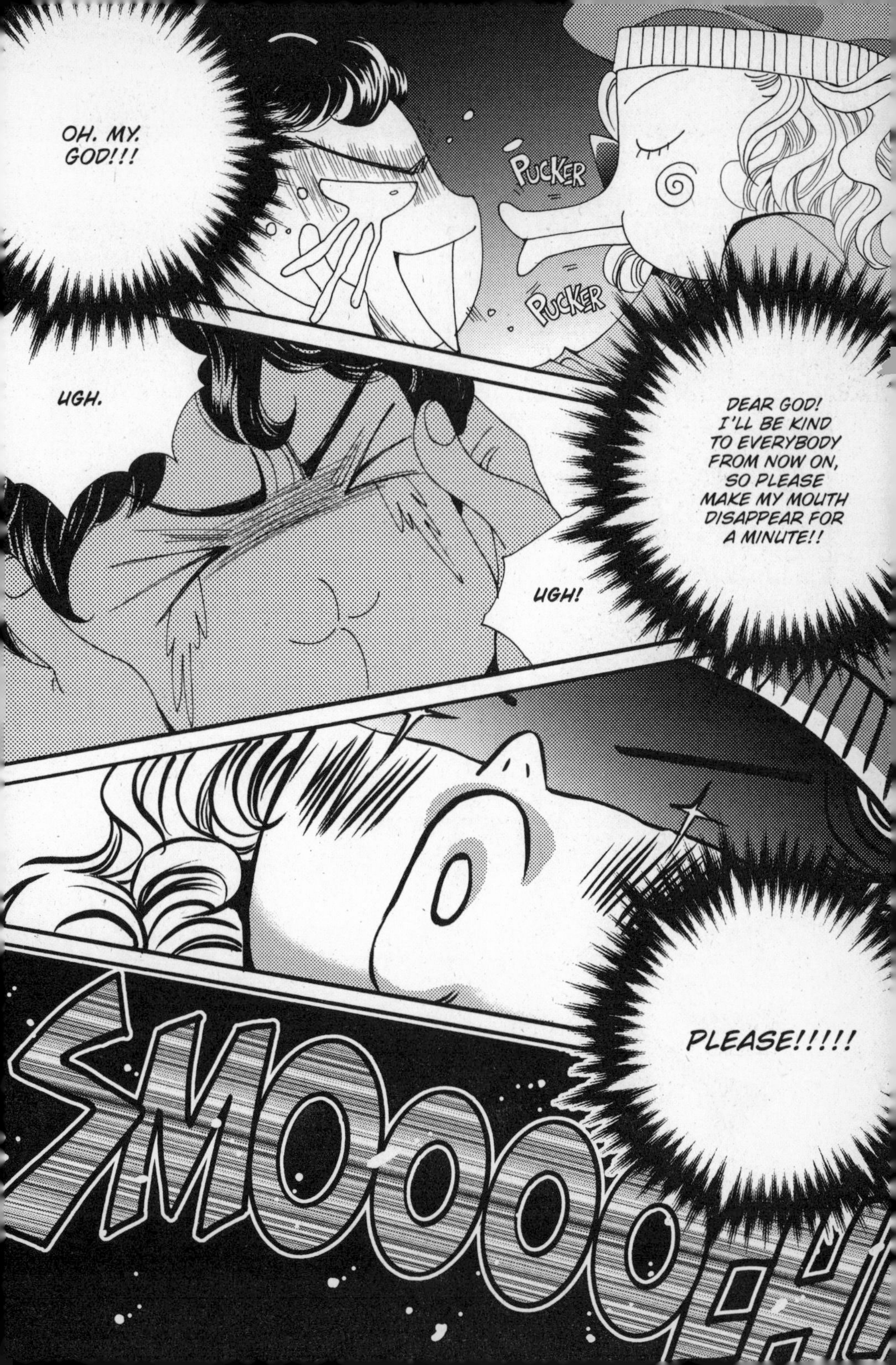
OH. MY. GOD!!!
PUCKER
PUCKER
UGH.
DEAR GOD! I'LL BE KIND TO EVERYBODY FROM NOW ON, SO PLEASE MAKE MY MOUTH DISAPPEAR FOR A MINUTE!!
UGH!
PLEASE!!!!!
SMOOOO

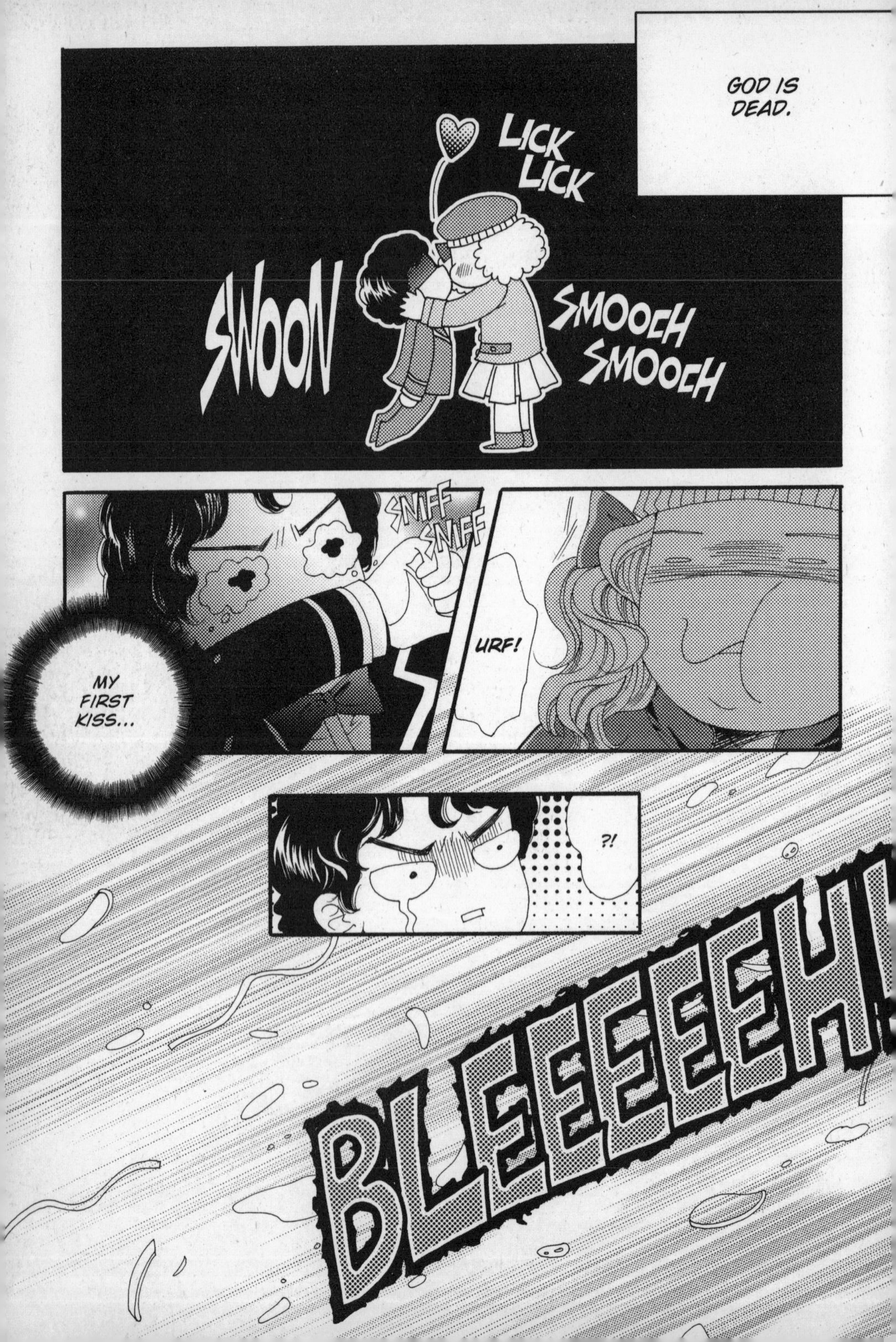
GOD IS DEAD.
LICK LICK
SWOON
SMOOCH SMOOCH
SNIFF SNIFF
MY FIRST KISS...
URF!
?!
BLEEEEEH!

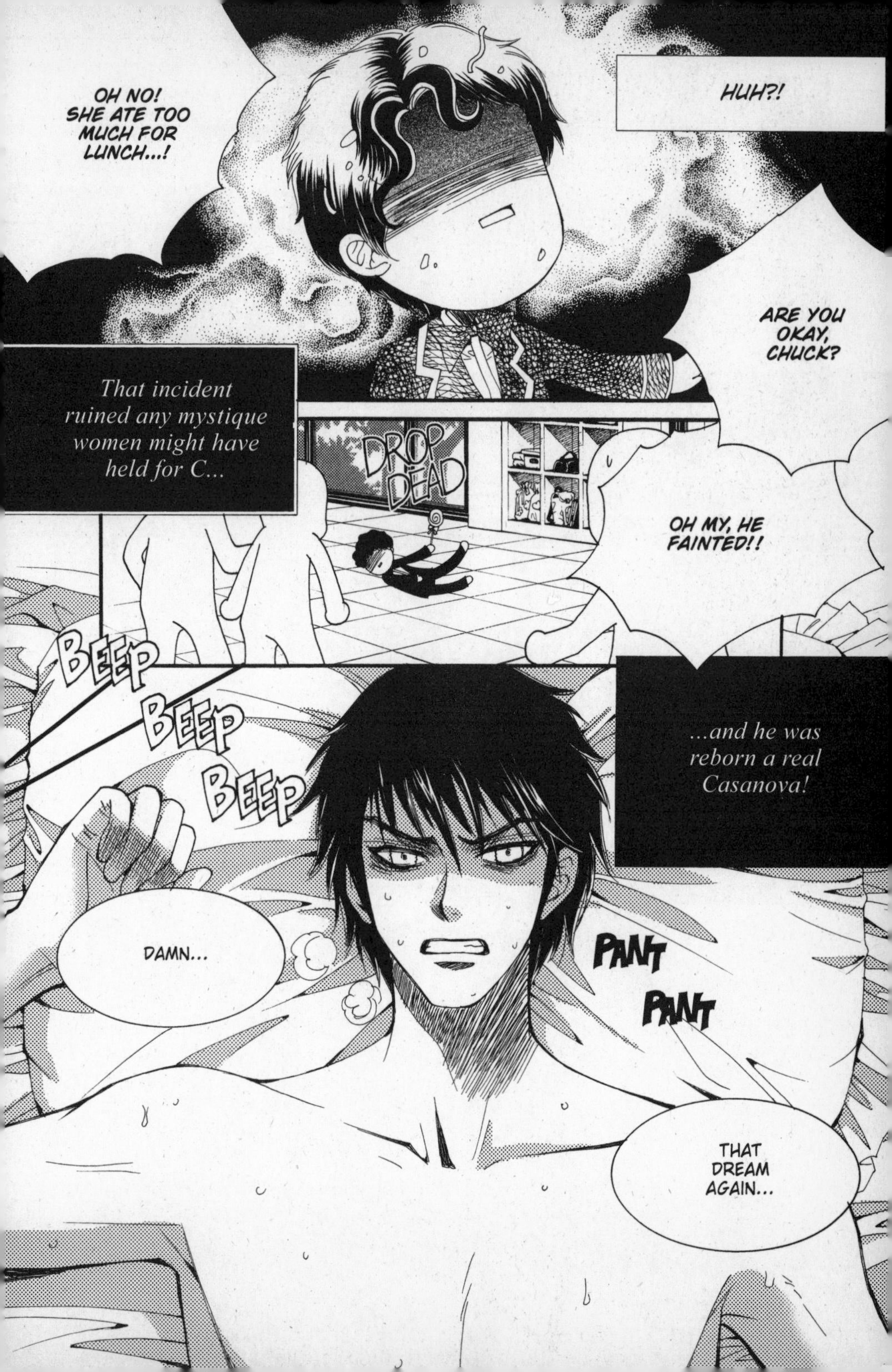

OH NO! SHE ATE TOO MUCH FOR LUNCH...!
HUH?!
ARE YOU OKAY, CHUCK?
That incident ruined any mystique women might have held for C...
DROP DEAD
OH MY, HE FAINTED!!
BEEP
BEEP
BEEP
...and he was reborn a real Casanova!
DAMN...
PANT
PANT
THAT DREAM AGAIN...

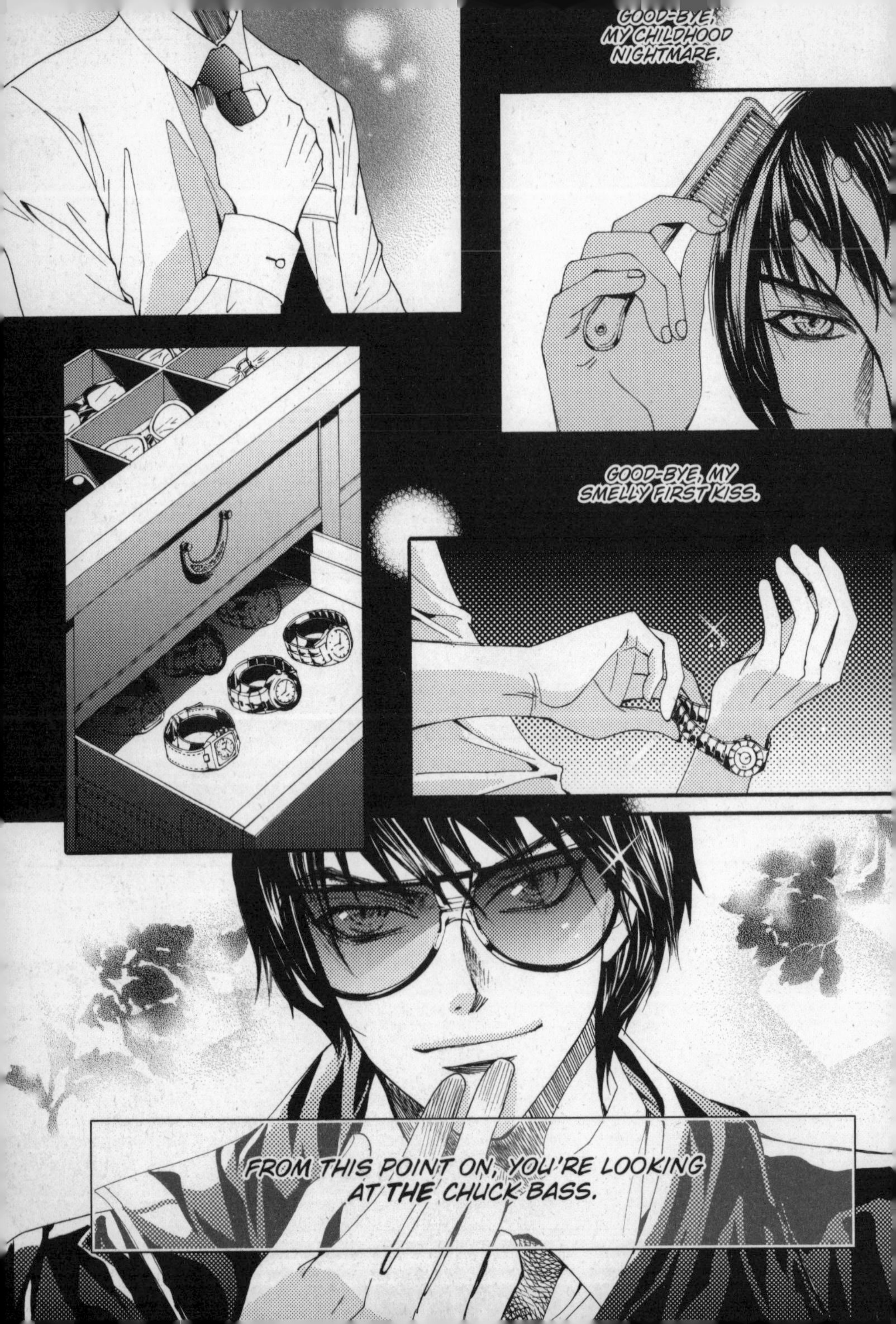
GOOD-BYE, MY CHILDHOOD NIGHTMARE.
GOOD-BYE, MY SMELLY FIRST KISS.
FROM THIS POINT ON, YOU'RE LOOKING AT THE CHUCK BASS.

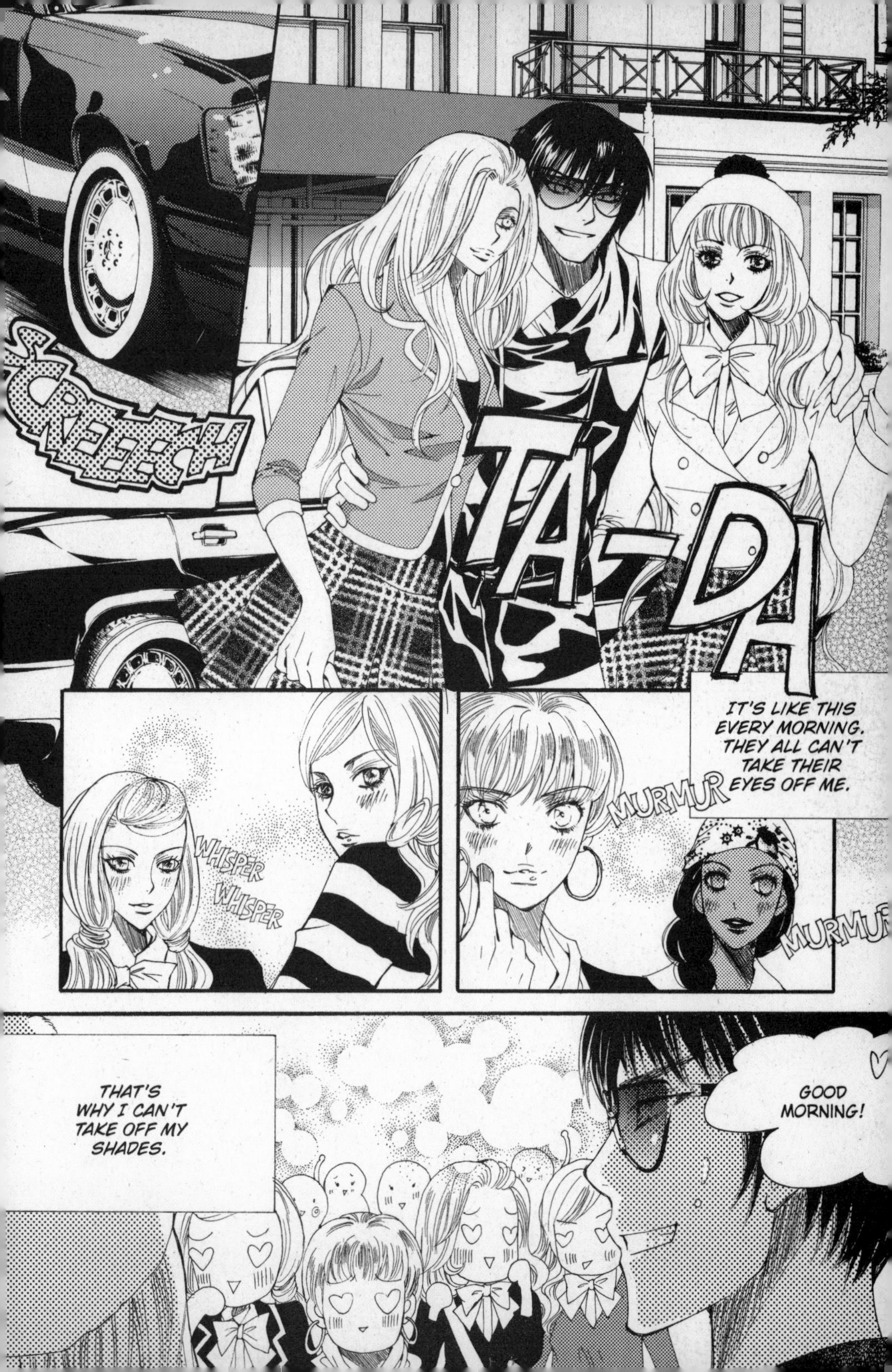
SCREEECH
TA-DA
WHISPER
WHISPER
IT'S LIKE THIS EVERY MORNING. THEY ALL CAN'T TAKE THEIR EYES OFF ME.
MURMUR
MURMUR
THAT'S WHY I CAN'T TAKE OFF MY SHADES.
GOOD MORNING!

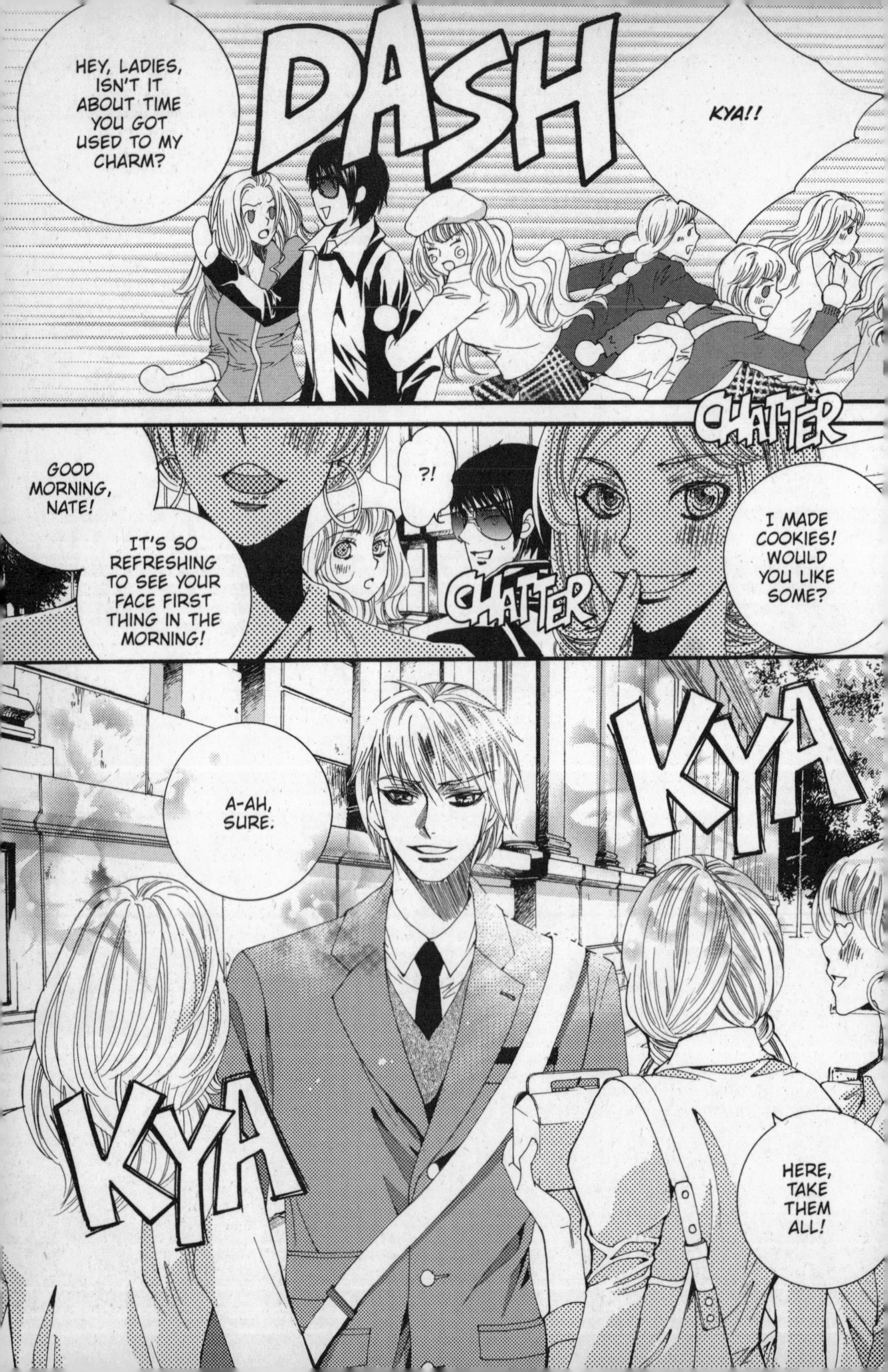
HEY, LADIES, ISN'T IT ABOUT TIME YOU GOT USED TO MY CHARM?
DASH
KYA!!
GOOD MORNING, NATE!
IT'S SO REFRESHING TO SEE YOUR FACE FIRST THING IN THE MORNING!
?!
CHATTER
CHATTER
I MADE COOKIES! WOULD YOU LIKE SOME?
A-AH, SURE.
KYA
KYA
HERE, TAKE THEM ALL!

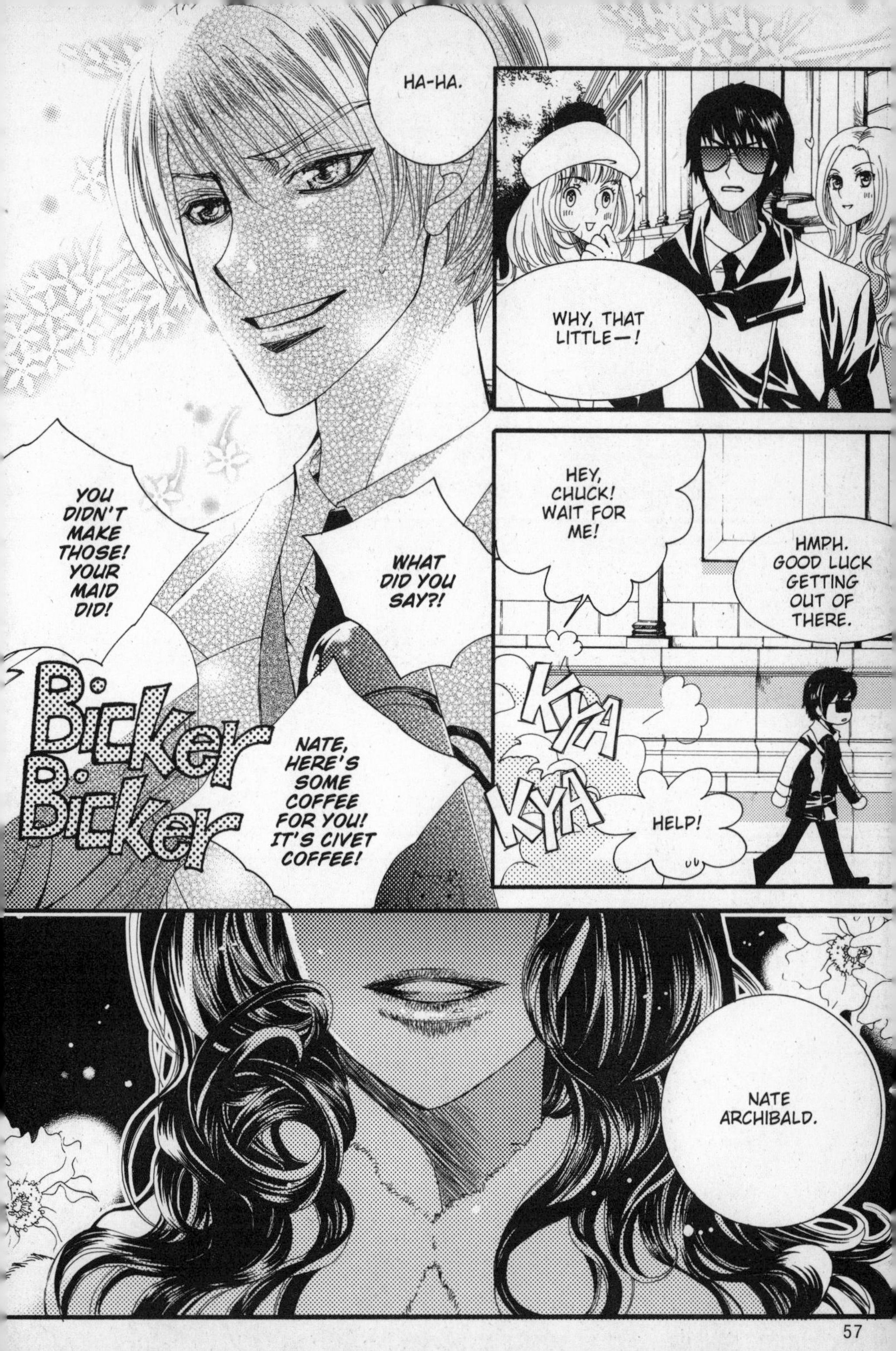
HA-HA.
YOU DIDN'T MAKE THOSE! YOUR MAID DID!
WHAT DID YOU SAY?!
Bicker Bicker
NATE, HERE'S SOME COFFEE FOR YOU! IT'S CIVET COFFEE!
WHY, THAT LITTLE—!
HEY, CHUCK! WAIT FOR ME!
HMPH. GOOD LUCK GETTING OUT OF THERE.
KYA
KYA
HELP!
NATE ARCHIBALD.

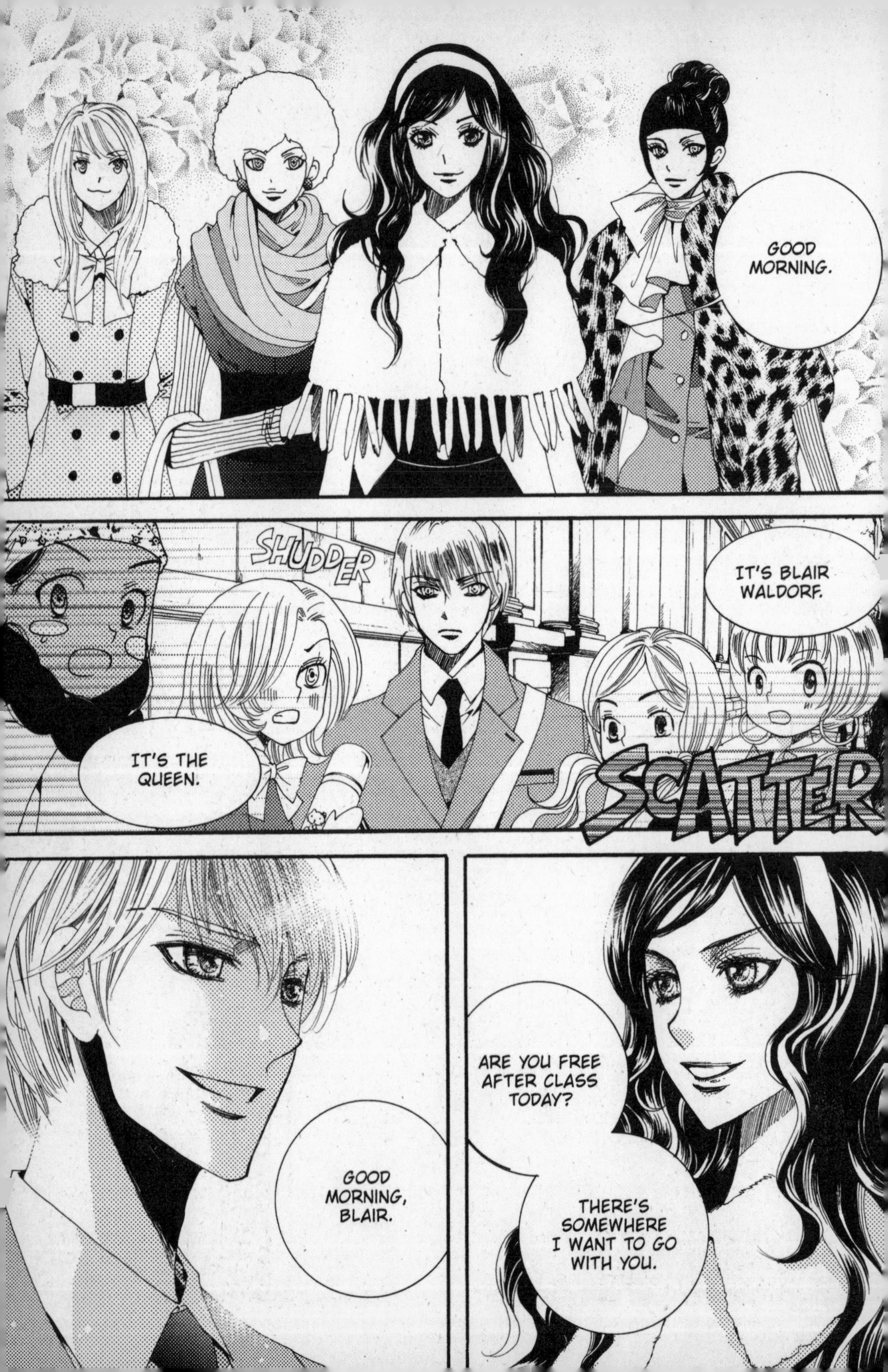
GOOD MORNING.
SHUDDER
IT'S THE QUEEN.
IT'S BLAIR WALDORF.
SCATTER
GOOD MORNING, BLAIR.
ARE YOU FREE AFTER CLASS TODAY?
THERE'S SOMEWHERE I WANT TO GO WITH YOU.

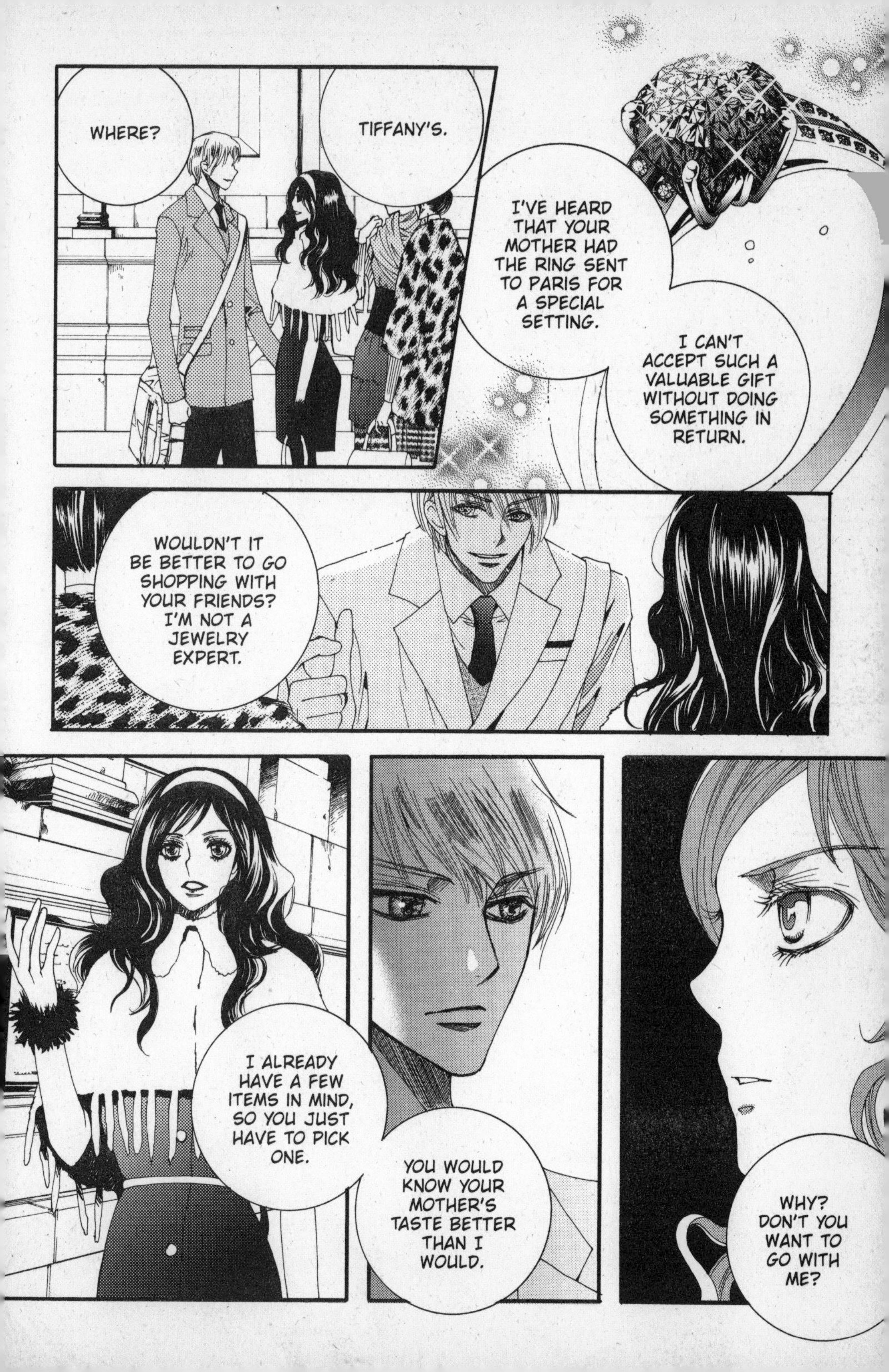
WHERE?
TIFFANY'S.
I'VE HEARD THAT YOUR MOTHER HAD THE RING SENT TO PARIS FOR A SPECIAL SETTING.
I CAN'T ACCEPT SUCH A VALUABLE GIFT WITHOUT DOING SOMETHING IN RETURN.
WOULDN'T IT BE BETTER TO GO SHOPPING WITH YOUR FRIENDS? I'M NOT A JEWELRY EXPERT.
I ALREADY HAVE A FEW ITEMS IN MIND, SO YOU JUST HAVE TO PICK ONE.
YOU WOULD KNOW YOUR MOTHER'S TASTE BETTER THAN I WOULD.
WHY? DON'T YOU WANT TO GO WITH ME?

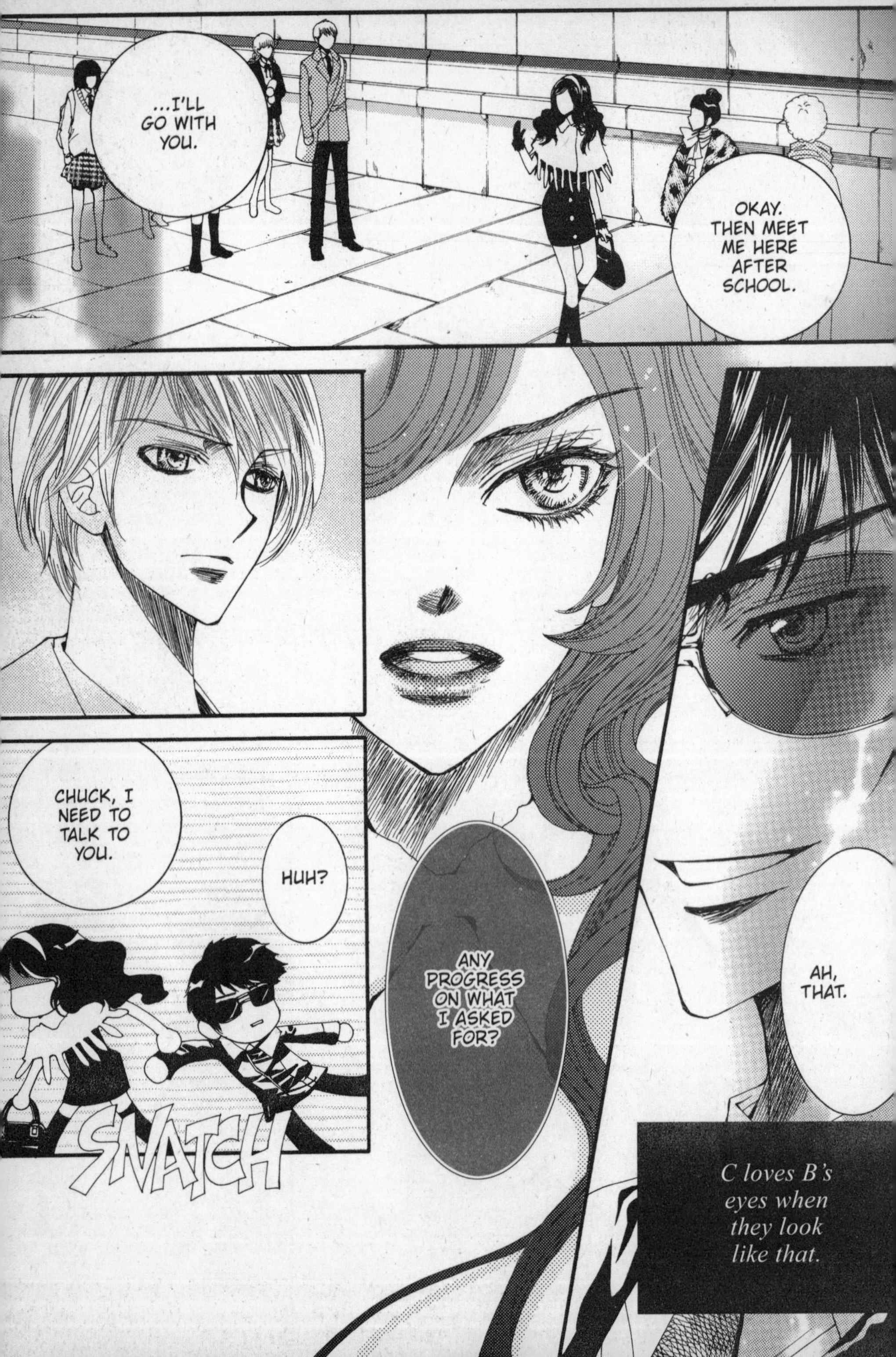
...I'LL GO WITH YOU.
OKAY. THEN MEET ME HERE AFTER SCHOOL.
CHUCK, I NEED TO TALK TO YOU.
HUH?
SNATCH
ANY PROGRESS ON WHAT I ASKED FOR?
AH, THAT.
C loves B's eyes when they look like that.

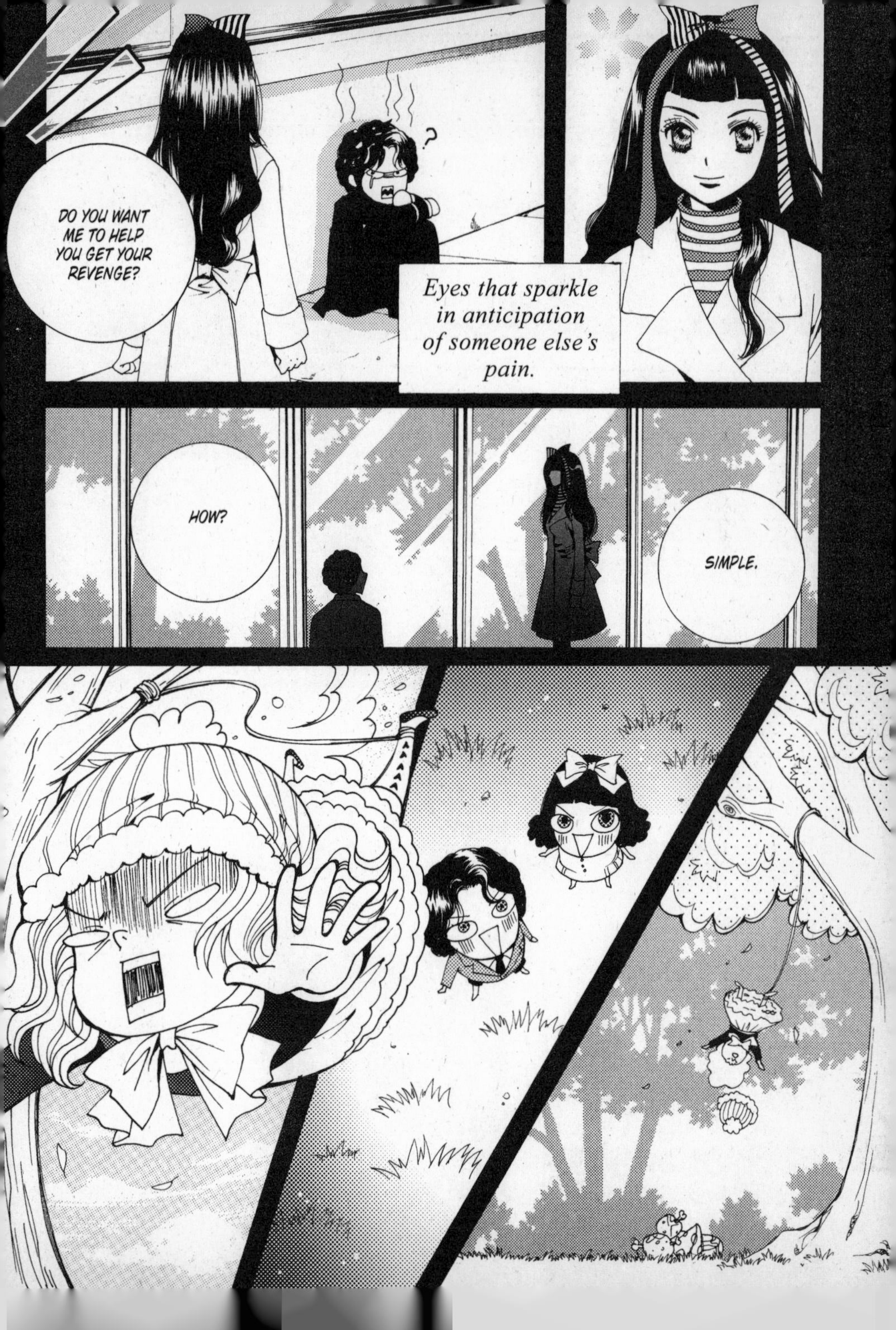
DO YOU WANT ME TO HELP YOU GET YOUR REVENGE?
?
Eyes that sparkle in anticipation of someone else's pain.
HOW?
SIMPLE.

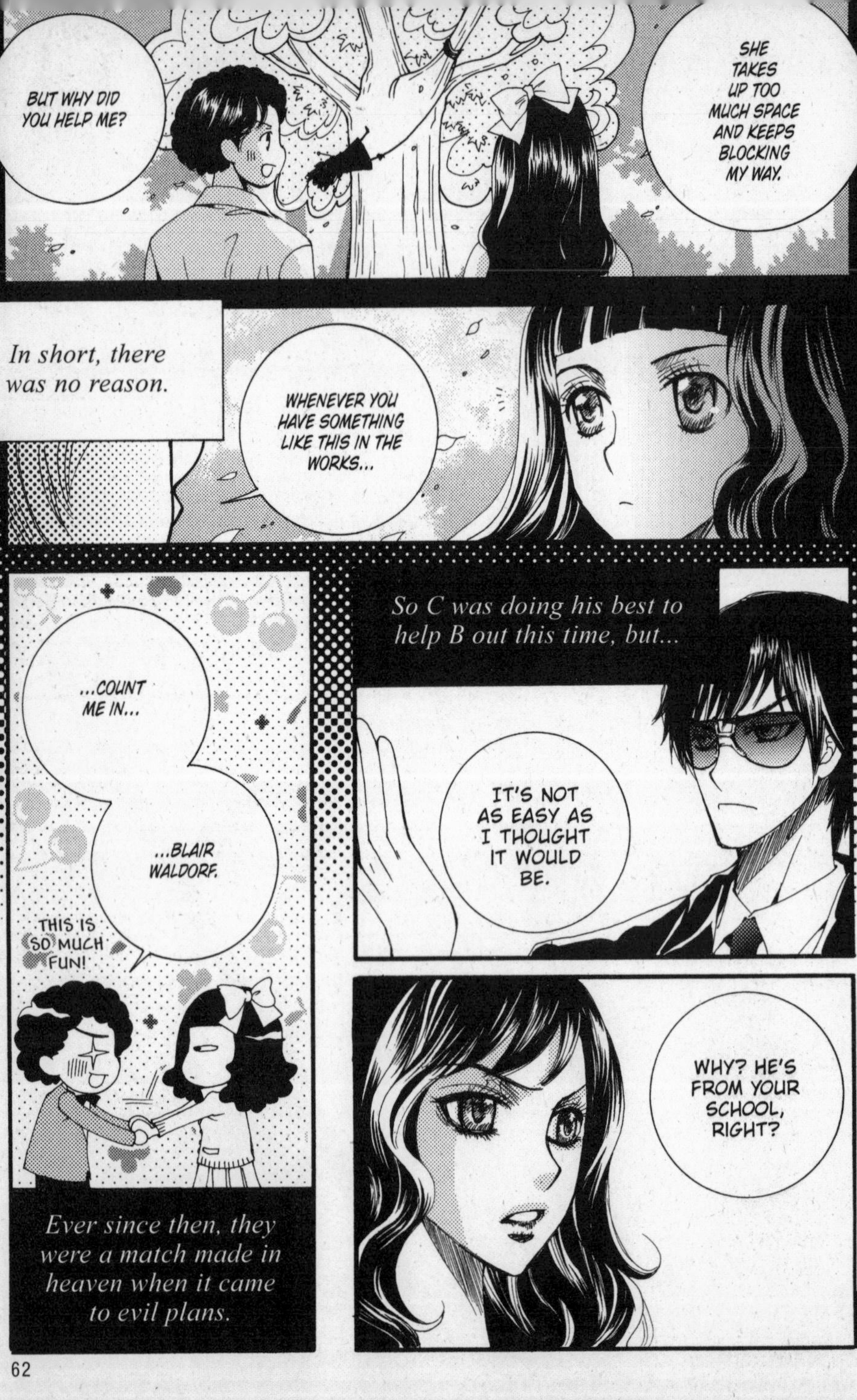
BUT WHY DID YOU HELP ME?
SHE TAKES UP TOO MUCH SPACE AND KEEPS BLOCKING MY WAY.
In short, there was no reason.
WHENEVER YOU HAVE SOMETHING LIKE THIS IN THE WORKS...
...COUNT ME IN...
...BLAIR WALDORF.
THIS IS SO MUCH FUN!
Ever since then, they were a match made in heaven when it came to evil plans.
So C was doing his best to help B out this time, but...
IT'S NOT AS EASY AS I THOUGHT IT WOULD BE.
WHY? HE'S FROM YOUR SCHOOL, RIGHT?

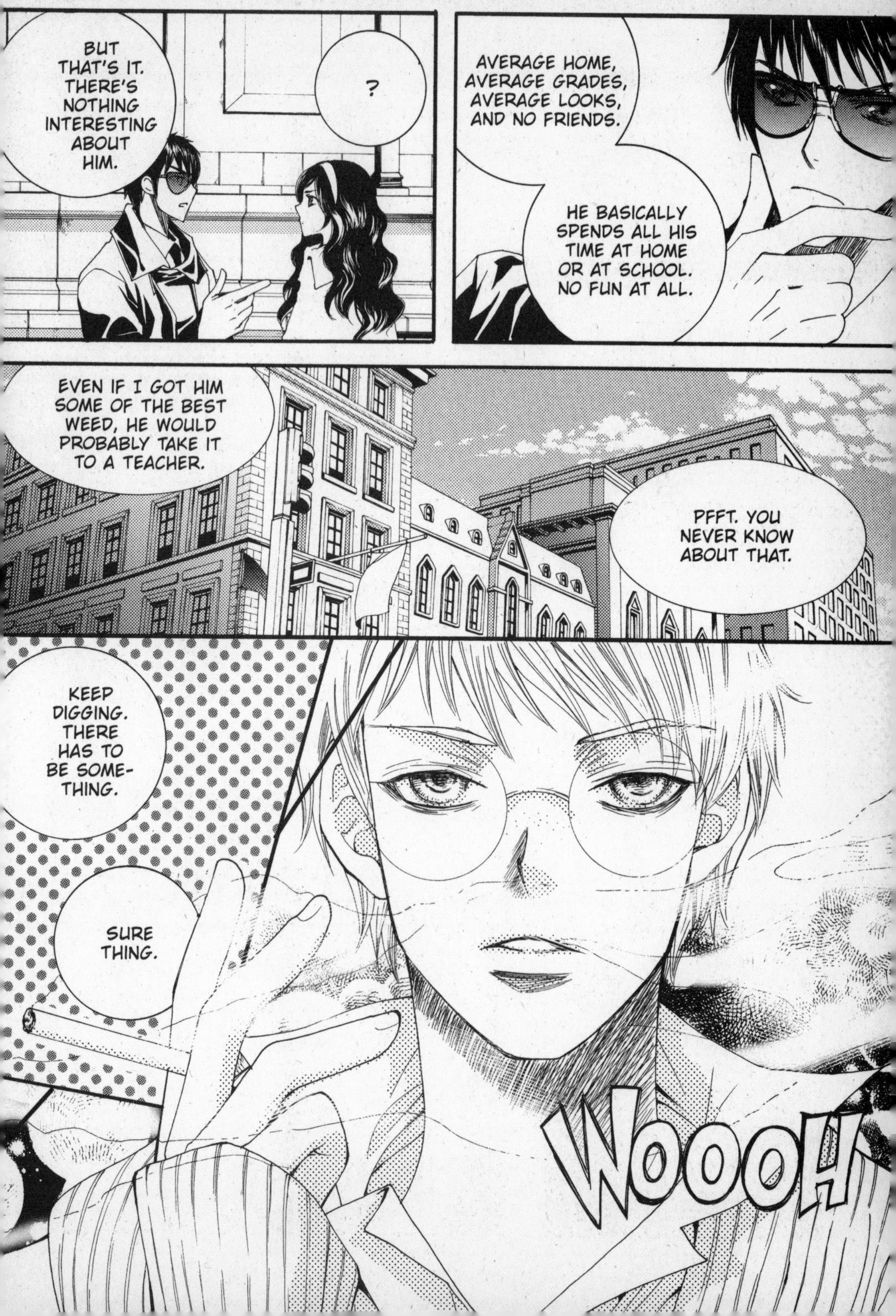
BUT THAT'S IT. THERE'S NOTHING INTERESTING ABOUT HIM.
?
AVERAGE HOME, AVERAGE GRADES, AVERAGE LOOKS, AND NO FRIENDS.
HE BASICALLY SPENDS ALL HIS TIME AT HOME OR AT SCHOOL. NO FUN AT ALL.
EVEN IF I GOT HIM SOME OF THE BEST WEED, HE WOULD PROBABLY TAKE IT TO A TEACHER.
PFFT. YOU NEVER KNOW ABOUT THAT.
KEEP DIGGING. THERE HAS TO BE SOME-THING.
SURE THING.
WOOOH

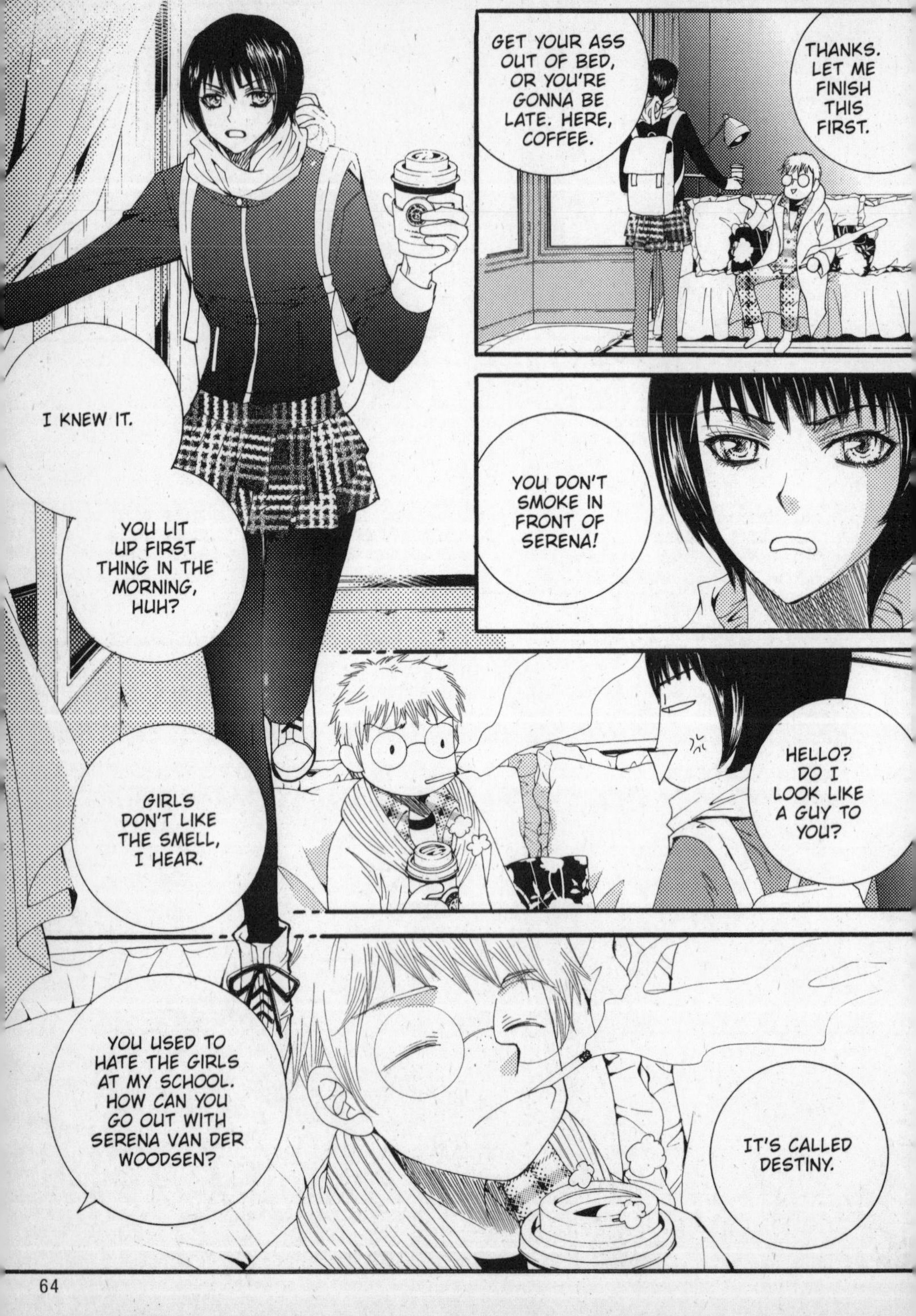
I KNEW IT.
YOU LIT UP FIRST THING IN THE MORNING, HUH?
GIRLS DON'T LIKE THE SMELL, I HEAR.
GET YOUR ASS OUT OF BED, OR YOU'RE GONNA BE LATE. HERE, COFFEE.
THANKS. LET ME FINISH THIS FIRST.
YOU DON'T SMOKE IN FRONT OF SERENA!
HELLO? DO I LOOK LIKE A GUY TO YOU?
YOU USED TO HATE THE GIRLS AT MY SCHOOL. HOW CAN YOU GO OUT WITH SERENA VAN DER WOODSEN?
IT'S CALLED DESTINY.

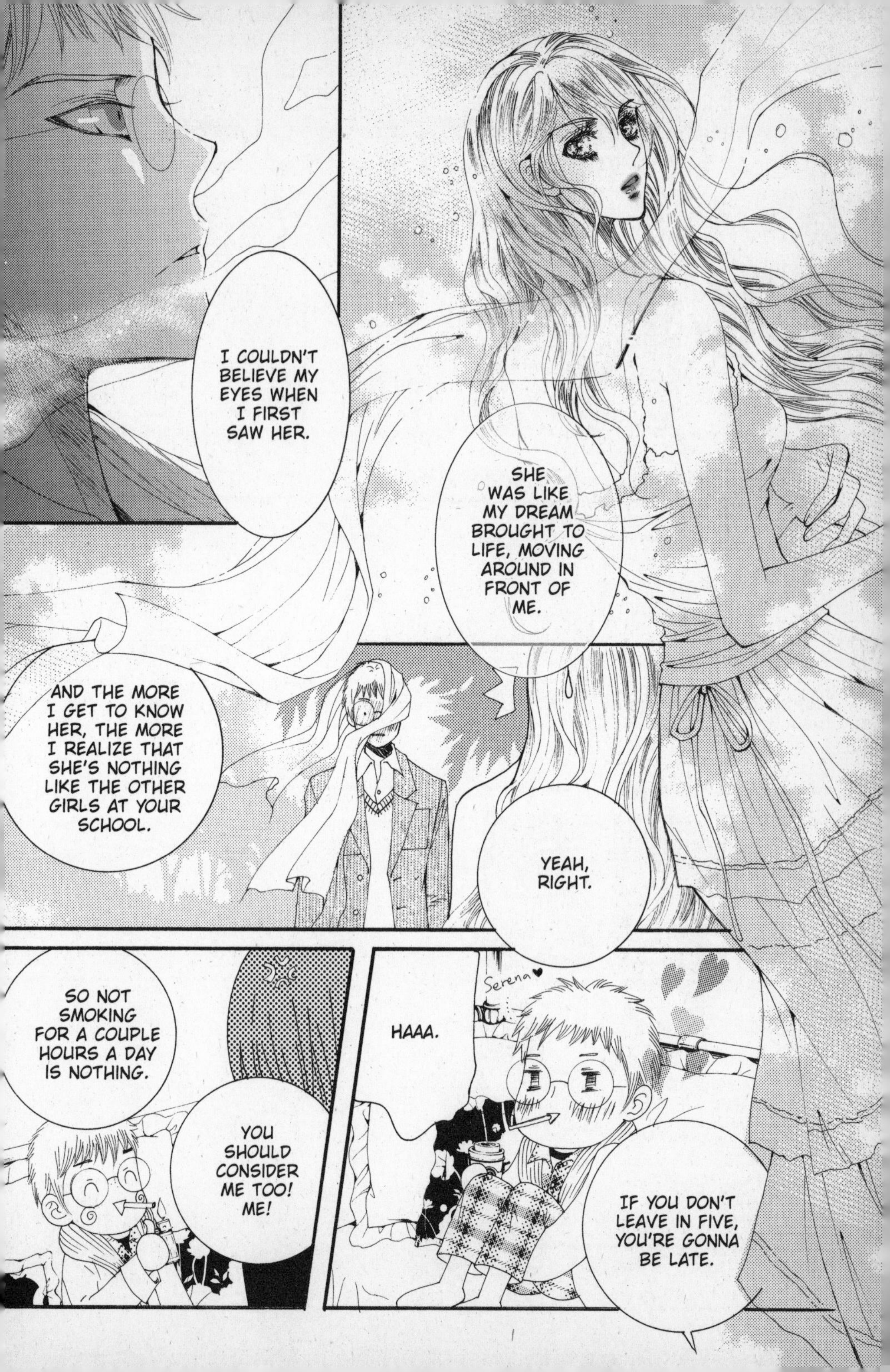
I COULDN'T BELIEVE MY EYES WHEN I FIRST SAW HER.
SHE WAS LIKE MY DREAM BROUGHT TO LIFE, MOVING AROUND IN FRONT OF ME.
AND THE MORE I GET TO KNOW HER, THE MORE I REALIZE THAT SHE'S NOTHING LIKE THE OTHER GIRLS AT YOUR SCHOOL.
YEAH, RIGHT.
SO NOT SMOKING FOR A COUPLE HOURS A DAY IS NOTHING.
YOU SHOULD CONSIDER ME TOO! ME!
Serena♥
HAAA.
IF YOU DON'T LEAVE IN FIVE, YOU'RE GONNA BE LATE.

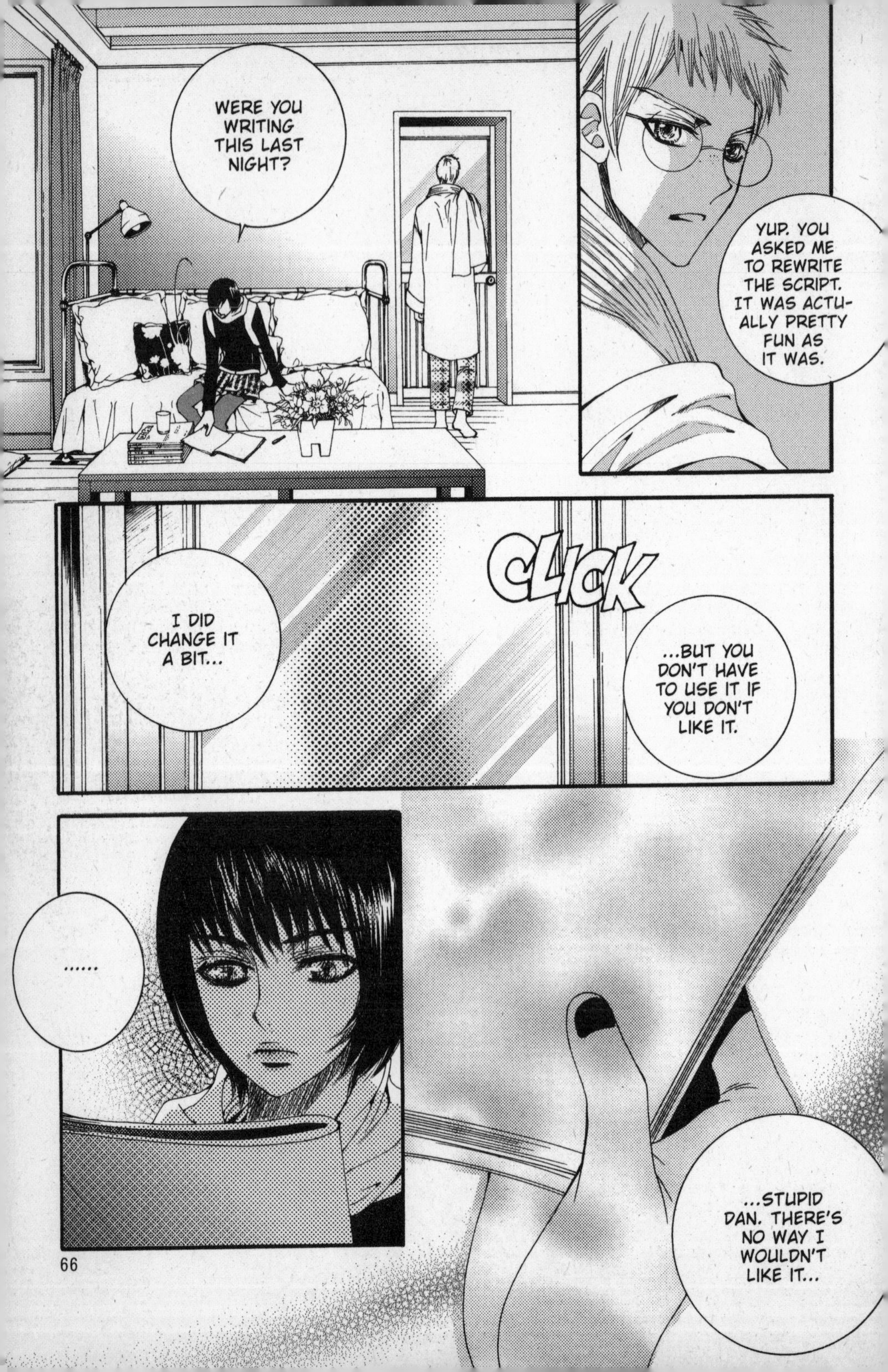
WERE YOU WRITING THIS LAST NIGHT?
YUP. YOU ASKED ME TO REWRITE THE SCRIPT. IT WAS ACTU-ALLY PRETTY FUN AS IT WAS.
I DID CHANGE IT A BIT...
CLICK
...BUT YOU DON'T HAVE TO USE IT IF YOU DON'T LIKE IT.
......
...STUPID DAN. THERE'S NO WAY I WOULDN'T LIKE IT...

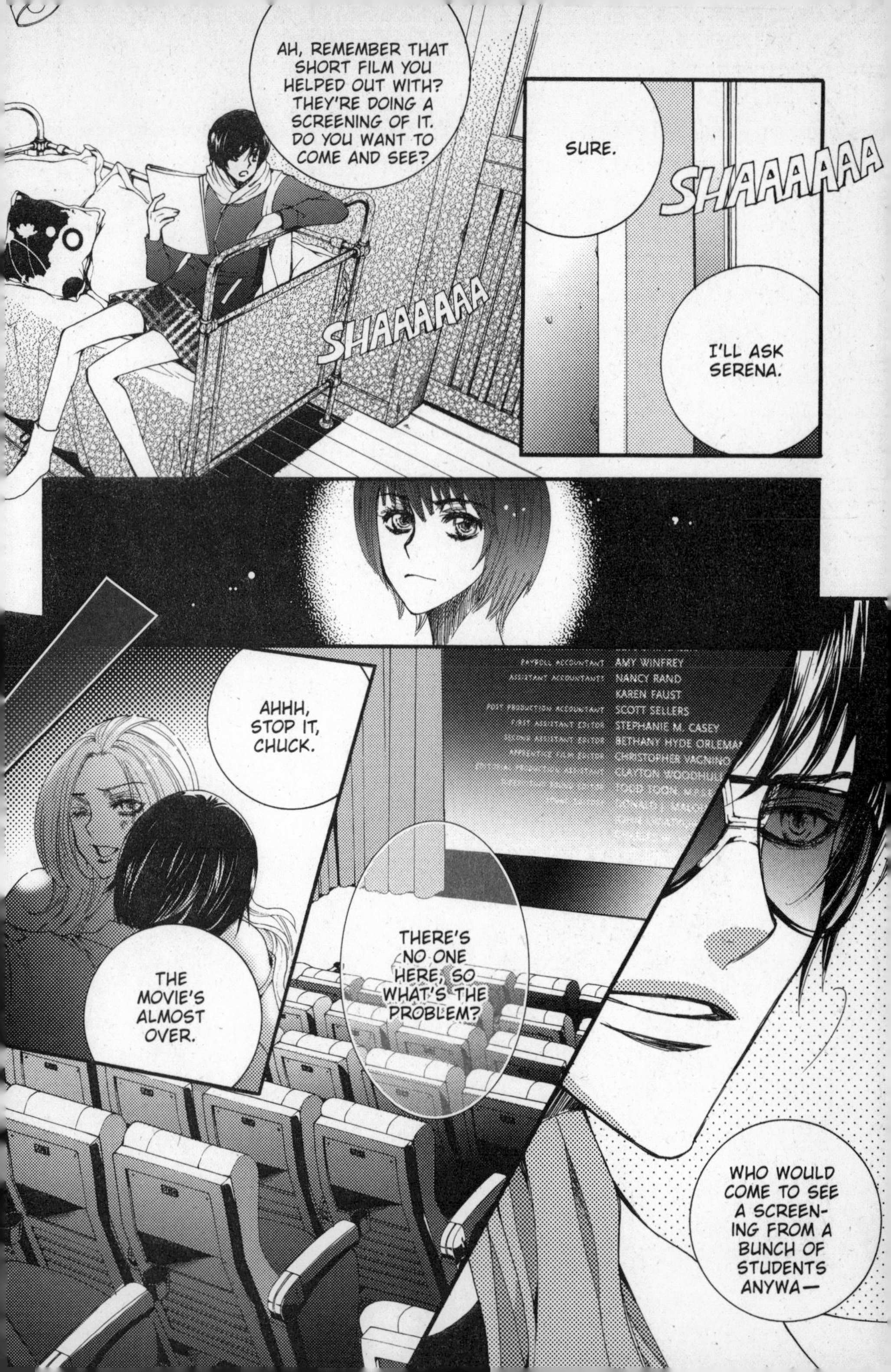
AH, REMEMBER THAT SHORT FILM YOU HELPED OUT WITH? THEY'RE DOING A SCREENING OF IT. DO YOU WANT TO COME AND SEE?
SHAAAAAA
SURE.
SHAAAAAAA
I'LL ASK SERENA.
AHHH, STOP IT, CHUCK.
THE MOVIE'S ALMOST OVER.
AMY WINFREY
NANCY RAND
KAREN FAUST
SCOTT SELLERS
STEPHANIE M. CASEY
THERE'S NO ONE HERE, SO WHAT'S THE PROBLEM?
WHO WOULD COME TO SEE A SCREEN-ING FROM A BUNCH OF STUDENTS ANYWA—

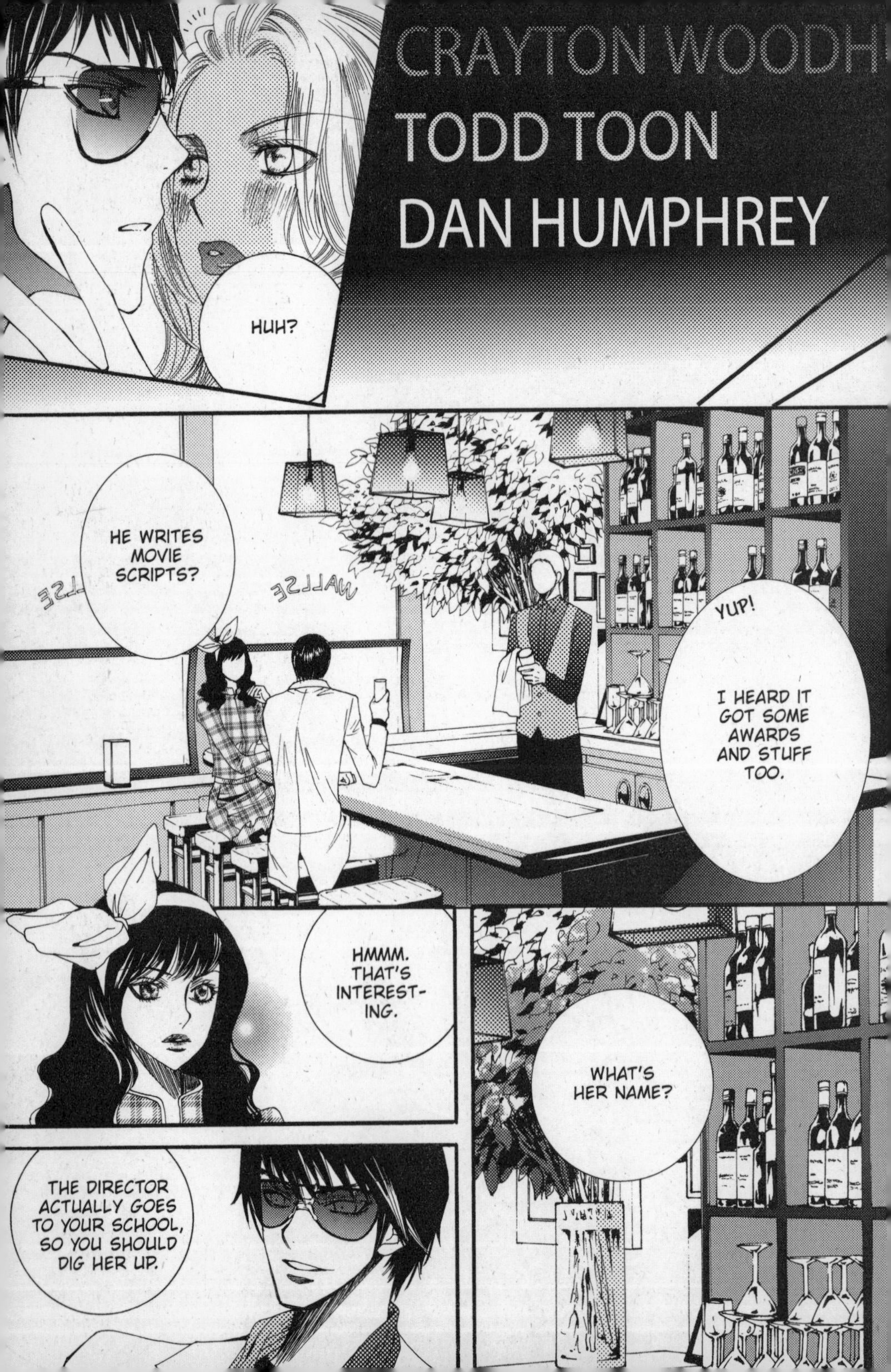
HUH?
CRAYTON WOODH
TODD TOON
DAN HUMPHREY
HE WRITES MOVIE SCRIPTS?
YUP!
I HEARD IT GOT SOME AWARDS AND STUFF TOO.
HMMM. THAT'S INTEREST-ING.
THE DIRECTOR ACTUALLY GOES TO YOUR SCHOOL, SO YOU SHOULD DIG HER UP.
WHAT'S HER NAME?

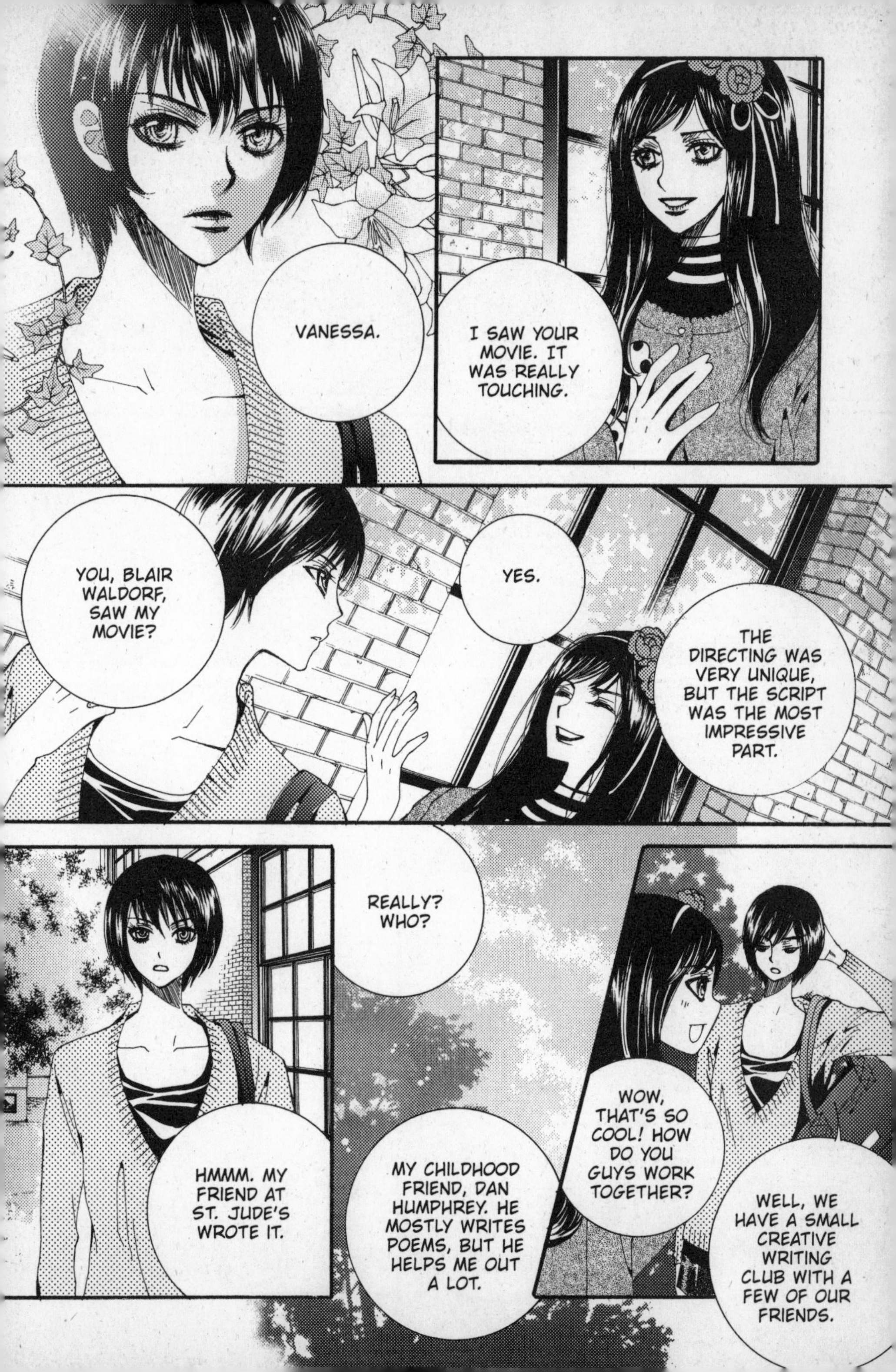
VANESSA.
I SAW YOUR MOVIE. IT WAS REALLY TOUCHING.
YOU, BLAIR WALDORF, SAW MY MOVIE?
YES.
THE DIRECTING WAS VERY UNIQUE, BUT THE SCRIPT WAS THE MOST IMPRESSIVE PART.
REALLY? WHO?
HMMM. MY FRIEND AT ST. JUDE'S WROTE IT.
MY CHILDHOOD FRIEND, DAN HUMPHREY. HE MOSTLY WRITES POEMS, BUT HE HELPS ME OUT A LOT.
WOW, THAT'S SO COOL! HOW DO YOU GUYS WORK TOGETHER?
WELL, WE HAVE A SMALL CREATIVE WRITING CLUB WITH A FEW OF OUR FRIENDS.

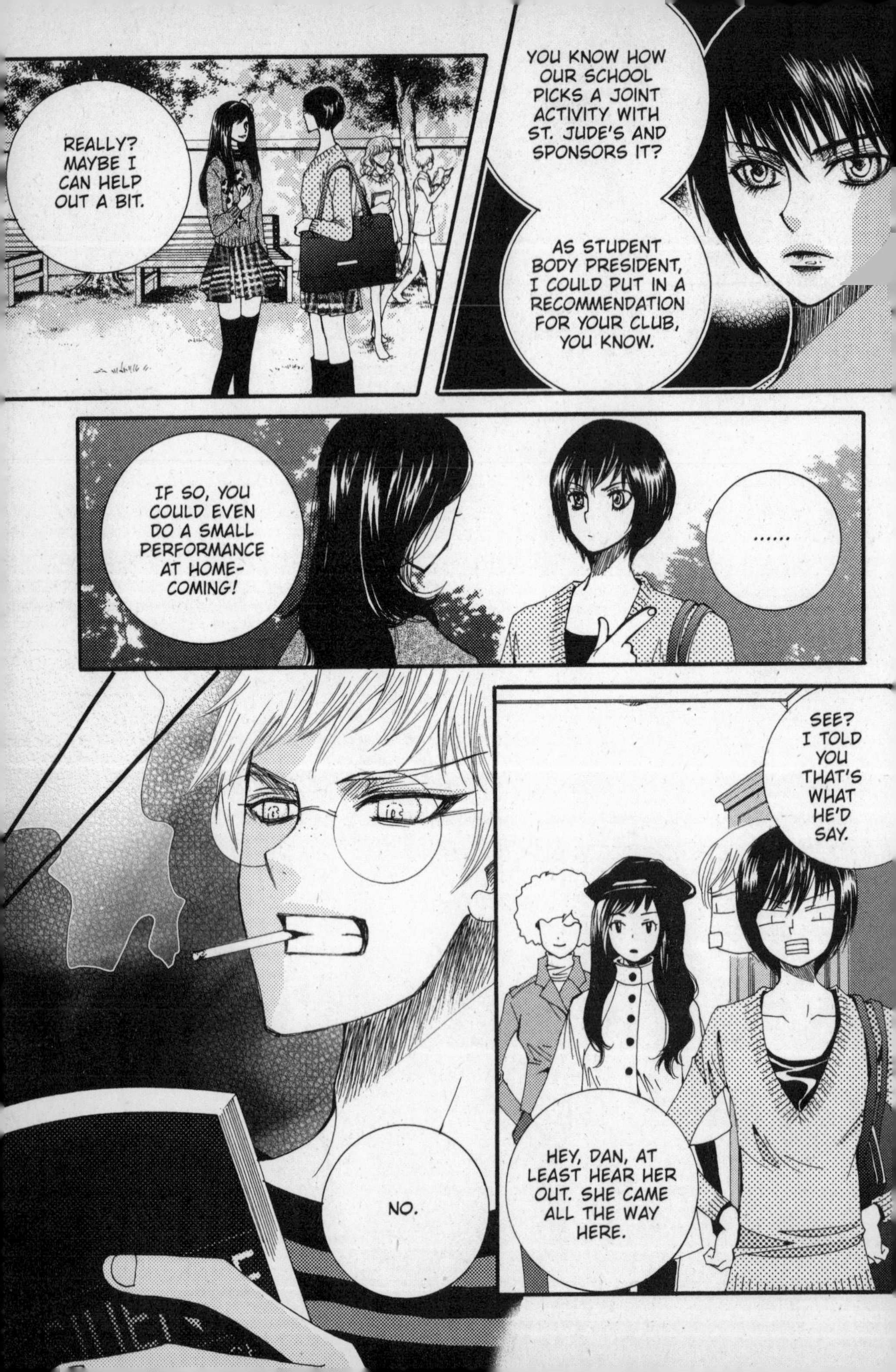
REALLY? MAYBE I CAN HELP OUT A BIT.
YOU KNOW HOW OUR SCHOOL PICKS A JOINT ACTIVITY WITH ST. JUDE'S AND SPONSORS IT?
AS STUDENT BODY PRESIDENT, I COULD PUT IN A RECOMMENDATION FOR YOUR CLUB, YOU KNOW.
IF SO, YOU COULD EVEN DO A SMALL PERFORMANCE AT HOME-COMING!
......
NO.
SEE? I TOLD YOU THAT'S WHAT HE'D SAY.
HEY, DAN, AT LEAST HEAR HER OUT. SHE CAME ALL THE WAY HERE.

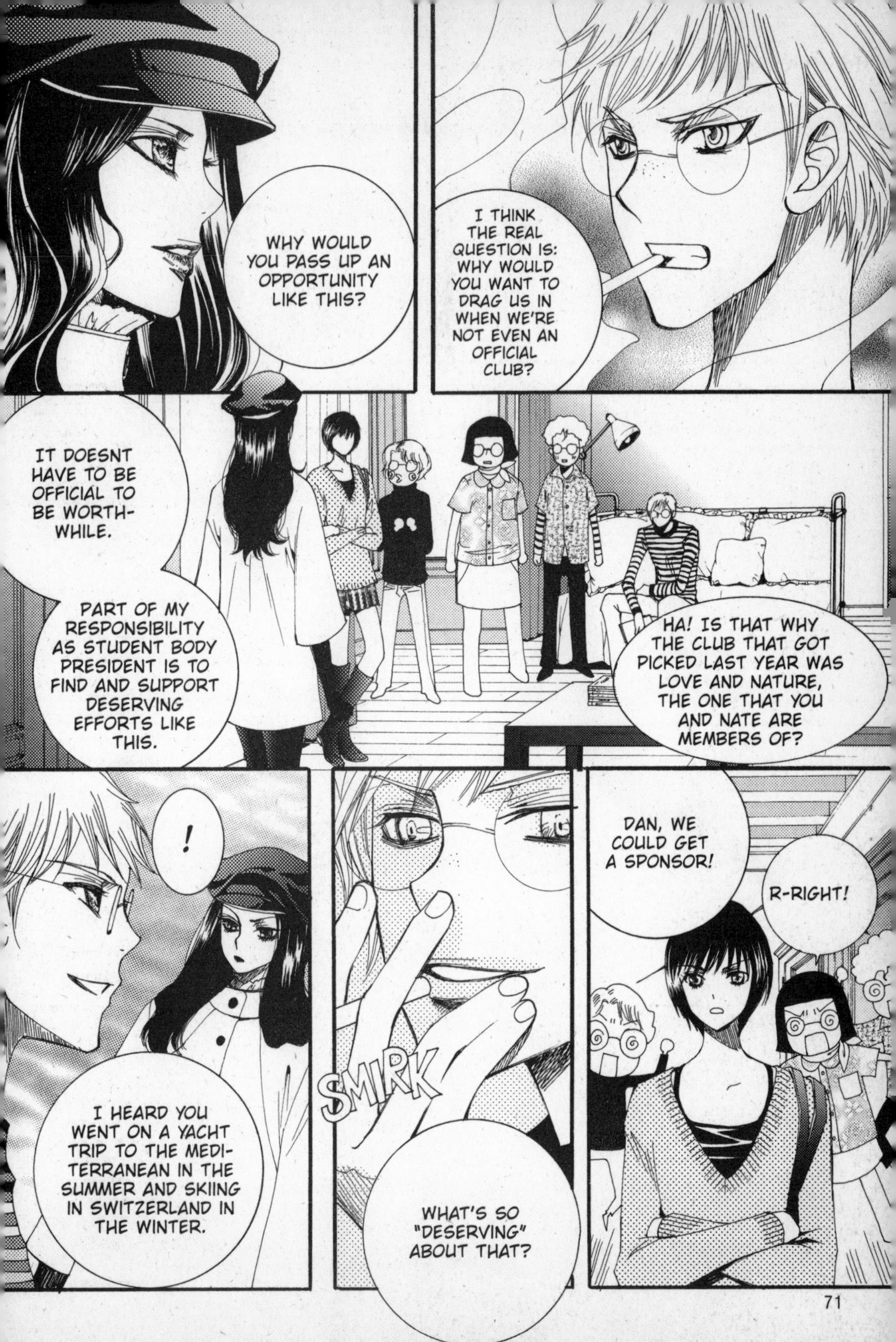
WHY WOULD YOU PASS UP AN OPPORTUNITY LIKE THIS?
I THINK THE REAL QUESTION IS: WHY WOULD YOU WANT TO DRAG US IN WHEN WE'RE NOT EVEN AN OFFICIAL CLUB?
IT DOESNT HAVE TO BE OFFICIAL TO BE WORTH-WHILE.
PART OF MY RESPONSIBILITY AS STUDENT BODY PRESIDENT IS TO FIND AND SUPPORT DESERVING EFFORTS LIKE THIS.
HA! IS THAT WHY THE CLUB THAT GOT PICKED LAST YEAR WAS LOVE AND NATURE, THE ONE THAT YOU AND NATE ARE MEMBERS OF?
!
I HEARD YOU WENT ON A YACHT TRIP TO THE MEDI-TERRANEAN IN THE SUMMER AND SKIING IN SWITZERLAND IN THE WINTER.
SMIRK
WHAT'S SO "DESERVING" ABOUT THAT?
DAN, WE COULD GET A SPONSOR!
R-RIGHT!

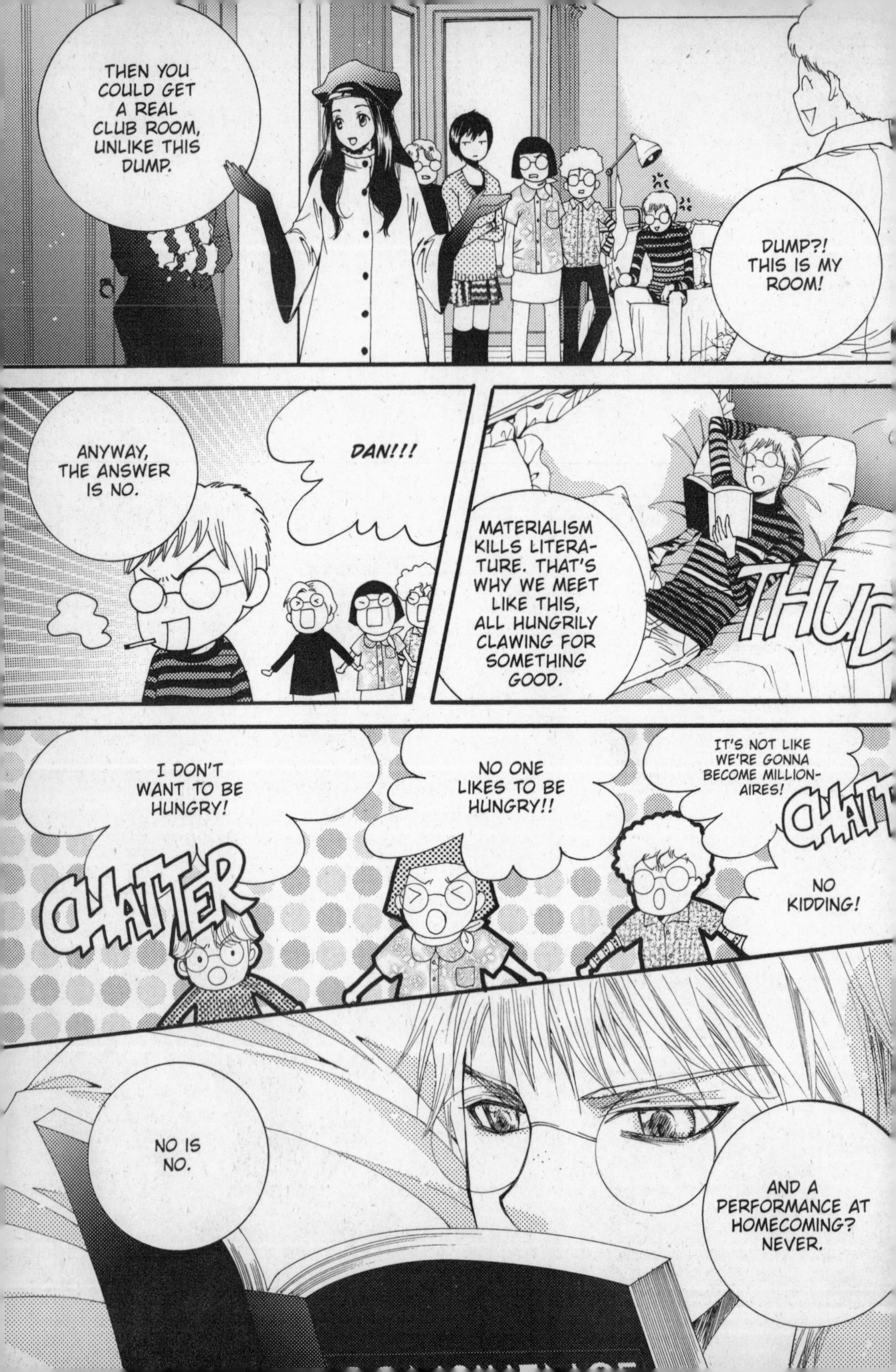
THEN YOU COULD GET A REAL CLUB ROOM, UNLIKE THIS DUMP.
DUMP?! THIS IS MY ROOM!
ANYWAY, THE ANSWER IS NO.
DAN!!!
MATERIALISM KILLS LITERA-TURE. THAT'S WHY WE MEET LIKE THIS, ALL HUNGRILY CLAWING FOR SOMETHING GOOD.
THUD
I DON'T WANT TO BE HUNGRY!
NO ONE LIKES TO BE HUNGRY!!
IT'S NOT LIKE WE'RE GONNA BECOME MILLION-AIRES!
CHATTER
CHATTER
NO KIDDING!
NO IS NO.
AND A PERFORMANCE AT HOMECOMING? NEVER.

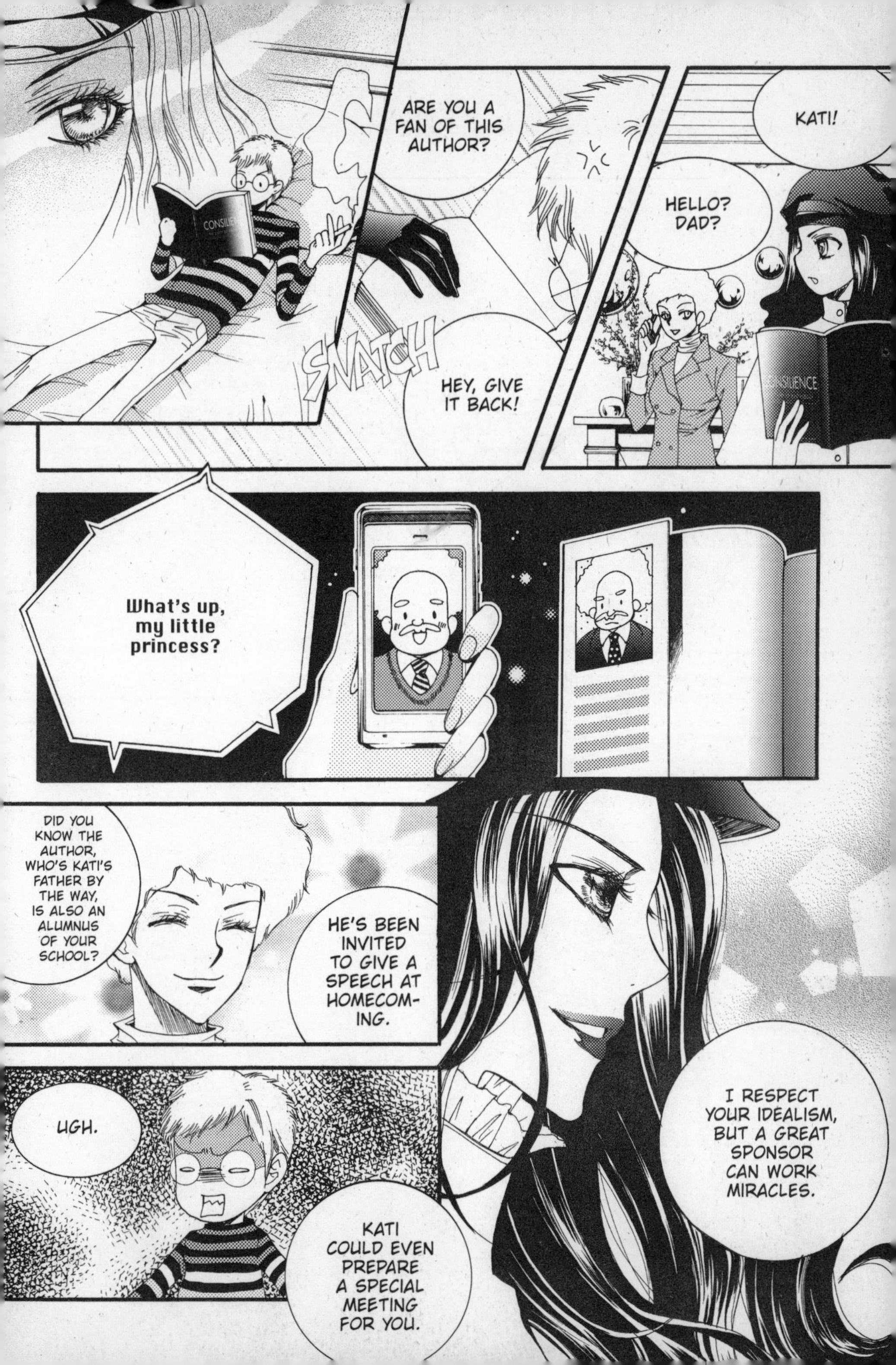
ARE YOU A FAN OF THIS AUTHOR?
SNATCH
HEY, GIVE IT BACK!
KATI!
HELLO? DAD?
What's up, my little princess?
DID YOU KNOW THE AUTHOR, WHO'S KATI'S FATHER BY THE WAY, IS ALSO AN ALUMNUS OF YOUR SCHOOL?
HE'S BEEN INVITED TO GIVE A SPEECH AT HOMECOM-ING.
UGH.
I RESPECT YOUR IDEALISM, BUT A GREAT SPONSOR CAN WORK MIRACLES.
KATI COULD EVEN PREPARE A SPECIAL MEETING FOR YOU.

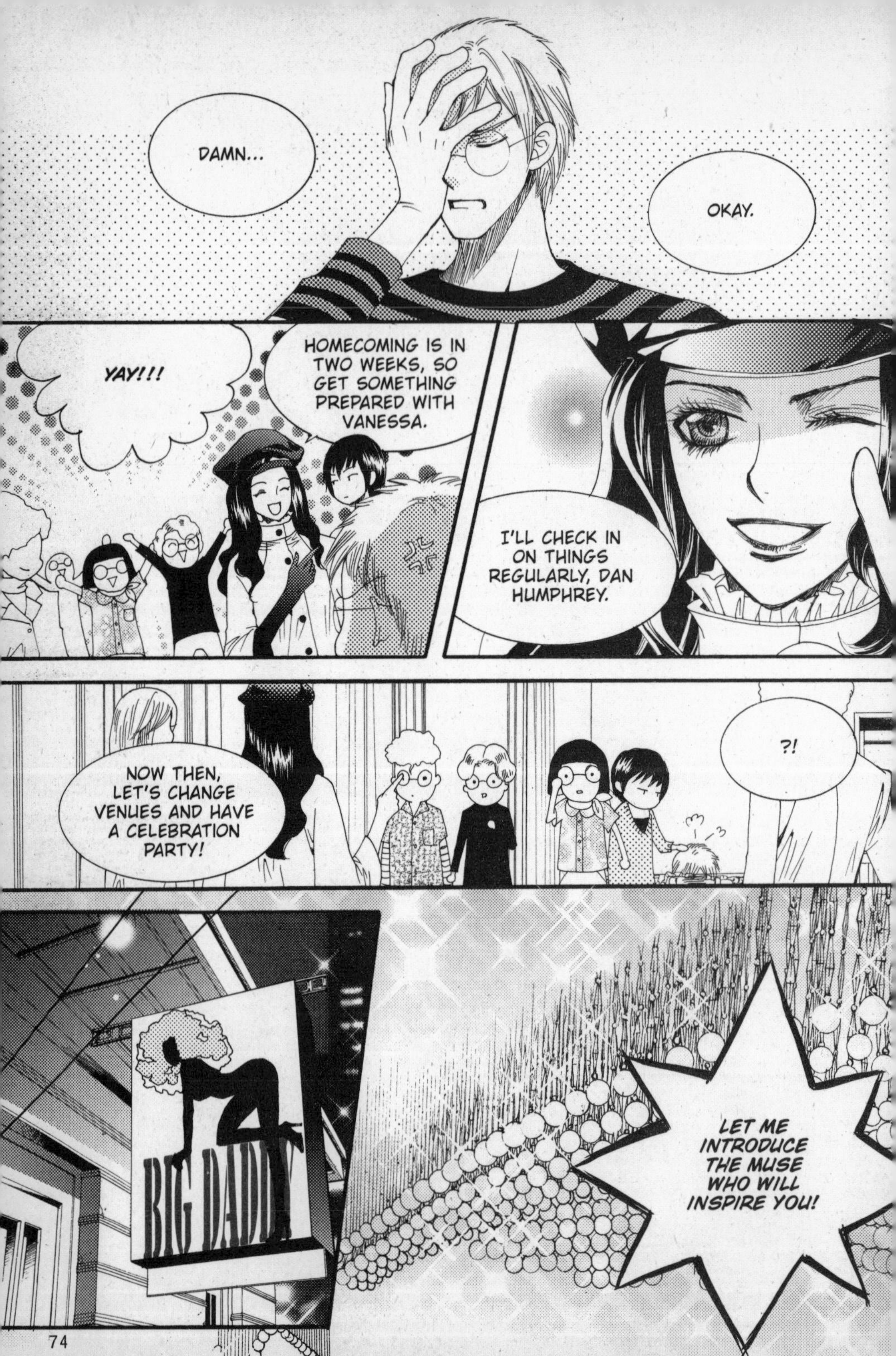
DAMN...
OKAY.
YAY!!!
HOMECOMING IS IN TWO WEEKS, SO GET SOMETHING PREPARED WITH VANESSA.
I'LL CHECK IN ON THINGS REGULARLY, DAN HUMPHREY.
NOW THEN, LET'S CHANGE VENUES AND HAVE A CELEBRATION PARTY!
?!
BIG DADDY
LET ME INTRODUCE THE MUSE WHO WILL INSPIRE YOU!

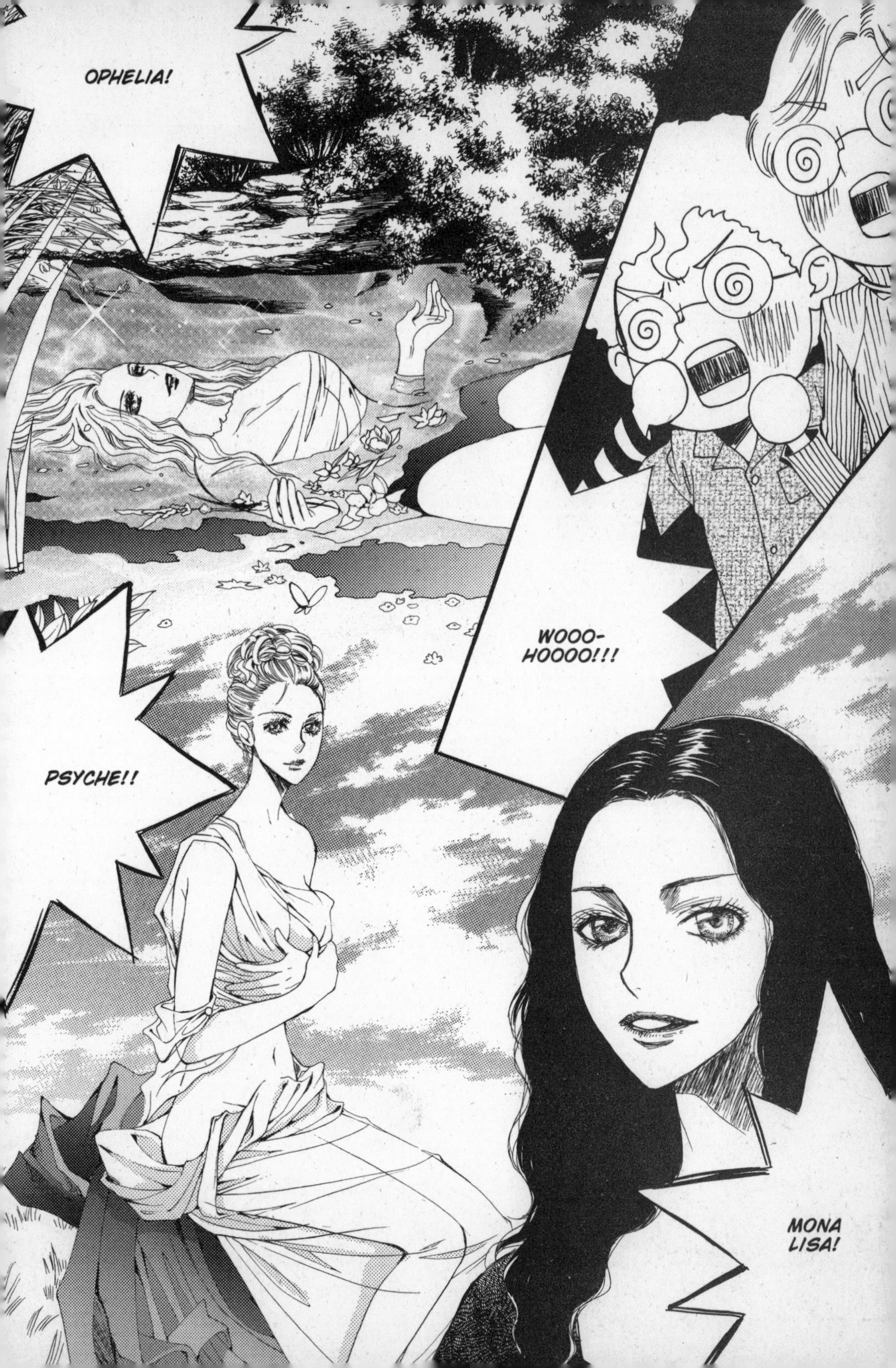
OPHELIA!
WOOO-HOOOO!!!
PSYCHE!!
MONA LISA!

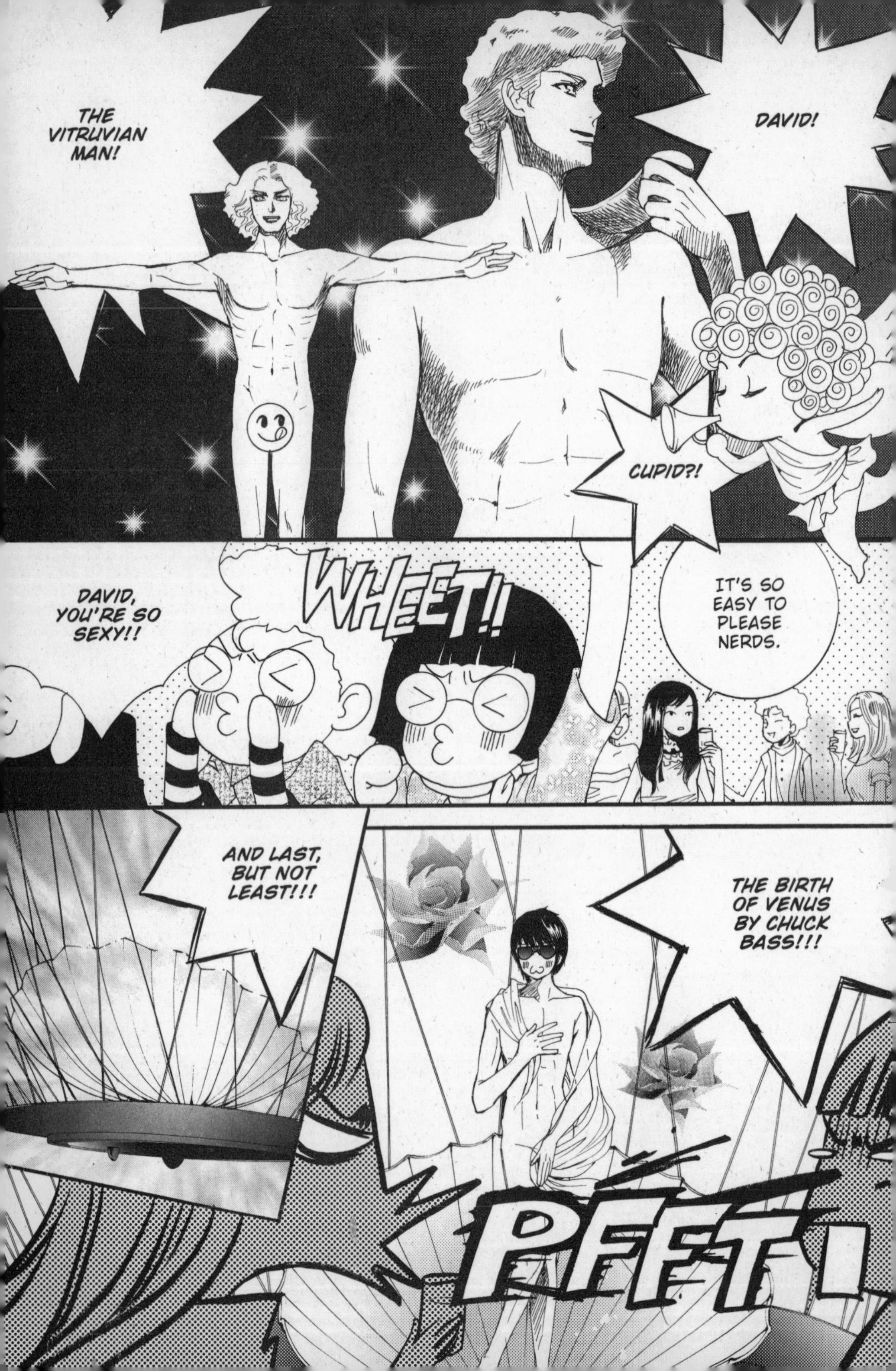
THE VITRUVIAN MAN!
DAVID!
CUPID?!
DAVID, YOU'RE SO SEXY!!
WHEET!!
IT'S SO EASY TO PLEASE NERDS.
AND LAST, BUT NOT LEAST!!!
THE BIRTH OF VENUS BY CHUCK BASS!!!
PFFT!

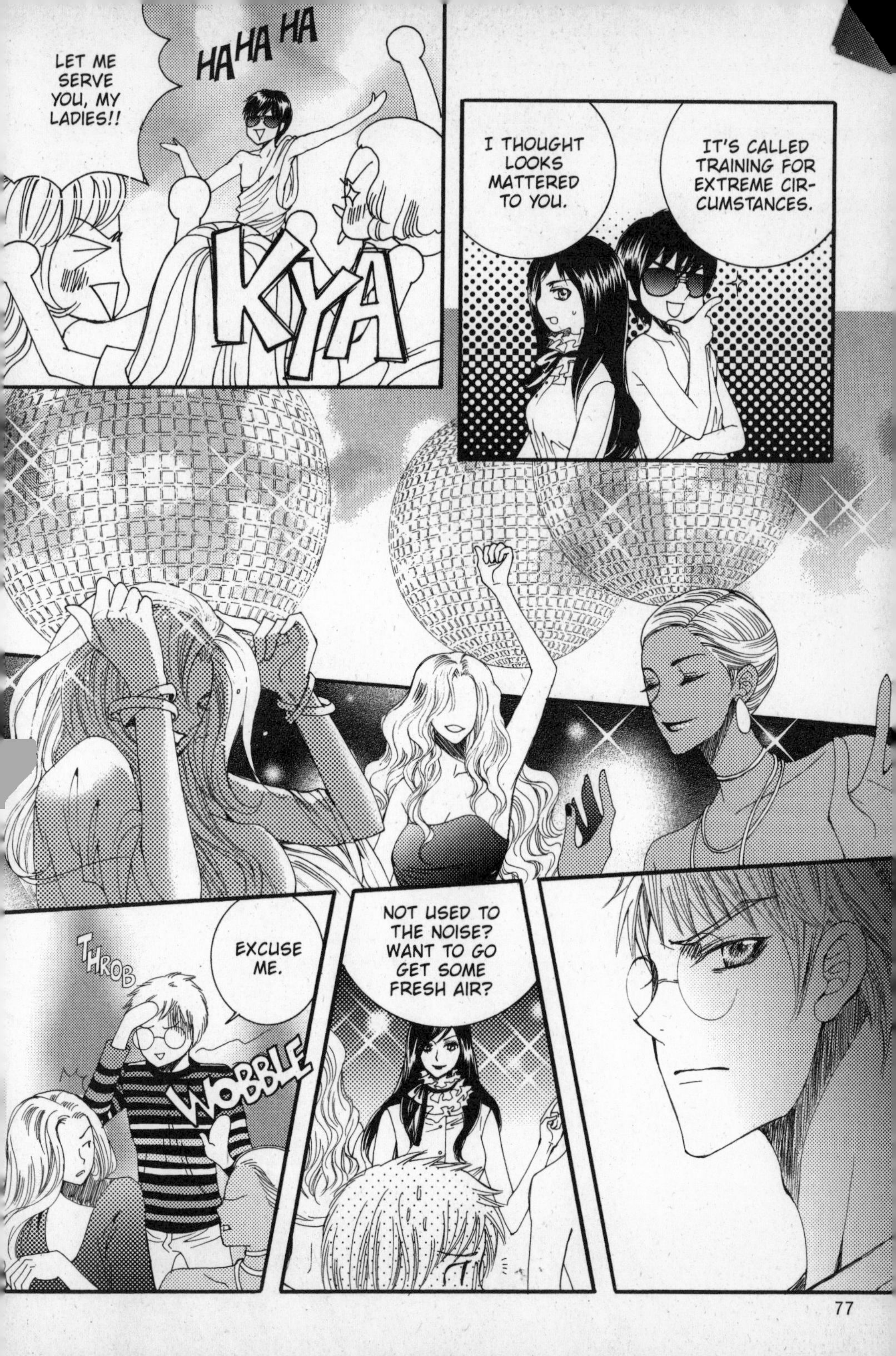
LET ME SERVE YOU, MY LADIES!!
HAHAHA HA
KYA
I THOUGHT LOOKS MATTERED TO YOU.
IT'S CALLED TRAINING FOR EXTREME CIR-CUMSTANCES.
THROB
EXCUSE ME.
WOBBLE
NOT USED TO THE NOISE? WANT TO GO GET SOME FRESH AIR?

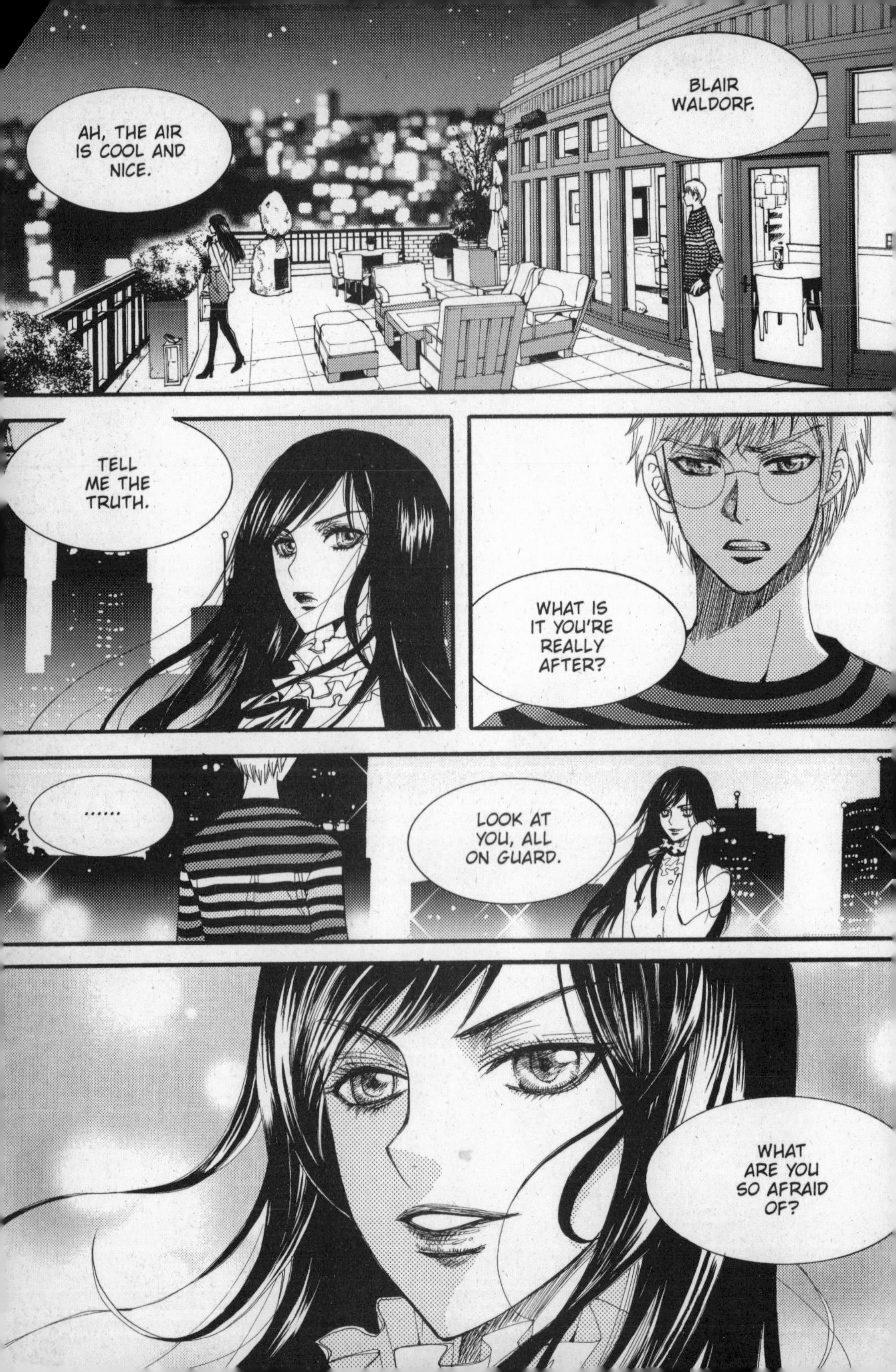
AH, THE AIR IS COOL AND NICE.
BLAIR WALDORF.
TELL ME THE TRUTH.
WHAT IS IT YOU'RE REALLY AFTER?
......
LOOK AT YOU, ALL ON GUARD.
WHAT ARE YOU SO AFRAID OF?

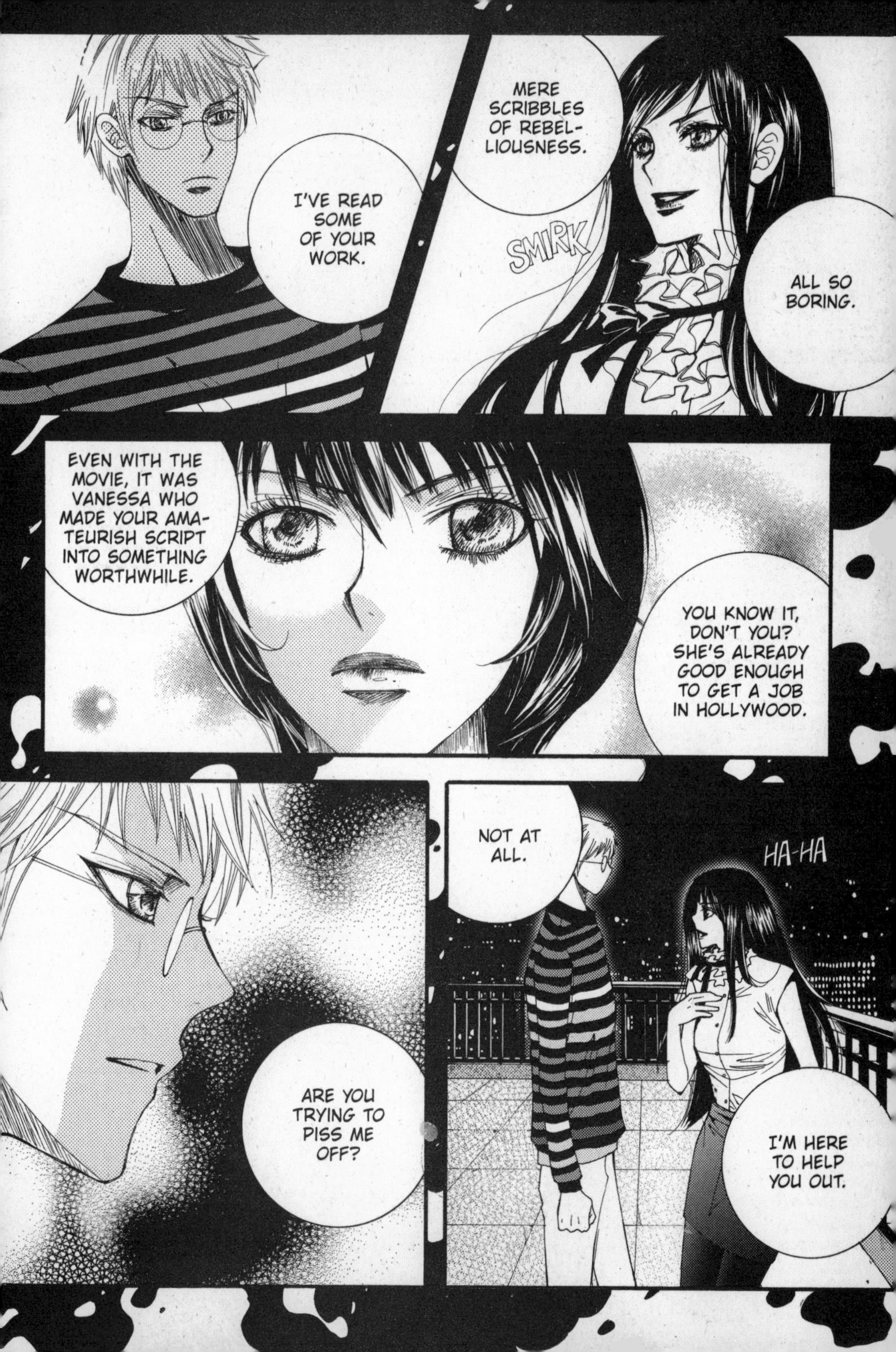
I'VE READ SOME OF YOUR WORK.
MERE SCRIBBLES OF REBEL-LIOUSNESS.
SMIRK
ALL SO BORING.
EVEN WITH THE MOVIE, IT WAS VANESSA WHO MADE YOUR AMA-TEURISH SCRIPT INTO SOMETHING WORTHWHILE.
YOU KNOW IT, DON'T YOU? SHE'S ALREADY GOOD ENOUGH TO GET A JOB IN HOLLYWOOD.
ARE YOU TRYING TO PISS ME OFF?
NOT AT ALL.
HA-HA
I'M HERE TO HELP YOU OUT.

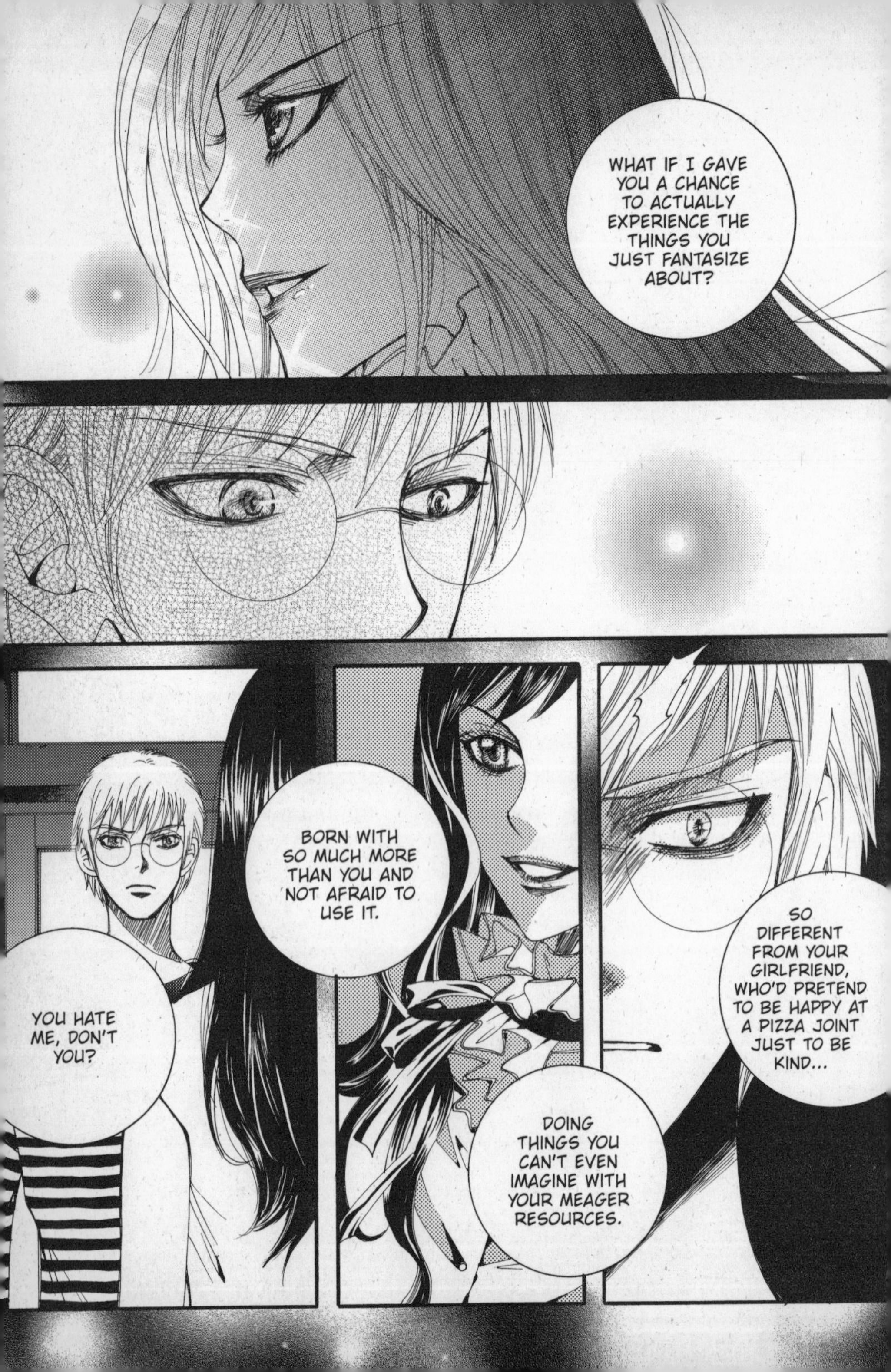
WHAT IF I GAVE YOU A CHANCE TO ACTUALLY EXPERIENCE THE THINGS YOU JUST FANTASIZE ABOUT?
YOU HATE ME, DON'T YOU?
BORN WITH SO MUCH MORE THAN YOU AND NOT AFRAID TO USE IT.
DOING THINGS YOU CAN'T EVEN IMAGINE WITH YOUR MEAGER RESOURCES.
SO DIFFERENT FROM YOUR GIRLFRIEND, WHO'D PRETEND TO BE HAPPY AT A PIZZA JOINT JUST TO BE KIND...

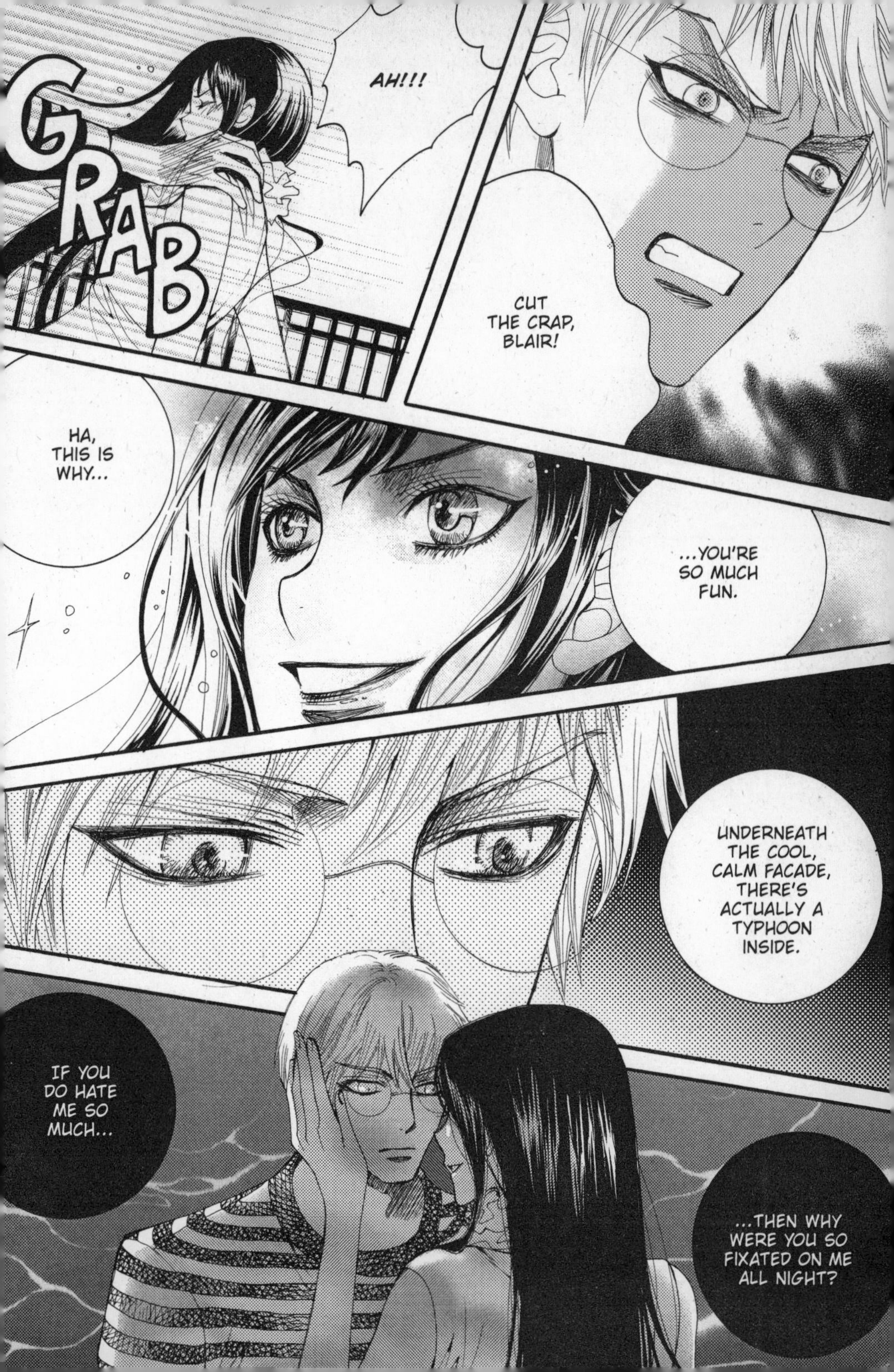
GRAB
AH!!!
CUT THE CRAP, BLAIR!
HA, THIS IS WHY...
...YOU'RE SO MUCH FUN.
UNDERNEATH THE COOL, CALM FACADE, THERE'S ACTUALLY A TYPHOON INSIDE.
IF YOU DO HATE ME SO MUCH...
...THEN WHY WERE YOU SO FIXATED ON ME ALL NIGHT?

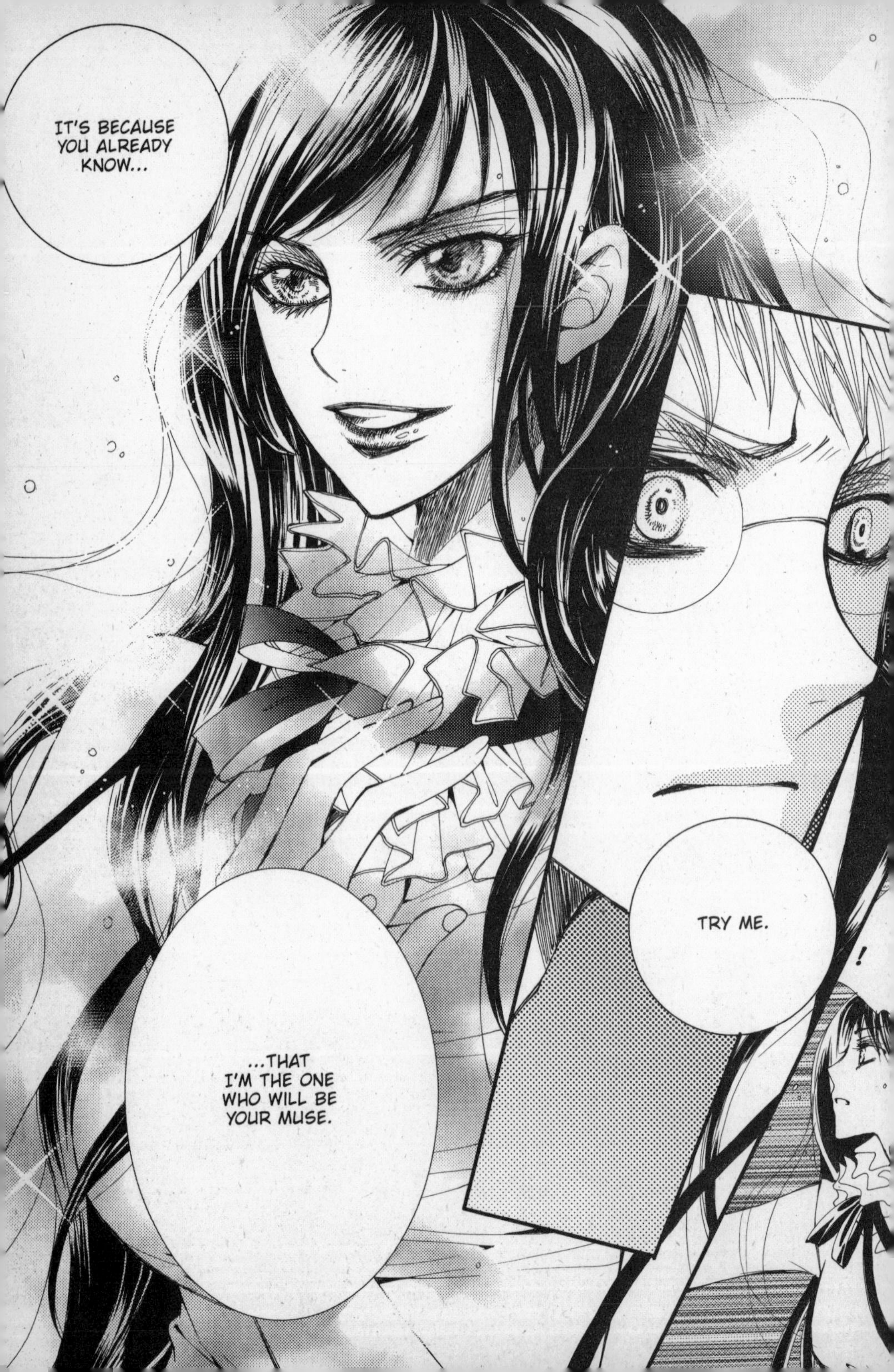
IT'S BECAUSE YOU ALREADY KNOW...
...THAT I'M THE ONE WHO WILL BE YOUR MUSE.
TRY ME.
!

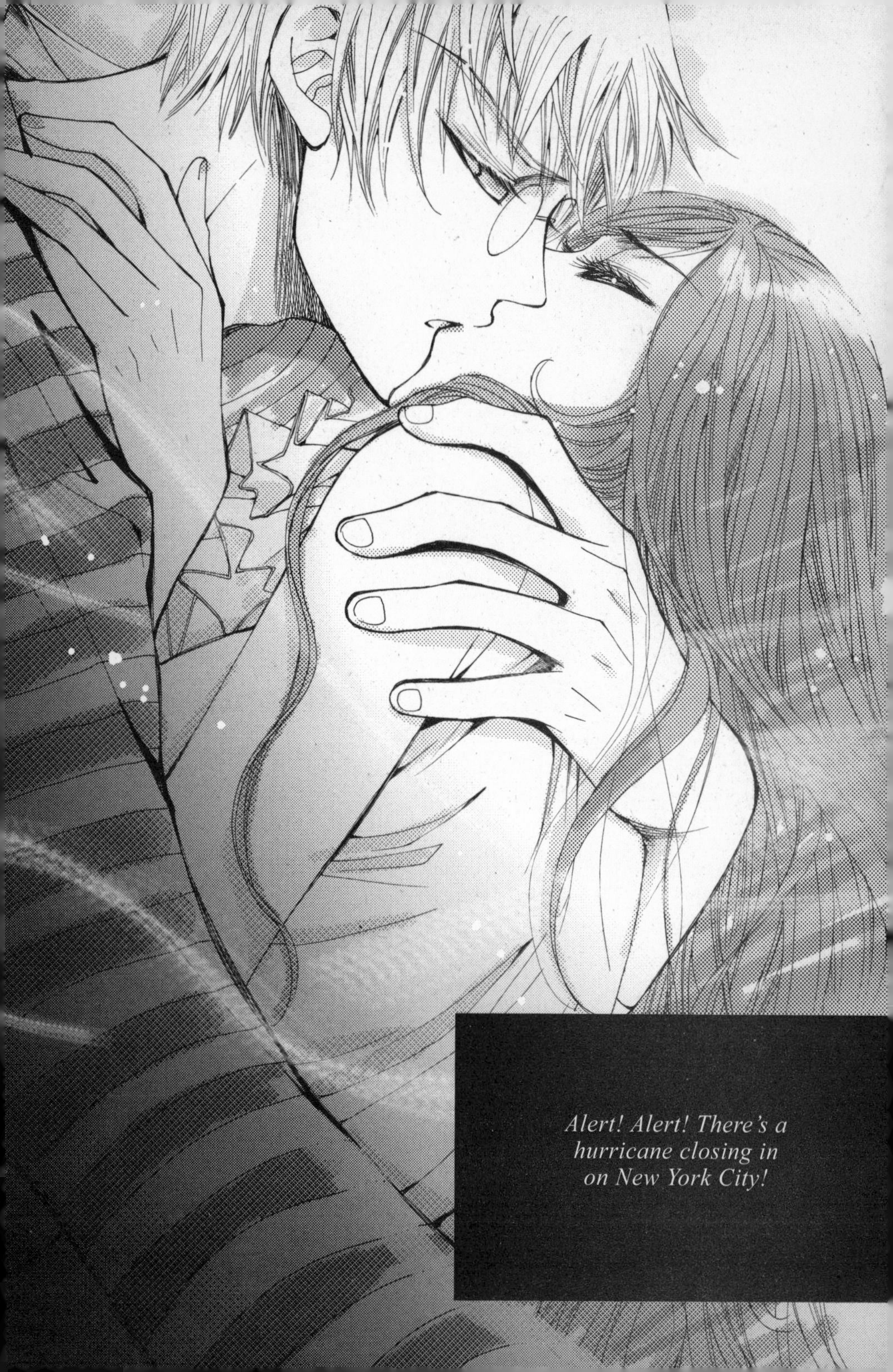
Alert! Alert! There's a hurricane closing in on New York City!

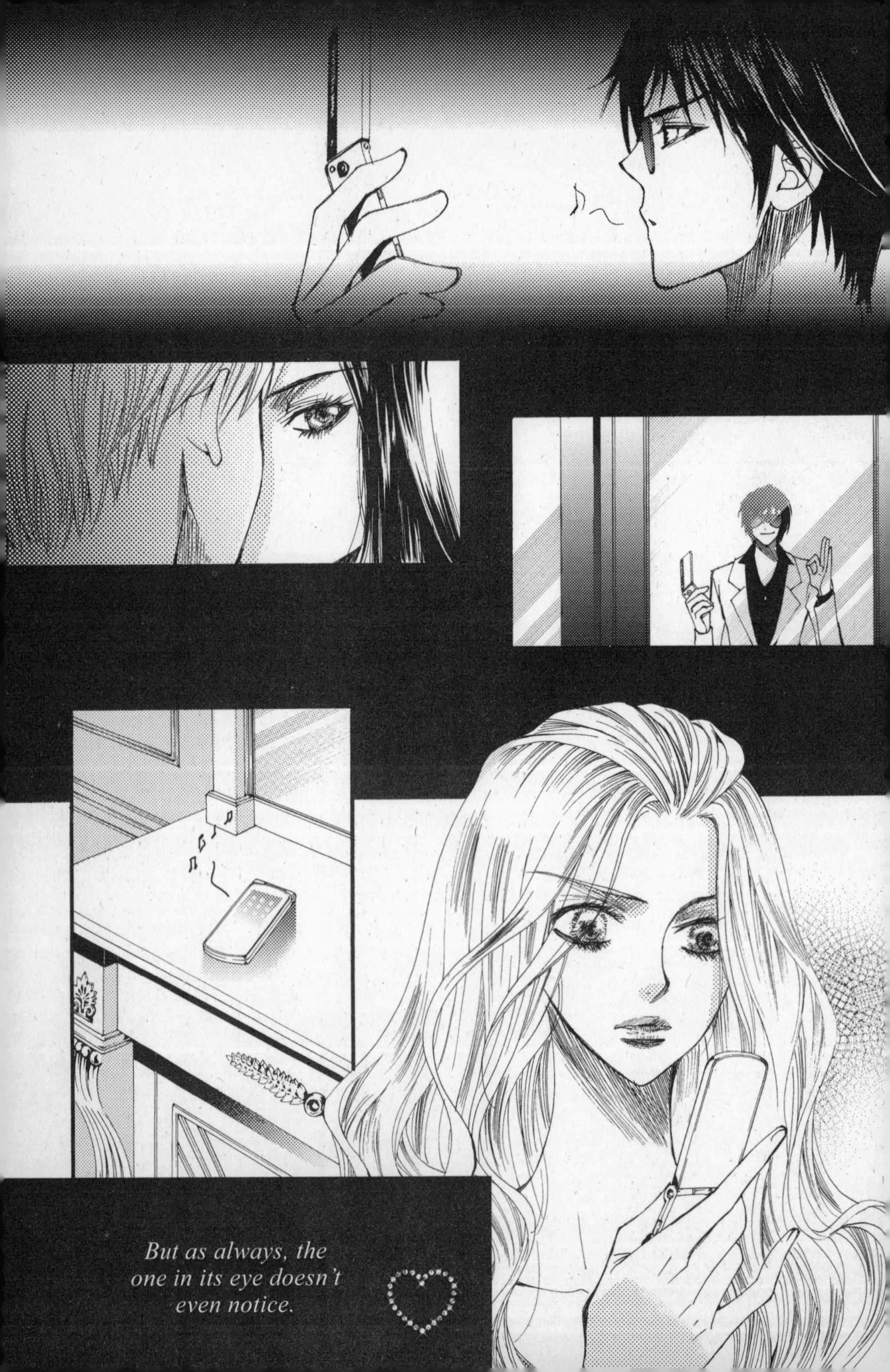
But as always, the one in its eye doesn't even notice.

gossip girl

FOR YOUR EYES ONLY

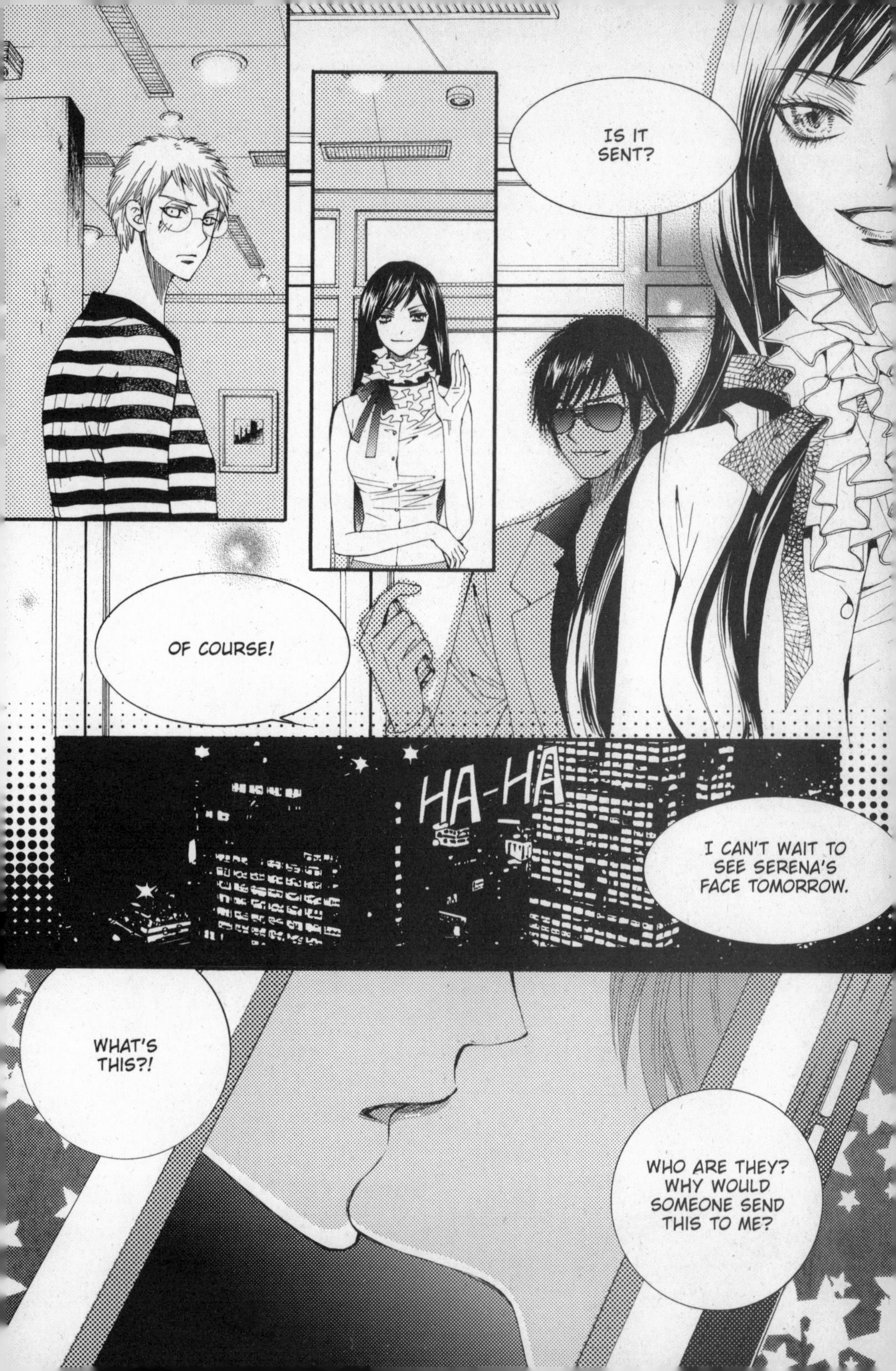
IS IT SENT?
OF COURSE!
HA-HA
I CAN'T WAIT TO SEE SERENA'S FACE TOMORROW.
WHAT'S THIS?!
WHO ARE THEY? WHY WOULD SOMEONE SEND THIS TO ME?

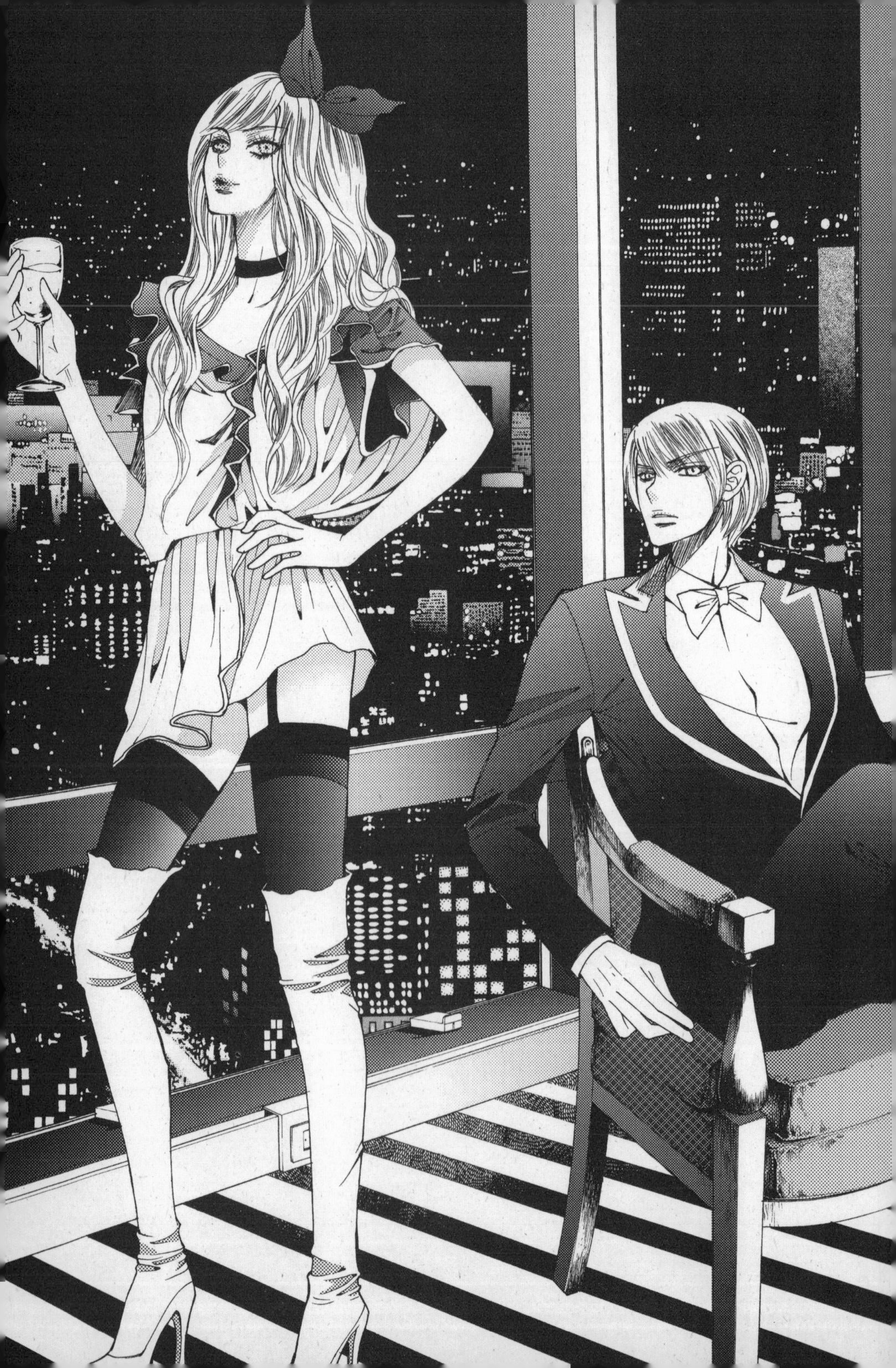

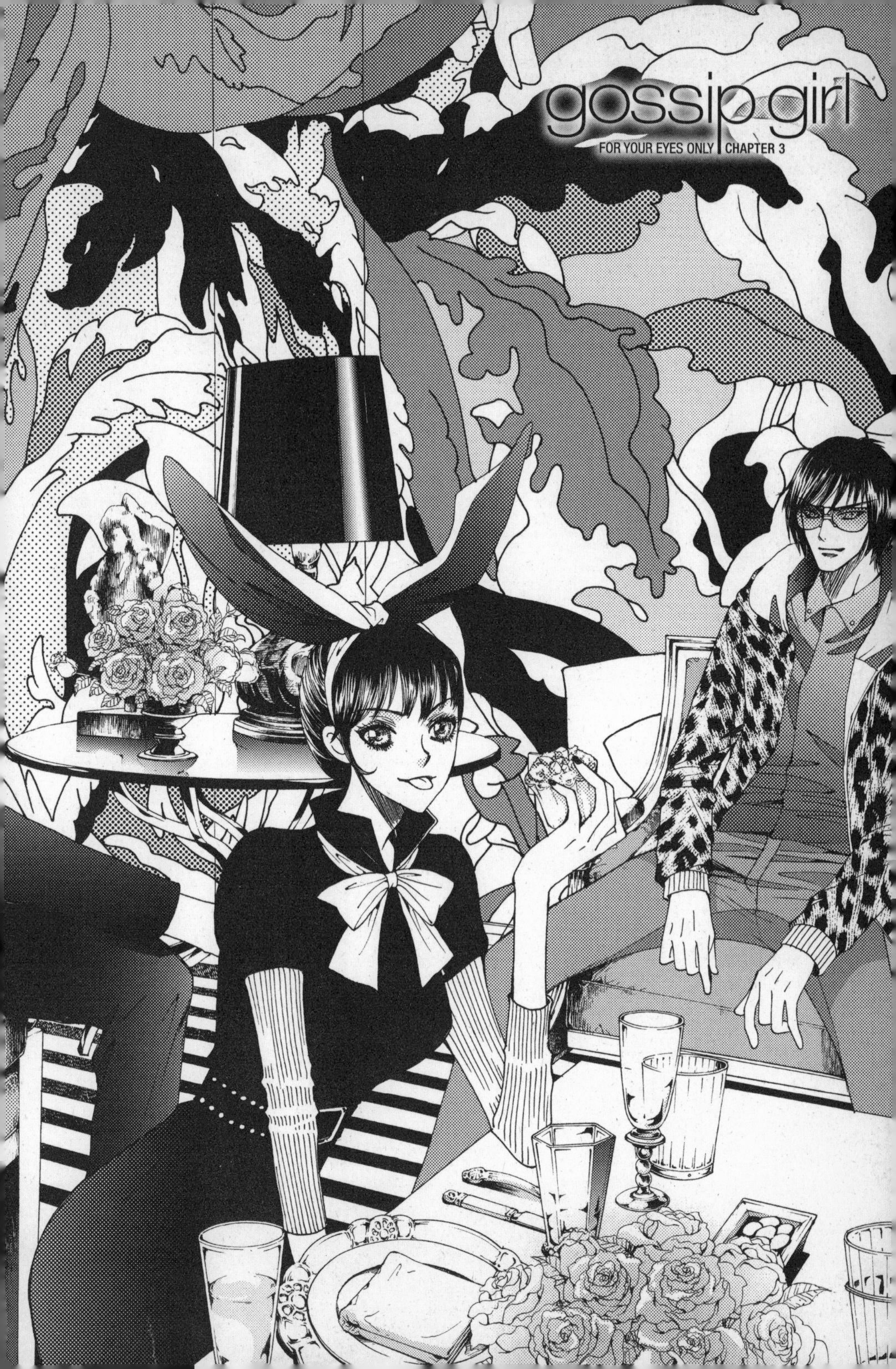
gossip girl
FOR YOUR EYES ONLY | CHAPTER 3

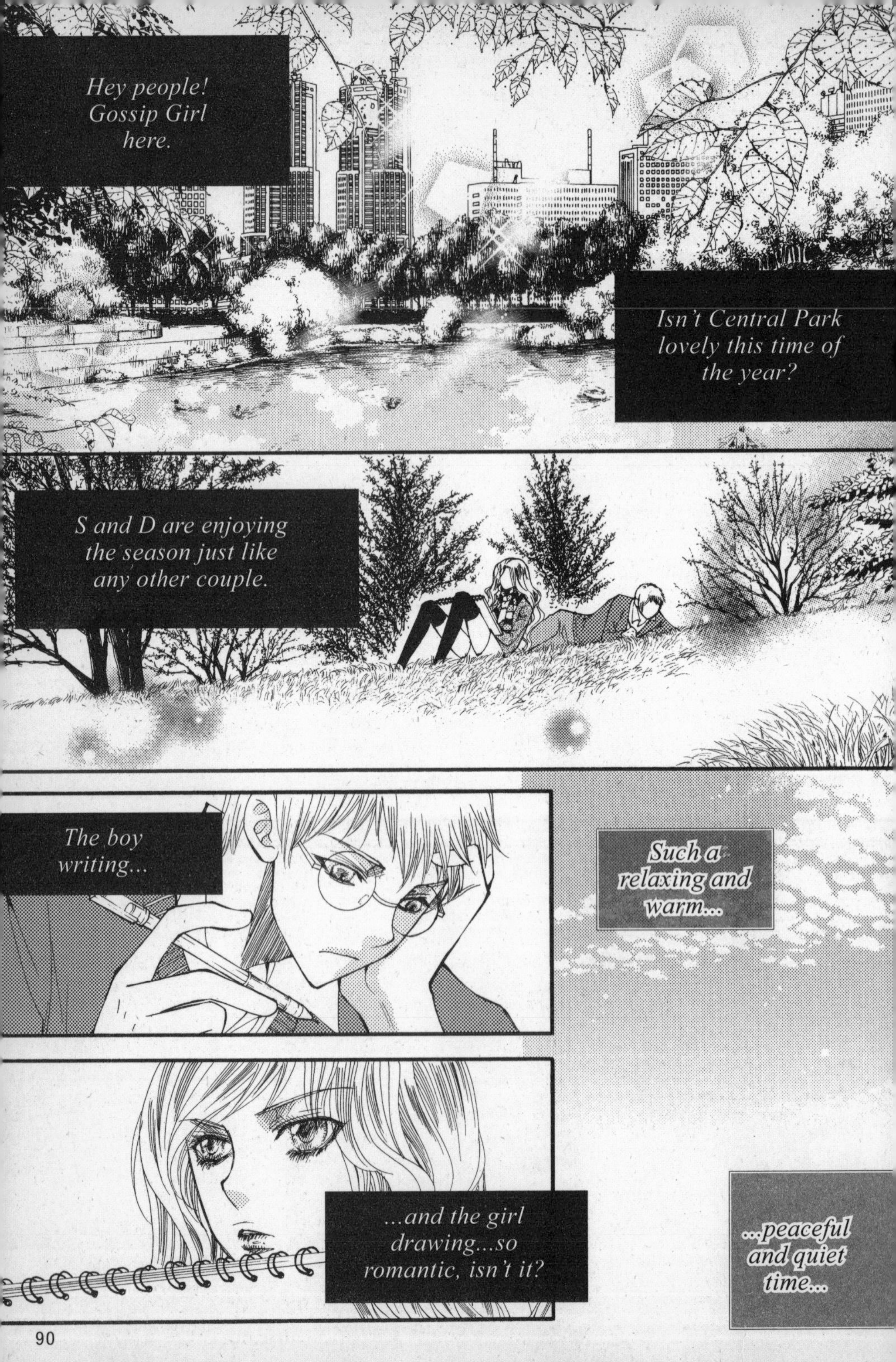
Hey people! Gossip Girl here.
Isn't Central Park lovely this time of the year?
S and D are enjoying the season just like any other couple.
The boy writing...
Such a relaxing and warm...
...and the girl drawing...so romantic, isn't it?
...peaceful and quiet time...

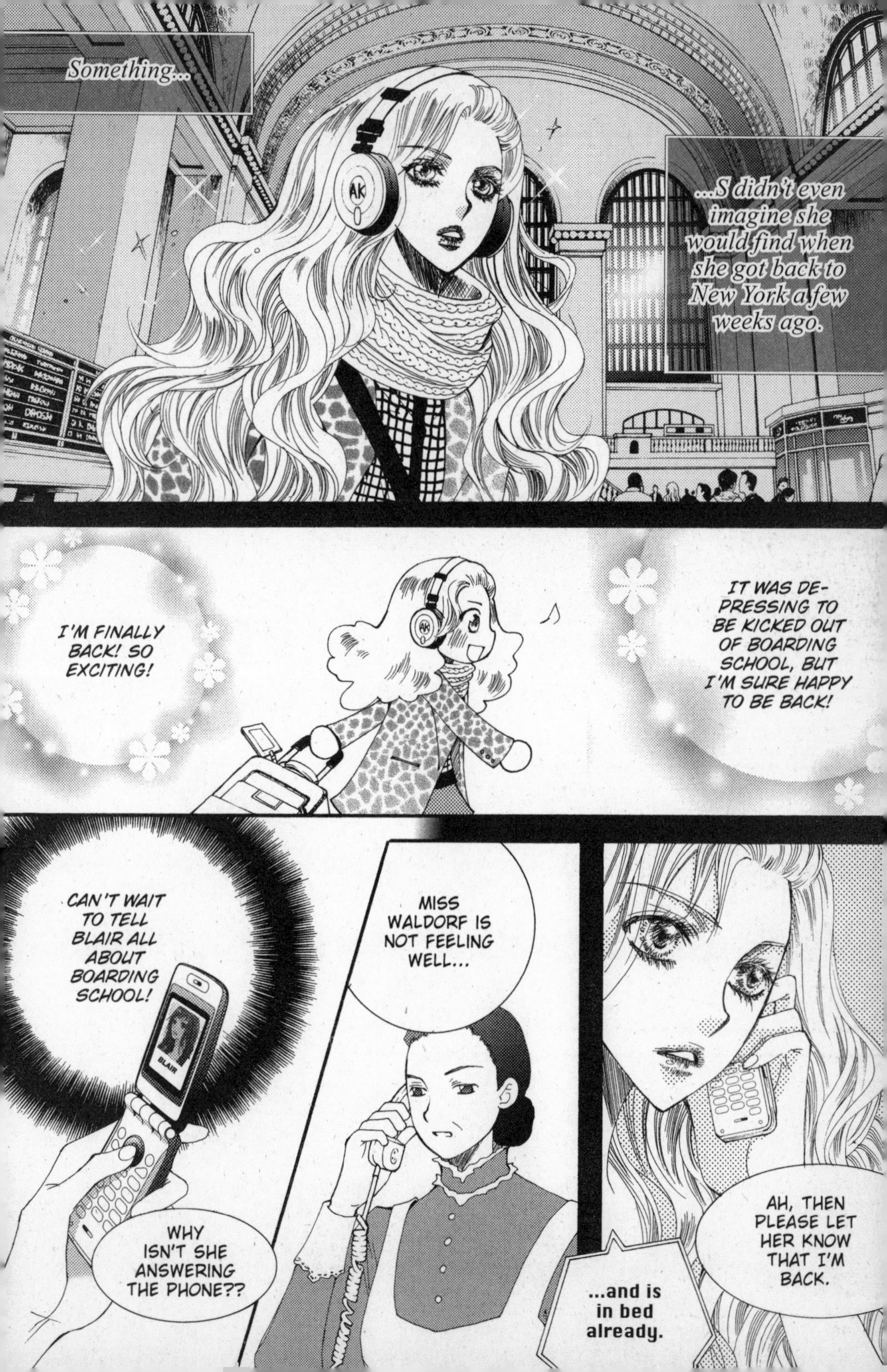
Something...
...S didn't even imagine she would find when she got back to New York a few weeks ago.
I'M FINALLY BACK! SO EXCITING!
IT WAS DE-PRESSING TO BE KICKED OUT OF BOARDING SCHOOL, BUT I'M SURE HAPPY TO BE BACK!
CAN'T WAIT TO TELL BLAIR ALL ABOUT BOARDING SCHOOL!
BLAIR
WHY ISN'T SHE ANSWERING THE PHONE??
MISS WALDORF IS NOT FEELING WELL...
...and is in bed already.
AH, THEN PLEASE LET HER KNOW THAT I'M BACK.

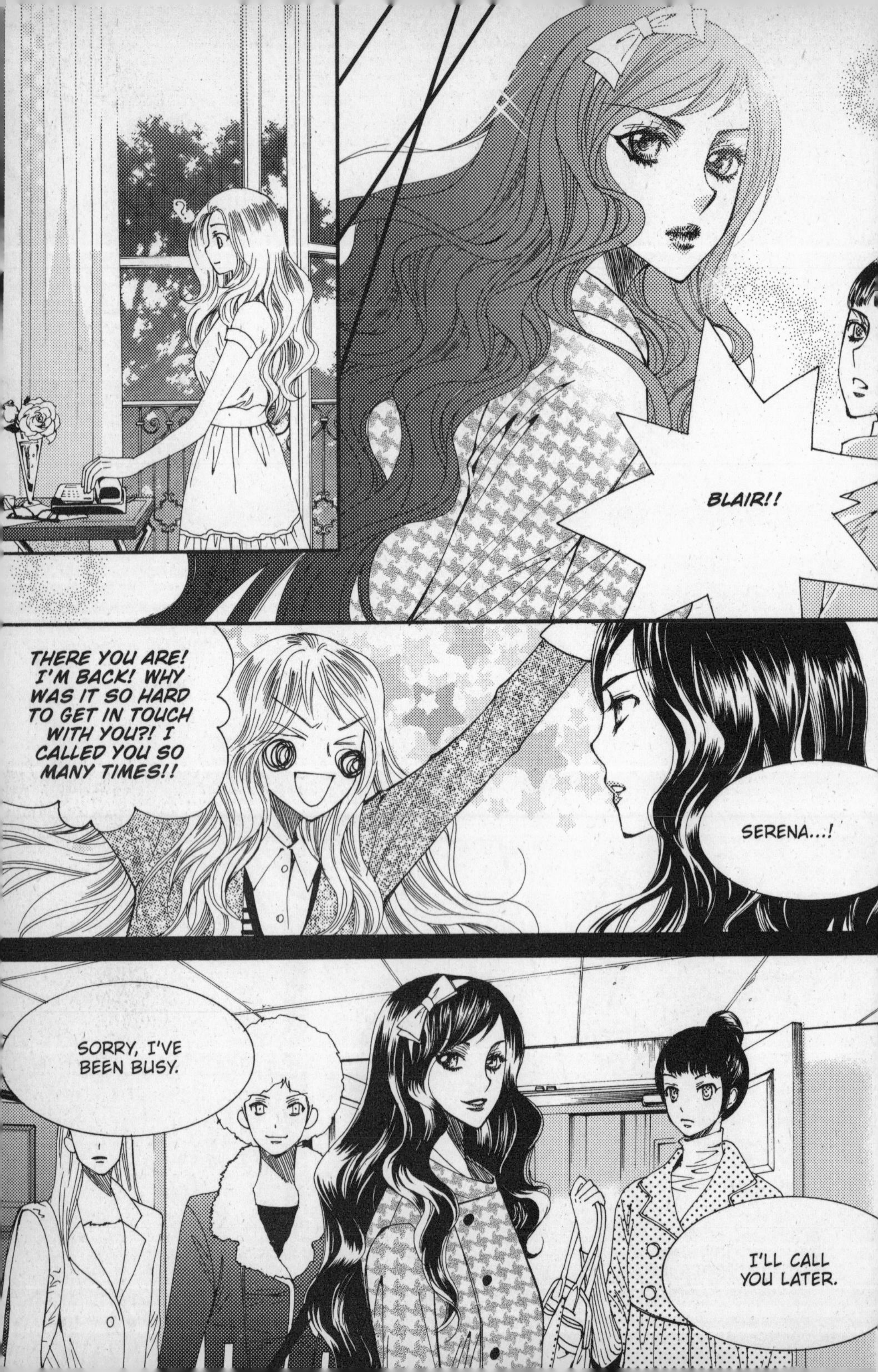
BLAIR!!
THERE YOU ARE! I'M BACK! WHY WAS IT SO HARD TO GET IN TOUCH WITH YOU?! I CALLED YOU SO MANY TIMES!!
SERENA...!
SORRY, I'VE BEEN BUSY.
I'LL CALL YOU LATER.

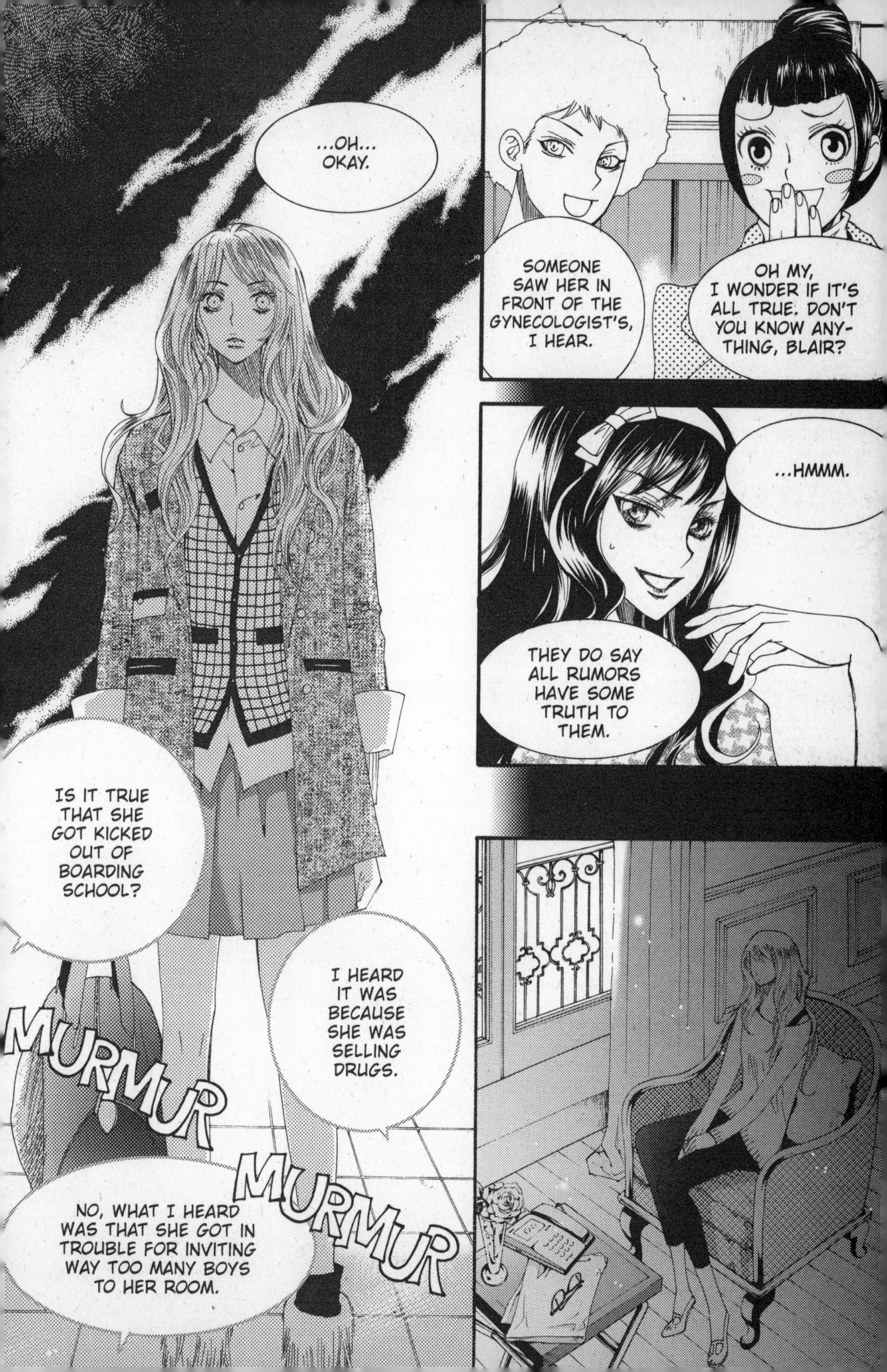
...OH... OKAY.
IS IT TRUE THAT SHE GOT KICKED OUT OF BOARDING SCHOOL?
MURMUR
I HEARD IT WAS BECAUSE SHE WAS SELLING DRUGS.
MURMUR
NO, WHAT I HEARD WAS THAT SHE GOT IN TROUBLE FOR INVITING WAY TOO MANY BOYS TO HER ROOM.
SOMEONE SAW HER IN FRONT OF THE GYNECOLOGIST'S, I HEAR.
OH MY, I WONDER IF IT'S ALL TRUE. DON'T YOU KNOW ANY-THING, BLAIR?
...HMMM.
THEY DO SAY ALL RUMORS HAVE SOME TRUTH TO THEM.

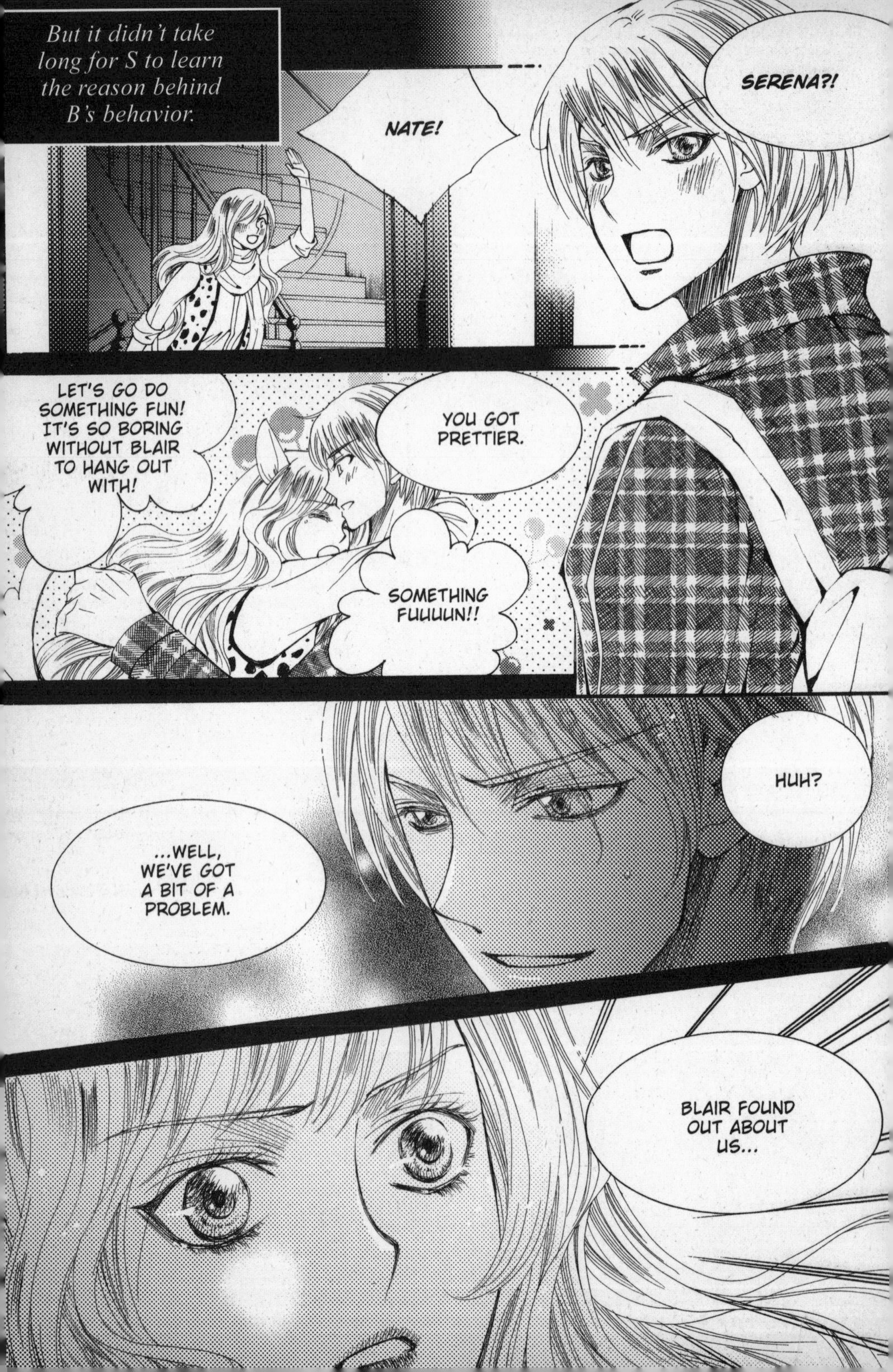

But it didn't take long for S to learn the reason behind B's behavior.
NATE!
SERENA?!
LET'S GO DO SOMETHING FUN! IT'S SO BORING WITHOUT BLAIR TO HANG OUT WITH!
YOU GOT PRETTIER.
SOMETHING FUUUUN!!
...WELL, WE'VE GOT A BIT OF A PROBLEM.
HUH?
BLAIR FOUND OUT ABOUT US...

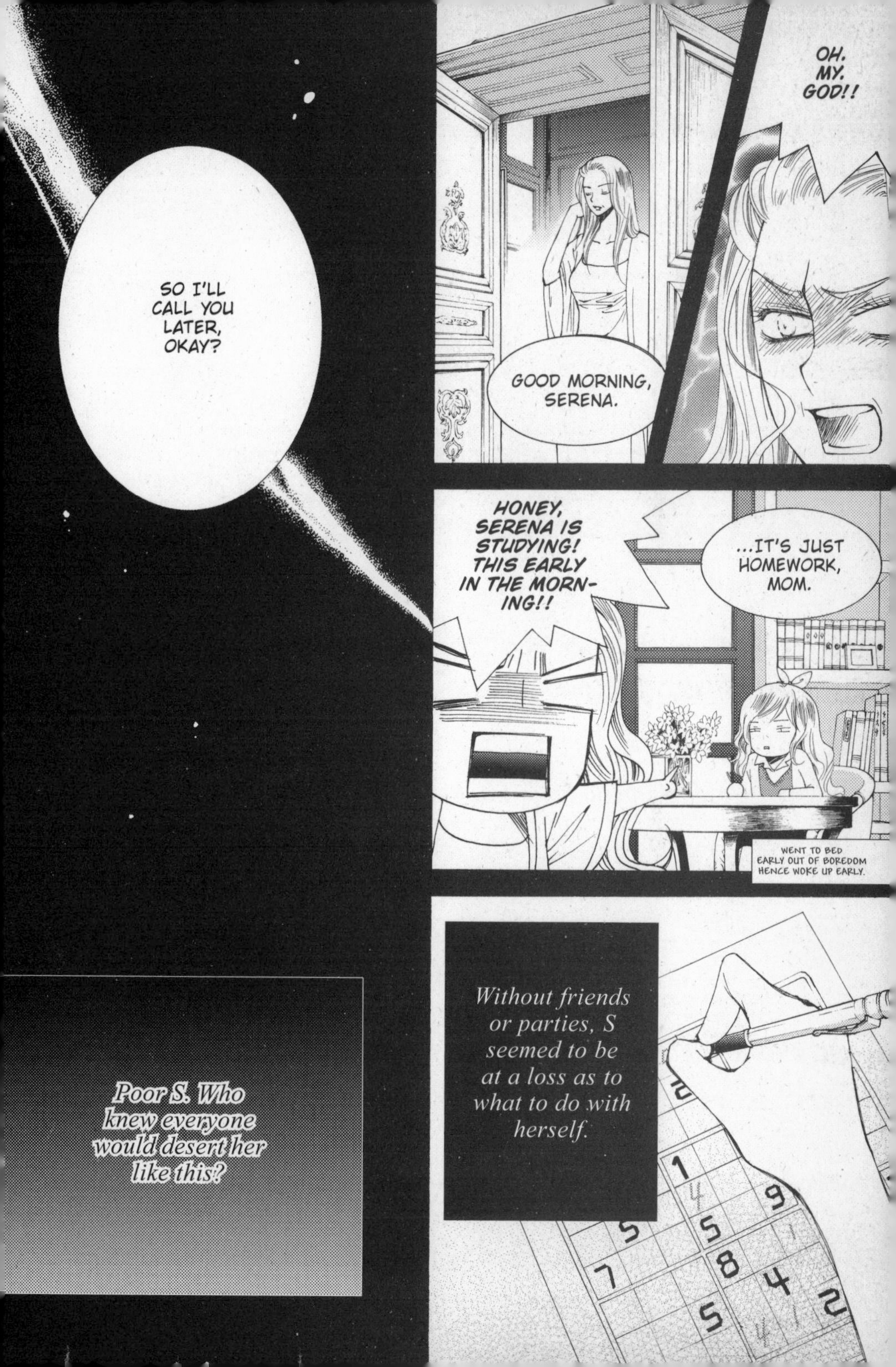
SO I'LL CALL YOU LATER, OKAY?
Poor S. Who knew everyone would desert her like this?
GOOD MORNING, SERENA.
OH. MY. GOD!!
HONEY, SERENA IS STUDYING! THIS EARLY IN THE MORN-ING!!
...IT'S JUST HOMEWORK, MOM.
WENT TO BED EARLY OUT OF BOREDOM HENCE WOKE UP EARLY.
Without friends or parties, S seemed to be at a loss as to what to do with herself.

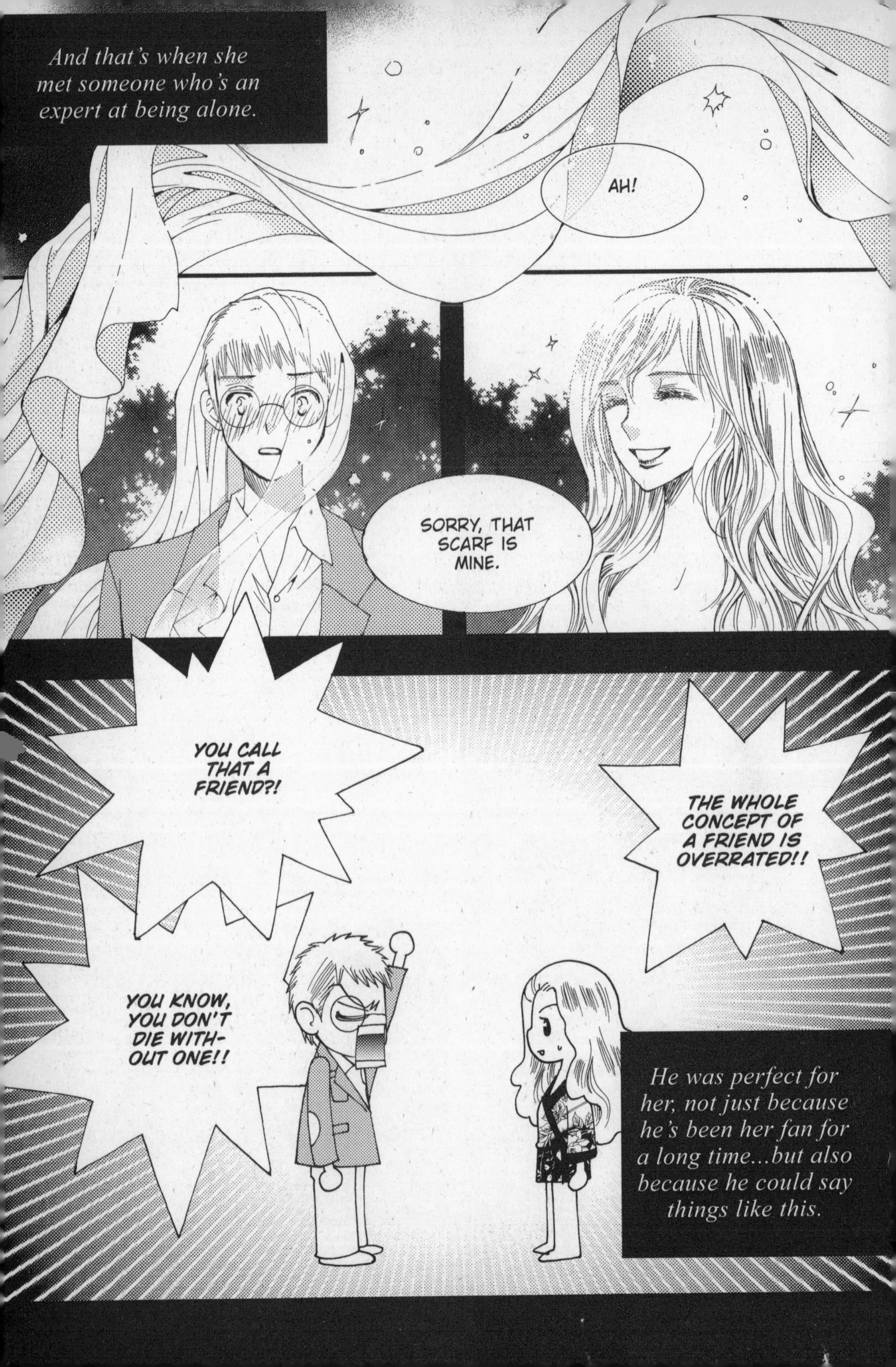
And that's when she met someone who's an expert at being alone.
AH!
SORRY, THAT SCARF IS MINE.
YOU CALL THAT A FRIEND?!
YOU KNOW, YOU DON'T DIE WITH-OUT ONE!!
THE WHOLE CONCEPT OF A FRIEND IS OVERRATED!!
He was perfect for her, not just because he's been her fan for a long time...but also because he could say things like this.

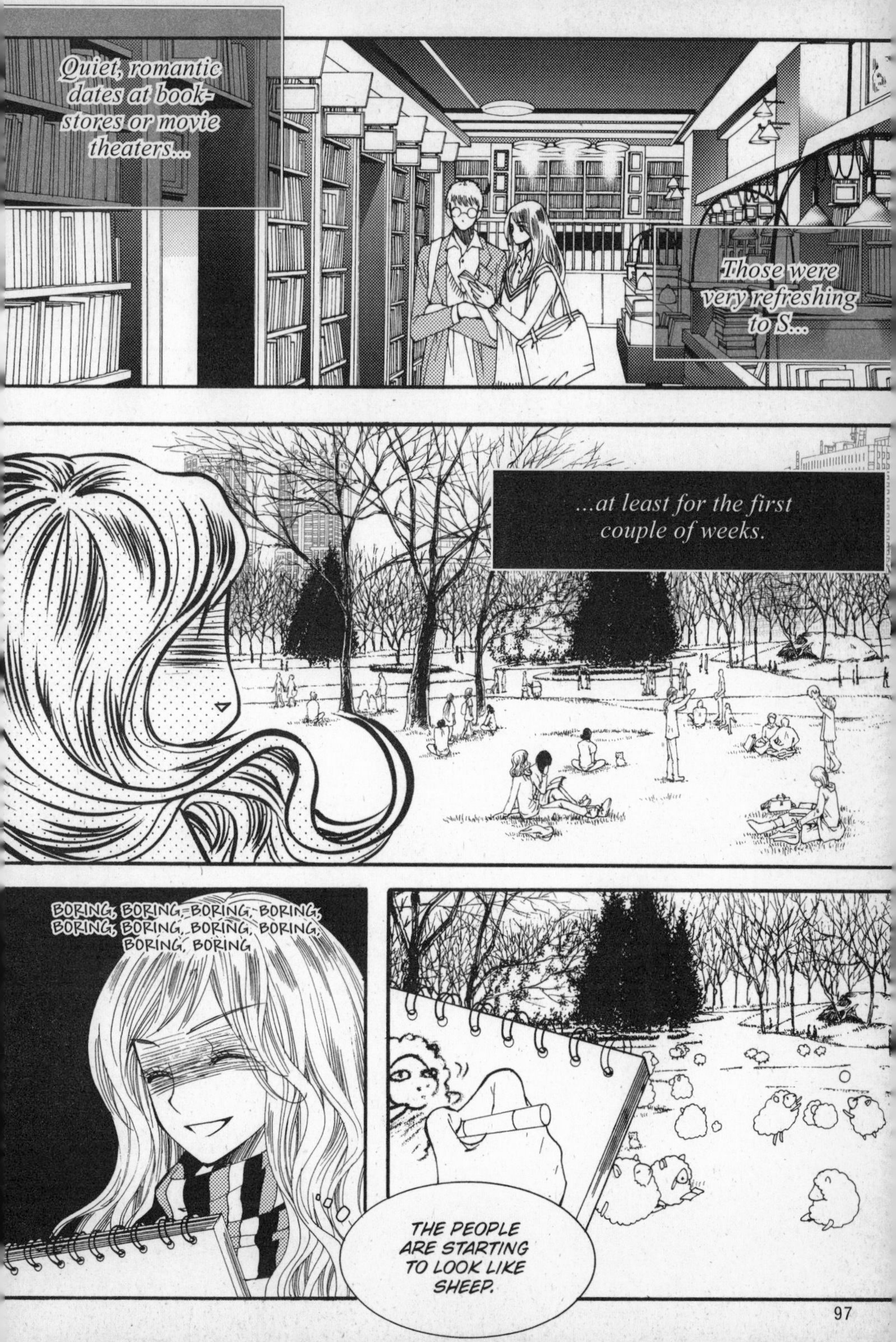

Quiet, romantic dates at book-stores or movie theaters...
Those were very refreshing to S...
...at least for the first couple of weeks.
BORING, BORING, BORING, BORING, BORING, BORING, BORING, BORING, BORING, BORING
THE PEOPLE ARE STARTING TO LOOK LIKE SHEEP.

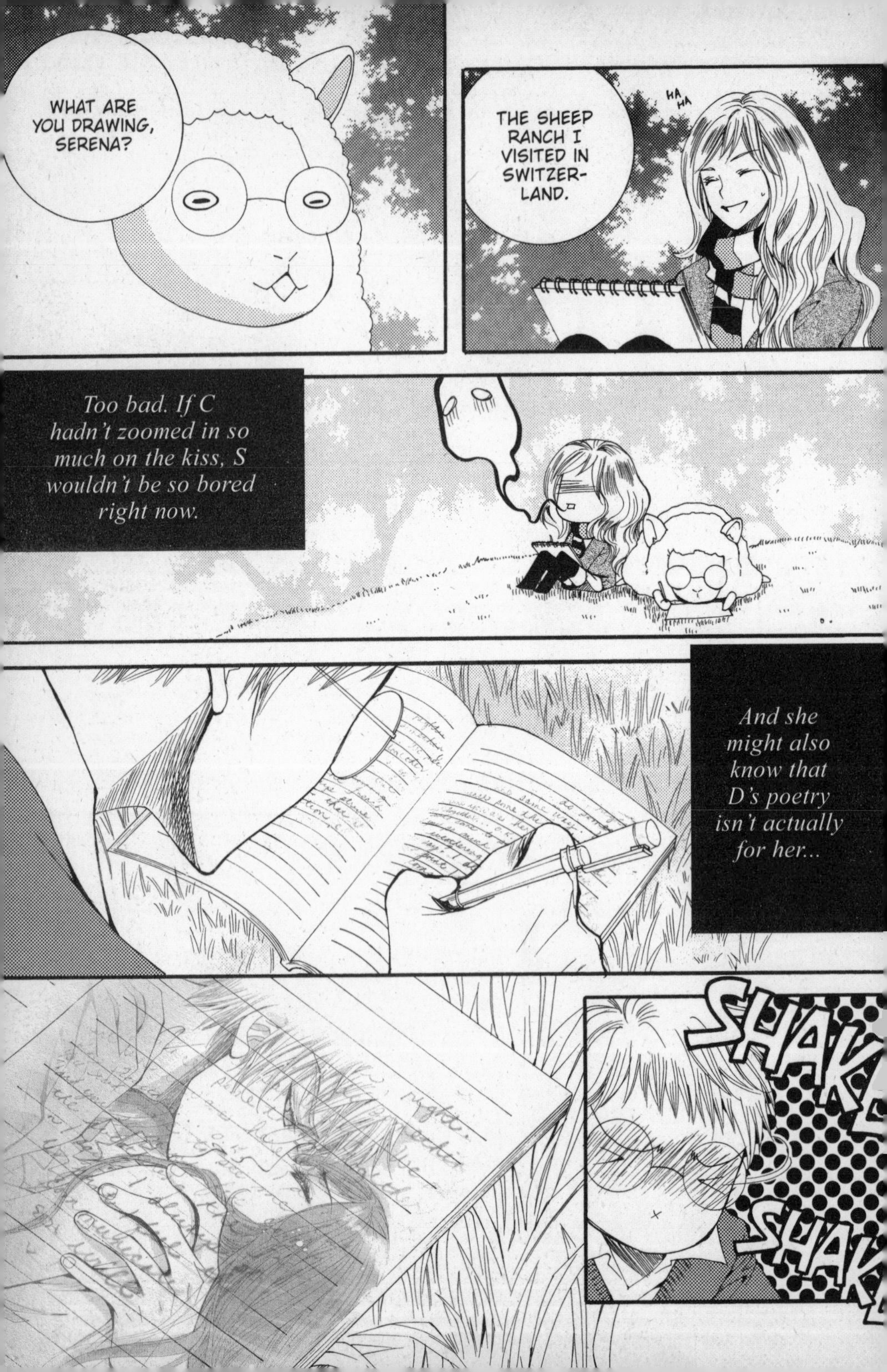
WHAT ARE YOU DRAWING, SERENA?
HA HA
THE SHEEP RANCH I VISITED IN SWITZER-LAND.
Too bad. If C hadn't zoomed in so much on the kiss, S wouldn't be so bored right now.
And she might also know that D's poetry isn't actually for her...
SHAKE
SHAKE

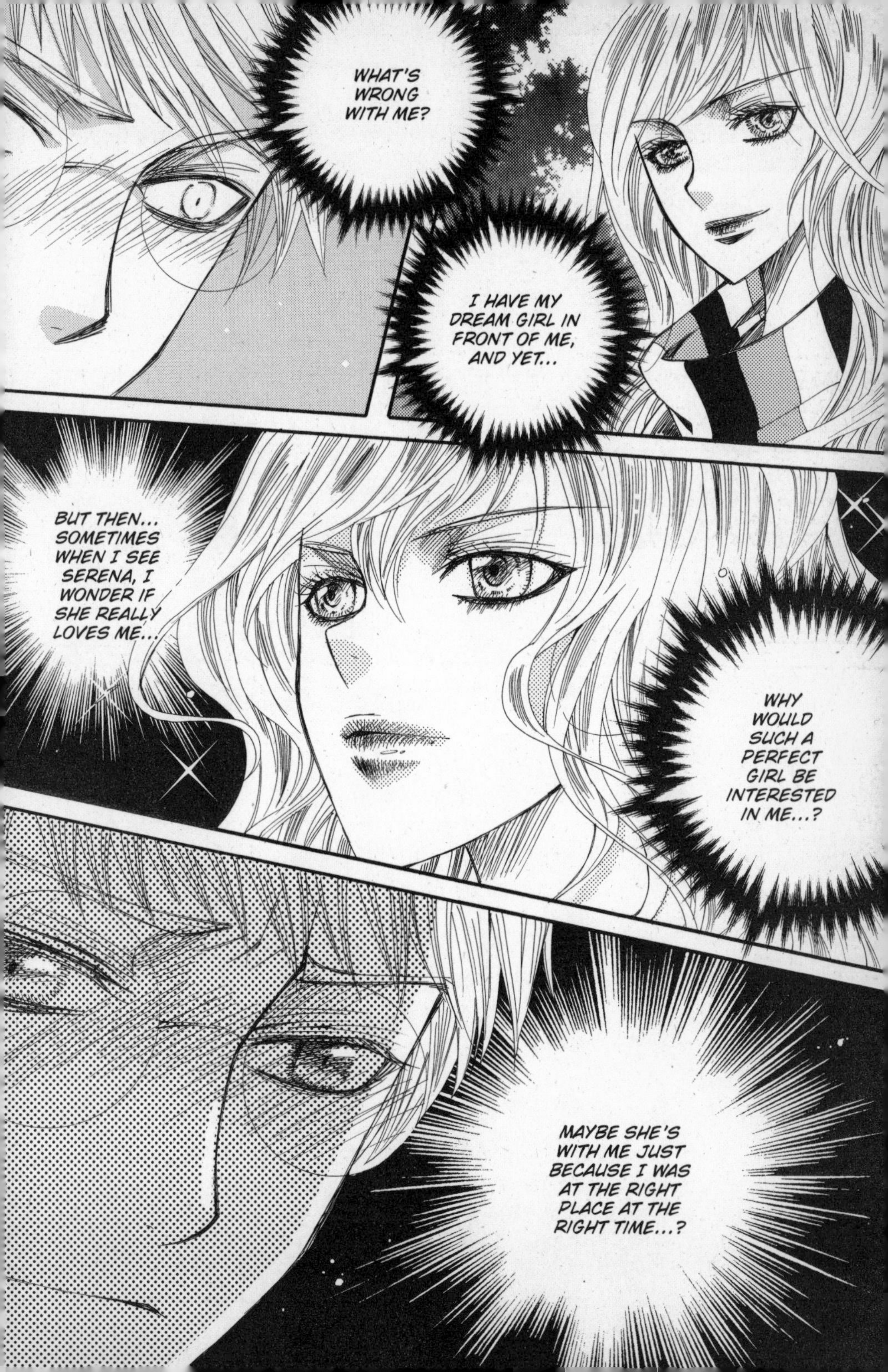
WHAT'S WRONG WITH ME?
I HAVE MY DREAM GIRL IN FRONT OF ME, AND YET...
BUT THEN... SOMETIMES WHEN I SEE SERENA, I WONDER IF SHE REALLY LOVES ME...
WHY WOULD SUCH A PERFECT GIRL BE INTERESTED IN ME...?
MAYBE SHE'S WITH ME JUST BECAUSE I WAS AT THE RIGHT PLACE AT THE RIGHT TIME...?

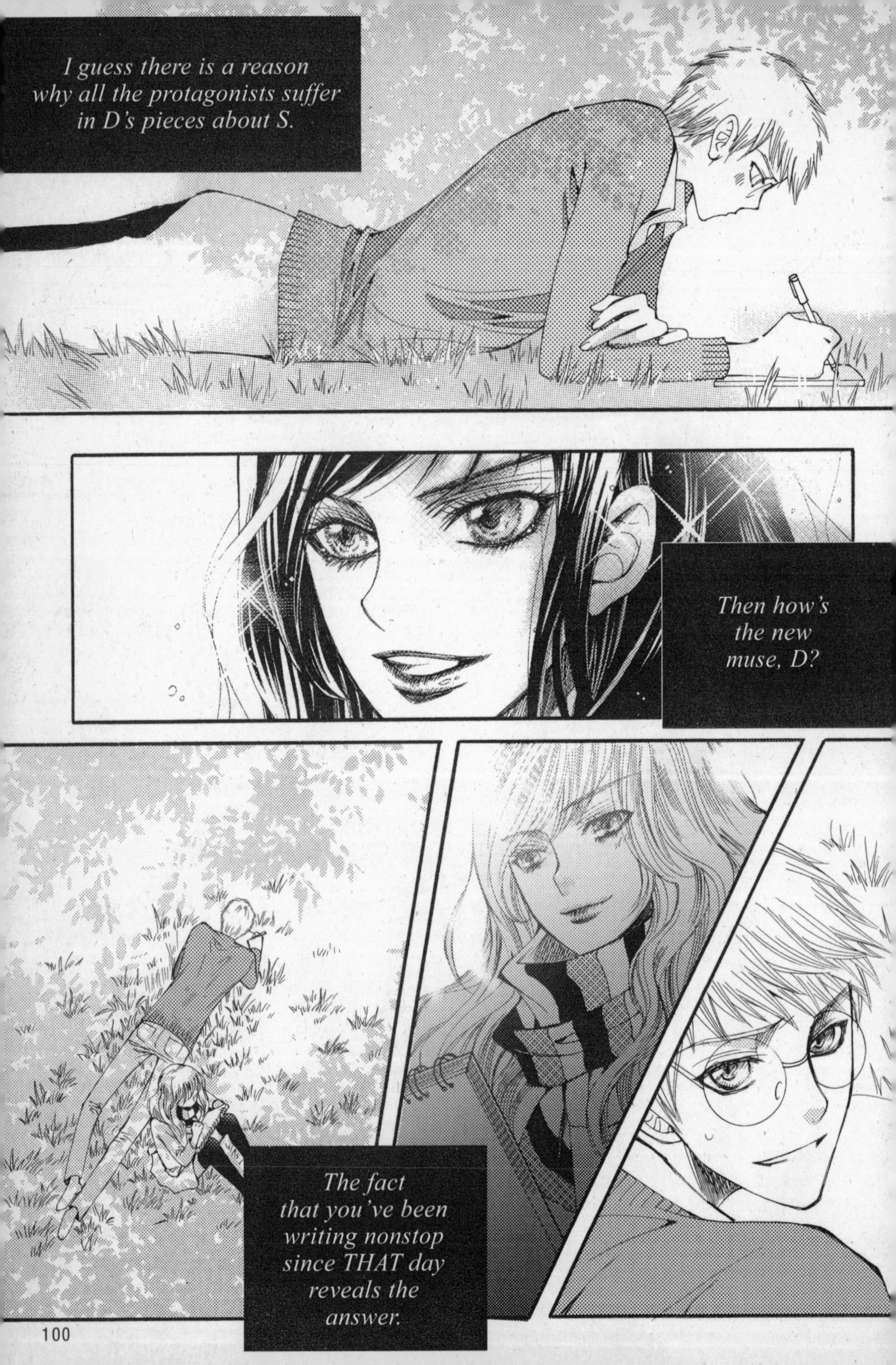
I guess there is a reason why all the protagonists suffer in D's pieces about S.
Then how's the new muse, D?
The fact that you've been writing nonstop since THAT day reveals the answer.

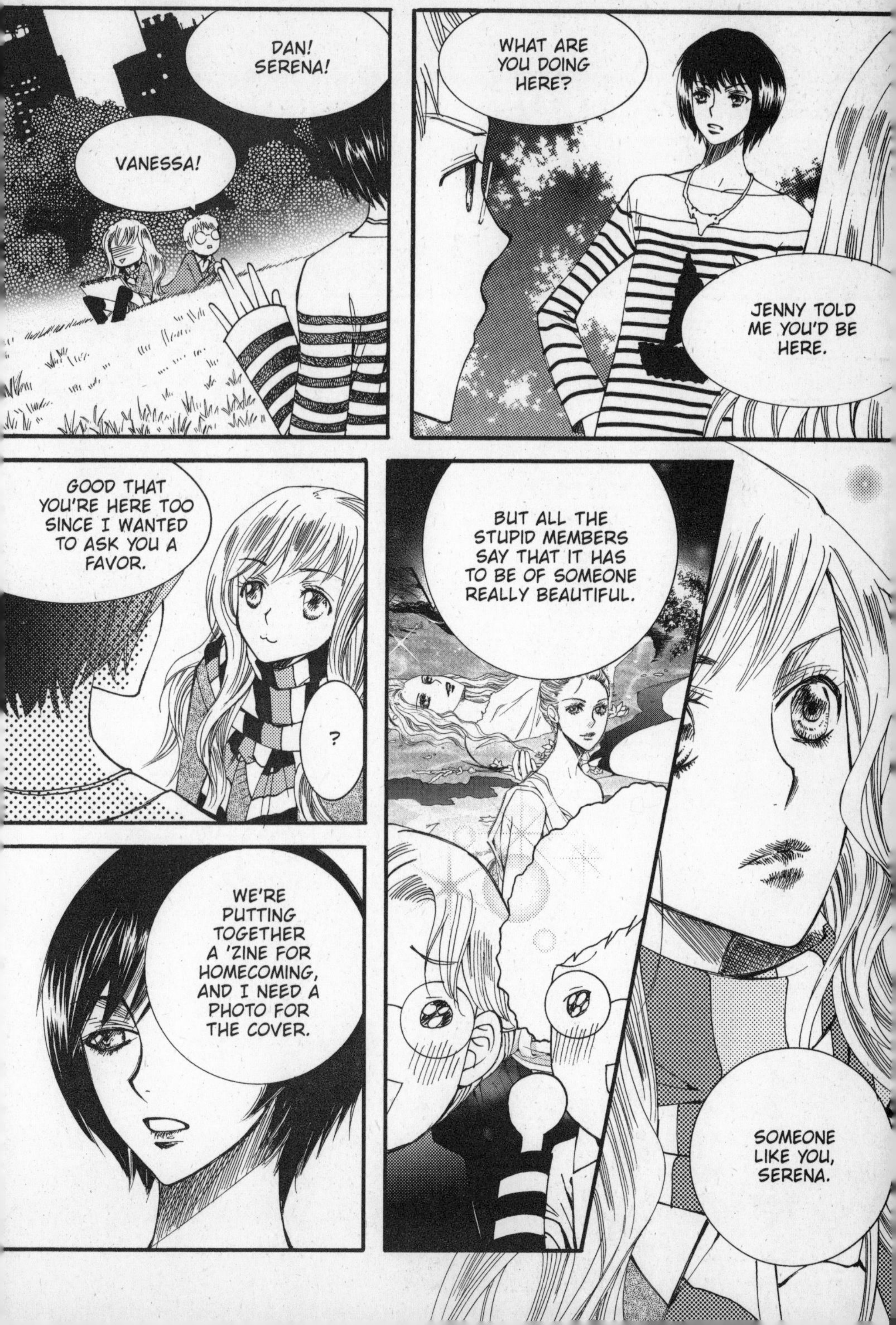
DAN! SERENA!
VANESSA!
WHAT ARE YOU DOING HERE?
JENNY TOLD ME YOU'D BE HERE.
GOOD THAT YOU'RE HERE TOO SINCE I WANTED TO ASK YOU A FAVOR.
?
WE'RE PUTTING TOGETHER A 'ZINE FOR HOMECOMING, AND I NEED A PHOTO FOR THE COVER.
BUT ALL THE STUPID MEMBERS SAY THAT IT HAS TO BE OF SOMEONE REALLY BEAUTIFUL.
SOMEONE LIKE YOU, SERENA.

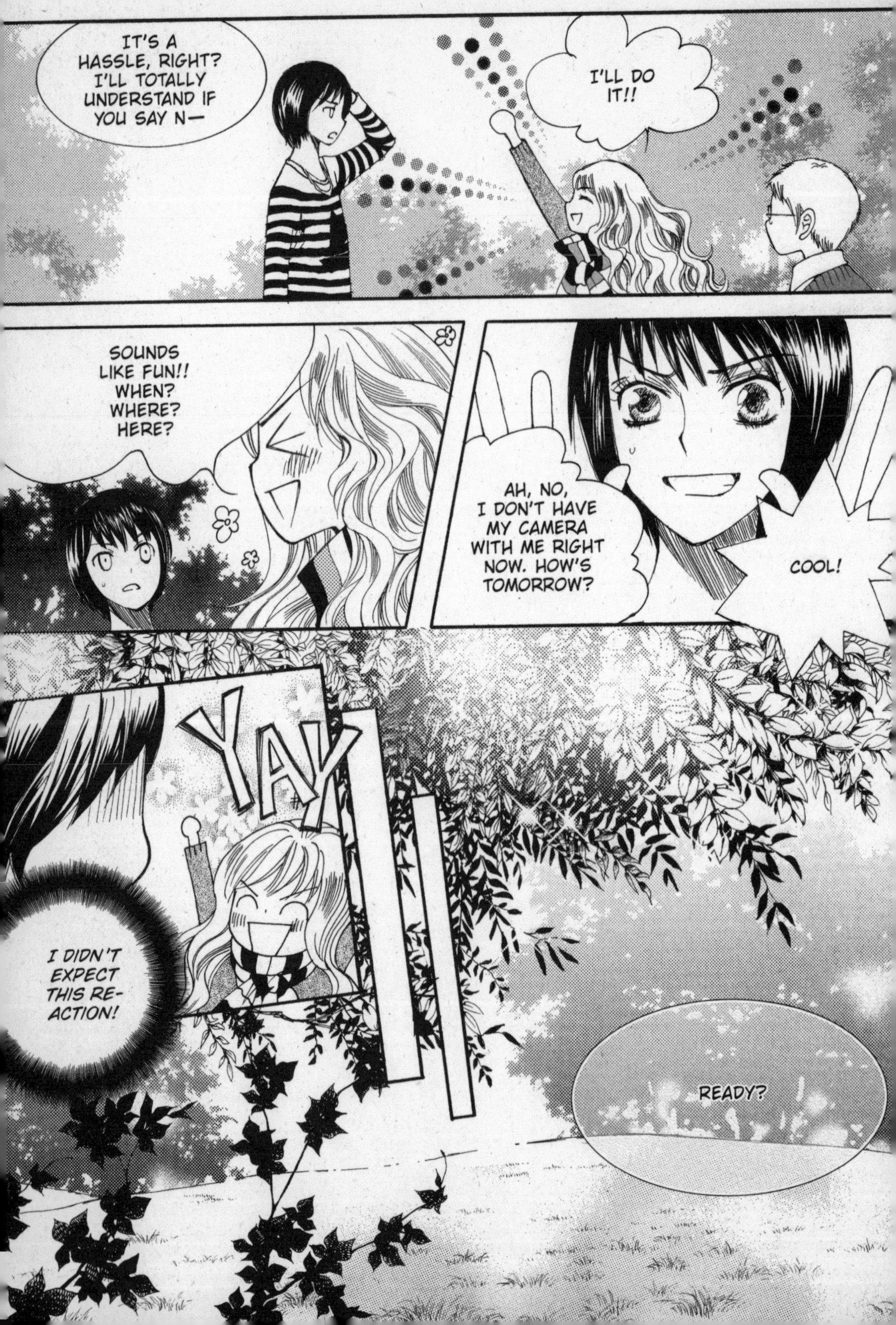
IT'S A HASSLE, RIGHT? I'LL TOTALLY UNDERSTAND IF YOU SAY N—
I'LL DO IT!!
SOUNDS LIKE FUN!! WHEN? WHERE? HERE?
AH, NO, I DON'T HAVE MY CAMERA WITH ME RIGHT NOW. HOW'S TOMORROW?
COOL!
YAY
I DIDN'T EXPECT THIS RE-ACTION!
READY?

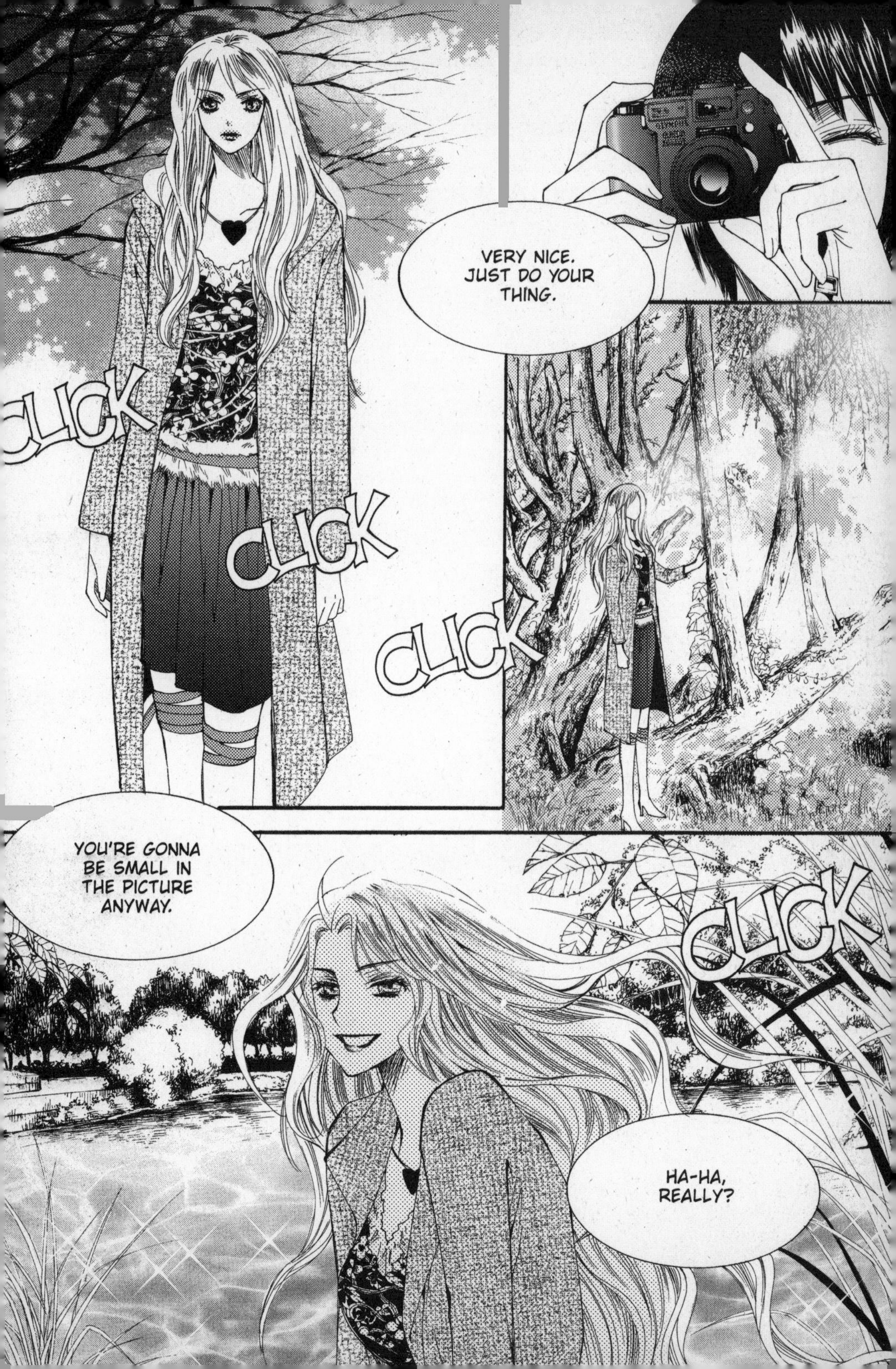
CLICK
CLICK
VERY NICE. JUST DO YOUR THING.
CLICK
YOU'RE GONNA BE SMALL IN THE PICTURE ANYWAY.
CLICK
HA-HA, REALLY?

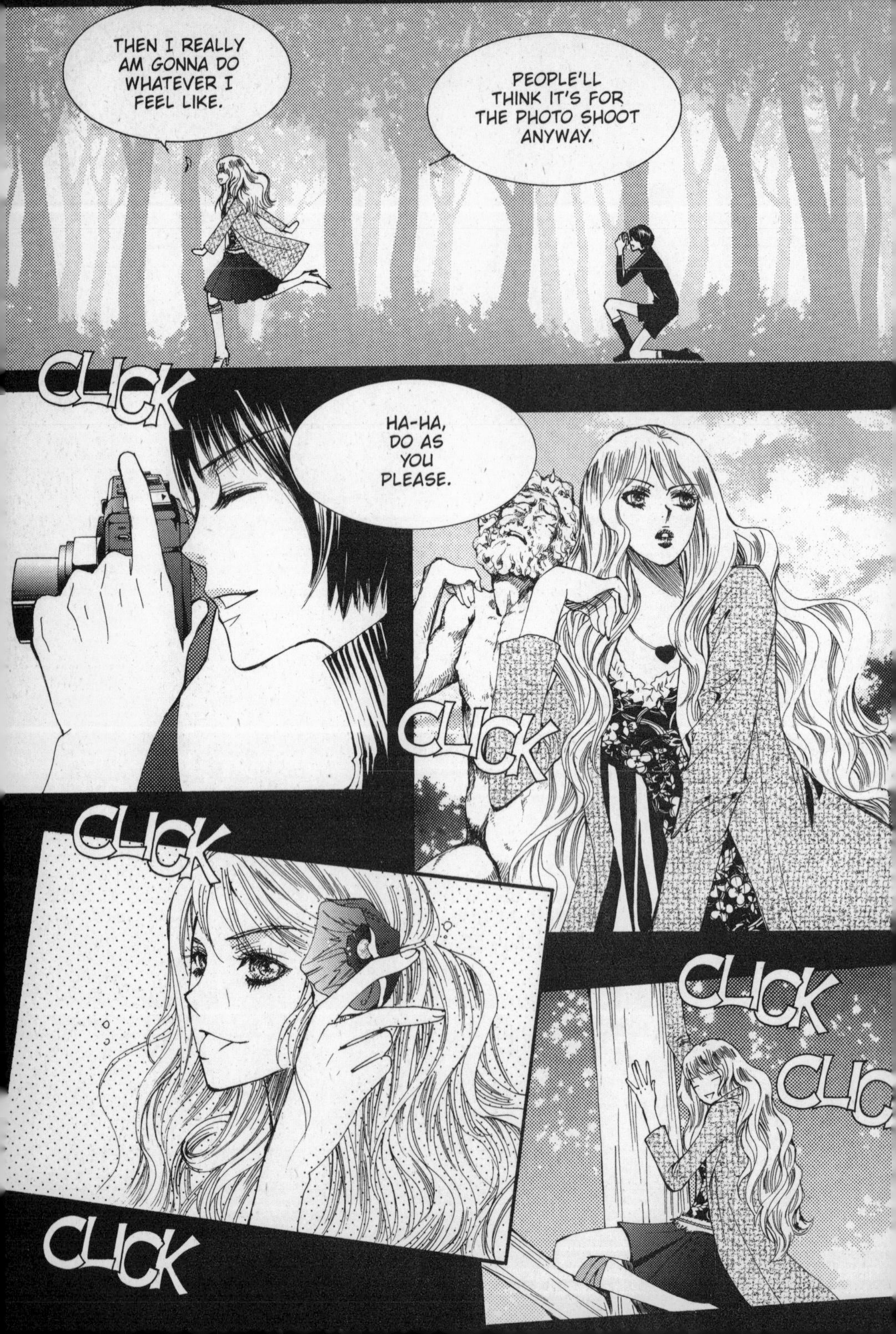
THEN I REALLY AM GONNA DO WHATEVER I FEEL LIKE.
PEOPLE'LL THINK IT'S FOR THE PHOTO SHOOT ANYWAY.
CLICK
HA-HA, DO AS YOU PLEASE.
CLICK
CLICK
CLICK
CLICK
CLICK
CLIC

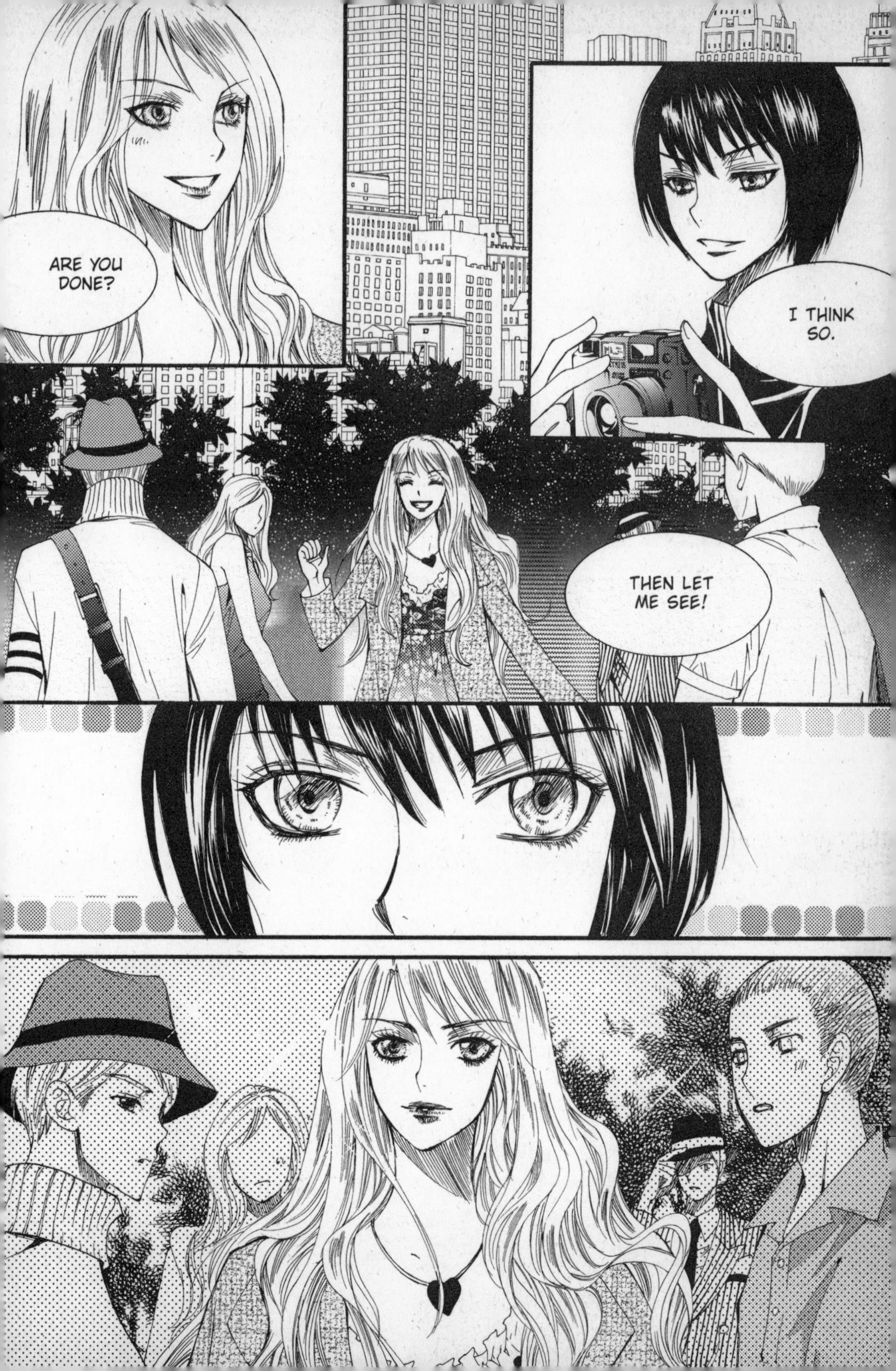

ARE YOU DONE?
I THINK SO.
THEN LET ME SEE!

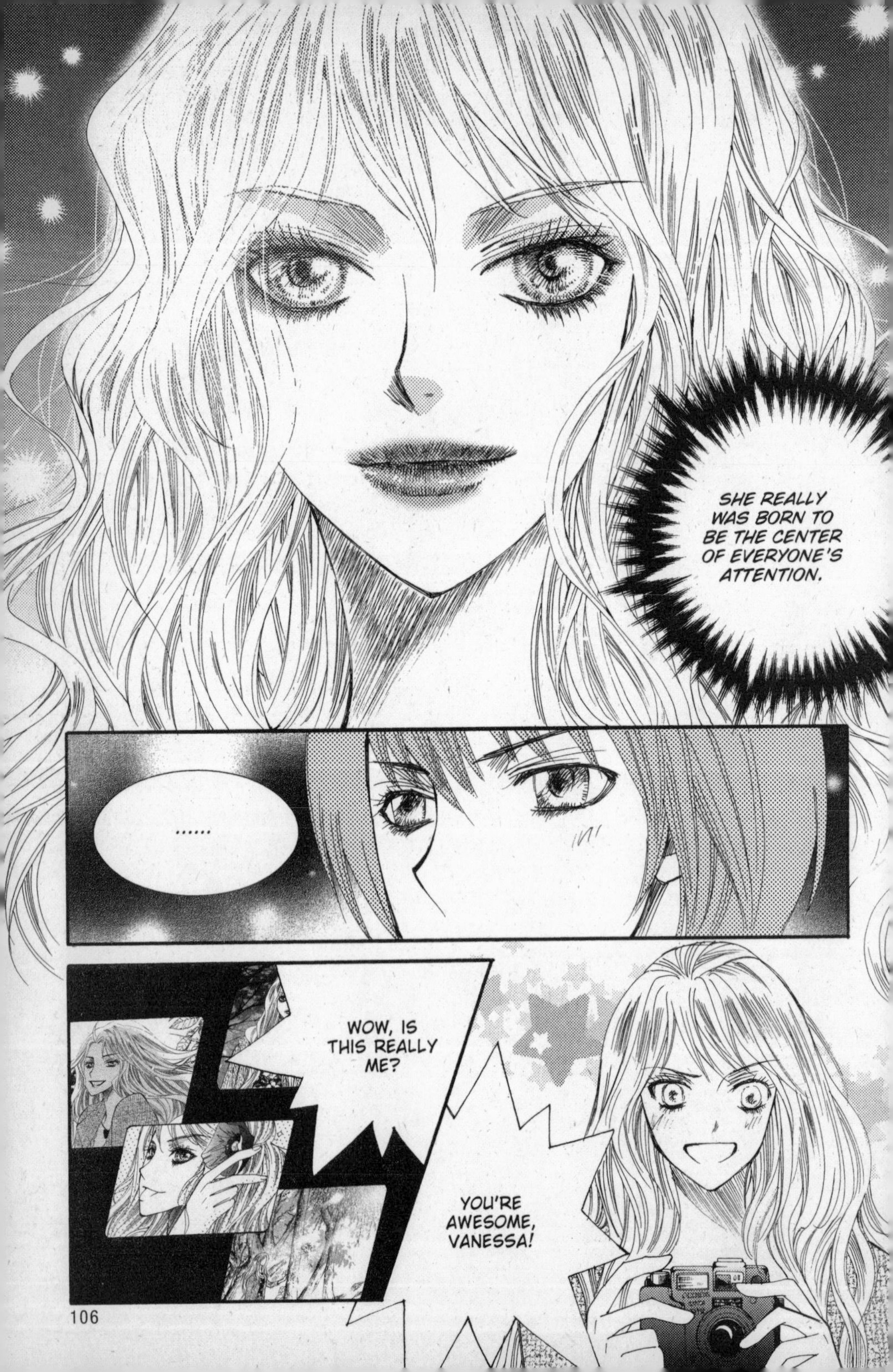
SHE REALLY WAS BORN TO BE THE CENTER OF EVERYONE'S ATTENTION.
......
WOW, IS THIS REALLY ME?
YOU'RE AWESOME, VANESSA!

HONESTLY, I COULDN'T FOLLOW YOUR MOVIE AT ALL, BUT THESE ARE COOL!

AH... IS THAT SO...

IS THIS THE SAME SERENA WHO EVERYBODY'S GOSSIPING ABOUT AT SCHOOL?

EXCUSE ME, BUT WOULD IT BE OKAY IF WE TAKE A SHOT OF YOU, MISS?

WHO ARE THESE GUYS? PERVERTED OLD MEN?

ACTUALLY, WE SHOULD GET GOIN—

WE'VE BEEN WATCHING, AND IT SEEMS LIKE YOU HAVE TALENT AS A MODEL.

I'LL DO IT!

HUH?!

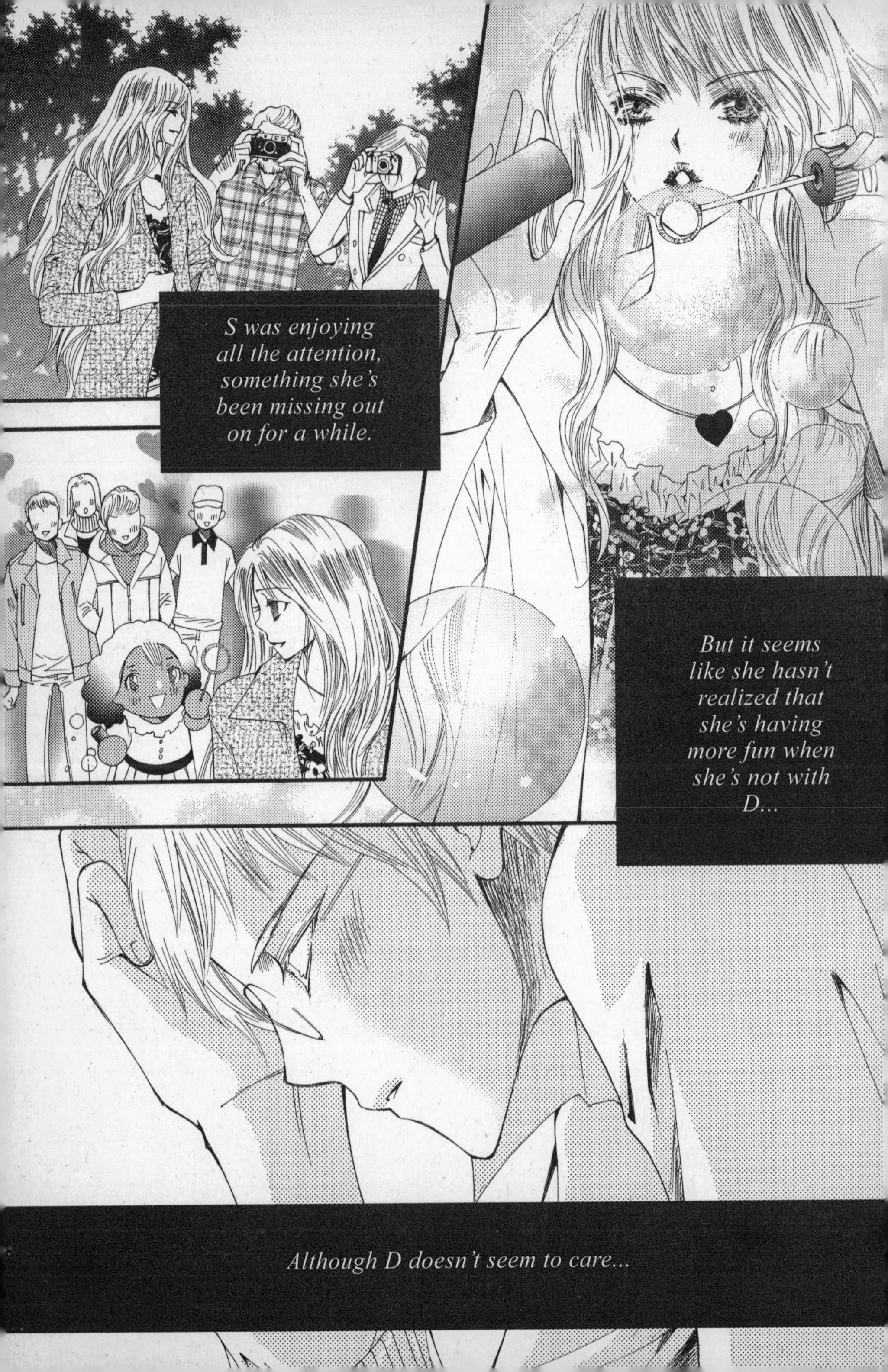
S was enjoying all the attention, something she's been missing out on for a while.
But it seems like she hasn't realized that she's having more fun when she's not with D...
Although D doesn't seem to care...

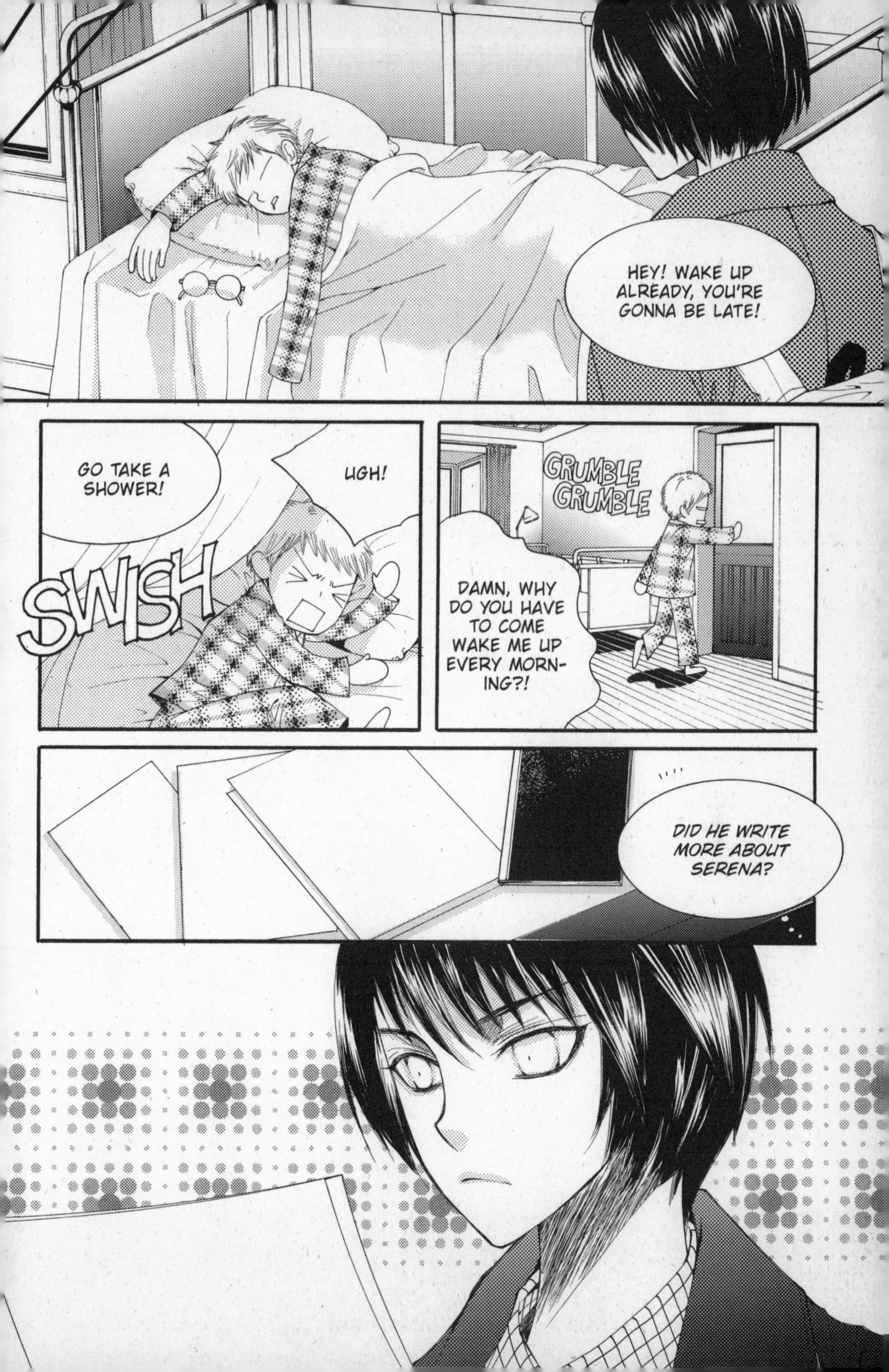
HEY! WAKE UP ALREADY, YOU'RE GONNA BE LATE!
GO TAKE A SHOWER!
UGH!
SWISH
GRUMBLE GRUMBLE
DAMN, WHY DO YOU HAVE TO COME WAKE ME UP EVERY MORN-ING?!
DID HE WRITE MORE ABOUT SERENA?

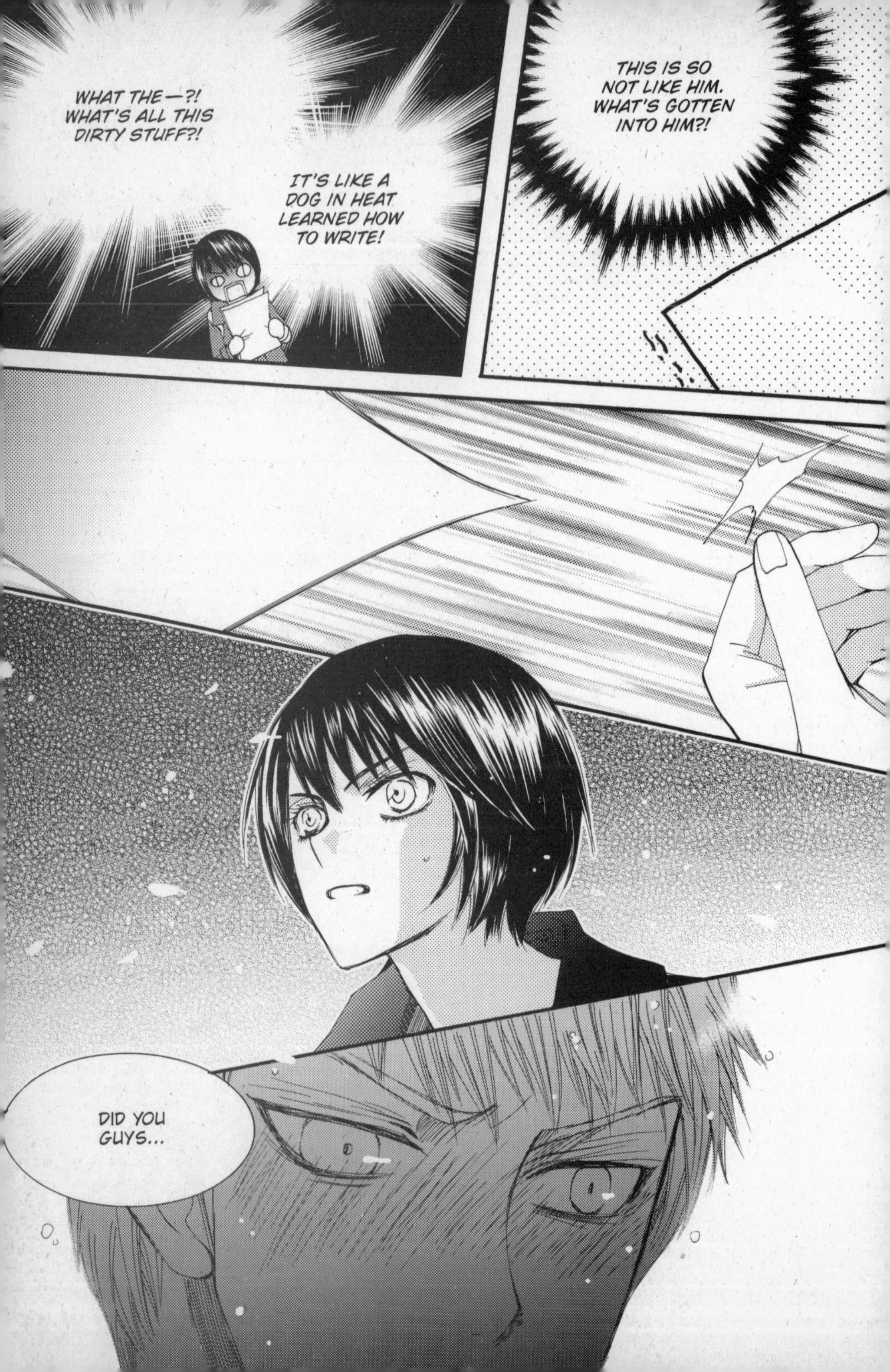
WHAT THE—?! WHAT'S ALL THIS DIRTY STUFF?!
IT'S LIKE A DOG IN HEAT LEARNED HOW TO WRITE!
THIS IS SO NOT LIKE HIM. WHAT'S GOTTEN INTO HIM?!
DID YOU GUYS...

...SLEEP TOGETHER??!

ARE YOU CRAZY?!

THEN WHY ARE YOU SUDDENLY BUYING HIM ARMANI?

EVERYTHING NEEDS TO BE PERFECT, THAT'S ALL.

HUH?

IF A CERTAIN SOMEONE HAD DONE HIS JOB RIGHT, I WOULDN'T BE GOING THROUGH ALL THIS.

SINCE THAT STUPID SOMEONE HAD TO TAKE A PICTURE OF JUST THE LIPS, NOW I'M STUCK WITH DAN, AND OF COURSE HE'S FALLING MORE AND MORE FOR ME BY THE MINUTE!

MY MAILBOX IS FILLED WITH TONS OF FILTHY POEMS HE WROTE.

THAT'S HILARIOUS!

I'M THIS CLOSE TO REPORTING HIM FOR SEXUAL HARASSMENT!

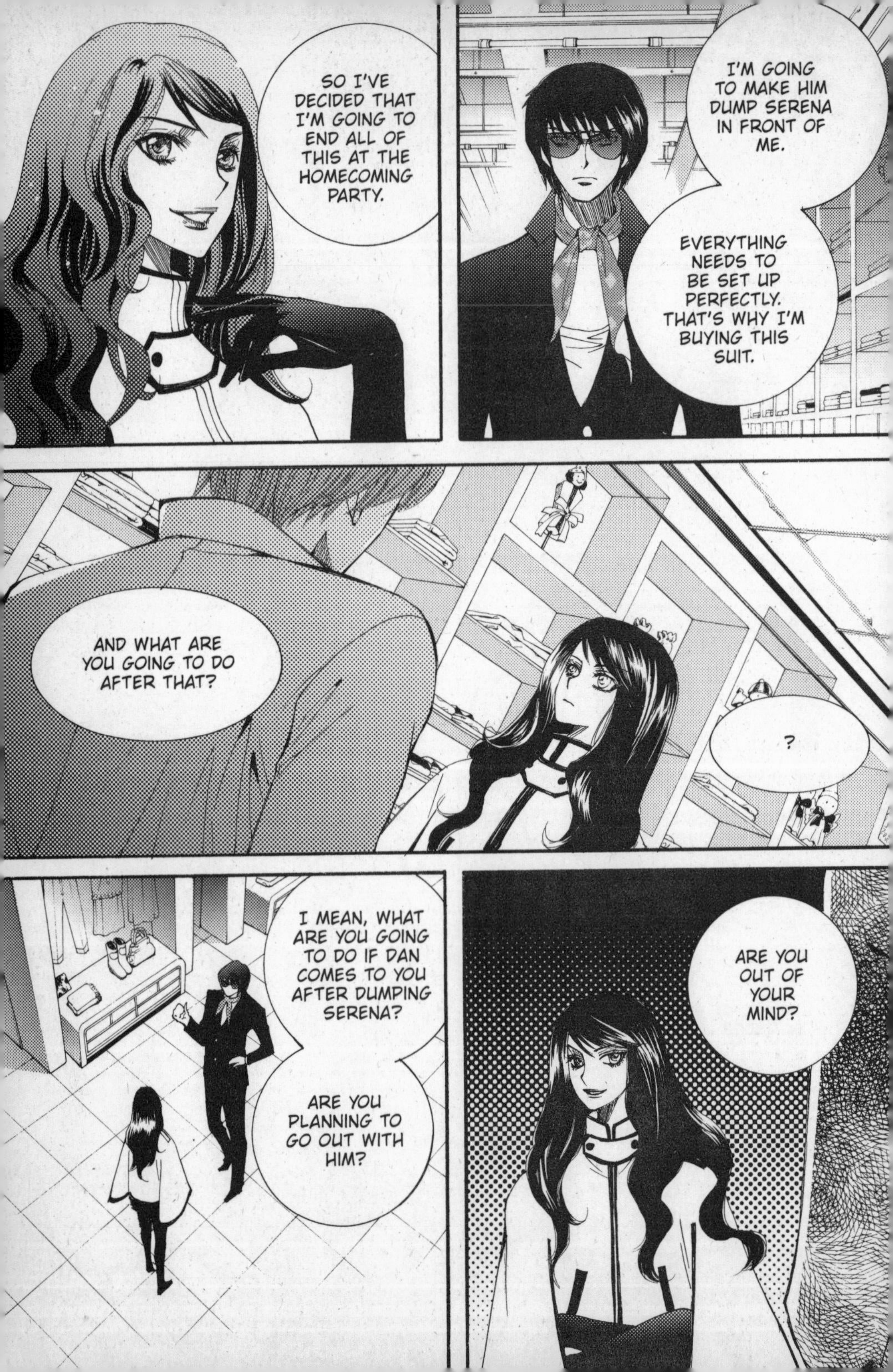
SO I'VE DECIDED THAT I'M GOING TO END ALL OF THIS AT THE HOMECOMING PARTY.
I'M GOING TO MAKE HIM DUMP SERENA IN FRONT OF ME.
EVERYTHING NEEDS TO BE SET UP PERFECTLY. THAT'S WHY I'M BUYING THIS SUIT.
AND WHAT ARE YOU GOING TO DO AFTER THAT?
?
I MEAN, WHAT ARE YOU GOING TO DO IF DAN COMES TO YOU AFTER DUMPING SERENA?
ARE YOU PLANNING TO GO OUT WITH HIM?
ARE YOU OUT OF YOUR MIND?

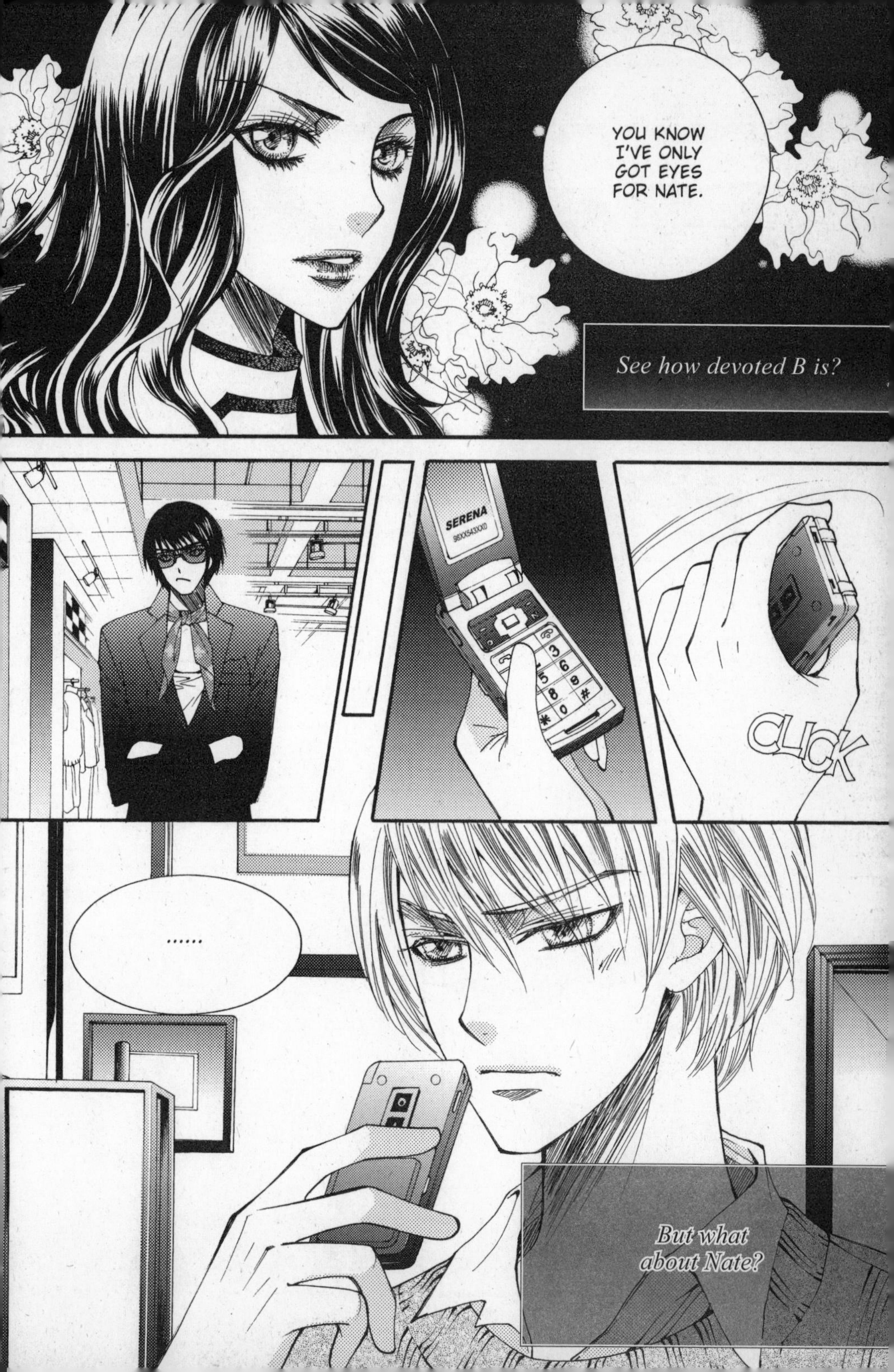
YOU KNOW I'VE ONLY GOT EYES FOR NATE.
See how devoted B is?
SERENA
CLICK
......
But what about Nate?

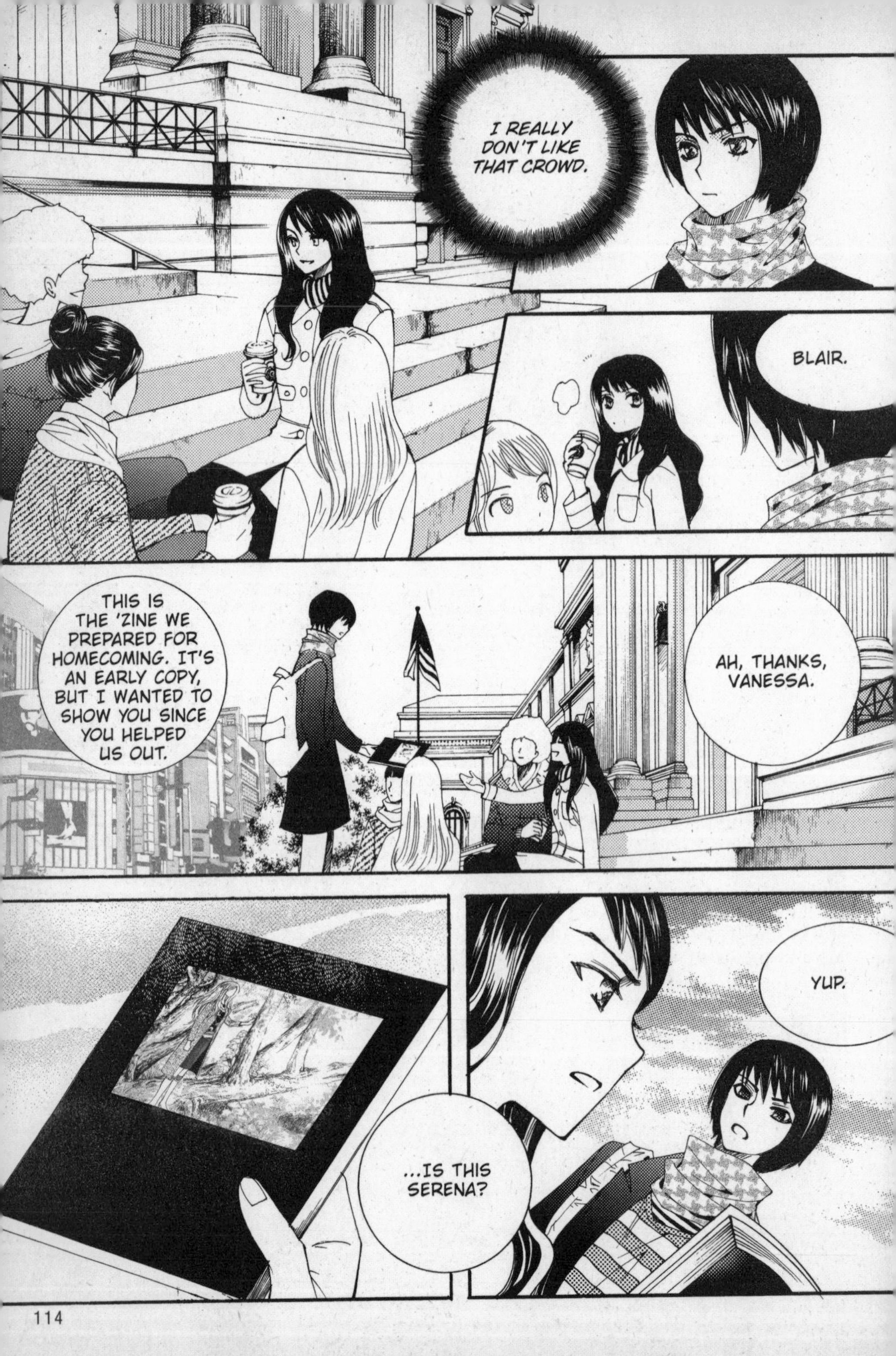
I REALLY DON'T LIKE THAT CROWD.
BLAIR.
THIS IS THE 'ZINE WE PREPARED FOR HOMECOMING. IT'S AN EARLY COPY, BUT I WANTED TO SHOW YOU SINCE YOU HELPED US OUT.
AH, THANKS, VANESSA.
...IS THIS SERENA?
YUP.

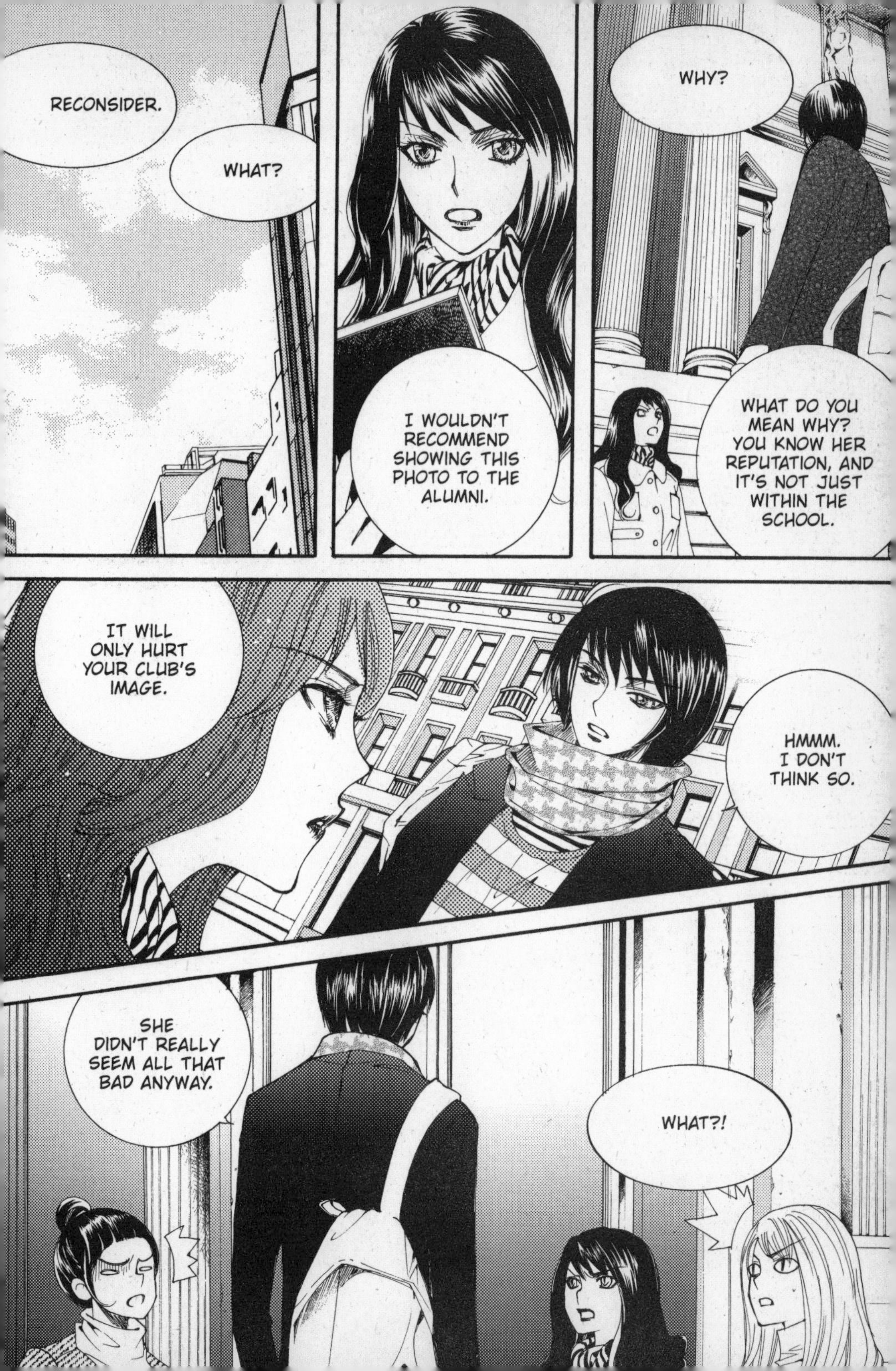
RECONSIDER.
WHAT?
I WOULDN'T RECOMMEND SHOWING THIS PHOTO TO THE ALUMNI.
WHY?
WHAT DO YOU MEAN WHY? YOU KNOW HER REPUTATION, AND IT'S NOT JUST WITHIN THE SCHOOL.
IT WILL ONLY HURT YOUR CLUB'S IMAGE.
HMMM. I DON'T THINK SO.
SHE DIDN'T REALLY SEEM ALL THAT BAD ANYWAY.
WHAT?!

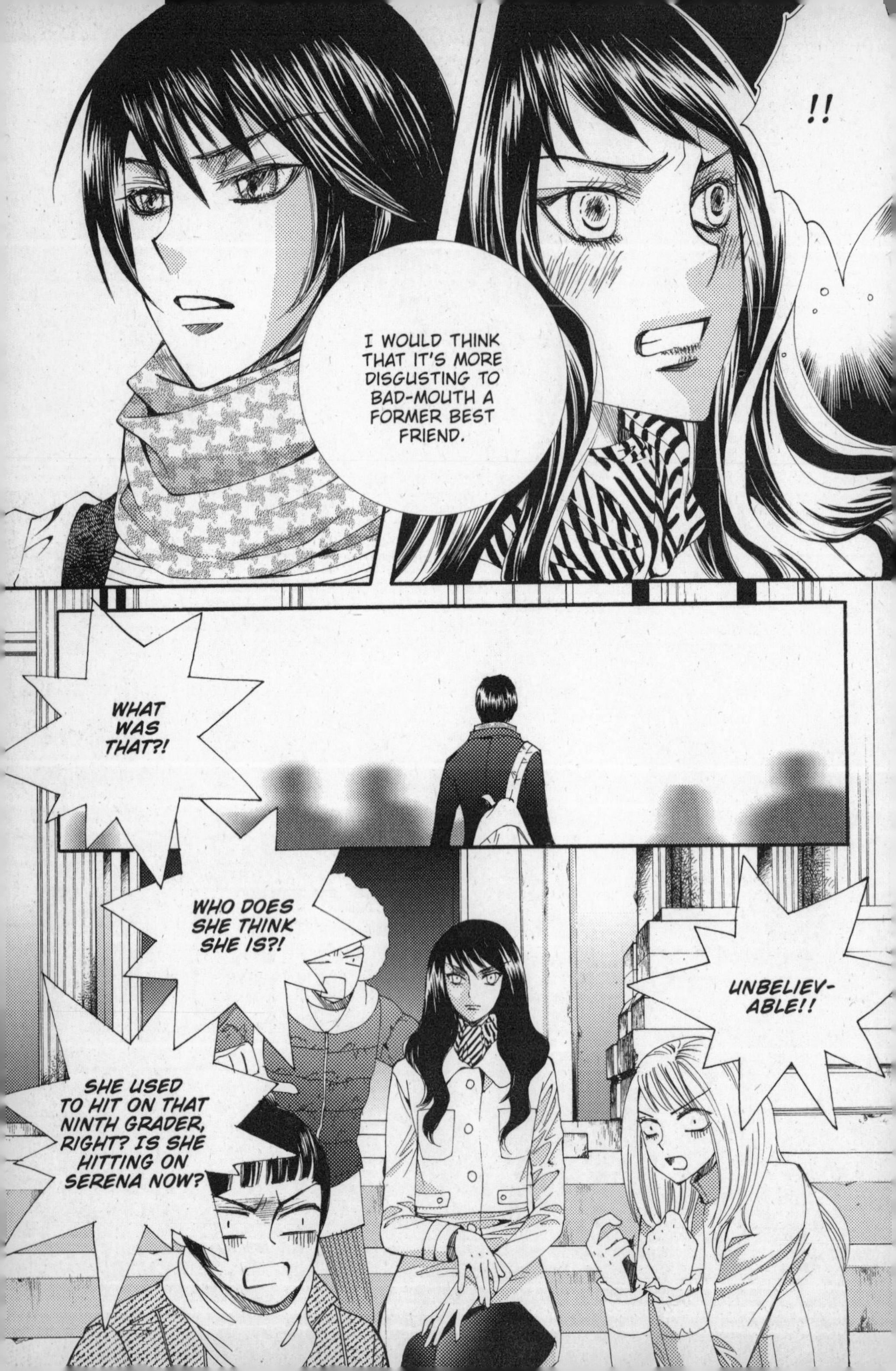
!!
I WOULD THINK THAT IT'S MORE DISGUSTING TO BAD-MOUTH A FORMER BEST FRIEND.
WHAT WAS THAT?!
WHO DOES SHE THINK SHE IS?!
UNBELIEV-ABLE!!
SHE USED TO HIT ON THAT NINTH GRADER, RIGHT? IS SHE HITTING ON SERENA NOW?

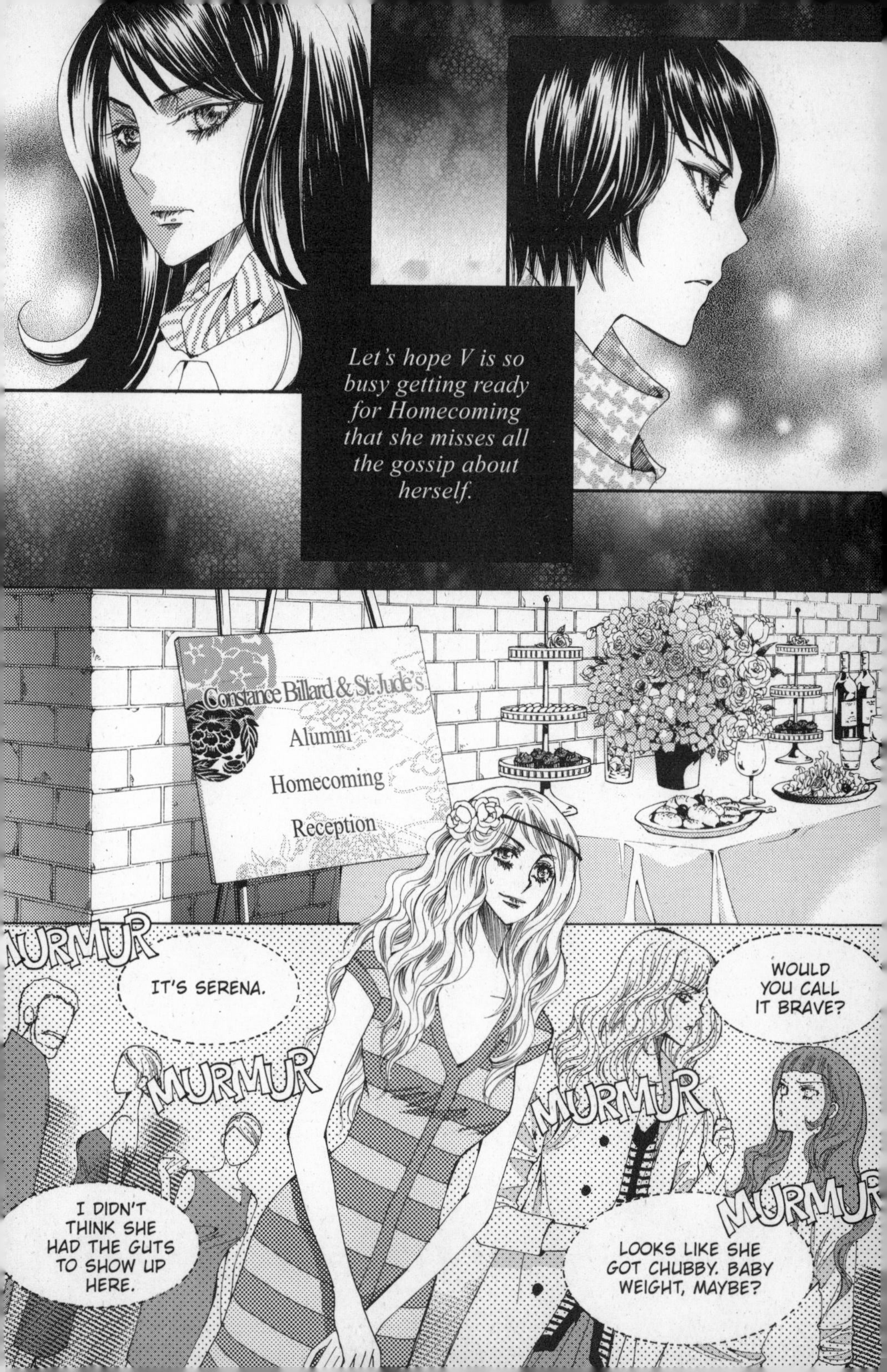
Let's hope V is so busy getting ready for Homecoming that she misses all the gossip about herself.
Constance Billard & St. Jude's
Alumni
Homecoming
Reception
MURMUR
IT'S SERENA.
WOULD YOU CALL IT BRAVE?
MURMUR
MURMUR
I DIDN'T THINK SHE HAD THE GUTS TO SHOW UP HERE.
MURMUR
LOOKS LIKE SHE GOT CHUBBY. BABY WEIGHT, MAYBE?

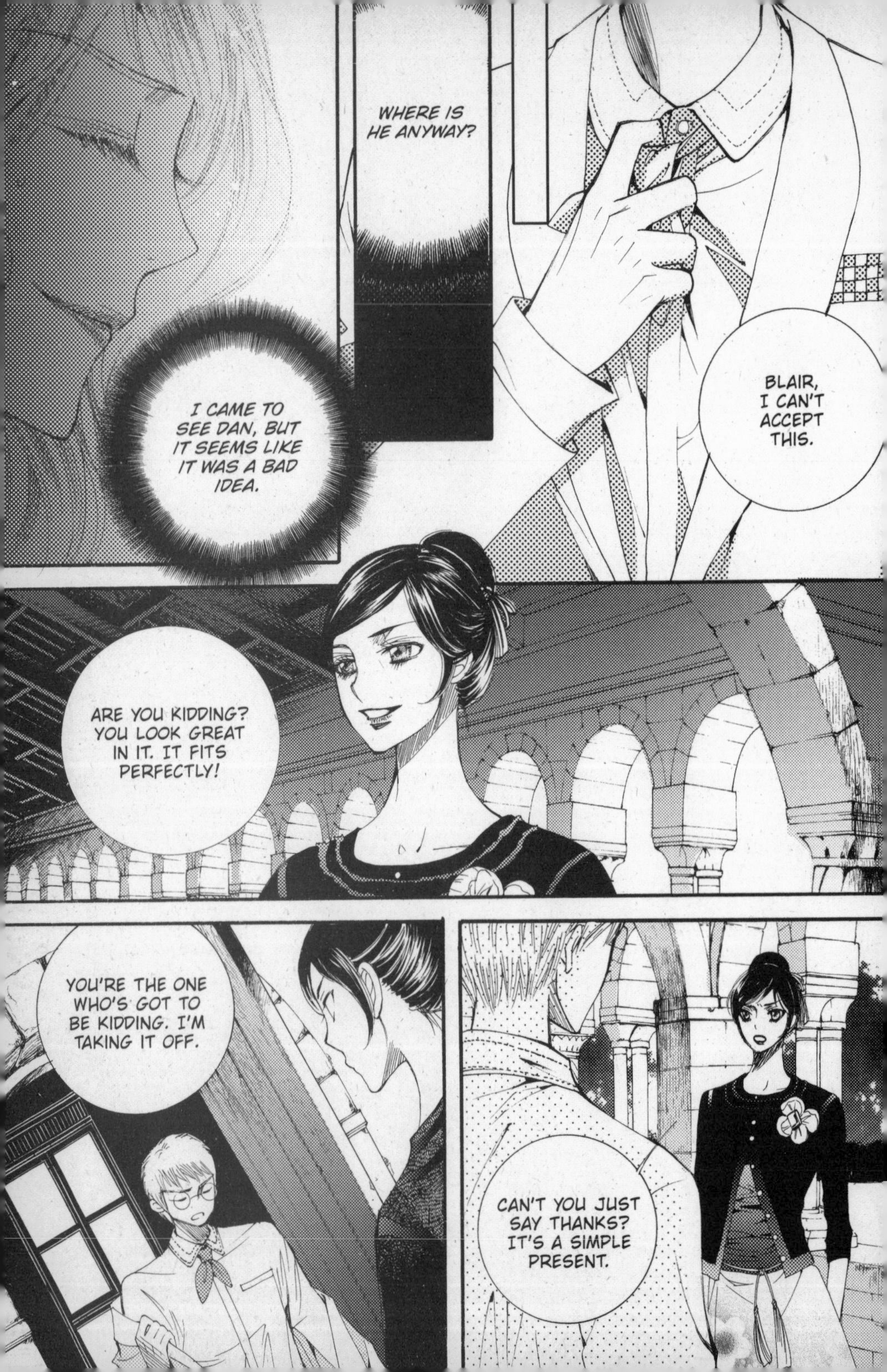
I CAME TO SEE DAN, BUT IT SEEMS LIKE IT WAS A BAD IDEA.
WHERE IS HE ANYWAY?
BLAIR, I CAN'T ACCEPT THIS.
ARE YOU KIDDING? YOU LOOK GREAT IN IT. IT FITS PERFECTLY!
YOU'RE THE ONE WHO'S GOT TO BE KIDDING. I'M TAKING IT OFF.
CAN'T YOU JUST SAY THANKS? IT'S A SIMPLE PRESENT.

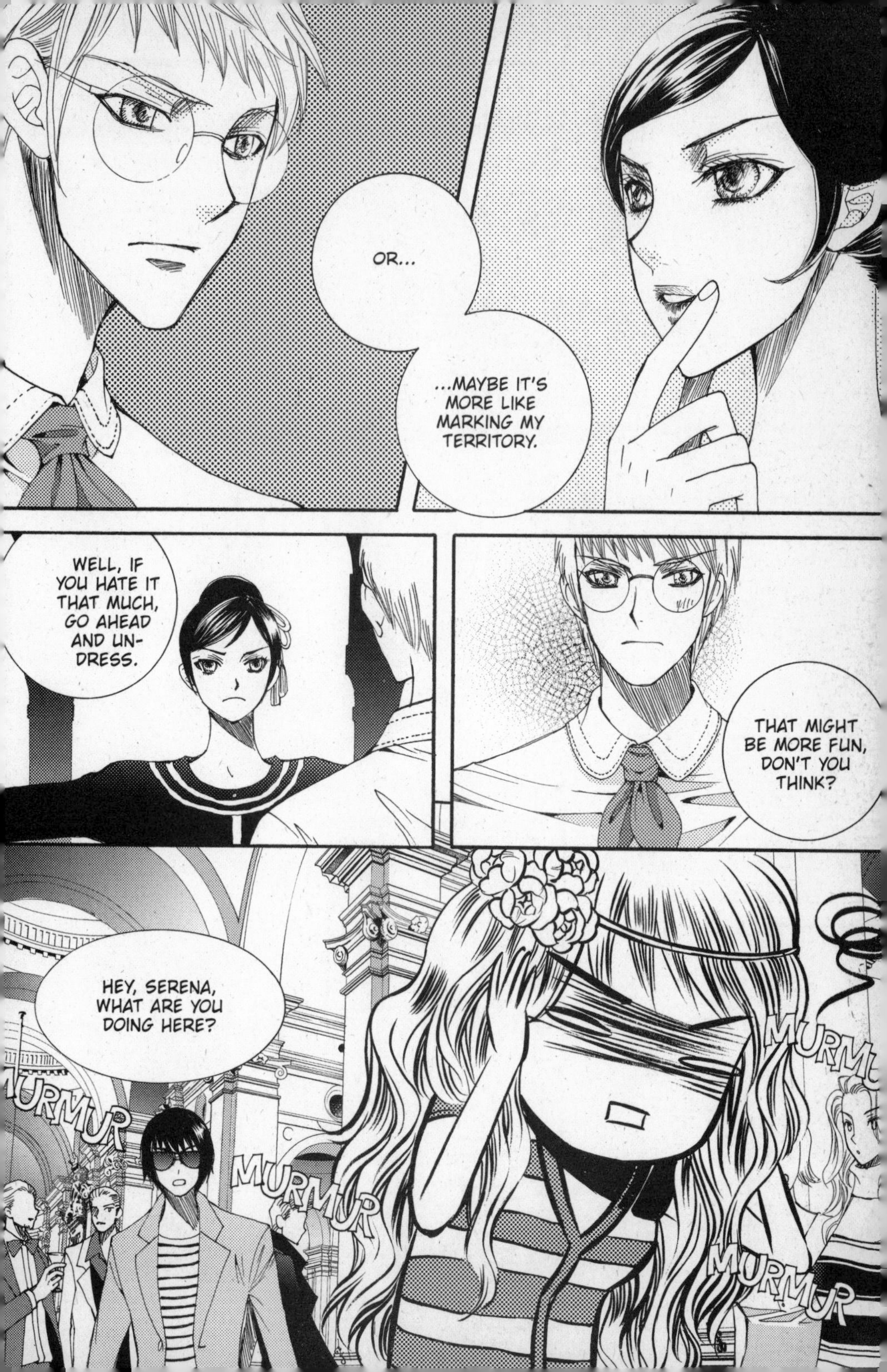
OR...
...MAYBE IT'S MORE LIKE MARKING MY TERRITORY.
WELL, IF YOU HATE IT THAT MUCH, GO AHEAD AND UN-DRESS.
THAT MIGHT BE MORE FUN, DON'T YOU THINK?
HEY, SERENA, WHAT ARE YOU DOING HERE?
MURMUR
MURMUR
MURMUR
MURMUR
MURMUR

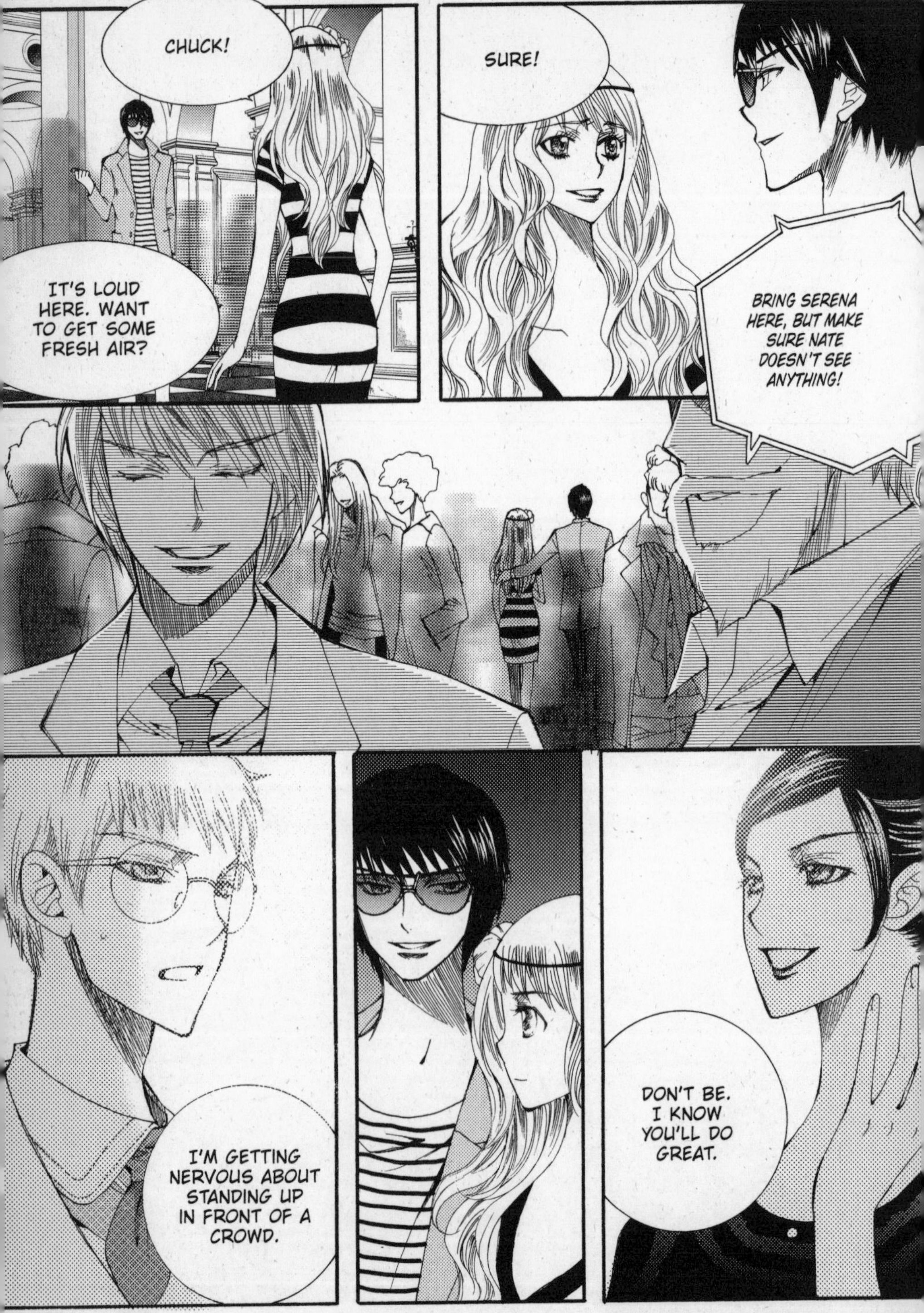
CHUCK!
IT'S LOUD HERE. WANT TO GET SOME FRESH AIR?
SURE!
BRING SERENA HERE, BUT MAKE SURE NATE DOESN'T SEE ANYTHING!
I'M GETTING NERVOUS ABOUT STANDING UP IN FRONT OF A CROWD.
DON'T BE. I KNOW YOU'LL DO GREAT.

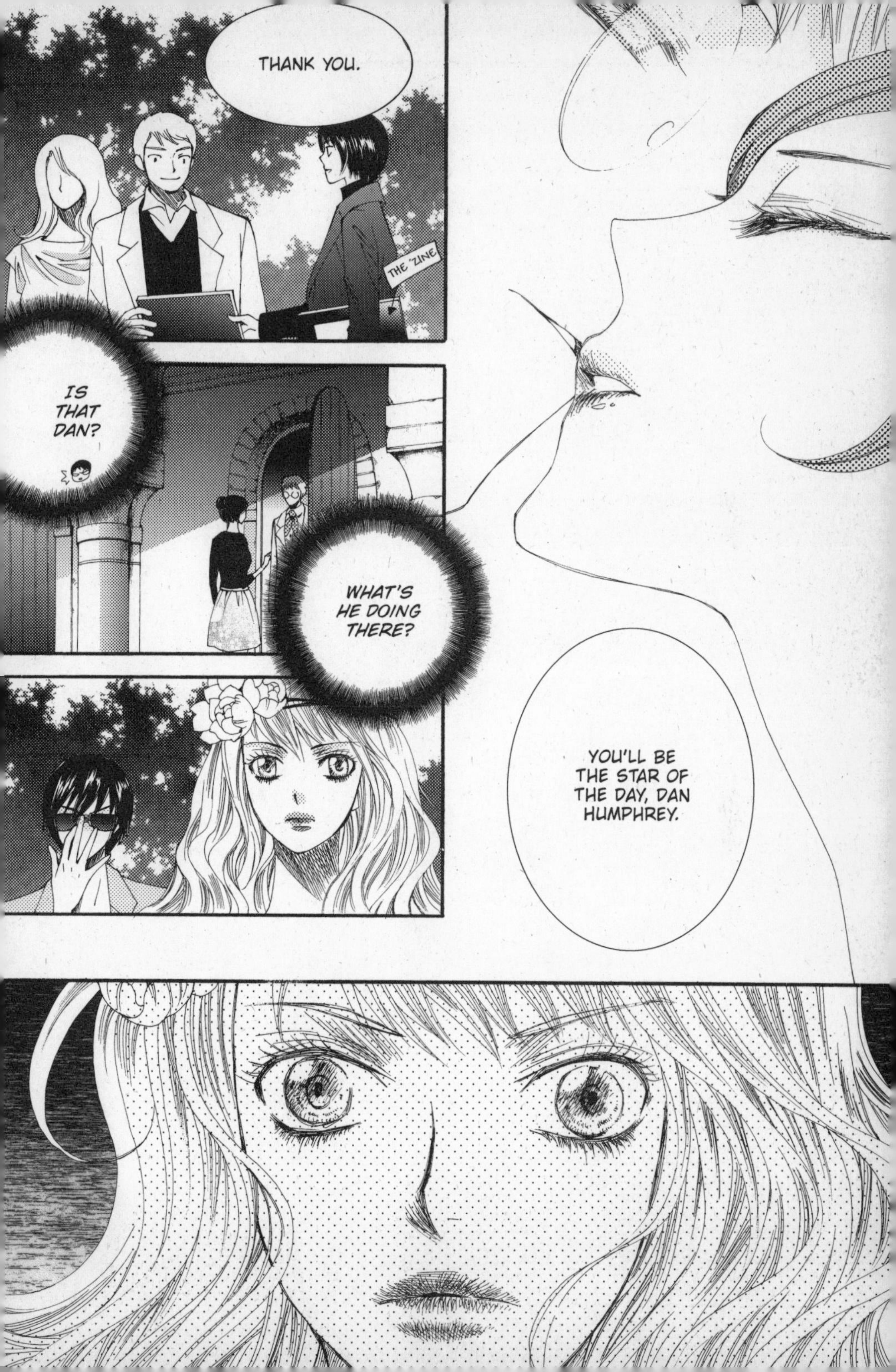
THANK YOU.
THE 'ZINE
IS THAT DAN?
WHAT'S HE DOING THERE?
YOU'LL BE THE STAR OF THE DAY, DAN HUMPHREY.

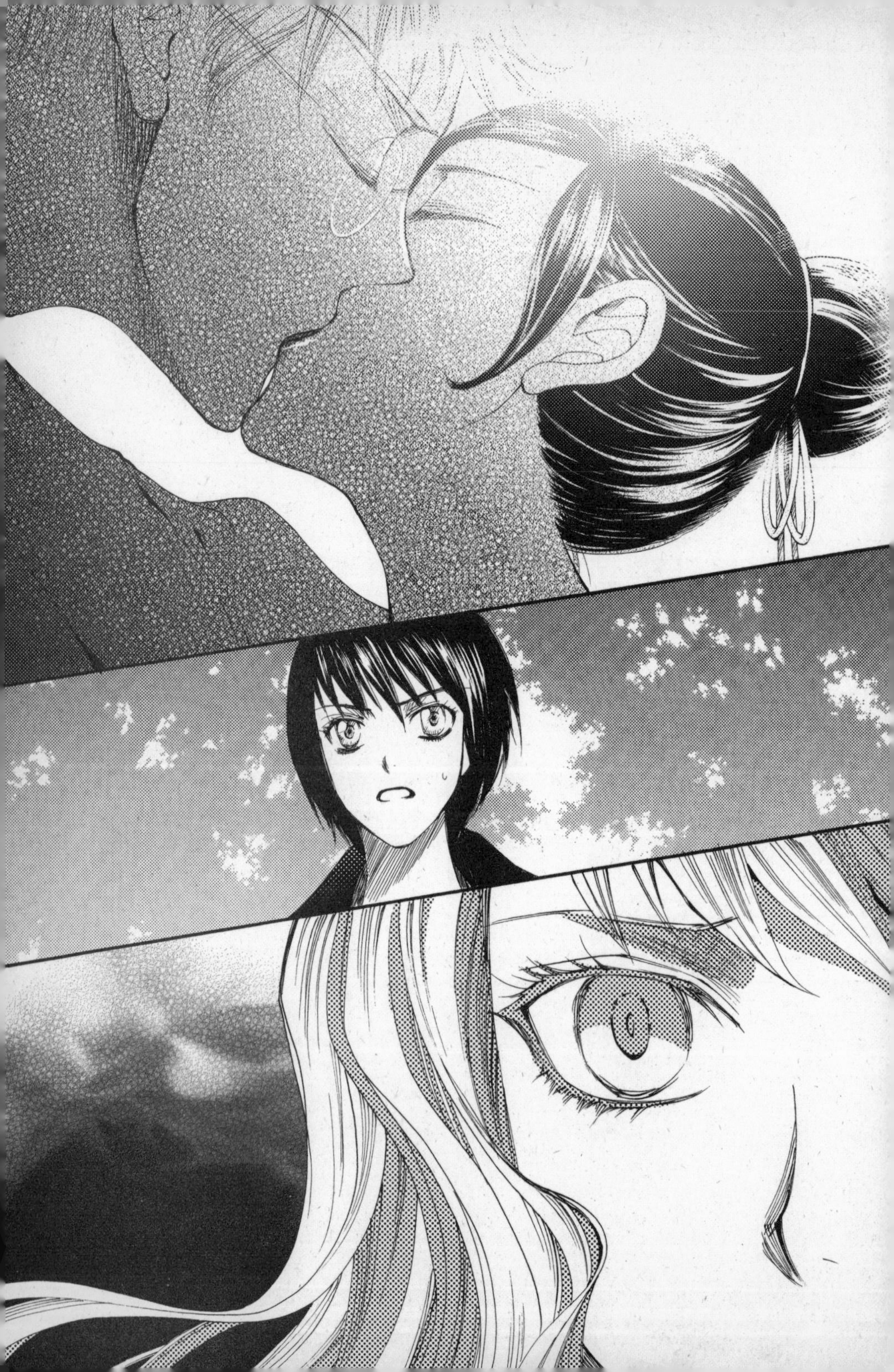

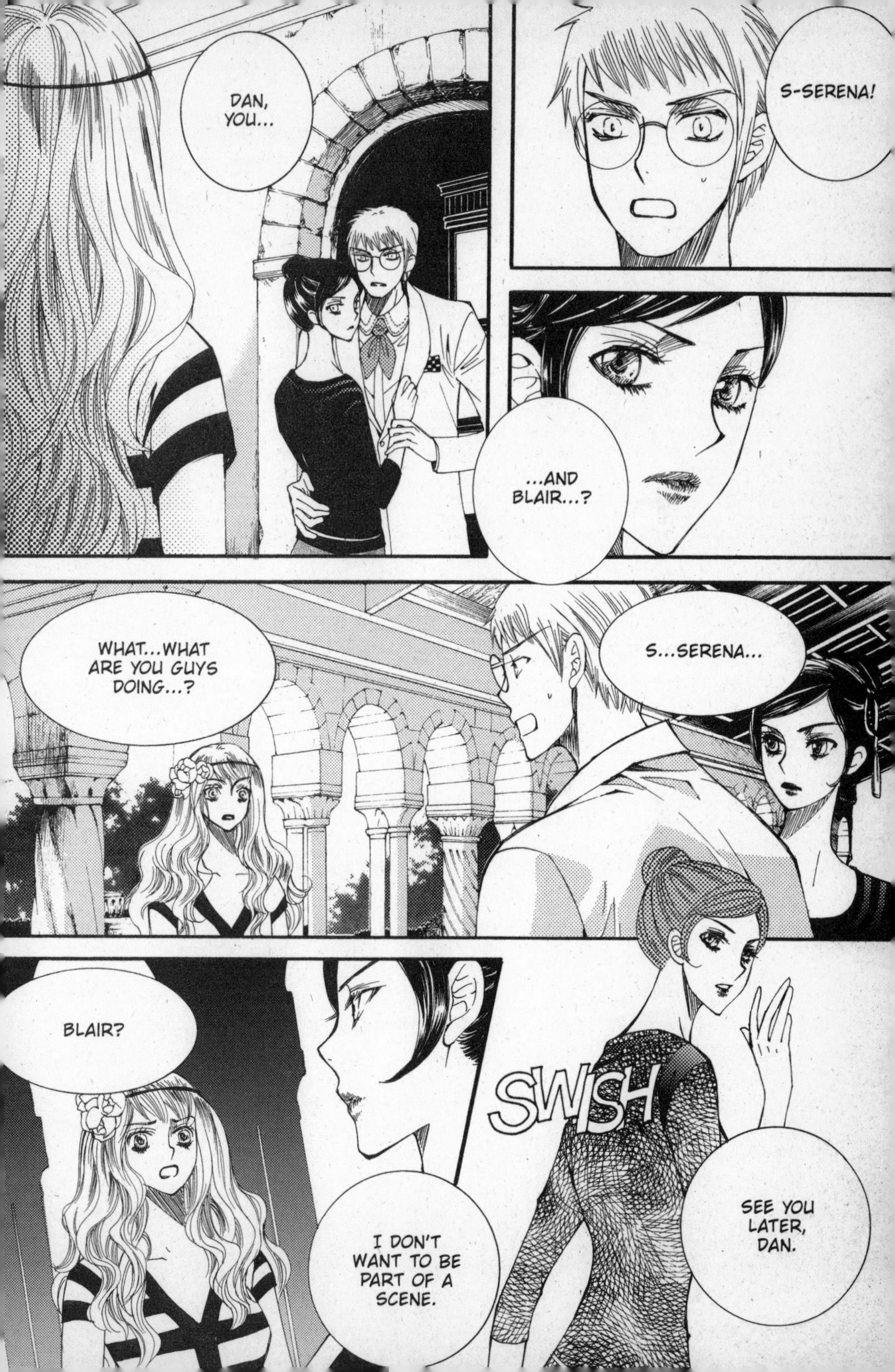
DAN, YOU...
S-SERENA!
...AND BLAIR...?
WHAT...WHAT ARE YOU GUYS DOING...?
S...SERENA...
BLAIR?
I DON'T WANT TO BE PART OF A SCENE.
SWISH
SEE YOU LATER, DAN.

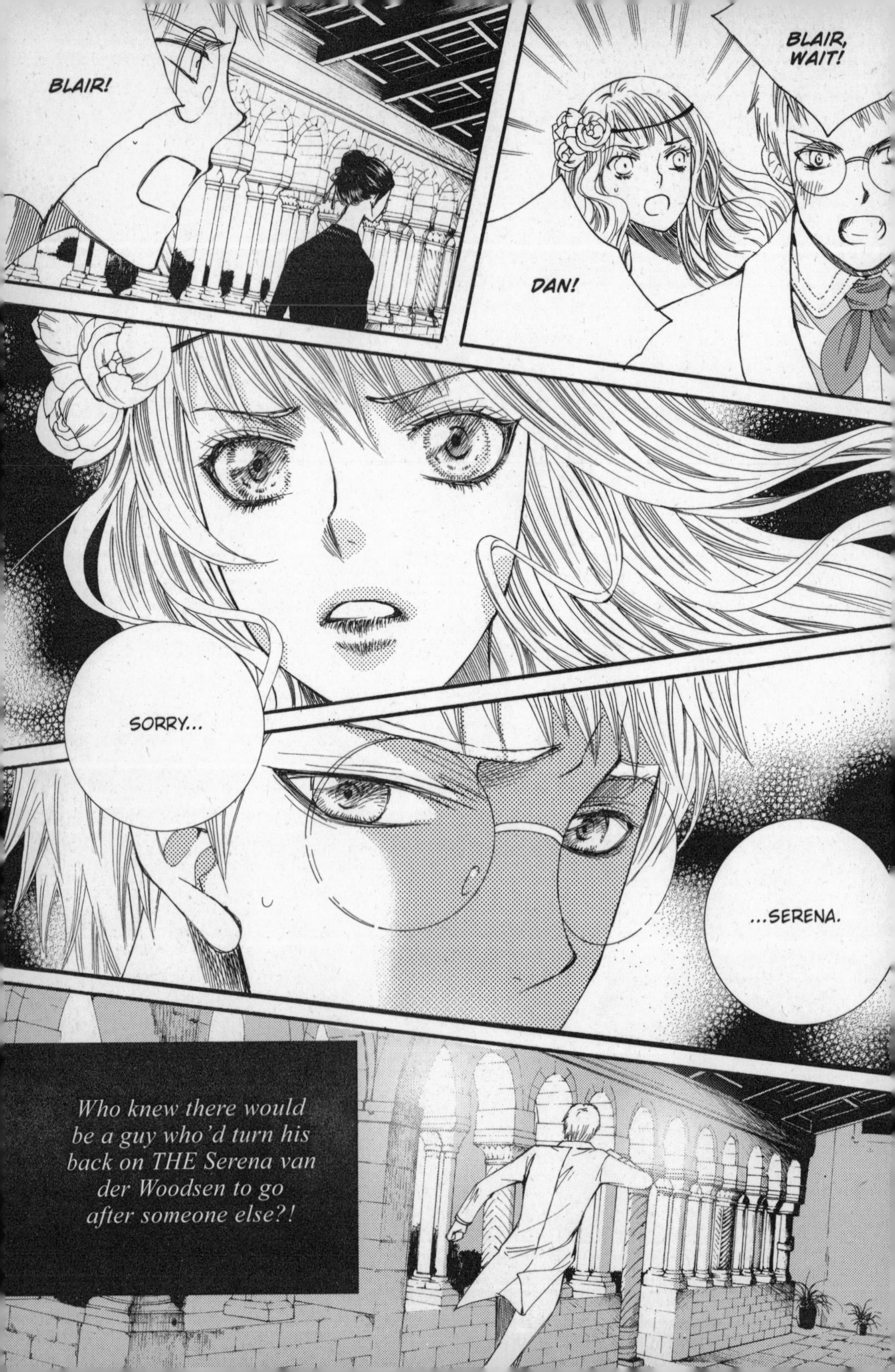
BLAIR!
BLAIR, WAIT!
DAN!
SORRY...
...SERENA.
Who knew there would be a guy who'd turn his back on THE Serena van der Woodsen to go after someone else?!

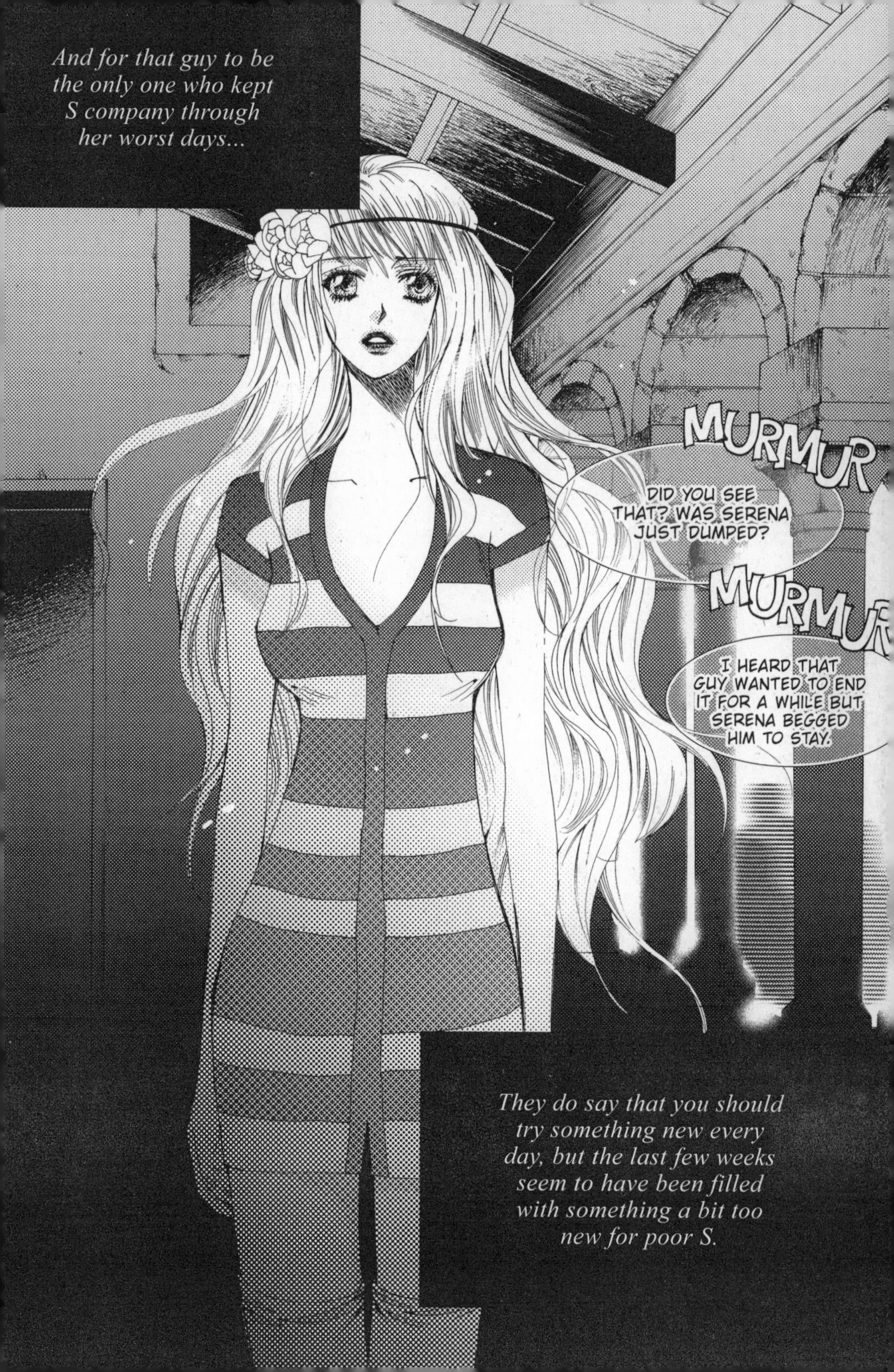
And for that guy to be the only one who kept S company through her worst days...
MURMUR
DID YOU SEE THAT? WAS SERENA JUST DUMPED?
MURMUR
I HEARD THAT GUY WANTED TO END IT FOR A WHILE BUT SERENA BEGGED HIM TO STAY.
They do say that you should try something new every day, but the last few weeks seem to have been filled with something a bit too new for poor S.

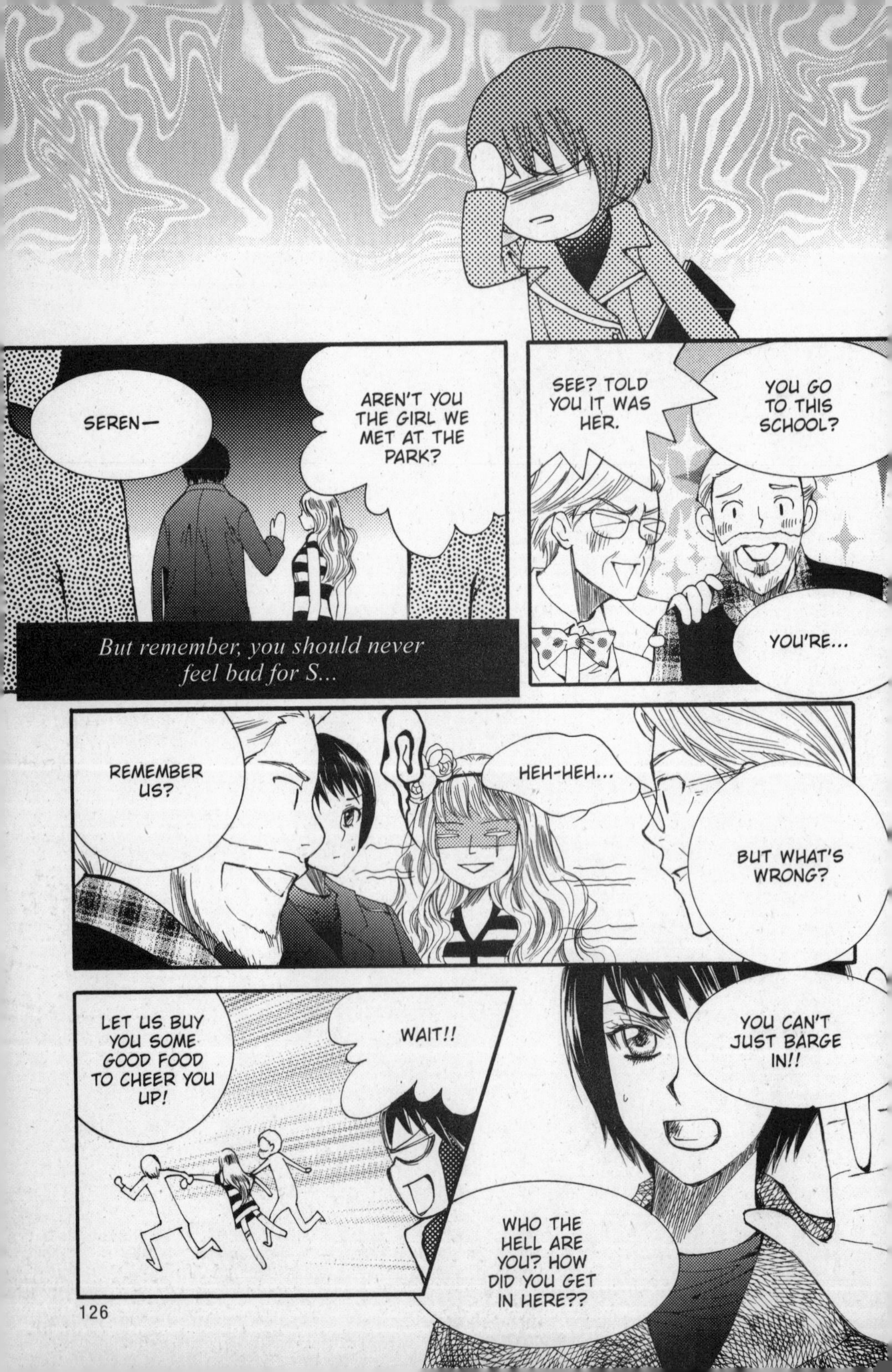
SEREN—
AREN'T YOU THE GIRL WE MET AT THE PARK?
But remember, you should never feel bad for S...
SEE? TOLD YOU IT WAS HER.
YOU GO TO THIS SCHOOL?
YOU'RE...
REMEMBER US?
HEH-HEH...
BUT WHAT'S WRONG?
LET US BUY YOU SOME GOOD FOOD TO CHEER YOU UP!
WAIT!!
YOU CAN'T JUST BARGE IN!!
WHO THE HELL ARE YOU? HOW DID YOU GET IN HERE??

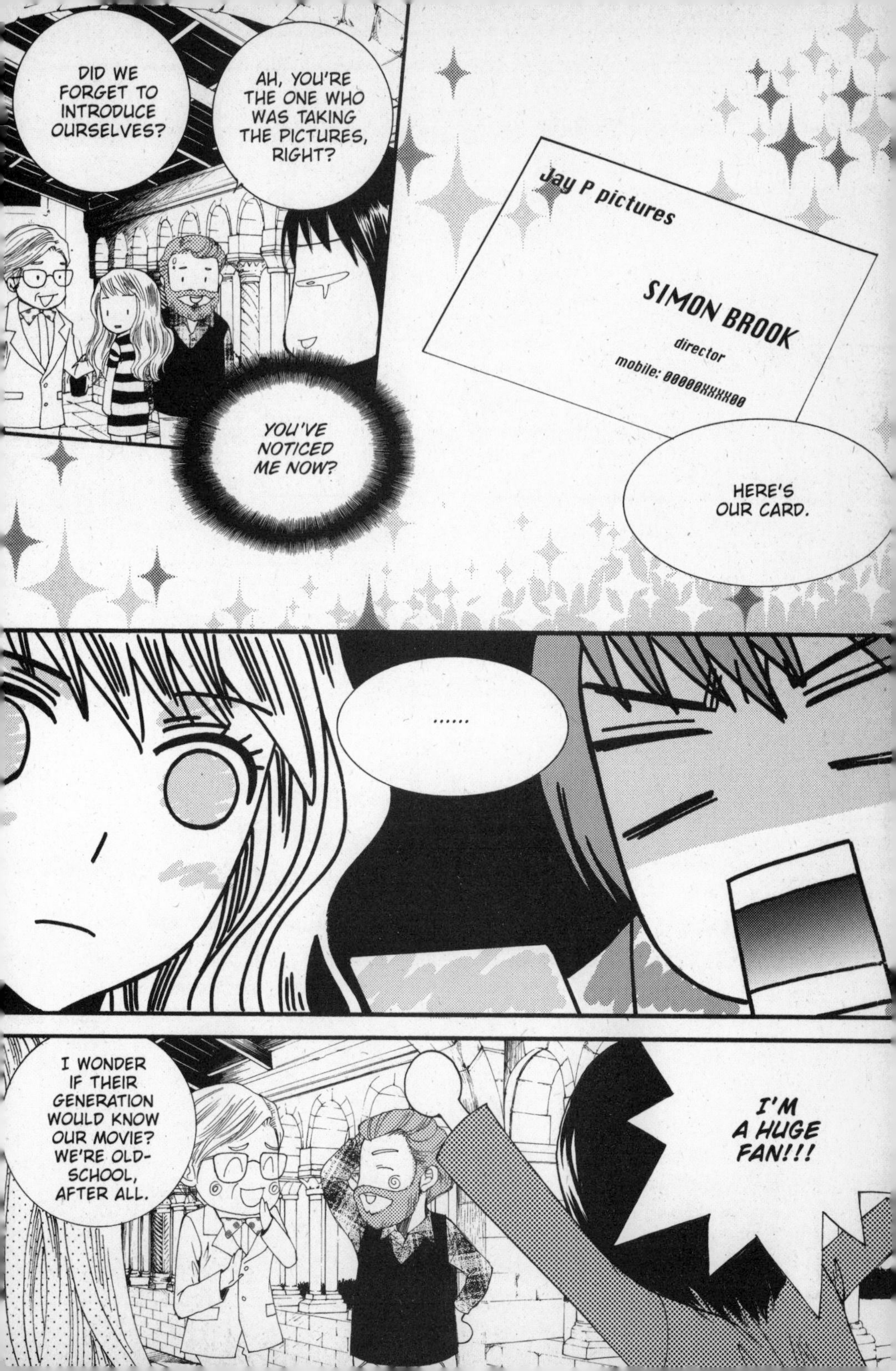
DID WE FORGET TO INTRODUCE OURSELVES?
AH, YOU'RE THE ONE WHO WAS TAKING THE PICTURES, RIGHT?
YOU'VE NOTICED ME NOW?
Jay P pictures
SIMON BROOK
director
mobile: 00000XXXX00
HERE'S OUR CARD.
......
I WONDER IF THEIR GENERATION WOULD KNOW OUR MOVIE? WE'RE OLD-SCHOOL, AFTER ALL.
I'M A HUGE FAN!!!

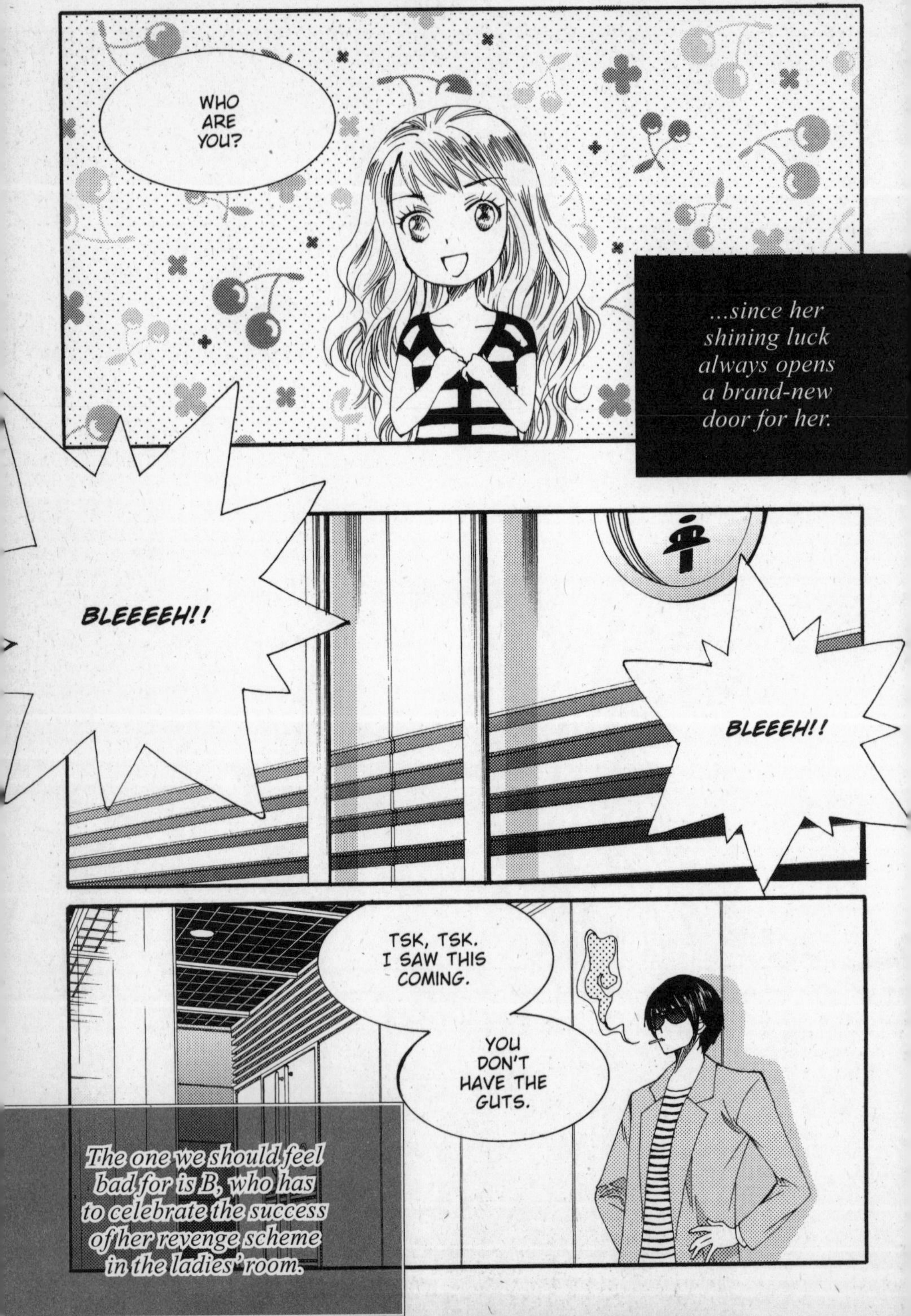
WHO ARE YOU?
...since her shining luck always opens a brand-new door for her.
BLEEEEH!!
BLEEEH!!
TSK, TSK. I SAW THIS COMING.
YOU DON'T HAVE THE GUTS.
The one we should feel bad for is B, who has to celebrate the success of her revenge scheme in the ladies' room.

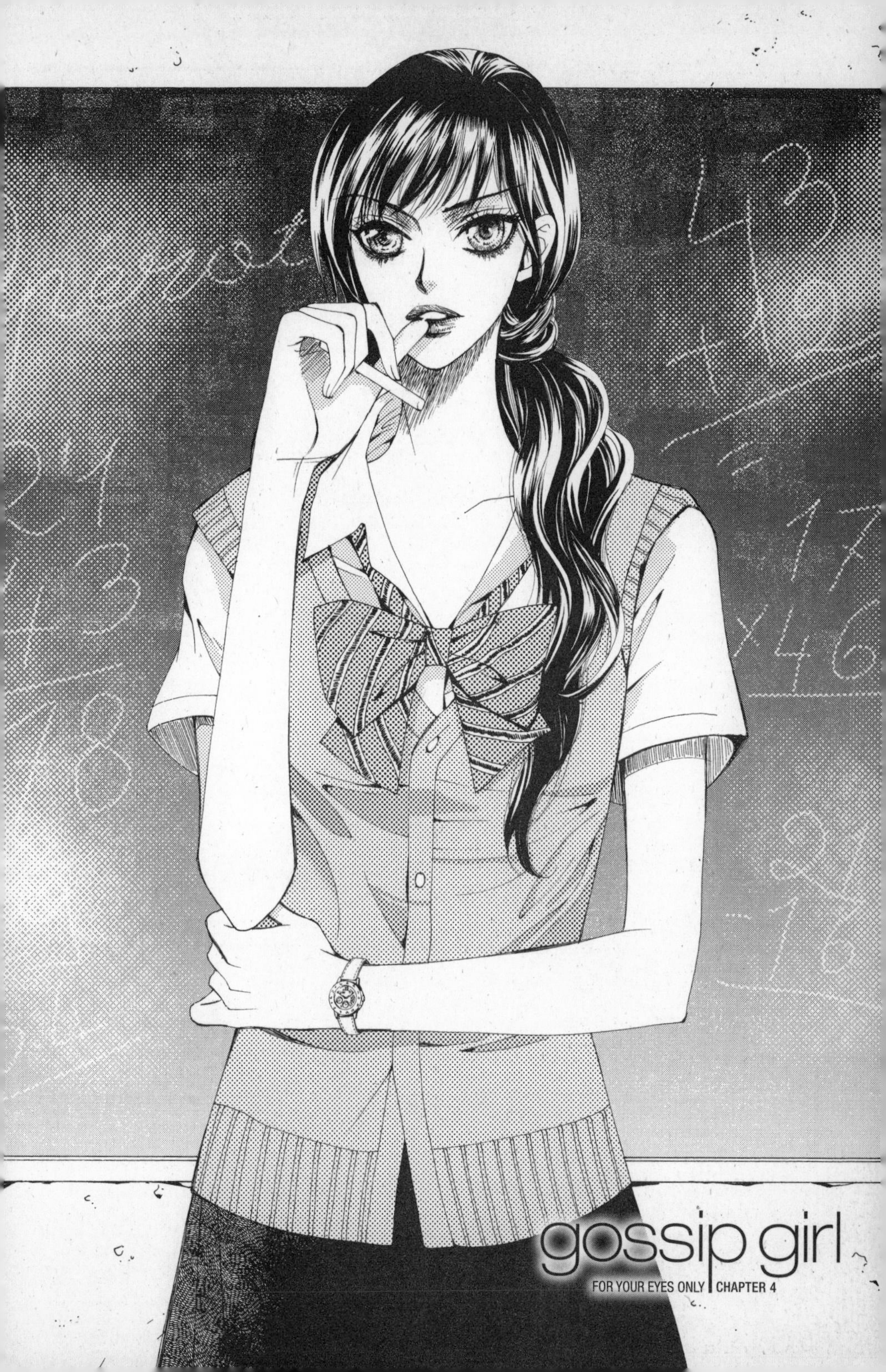
gossip girl
FOR YOUR EYES ONLY
CHAPTER 4

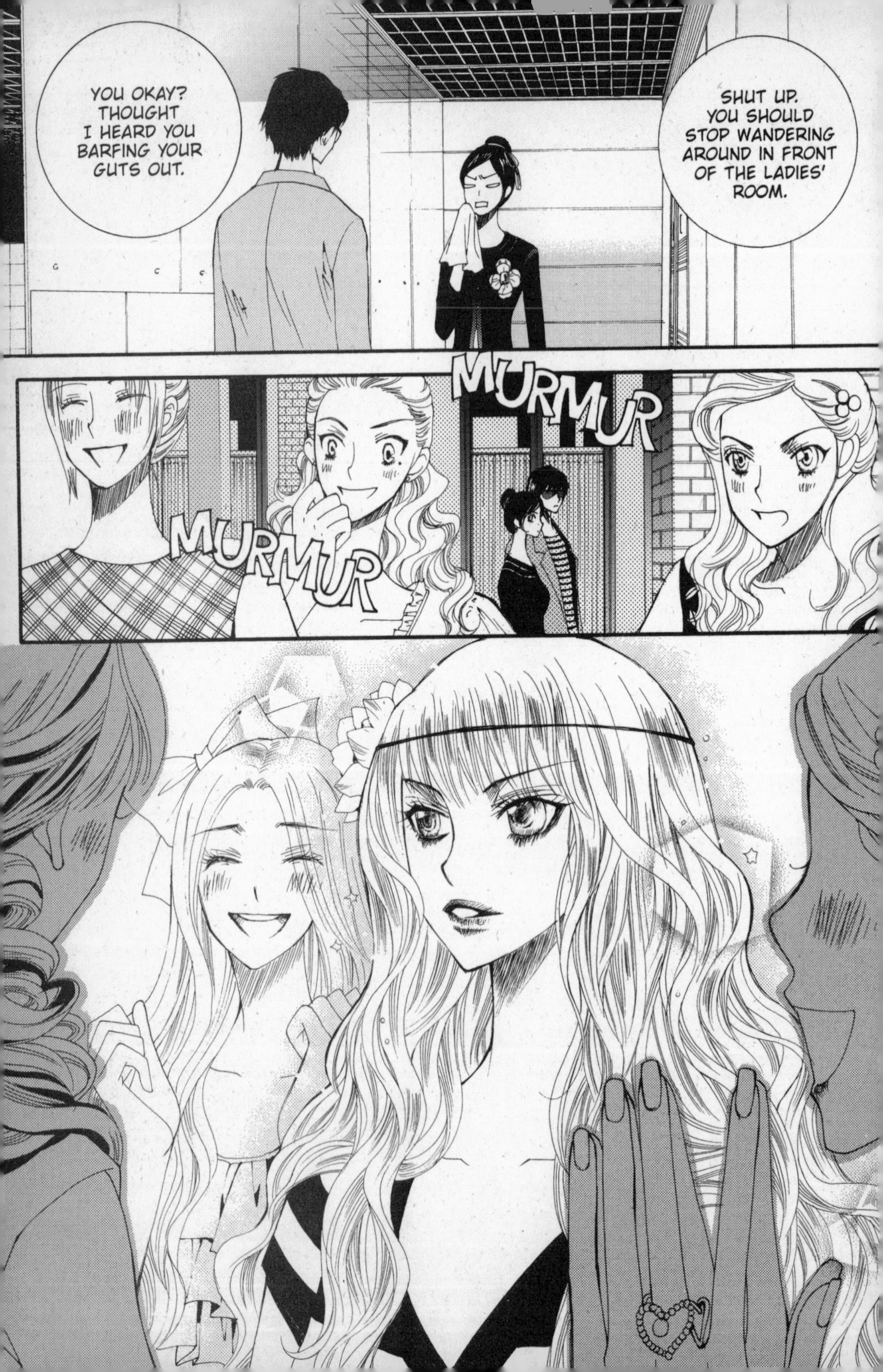
YOU OKAY? THOUGHT I HEARD YOU BARFING YOUR GUTS OUT.
SHUT UP. YOU SHOULD STOP WANDERING AROUND IN FRONT OF THE LADIES' ROOM.
MURMUR
MURMUR

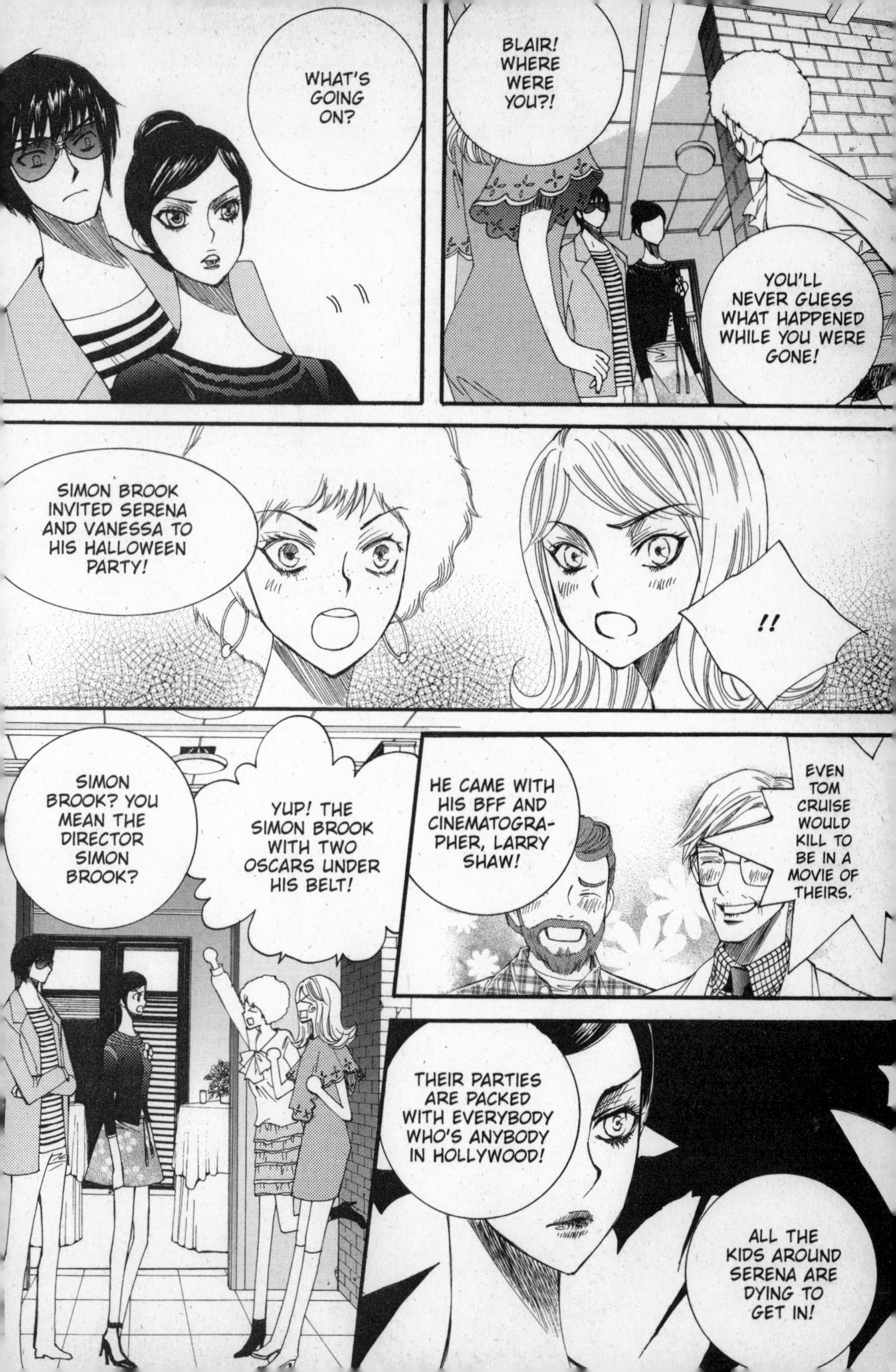
WHAT'S GOING ON?
BLAIR! WHERE WERE YOU?!
YOU'LL NEVER GUESS WHAT HAPPENED WHILE YOU WERE GONE!
SIMON BROOK INVITED SERENA AND VANESSA TO HIS HALLOWEEN PARTY!
!!
SIMON BROOK? YOU MEAN THE DIRECTOR SIMON BROOK?
YUP! THE SIMON BROOK WITH TWO OSCARS UNDER HIS BELT!
HE CAME WITH HIS BFF AND CINEMATOGRAPHER, LARRY SHAW!
EVEN TOM CRUISE WOULD KILL TO BE IN A MOVIE OF THEIRS.
THEIR PARTIES ARE PACKED WITH EVERYBODY WHO'S ANYBODY IN HOLLYWOOD!
ALL THE KIDS AROUND SERENA ARE DYING TO GET IN!

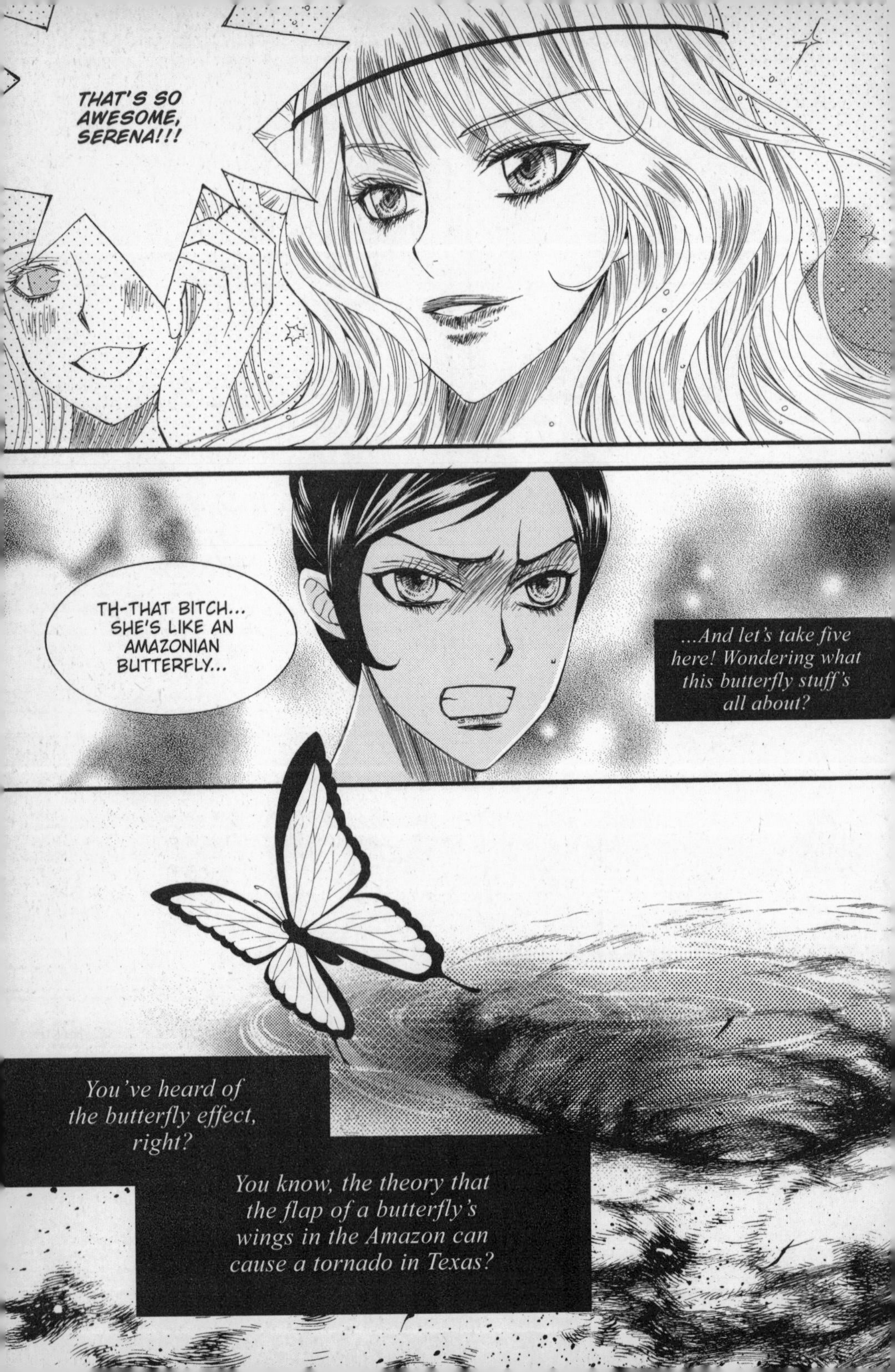
THAT'S SO AWESOME, SERENA!!!
TH-THAT BITCH... SHE'S LIKE AN AMAZONIAN BUTTERFLY...
...And let's take five here! Wondering what this butterfly stuff's all about?
You've heard of the butterfly effect, right?
You know, the theory that the flap of a butterfly's wings in the Amazon can cause a tornado in Texas?

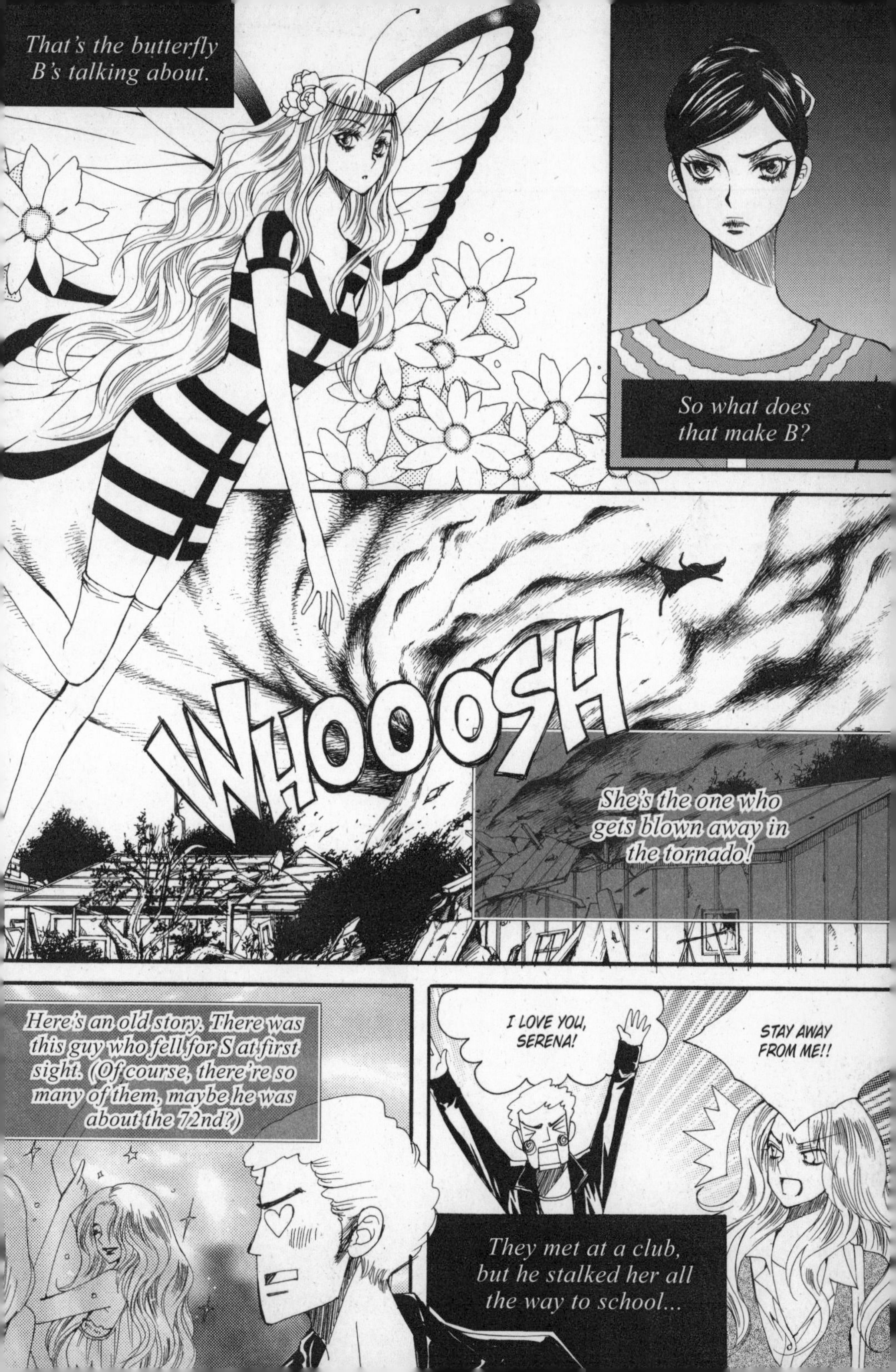
That's the butterfly B's talking about.
So what does that make B?
WHOOOSH
She's the one who gets blown away in the tornado!
Here's an old story. There was this guy who fell for S at first sight. (Of course, there're so many of them, maybe he was about the 72nd?)
I LOVE YOU, SERENA!
STAY AWAY FROM ME!!
They met at a club, but he stalked her all the way to school...

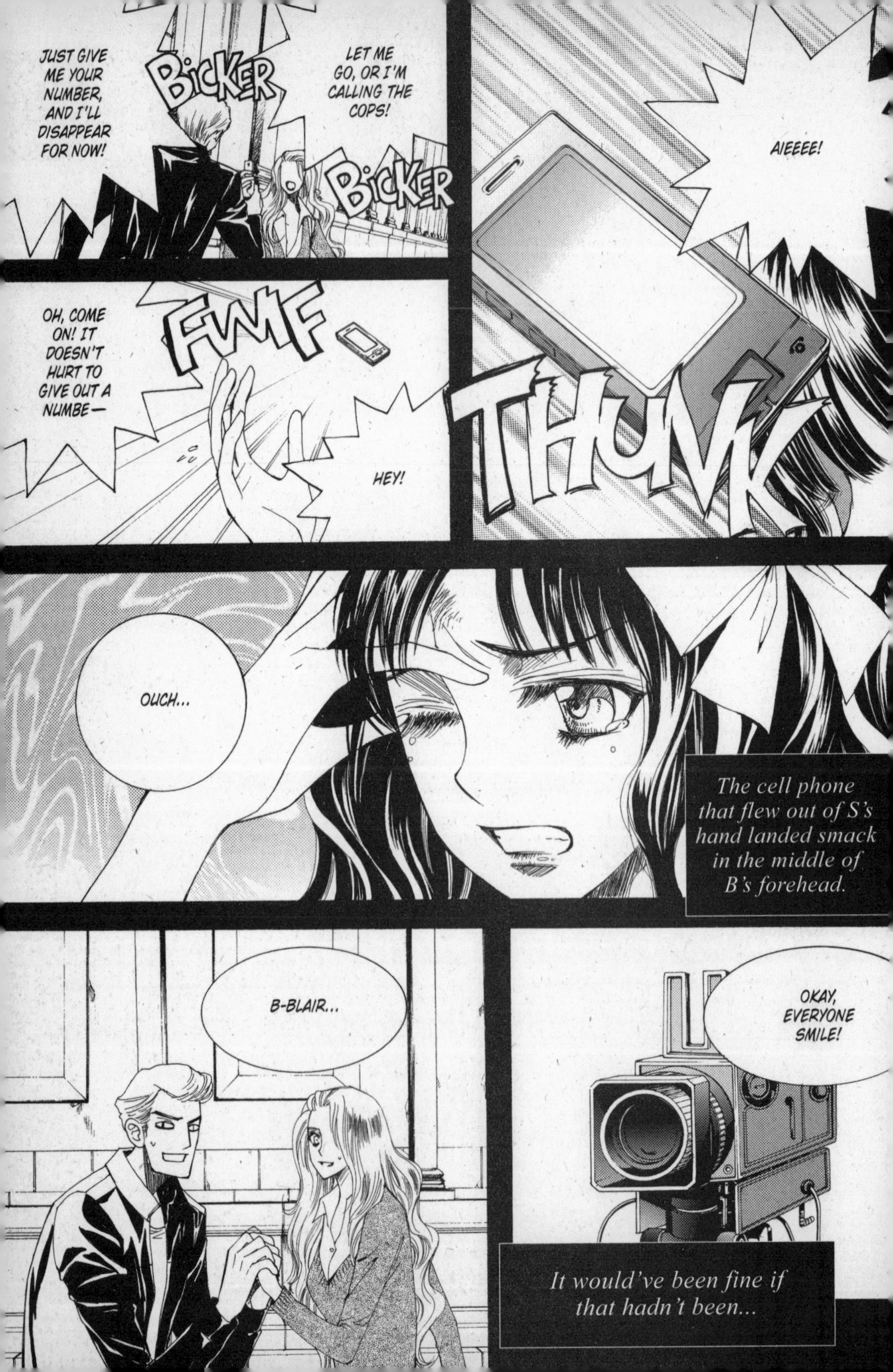
JUST GIVE ME YOUR NUMBER, AND I'LL DISAPPEAR FOR NOW!
BICKER
LET ME GO, OR I'M CALLING THE COPS!
BICKER
OH, COME ON! IT DOESN'T HURT TO GIVE OUT A NUMBE—
FWIF
HEY!
AIEEEE!
THUNK
OUCH...
The cell phone that flew out of S's hand landed smack in the middle of B's forehead.
B-BLAIR...
OKAY, EVERYONE SMILE!
It would've been fine if that hadn't been...

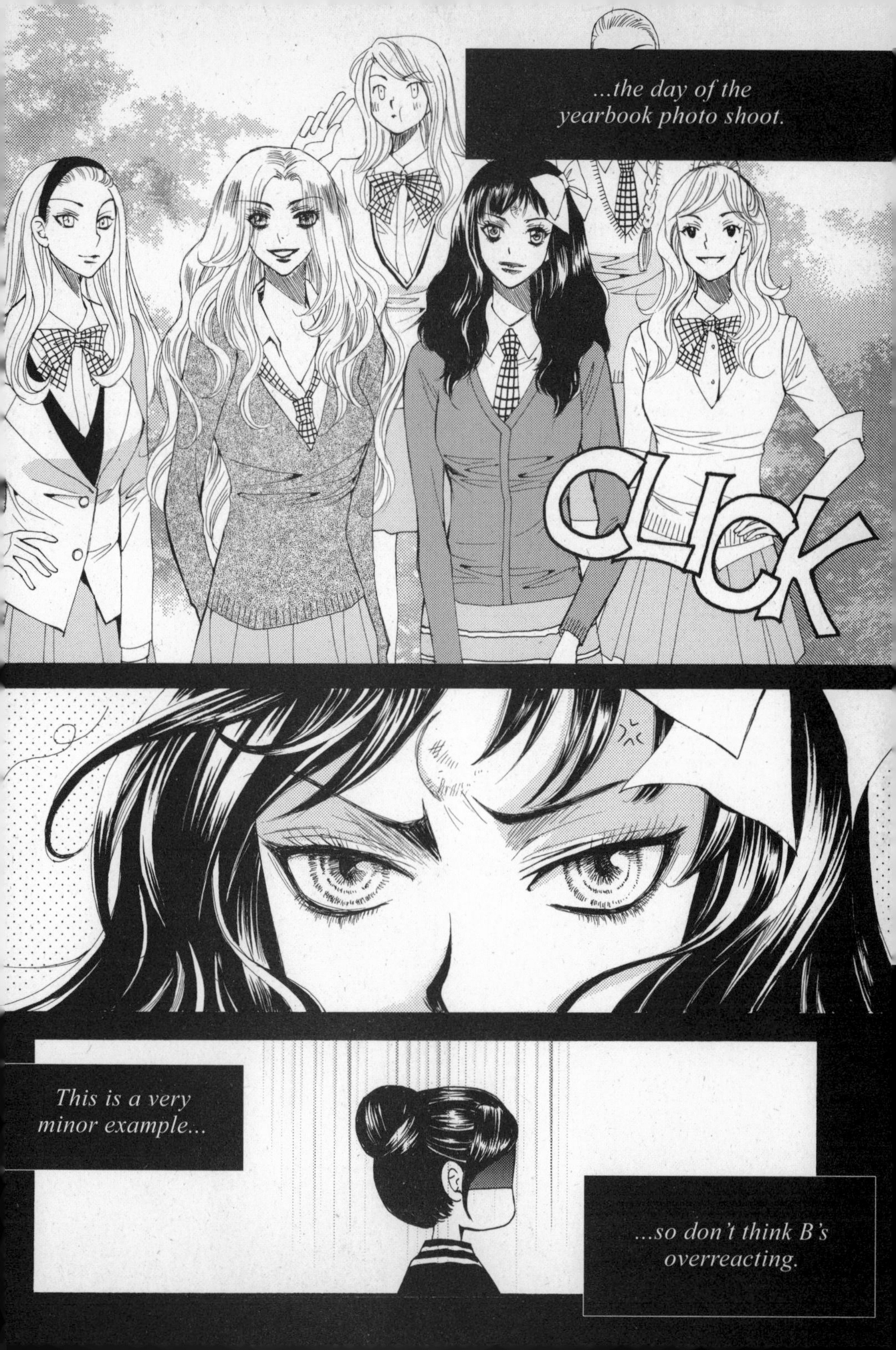
...the day of the yearbook photo shoot.
CLICK
This is a very minor example...
...so don't think B's overreacting.

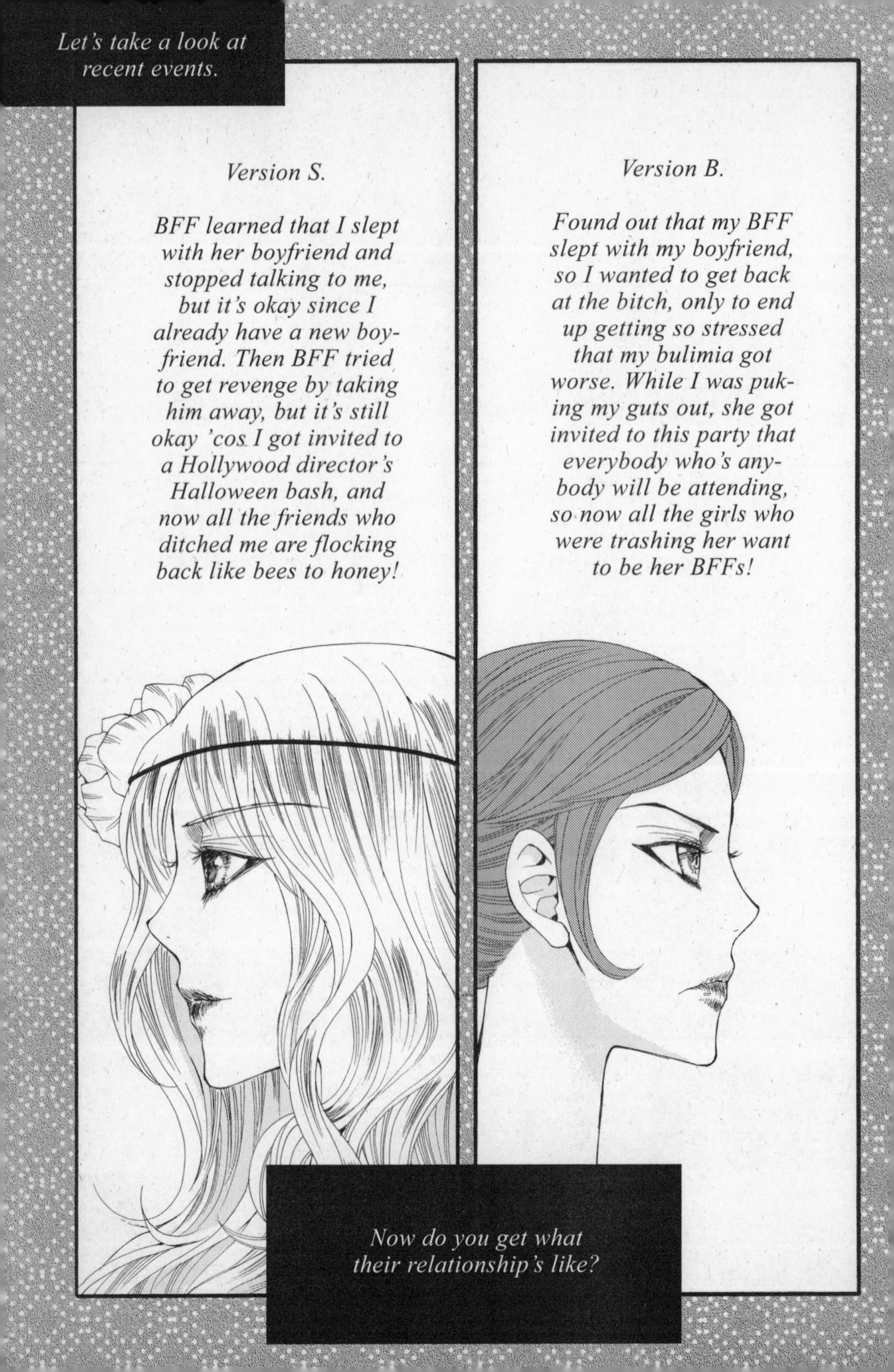
Let's take a look at recent events.
Version S.
BFF learned that I slept with her boyfriend and stopped talking to me, but it's okay since I already have a new boy-friend. Then BFF tried to get revenge by taking him away, but it's still okay 'cos I got invited to a Hollywood director's Halloween bash, and now all the friends who ditched me are flocking back like bees to honey!
Version B.
Found out that my BFF slept with my boyfriend, so I wanted to get back at the bitch, only to end up getting so stressed that my bulimia got worse. While I was puk-ing my guts out, she got invited to this party that everybody who's any-body will be attending, so now all the girls who were trashing her want to be her BFFs!
Now do you get what their relationship's like?

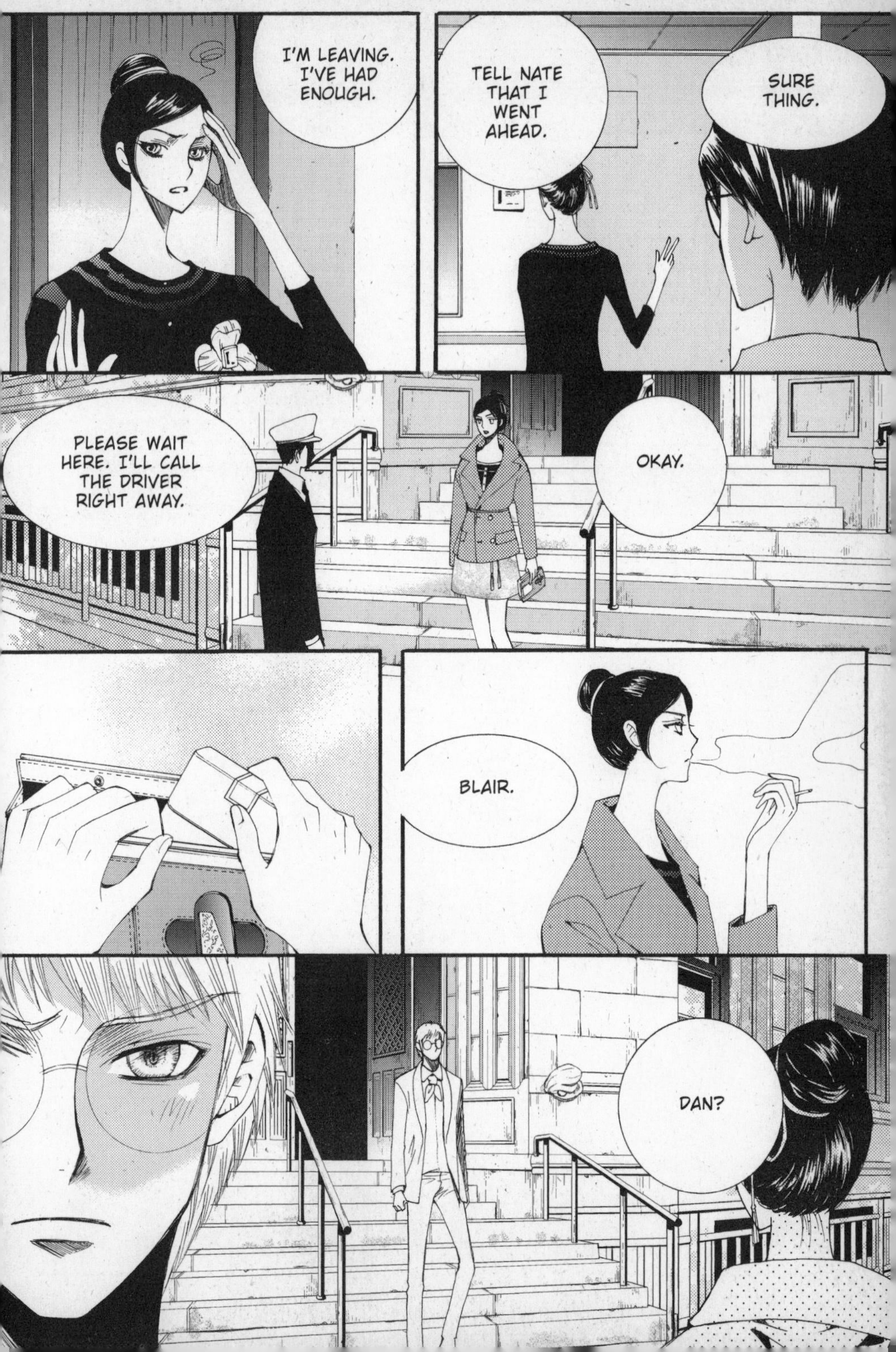
I'M LEAVING. I'VE HAD ENOUGH.
TELL NATE THAT I WENT AHEAD.
SURE THING.
PLEASE WAIT HERE. I'LL CALL THE DRIVER RIGHT AWAY.
OKAY.
BLAIR.
DAN?

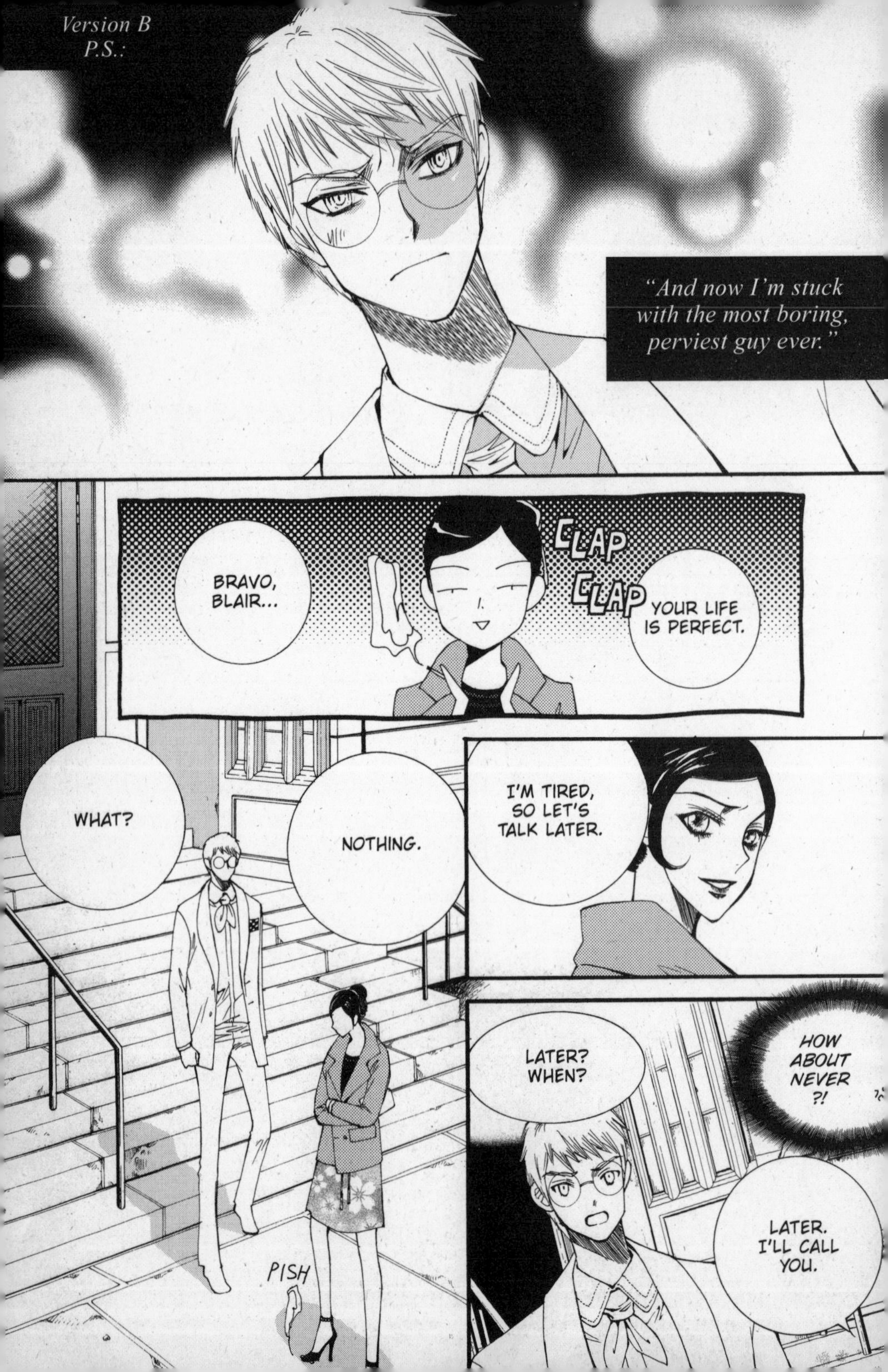
Version B
P.S.:
"And now I'm stuck with the most boring, perviest guy ever."
BRAVO, BLAIR...
CLAP CLAP
YOUR LIFE IS PERFECT.
WHAT?
NOTHING.
PISH
I'M TIRED, SO LET'S TALK LATER.
LATER? WHEN?
HOW ABOUT NEVER ?!
LATER. I'LL CALL YOU.

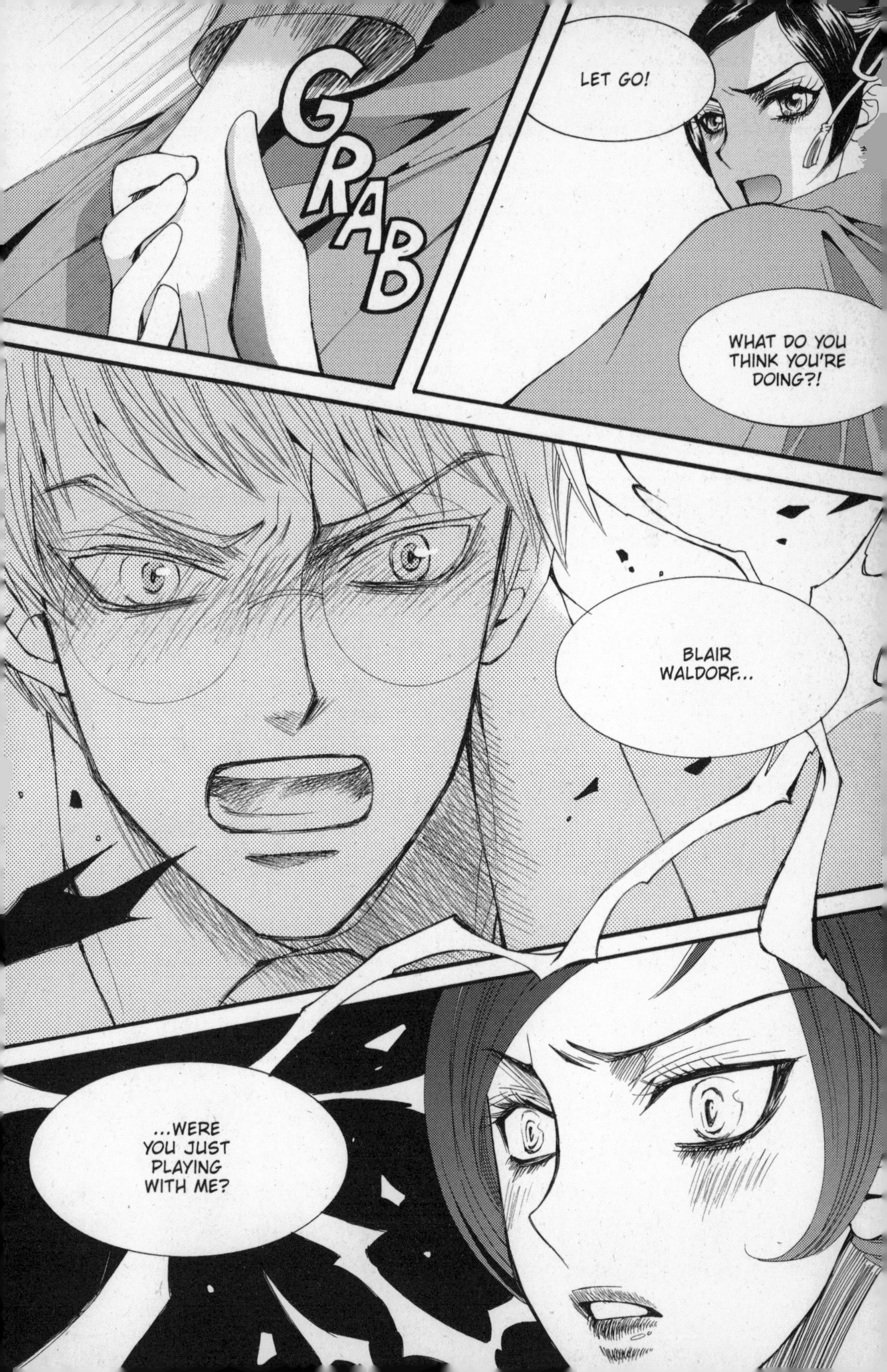
GRAB
LET GO!
WHAT DO YOU THINK YOU'RE DOING?!
BLAIR WALDORF...
...WERE YOU JUST PLAYING WITH ME?

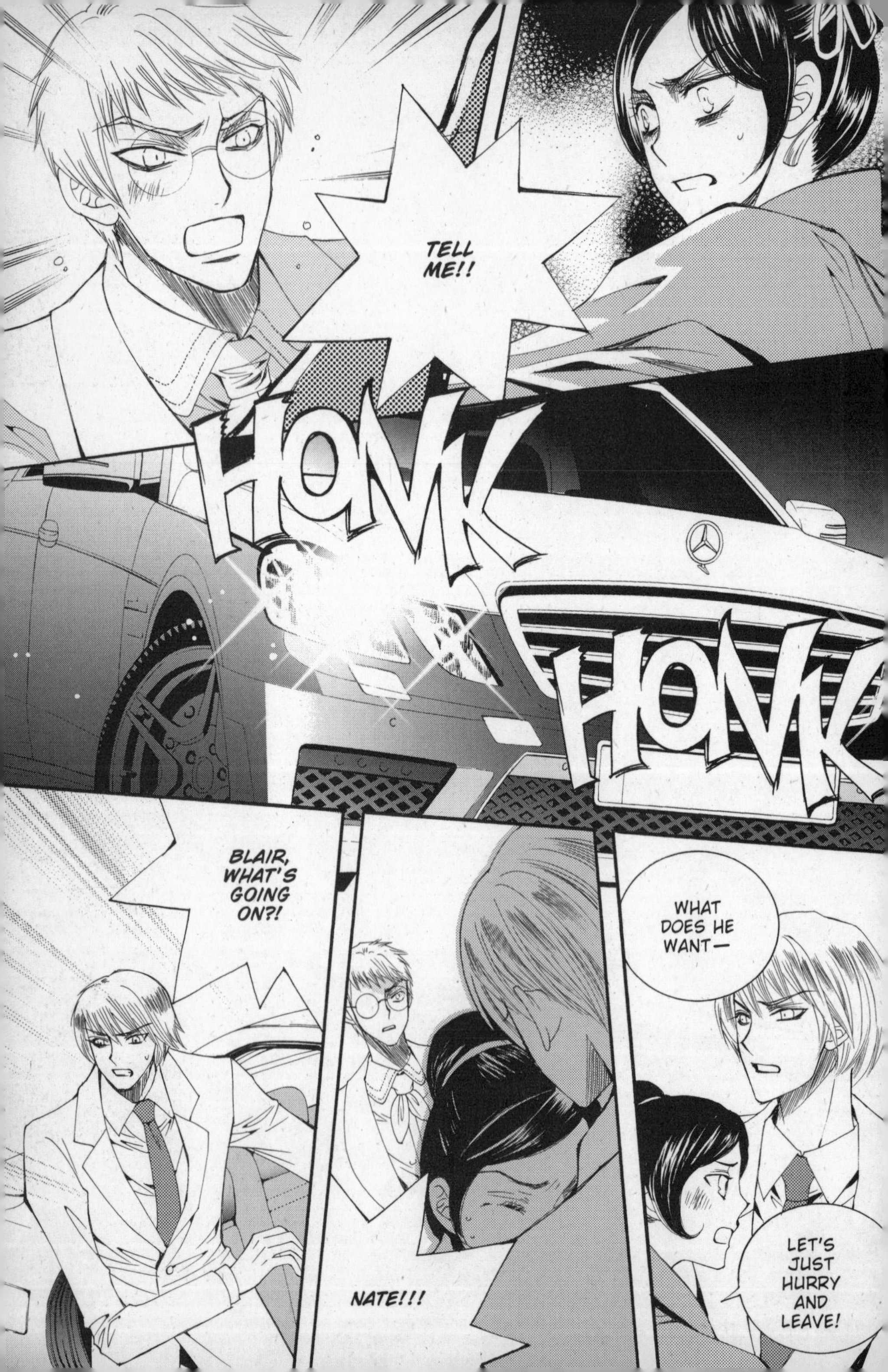
TELL ME!!
HONK
HONK
BLAIR, WHAT'S GOING ON?!
NATE!!!
WHAT DOES HE WANT—
LET'S JUST HURRY AND LEAVE!

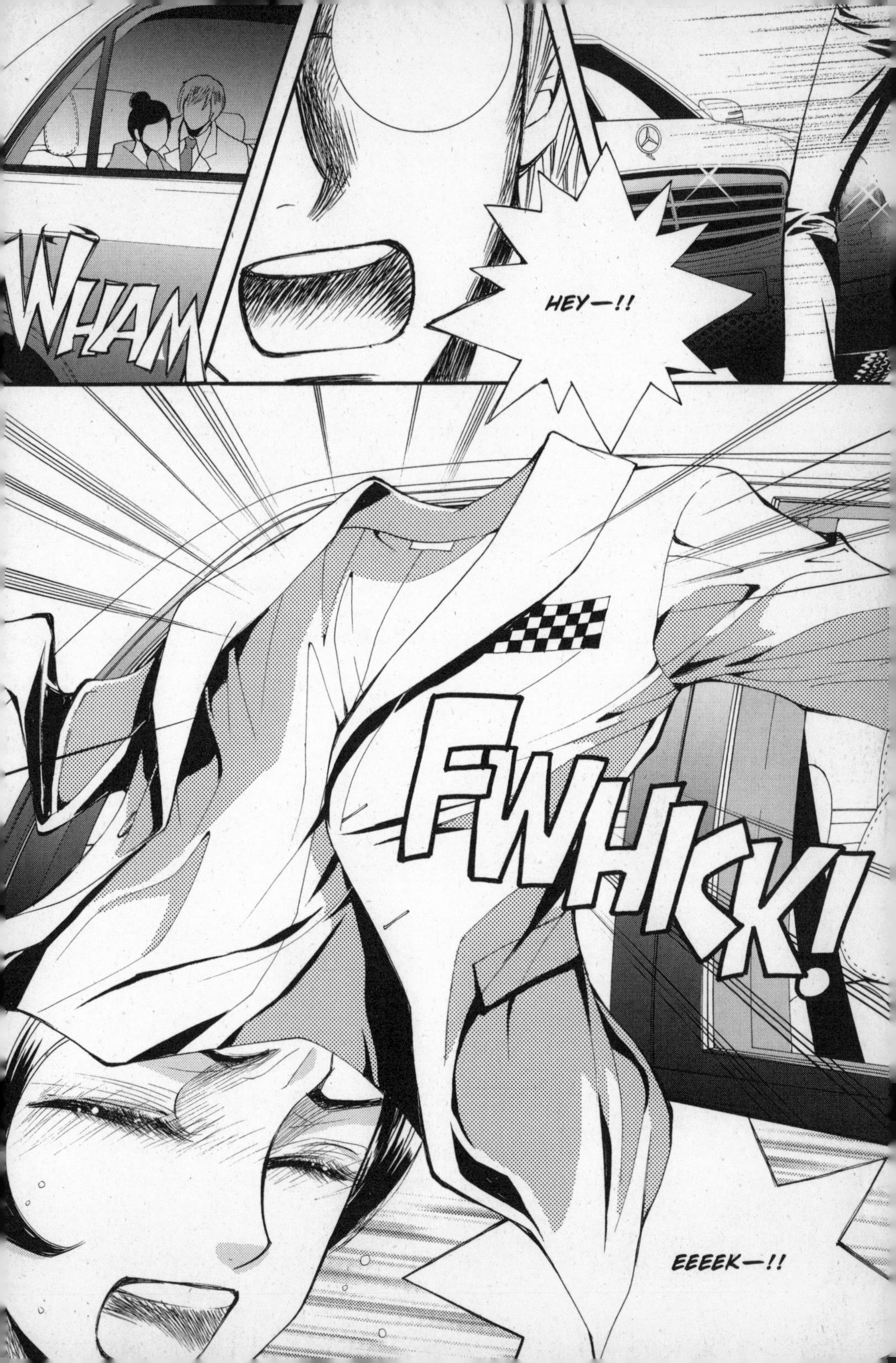
WHAM
HEY—!!
FWHICK!
EEEEK—!!

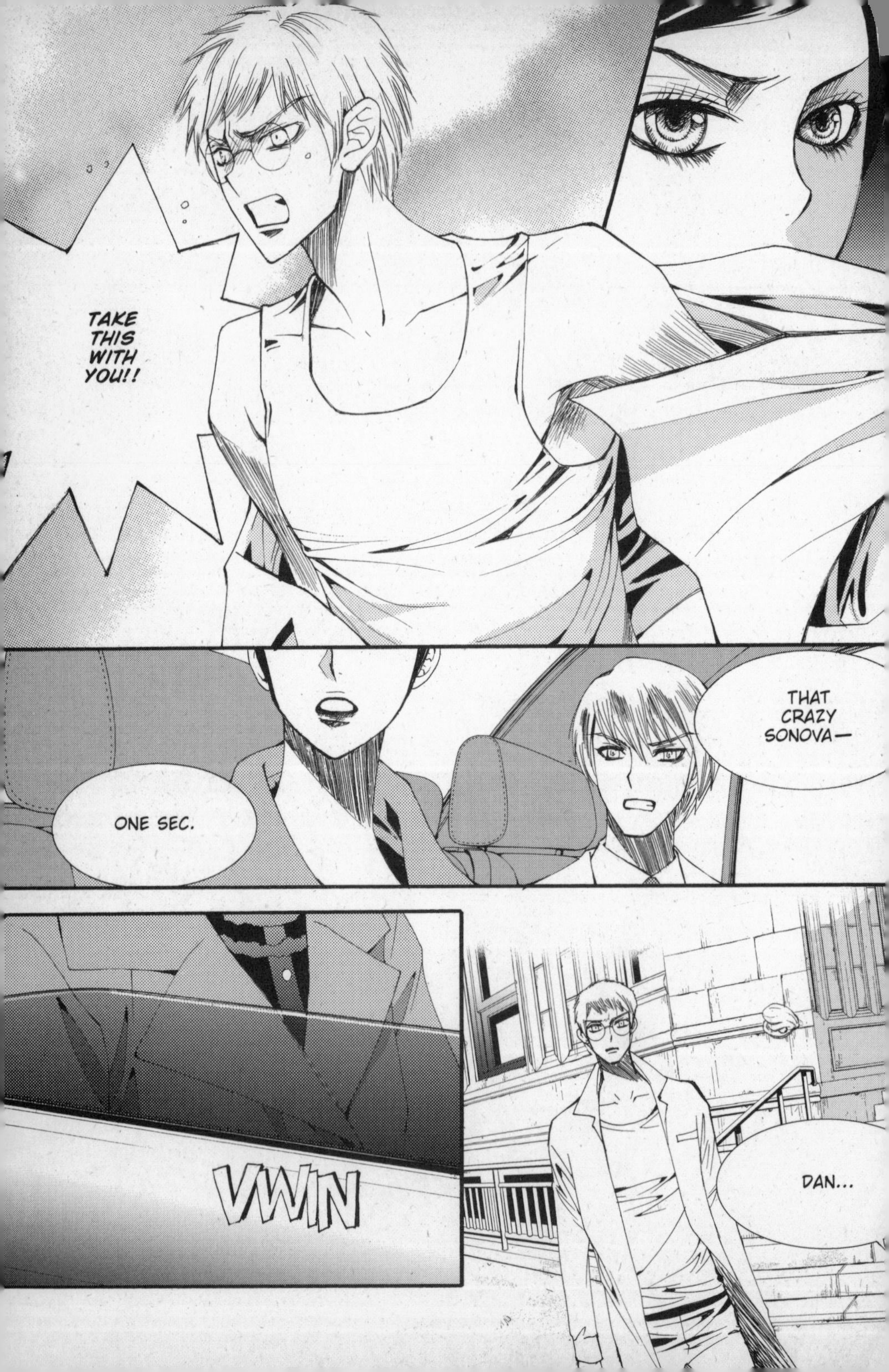
TAKE THIS WITH YOU!!
ONE SEC.
THAT CRAZY SONOVA—
VWIN
DAN...

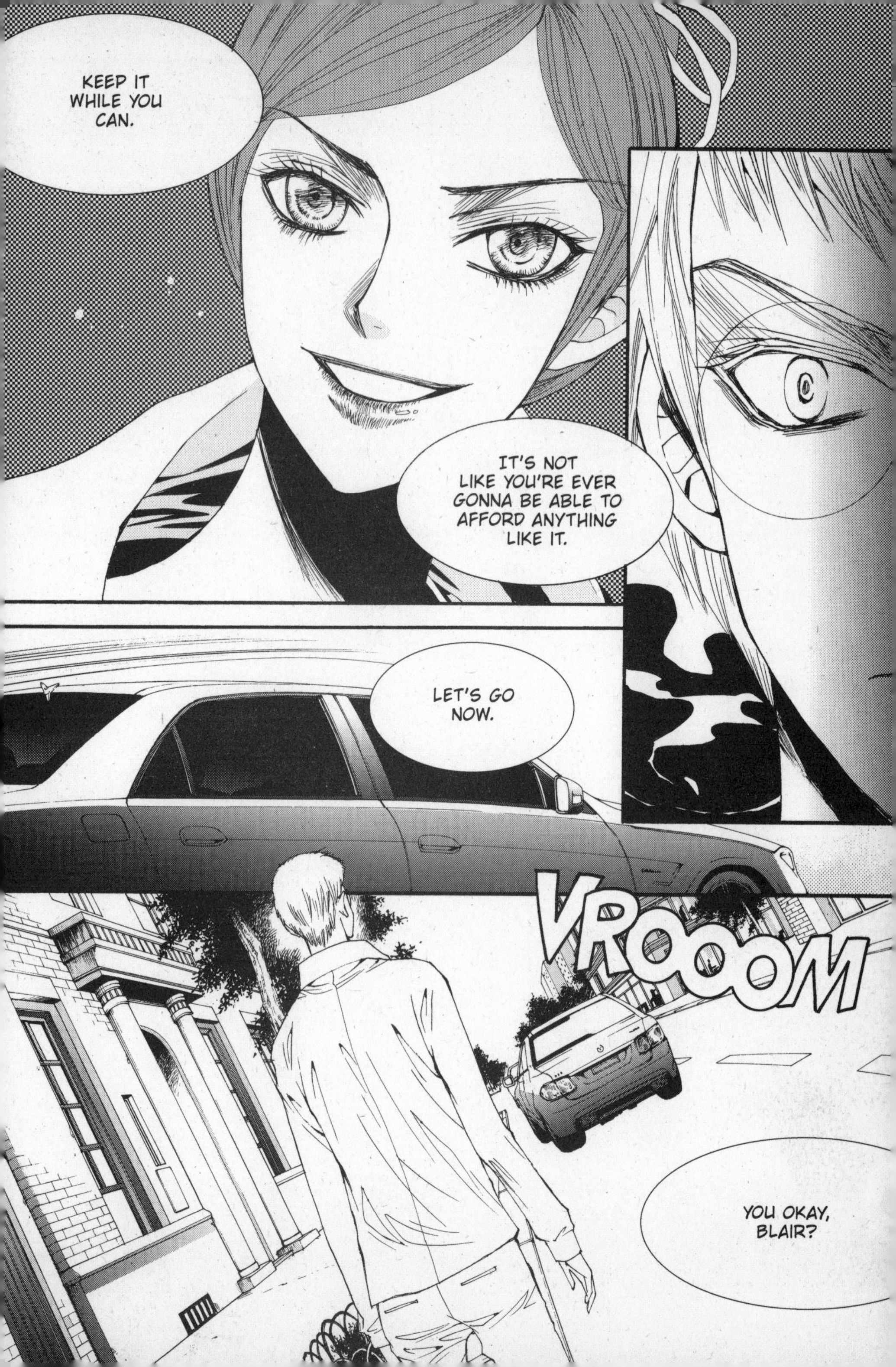
KEEP IT WHILE YOU CAN.
IT'S NOT LIKE YOU'RE EVER GONNA BE ABLE TO AFFORD ANYTHING LIKE IT.
LET'S GO NOW.
VROOOOM
YOU OKAY, BLAIR?

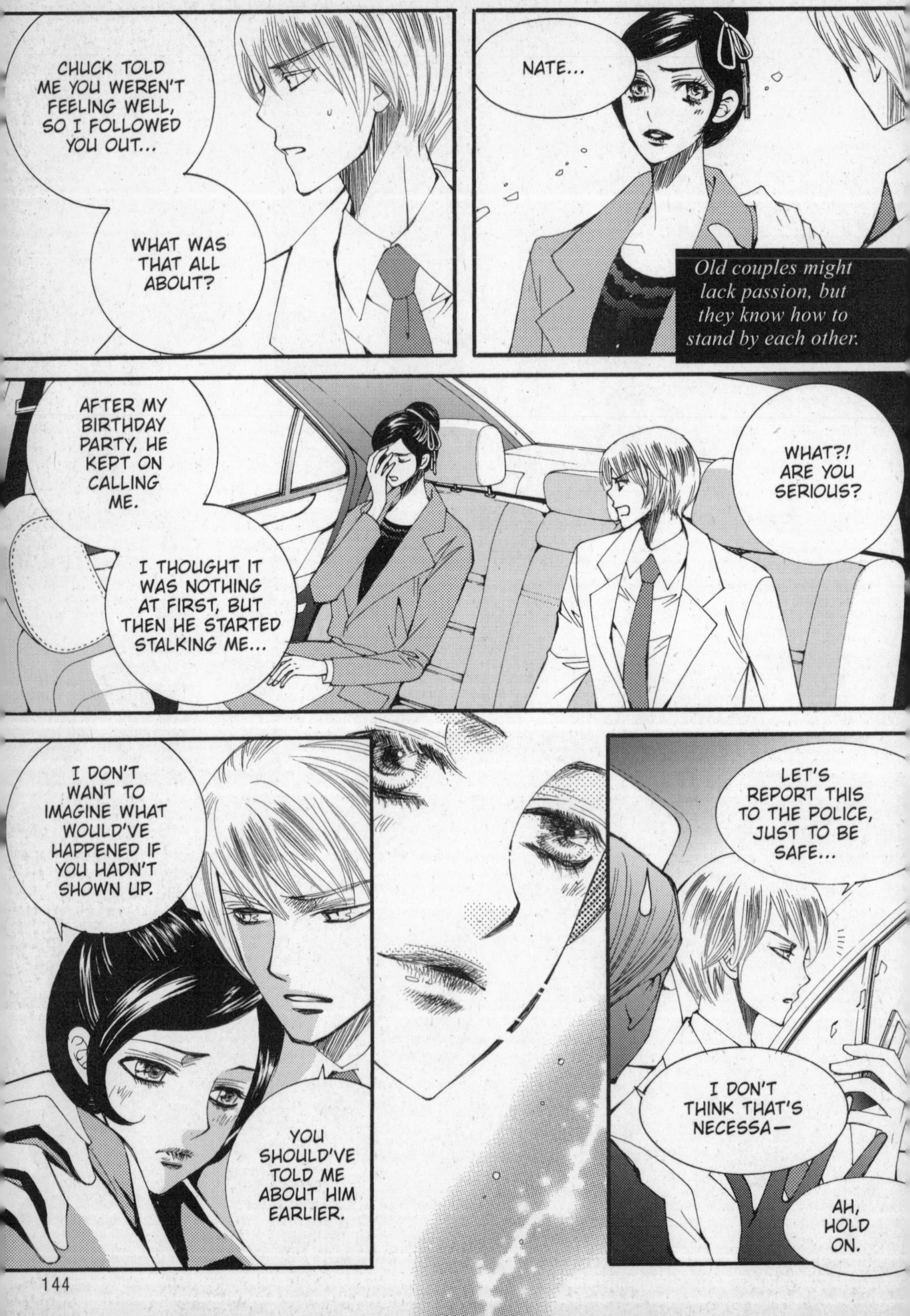
CHUCK TOLD ME YOU WEREN'T FEELING WELL, SO I FOLLOWED YOU OUT...
WHAT WAS THAT ALL ABOUT?
NATE...
Old couples might lack passion, but they know how to stand by each other.
AFTER MY BIRTHDAY PARTY, HE KEPT ON CALLING ME.
I THOUGHT IT WAS NOTHING AT FIRST, BUT THEN HE STARTED STALKING ME...
WHAT?! ARE YOU SERIOUS?
I DON'T WANT TO IMAGINE WHAT WOULD'VE HAPPENED IF YOU HADN'T SHOWN UP.
YOU SHOULD'VE TOLD ME ABOUT HIM EARLIER.
LET'S REPORT THIS TO THE POLICE, JUST TO BE SAFE...
I DON'T THINK THAT'S NECESSA—
AH, HOLD ON.

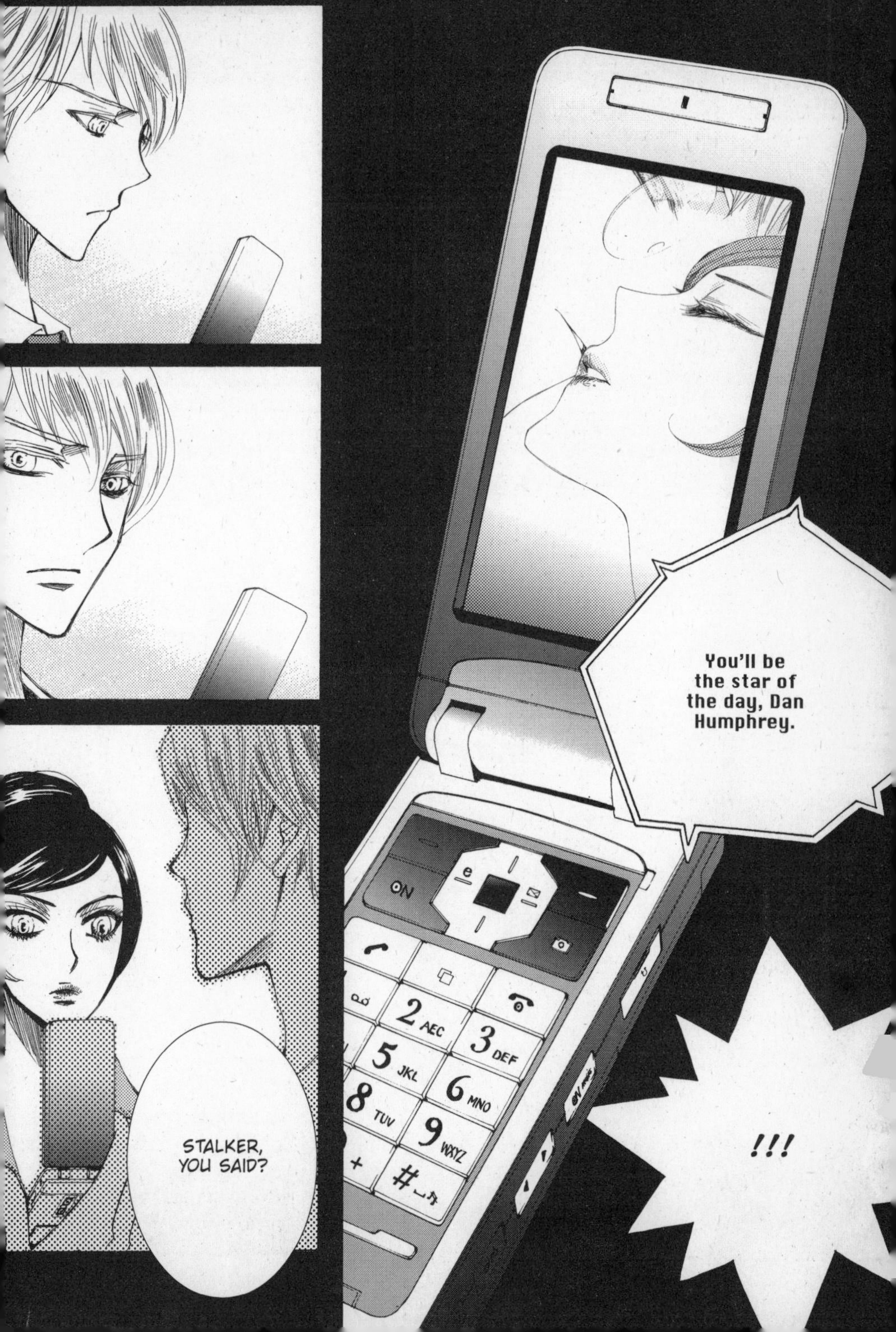
STALKER, YOU SAID?
You'll be the star of the day, Dan Humphrey.
!!!

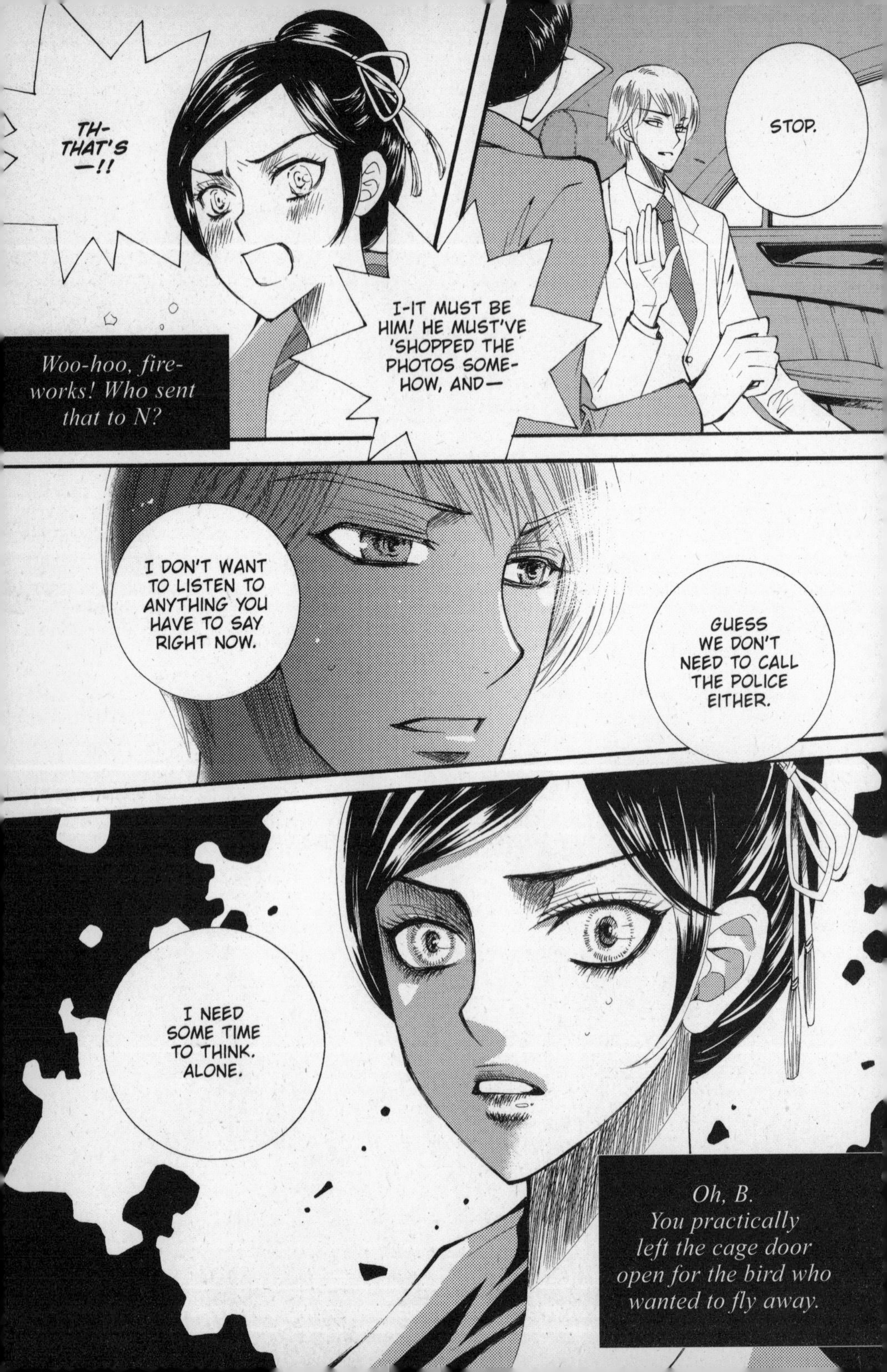
TH-THAT'S—!!
Woo-hoo, fire-works! Who sent that to N?
I-IT MUST BE HIM! HE MUST'VE 'SHOPPED THE PHOTOS SOMEHOW, AND—
STOP.
I DON'T WANT TO LISTEN TO ANYTHING YOU HAVE TO SAY RIGHT NOW.
GUESS WE DON'T NEED TO CALL THE POLICE EITHER.
I NEED SOME TIME TO THINK. ALONE.
Oh, B. You practically left the cage door open for the bird who wanted to fly away.

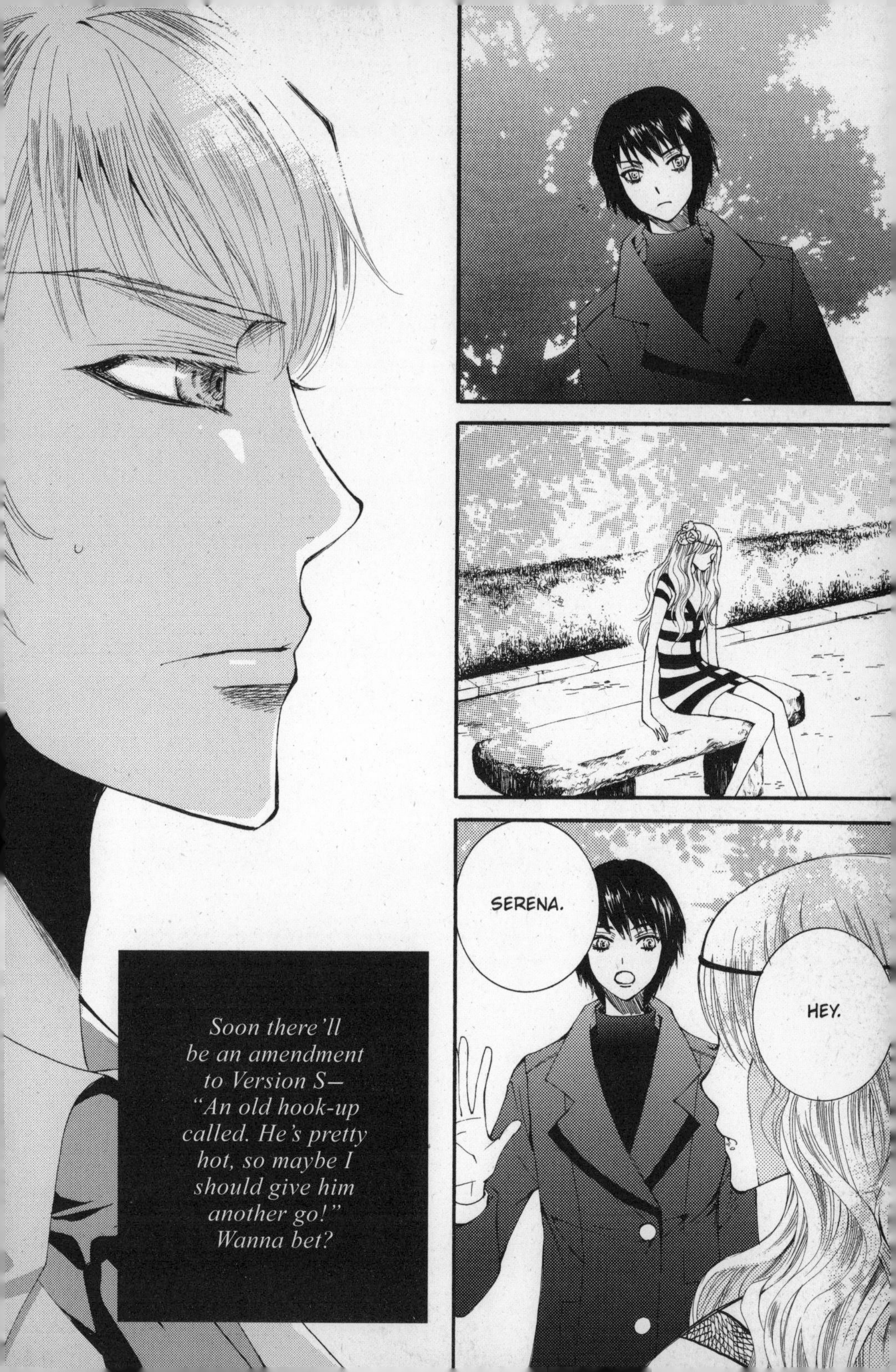
Soon there'll be an amendment to Version S— "An old hook-up called. He's pretty hot, so maybe I should give him another go!" Wanna bet?
SERENA.
HEY.

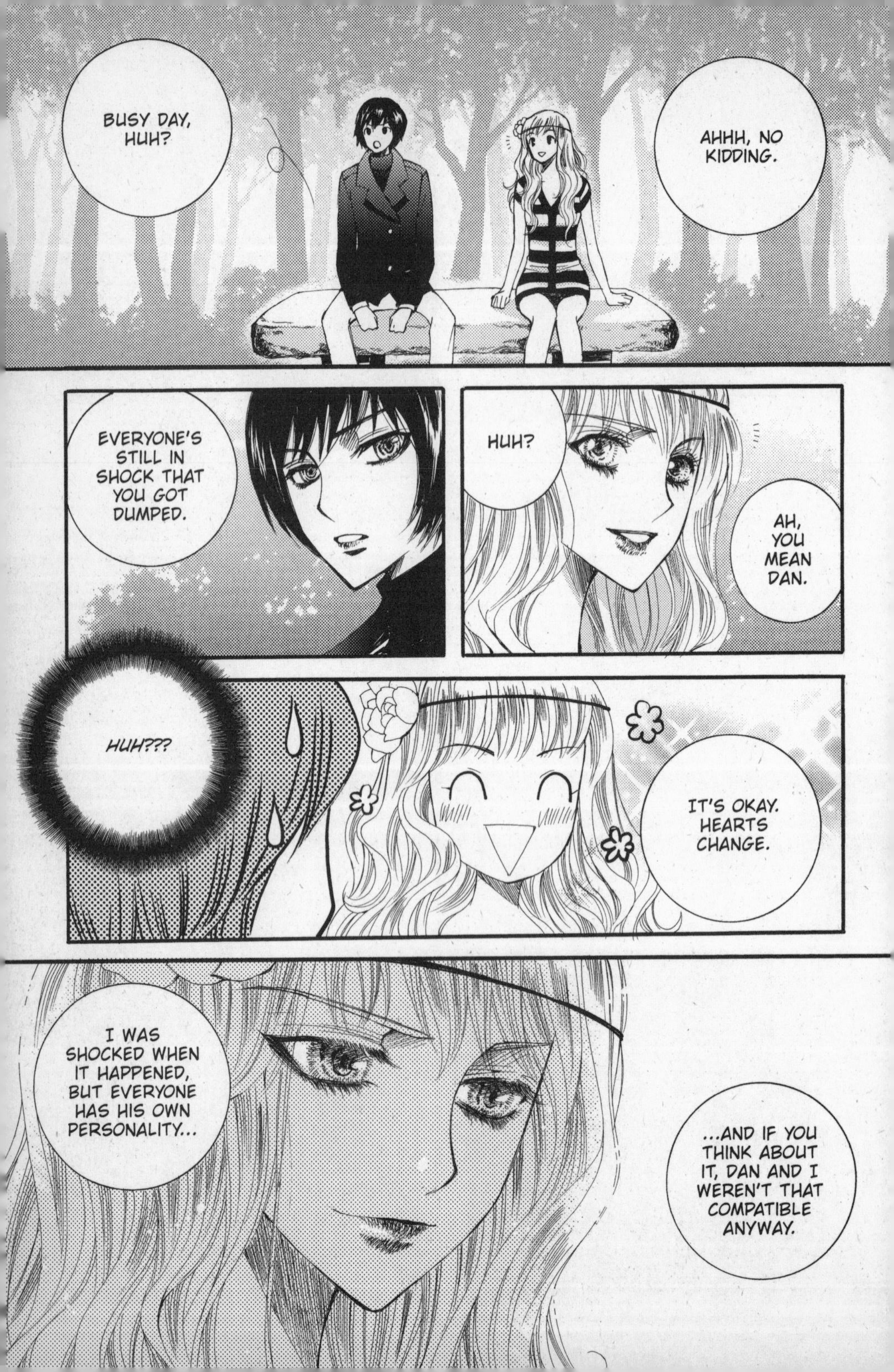
BUSY DAY, HUH?
AHHH, NO KIDDING.
EVERYONE'S STILL IN SHOCK THAT YOU GOT DUMPED.
HUH?
AH, YOU MEAN DAN.
HUH???
IT'S OKAY. HEARTS CHANGE.
I WAS SHOCKED WHEN IT HAPPENED, BUT EVERYONE HAS HIS OWN PERSONALITY...
...AND IF YOU THINK ABOUT IT, DAN AND I WEREN'T THAT COMPATIBLE ANYWAY.

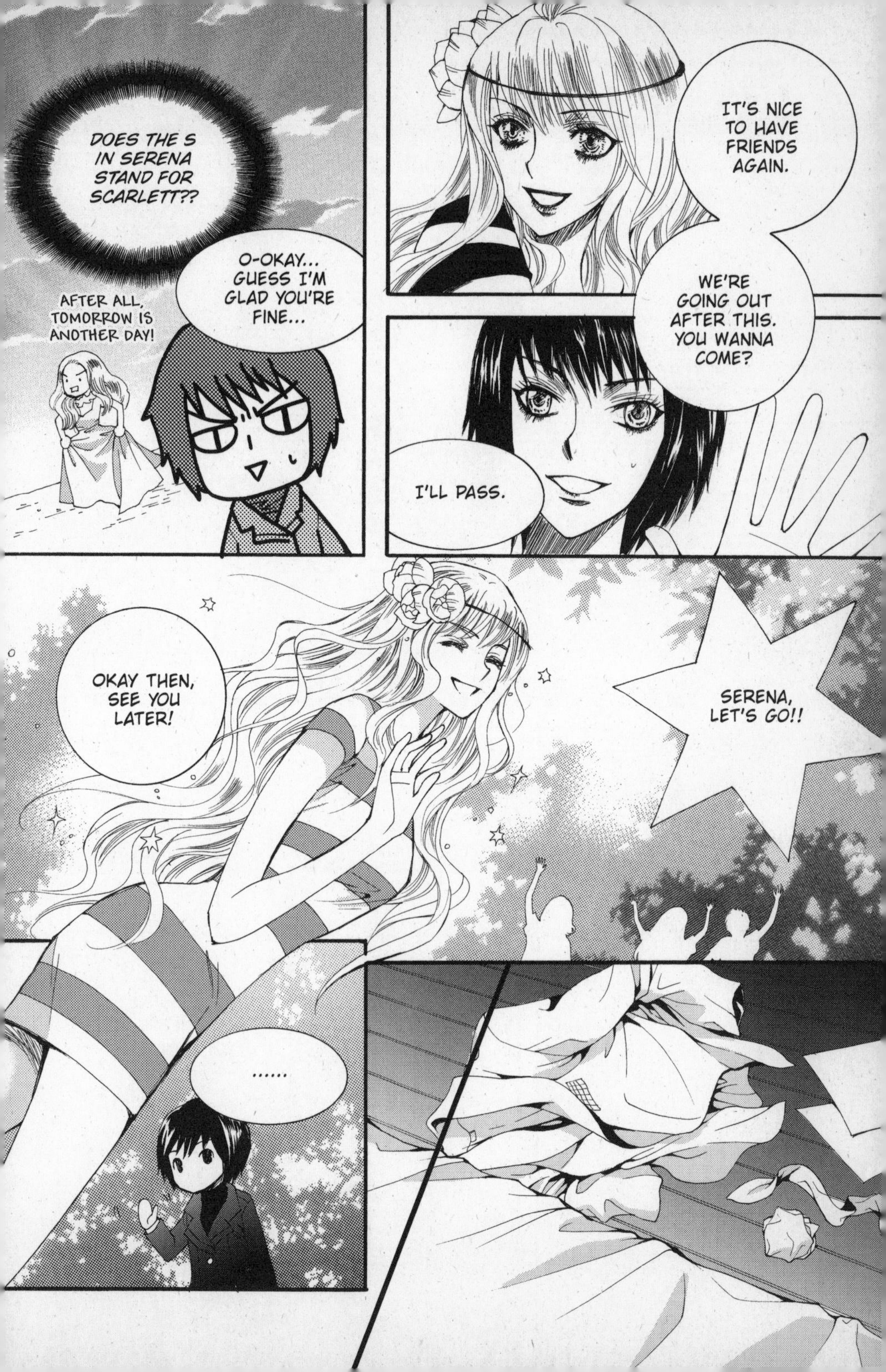
DOES THE S IN SERENA STAND FOR SCARLETT??
AFTER ALL, TOMORROW IS ANOTHER DAY!
O-OKAY... GUESS I'M GLAD YOU'RE FINE...
IT'S NICE TO HAVE FRIENDS AGAIN.
WE'RE GOING OUT AFTER THIS. YOU WANNA COME?
I'LL PASS.
OKAY THEN, SEE YOU LATER!
SERENA, LET'S GO!!
......

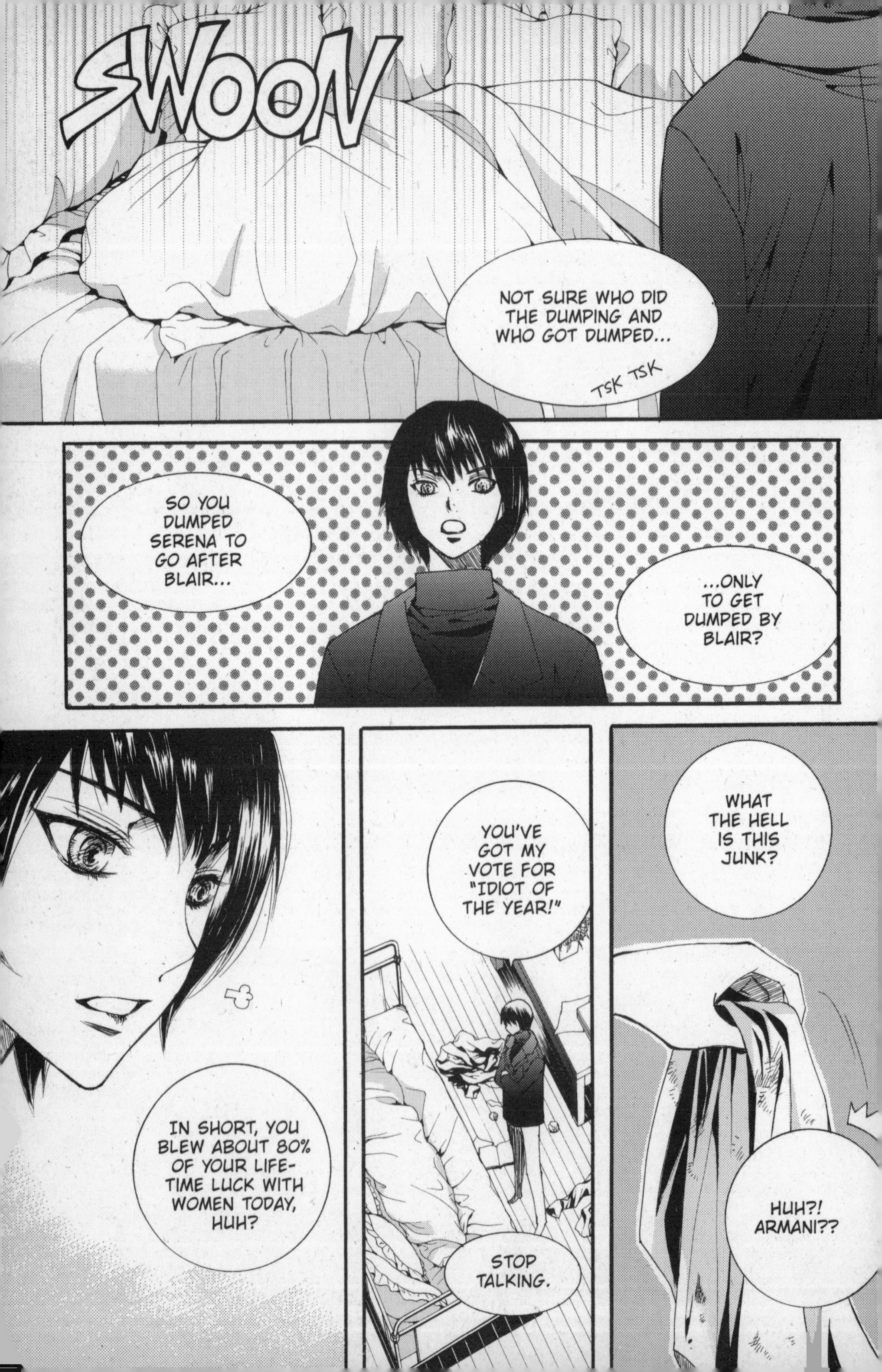
SWOON
NOT SURE WHO DID THE DUMPING AND WHO GOT DUMPED...
TSK TSK
SO YOU DUMPED SERENA TO GO AFTER BLAIR...
...ONLY TO GET DUMPED BY BLAIR?
IN SHORT, YOU BLEW ABOUT 80% OF YOUR LIFE-TIME LUCK WITH WOMEN TODAY, HUH?
YOU'VE GOT MY VOTE FOR "IDIOT OF THE YEAR!"
STOP TALKING.
WHAT THE HELL IS THIS JUNK?
HUH?! ARMANI??

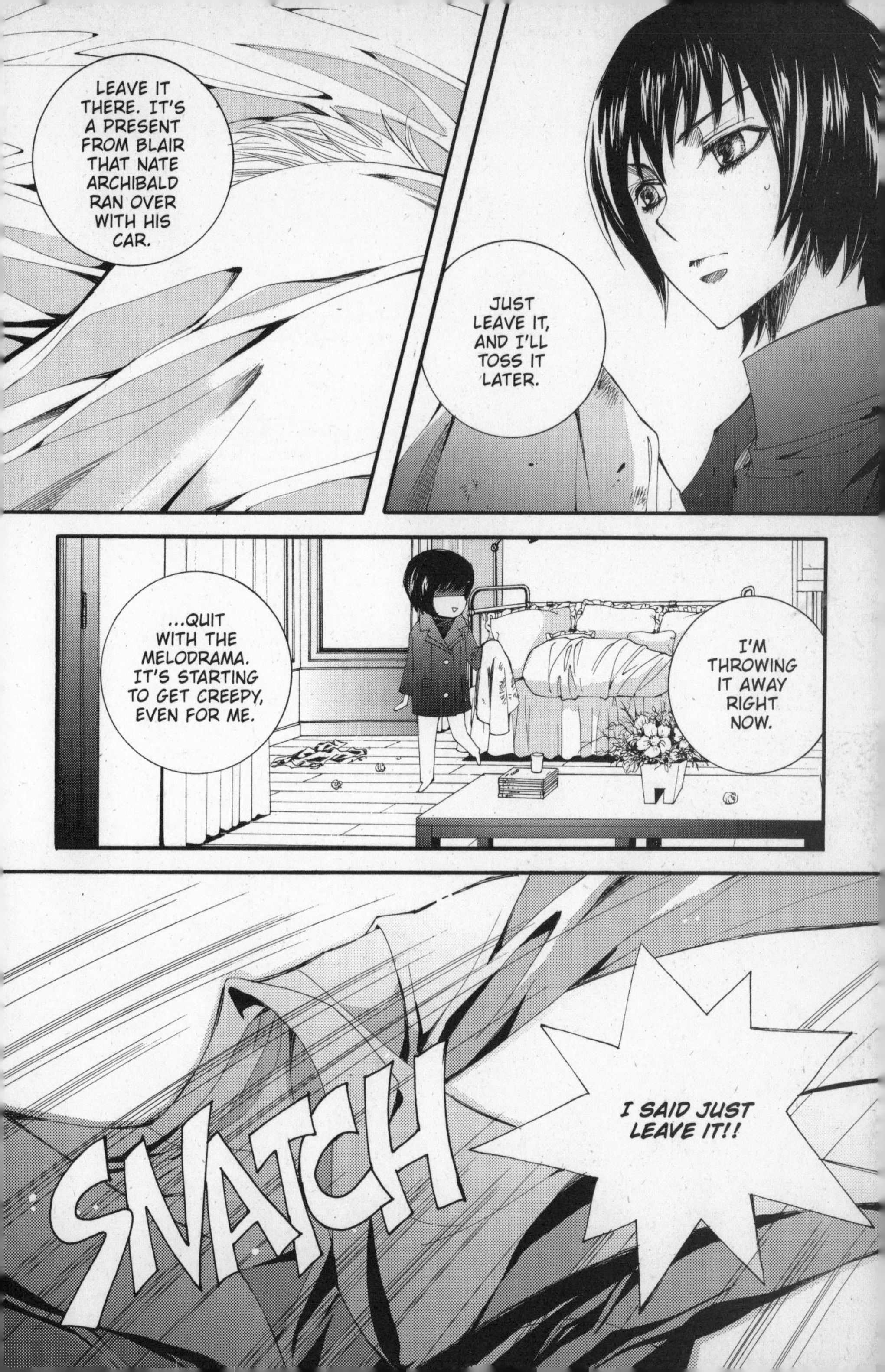
LEAVE IT THERE. IT'S A PRESENT FROM BLAIR THAT NATE ARCHIBALD RAN OVER WITH HIS CAR.
JUST LEAVE IT, AND I'LL TOSS IT LATER.
...QUIT WITH THE MELODRAMA. IT'S STARTING TO GET CREEPY, EVEN FOR ME.
I'M THROWING IT AWAY RIGHT NOW.
SNATCH
I SAID JUST LEAVE IT!!

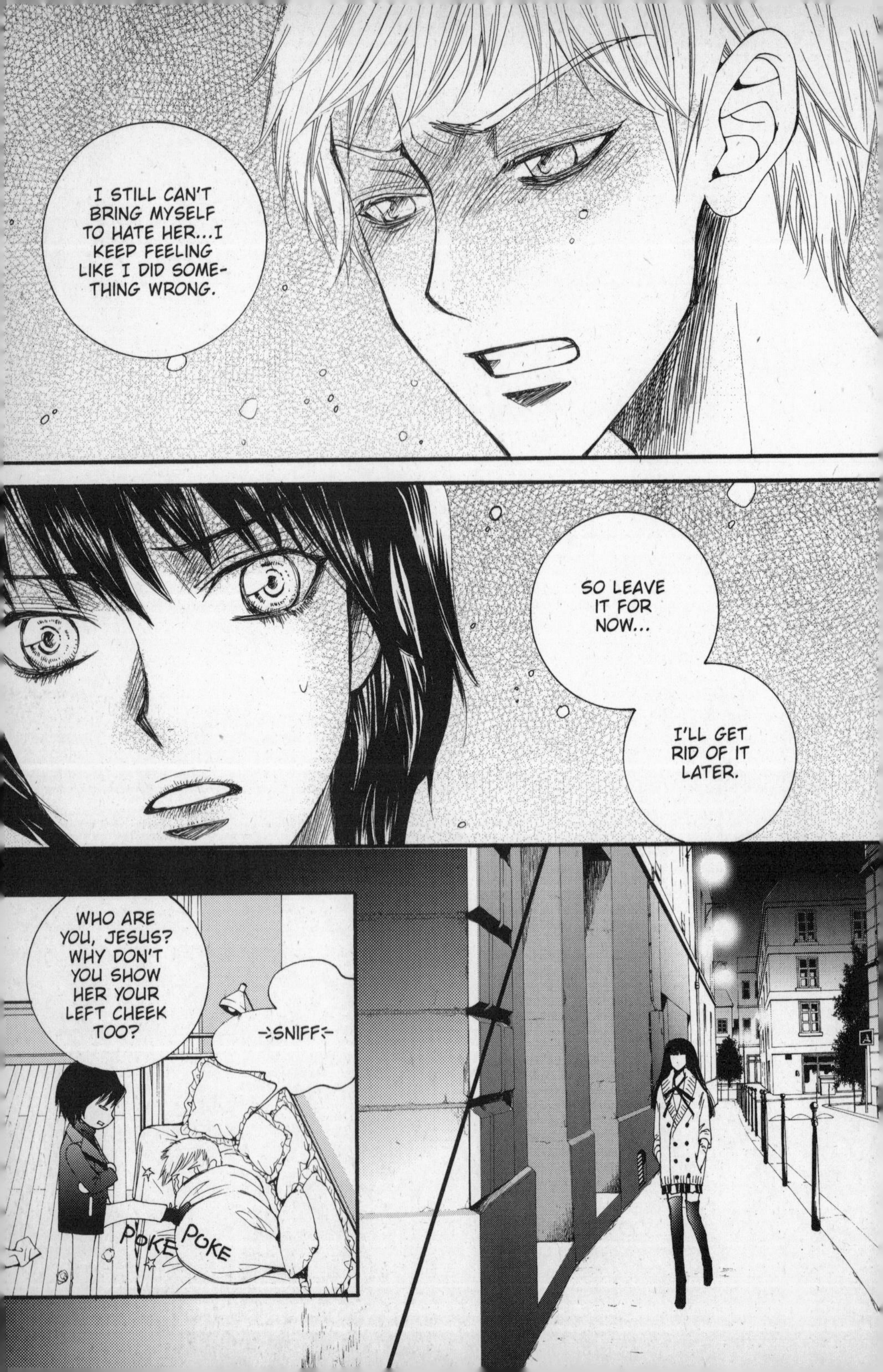
I STILL CAN'T BRING MYSELF TO HATE HER...I KEEP FEELING LIKE I DID SOME-THING WRONG.
SO LEAVE IT FOR NOW...
I'LL GET RID OF IT LATER.
WHO ARE YOU, JESUS? WHY DON'T YOU SHOW HER YOUR LEFT CHEEK TOO?
SNIFF
POKE
POKE

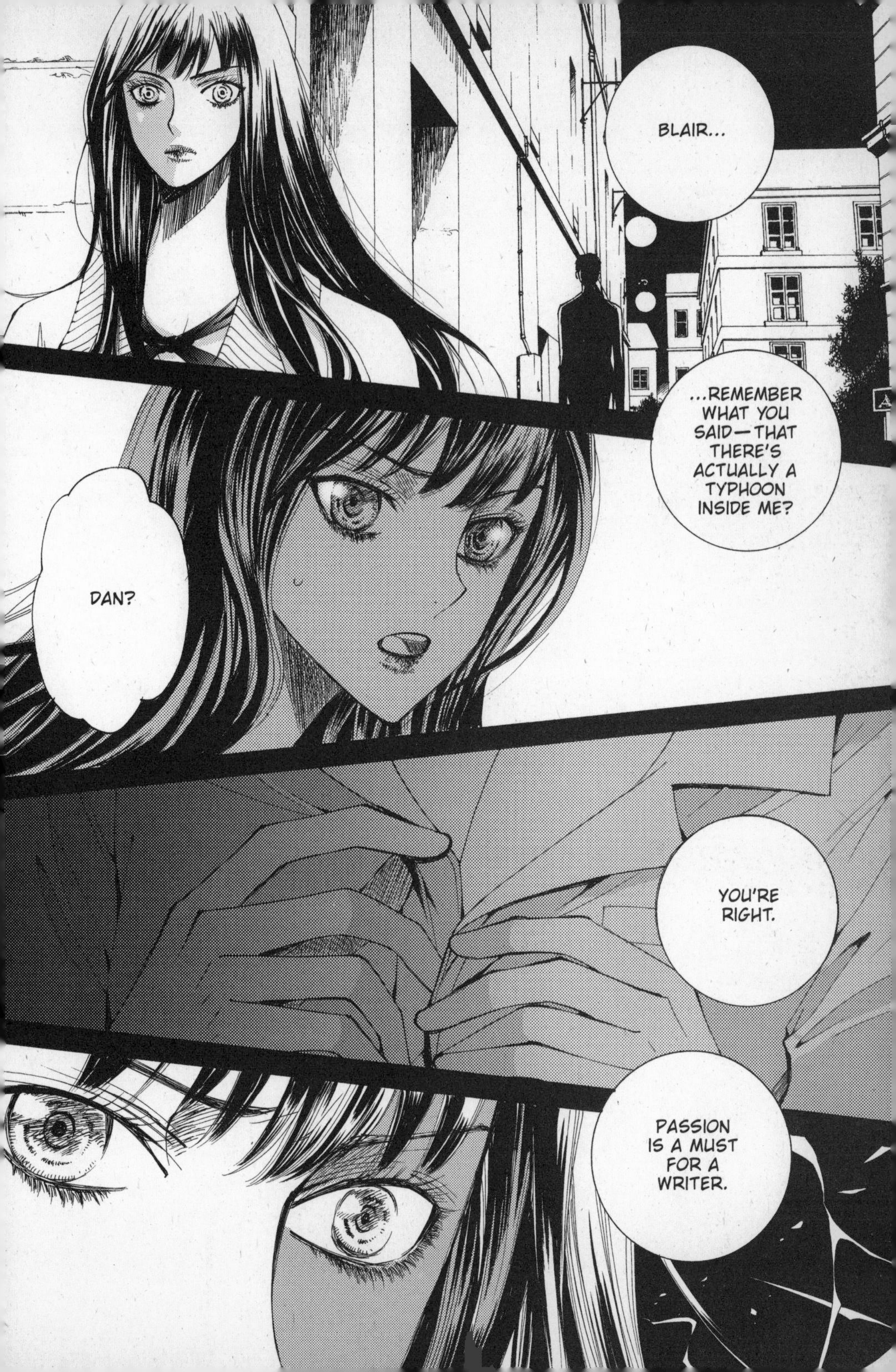
BLAIR...
...REMEMBER WHAT YOU SAID—THAT THERE'S ACTUALLY A TYPHOON INSIDE ME?
DAN?
YOU'RE RIGHT.
PASSION IS A MUST FOR A WRITER.

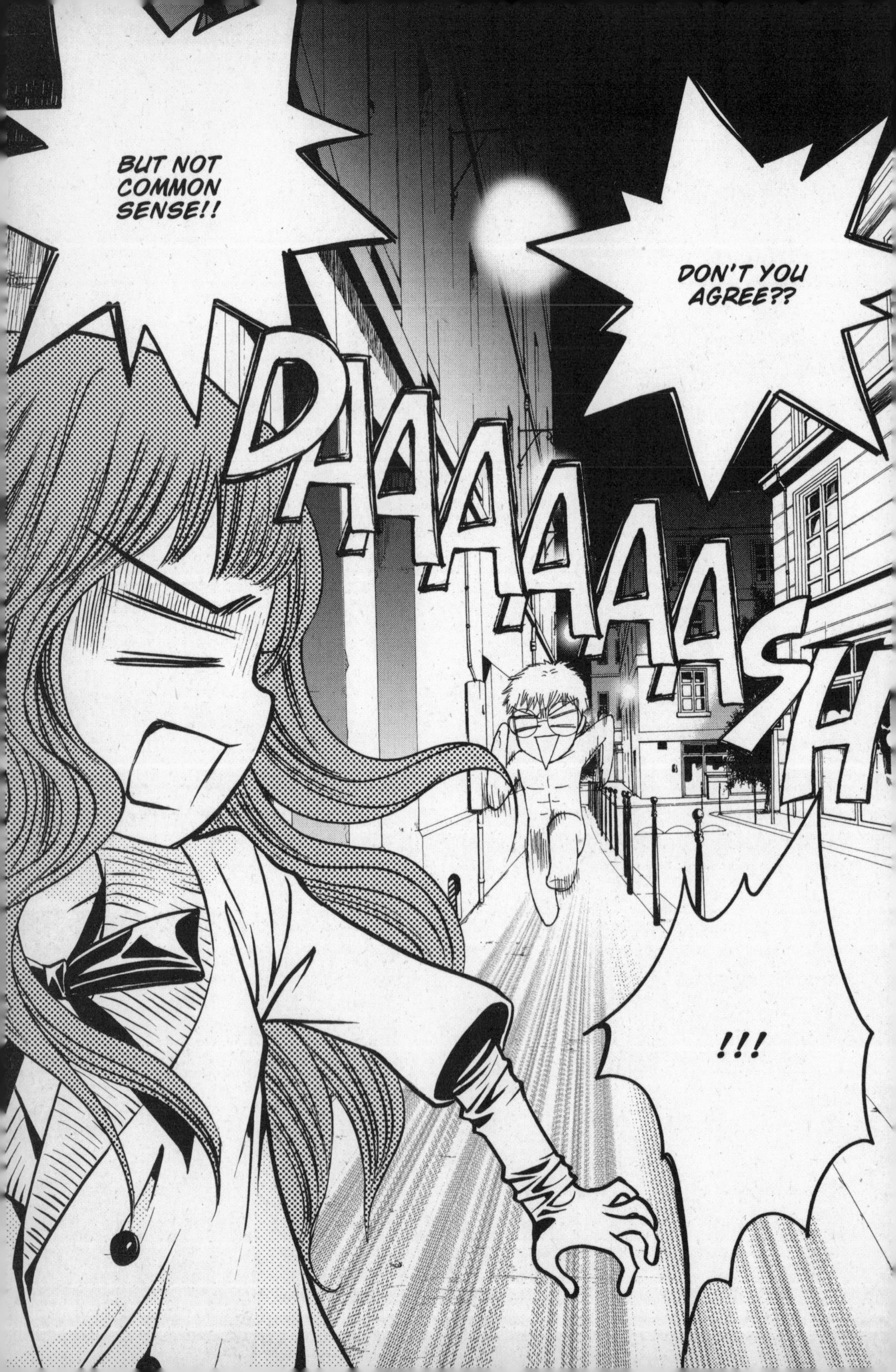
BUT NOT COMMON SENSE!!
DON'T YOU AGREE??
DAAAAAASH
!!!

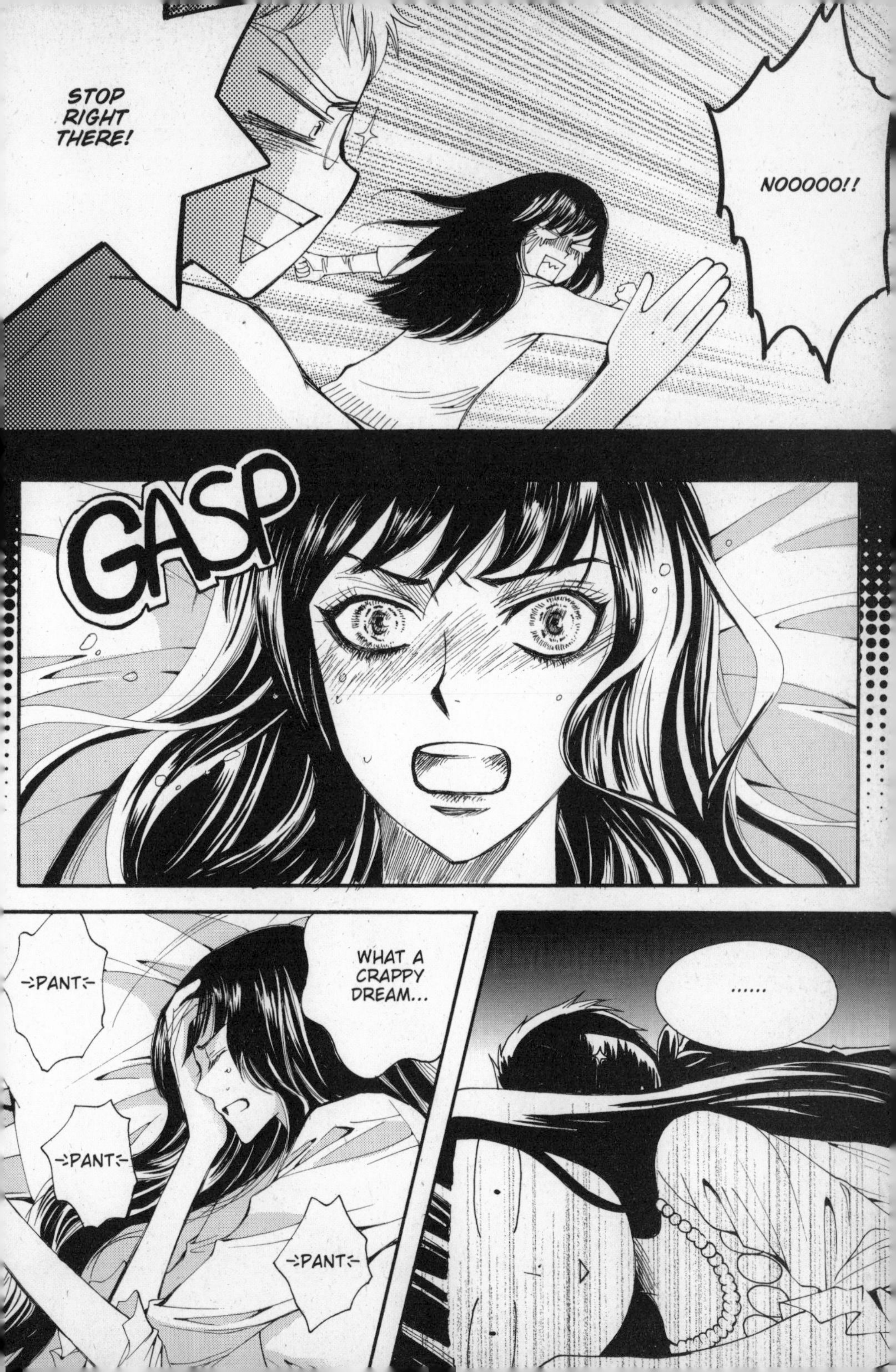
STOP RIGHT THERE!
NOOOOO!!
GASP
-PANT-
WHAT A CRAPPY DREAM...
-PANT-
-PANT-
......

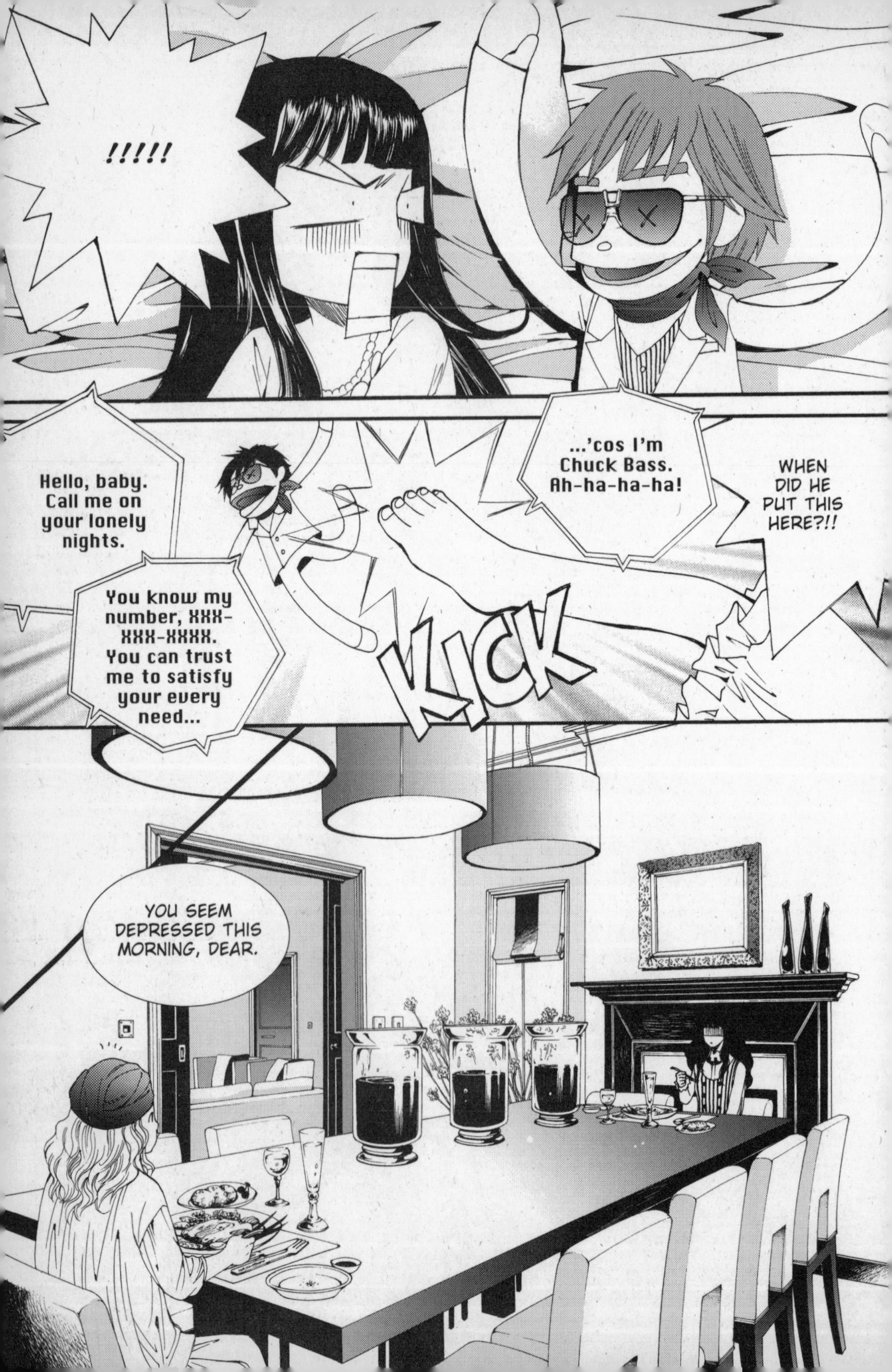
!!!!!
Hello, baby. Call me on your lonely nights.
You know my number, XXX-XXX-XXXX. You can trust me to satisfy your every need...
...'cos I'm Chuck Bass. Ah-ha-ha-ha!
WHEN DID HE PUT THIS HERE?!!
KICK
YOU SEEM DEPRESSED THIS MORNING, DEAR.

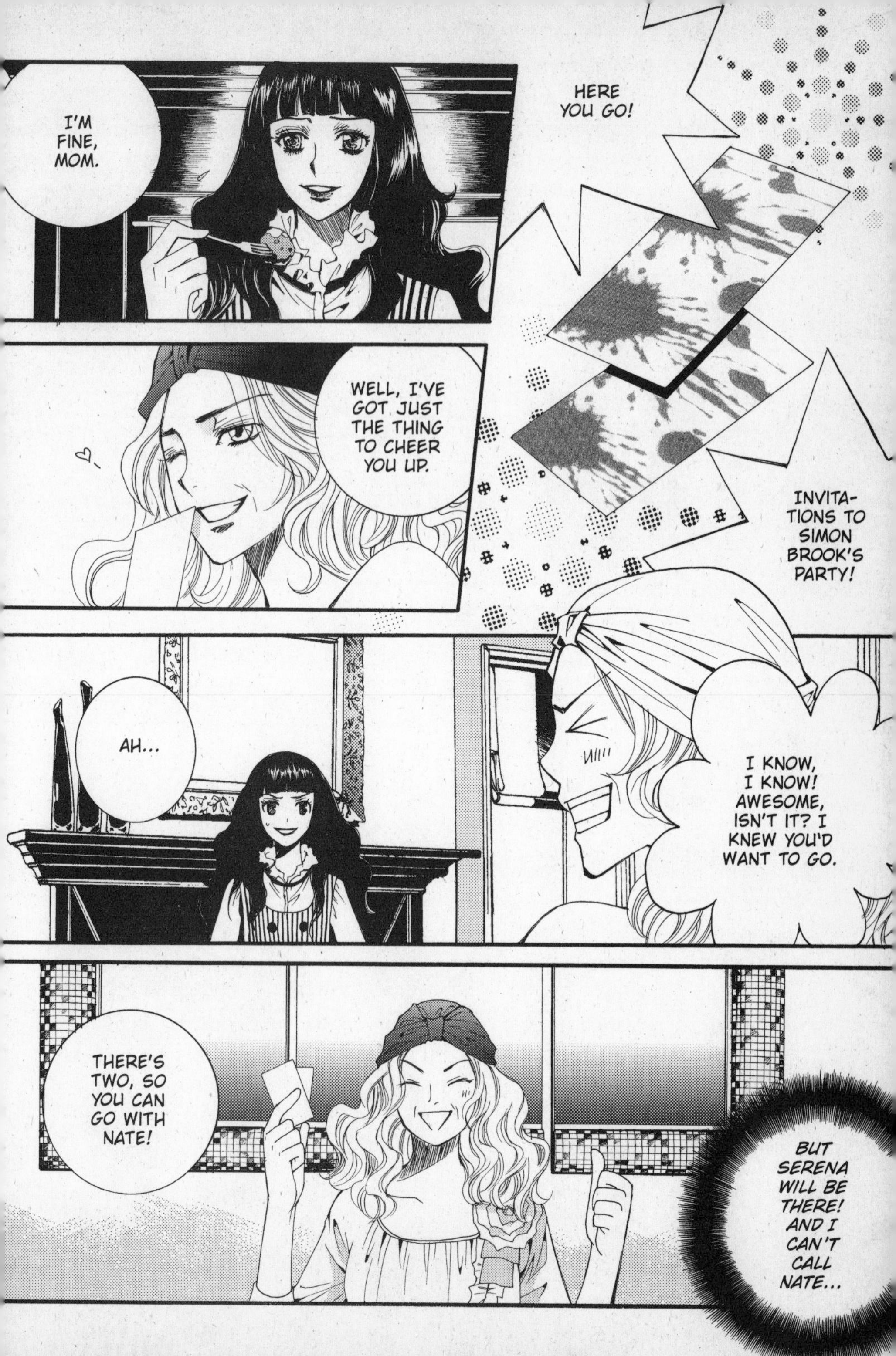
I'M FINE, MOM.
WELL, I'VE GOT JUST THE THING TO CHEER YOU UP.
HERE YOU GO!
INVITATIONS TO SIMON BROOK'S PARTY!
AH...
I KNOW, I KNOW! AWESOME, ISN'T IT? I KNEW YOU'D WANT TO GO.
THERE'S TWO, SO YOU CAN GO WITH NATE!
BUT SERENA WILL BE THERE! AND I CAN'T CALL NATE...

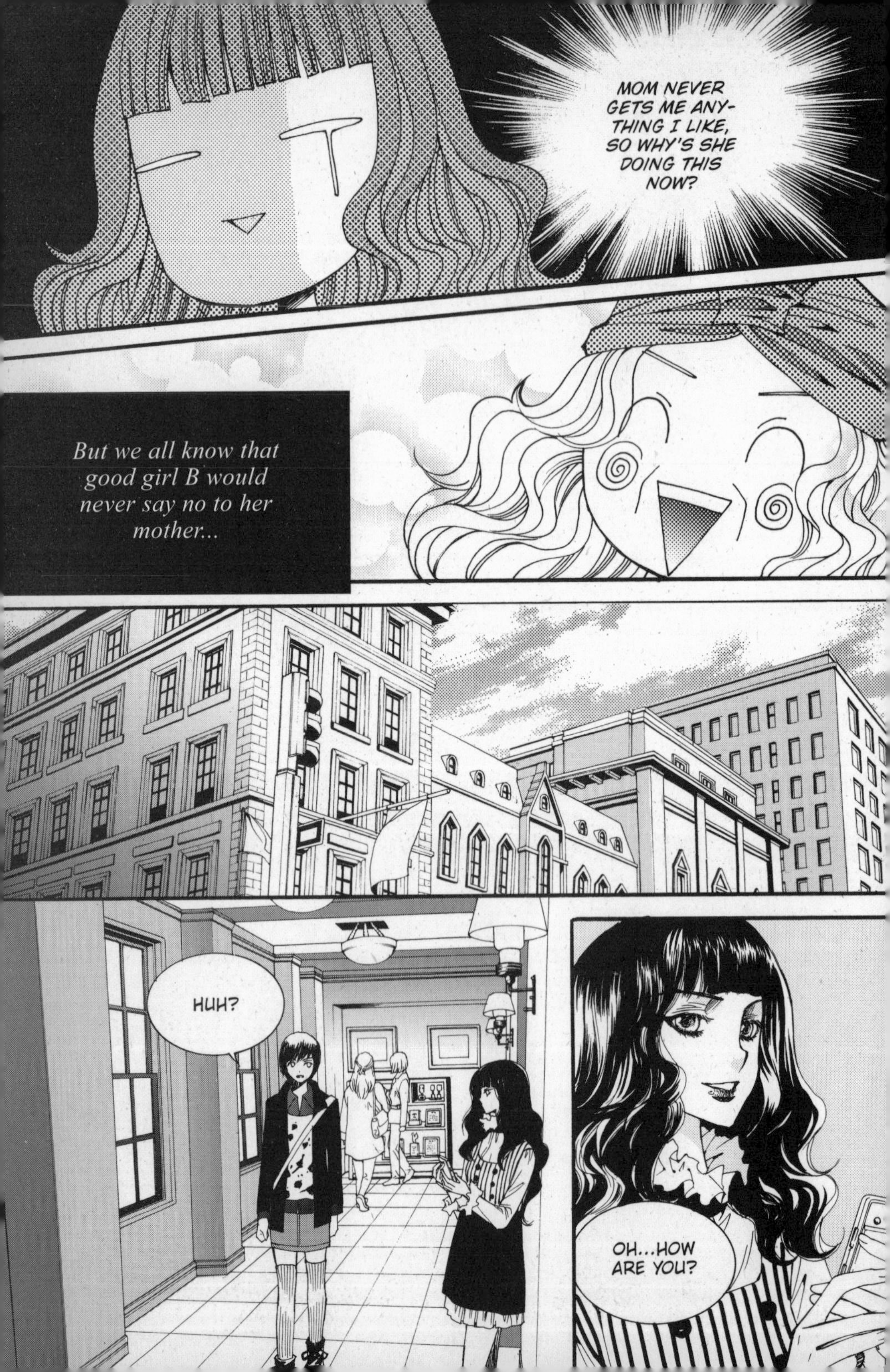
MOM NEVER GETS ME ANYTHING I LIKE, SO WHY'S SHE DOING THIS NOW?
But we all know that good girl B would never say no to her mother...
HUH?
OH...HOW ARE YOU?

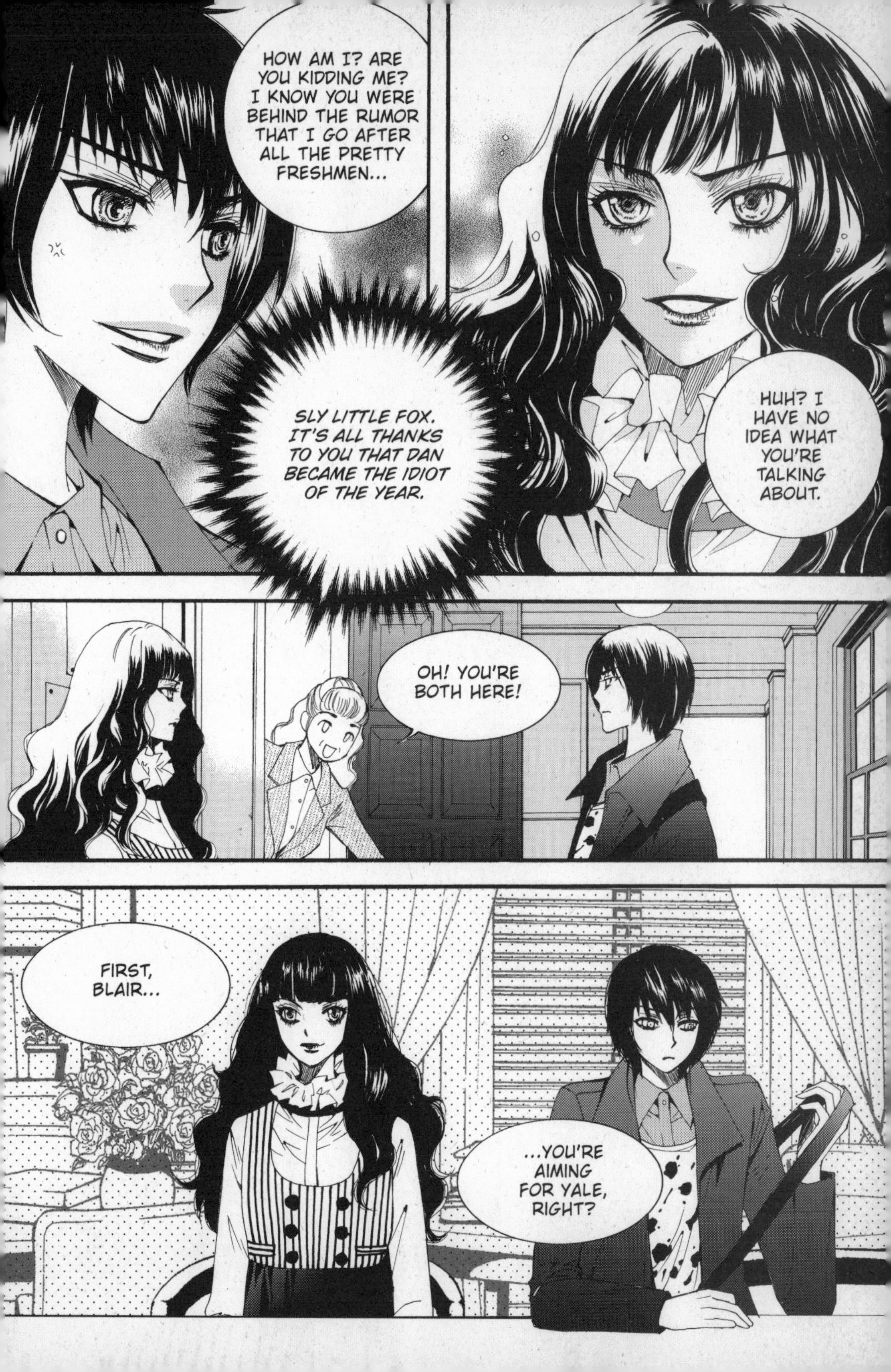
HOW AM I? ARE YOU KIDDING ME? I KNOW YOU WERE BEHIND THE RUMOR THAT I GO AFTER ALL THE PRETTY FRESHMEN...
SLY LITTLE FOX. IT'S ALL THANKS TO YOU THAT DAN BECAME THE IDIOT OF THE YEAR.
HUH? I HAVE NO IDEA WHAT YOU'RE TALKING ABOUT.
OH! YOU'RE BOTH HERE!
FIRST, BLAIR...
...YOU'RE AIMING FOR YALE, RIGHT?

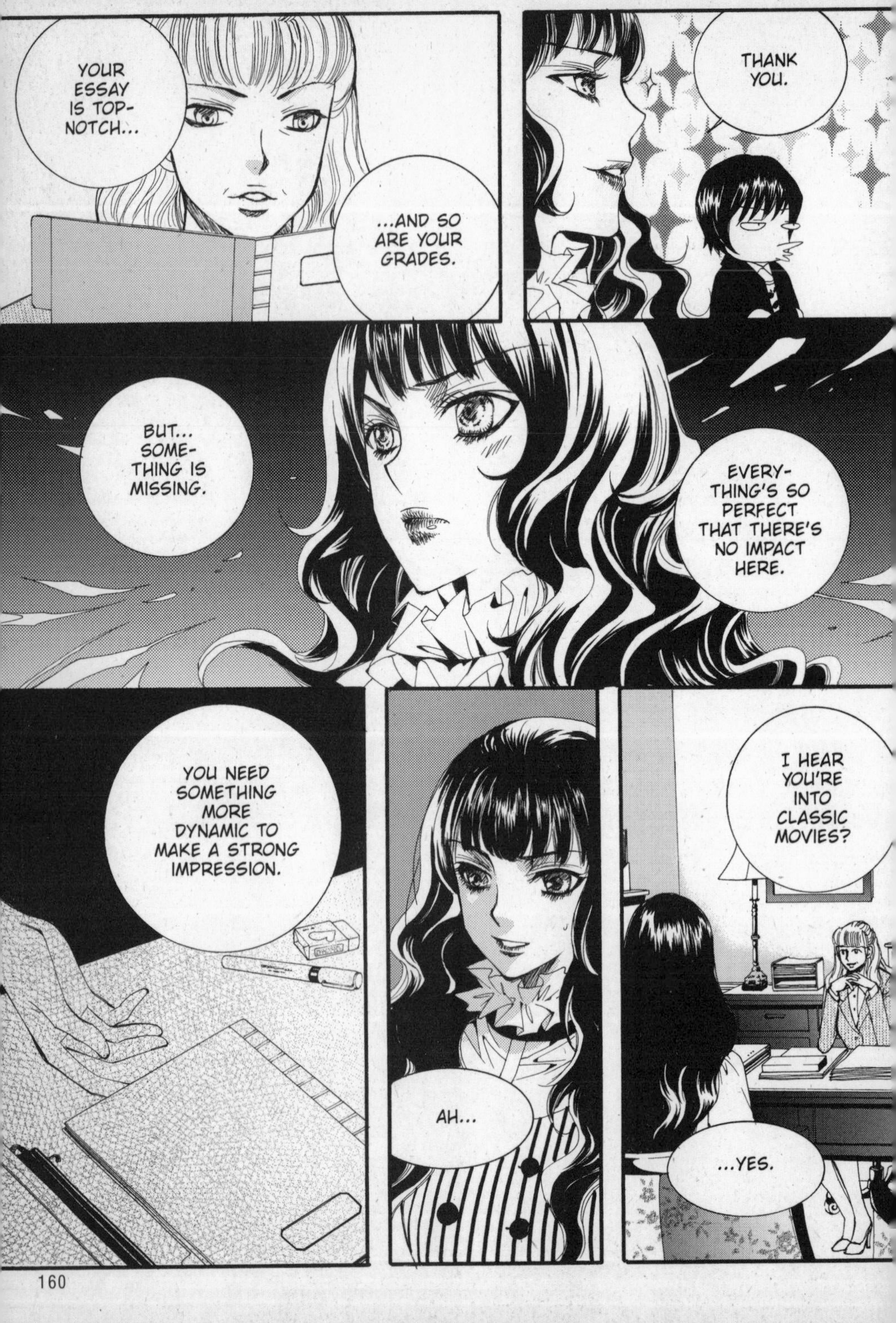
YOUR ESSAY IS TOP-NOTCH...
...AND SO ARE YOUR GRADES.
THANK YOU.
BUT... SOME-THING IS MISSING.
EVERY-THING'S SO PERFECT THAT THERE'S NO IMPACT HERE.
YOU NEED SOMETHING MORE DYNAMIC TO MAKE A STRONG IMPRESSION.
AH...
I HEAR YOU'RE INTO CLASSIC MOVIES?
...YES.

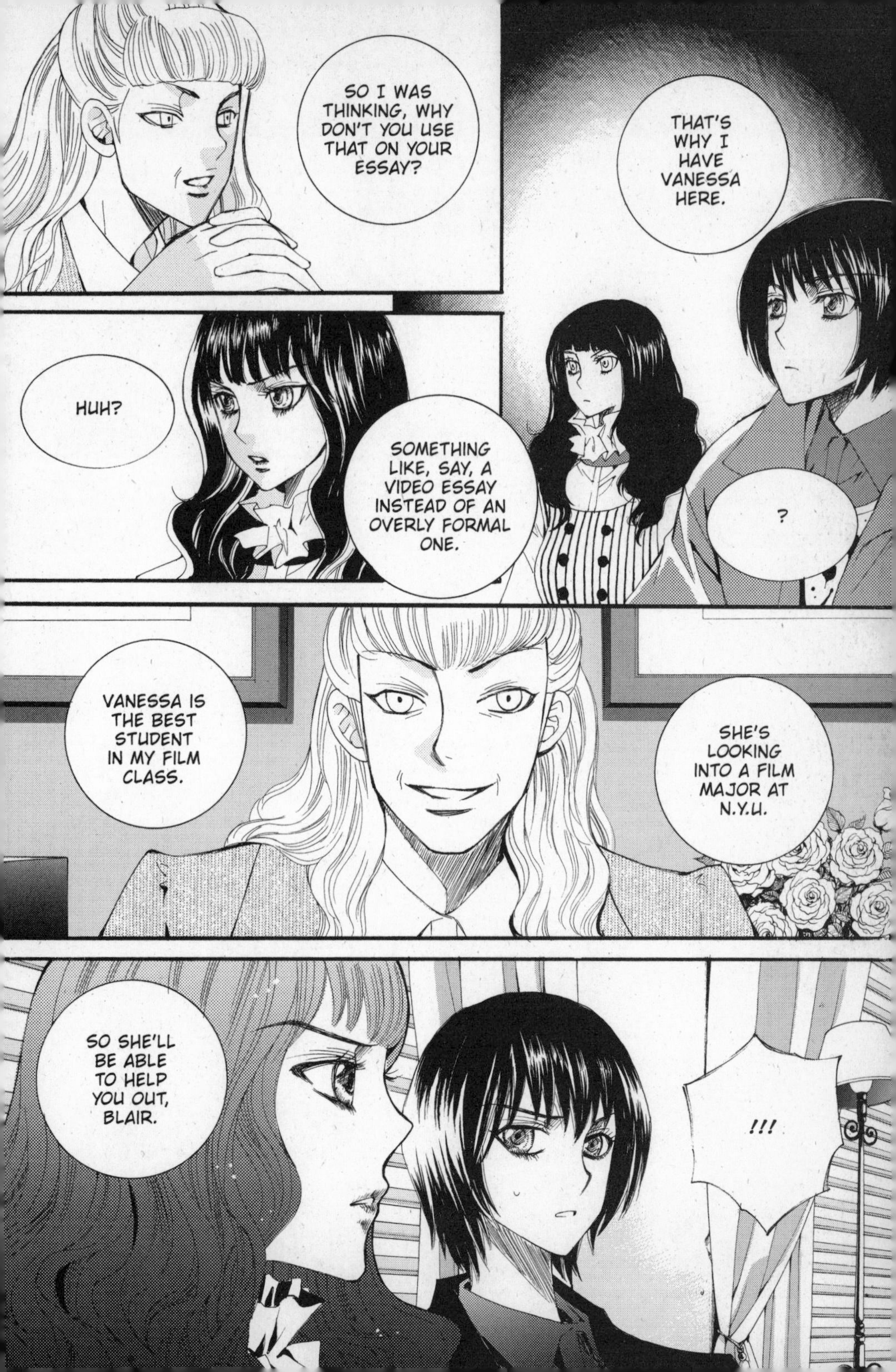
SO I WAS THINKING, WHY DON'T YOU USE THAT ON YOUR ESSAY?
HUH?
SOMETHING LIKE, SAY, A VIDEO ESSAY INSTEAD OF AN OVERLY FORMAL ONE.
THAT'S WHY I HAVE VANESSA HERE.
?
VANESSA IS THE BEST STUDENT IN MY FILM CLASS.
SHE'S LOOKING INTO A FILM MAJOR AT N.Y.U.
SO SHE'LL BE ABLE TO HELP YOU OUT, BLAIR.
!!!

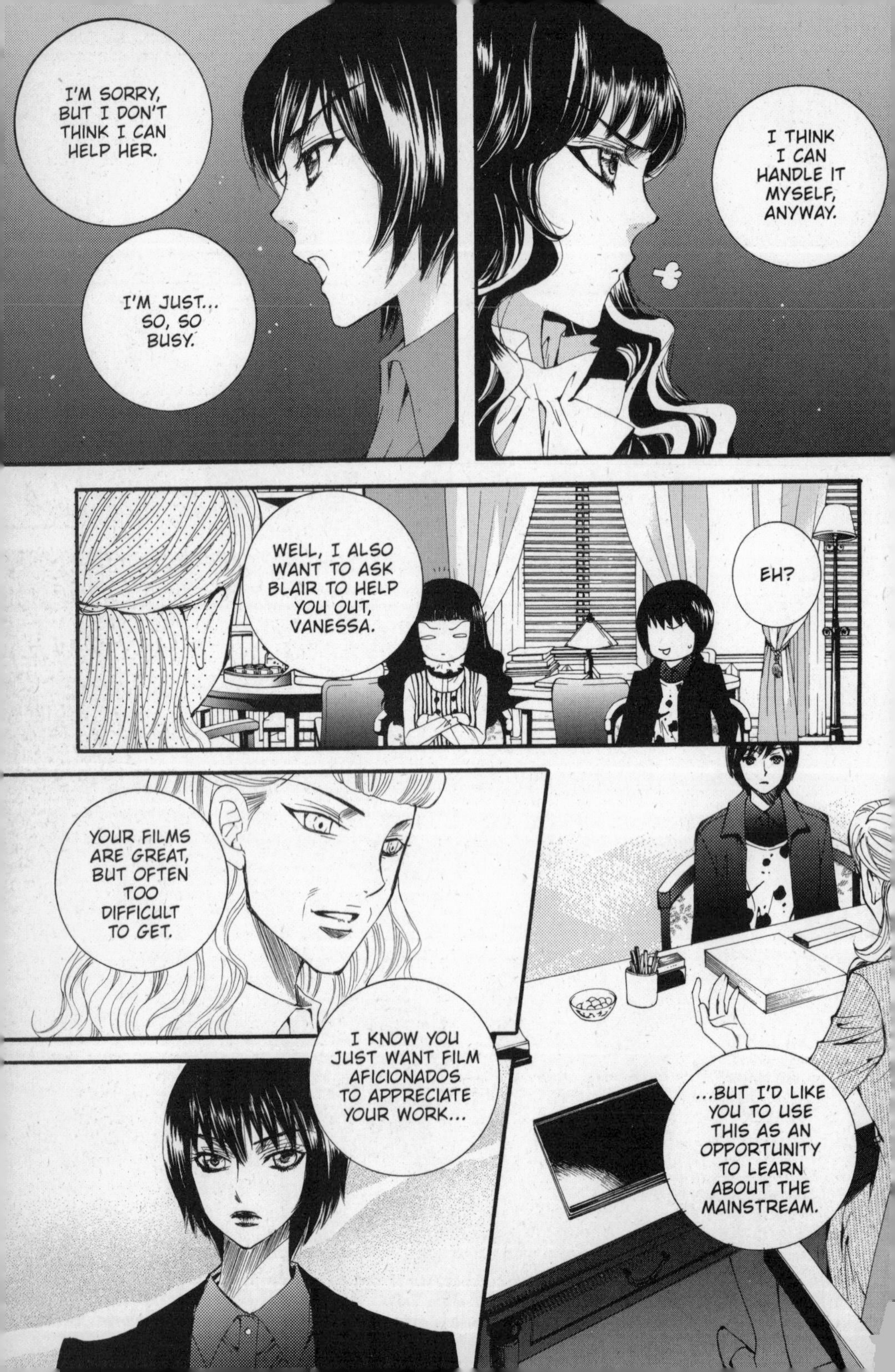
I'M SORRY, BUT I DON'T THINK I CAN HELP HER.
I'M JUST... SO, SO BUSY.
I THINK I CAN HANDLE IT MYSELF, ANYWAY.
WELL, I ALSO WANT TO ASK BLAIR TO HELP YOU OUT, VANESSA.
EH?
YOUR FILMS ARE GREAT, BUT OFTEN TOO DIFFICULT TO GET.
I KNOW YOU JUST WANT FILM AFICIONADOS TO APPRECIATE YOUR WORK...
...BUT I'D LIKE YOU TO USE THIS AS AN OPPORTUNITY TO LEARN ABOUT THE MAINSTREAM.

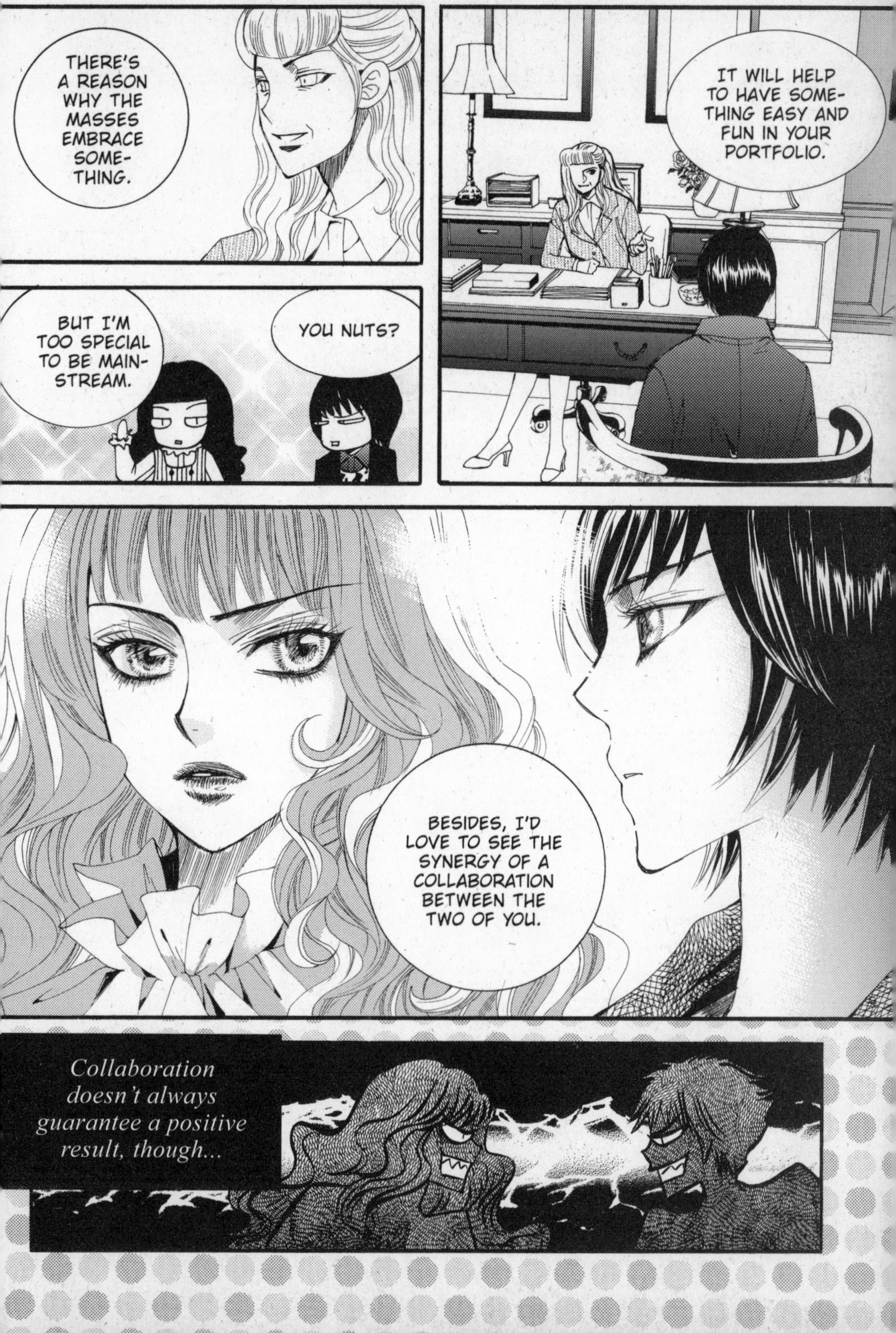
THERE'S A REASON WHY THE MASSES EMBRACE SOME-THING.
IT WILL HELP TO HAVE SOME-THING EASY AND FUN IN YOUR PORTFOLIO.
BUT I'M TOO SPECIAL TO BE MAIN-STREAM.
YOU NUTS?
BESIDES, I'D LOVE TO SEE THE SYNERGY OF A COLLABORATION BETWEEN THE TWO OF YOU.
Collaboration doesn't always guarantee a positive result, though...

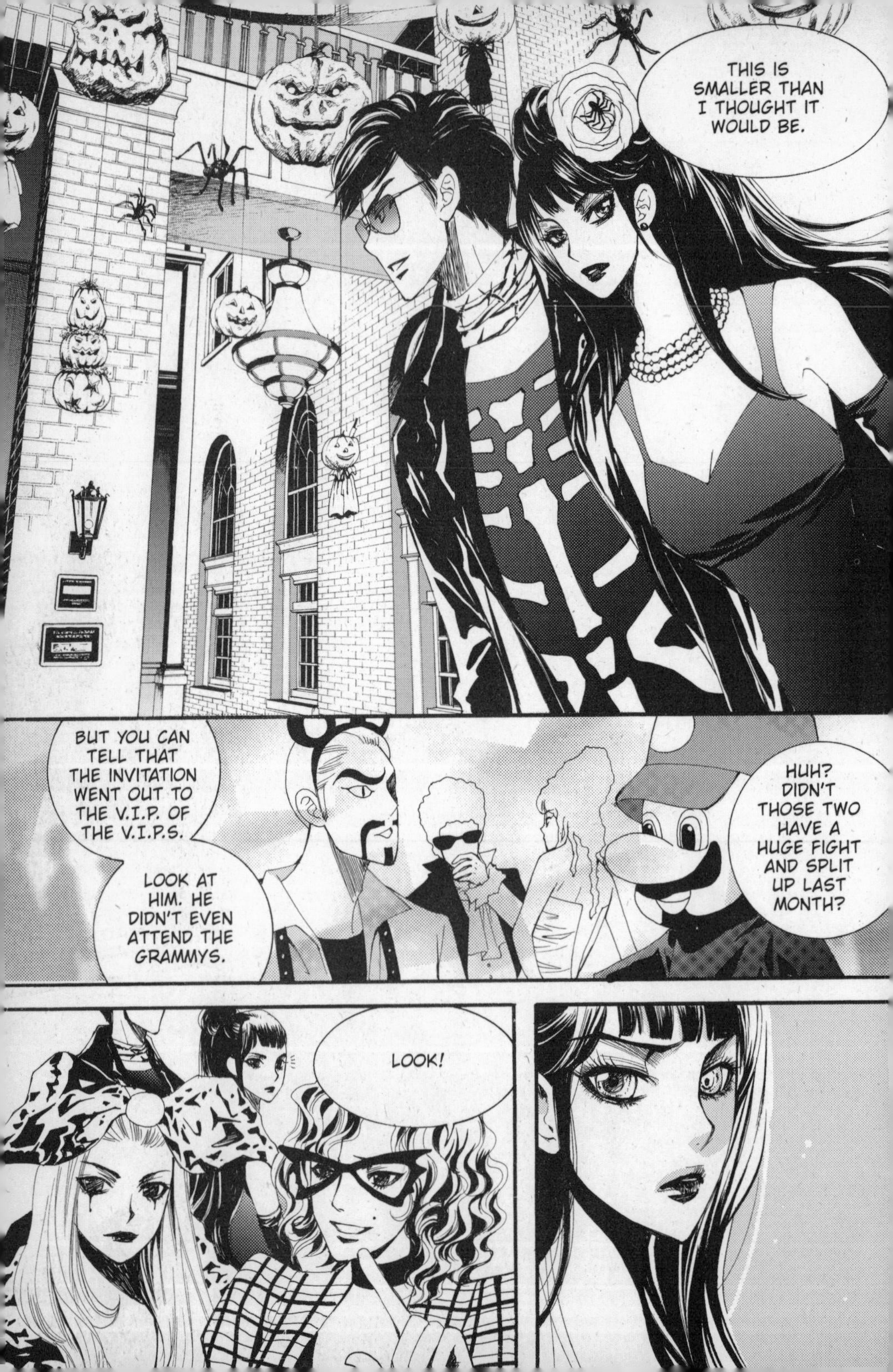

THIS IS SMALLER THAN I THOUGHT IT WOULD BE.
BUT YOU CAN TELL THAT THE INVITATION WENT OUT TO THE V.I.P. OF THE V.I.P.S.
LOOK AT HIM. HE DIDN'T EVEN ATTEND THE GRAMMYS.
HUH? DIDN'T THOSE TWO HAVE A HUGE FIGHT AND SPLIT UP LAST MONTH?
LOOK!

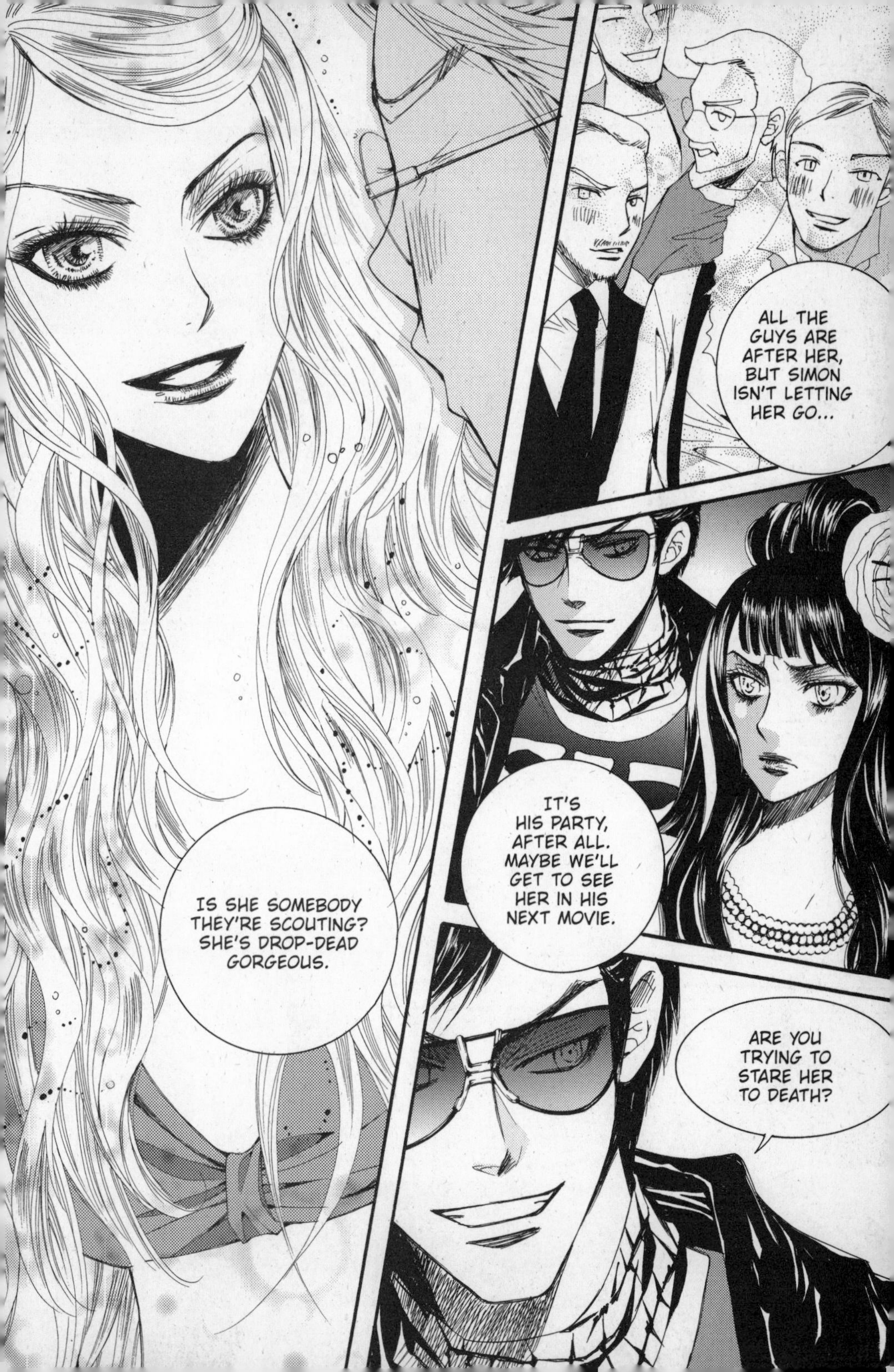
IS SHE SOMEBODY THEY'RE SCOUTING? SHE'S DROP-DEAD GORGEOUS.
ALL THE GUYS ARE AFTER HER, BUT SIMON ISN'T LETTING HER GO...
IT'S HIS PARTY, AFTER ALL. MAYBE WE'LL GET TO SEE HER IN HIS NEXT MOVIE.
ARE YOU TRYING TO STARE HER TO DEATH?

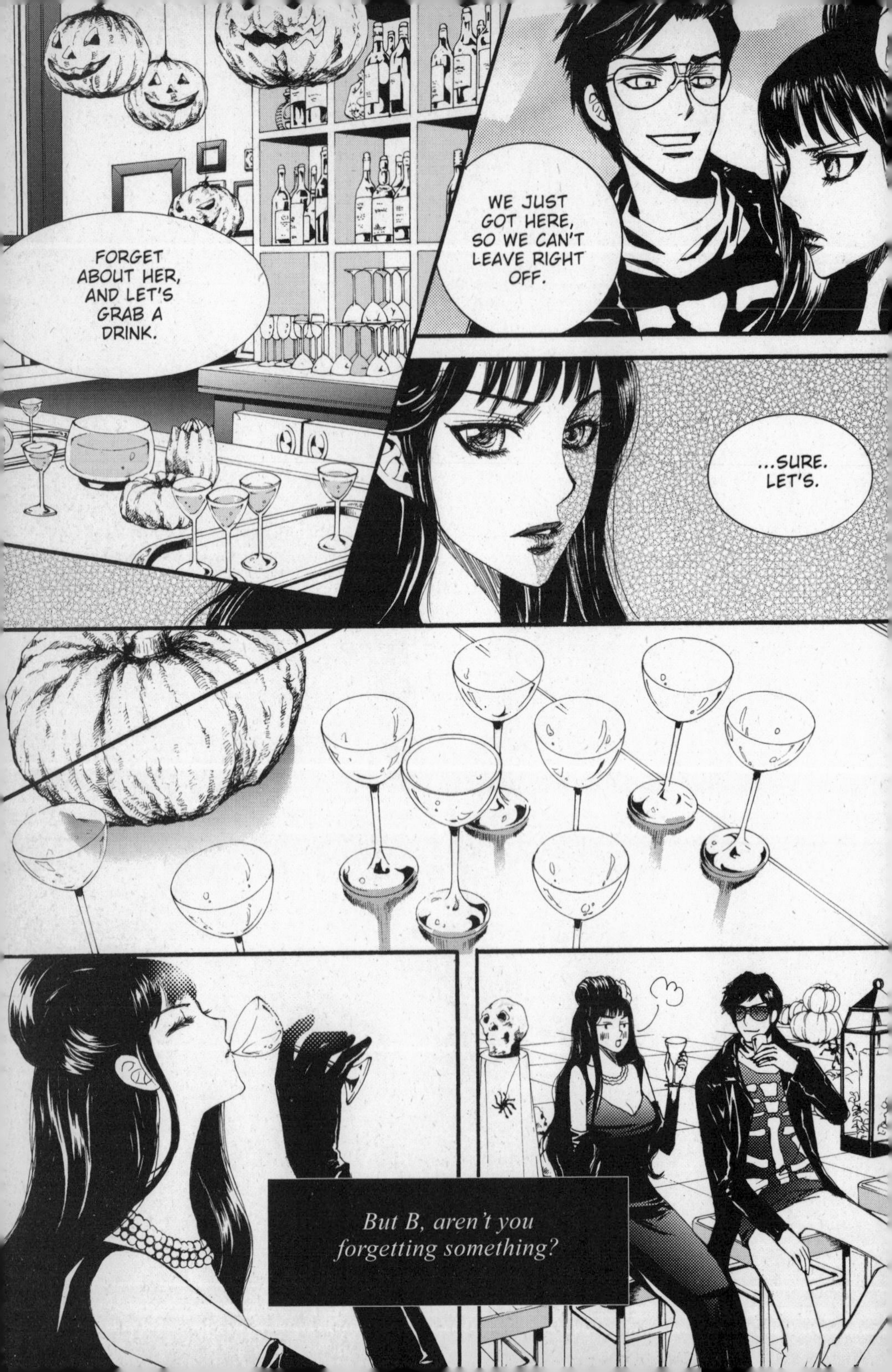
FORGET ABOUT HER, AND LET'S GRAB A DRINK.
WE JUST GOT HERE, SO WE CAN'T LEAVE RIGHT OFF.
...SURE. LET'S.
But B, aren't you forgetting something?

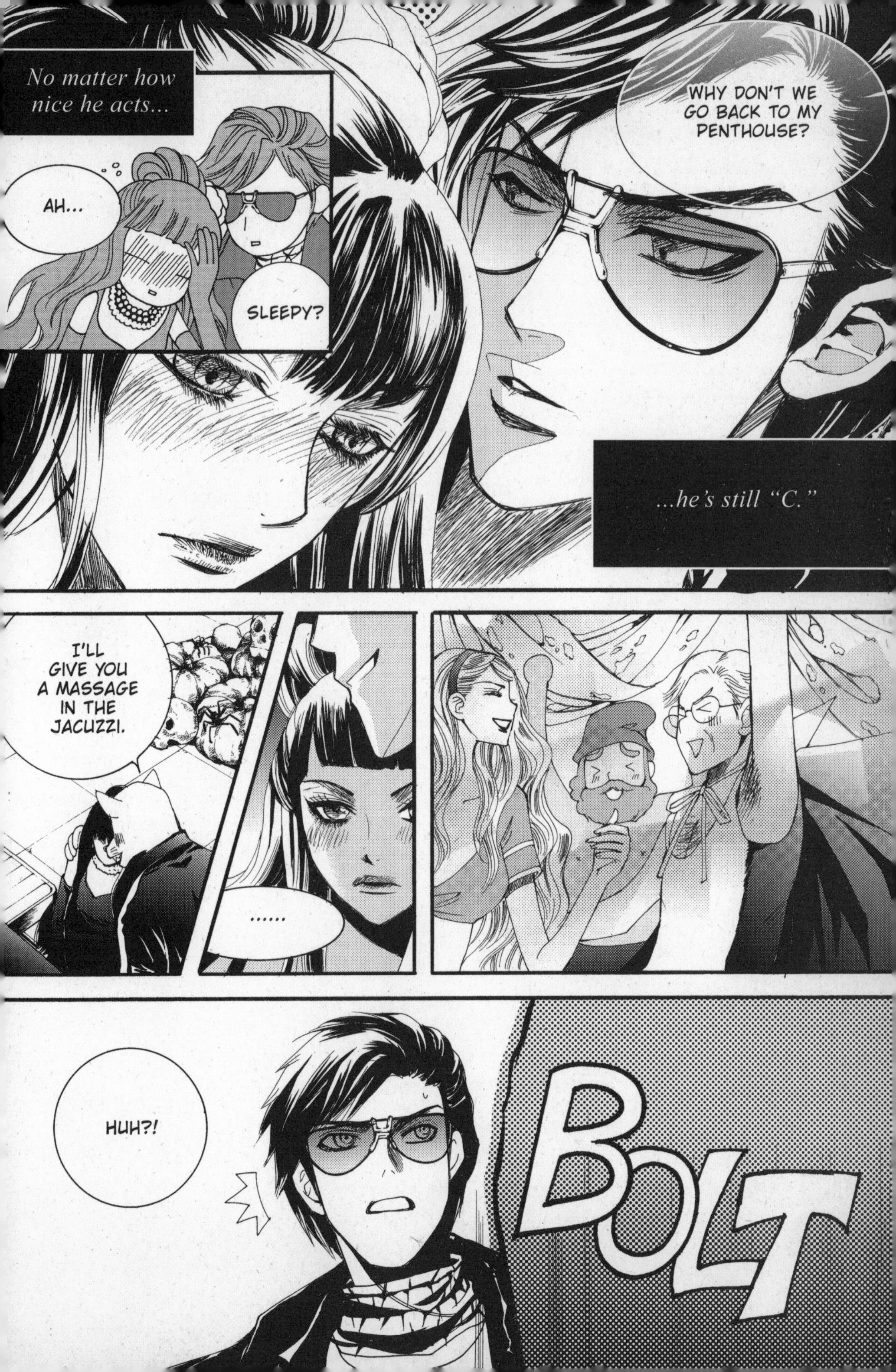

No matter how nice he acts...
AH...
SLEEPY?
WHY DON'T WE GO BACK TO MY PENTHOUSE?
...he's still "C."
I'LL GIVE YOU A MASSAGE IN THE JACUZZI.
......
HUH?!
BOLT

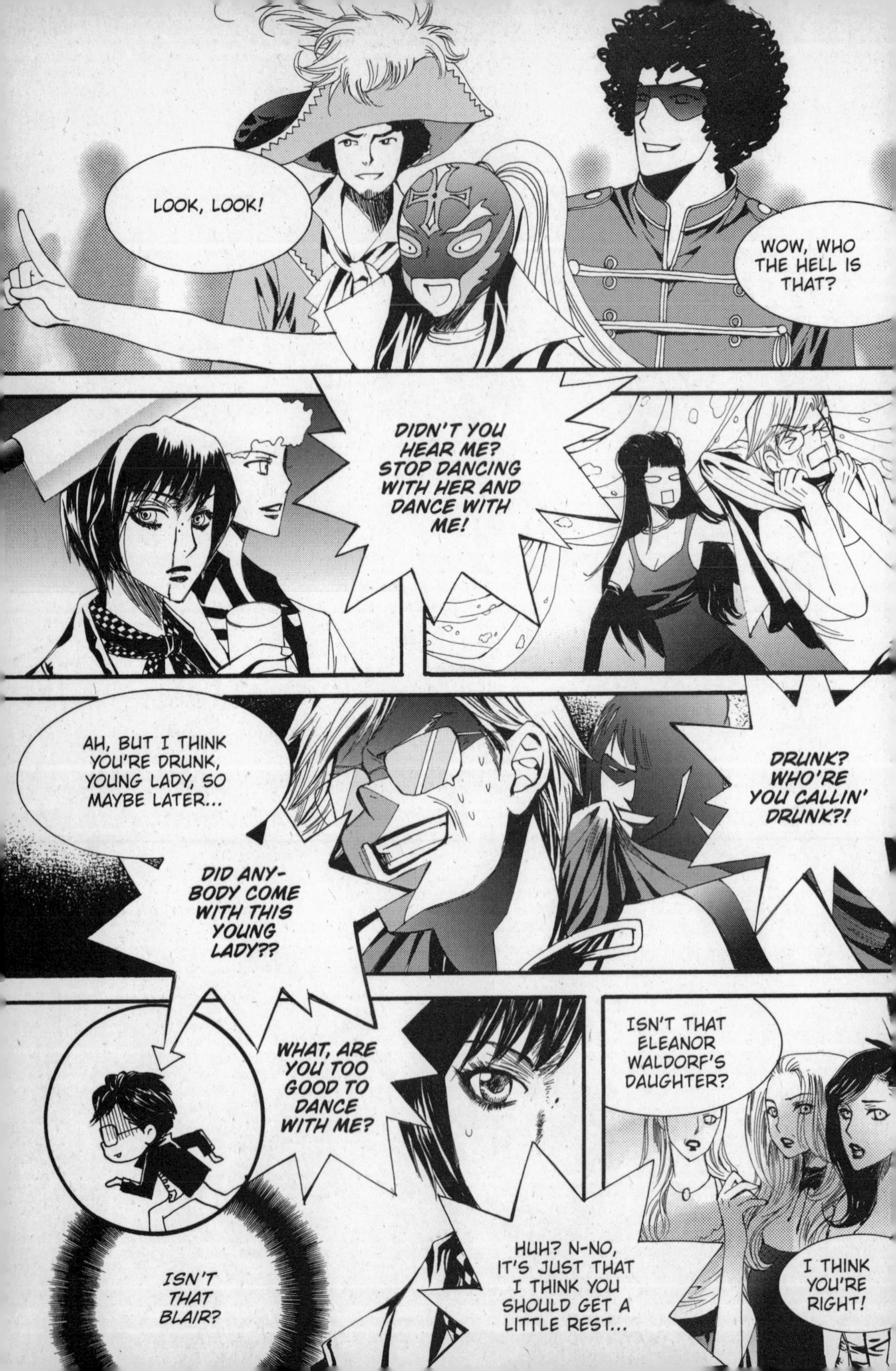
LOOK, LOOK!
WOW, WHO THE HELL IS THAT?
DIDN'T YOU HEAR ME? STOP DANCING WITH HER AND DANCE WITH ME!
AH, BUT I THINK YOU'RE DRUNK, YOUNG LADY, SO MAYBE LATER...
DRUNK? WHO'RE YOU CALLIN' DRUNK?!
DID ANY-BODY COME WITH THIS YOUNG LADY??
ISN'T THAT BLAIR?
WHAT, ARE YOU TOO GOOD TO DANCE WITH ME?
HUH? N-NO, IT'S JUST THAT I THINK YOU SHOULD GET A LITTLE REST...
ISN'T THAT ELEANOR WALDORF'S DAUGHTER?
I THINK YOU'RE RIGHT!

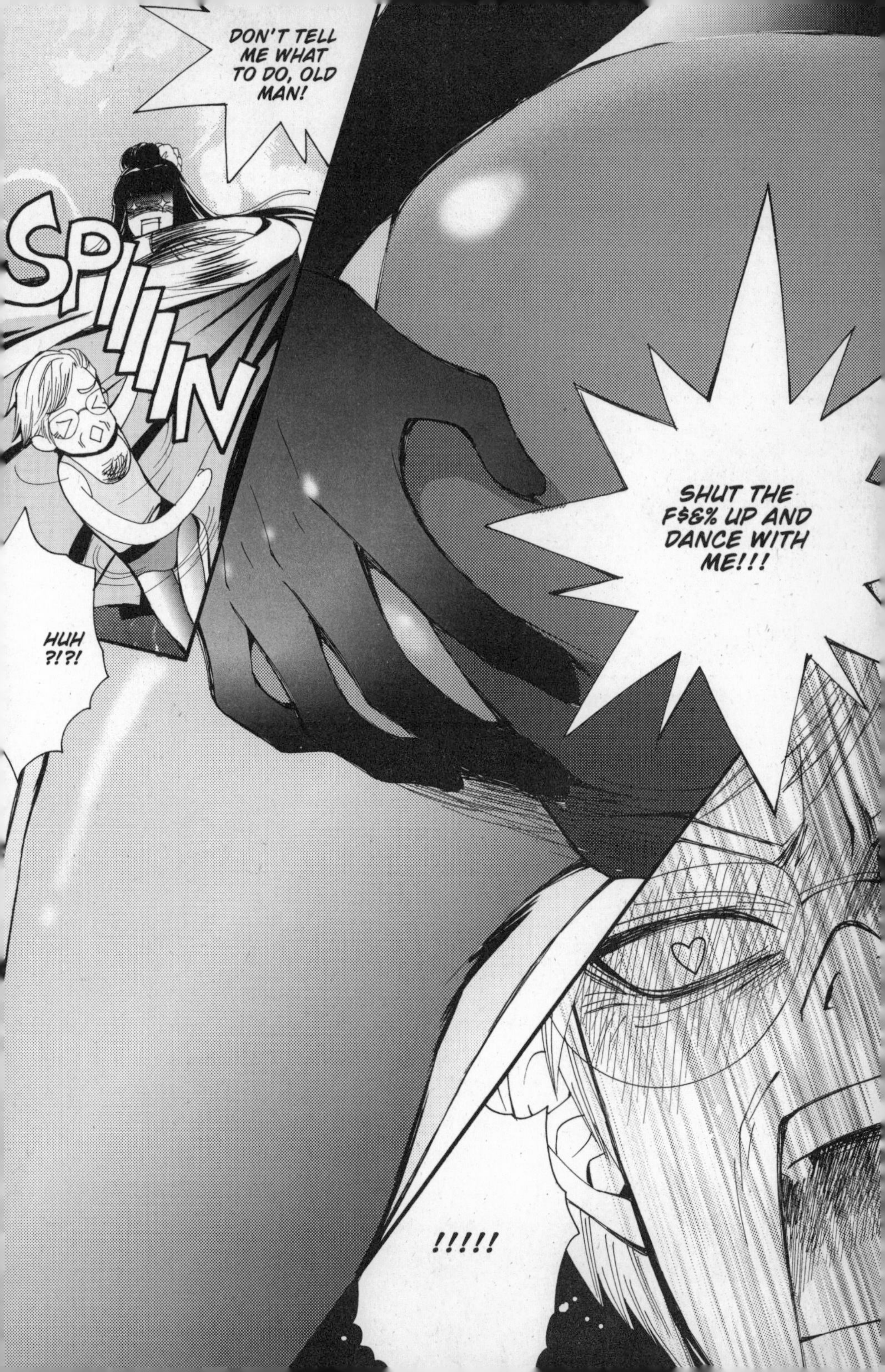
DON'T TELL ME WHAT TO DO, OLD MAN!
SPIIIIIN
HUH ?!?!
SHUT THE F$&% UP AND DANCE WITH ME!!!
!!!!!

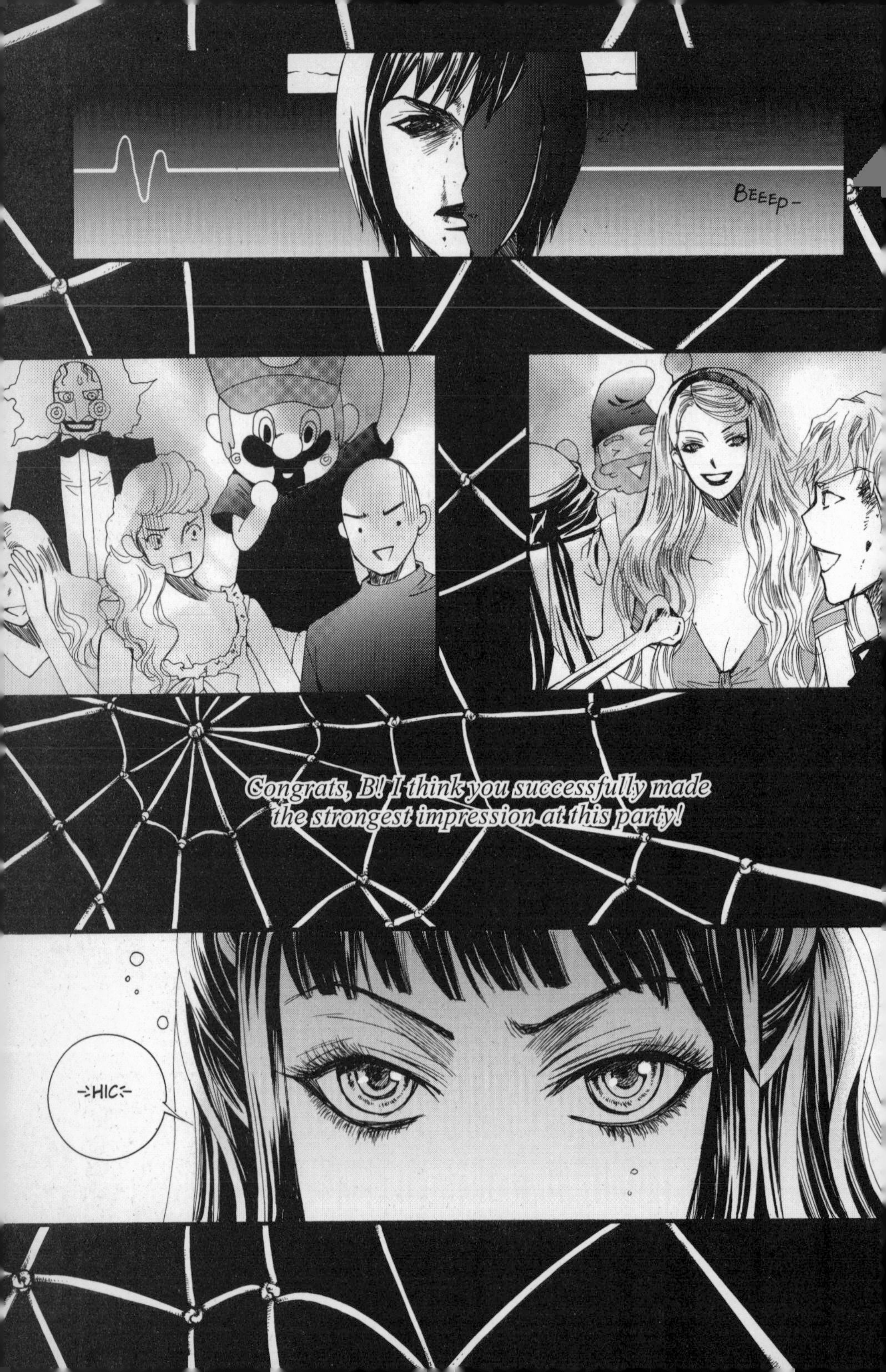
BEEEP-
Congrats, B! I think you successfully made the strongest impression at this party!
-HIC-

gossip girl

FOR YOUR EYES ONLY

gossip girl

FOR YOUR EYES ONLY | CHAPTER 5

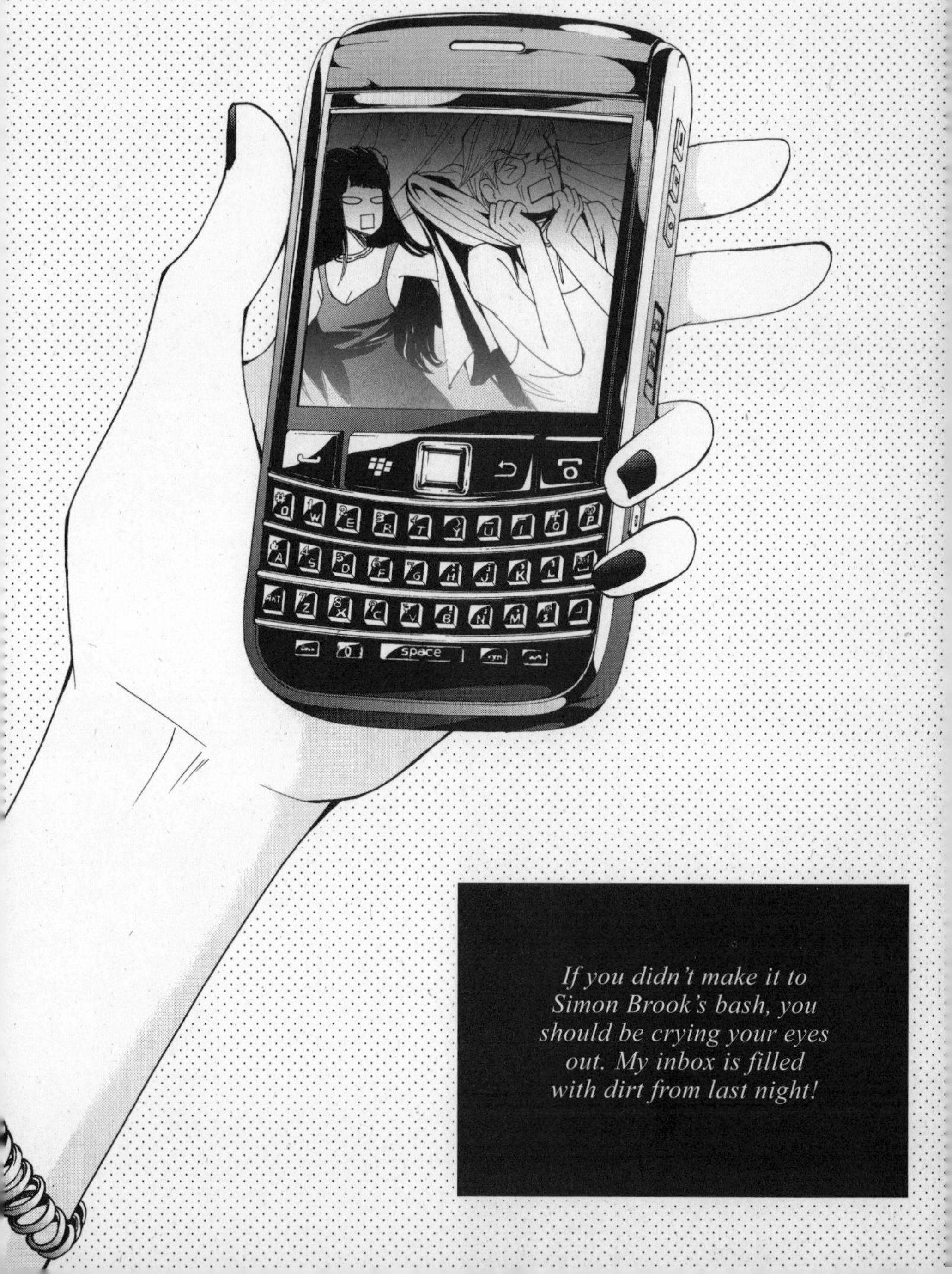
If you didn't make it to Simon Brook's bash, you should be crying your eyes out. My inbox is filled with dirt from last night!

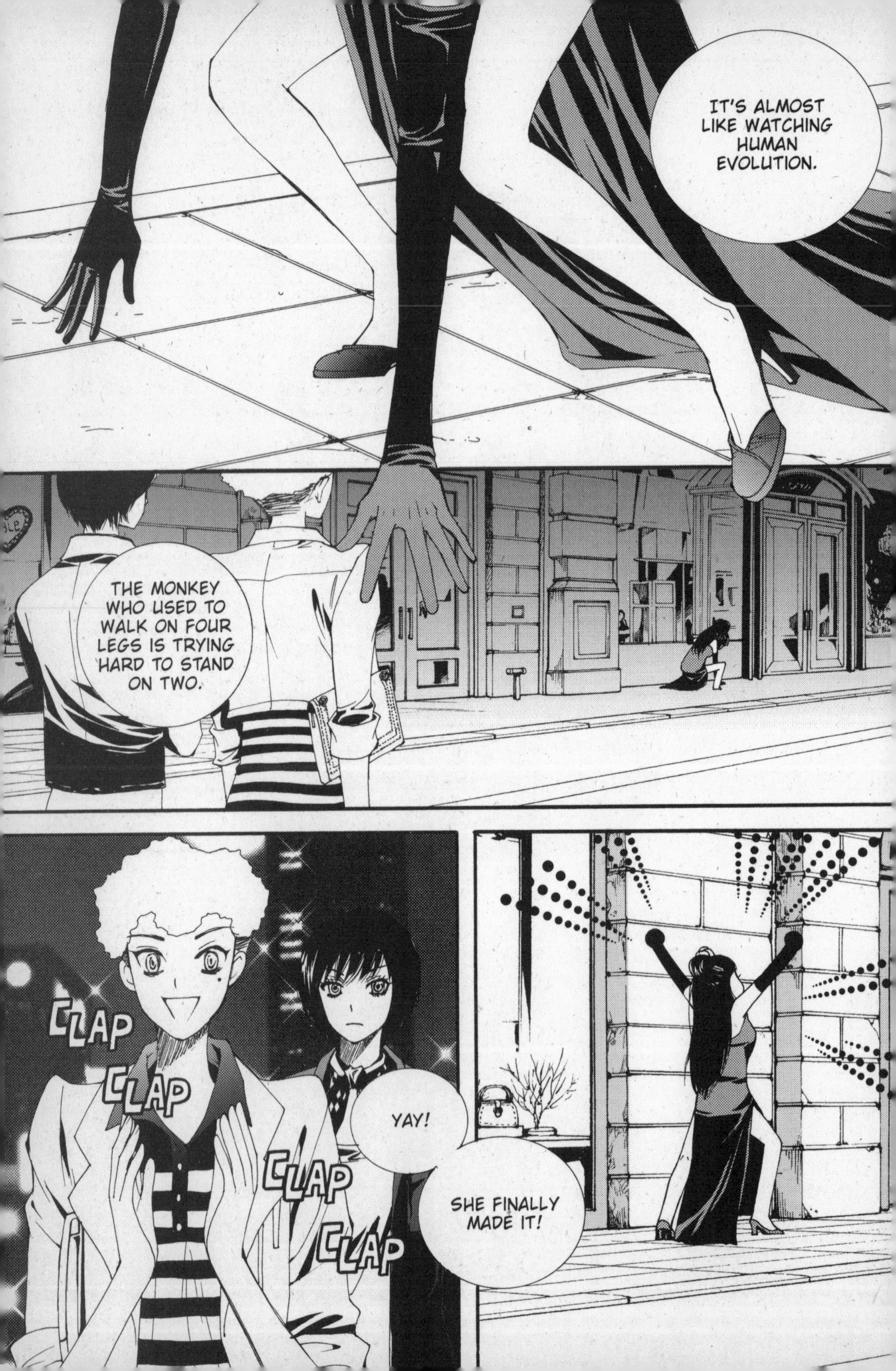
IT'S ALMOST LIKE WATCHING HUMAN EVOLUTION.
THE MONKEY WHO USED TO WALK ON FOUR LEGS IS TRYING HARD TO STAND ON TWO.
CLAP
CLAP
CLAP
CLAP
YAY!
SHE FINALLY MADE IT!

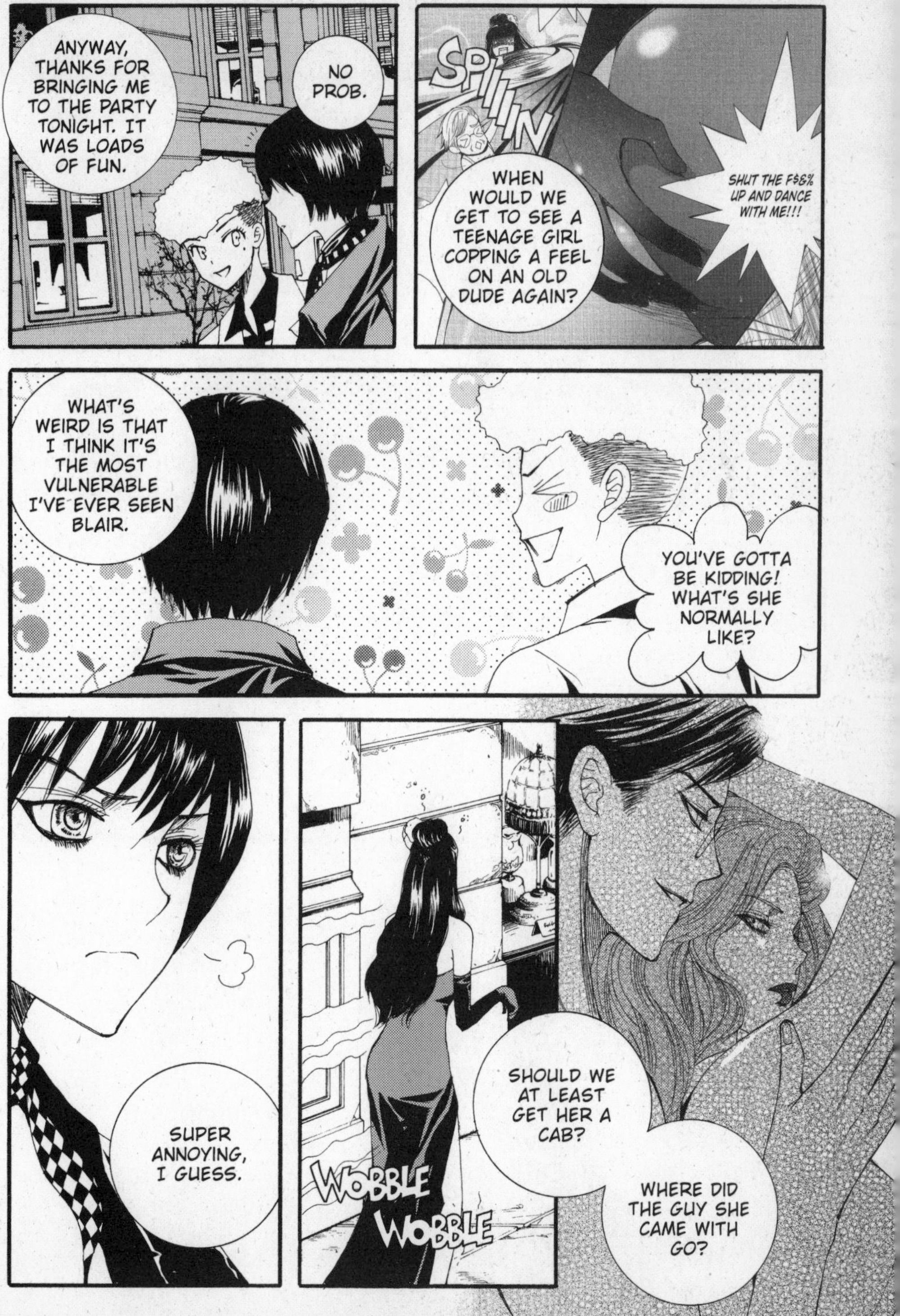
ANYWAY, THANKS FOR BRINGING ME TO THE PARTY TONIGHT. IT WAS LOADS OF FUN.
NO PROB.
SPIIIIN
WHEN WOULD WE GET TO SEE A TEENAGE GIRL COPPING A FEEL ON AN OLD DUDE AGAIN?
SHUT THE F$&% UP AND DANCE WITH ME!!!
WHAT'S WEIRD IS THAT I THINK IT'S THE MOST VULNERABLE I'VE EVER SEEN BLAIR.
YOU'VE GOTTA BE KIDDING! WHAT'S SHE NORMALLY LIKE?
SUPER ANNOYING, I GUESS.
WOBBLE
WOBBLE
SHOULD WE AT LEAST GET HER A CAB?
WHERE DID THE GUY SHE CAME WITH GO?

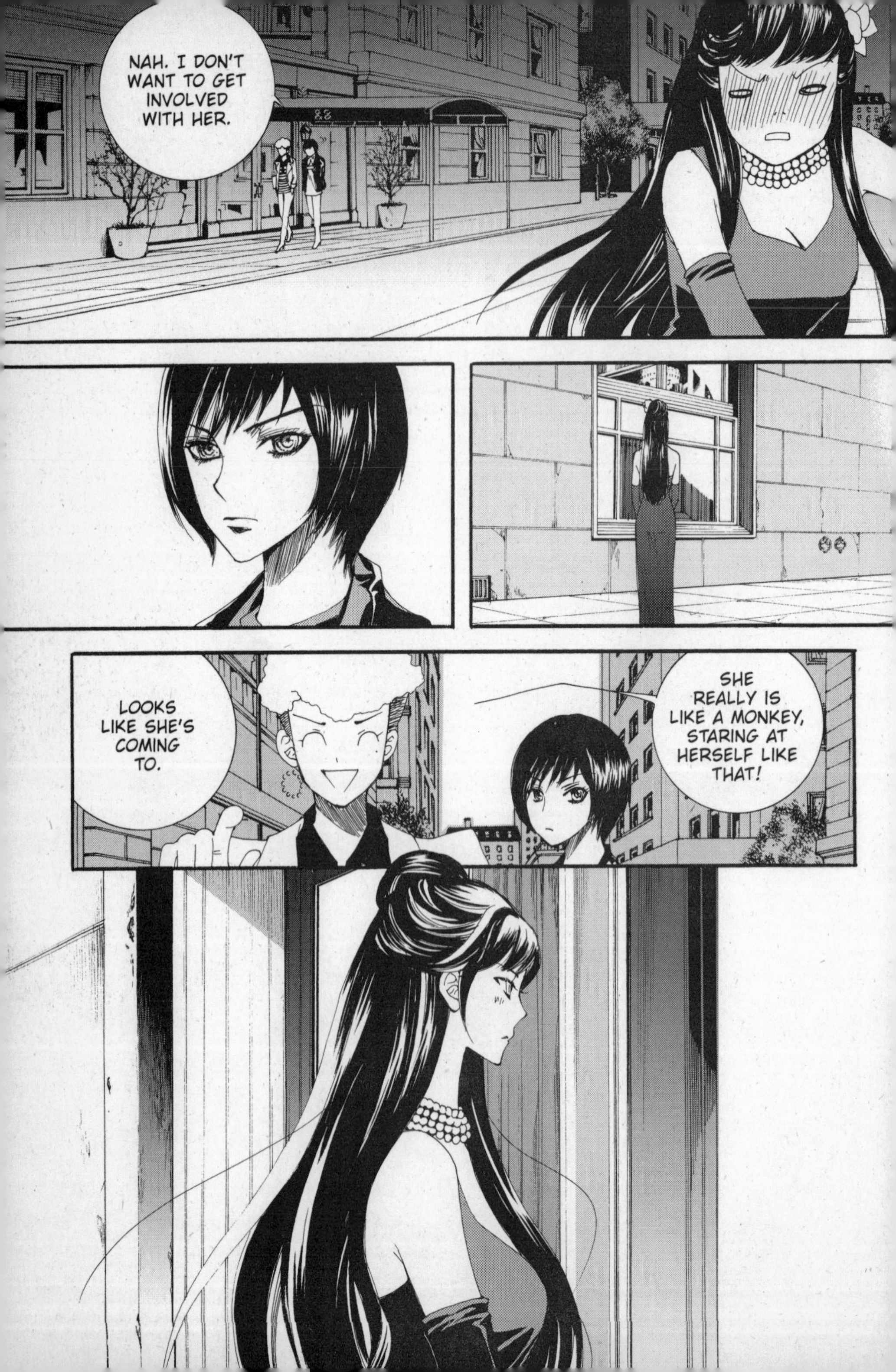
NAH. I DON'T WANT TO GET INVOLVED WITH HER.
LOOKS LIKE SHE'S COMING TO.
SHE REALLY IS LIKE A MONKEY, STARING AT HERSELF LIKE THAT!

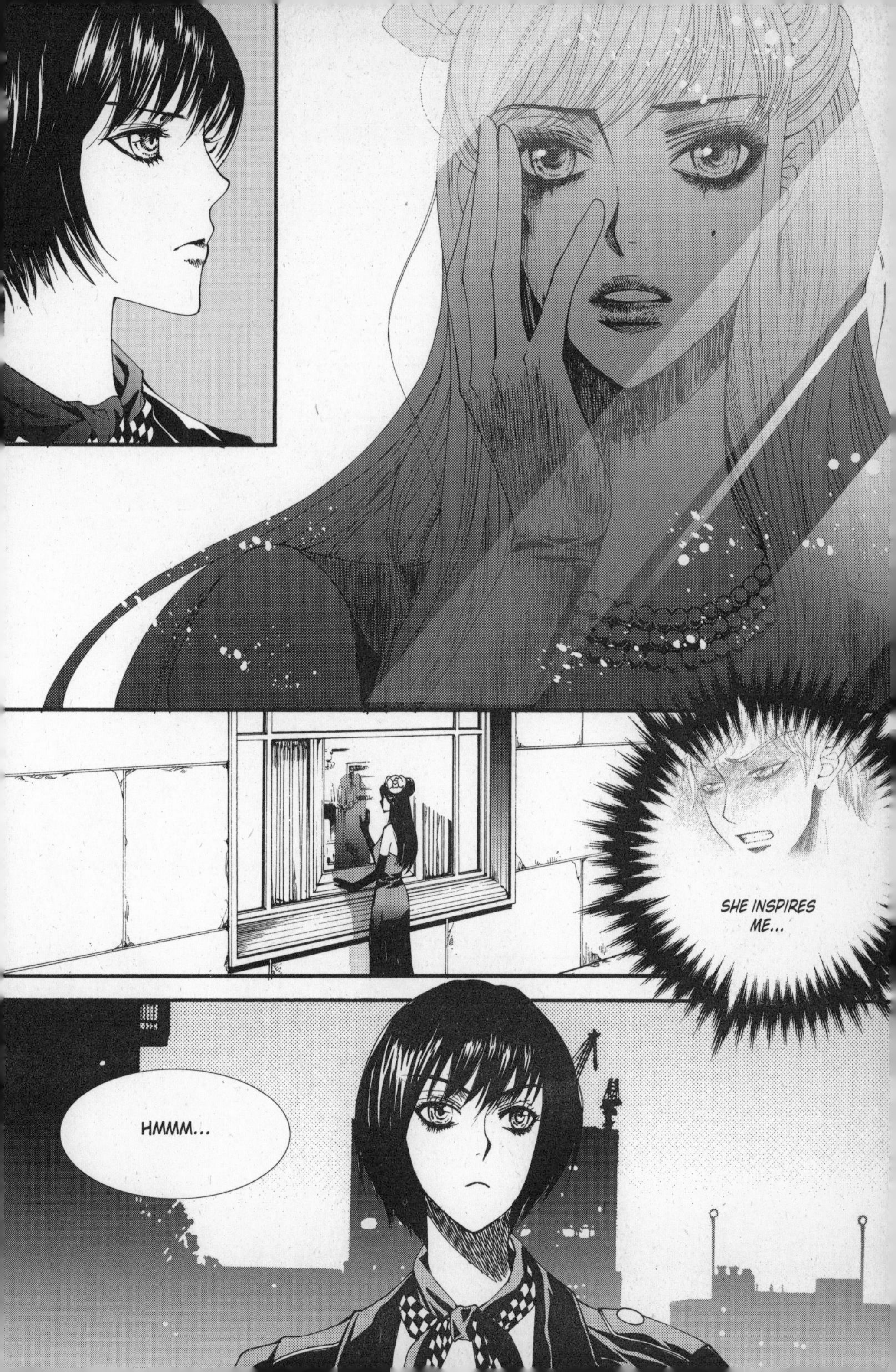
SHE INSPIRES ME...
HMMM...

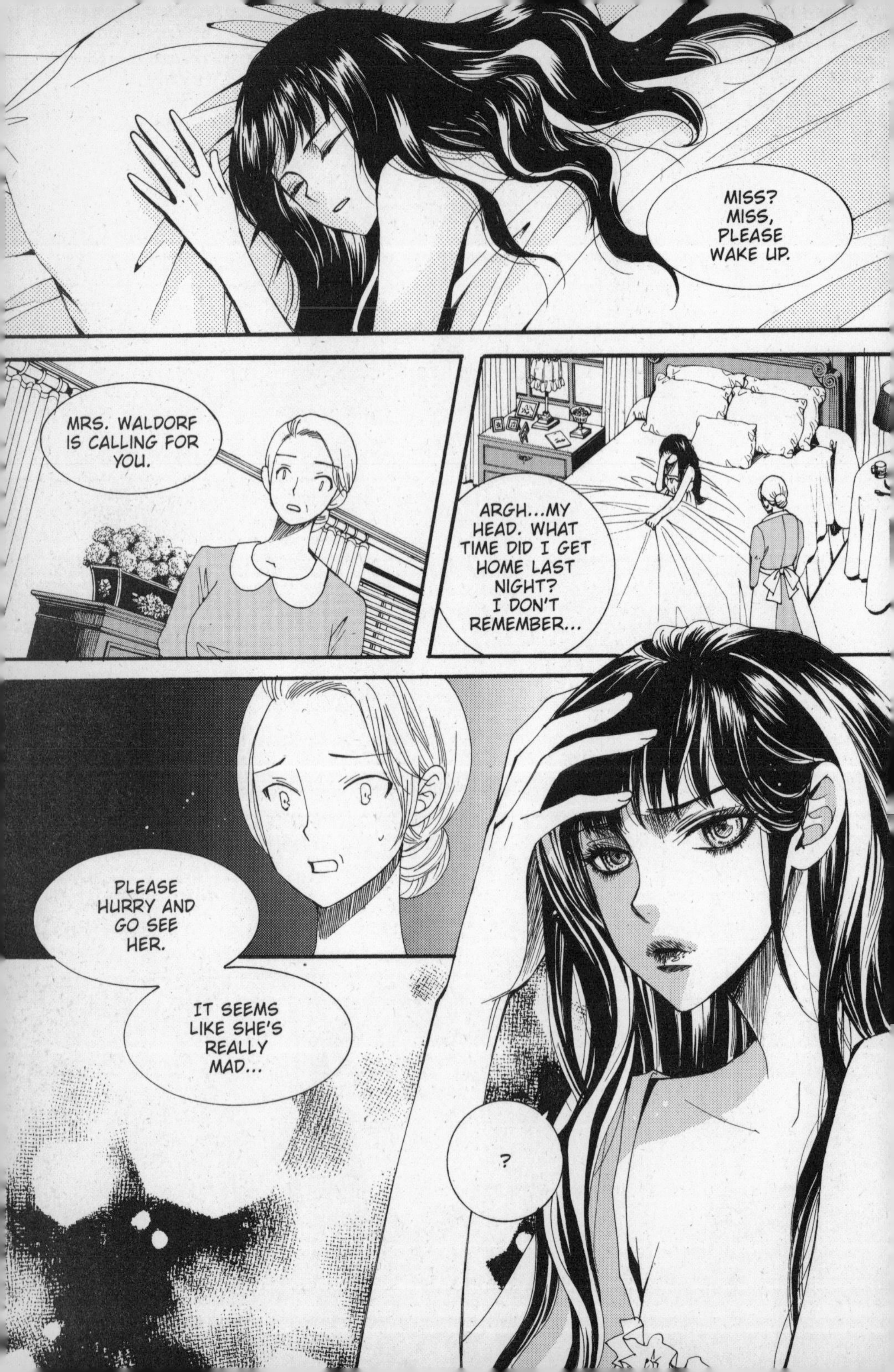
MISS? MISS, PLEASE WAKE UP.
MRS. WALDORF IS CALLING FOR YOU.
ARGH...MY HEAD. WHAT TIME DID I GET HOME LAST NIGHT? I DON'T REMEMBER...
PLEASE HURRY AND GO SEE HER.
IT SEEMS LIKE SHE'S REALLY MAD...
?

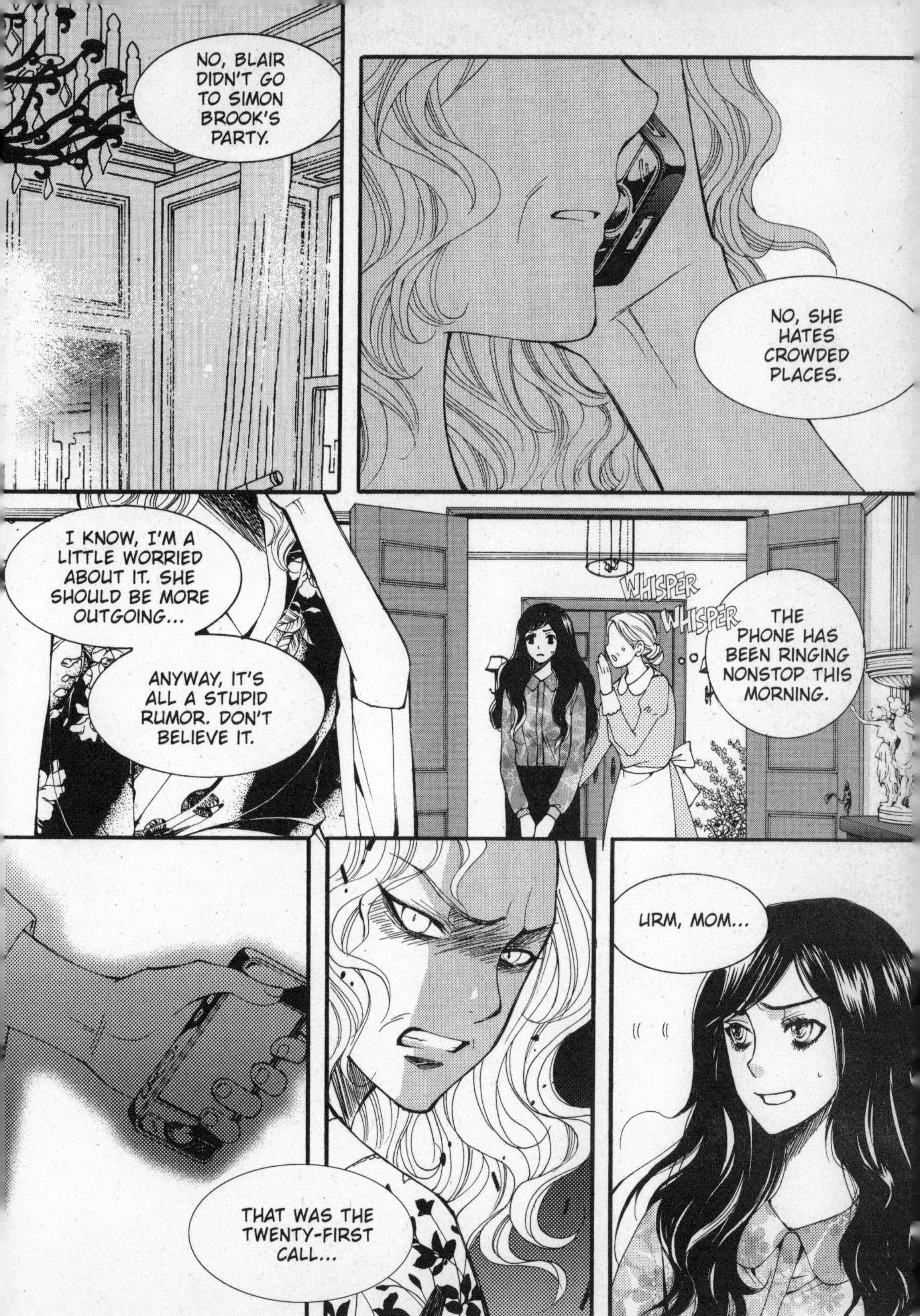

NO, BLAIR DIDN'T GO TO SIMON BROOK'S PARTY.
NO, SHE HATES CROWDED PLACES.
I KNOW, I'M A LITTLE WORRIED ABOUT IT. SHE SHOULD BE MORE OUTGOING...
ANYWAY, IT'S ALL A STUPID RUMOR. DON'T BELIEVE IT.
WHISPER
WHISPER
THE PHONE HAS BEEN RINGING NONSTOP THIS MORNING.
THAT WAS THE TWENTY-FIRST CALL...
URM, MOM...

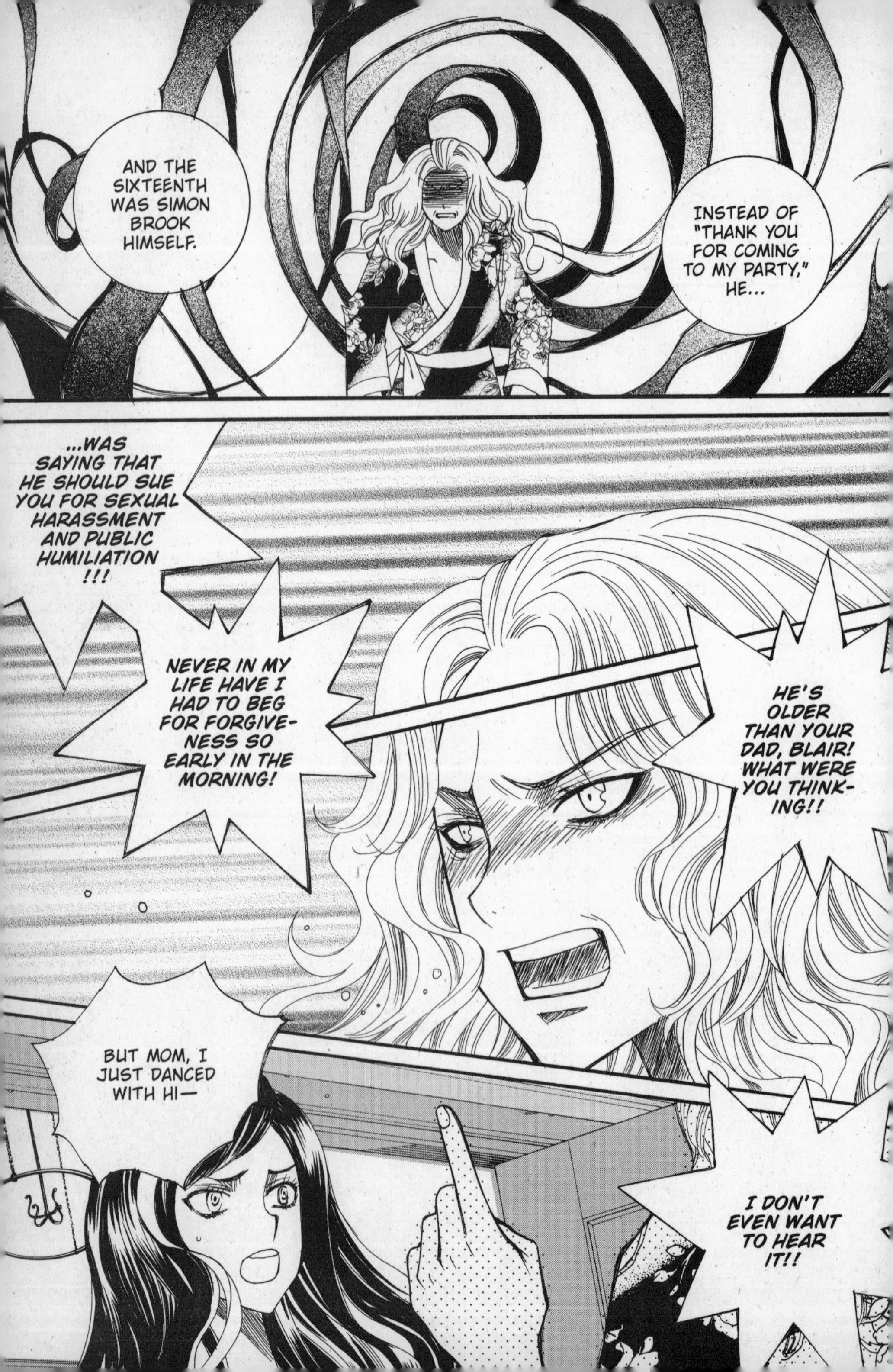
AND THE SIXTEENTH WAS SIMON BROOK HIMSELF.
INSTEAD OF "THANK YOU FOR COMING TO MY PARTY," HE...
...WAS SAYING THAT HE SHOULD SUE YOU FOR SEXUAL HARASSMENT AND PUBLIC HUMILIATION !!!
NEVER IN MY LIFE HAVE I HAD TO BEG FOR FORGIVE-NESS SO EARLY IN THE MORNING!
HE'S OLDER THAN YOUR DAD, BLAIR! WHAT WERE YOU THINK-ING!!
BUT MOM, I JUST DANCED WITH HI—
I DON'T EVEN WANT TO HEAR IT!!

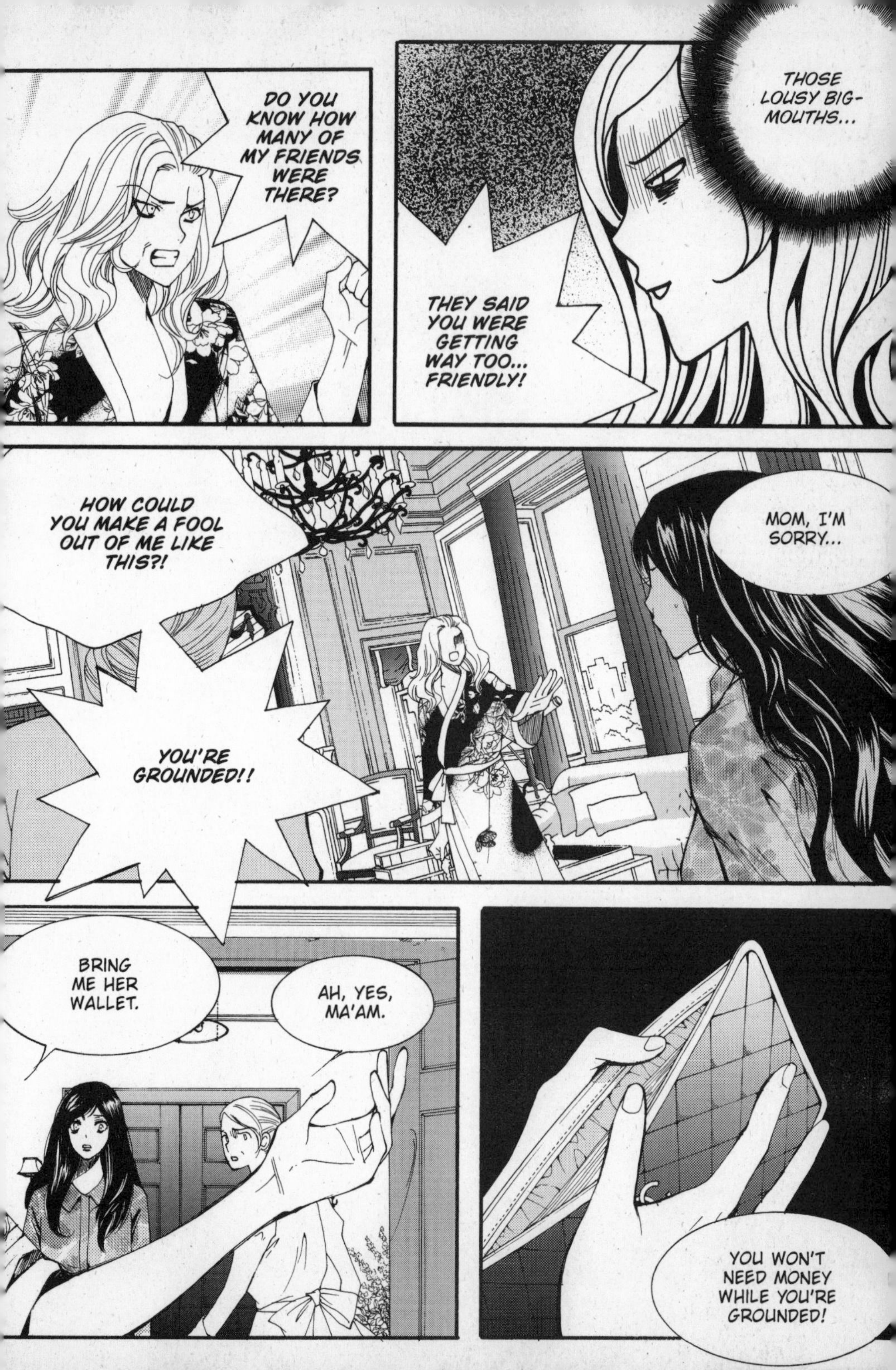
DO YOU KNOW HOW MANY OF MY FRIENDS WERE THERE?
THEY SAID YOU WERE GETTING WAY TOO... FRIENDLY!
THOSE LOUSY BIG-MOUTHS...
HOW COULD YOU MAKE A FOOL OUT OF ME LIKE THIS?!
YOU'RE GROUNDED!!
MOM, I'M SORRY...
BRING ME HER WALLET.
AH, YES, MA'AM.
YOU WON'T NEED MONEY WHILE YOU'RE GROUNDED!

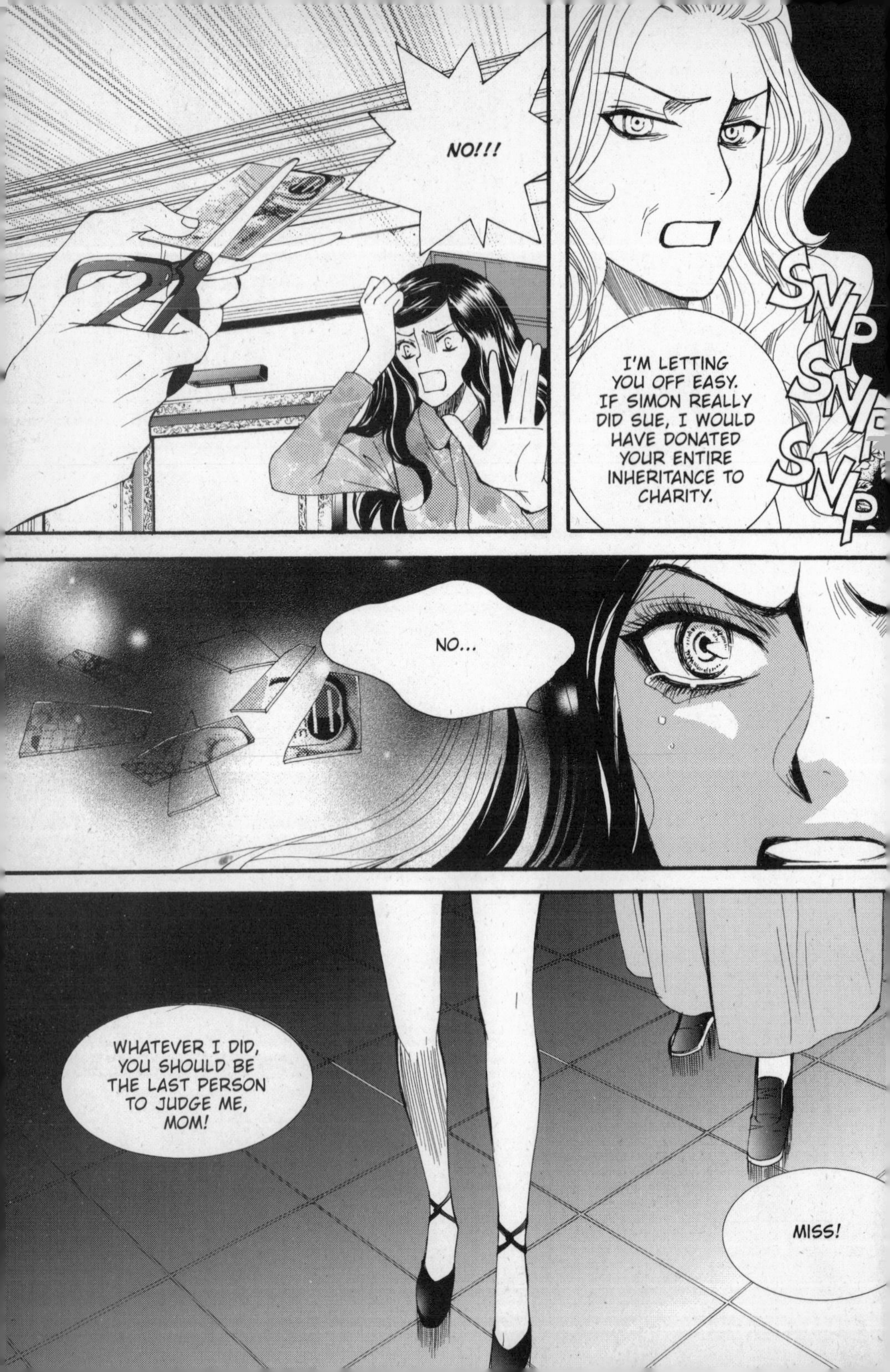
NO!!!
I'M LETTING YOU OFF EASY. IF SIMON REALLY DID SUE, I WOULD HAVE DONATED YOUR ENTIRE INHERITANCE TO CHARITY.
SNIP SNIP SNIP
NO...
WHATEVER I DID, YOU SHOULD BE THE LAST PERSON TO JUDGE ME, MOM!
MISS!

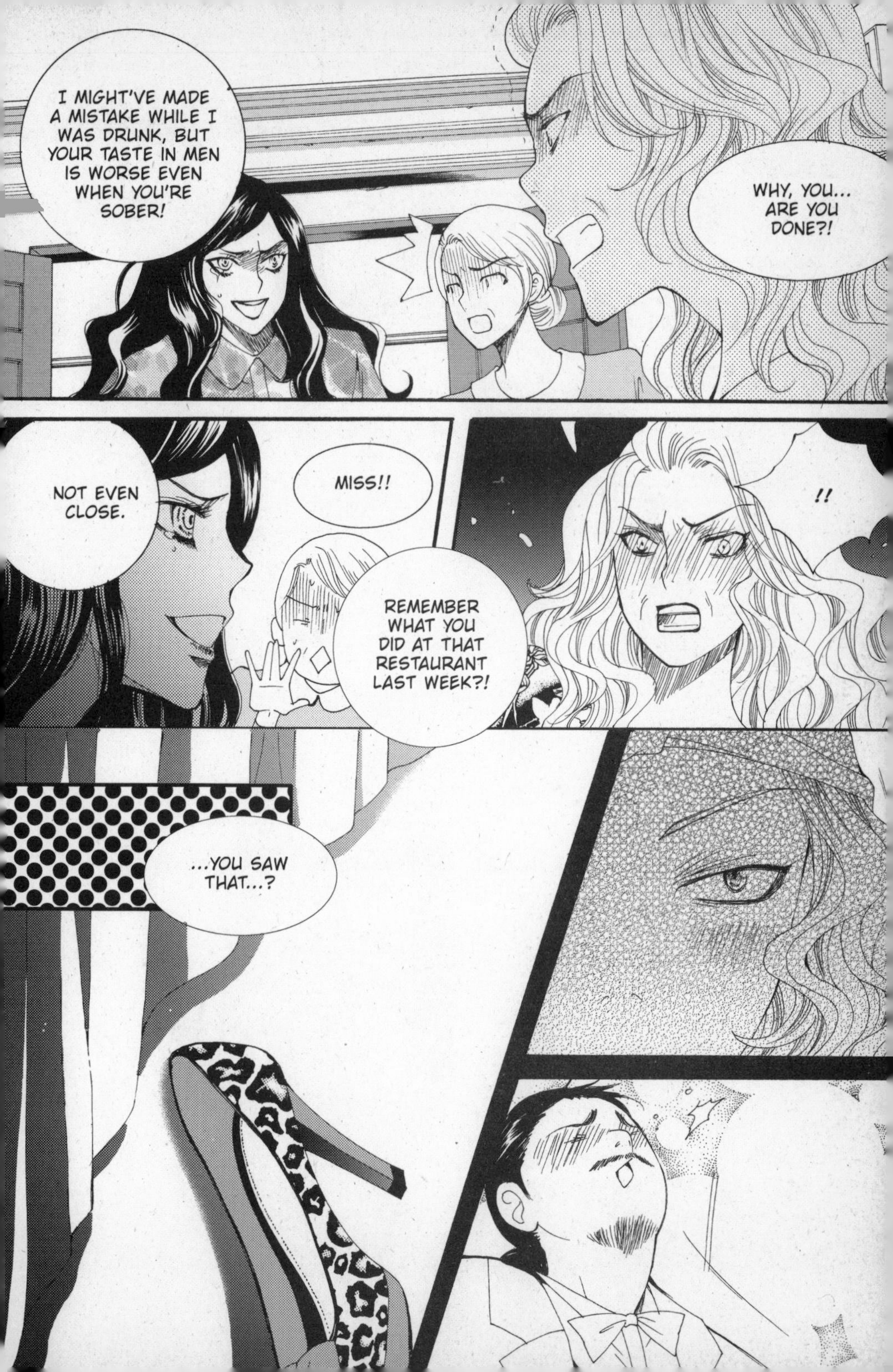

I MIGHT'VE MADE A MISTAKE WHILE I WAS DRUNK, BUT YOUR TASTE IN MEN IS WORSE EVEN WHEN YOU'RE SOBER!
WHY, YOU... ARE YOU DONE?!
NOT EVEN CLOSE.
MISS!!
REMEMBER WHAT YOU DID AT THAT RESTAURANT LAST WEEK?!
!!
...YOU SAW THAT...?

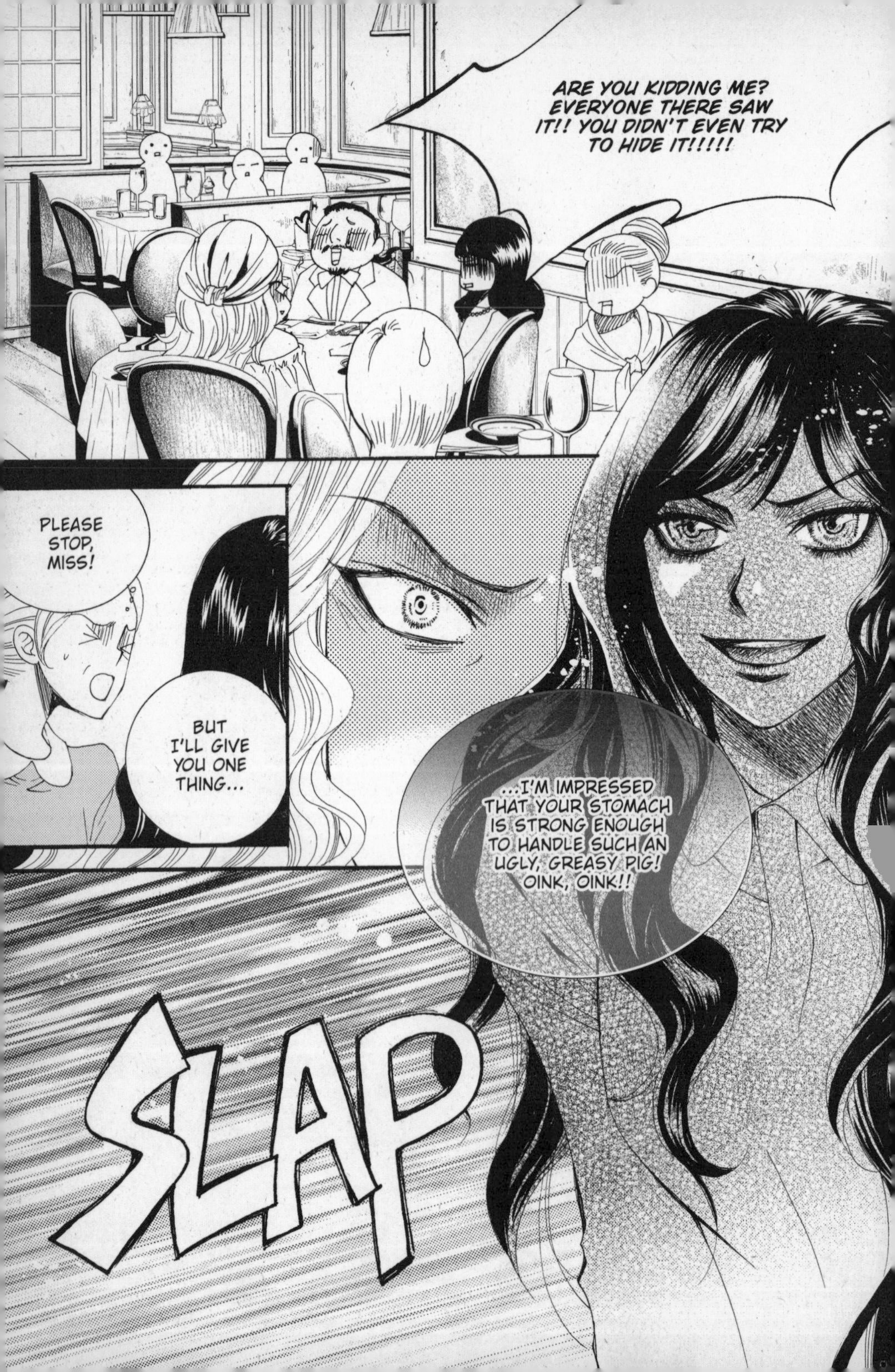
ARE YOU KIDDING ME? EVERYONE THERE SAW IT!! YOU DIDN'T EVEN TRY TO HIDE IT!!!!!
PLEASE STOP, MISS!
BUT I'LL GIVE YOU ONE THING...
...I'M IMPRESSED THAT YOUR STOMACH IS STRONG ENOUGH TO HANDLE SUCH AN UGLY, GREASY PIG! OINK, OINK!!
SLAP

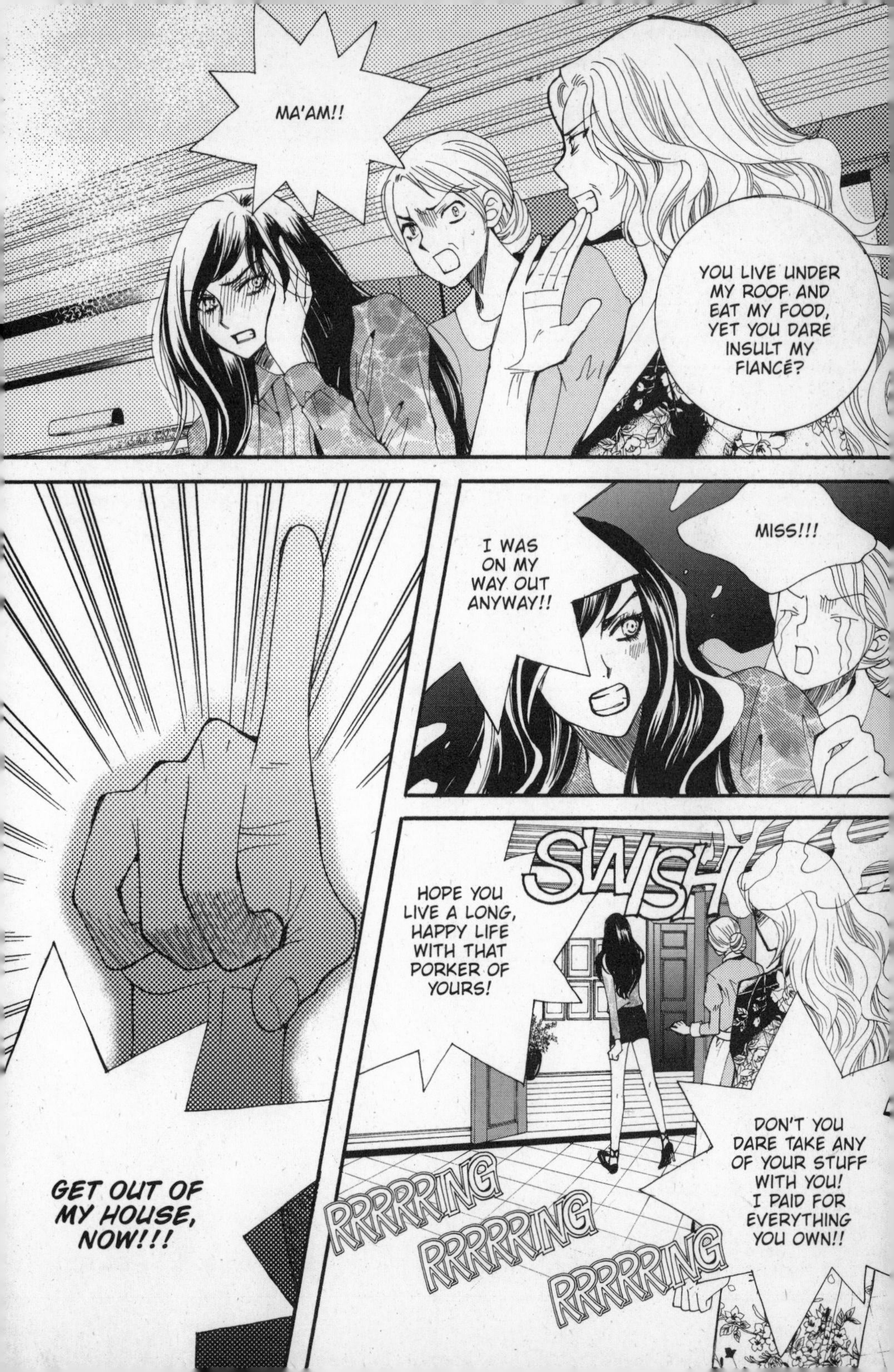

MA'AM!!
YOU LIVE UNDER MY ROOF AND EAT MY FOOD, YET YOU DARE INSULT MY FIANCÉ?
GET OUT OF MY HOUSE, NOW!!!
I WAS ON MY WAY OUT ANYWAY!!
MISS!!!
SWISH
HOPE YOU LIVE A LONG, HAPPY LIFE WITH THAT PORKER OF YOURS!
DON'T YOU DARE TAKE ANY OF YOUR STUFF WITH YOU! I PAID FOR EVERYTHING YOU OWN!!
RRRRRING
RRRRRING
RRRRRING

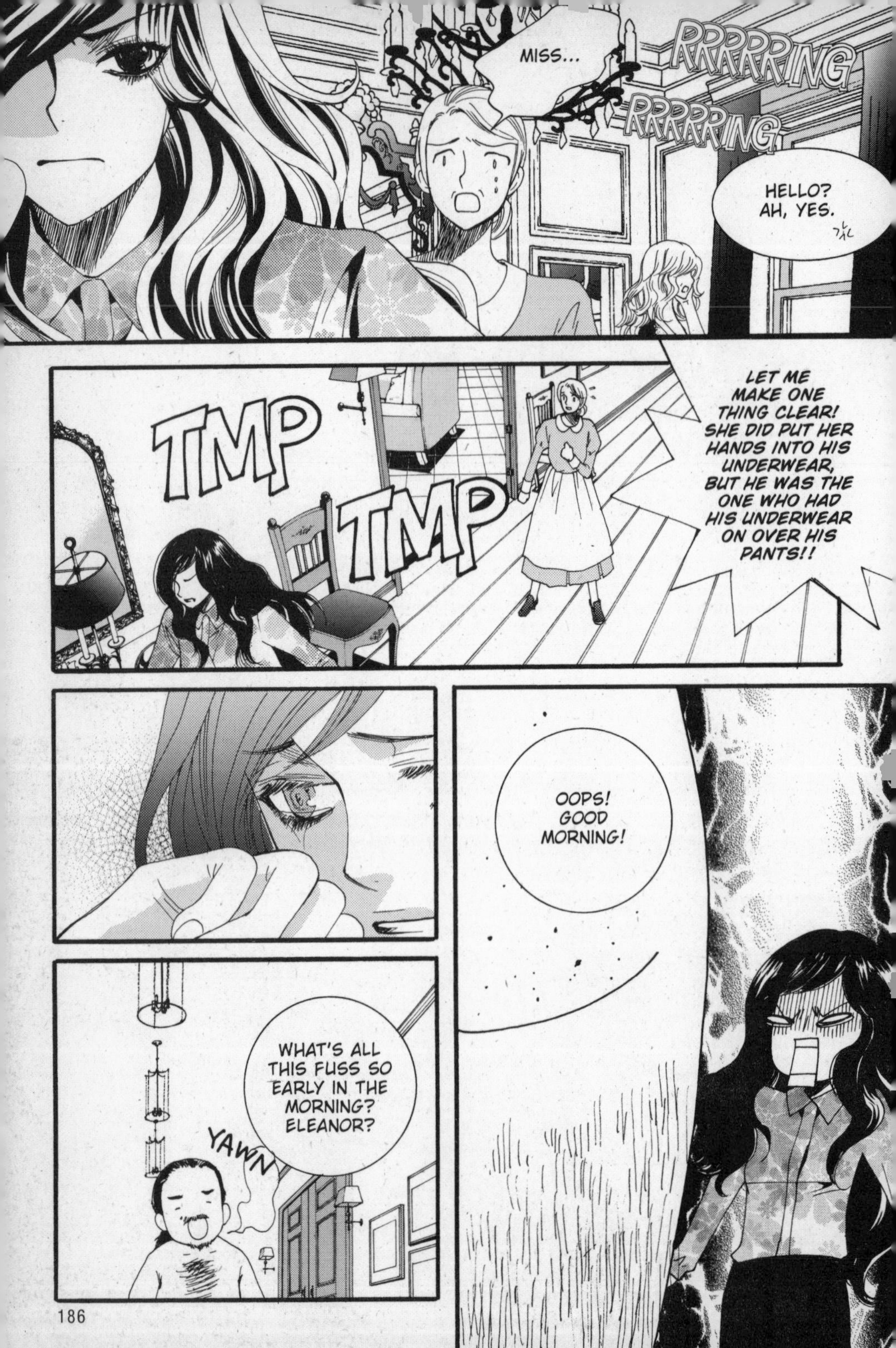
MISS...
RRRRRING
RRRRRING
HELLO? AH, YES.
TMP
TMP
LET ME MAKE ONE THING CLEAR! SHE DID PUT HER HANDS INTO HIS UNDERWEAR, BUT HE WAS THE ONE WHO HAD HIS UNDERWEAR ON OVER HIS PANTS!!
WHAT'S ALL THIS FUSS SO EARLY IN THE MORNING? ELEANOR?
YAWN
OOPS! GOOD MORNING!

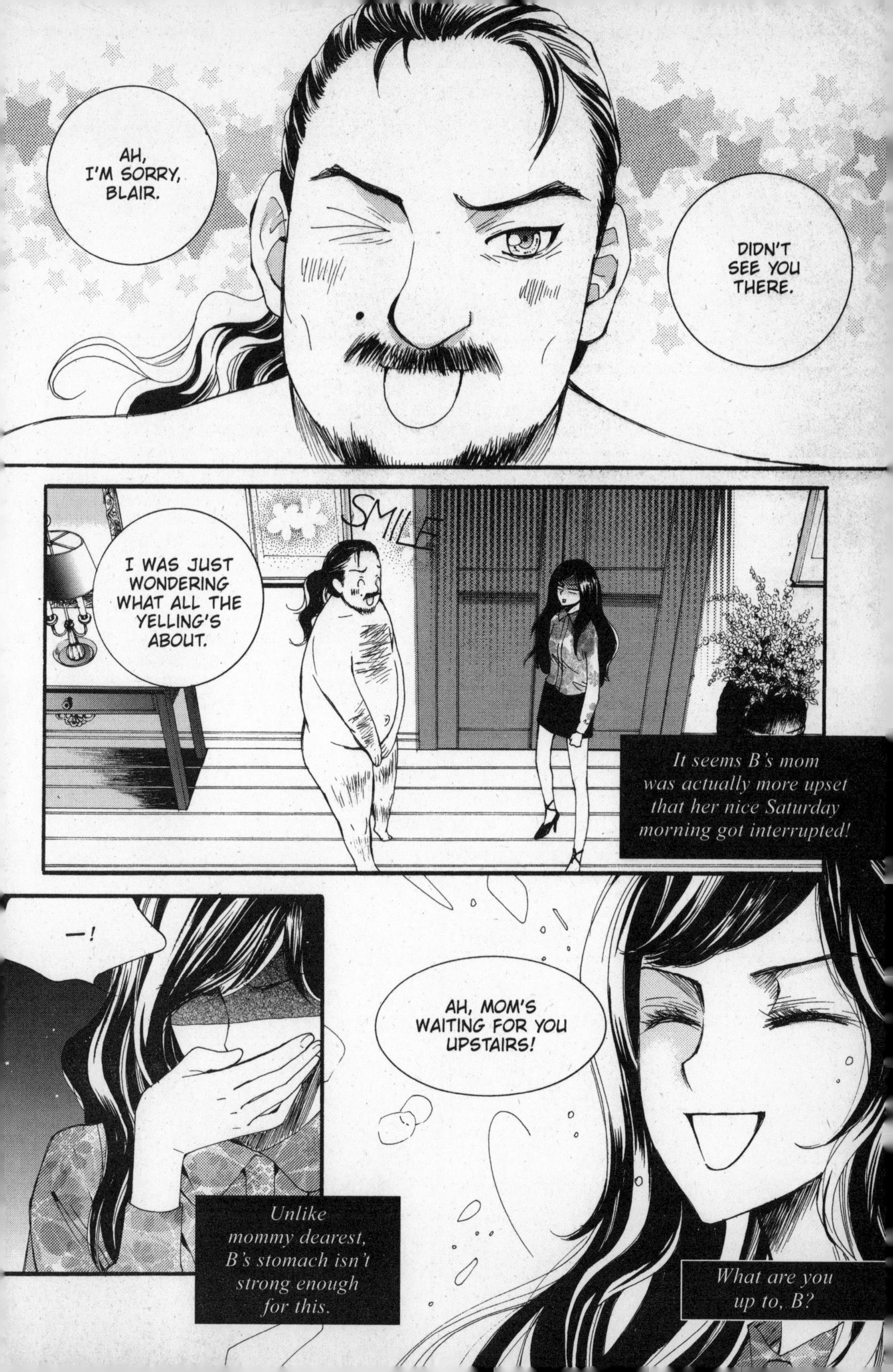
AH, I'M SORRY, BLAIR.
DIDN'T SEE YOU THERE.
SMILE
I WAS JUST WONDERING WHAT ALL THE YELLING'S ABOUT.
It seems B's mom was actually more upset that her nice Saturday morning got interrupted!
—!
Unlike mommy dearest, B's stomach isn't strong enough for this.
AH, MOM'S WAITING FOR YOU UPSTAIRS!
What are you up to, B?

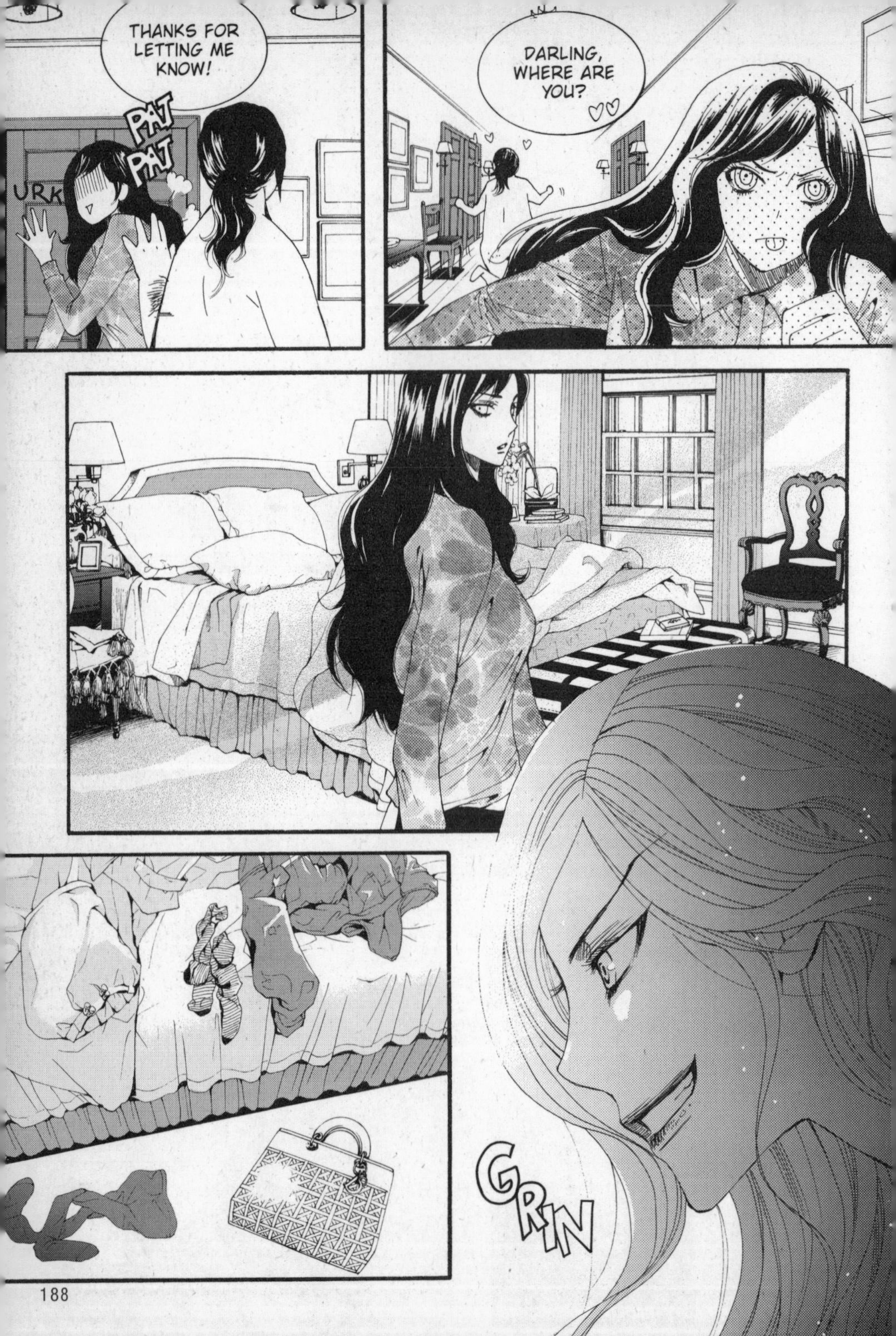
THANKS FOR LETTING ME KNOW!
PAT PAT
URK
DARLING, WHERE ARE YOU?
GRIN

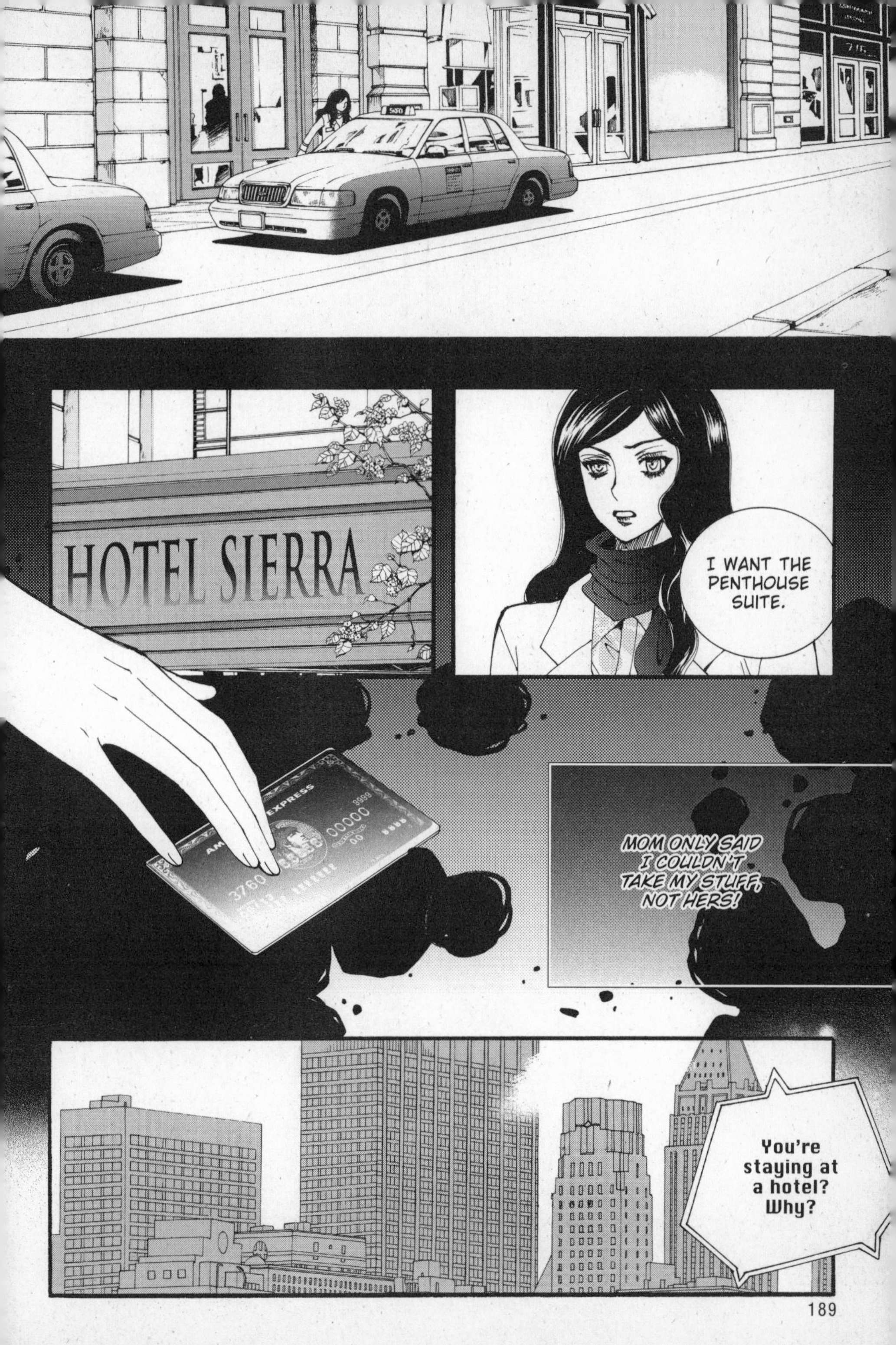
HOTEL SIERRA
I WANT THE PENTHOUSE SUITE.
MOM ONLY SAID I COULDN'T TAKE MY STUFF, NOT HERS!
You're staying at a hotel? Why?

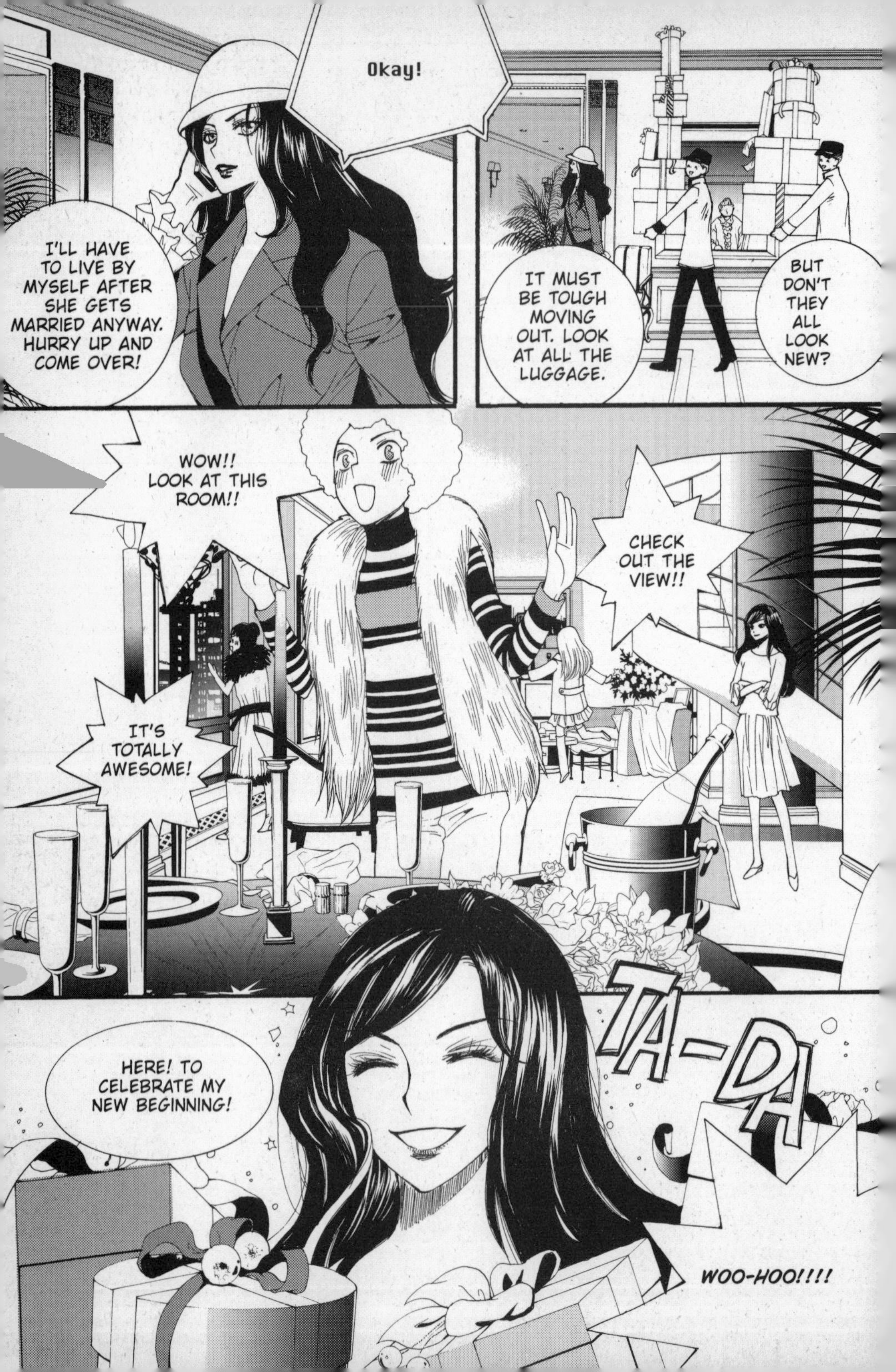
Okay!
I'LL HAVE TO LIVE BY MYSELF AFTER SHE GETS MARRIED ANYWAY. HURRY UP AND COME OVER!
IT MUST BE TOUGH MOVING OUT. LOOK AT ALL THE LUGGAGE.
BUT DON'T THEY ALL LOOK NEW?
WOW!! LOOK AT THIS ROOM!!
IT'S TOTALLY AWESOME!
CHECK OUT THE VIEW!!
HERE! TO CELEBRATE MY NEW BEGINNING!
TA-DA
WOO-HOO!!!!

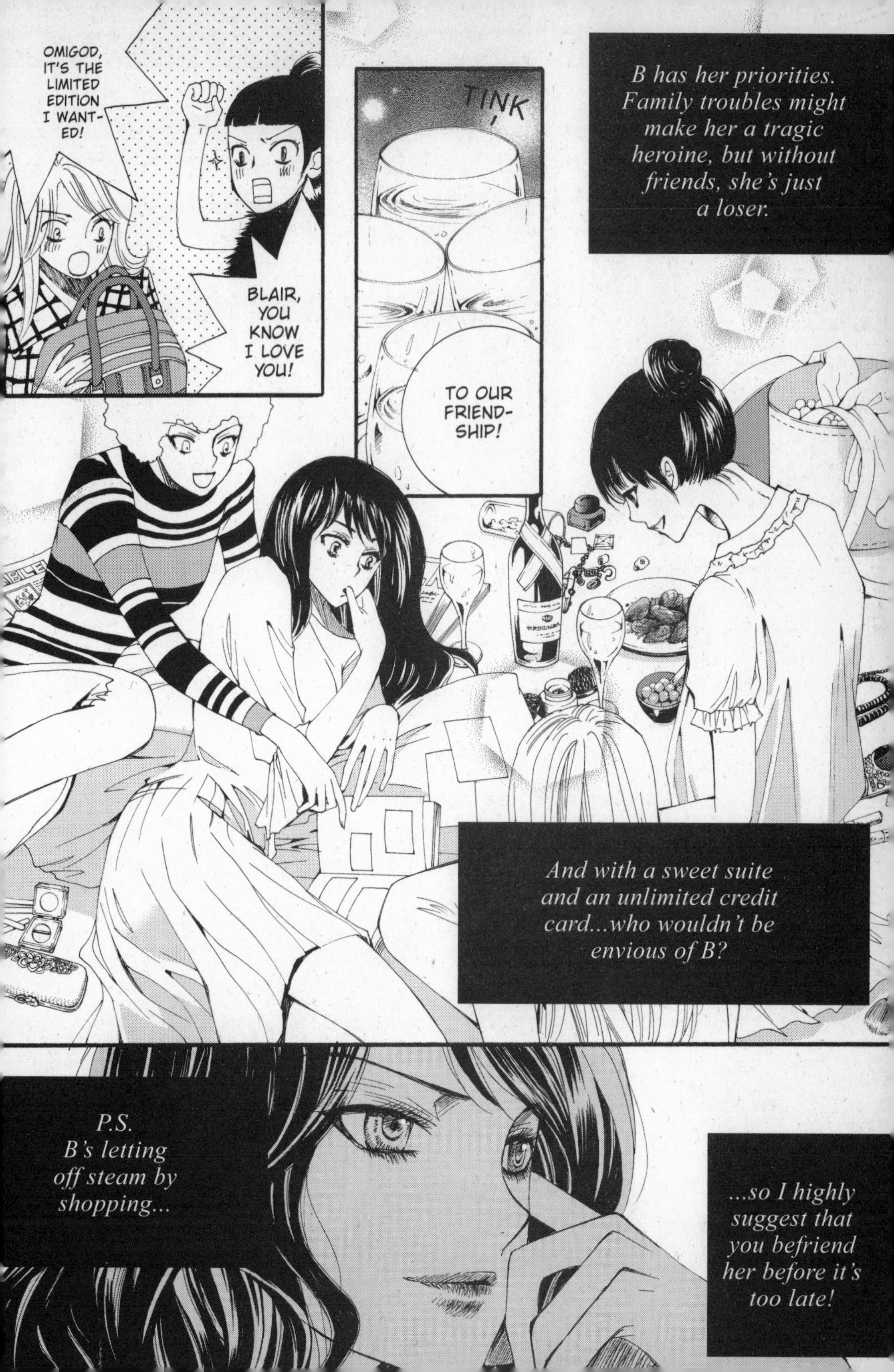
OMIGOD, IT'S THE LIMITED EDITION I WANT-ED!
BLAIR, YOU KNOW I LOVE YOU!
TINK
TO OUR FRIEND-SHIP!
B has her priorities. Family troubles might make her a tragic heroine, but without friends, she's just a loser.
And with a sweet suite and an unlimited credit card...who wouldn't be envious of B?
P.S. B's letting off steam by shopping...
...so I highly suggest that you befriend her before it's too late!

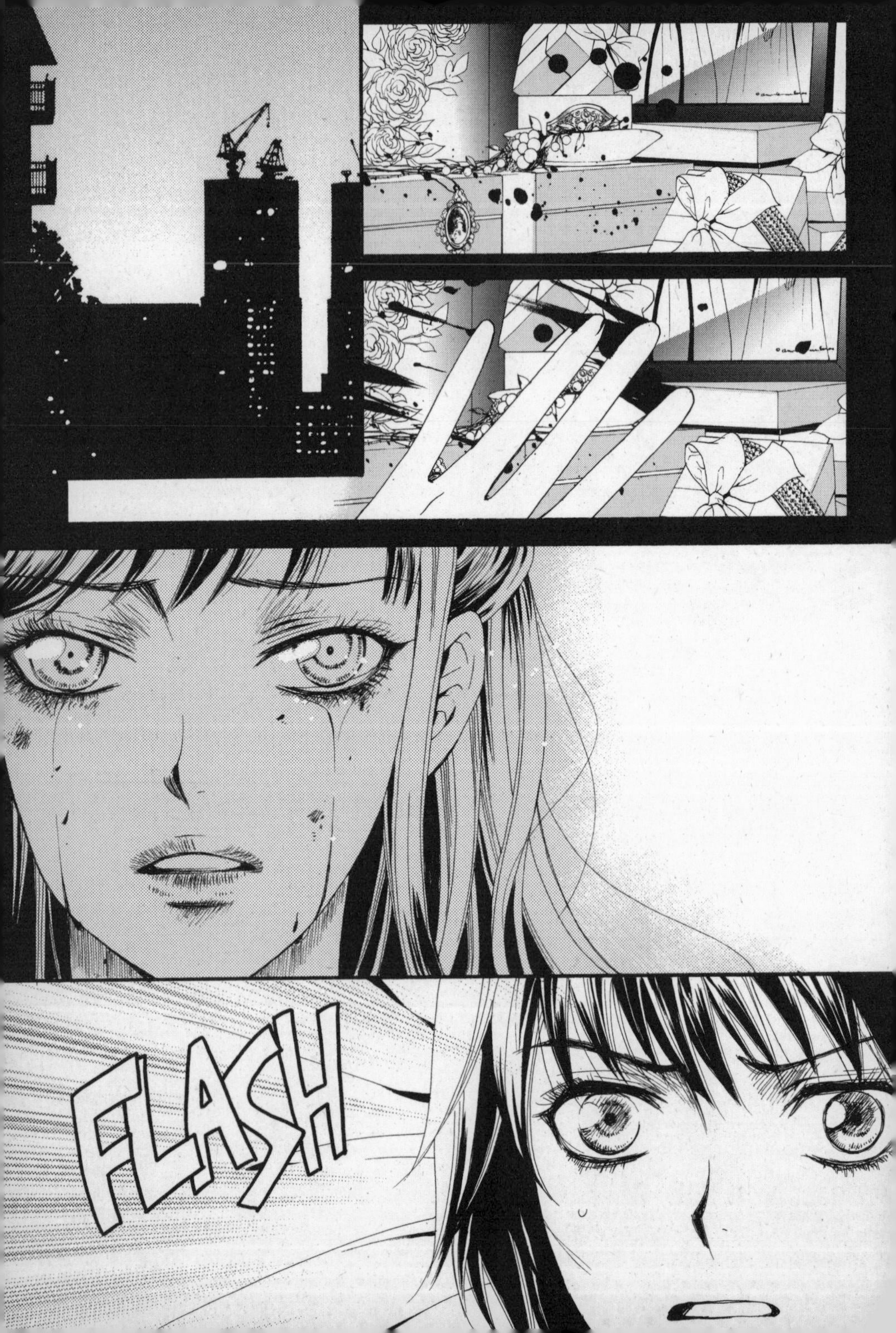
FLASH

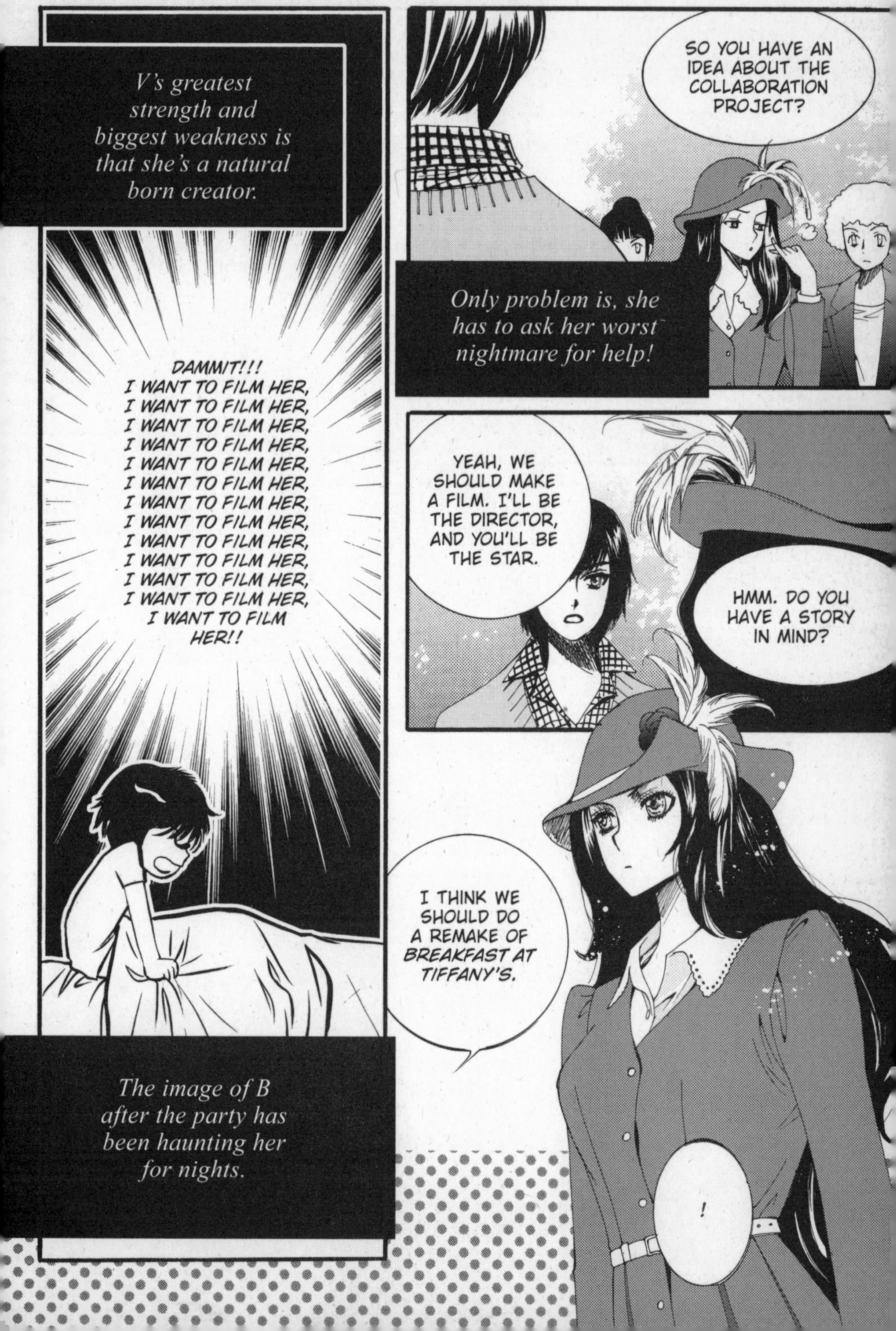
V's greatest strength and biggest weakness is that she's a natural born creator.
DAMMIT!!! I WANT TO FILM HER, I WANT TO FILM HER, I WANT TO FILM HER, I WANT TO FILM HER, I WANT TO FILM HER, I WANT TO FILM HER, I WANT TO FILM HER, I WANT TO FILM HER, I WANT TO FILM HER, I WANT TO FILM HER, I WANT TO FILM HER, I WANT TO FILM HER, I WANT TO FILM HER!!
The image of B after the party has been haunting her for nights.
SO YOU HAVE AN IDEA ABOUT THE COLLABORATION PROJECT?
Only problem is, she has to ask her worst nightmare for help!
YEAH, WE SHOULD MAKE A FILM. I'LL BE THE DIRECTOR, AND YOU'LL BE THE STAR.
HMM. DO YOU HAVE A STORY IN MIND?
I THINK WE SHOULD DO A REMAKE OF *BREAKFAST AT TIFFANY'S.*
!

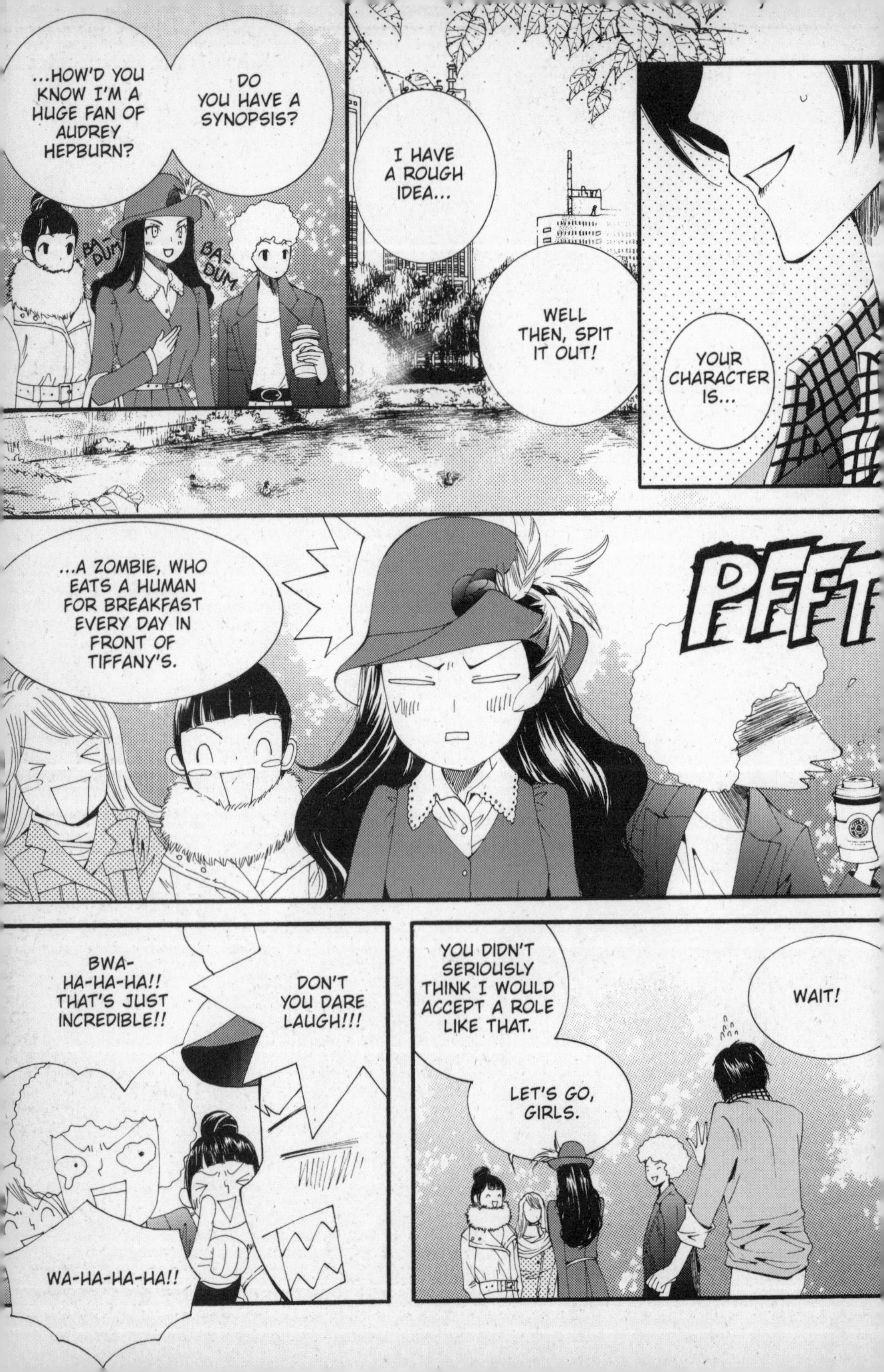
...HOW'D YOU KNOW I'M A HUGE FAN OF AUDREY HEPBURN?
DO YOU HAVE A SYNOPSIS?
BA-DUM
BA-DUM
I HAVE A ROUGH IDEA...
WELL THEN, SPIT IT OUT!
YOUR CHARACTER IS...
...A ZOMBIE, WHO EATS A HUMAN FOR BREAKFAST EVERY DAY IN FRONT OF TIFFANY'S.
PFFT
BWA-HA-HA-HA!! THAT'S JUST INCREDIBLE!!
DON'T YOU DARE LAUGH!!!
WA-HA-HA-HA!!
YOU DIDN'T SERIOUSLY THINK I WOULD ACCEPT A ROLE LIKE THAT.
LET'S GO, GIRLS.
WAIT!

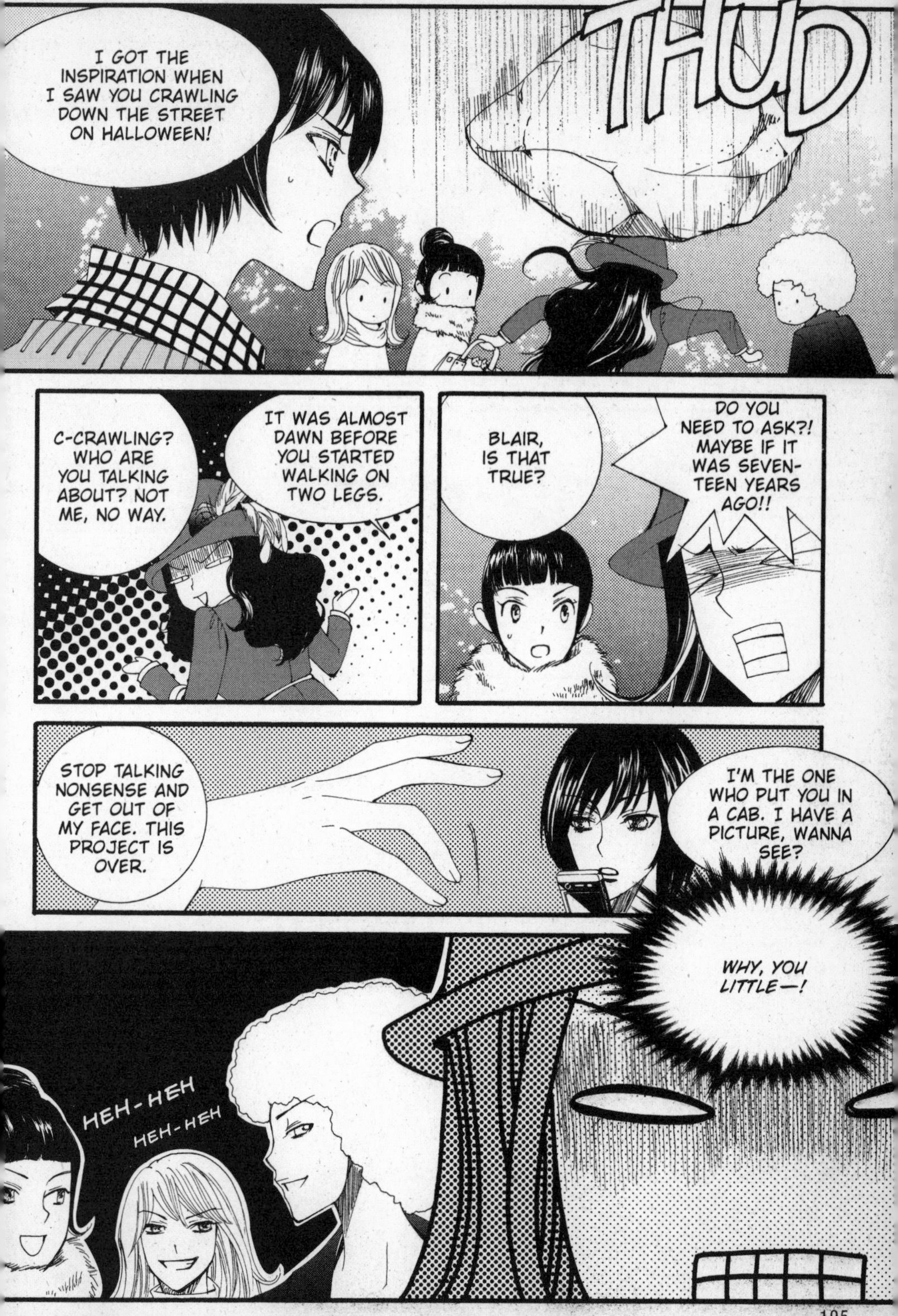
I GOT THE INSPIRATION WHEN I SAW YOU CRAWLING DOWN THE STREET ON HALLOWEEN!
THUD
C-CRAWLING? WHO ARE YOU TALKING ABOUT? NOT ME, NO WAY.
IT WAS ALMOST DAWN BEFORE YOU STARTED WALKING ON TWO LEGS.
BLAIR, IS THAT TRUE?
DO YOU NEED TO ASK?! MAYBE IF IT WAS SEVENTEEN YEARS AGO!!
STOP TALKING NONSENSE AND GET OUT OF MY FACE. THIS PROJECT IS OVER.
I'M THE ONE WHO PUT YOU IN A CAB. I HAVE A PICTURE, WANNA SEE?
WHY, YOU LITTLE—!
HEH-HEH
HEH-HEH

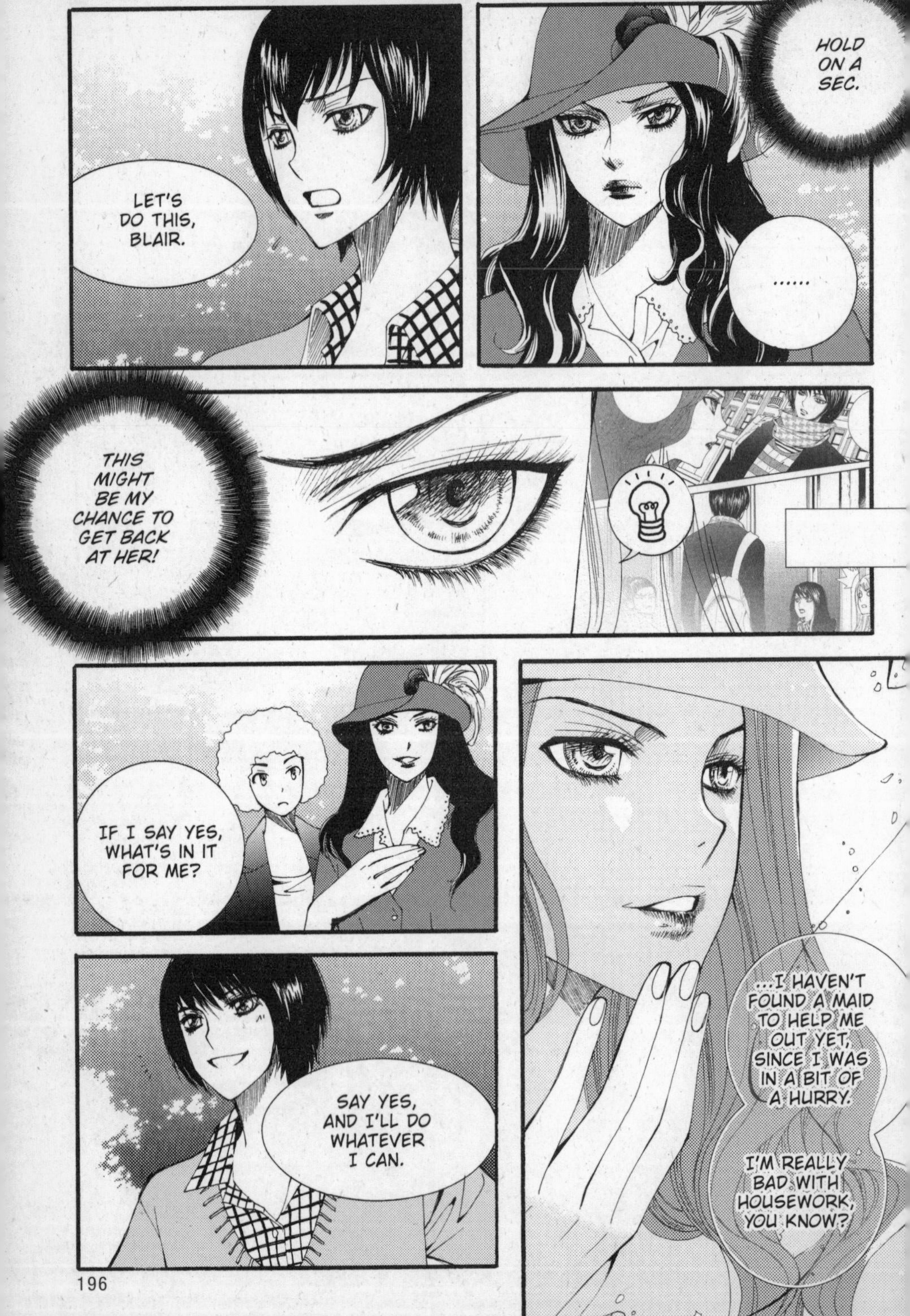
LET'S DO THIS, BLAIR.
HOLD ON A SEC.
......
THIS MIGHT BE MY CHANCE TO GET BACK AT HER!
IF I SAY YES, WHAT'S IN IT FOR ME?
SAY YES, AND I'LL DO WHATEVER I CAN.
...I HAVEN'T FOUND A MAID TO HELP ME OUT YET, SINCE I WAS IN A BIT OF A HURRY.
I'M REALLY BAD WITH HOUSEWORK, YOU KNOW?

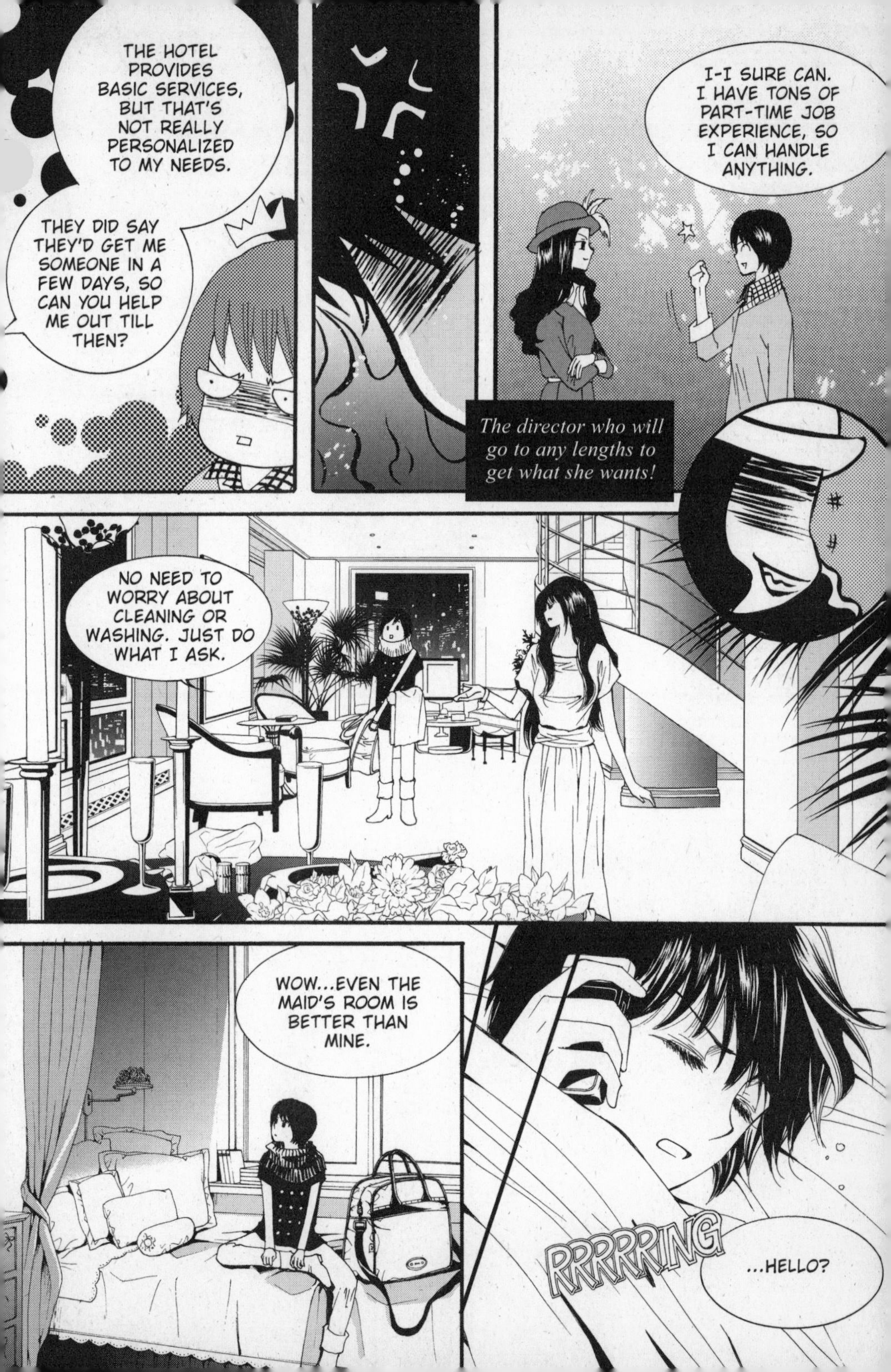
THE HOTEL PROVIDES BASIC SERVICES, BUT THAT'S NOT REALLY PERSONALIZED TO MY NEEDS.
THEY DID SAY THEY'D GET ME SOMEONE IN A FEW DAYS, SO CAN YOU HELP ME OUT TILL THEN?
I-I SURE CAN. I HAVE TONS OF PART-TIME JOB EXPERIENCE, SO I CAN HANDLE ANYTHING.
The director who will go to any lengths to get what she wants!
NO NEED TO WORRY ABOUT CLEANING OR WASHING. JUST DO WHAT I ASK.
WOW...EVEN THE MAID'S ROOM IS BETTER THAN MINE.
RRRRRING
...HELLO?

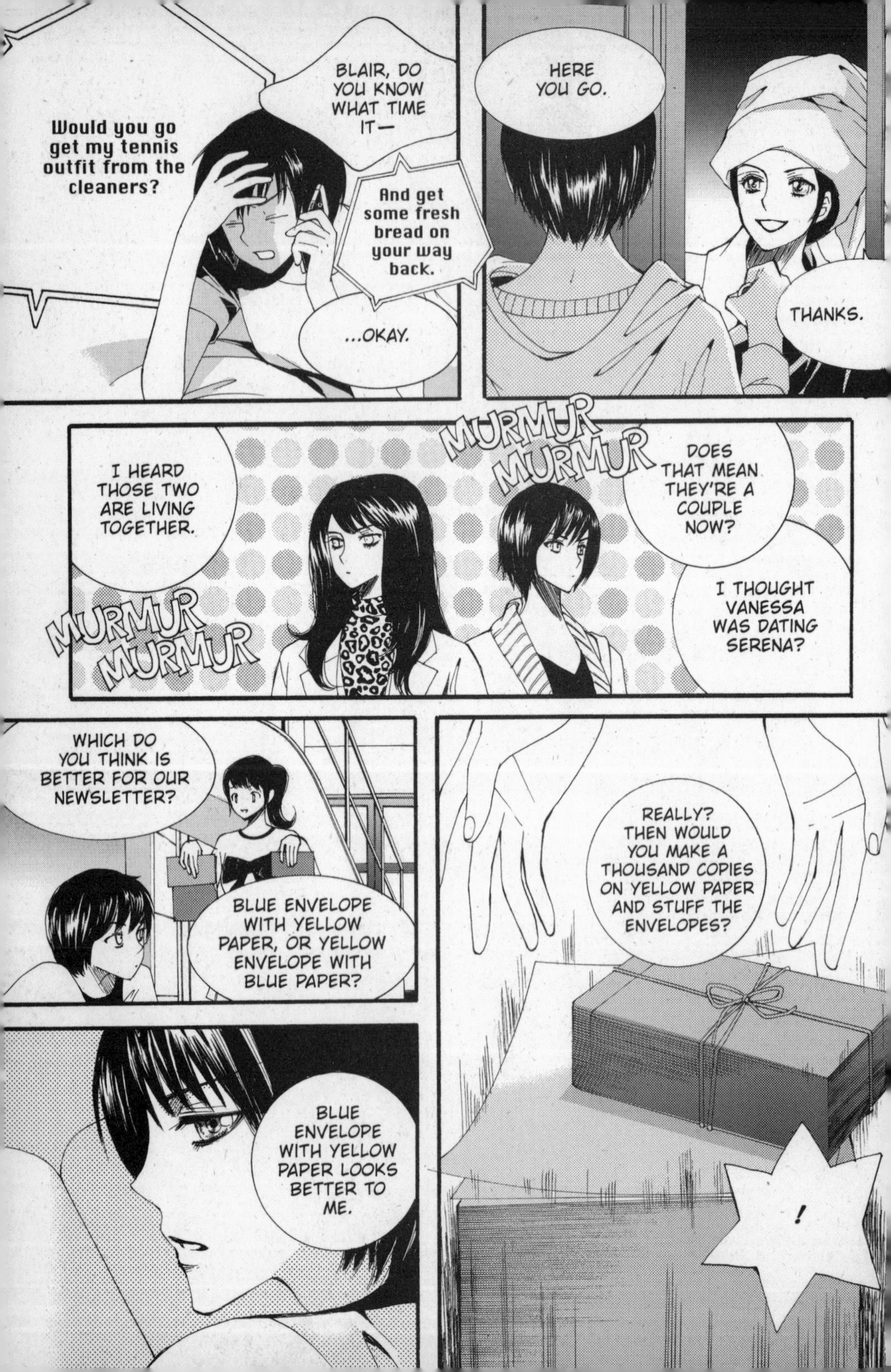
Would you go get my tennis outfit from the cleaners?
BLAIR, DO YOU KNOW WHAT TIME IT—
And get some fresh bread on your way back.
...OKAY.
HERE YOU GO.
THANKS.
I HEARD THOSE TWO ARE LIVING TOGETHER.
MURMUR MURMUR
MURMUR MURMUR
DOES THAT MEAN THEY'RE A COUPLE NOW?
I THOUGHT VANESSA WAS DATING SERENA?
WHICH DO YOU THINK IS BETTER FOR OUR NEWSLETTER?
BLUE ENVELOPE WITH YELLOW PAPER, OR YELLOW ENVELOPE WITH BLUE PAPER?
REALLY? THEN WOULD YOU MAKE A THOUSAND COPIES ON YELLOW PAPER AND STUFF THE ENVELOPES?
BLUE ENVELOPE WITH YELLOW PAPER LOOKS BETTER TO ME.
!

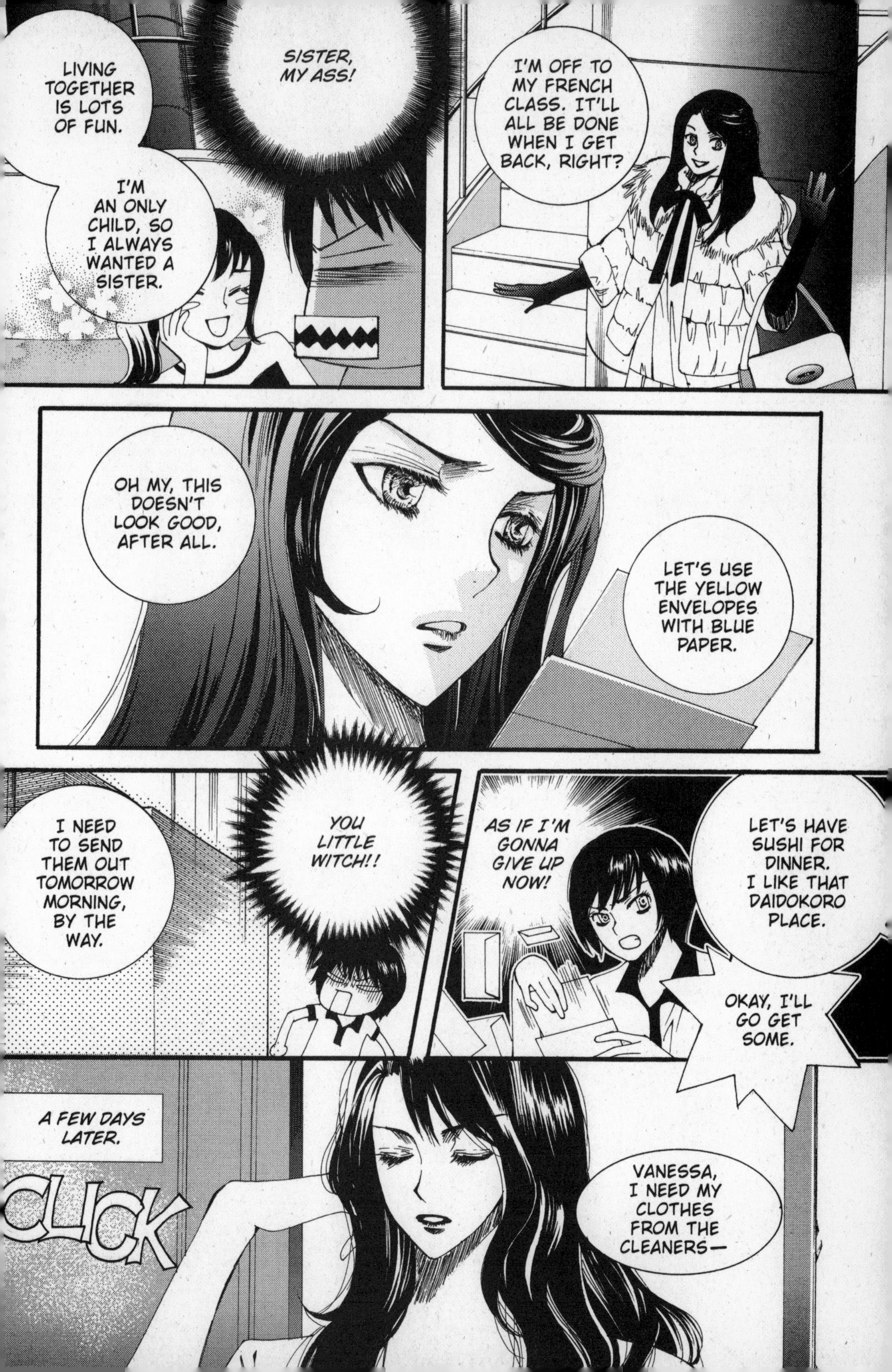

LIVING TOGETHER IS LOTS OF FUN.
I'M AN ONLY CHILD, SO I ALWAYS WANTED A SISTER.
SISTER, MY ASS!
I'M OFF TO MY FRENCH CLASS. IT'LL ALL BE DONE WHEN I GET BACK, RIGHT?
OH MY, THIS DOESN'T LOOK GOOD, AFTER ALL.
LET'S USE THE YELLOW ENVELOPES WITH BLUE PAPER.
I NEED TO SEND THEM OUT TOMORROW MORNING, BY THE WAY.
YOU LITTLE WITCH!!
AS IF I'M GONNA GIVE UP NOW!
LET'S HAVE SUSHI FOR DINNER. I LIKE THAT DAIDOKORO PLACE.
OKAY, I'LL GO GET SOME.
A FEW DAYS LATER.
CLICK
VANESSA, I NEED MY CLOTHES FROM THE CLEANERS—

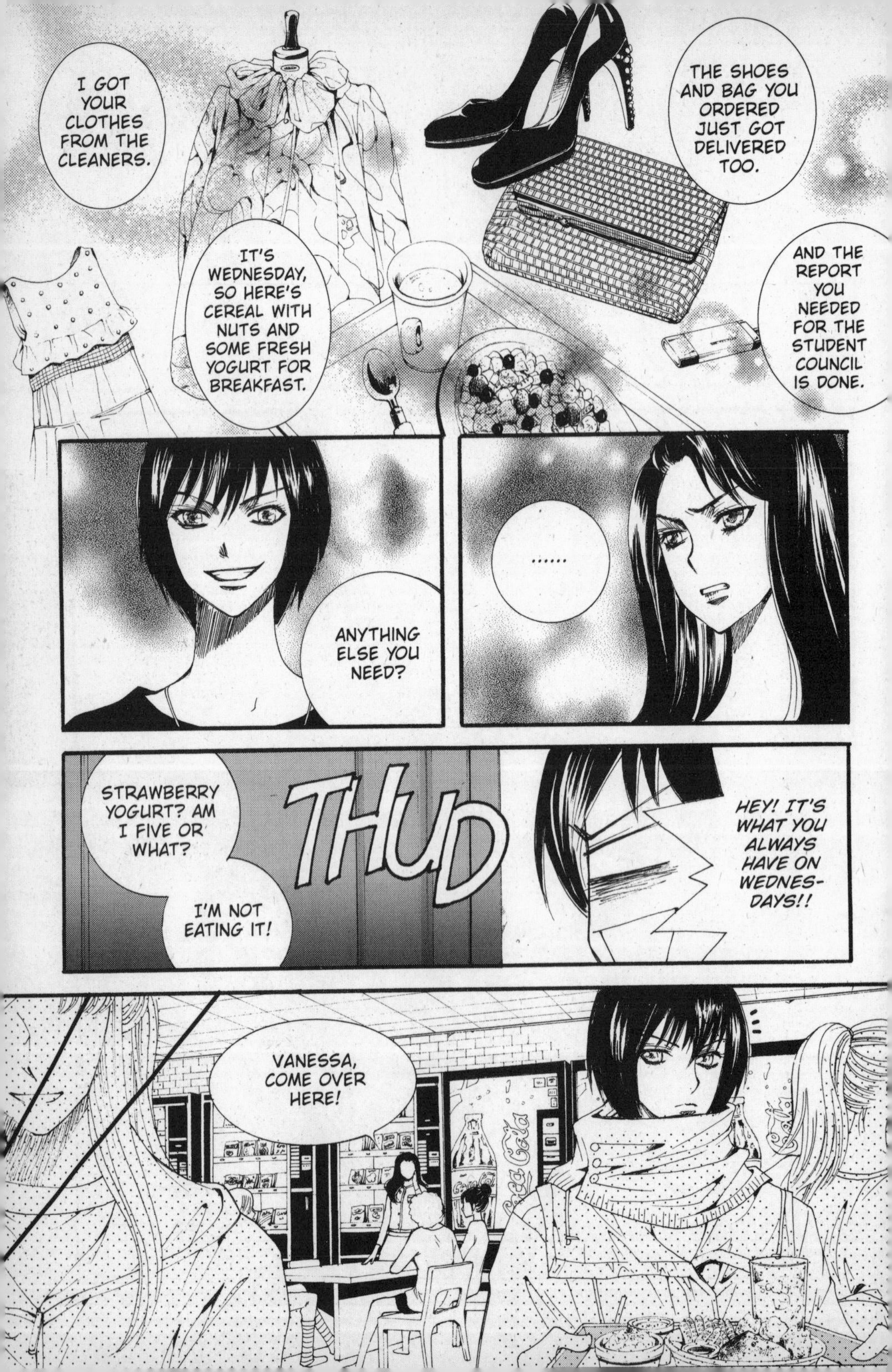
I GOT YOUR CLOTHES FROM THE CLEANERS.
THE SHOES AND BAG YOU ORDERED JUST GOT DELIVERED TOO.
IT'S WEDNESDAY, SO HERE'S CEREAL WITH NUTS AND SOME FRESH YOGURT FOR BREAKFAST.
AND THE REPORT YOU NEEDED FOR THE STUDENT COUNCIL IS DONE.
ANYTHING ELSE YOU NEED?
......
STRAWBERRY YOGURT? AM I FIVE OR WHAT?
I'M NOT EATING IT!
THUD
HEY! IT'S WHAT YOU ALWAYS HAVE ON WEDNES-DAYS!!
VANESSA, COME OVER HERE!

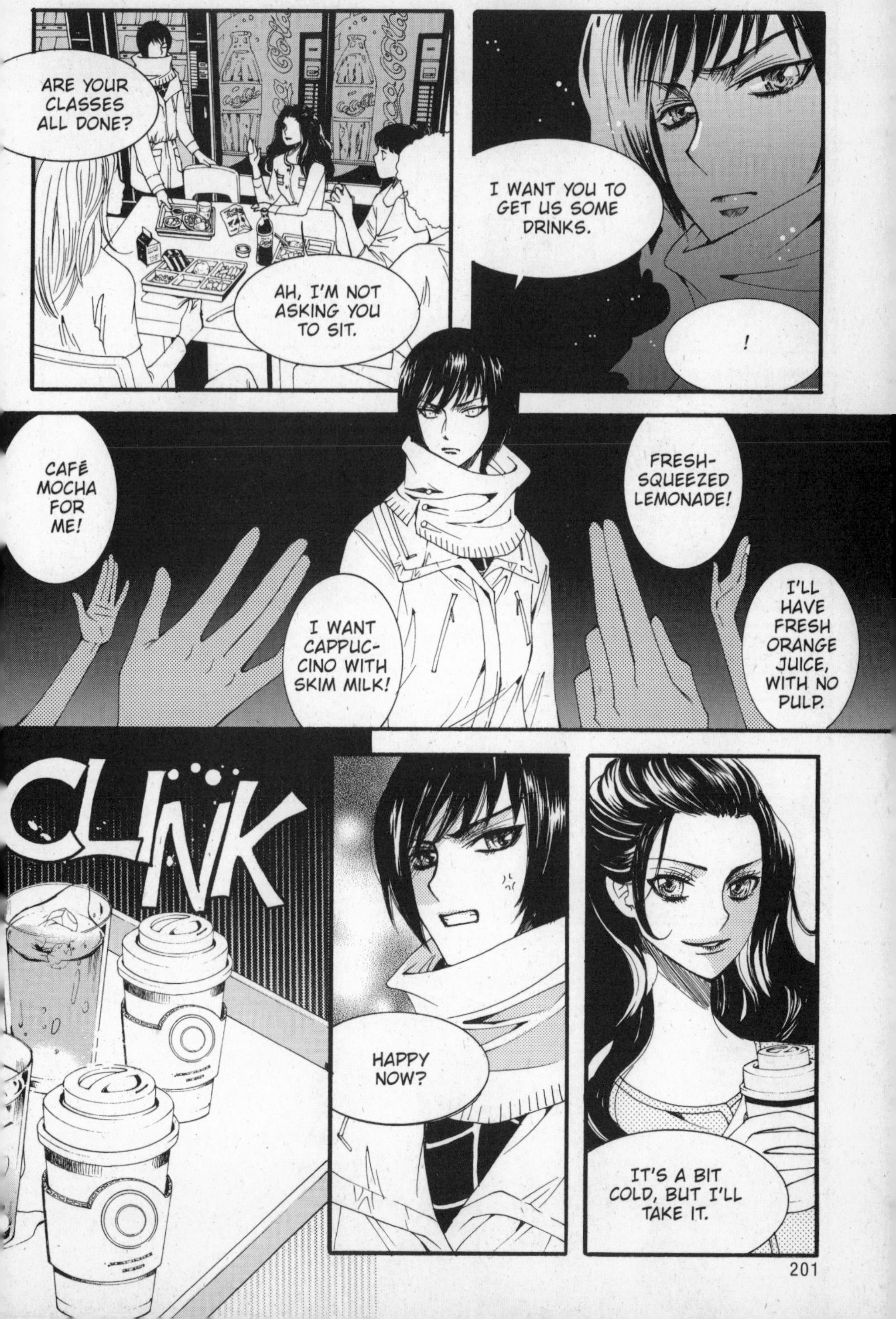
ARE YOUR CLASSES ALL DONE?
AH, I'M NOT ASKING YOU TO SIT.
I WANT YOU TO GET US SOME DRINKS.
!
CAFÉ MOCHA FOR ME!
I WANT CAPPUC-CINO WITH SKIM MILK!
FRESH-SQUEEZED LEMONADE!
I'LL HAVE FRESH ORANGE JUICE, WITH NO PULP.
CLINK
HAPPY NOW?
IT'S A BIT COLD, BUT I'LL TAKE IT.

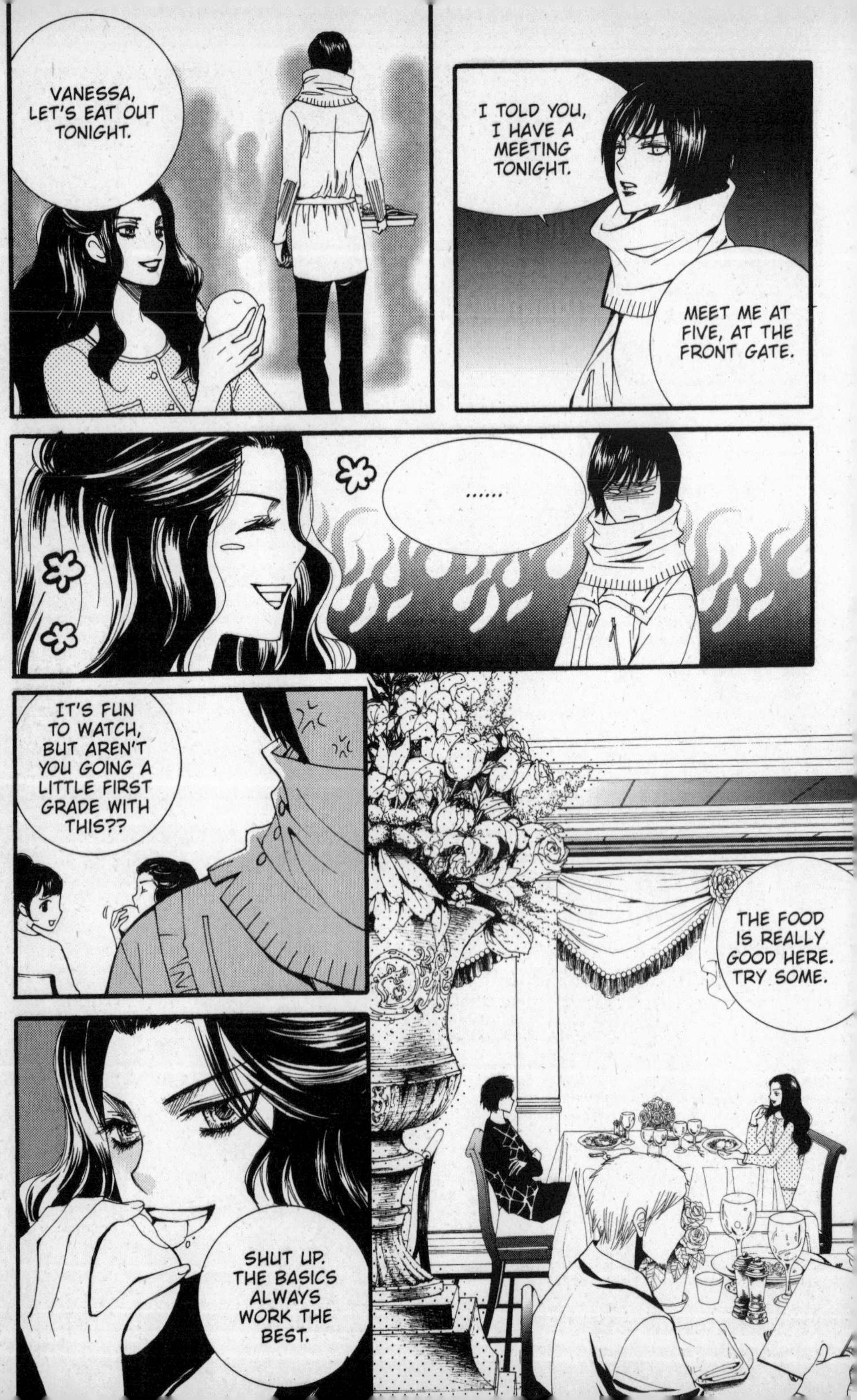
VANESSA, LET'S EAT OUT TONIGHT.
I TOLD YOU, I HAVE A MEETING TONIGHT.
MEET ME AT FIVE, AT THE FRONT GATE.
......
IT'S FUN TO WATCH, BUT AREN'T YOU GOING A LITTLE FIRST GRADE WITH THIS??
SHUT UP. THE BASICS ALWAYS WORK THE BEST.
THE FOOD IS REALLY GOOD HERE. TRY SOME.

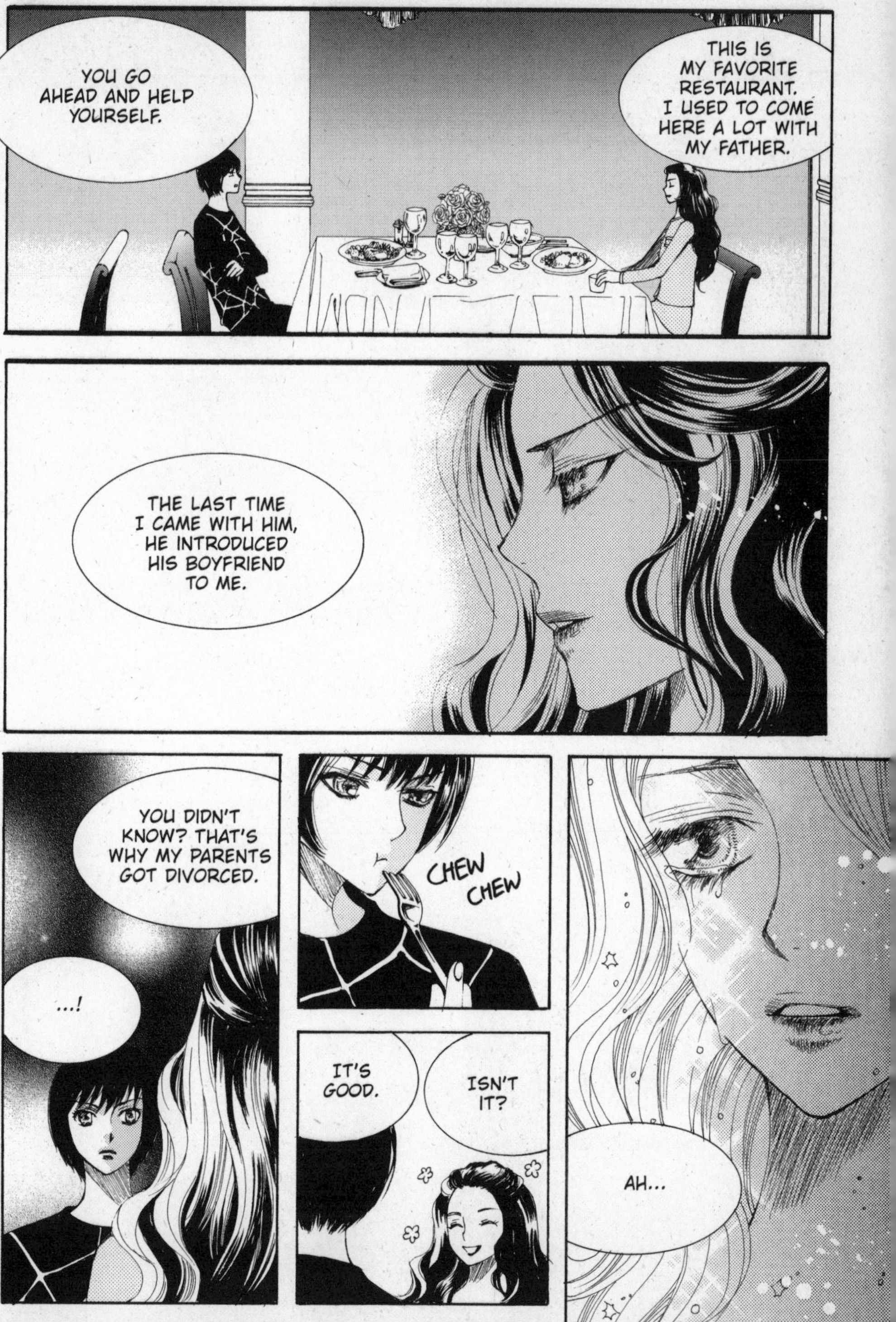
YOU GO AHEAD AND HELP YOURSELF.
THIS IS MY FAVORITE RESTAURANT. I USED TO COME HERE A LOT WITH MY FATHER.
THE LAST TIME I CAME WITH HIM, HE INTRODUCED HIS BOYFRIEND TO ME.
YOU DIDN'T KNOW? THAT'S WHY MY PARENTS GOT DIVORCED.
...!
CHEW CHEW
IT'S GOOD.
ISN'T IT?
AH...

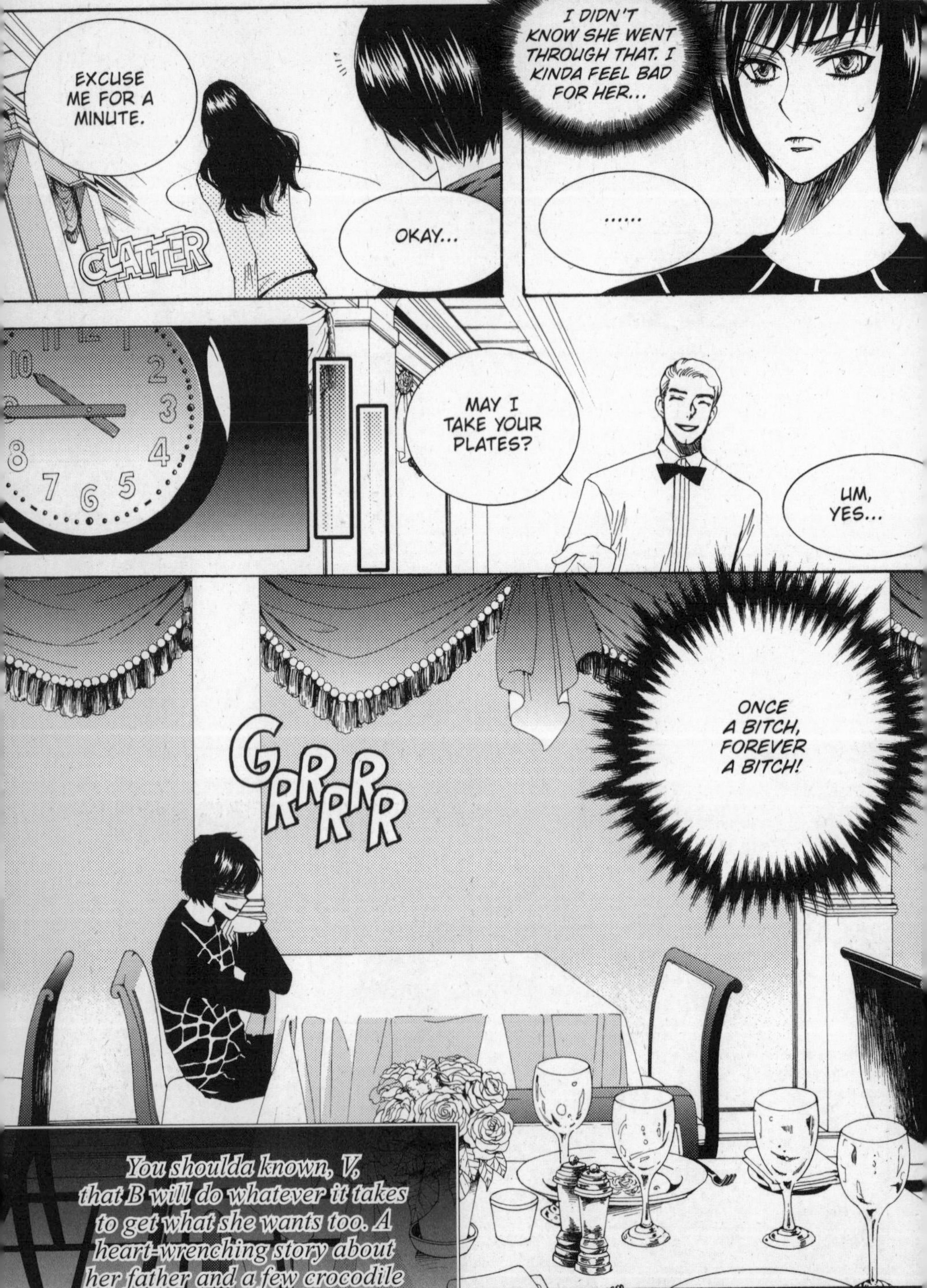
EXCUSE ME FOR A MINUTE.
CLATTER
OKAY...
I DIDN'T KNOW SHE WENT THROUGH THAT. I KINDA FEEL BAD FOR HER...
......
MAY I TAKE YOUR PLATES?
UM, YES...
GRRRRR
ONCE A BITCH, FOREVER A BITCH!
You shoulda known, V, that B will do whatever it takes to get what she wants too. A heart-wrenching story about her father and a few crocodile tears — it's a classic!

gossip girl

FOR YOUR EYES ONLY

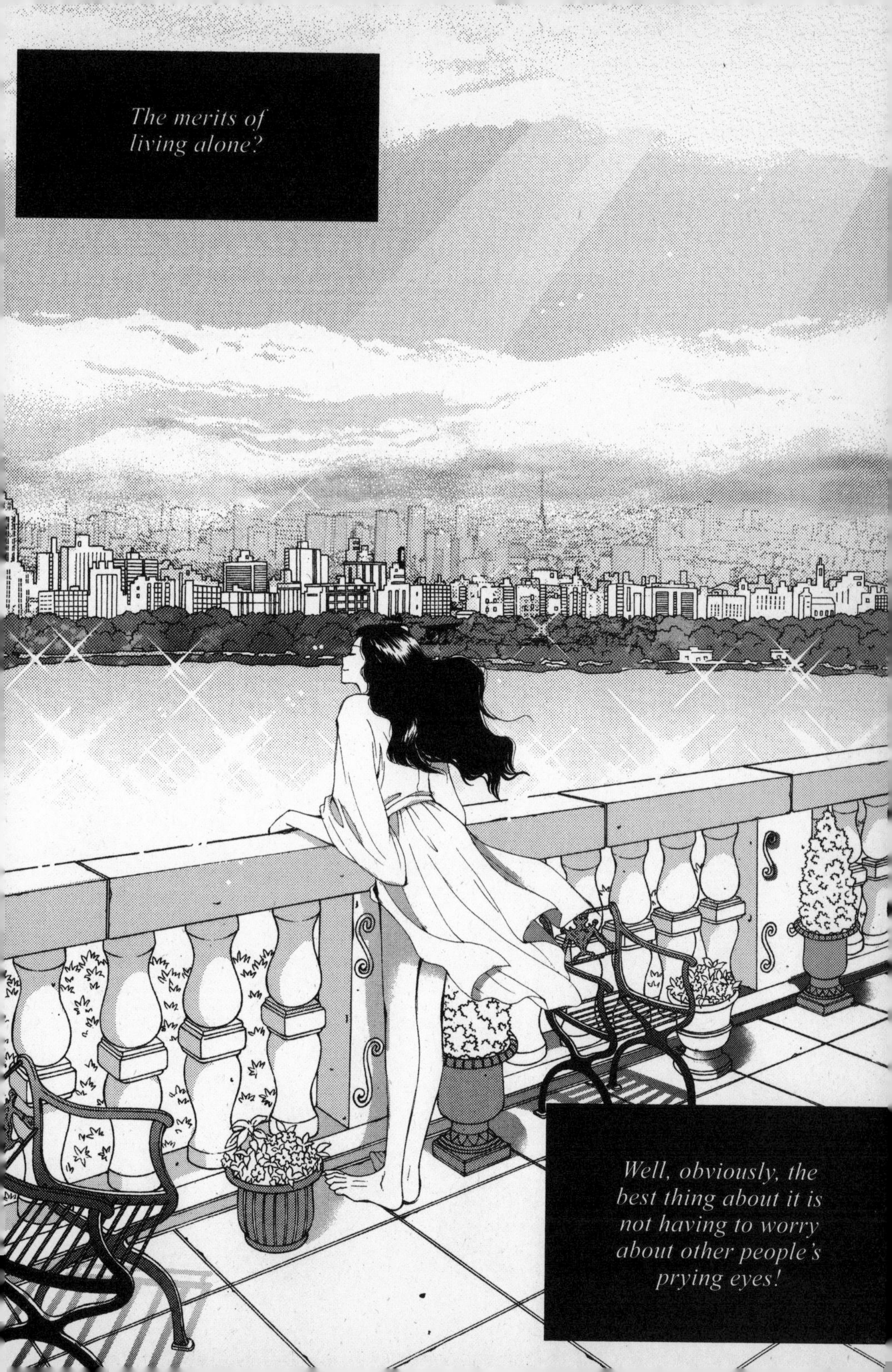
The merits of living alone?
Well, obviously, the best thing about it is not having to worry about other people's prying eyes!

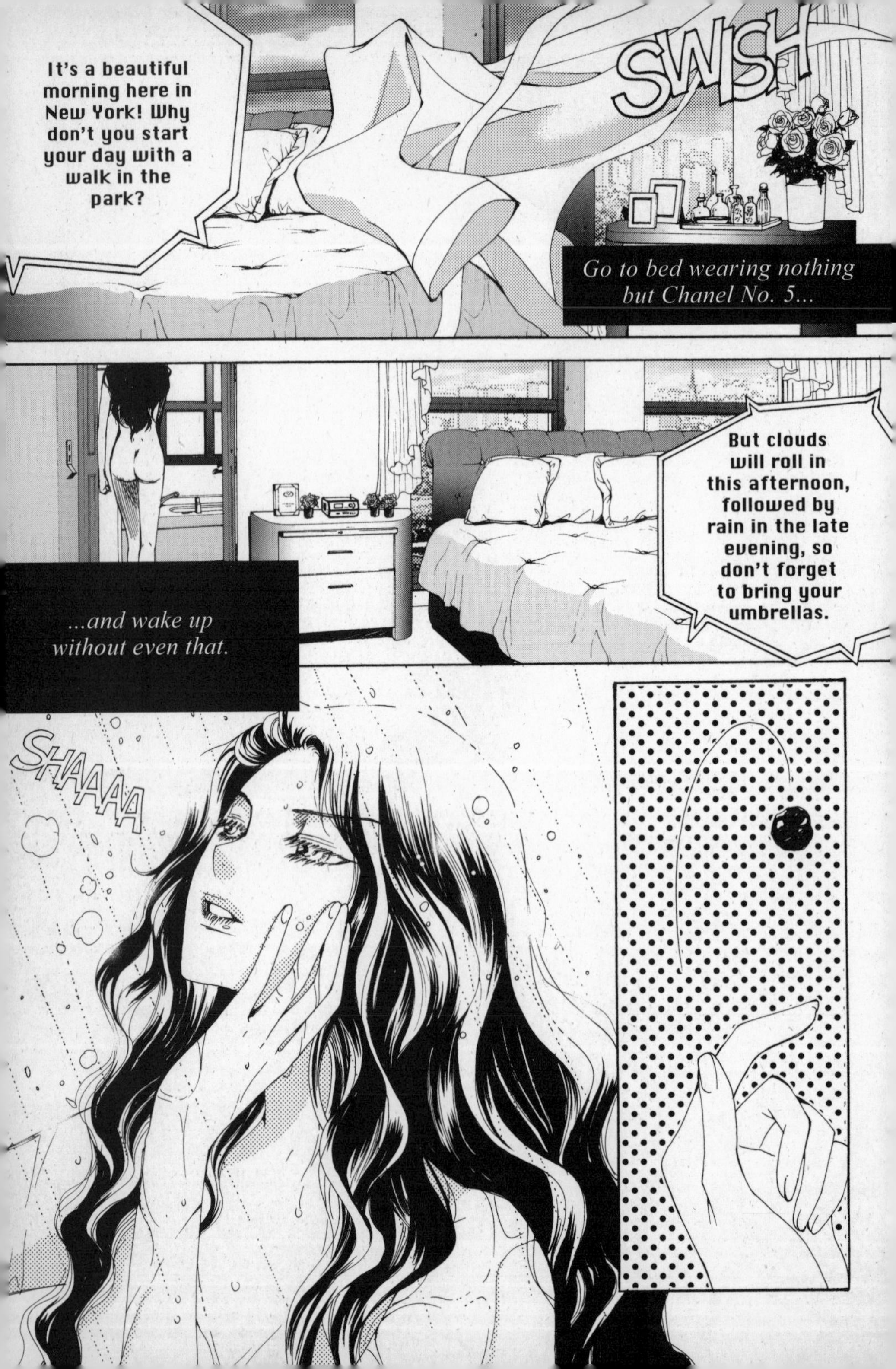

It's a beautiful morning here in New York! Why don't you start your day with a walk in the park?
SWISH
Go to bed wearing nothing but Chanel No. 5...
...and wake up without even that.
But clouds will roll in this afternoon, followed by rain in the late evening, so don't forget to bring your umbrellas.
SHAAAAA

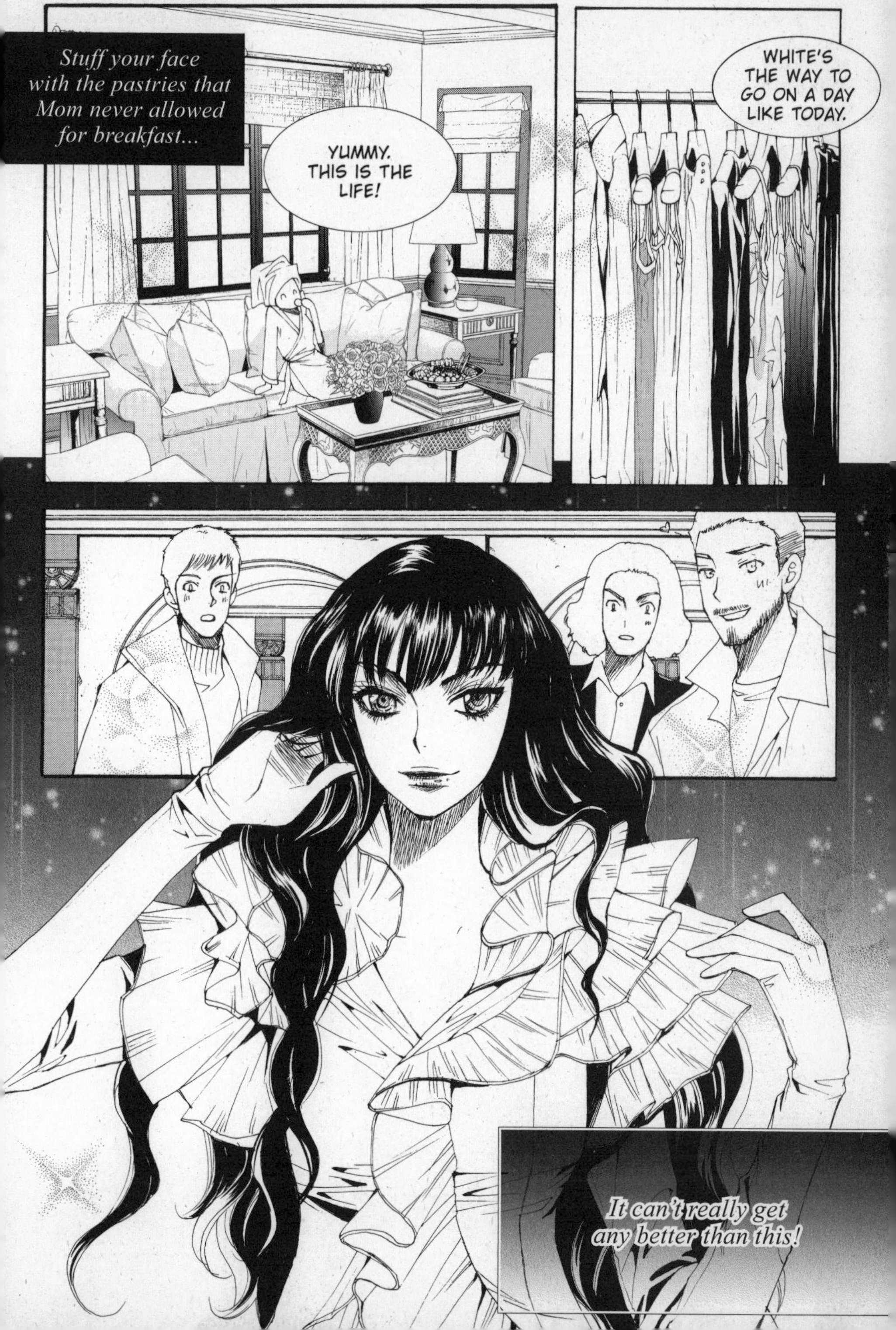
Stuff your face with the pastries that Mom never allowed for breakfast...
YUMMY. THIS IS THE LIFE!
WHITE'S THE WAY TO GO ON A DAY LIKE TODAY.
It can't really get any better than this!

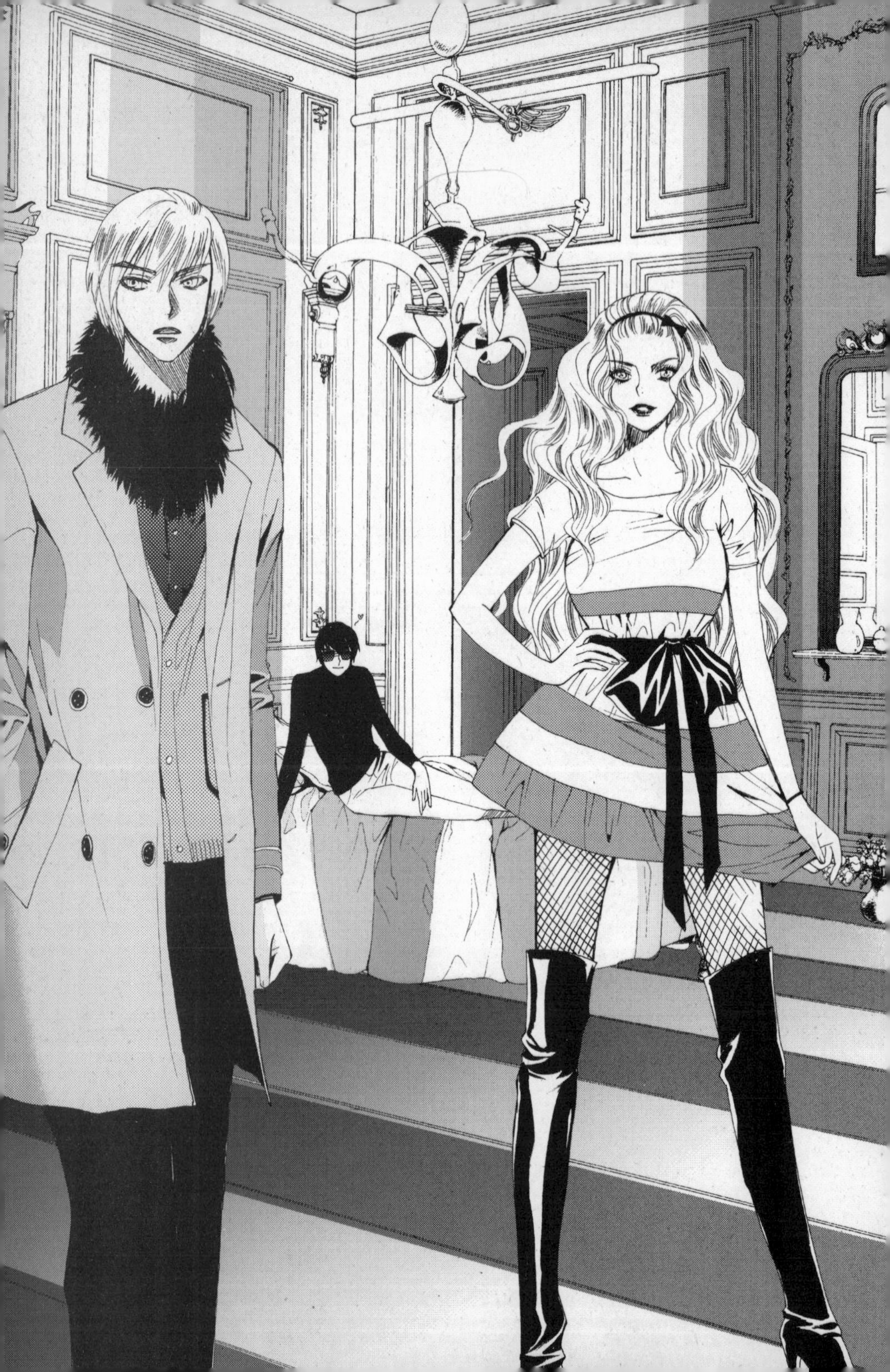

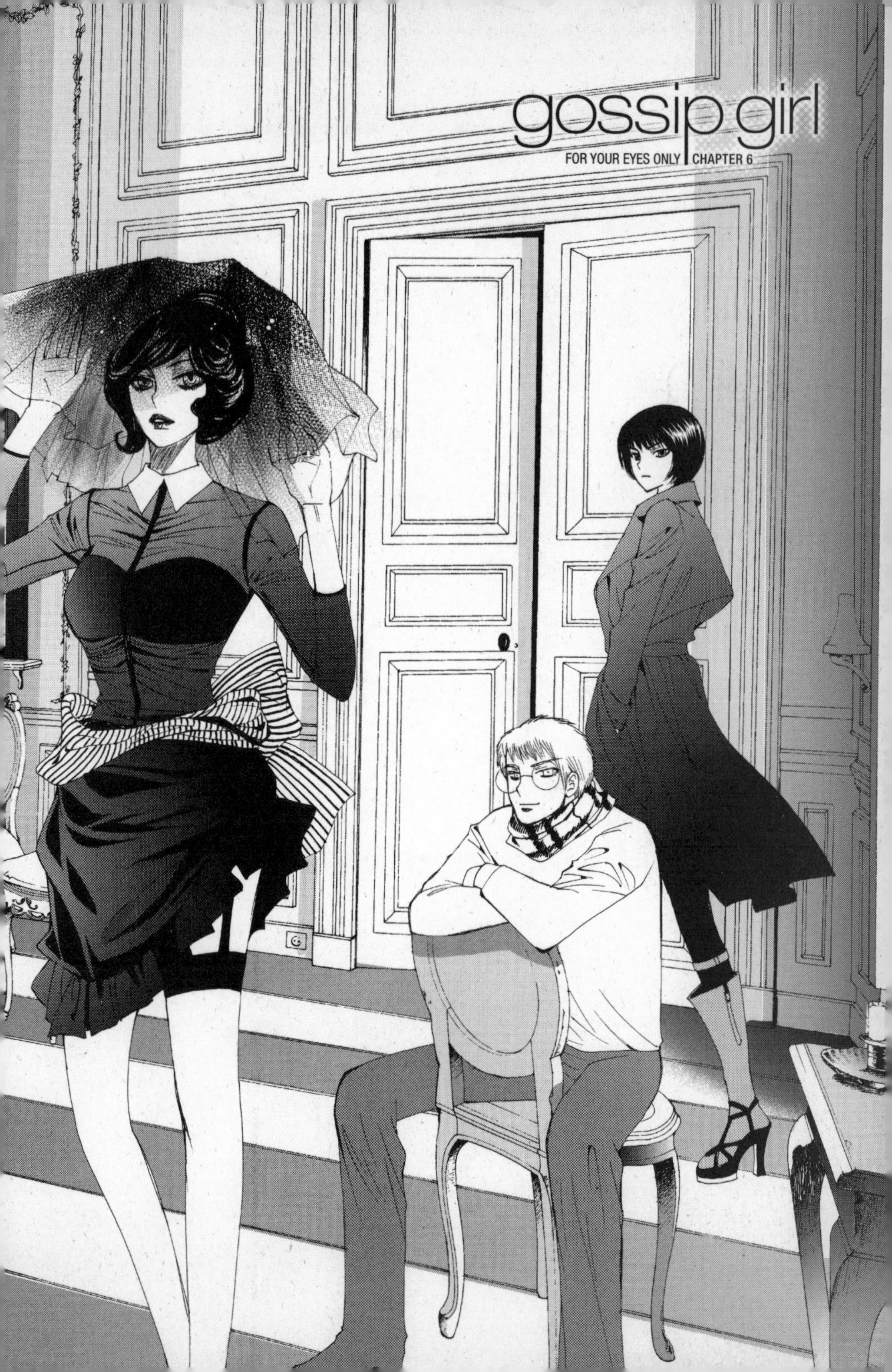
gossip girl
FOR YOUR EYES ONLY | CHAPTER 6

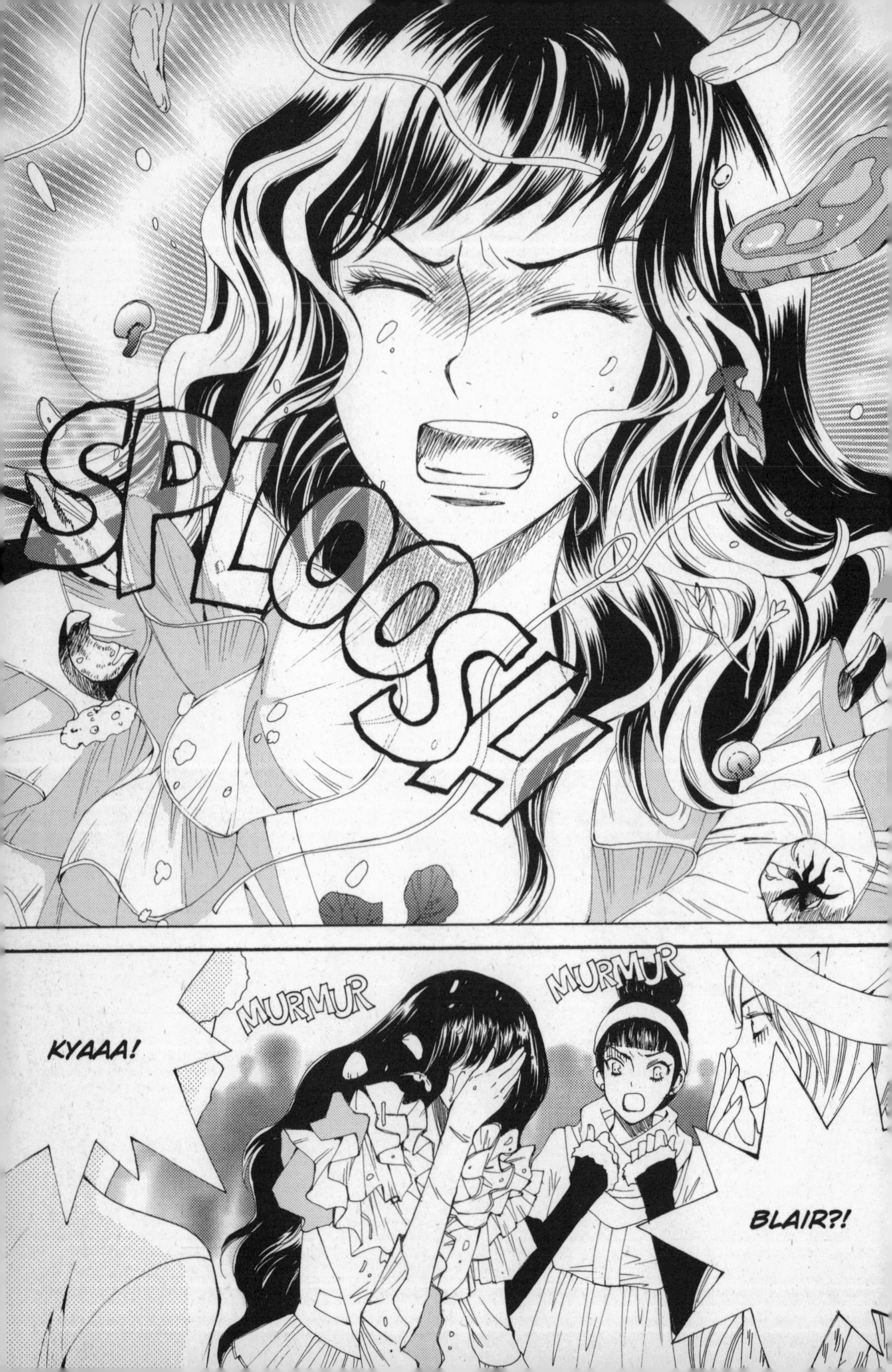
SPLOOSH!
KYAAA!
MURMUR
MURMUR
BLAIR?!

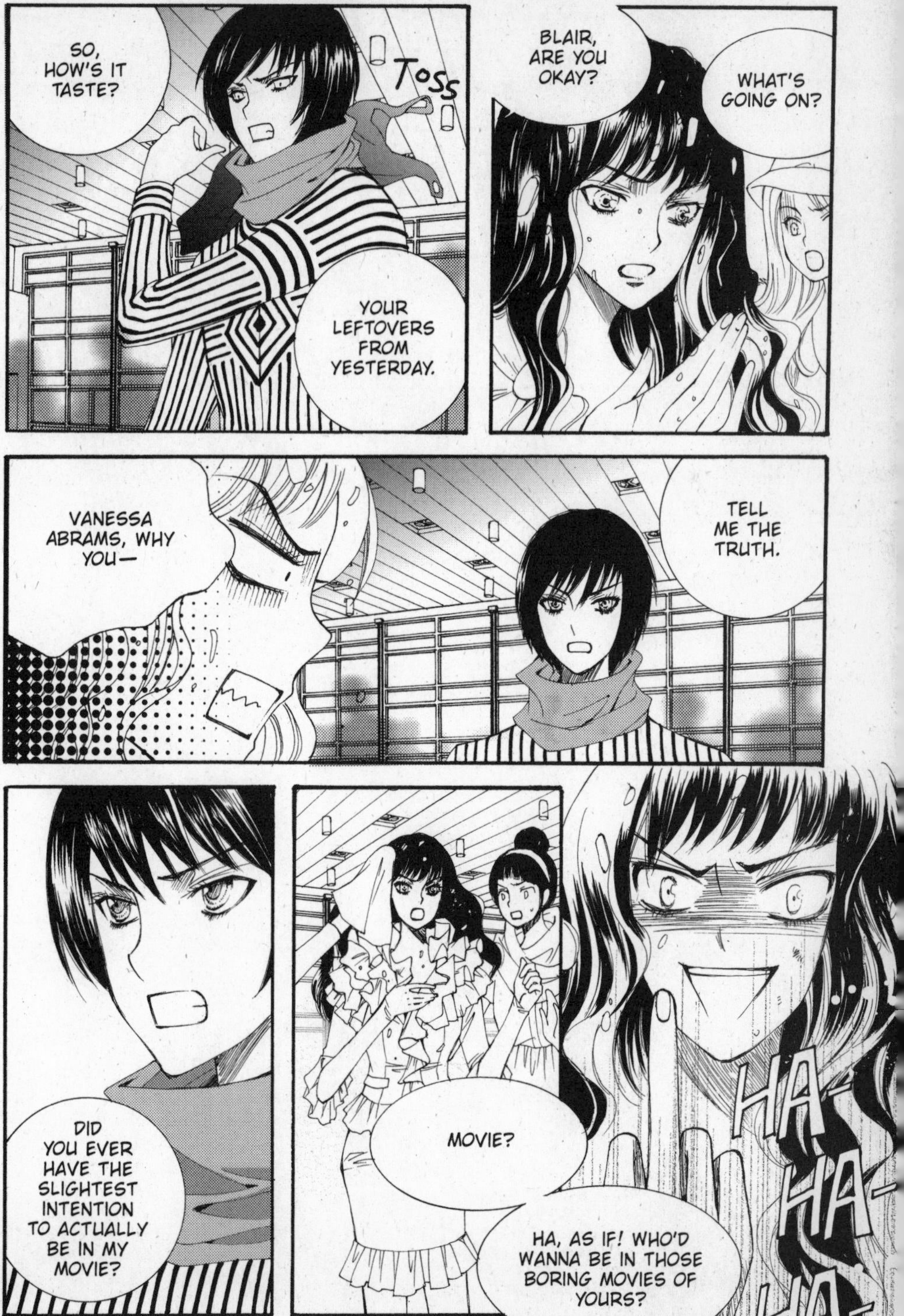
SO, HOW'S IT TASTE?
TOSS
YOUR LEFTOVERS FROM YESTERDAY.
BLAIR, ARE YOU OKAY?
WHAT'S GOING ON?
VANESSA ABRAMS, WHY YOU—
TELL ME THE TRUTH.
DID YOU EVER HAVE THE SLIGHTEST INTENTION TO ACTUALLY BE IN MY MOVIE?
MOVIE?
HA, AS IF! WHO'D WANNA BE IN THOSE BORING MOVIES OF YOURS?
HA- HA- HA-

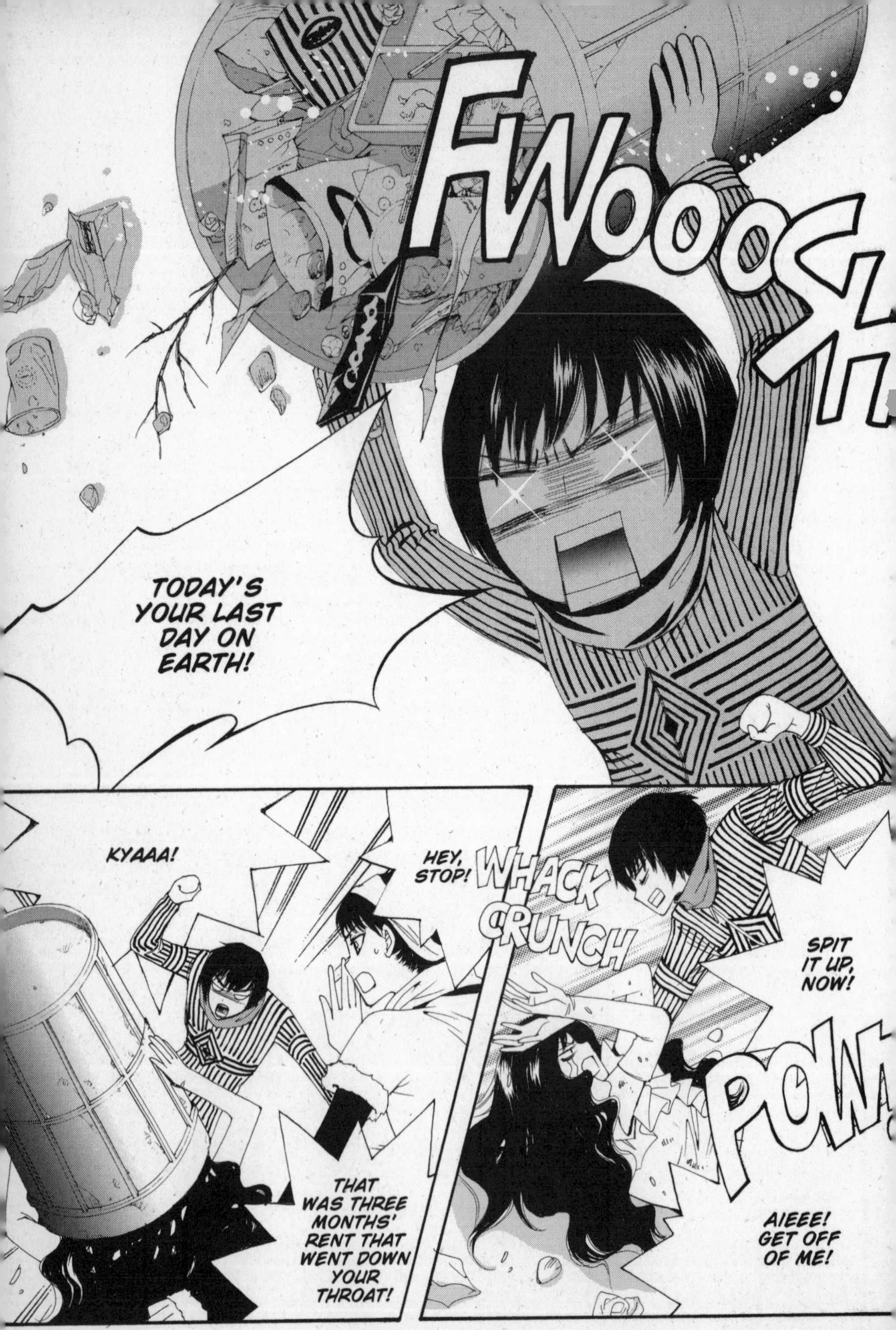
FWOOOSH
TODAY'S YOUR LAST DAY ON EARTH!
KYAAA!
HEY, STOP!
THAT WAS THREE MONTHS' RENT THAT WENT DOWN YOUR THROAT!
WHACK
CRUNCH
SPIT IT UP, NOW!
POW
AIEEE! GET OFF OF ME!

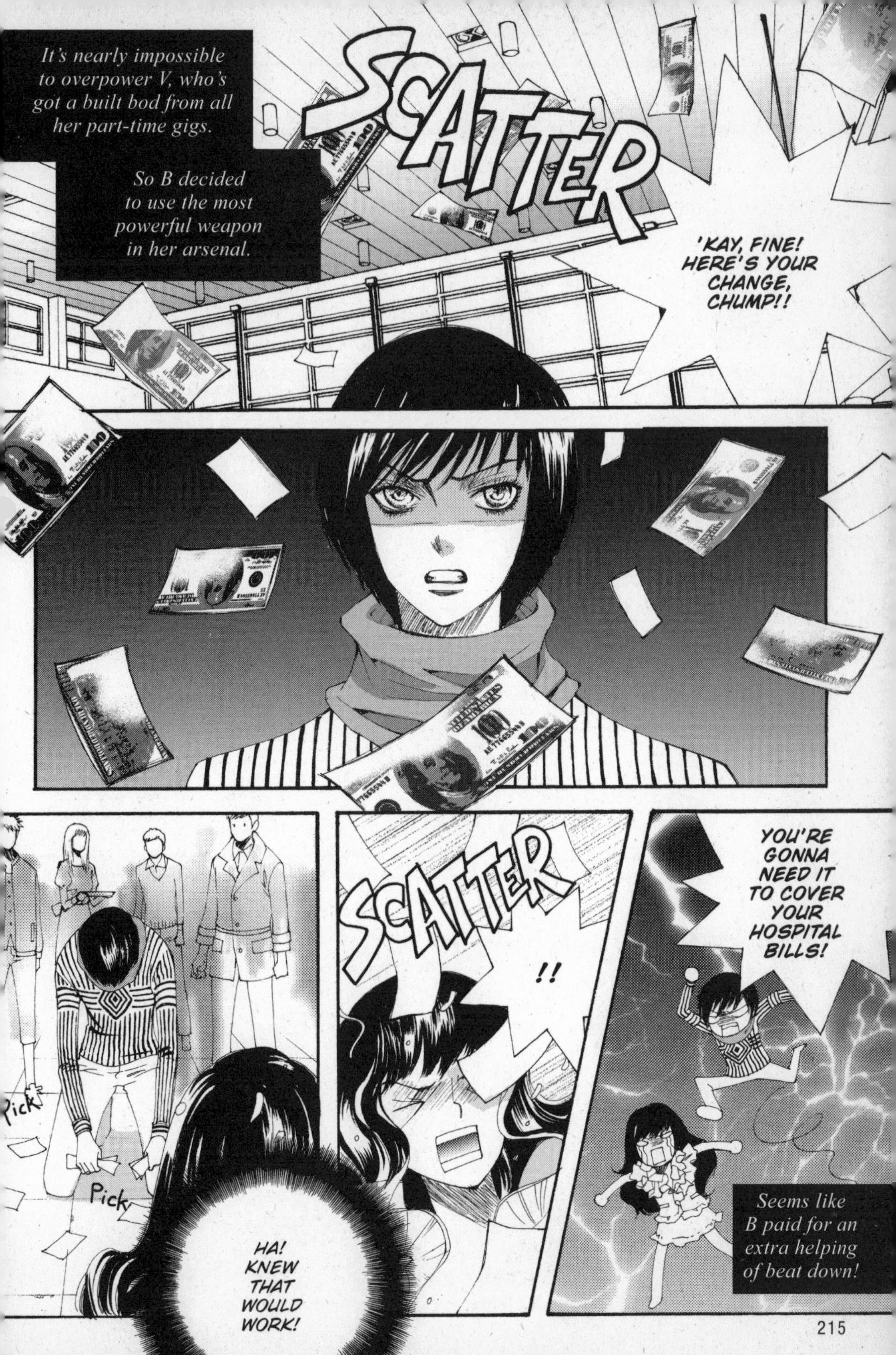

It's nearly impossible to overpower V, who's got a built bod from all her part-time gigs.
So B decided to use the most powerful weapon in her arsenal.
SCATTER
'KAY, FINE! HERE'S YOUR CHANGE, CHUMP!!
Pick
Pick
HA! KNEW THAT WOULD WORK!
SCATTER
!!
YOU'RE GONNA NEED IT TO COVER YOUR HOSPITAL BILLS!
Seems like B paid for an extra helping of beat down!

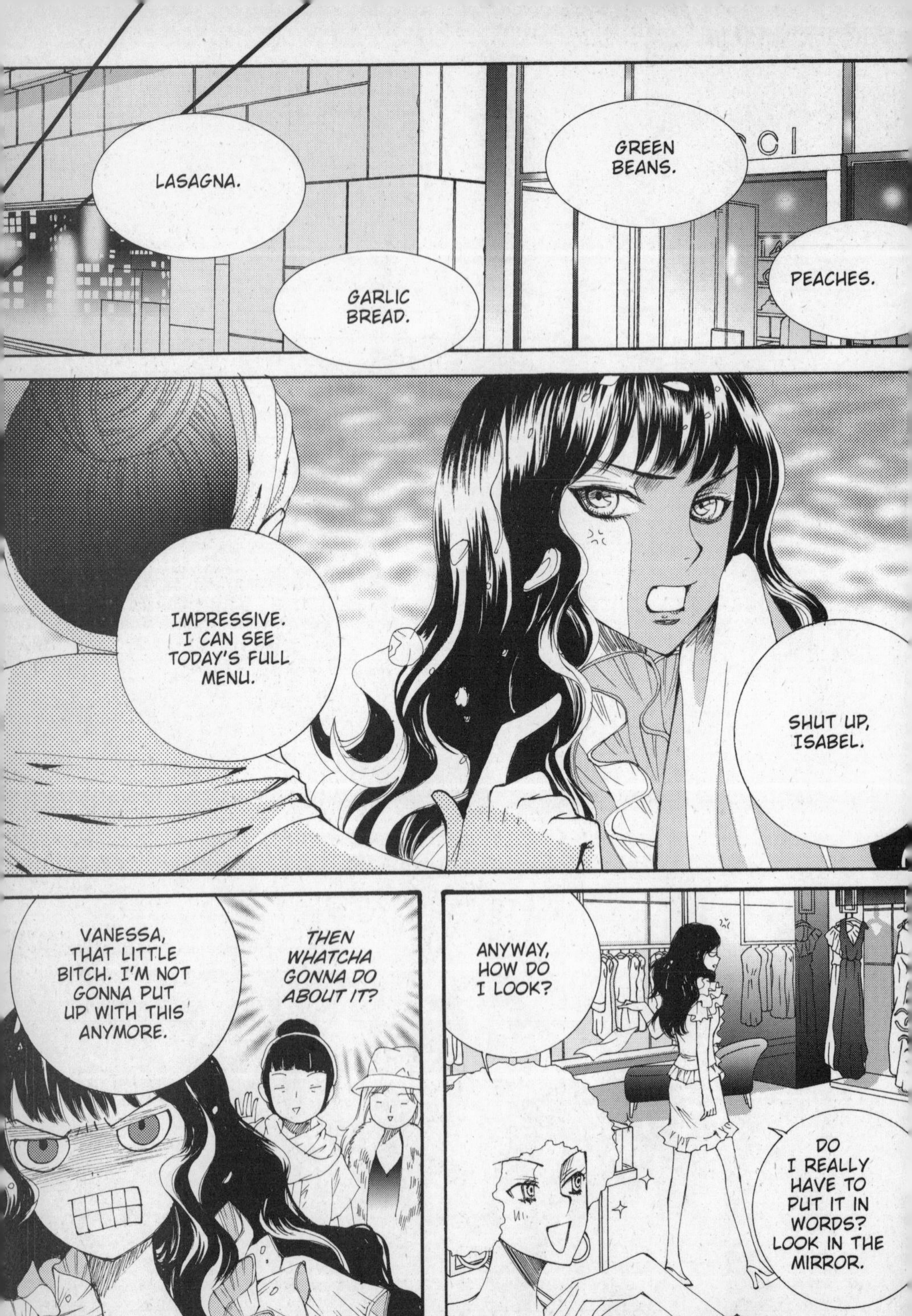
LASAGNA.
GARLIC BREAD.
GREEN BEANS.
PEACHES.
IMPRESSIVE. I CAN SEE TODAY'S FULL MENU.
SHUT UP, ISABEL.
VANESSA, THAT LITTLE BITCH. I'M NOT GONNA PUT UP WITH THIS ANYMORE.
THEN WHATCHA GONNA DO ABOUT IT?
ANYWAY, HOW DO I LOOK?
DO I REALLY HAVE TO PUT IT IN WORDS? LOOK IN THE MIRROR.

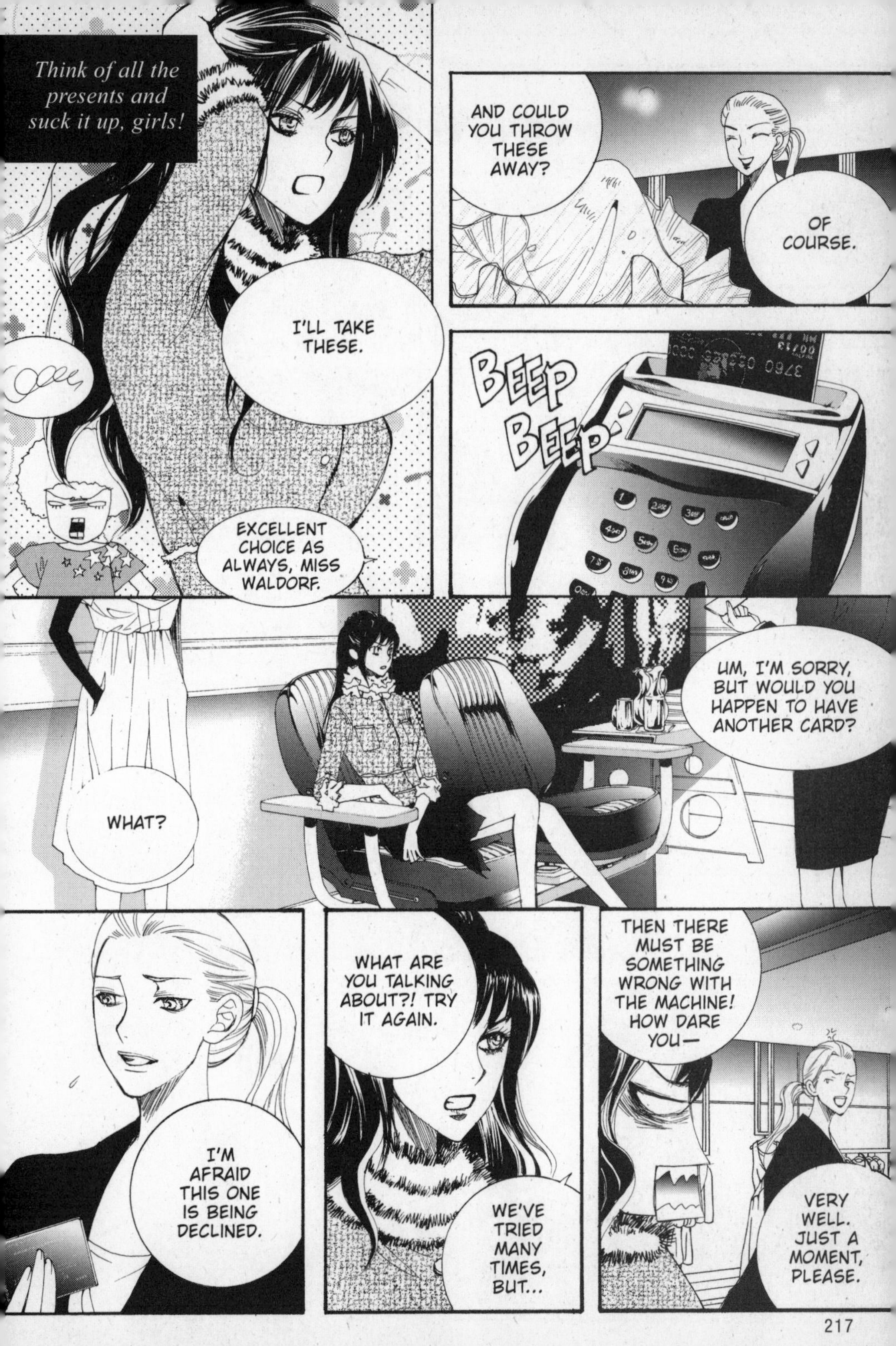
Think of all the presents and suck it up, girls!
I'LL TAKE THESE.
EXCELLENT CHOICE AS ALWAYS, MISS WALDORF.
AND COULD YOU THROW THESE AWAY?
OF COURSE.
BEEP BEEP
WHAT?
UM, I'M SORRY, BUT WOULD YOU HAPPEN TO HAVE ANOTHER CARD?
I'M AFRAID THIS ONE IS BEING DECLINED.
WHAT ARE YOU TALKING ABOUT?! TRY IT AGAIN.
WE'VE TRIED MANY TIMES, BUT...
THEN THERE MUST BE SOMETHING WRONG WITH THE MACHINE! HOW DARE YOU—
VERY WELL. JUST A MOMENT, PLEASE.

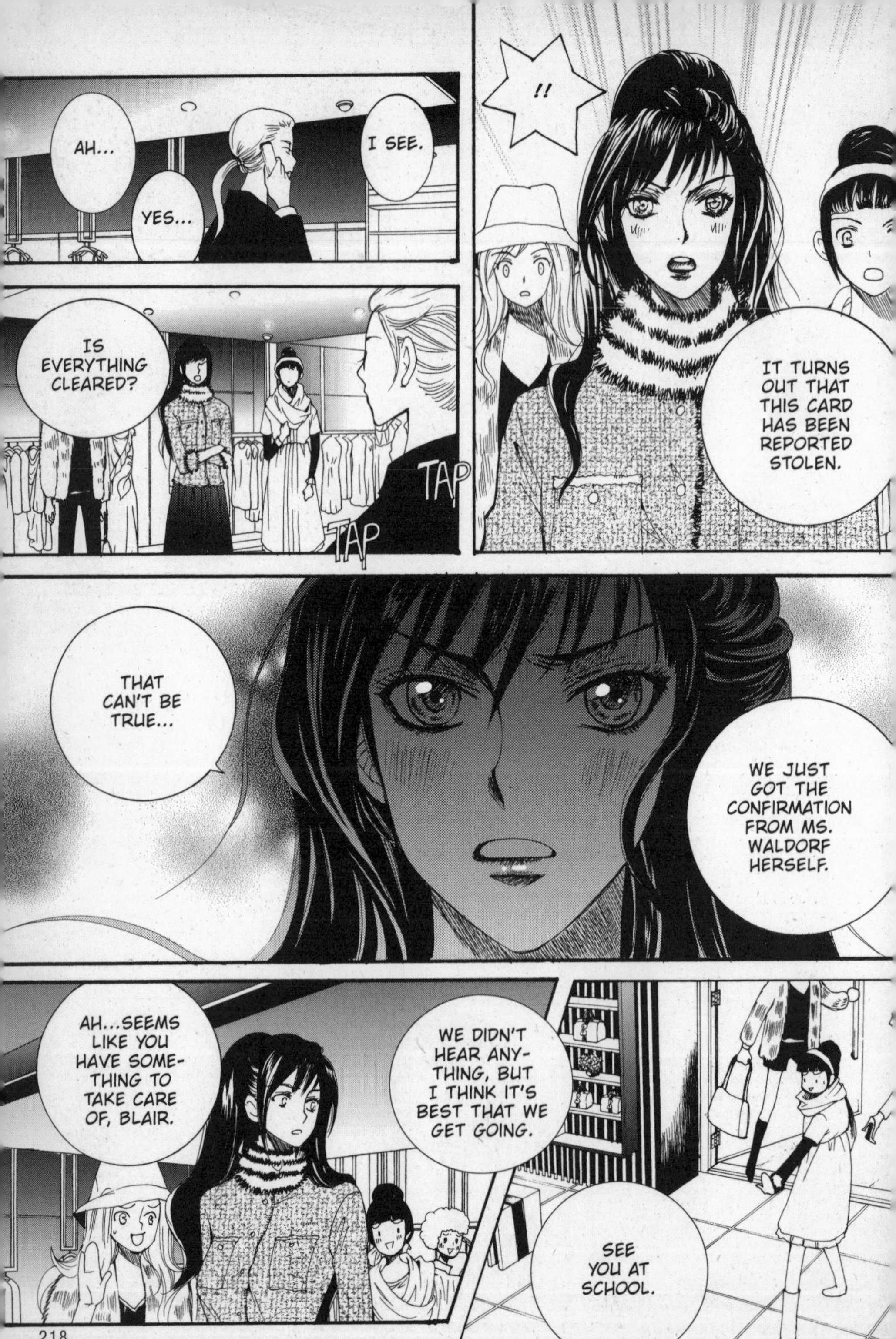
AH...
YES...
I SEE.
IS EVERYTHING CLEARED?
TAP
TAP
!!
IT TURNS OUT THAT THIS CARD HAS BEEN REPORTED STOLEN.
THAT CAN'T BE TRUE...
WE JUST GOT THE CONFIRMATION FROM MS. WALDORF HERSELF.
AH...SEEMS LIKE YOU HAVE SOME-THING TO TAKE CARE OF, BLAIR.
WE DIDN'T HEAR ANY-THING, BUT I THINK IT'S BEST THAT WE GET GOING.
SEE YOU AT SCHOOL.

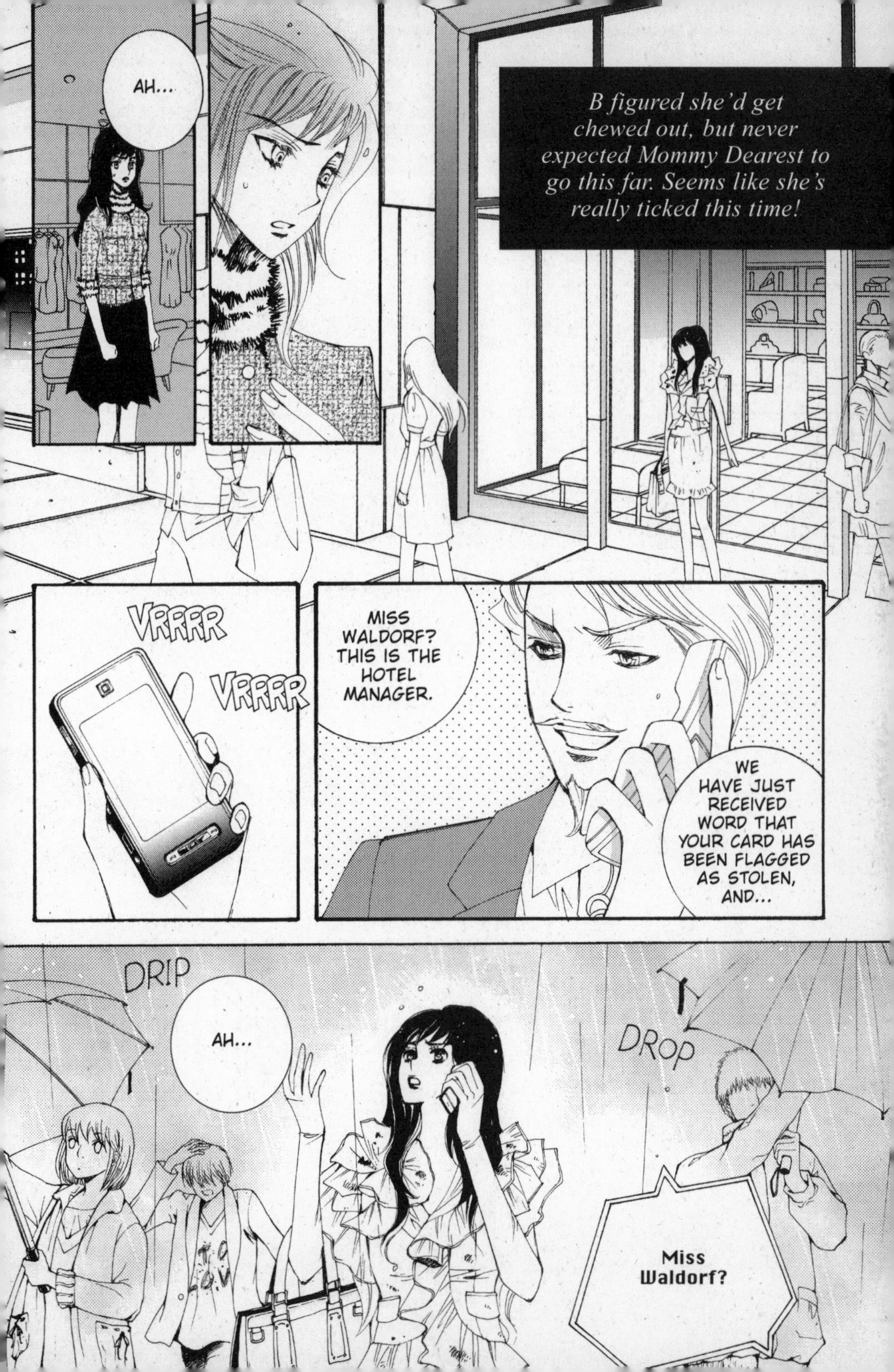
AH...
B figured she'd get chewed out, but never expected Mommy Dearest to go this far. Seems like she's really ticked this time!
VRRRR
VRRRR
MISS WALDORF? THIS IS THE HOTEL MANAGER.
WE HAVE JUST RECEIVED WORD THAT YOUR CARD HAS BEEN FLAGGED AS STOLEN, AND...
DRIP
AH...
DROP
Miss Waldorf?

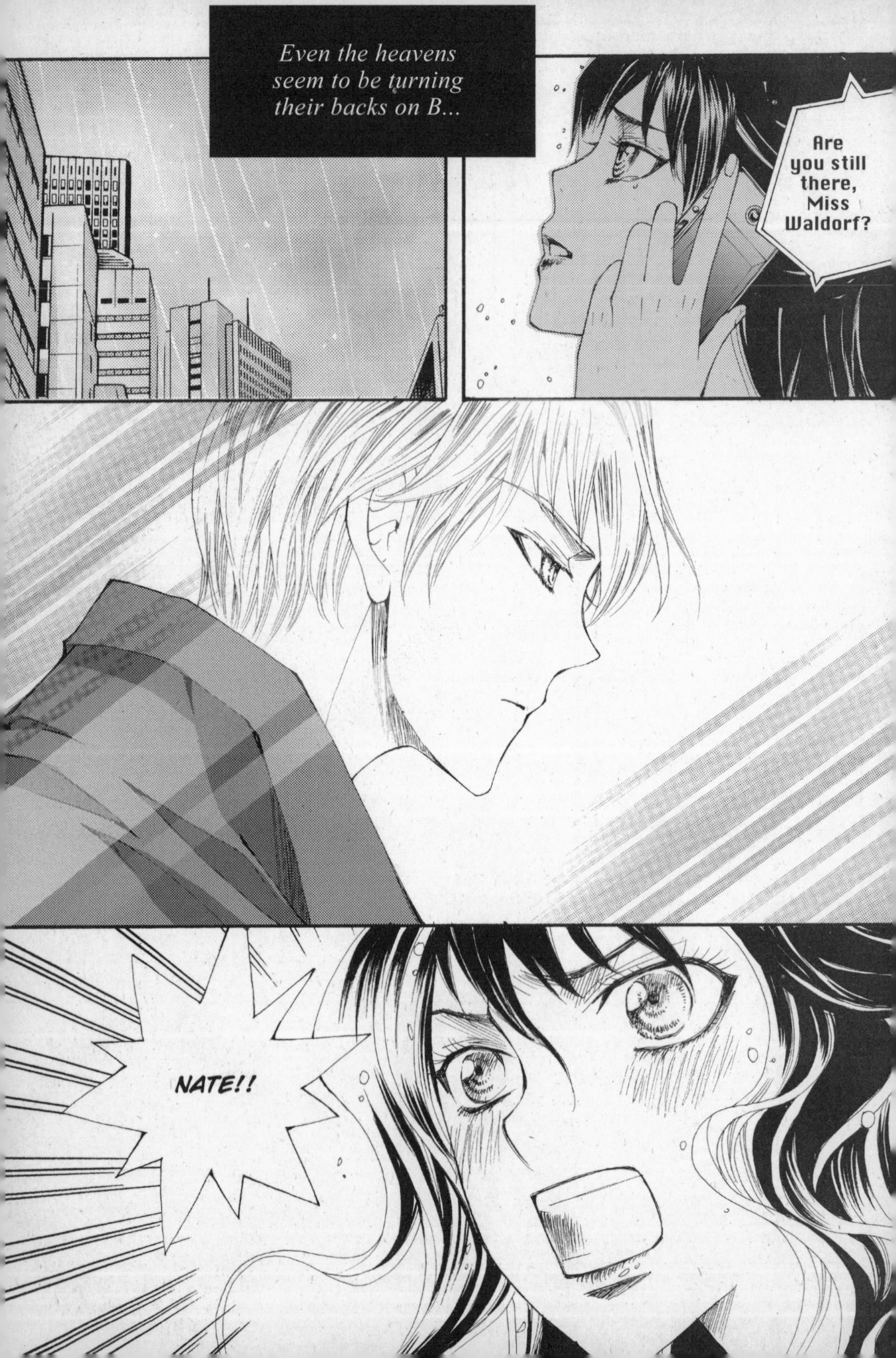
Even the heavens seem to be turning their backs on B...
Are you still there, Miss Waldorf?
NATE!!

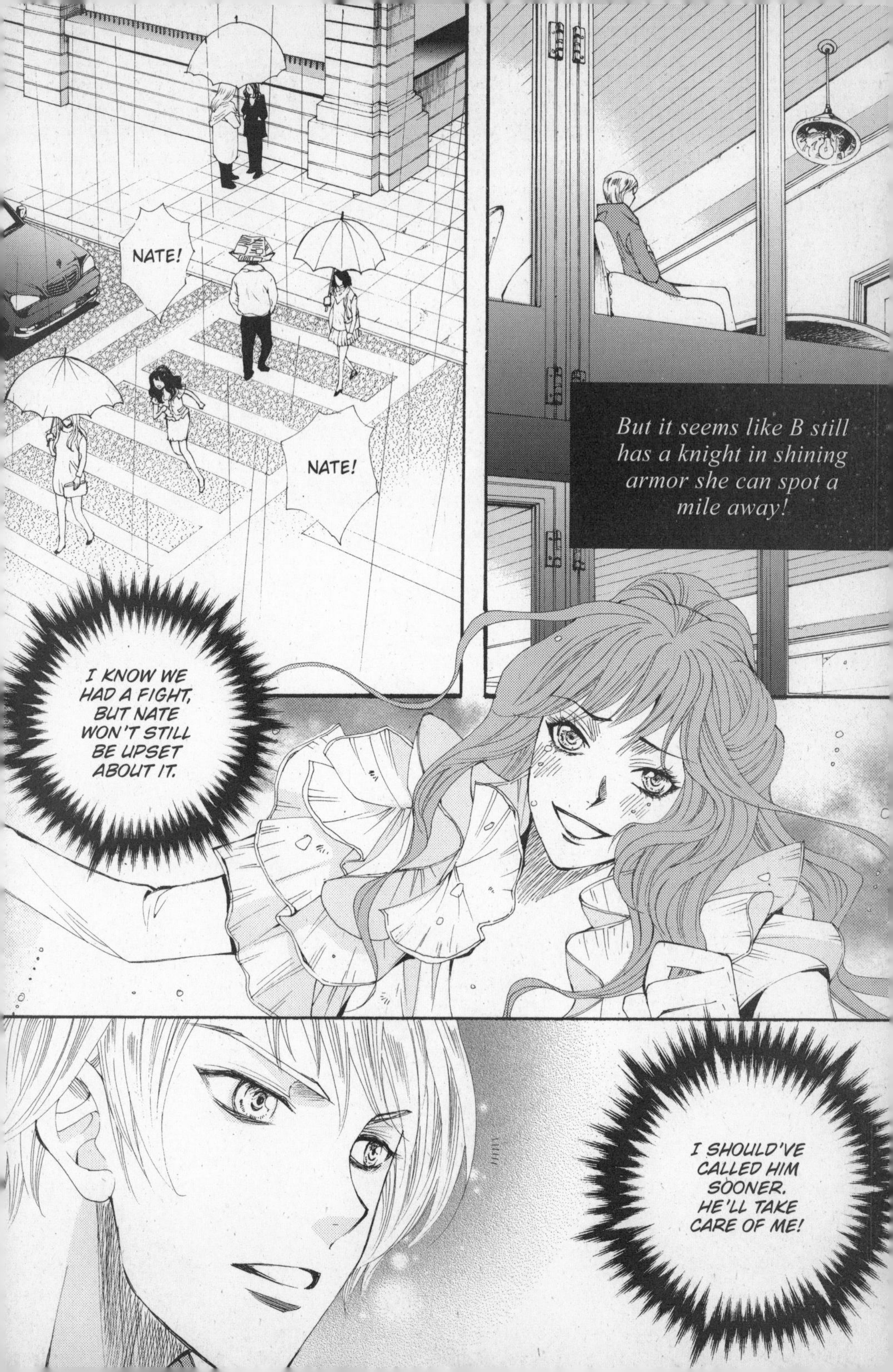
NATE!
NATE!
But it seems like B still has a knight in shining armor she can spot a mile away!
I KNOW WE HAD A FIGHT, BUT NATE WON'T STILL BE UPSET ABOUT IT.
I SHOULD'VE CALLED HIM SOONER. HE'LL TAKE CARE OF ME!

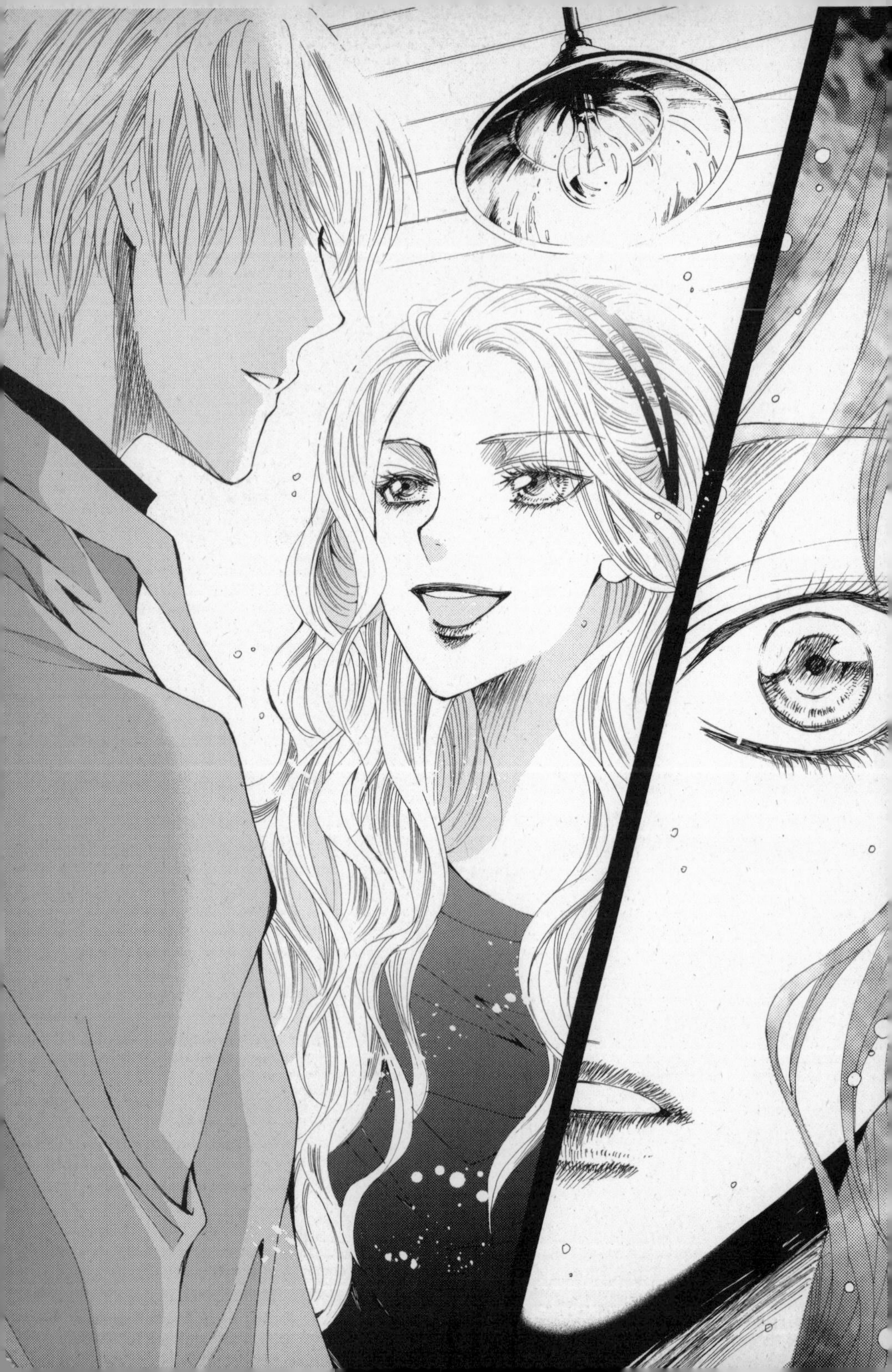

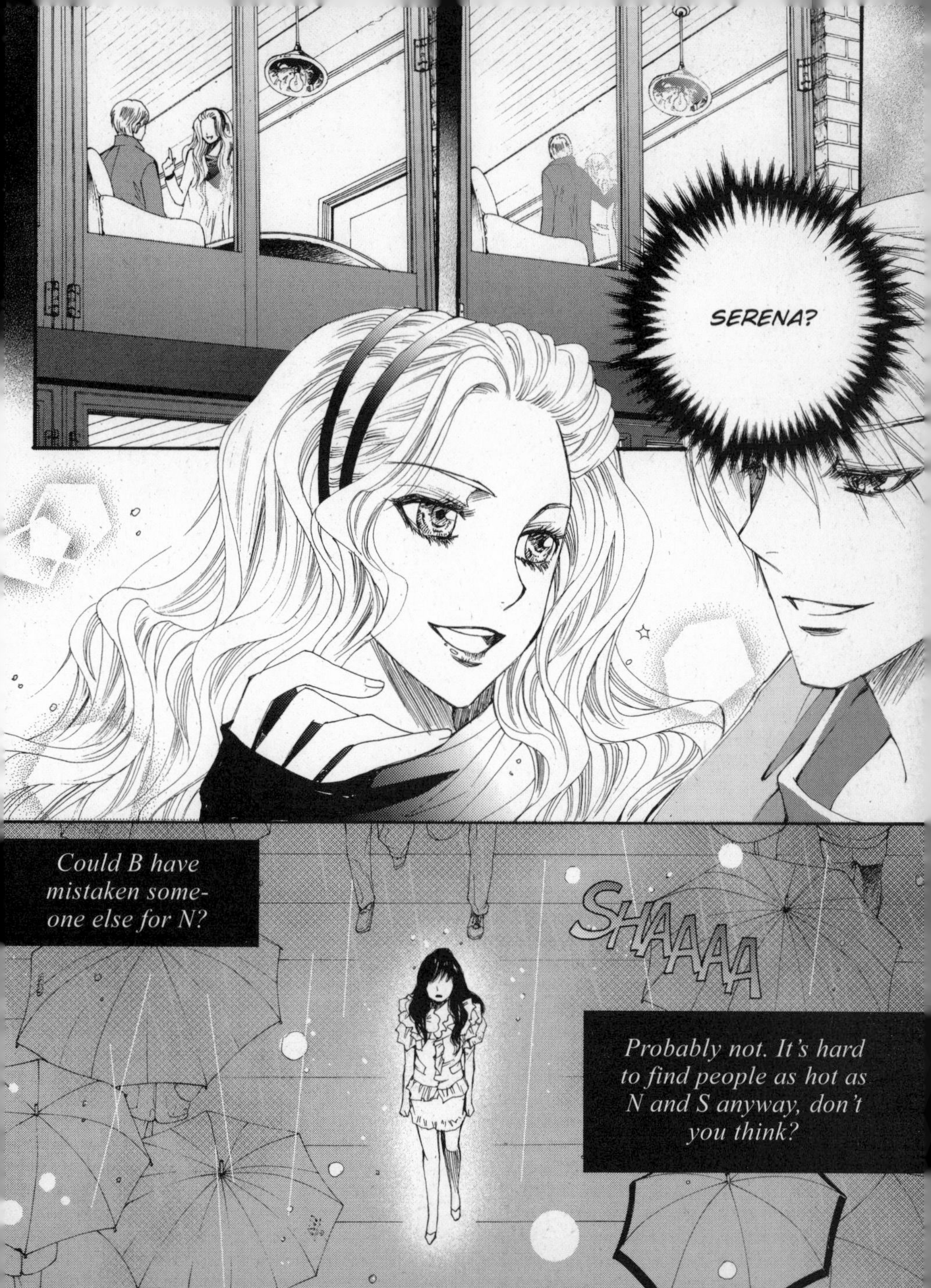
SERENA?
Could B have mistaken some-one else for N?
SHAAAA
Probably not. It's hard to find people as hot as N and S anyway, don't you think?

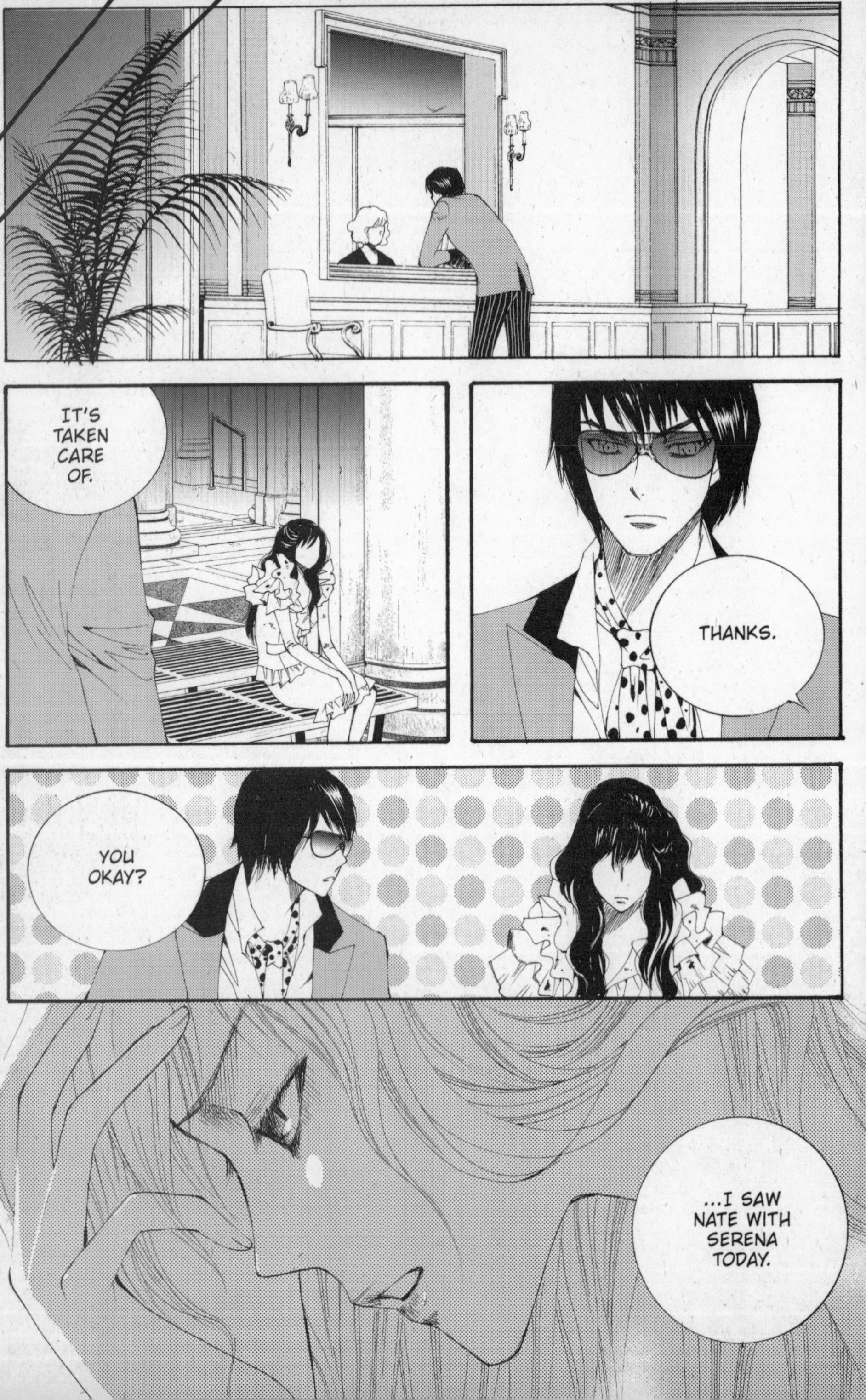
IT'S TAKEN CARE OF.
THANKS.
YOU OKAY?
...I SAW NATE WITH SERENA TODAY.

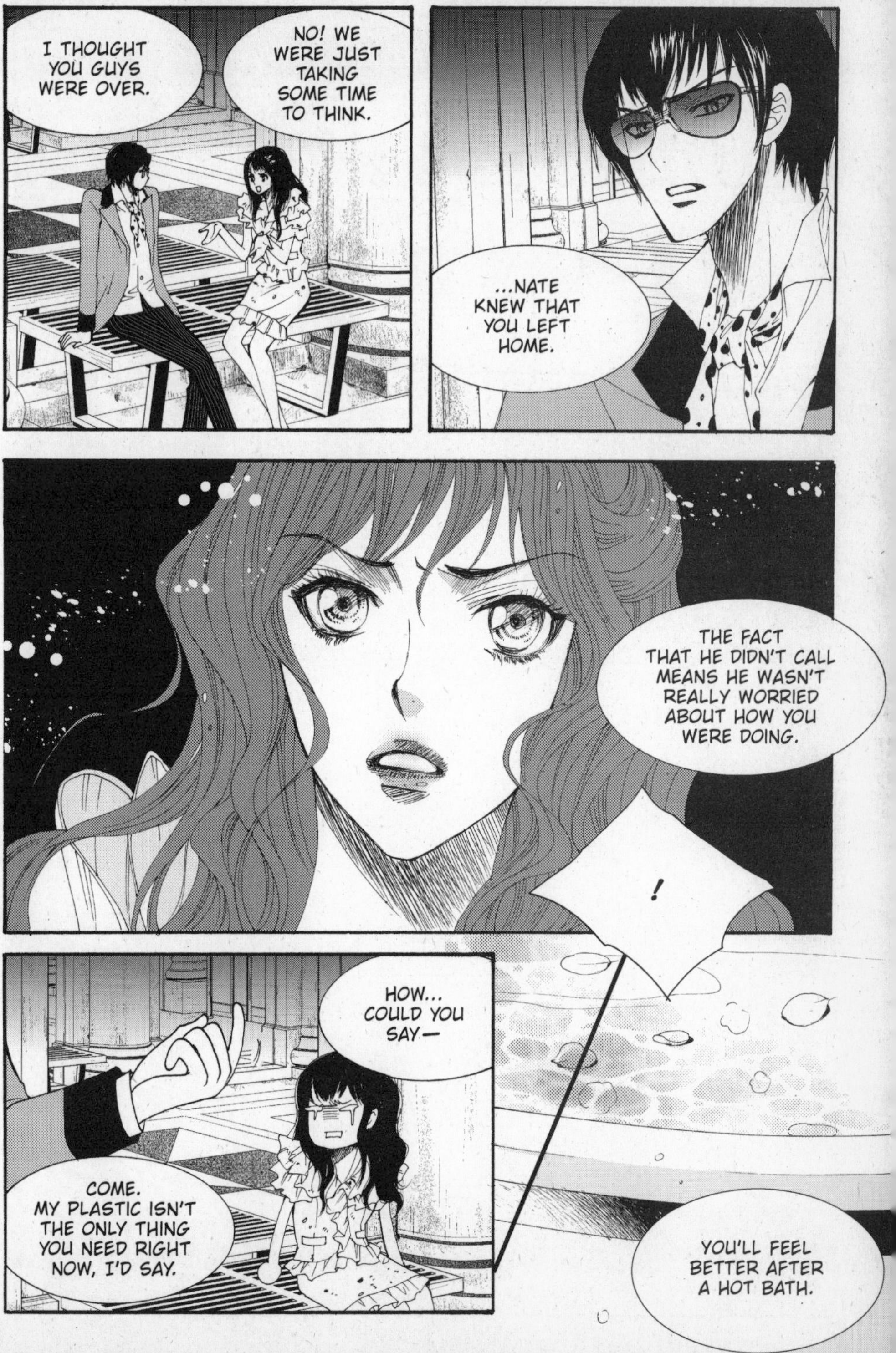
I THOUGHT YOU GUYS WERE OVER.
NO! WE WERE JUST TAKING SOME TIME TO THINK.
...NATE KNEW THAT YOU LEFT HOME.
THE FACT THAT HE DIDN'T CALL MEANS HE WASN'T REALLY WORRIED ABOUT HOW YOU WERE DOING.
!
HOW... COULD YOU SAY—
COME. MY PLASTIC ISN'T THE ONLY THING YOU NEED RIGHT NOW, I'D SAY.
YOU'LL FEEL BETTER AFTER A HOT BATH.

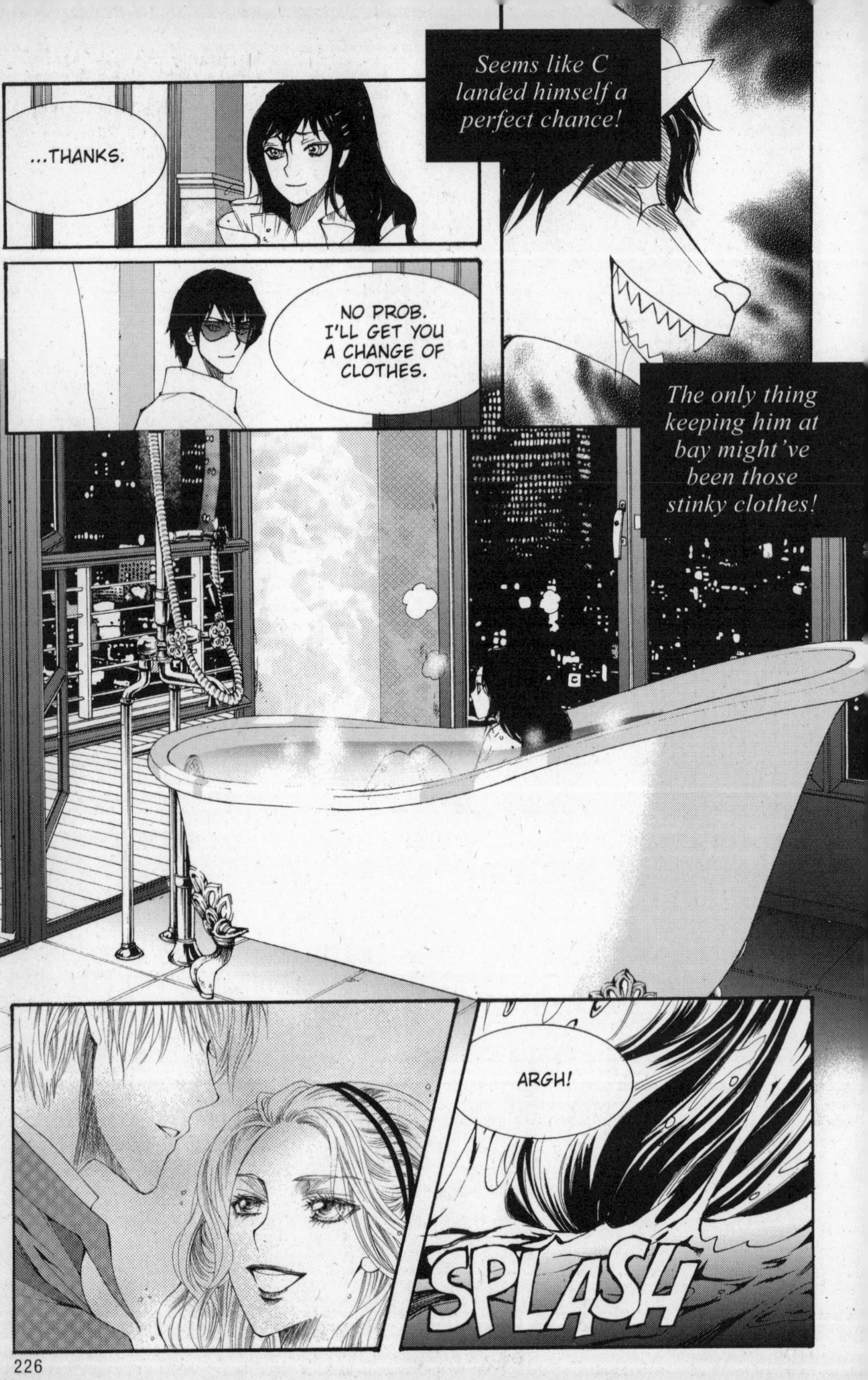

...THANKS.
NO PROB. I'LL GET YOU A CHANGE OF CLOTHES.
Seems like C landed himself a perfect chance!
The only thing keeping him at bay might've been those stinky clothes!
ARGH!
SPLASH

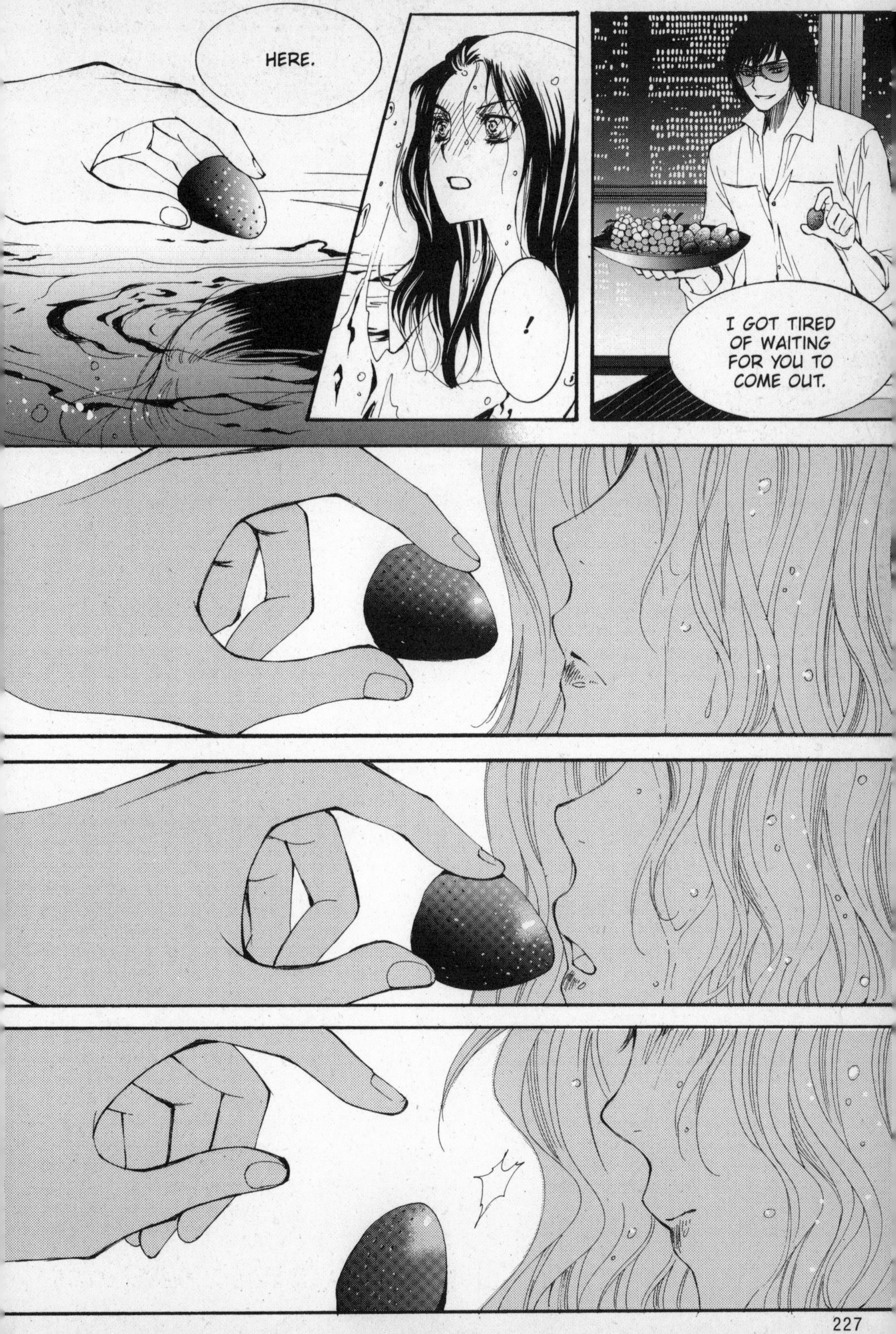
HERE.
!
I GOT TIRED OF WAITING FOR YOU TO COME OUT.

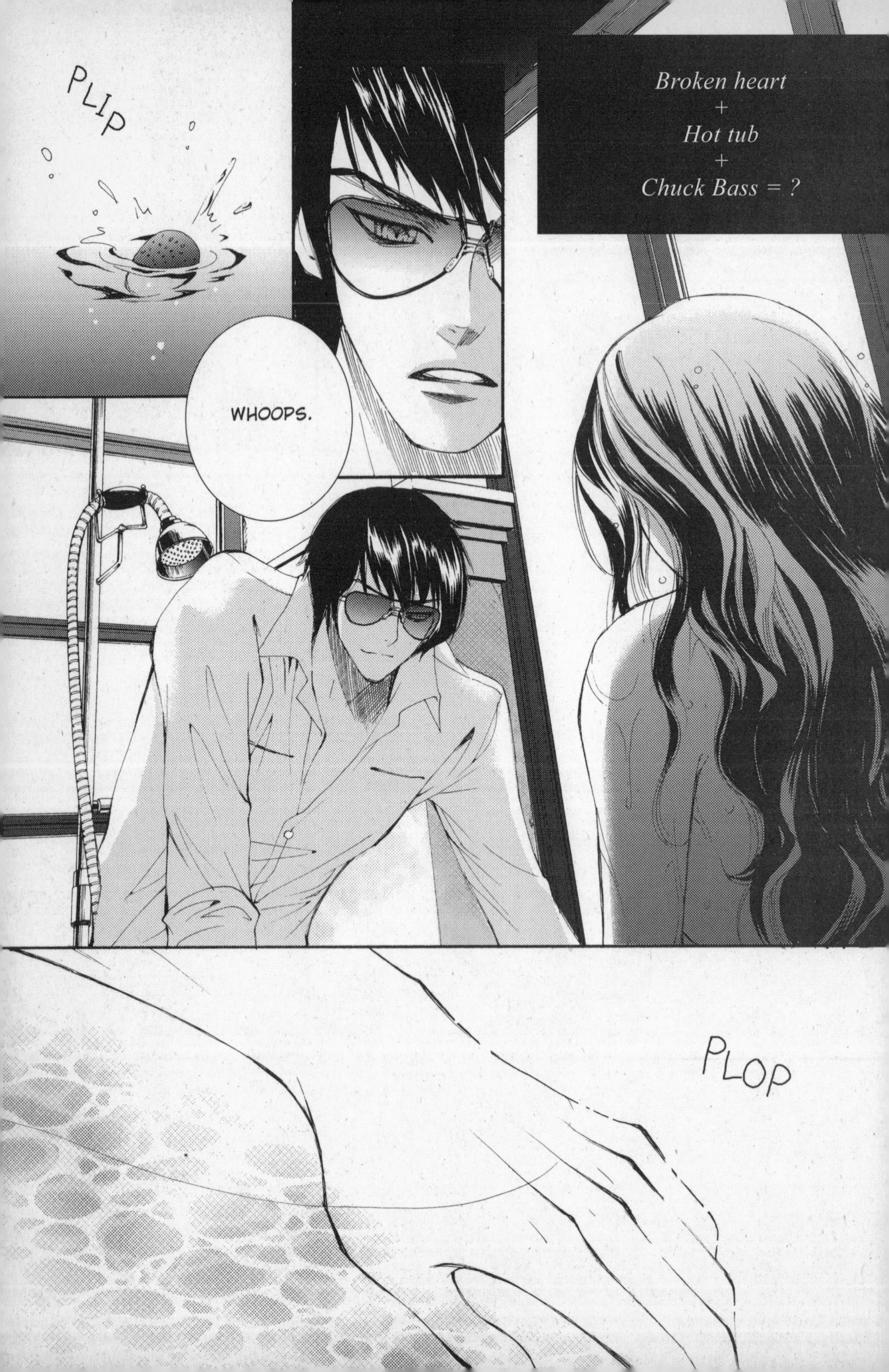
PLIP
Broken heart
+
Hot tub
+
Chuck Bass = ?
WHOOPS.
PLOP

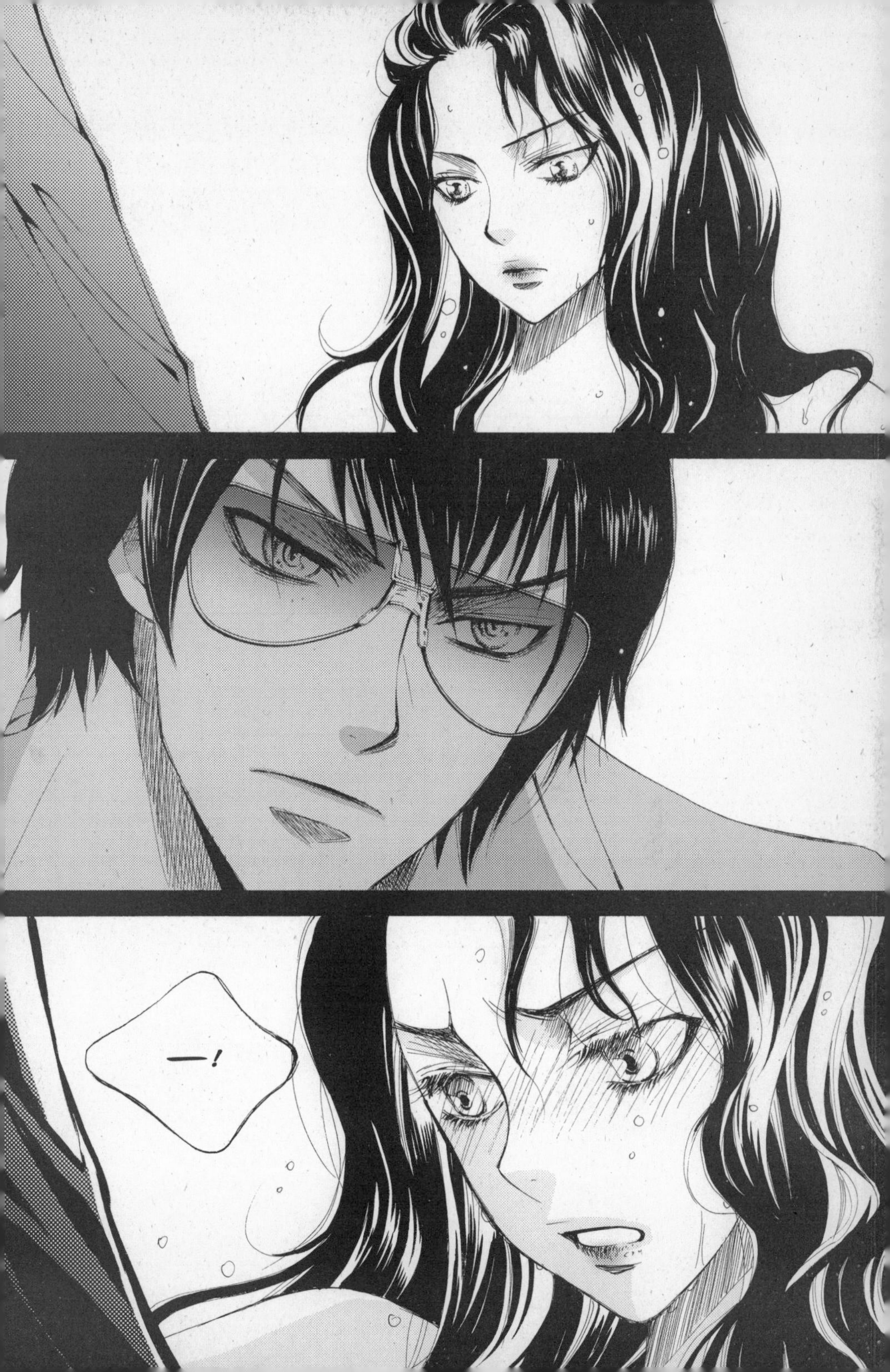
—!

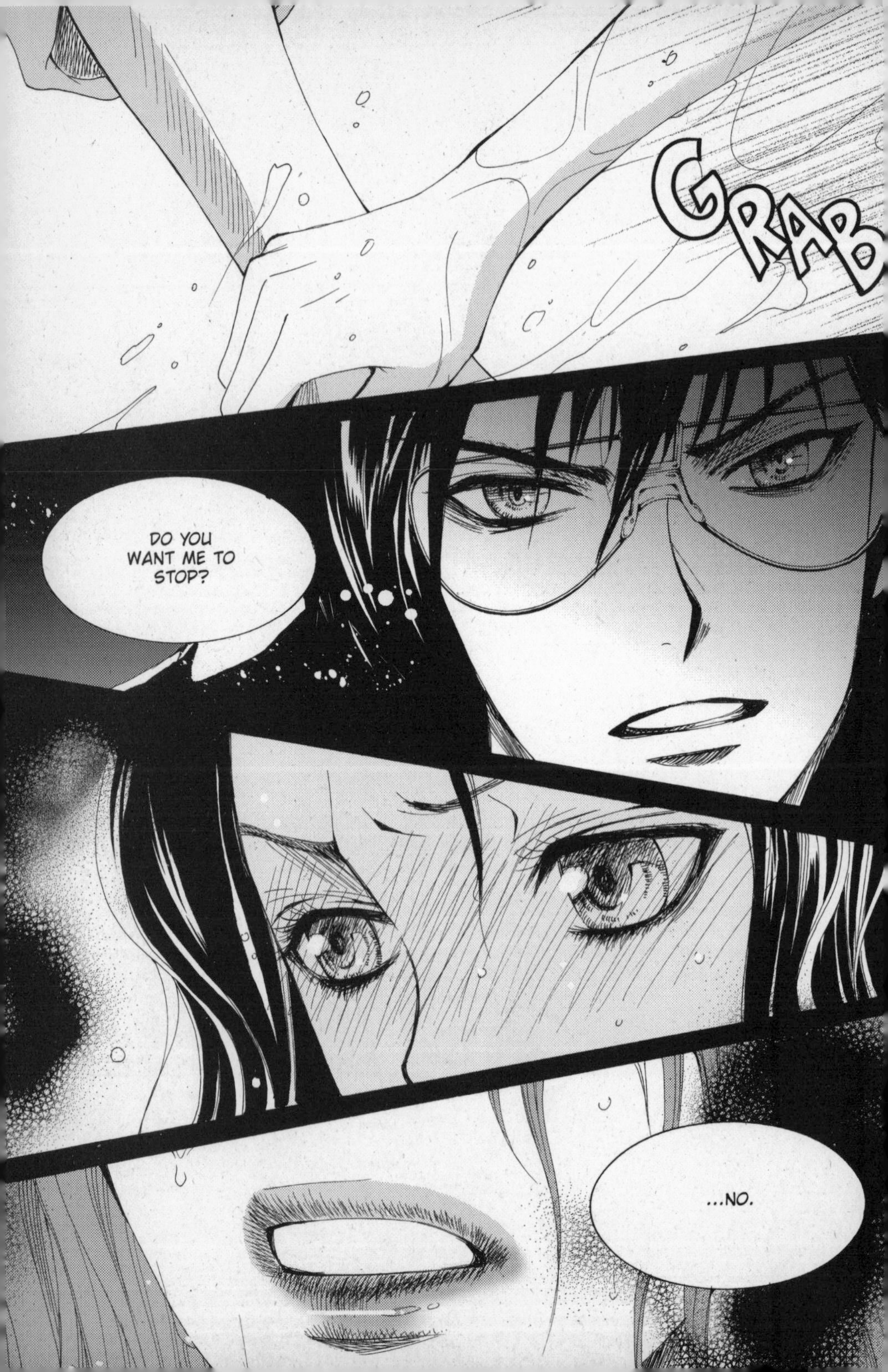
GRAB
DO YOU WANT ME TO STOP?
...NO.

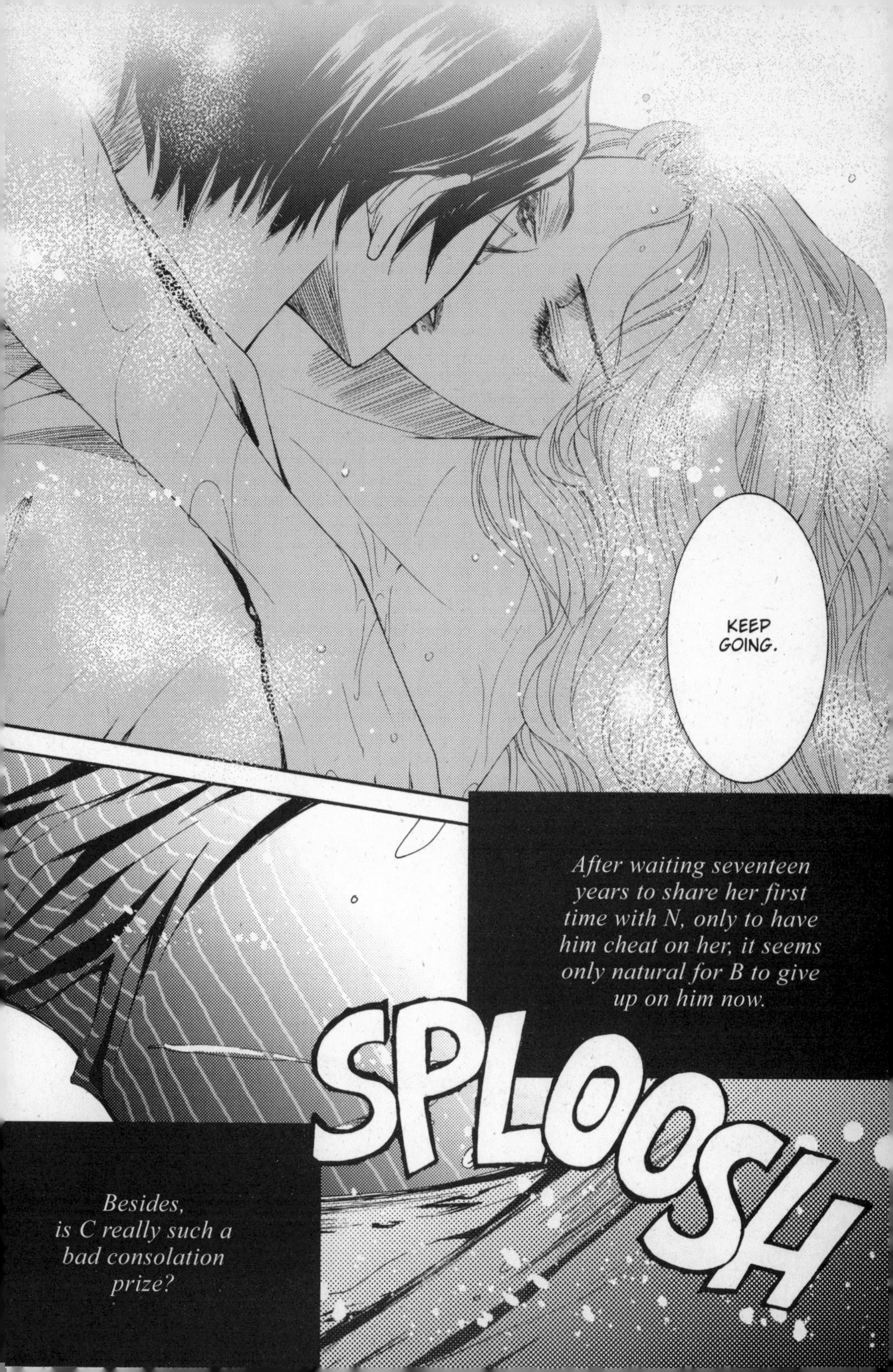
KEEP GOING.
After waiting seventeen years to share her first time with N, only to have him cheat on her, it seems only natural for B to give up on him now.
SPLOOSH
Besides, is C really such a bad consolation prize?

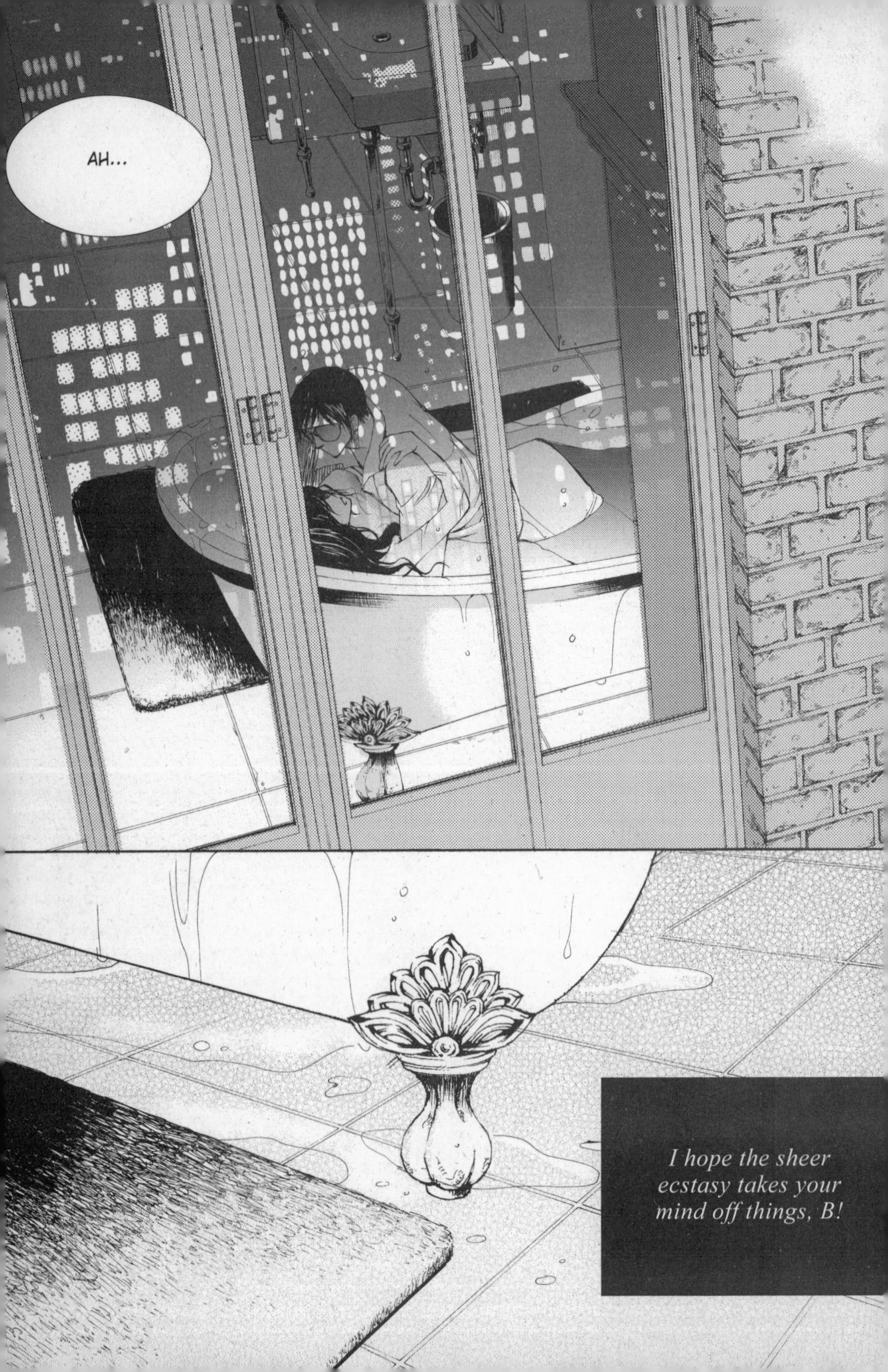
AH...
I hope the sheer ecstasy takes your mind off things, B!

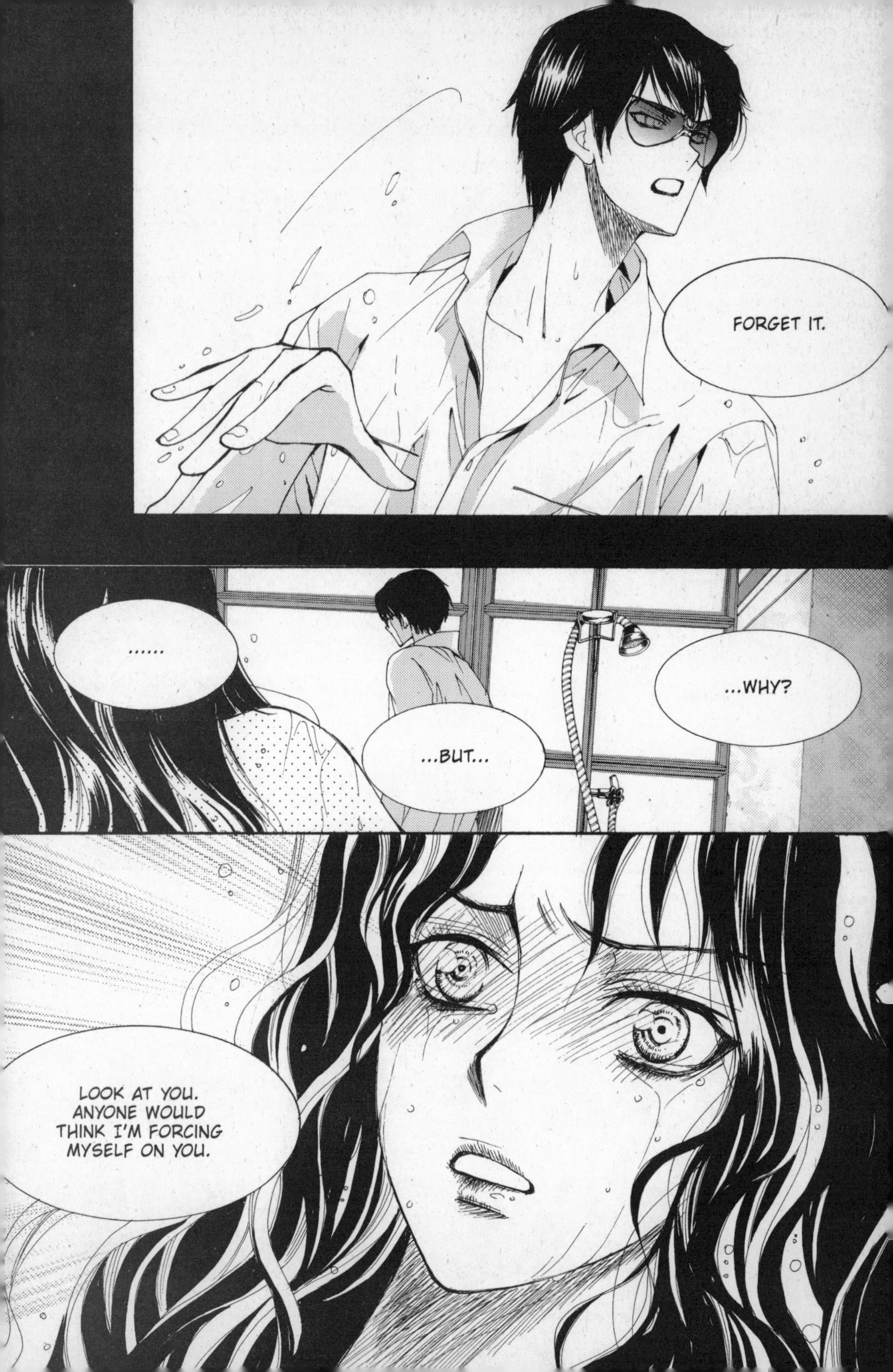
FORGET IT.
......
...BUT...
...WHY?
LOOK AT YOU. ANYONE WOULD THINK I'M FORCING MYSELF ON YOU.

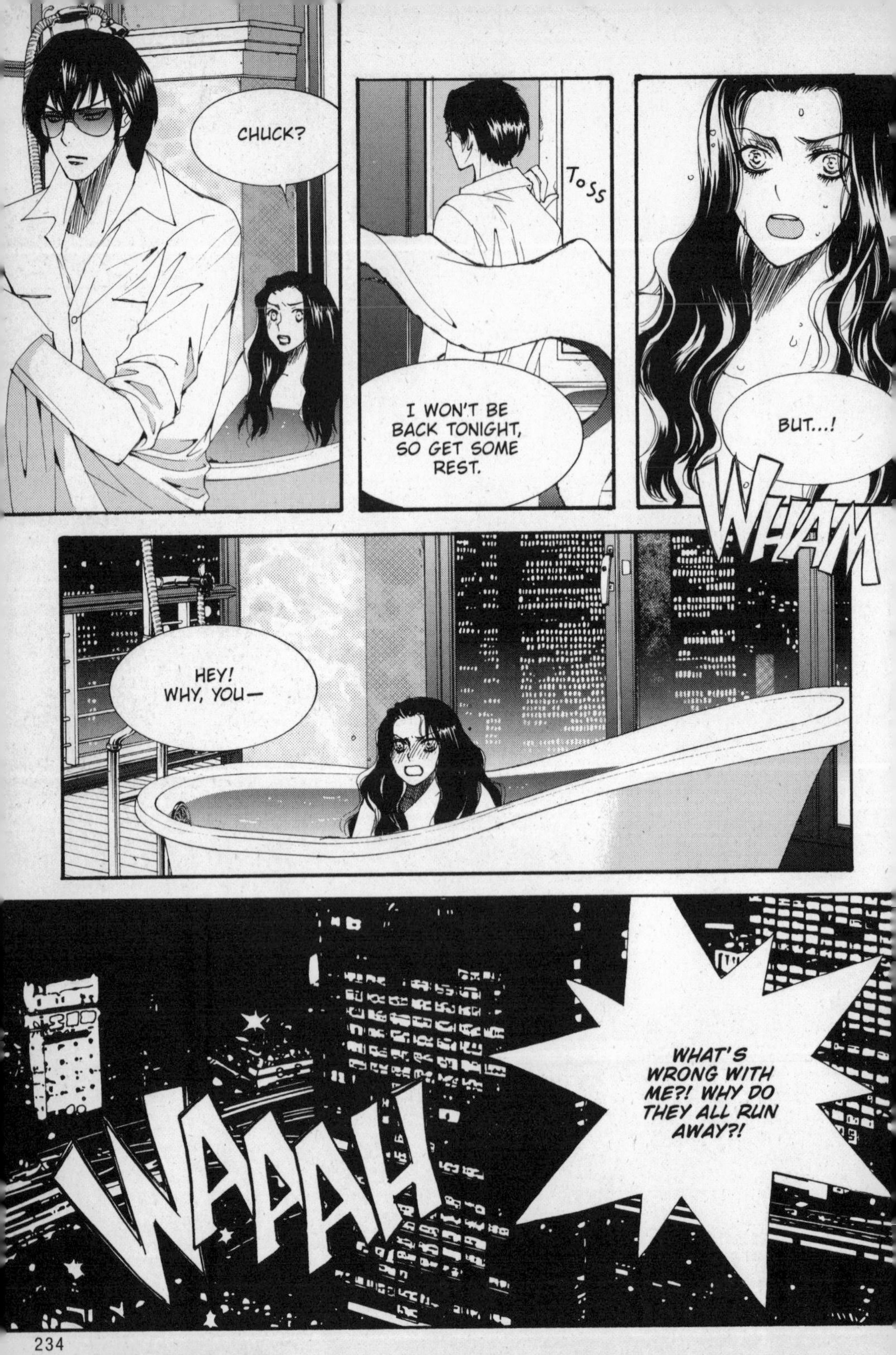
CHUCK?
TOSS
I WON'T BE BACK TONIGHT, SO GET SOME REST.
BUT...!
WHAM
HEY! WHY, YOU—
WAPAH
WHAT'S WRONG WITH ME?! WHY DO THEY ALL RUN AWAY?!

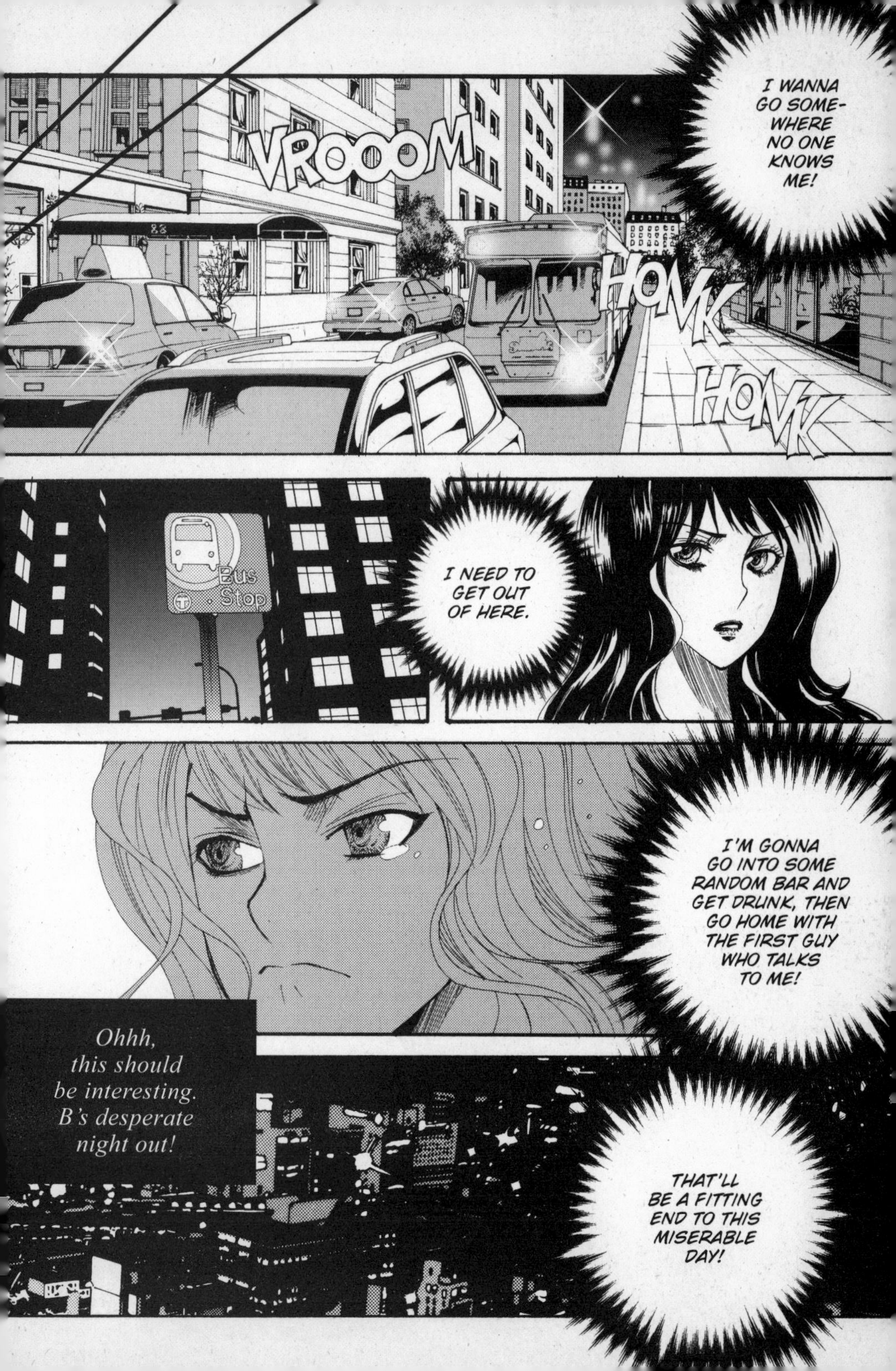
VROOOM
I WANNA GO SOME-WHERE NO ONE KNOWS ME!
HONK
HONK
Bus Stop
I NEED TO GET OUT OF HERE.
I'M GONNA GO INTO SOME RANDOM BAR AND GET DRUNK, THEN GO HOME WITH THE FIRST GUY WHO TALKS TO ME!
Ohhh, this should be interesting. B's desperate night out!
THAT'LL BE A FITTING END TO THIS MISERABLE DAY!

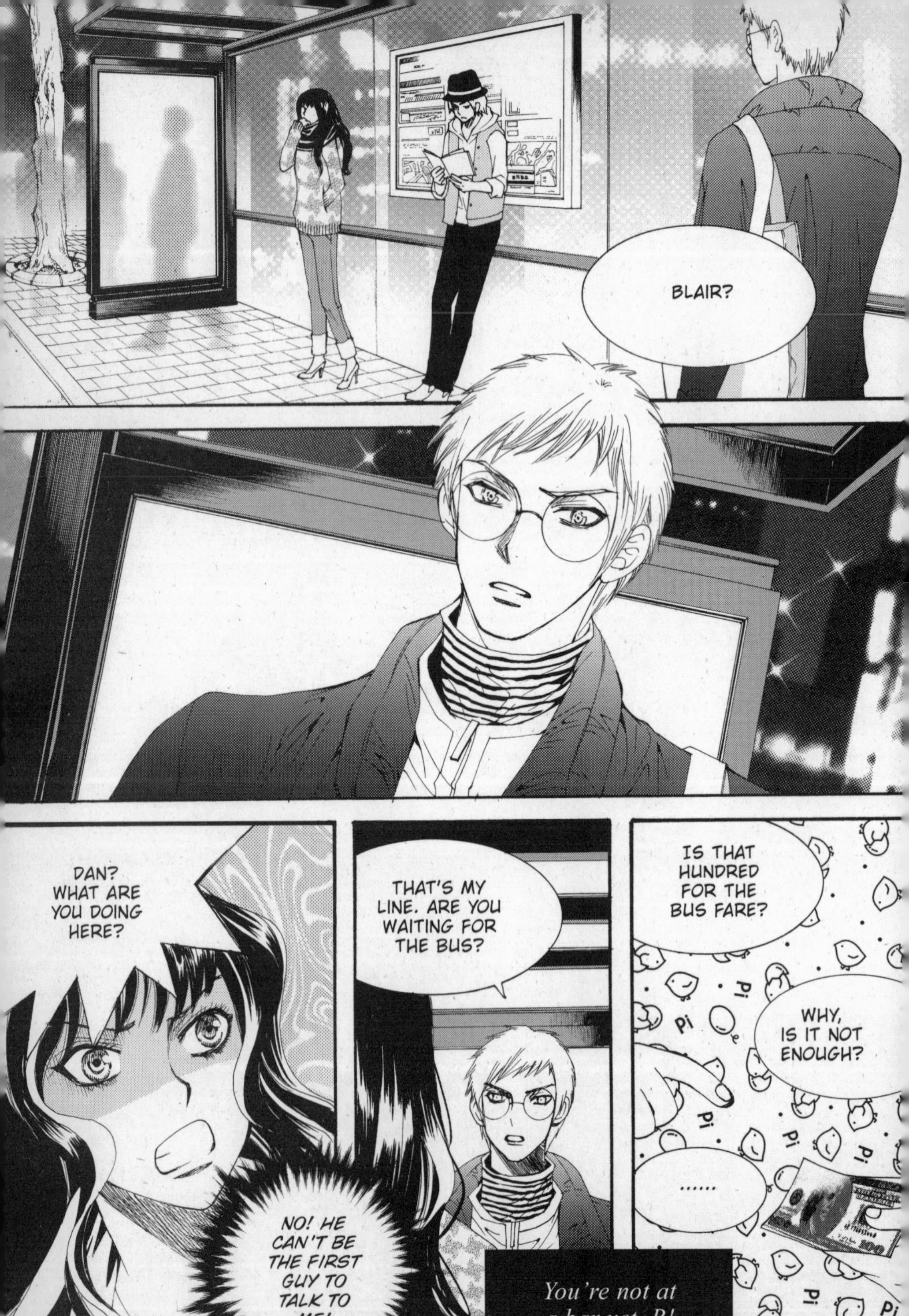
BLAIR?
DAN? WHAT ARE YOU DOING HERE?
NO! HE CAN'T BE THE FIRST GUY TO TALK TO ME!
THAT'S MY LINE. ARE YOU WAITING FOR THE BUS?
You're not at a bar yet, B!
IS THAT HUNDRED FOR THE BUS FARE?
WHY, IS IT NOT ENOUGH?
......
Pi
Pi
Pi
Pi
Pi
Pi
Pi

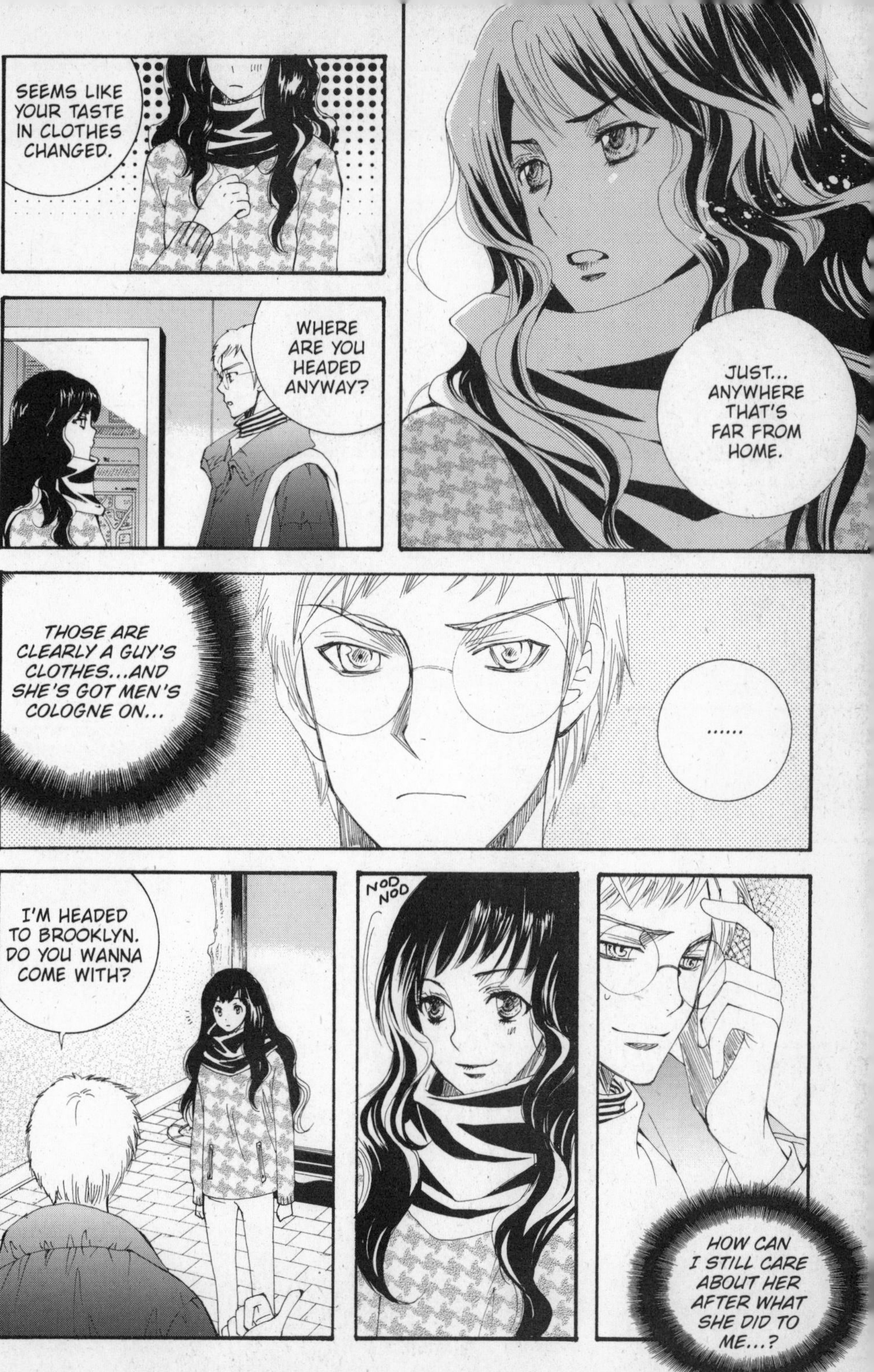
SEEMS LIKE YOUR TASTE IN CLOTHES CHANGED.
WHERE ARE YOU HEADED ANYWAY?
JUST... ANYWHERE THAT'S FAR FROM HOME.
THOSE ARE CLEARLY A GUY'S CLOTHES...AND SHE'S GOT MEN'S COLOGNE ON...
......
I'M HEADED TO BROOKLYN. DO YOU WANNA COME WITH?
NOD NOD
HOW CAN I STILL CARE ABOUT HER AFTER WHAT SHE DID TO ME...?

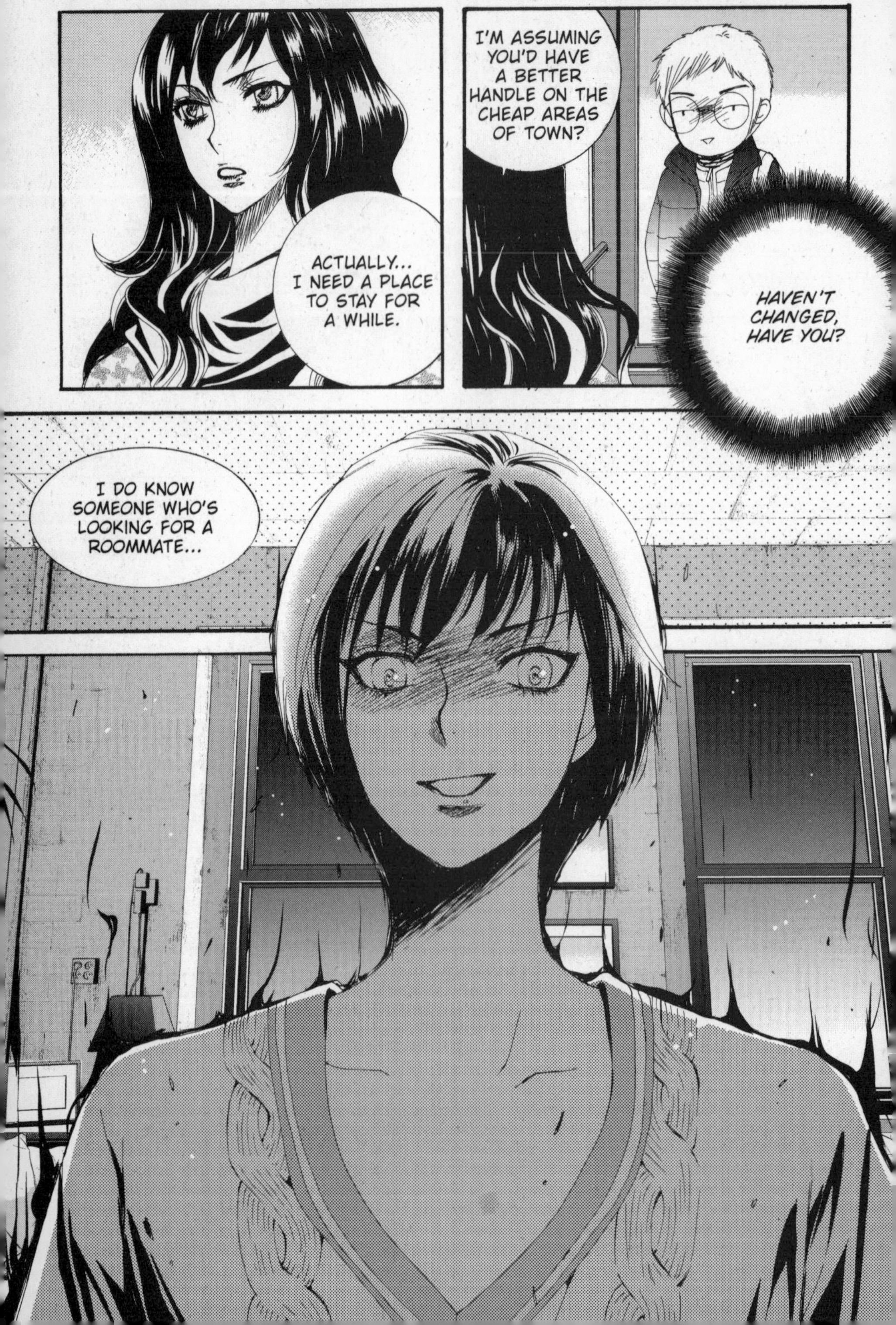
ACTUALLY... I NEED A PLACE TO STAY FOR A WHILE.
I'M ASSUMING YOU'D HAVE A BETTER HANDLE ON THE CHEAP AREAS OF TOWN?
HAVEN'T CHANGED, HAVE YOU?
I DO KNOW SOMEONE WHO'S LOOKING FOR A ROOMMATE...

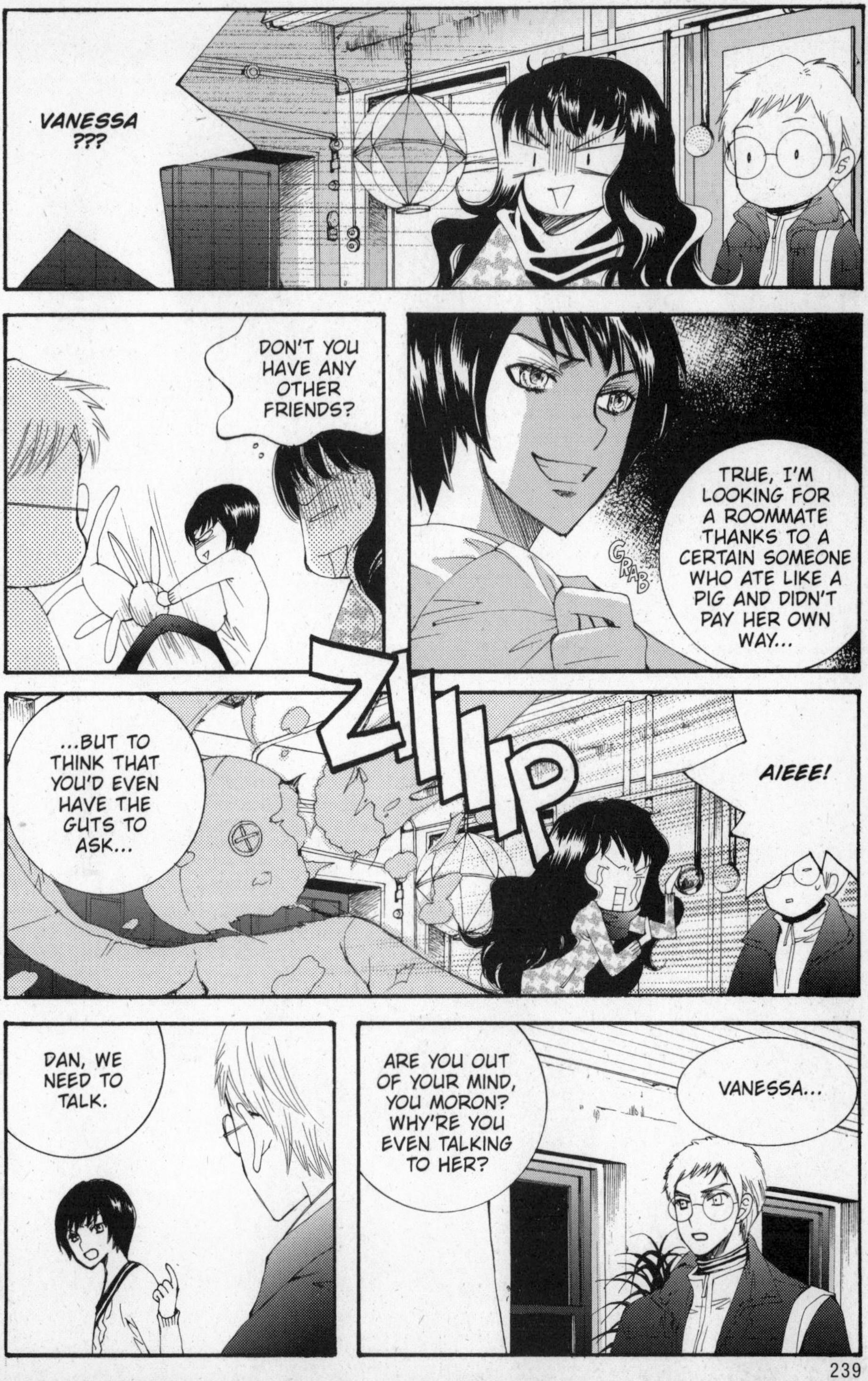
VANESSA ???
DON'T YOU HAVE ANY OTHER FRIENDS?
TRUE, I'M LOOKING FOR A ROOMMATE THANKS TO A CERTAIN SOMEONE WHO ATE LIKE A PIG AND DIDN'T PAY HER OWN WAY...
GRAB
ZIIIP
...BUT TO THINK THAT YOU'D EVEN HAVE THE GUTS TO ASK...
AIEEE!
DAN, WE NEED TO TALK.
ARE YOU OUT OF YOUR MIND, YOU MORON? WHY'RE YOU EVEN TALKING TO HER?
VANESSA...

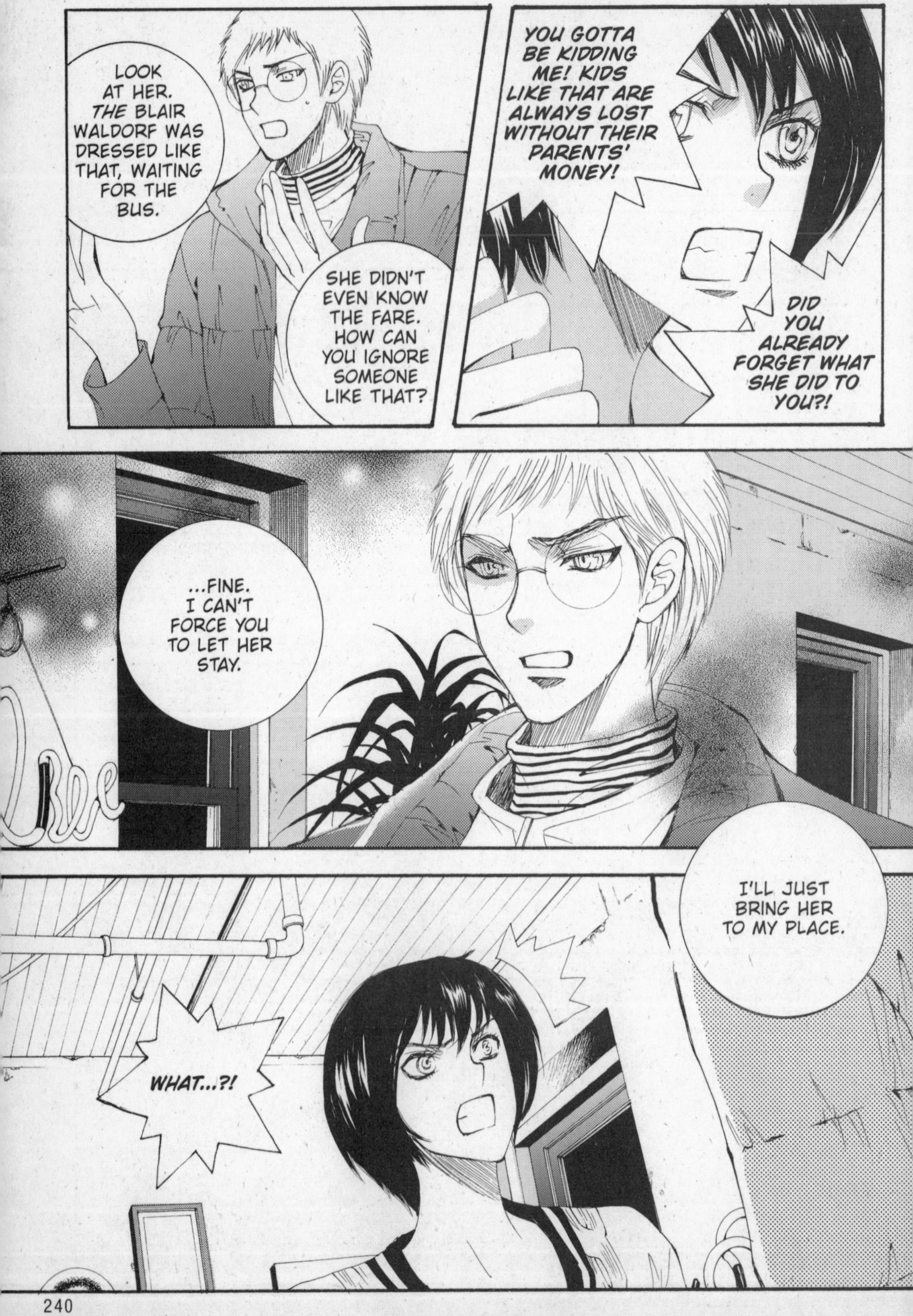
LOOK AT HER. THE BLAIR WALDORF WAS DRESSED LIKE THAT, WAITING FOR THE BUS.
SHE DIDN'T EVEN KNOW THE FARE. HOW CAN YOU IGNORE SOMEONE LIKE THAT?
YOU GOTTA BE KIDDING ME! KIDS LIKE THAT ARE ALWAYS LOST WITHOUT THEIR PARENTS' MONEY!
DID YOU ALREADY FORGET WHAT SHE DID TO YOU?!
...FINE. I CAN'T FORCE YOU TO LET HER STAY.
I'LL JUST BRING HER TO MY PLACE.
WHAT...?!

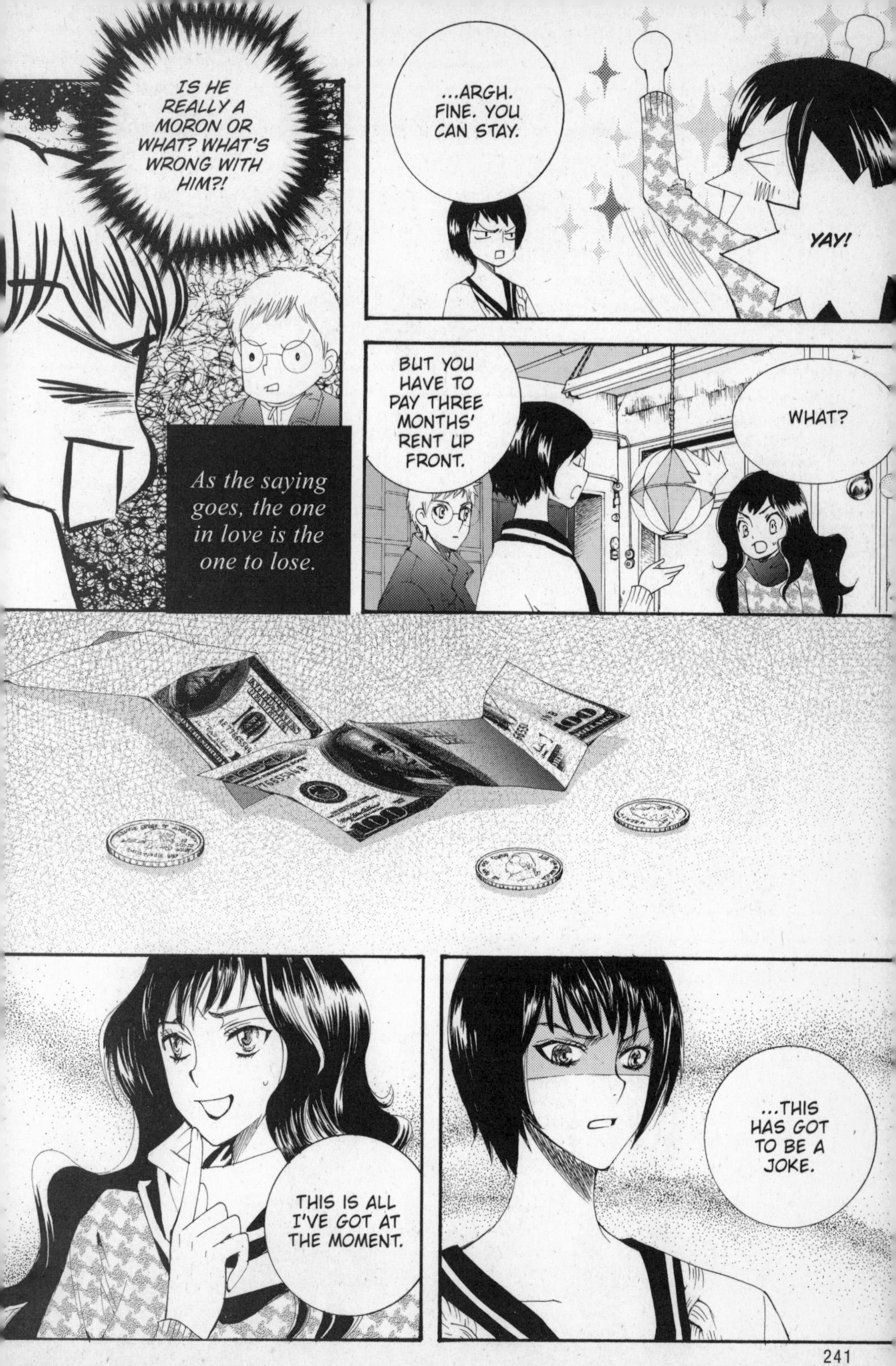
IS HE REALLY A MORON OR WHAT? WHAT'S WRONG WITH HIM?!
As the saying goes, the one in love is the one to lose.
...ARGH. FINE. YOU CAN STAY.
YAY!
BUT YOU HAVE TO PAY THREE MONTHS' RENT UP FRONT.
WHAT?
THIS IS ALL I'VE GOT AT THE MOMENT.
...THIS HAS GOT TO BE A JOKE.

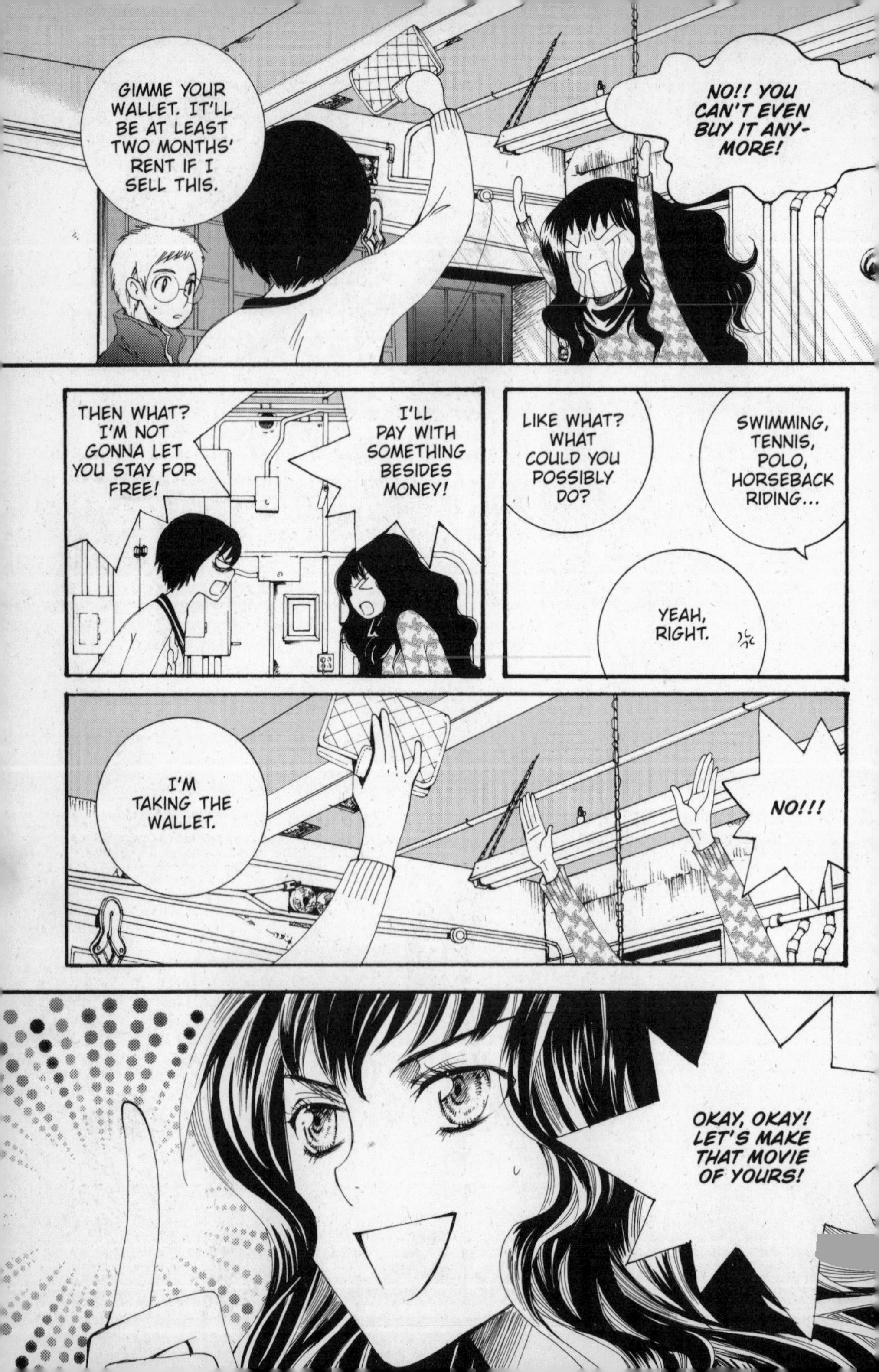
GIMME YOUR WALLET. IT'LL BE AT LEAST TWO MONTHS' RENT IF I SELL THIS.
NO!! YOU CAN'T EVEN BUY IT ANY-MORE!
THEN WHAT? I'M NOT GONNA LET YOU STAY FOR FREE!
I'LL PAY WITH SOMETHING BESIDES MONEY!
LIKE WHAT? WHAT COULD YOU POSSIBLY DO?
SWIMMING, TENNIS, POLO, HORSEBACK RIDING...
YEAH, RIGHT.
I'M TAKING THE WALLET.
NO!!!
OKAY, OKAY! LET'S MAKE THAT MOVIE OF YOURS!

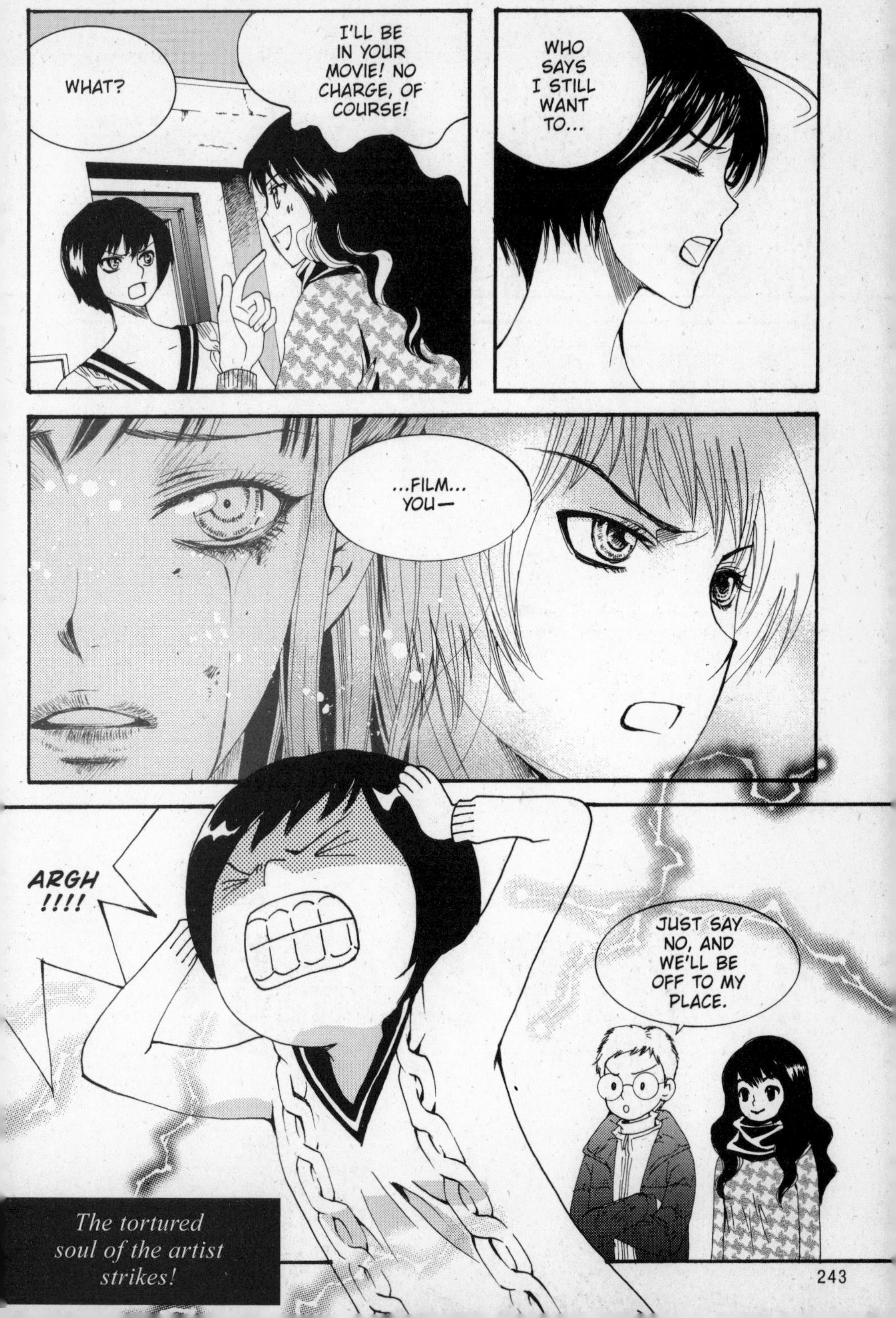
WHAT?
I'LL BE IN YOUR MOVIE! NO CHARGE, OF COURSE!
WHO SAYS I STILL WANT TO...
...FILM... YOU—
ARGH !!!!
JUST SAY NO, AND WE'LL BE OFF TO MY PLACE.
The tortured soul of the artist strikes!

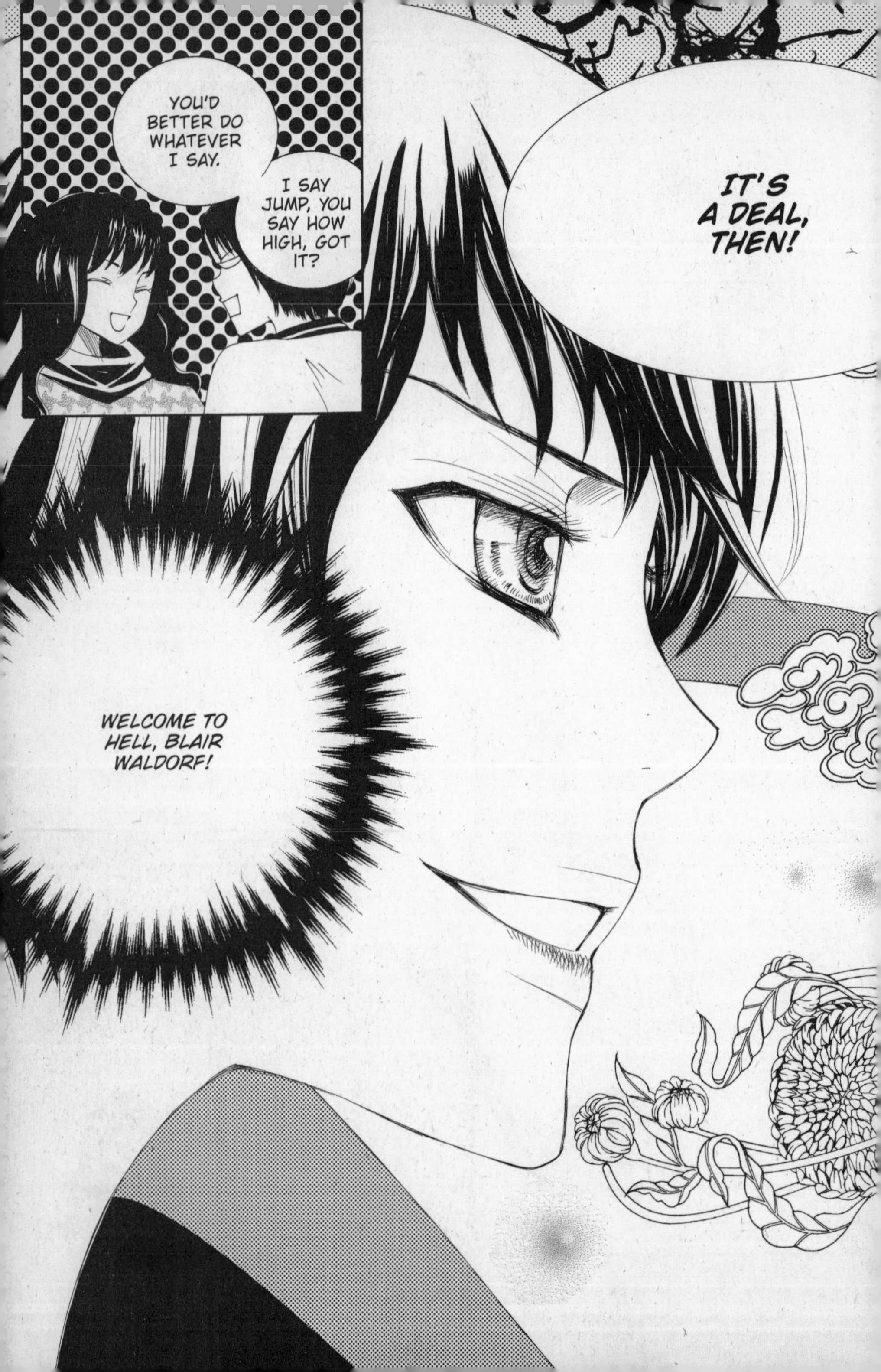
YOU'D BETTER DO WHATEVER I SAY.
I SAY JUMP, YOU SAY HOW HIGH, GOT IT?
IT'S A DEAL, THEN!
WELCOME TO HELL, BLAIR WALDORF!

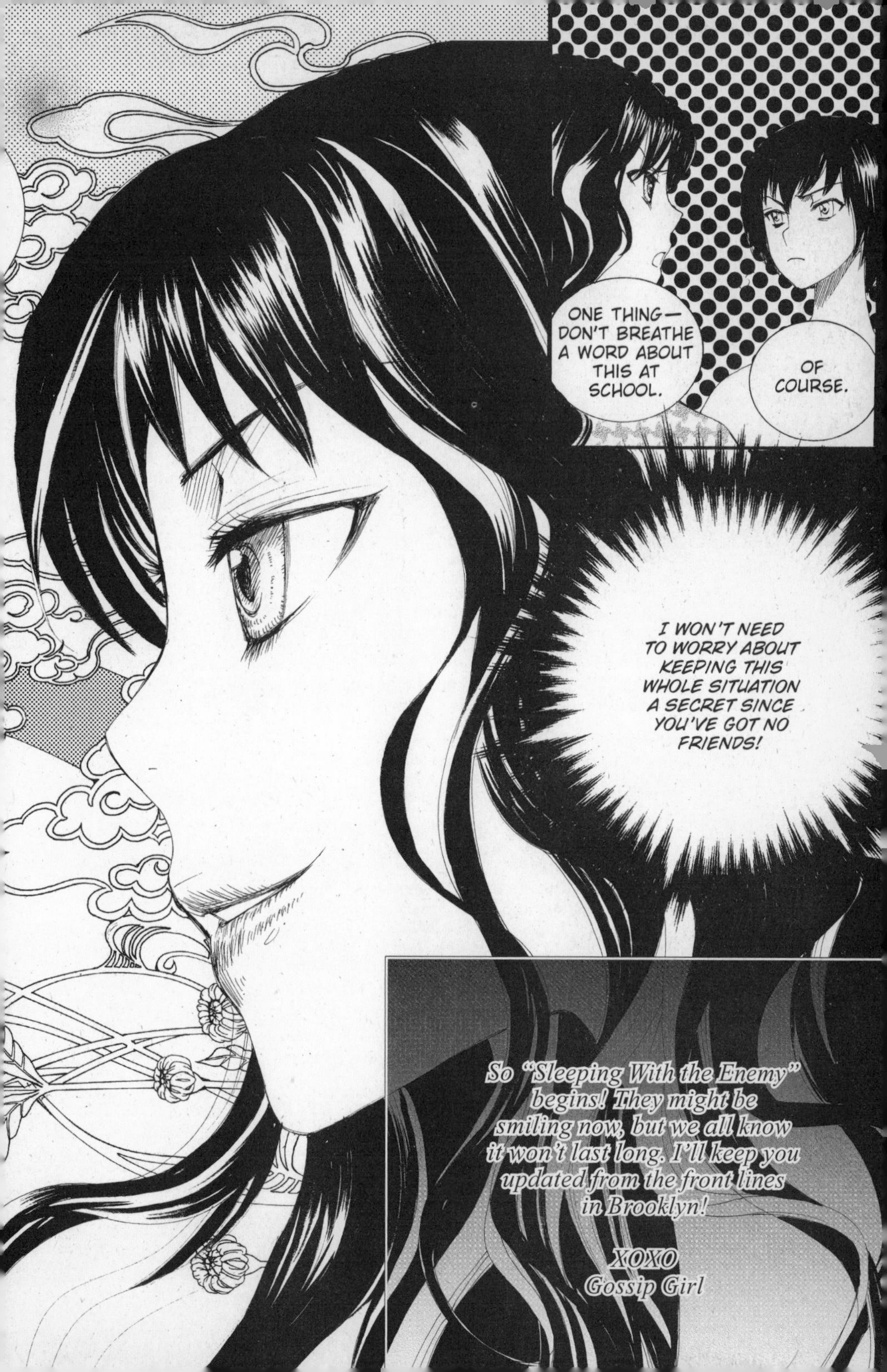
ONE THING—DON'T BREATHE A WORD ABOUT THIS AT SCHOOL.
OF COURSE.
I WON'T NEED TO WORRY ABOUT KEEPING THIS WHOLE SITUATION A SECRET SINCE YOU'VE GOT NO FRIENDS!
So "Sleeping With the Enemy" begins! They might be smiling now, but we all know it won't last long. I'll keep you updated from the front lines in Brooklyn!
XOXO
Gossip Girl

gossip girl

FOR YOUR EYES ONLY | VOLUME 1

Based on the GOSSIP GIRL novels
written by Cecily von Ziegesar

Art and Adaptation: HyeKyung Baek

Text and Illustrations Copyright © 2010
by Hachette Book Group, Inc.

Yen Press
Hachette Book Group
237 Park Avenue
New York, NY 10017

www.HachetteBookGroup.com
www.YenPress.com

Yen Press is an imprint of Hachette Book Group, Inc. The Yen
Press name and logo are trademarks of Hachette Book Group,
Inc.

alloyentertainment

151 West 26th Street, New York, NY 10001
alloyentertainment.com

First Yen Press Edition: August 2010

ISBN: 978-0-7595-3026-3

10 9 8 7 6 5 4 3 2 1

BVG

Printed in the United States of America